Synergizing Islamic Finance for Sustainability

Muhammad Ridhwan Ab. Aziz
Universiti Sains Islam Malaysia, Malaysia

Ahmad Rafiki
https://orcid.org/0000-0002-6360-8131
Universitas Medan Area, Indonesia

Fuadah Johari
https://orcid.org/0000-0003-3264-0742
Universiti Sains Islam Malaysia, Malaysia

IGI Global
Scientific Publishing
Publishing Tomorrow's Research Today

Vice President of Editorial	Melissa Wagner
Director of Acquisitions	Mikaela Felty
Director of Book Development	Jocelynn Hessler
Production Manager	Mike Brehm
Cover Design	Jose Rosado

Published in the United States of America by
IGI Global Scientific Publishing
701 East Chocolate Avenue
Hershey, PA, 17033, USA
Tel: 717-533-8845 | Fax: 717-533-7115
Website: https://www.igi-global.com E-mail: cust@igi-global.com

Library of Congress Cataloging-in-Publication Data

LCCN: 2025021041 (CIP Data Pending)
ISBN13: 979-8-3373-1842-4
Isbn13Softcover: 979-8-3373-1843-1
EISBN13: 979-8-3373-1844-8
British Cataloguing in Publication Data
A Cataloguing in Publication record for this book is available from the British Library.

Table of Contents

Detailed Table of Contents

As resource depletion, climate change, and environmental degradation worsen, the global quest of sustainable development has become essential. Sustainability is now at the forefront of international policy thanks to the United Nations' 2030 Agenda for Sustainable Development and the Paris Agreement under the United Nations Framework Convention on Climate Change (UNFCCC), which calls for creative and inclusive financial solutions to solve urgent ecological and social issues (UNDP, 2022). By critically analysing the potential and difficulties present in Islamic green finance, this chapter seeks to investigate the relationship between Islamic finance and environmental sustainability. It starts by discussing the foundations of Islamic green finance. The instruments of Islamic green finance are then discussed, followed by the opportunities and key challenges of Islamic green finance. The chapter will also discussed important achievements of Islamic green finance before ends it with policy recommendations for strengthening the role of Islamic finance in promoting a green finance.

This chapter examines the innovative integration of waqf (Islamic endowment) with digital technology, specifically e-wallets, as an alternative funding mechanism for research and development (R&D) in Technical and Vocational Education and Training (TVET) institutions. TVET plays a crucial role in developing skilled human capital for Malaysia's economic advancement, yet these institutions face significant funding constraints that limit their research capabilities and innovation potential. The study synthesizes data from diverse sources, including literature reviews, government reports, and statistical analyses, to evaluate how technology-enabled waqf systems can address this funding gap. The analysis reveals that Malaysian

Other than political, economic, and social factors, the element of defence waqf was highly significant in the strengthening, strengthening, and stability of a government throughout the time of the Prophet, the companions, the Uthmaniyah government, and the Abbasiyyah government. This research will look at how defence waqf was implemented during the time of the Prophet, his companions, the Uthmaniyah government, and the Abbasiyyah government. This article's technique is qualitative, involving secondary investigation with academic references to describe the defence waqf during the war. The data was then analysed to determine the Prophet's and companions' contributions to armaments and welfare. The findings reveal that the weapons used by Allah's Messenger, his companions, the Uthmaniyah administration, and the Abbasiyyah government are powerful and sophisticated, capable of defeating the enemy. In terms of welfare, Islamic history demonstrates that the Muslim community has the potential to practise welfare.

The integration of Islamic Financial Literacy, social entrepreneurship, and social finance is positioned as an innovative path to inclusive and sustainable development. Islamic Financial Literacy provides an ethical basis and understanding in accordance with Sharia principles in financial management. So that economic decisions follow religious values. Social entrepreneurship emphasizes business models based on the combined impact of economic sustainability through the creation of social values. Social finance, including zakat, waqf and investment, has a sharia effect and serves as a means of mobilizing resources to strengthen our communities. The integration of these three pillars provides an integrated Islamic economic framework that not only expands financial capacity and inclusion, but also contributes to reducing socioeconomic inequalities. The findings of this study show the need to strengthen Islamic digital financial literacy and guidelines that support investment in impact on sharia. The Zakat Institute recommends expanding the productive zakat program to transform Mustahik with Muzakki, but entrepreneurs are expected to use social effects for business models. New research fields are open to academic aspects, such as the development of Islamic index development indexes, Islamic digital financial literacy, and a hybrid model between zakat and investment income. This integration is in line with the Sustainable Development Goals (SDGs) and Maqā id al-Sharī'ah and can become a new paradigm of just and more sustainable global development.

This chapter discusses the integration of financial literacy with Islamic ethical principles in the context of digital financial tools. The rise of fintech, mobile banking, blockchain, and AI has revolutionized financial management, offering both opportunities for inclusion and risks such as impulsive consumption, debt dependency, and cybersecurity threats. From an Islamic perspective, financial literacy goes beyond technical knowledge, emphasizing moral responsibility, with wealth considered an amanah (trust) from Allah. The chapter explores how digital financial platforms can adhere to Islamic principles, focusing on moderation, wealth purification through zakat and waqf, and the importance of Shariah compliance. Key themes include the foundation of financial literacy, the role of fintech in inclusion, building ethical financial habits, and aligning financial practices with sustainability and social justice, contributing to the collective good and ethical stewardship in the digital economy.

Governments are encountering substantial difficulties in funding essential care for disabled individuals. These challenges are compounded by pervasive social concerns associated with the reliance of those needing supplementary assistance, especially following the loss of their elderly carers. The ageing process of carers presents significant issues for parents with special needs children. This issue intensifies when the child's lifestyle and continuous care are closely connected to the income earned by their parents over time. This phenomenon is particularly common among larger Muslim families globally, where familial dynamics and financial strategies significantly influence the care of dependents. A proactive strategy is crucial during critical stages of a family's development, ensuring comprehensive estate planning is executed to meet future lifetime care needs.

Personal retirement saving is crucial to ensure financial security during old age. Saving is viewed as a holistic approach from the perspective of Islam, which is shaped by religious and ethical values as well as socioeconomic factors. Thus, this conceptual paper emerges to examine the four determinants of choosing Islamic personal saving for retirement which are religious obligation, Islamic financial literacy, motivation and financial inclusion. Additionally, this paper highlights the role of Maqasid al-Shariah in fostering responsible saving behavior and enhancing financial well-being. This contributes to the significance of structured personal

It is overcoming regulatory challenge and collaboration between the stakeholders which is important, and its done using digital technology such as blockchain and fintech that are enhancing efficiency and accessibility.

Strategic alliances are essential for attaining sustainability by promoting collaboration across enterprises to tackle shared difficulties and accomplish mutual objectives of Islamic organization. The evolution of strategic alliance is influenced by the communication with facilitating effective of operation and have good governance and accountability. The accountability helps build trust and commitment by eliminating the like hood of opportunism among partners. Due to lack of fund mobilization, BMT needs support from BAZNAS. On the other hand, BMT are still lack of accountability. This study aims to examine the extent of Zakat, Infak and Sadaqah disclosure-Baitul Maal in Baitul Maal Wat Tamwil Institution (BMTI) located in Indonesia. The results show that the level of disclosure of Baitul Maal in Indonesia is at low level. This study expects BMTI to certify the good governance in Baitul Maal activities that would attract the Baznas who have to support and provide funding to ensure the effectiveness of BMTIs in facing of crisis.

Islamic social finance plays a key role in promoting ethical wealth distribution and financial inclusion. Rooted in Maqasid al-Shariah, it aligns with Sustainable Development Goals (SDGs) and Environmental, Social, and Governance (ESG) principles. This study explores how zakat, waqf, sadaqah, qard al-hasan, sukuk sosial, and takaful contribute to poverty reduction, education, and economic growth. Despite its potential, challenges include inefficiencies in fund distribution and regulatory fragmentation. Leveraging fintech innovations, corporate waqf models, and standardized governance can enhance its impact. Case studies from Malaysia, UAE, and Sudan demonstrate successful implementations. Policy recommendations include harmonized regulations, ESG-based sukuk, and fintech integration. This research provides insights for policymakers and financial institutions to strengthen Islamic social finance for sustainable development.

Islamic micro finance has a high potential in advancing financial inclusion and social inclusion in Indonesia, especially for the poor. While this has potential, there remain obstacles: low levels of Islamic financial literacy, a lack of institutional penetration, and poor systems of Sharia supervision. This book chapter fills the research gap by discussing the four major issues namely the role of MFIs in social welfare, problems in community empowerment, the sustainability of Sharia implementation, and the contribution of MFIs in reducing poverty and inequality. The results underline that MFIs can be used as actuators of social, value-based financing, financial education and the use of social funds. The contribution of this chapter to academia is that it links Islamic economic theory with sustainable development strategies and provides practical suggestions regarding how to strengthen MFIs. It is original in the sense of being written in a post-Covid-19 world and drawing on both normative and empirical considerations in order to evaluate the true social value of Islamic microfinance at the grassroots.

Preface

INTRODUCTION

In recent decades, sustainability has shifted from a peripheral conversation to a non-negotiable strategic priority within global policy, finance, governance, and socio-economic development structures. Islamic finance — with its normative ethics, real economy orientation, and risk-sharing foundations — possesses unique potential to advance sustainability that is principled, impactful, and socially embedded. Yet, the global literature still lacks a consolidated, multi-dimensional and deeply integrative treatment of Islamic finance and sustainability across all core layers of instruments, institutional forms, behavioural drivers, risk governance architecture, modern digital finance, ESG alignment and SDG execution. That is the epistemic gap this volume was designed to close.

Synergizing Islamic Finance for Sustainability is therefore intentionally constructed as an edited reference volume that does not merely describe concepts — but operationalizes pathways, maps empirical evidence, observes implementation challenges, and shows how value-based ethics in Islam directly informs real world frameworks of sustainability, social finance, and financial well-being. Islamic finance cannot remain only theoretically righteous — it must become practically transformational. Contributors in this volume — both senior and emerging scholars — were selected specifically because they engage that exact translation from theory → instruments → socio-economic impact.

This book is also foundationally forward-looking. It assumes the world of finance is entering a structural transition — driven by digitalization, planetary boundary risk, demographic ageing, the rise of impact driven governance, emergent AI markets, and resilience planning post-pandemic. Islamic finance is strategically positioned to lead a new normative global sustainable finance paradigm — if its theoretical strengths are re-mobilized into new design, new research, and new institutions. This book is meant to accelerate that transition.

CHAPTER OVERVIEW

- **Chapter 1** establishes the philosophical foundations and contemporary realities of Islamic green finance, clarifying obstacles and proposing policy roadmaps.
- **Chapter 2** examines digital waqf integration through e-wallet innovation for TVET R&D funding — a future growth space with national competitiveness implications.
- **Chapter 3** develops and validates an Islamic Financial Literacy construct aligned to Islamic epistemic domains and empirically grounded in Malaysia.
- **Chapter 4** provides the historical archeology of defence waqf, demonstrating how Islamic history operationalized institutional resilience and public goods.
- **Chapter 5** integrates Islamic financial literacy, social entrepreneurship and social finance as a tri-architecture for inclusive sustainable development.
- **Chapter 6** analyses Islamic digital financial literacy in navigating wealth ethics, behavioural risks, and digital stewardship in the 21st century.
- **Chapter 7** focuses on Islamic retirement strategies for special needs families — a deeply under-studied, high sensitivity policy domain.
- **Chapter 8** explores determinants of Islamic personal saving for retirement grounded in *Maqasid al-Shariah.*
- **Chapter 9** interrogates e-wallet usage, detrimental consumption behaviour and financial well-being through a *Maqasid al-Shariah* analytical prism.
- **Chapter 10** synergizes Islamic finance and Islamic social finance as dual sustainable architecture for SDG compliance.
- **Chapter 11** evaluates accountability and disclosure in Baitul Maal and Baznas strategic alliances for sustainable resource mobilization.
- **Chapter 12** aligns Islamic social finance instruments with *Maqasid al-Shariah* and ESG convergence through policy and fintech pathways.
- **Chapter 13** investigates Islamic microfinance impact in Indonesia as a post-pandemic poverty alleviation and empowerment mechanism.

CONCLUSION

As editors, we view this book as a milestone in strategically advancing the next generation of Islamic finance scholarship — scholarship that is no longer siloed or reactive — but integrative, policy-relevant, behaviourally informed and institutionally reformative. This volume animates the fact that Islamic finance is not only a financial system — it is a moral architecture for social flourishing and planetary equilibrium. Sustainability must not be an imported overlay to Islamic finance — it is already embedded in its ethical DNA.

We therefore hope this book becomes a reference anchor for researchers, regulators, Shariah scholars, policymakers, institutions, graduate students and practitioners across the OIC and beyond — as a scaffold for ideation, model building, curriculum renewal, market innovation and new impact investment theses. It is our duty to continue expanding Islamic finance into areas that have been systematically neglected: ageing society structures, disability care, education tech, national defence, digital behavioural science, resilience portfolios, climate transition financing, non-bank social finance institutions, and transnational alliance governance.

Finally, this book is also a call for collective leadership. Islamic finance cannot wait to be invited into global sustainability frameworks — it must assert itself inside them, shape them, and elevate them. This book is the beginning of that future-oriented assertion. May Allah grant acceptance, benefit, wisdom, clarity, and *istiqamah.* And may this volume be a *khayr* instrument for scholars, industry and society for decades ahead.

Muhammad Ridhwan Ab. Aziz
Universiti Sains Islam Malaysia, Malaysia

Ahmad Rafiki
Universitas Medan Area, Indonesia

Fuadah Johari
Universiti Sains Islam Malaysia, Malaysia

Chapter 1
Bridging Faith and Sustainability:
Navigating the Challenges of Islamic Green Finance

Muhamad Azhari Wahid
https://orcid.org/0000-0002-9984-9412
Universiti Sains Islam Malaysia, Malaysia

ABSTRACT

As resource depletion, climate change, and environmental degradation worsen, the global quest of sustainable development has become essential. Sustainability is now at the forefront of international policy thanks to the United Nations' 2030 Agenda for Sustainable Development and the Paris Agreement under the United Nations Framework Convention on Climate Change (UNFCCC), which calls for creative and inclusive financial solutions to solve urgent ecological and social issues (UNDP, 2022). By critically analysing the potential and difficulties present in Islamic green finance, this chapter seeks to investigate the relationship between Islamic finance and environmental sustainability. It starts by discussing the foundations of Islamic green finance. The instruments of Islamic green finance are then discussed, followed by the opportunities and key challenges of Islamic green finance. The chapter will also discussed important achievements of Islamic green finance before ends it with policy recommendations for strengthening the role of Islamic finance in promoting a green finance.

DOI: 10.4018/979-8-3373-1842-4.ch001

INTRODUCTION

As resource depletion, climate change, and environmental degradation worsen, the global quest for sustainable development has become essential. Sustainability is now at the forefront of international policy, thanks to the United Nations' 2030 Agenda for Sustainable Development and the Paris Agreement under the United Nations Framework Convention on Climate Change (UNFCCC), which calls for creative and inclusive financial solutions to solve urgent ecological and social issues (UNDP, 2022). As a result, both developed and developing economies have seen a significant increase in green finance initiatives. The term 'green finance' can be defined as financial investments going into environmental products, sustainable development projects and initiatives, and policies that support the growth of a more sustainable economy (OECD, 2020).

In the midst of this worldwide trend, Islamic finance provides a distinctive and morally sound substitute that is inherently consistent with sustainable development goals. Islamic finance, which has its roots in Shariah, places a strong emphasis on economic equity, social justice, and environmental stewardship which are values that are closely aligned with sustainability objectives (Kamali, 2010; Laldin & Furqani, 2013). Together with the moral requirement of *maslahah* (public interest), the fundamental principles of Islamic finance such as the prohibition of interest (*riba*), the avoidance of excessive uncertainty (*gharar*), and the encouragement of risk-sharing could provide a strong ethical and legal foundation for the advancement of sustainable financial practices.

The emergence of Islamic green finance can be evidenced by the application of Islamic financial instruments and products to fund environmentally beneficial projects which has shown increasing interest in recent years. Initiatives such as green sukuk issuance, sustainable *waqf* (endowments), and Islamic ESG (environmental, social, and governance) funds signify a growing recognition of the compatibility between Islamic finance and environmental sustainability. Notably, countries like Malaysia and Indonesia have led the issuance of green *sukuk*, showcasing the potential of Shariah-compliant financial tools to mobilise capital for climate-related investments (Securities Commission Malaysia, 2017; Ministry of Finance Indonesia, 2022).

Notwithstanding its potential, Islamic green financing is underdeveloped in its wider acceptance and efficacy. This situation is due to a number of conceptual, legal, operational, and market-related issues. Other than that, the situation is worsen due to inadequate green taxonomies that are in line with both Islamic principles and international environmental standards, a lack of standardised Shariah interpretations of environmental sustainability, and a lack of technical capability within Islamic financial institutions (Adewale, 2022).

By critically analysing the potential and difficulties present in Islamic green finance, this chapter seeks to investigate the relationship between Islamic finance and environmental sustainability. It starts by discussing the foundations of Islamic green finance. The instruments of Islamic green finance are then discussed, followed by the opportunities and key challenges of Islamic green finance. The chapter will also discussed important achievements of Islamic green finance before ends it with policy recommendations for strengthening the role of Islamic finance in promoting a green finance.

By doing this, the chapter aims to close the gap between traditional Islamic rules and modern environmental imperatives, and it adds to the continuing conversation on faith-based approaches to sustainability. Islamic green finance may be better positioned to contribute significantly to the global sustainability goal by negotiating the complexity of this relationship.

FOUNDATIONS OF ISLAMIC GREEN FINANCE

The legal, ethical, and spiritual tenets of Islam are the fundamental ground of Islamic green finance. These pillars offer a framework for comprehending how financial operations might support wider moral and environmental obligations in addition to economic goals. It is not a new approach to combine Islamic finance with environmental sustainability; rather, it is a rediscovering of the Islamic worldview where the environment is viewed as a trust (*amanah*) and people as stewards (*khalifah*) of the planet.

Islamic Finance: Principles and Objectives

The ethical and legal tenets of Shariah drawn from the main sources of Islam which are the al-Qur'an, al-Sunnah, *ijmā* (consensus), and *qiyās* (analogical reasoning). These form the foundation of Islamic banking and finance industry. To ensure that all economic operations respect justice, transparency, and serve the public interest, it establishes what is permissible (*halal*) and forbidden (*haram*) in financial transactions. In contrast to conventional finance, which primarily uses interest-based methods, Islamic finance forbids *riba* (usury or interest), *gharar* (extreme uncertainty), and *maysir* (gambling or speculation). It also prohibits participation in non-Shari'ah compliance industries such as alcohol, tobacco, guns, and traditional financial derivatives that are considered detrimental or immoral.

Rather, Islamic banking advocates for a different ethical framework founded on contracts like sale-based contracts (e.g. *murabahah*), profit-sharing (*mudarabah* and *musharakah*), and *ijarah* (lease). These contracts form the foundation of Shariah-compliant products and financial instruments that reflect actual economic activity (El-Gamal, 2006; Ayub, 2007). With this framework, financial stability is enhanced, and speculative behaviour is curbed by the focus on tying money to material assets and real economic activities. This is due to the fact that Islamic banking and finance promote prudent resource usage, long-term value development, and fair wealth distribution. More importantly, these principles naturally connect with the aims of sustainable finance.

Islamic finance's foundational theory is further supported by the *maqā id al-sharī ah*, or higher purposes of Islamic law. The *maqā id al-sharī ah* seeks to uphold and safeguard the five fundamental components of religion (*ad-dīn*), life (*nafs*), intellect (*'aql*), lineage (*nasl*), and property (*māl*). These goals provide Islamic economic theory with its moral compass and provide the standardize framework for evaluating Islamic financial operations (Chapra, 2008; Dusuki & Abdullah, 2007).

In order to acknowledge the natural environment as a resource that Allah has entrusted to mankind (*khalifah*), modern academics have advocated for the extension of the *maqā id* framework to include environmental stewardship and intergenerational justice (Auda, 2008; Laldin & Furqani, 2013). Environmental protection's incorporation in the larger framework of *maslahah 'āmmah* (public interest) demonstrates how Islamic rules is flexible and adaptable when it comes to tackling new global issues. Because it promotes financial activities that lessen environmental harm, facilitate sustainability transitions, and foster climate resilience in line with Islamic teachings, this interpretation gives Islamic green finance a solid theological and ethical foundation.

Therefore, Islamic finance is a moral economy that strives for socioeconomic fairness, ecological balance, and spiritual welfare rather than just a collection of financial prohibitions or technical contracts. It offers a thorough ethical framework that may support international sustainability goals, such as the Sustainable Development Goals (SDGs) of the UN, especially those pertaining to clean energy, climate action, and responsible production and consumption (UNDP & IsDB, 2019).

Ethical and Theological Concepts Relevant to Sustainability

Several ethical and theological concepts in Islam offer a normative basis for environmental responsibility:

First is the concept of *khalīfah*. The concept of *khalīfah* (vicegerency or stewardship) is foundational in Islamic environmental ethics. In Surah al-Baqarah (2:30), Allah declares:

"Indeed, I will make upon the earth a khalifah (vicegerent)" (Al-Quran; 2:30)

The idea that humans are vicegerents on Earth suggests that there is a divine duty for us to manage natural resources in a just, moral, and responsible manner.

The ultimate Owner, Allah (*al-Mālik*), has given humans authority as trustees, not as absolute proprietors of the planet. Humans must act as stewards to preserve the ecological integrity of the planet, use resources sensibly, and refrain from exploitation that causes deterioration. Kamali (2010) asserts that *khalīfah* establishes a moral duty to protect the planet for present and future generations by signifying both power and accountability.

The goals of Islamic green finance, which aims to raise money for investments that are ecologically conscious and fulfil the obligation of stewardship, are in line with this religious tenet. Second is the concept of *amānah* (trust). The Quran states:

> *"Indeed, We offered the trust (amānah) to the heavens and the earth and the mountains, and they declined to bear it and feared it, but man undertook to bear it. Indeed, he was unjust and ignorant." (Al-Quran; 33:72)*

The vastness of the *amānah* refers to the need to obey divine commands, which include the prudent management of natural resources is poetically depicted in this passage. Accepting this confidence represents both the possibility of betrayal and abuse as well as the moral ability and duty of humans.

Amānah, as it relates to the environment, suggests that biodiversity, ecosystems, water, and air are all divine trusts rather than resources to be used for uncontrollable financial gain. A breach of this trust occurs when these resources are mismanaged. This ethical obligation must thus be reflected in the design of financial goods and investments, which is the justification for the development of Shariah-compliant green financial instruments like green *sukuk*.

The third concept is *mīzān* (balance). The Quran emphasizes the concept of balance and harmony in Surah al-Rahman:

> *"And the heaven He raised and imposed the balance (mīzān), that you not transgress within the balance. And establish weight in justice and do not make deficienct the balance." (Surah al-Rahman: 7-9)*

This verse emphasises a deep cosmic and ecological order that Allah created. Each element of nature was made with a specific function and in a measured proportion. Degradation of the ecosystem, climate change, and social injustice result from the disruption of this equilibrium, whether through pollution, excessive consumption, or deforestation.

Maintaining *mīzān* reflects a believer's knowledge of divine wisdom in creation and is not just an environmental obligation but also a spiritual practice. This Qur'anic requirement is in conflict with financial strategies that encourage unbridled consumerism or disregard environmental constraints. Therefore, investments in sustainable agriculture, renewable energy, and green infrastructure, all of which contribute to environmental balance, should be given top priority in Islamic green financing.

The Quran repeatedly warns against *fasad* (corruption), especially when in results in environmental damage. In al-Quran, Allah mentioned:

"Do not cause corruption on the earth after it has been set in order. And call upon Him in fear and aspiration. Indeed, the mercy of Allah is near to the doers of good" (Surah al-A'raf: 56).

Fasad includes all types of environmental, social, moral, and financial deterioration. According to modern academics, it encompasses deforestation, industrial pollution, biodiversity loss, and climate change, especially when these consequences are brought on by greediness and unfair business practices (Abu-Sway, 1998). *Islah*, on the other hand, means restoration, renewal, and reform. It involves taking proactive steps to mend damage, restore natural systems, and advance ecological and social justice. *Islah* therefore emerges as a major theological driver of sustainability. By supporting initiatives that restore ecosystems, lower carbon footprints, and increase climate resilience, Islamic green finance actively promotes good (*maslahah*) rather than just avoiding damage (*darar*).

These moral and theological precepts offer a strong religious mandate for environmental preservation, establishing Islamic finance as a transformation tool for ecological stewardship as well as a legally compliant economic structure. As a result, including these principles within the framework of Islamic green finance guarantees both adherence to Shariah and applicability to current ecological issues.

Maqasid al-Shari'ah and the Sustainable Development Goals (SDGs)

The *maqasid al-Shari'ah* framework has gained prominence in recent years as a tool for aligning Islamic financial practices with global development agendas. The values embedded in *maqasid*, which are to preserve and promote human well-being (*maslahah*), echoed with the 17 Sustainable Development Goals (SDGs) established by the United Nations (UN) in 2015.

For instance, several SDGs such as SDG 1 (No Poverty), SDG 2 (Zero Hunger), SDG 3 (Good Health and Well-Being), SDG 6 (Clean Water and Sanitation) are aligned with the objective of *hifz al-Nafs* (preservation of life). Similarly, SDG 4 (Quality Education) is aligned to the objective of *hifz al-'Aql* (preservation of intellect). While SDG 1 (No Poverty), SDG 7 (Affordable and Clean Energy), SDG 8 (Decent Work and Economic Growth), SDG 9 (Industry, Innovation and Infrastructure), SDG 10 (Reduced Inequality), SDG 11 (Sustainable Cities and Communities), SDG 12 (Responsible Consumption and Production) and SDG 13 (Climate Action) are aligned with the objective of *hifz al-Mal* (preservation of wealth).

As such, Islamic green finance can serve as a means of actualising the *maqasid al-Shari'ah* in contemporary socioeconomic contexts (Dusuki & Abozaid, 2007; Asutay, 2012). By embedding sustainability into the *maqasid al-Shari'ah* framework, Islamic finance moves beyond mere compliance and becomes a value-based system capable of promoting long-term ecological and social well-being. This convergence is not only theologically sound but also strategically necessary, especially as Muslim-majority countries face increasing exposure to climate-related risks.

THE INSTRUMENTS OF ISLAMIC GREEN FINANCE

The purpose of Islamic green finance instruments is to direct Shariah-compliant funds towards environmentally beneficial initiatives. The main tools that are being developed or currently offered by Islamic finance as Figure 1:

Figure 1. Islamic green finance instruments

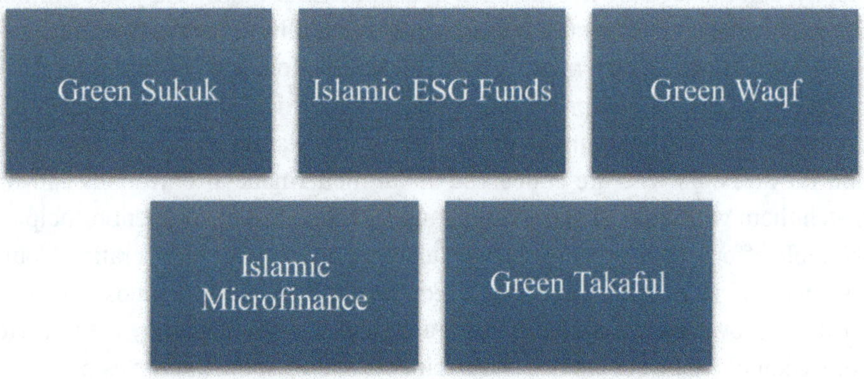

Green Sukuk

Shariah-compliant investment certificates known as "green sukuk" are used to fund ecologically friendly initiatives including waste management, clean transport, renewable energy, and climate-resilient infrastructure. Sukuk's asset-based or asset-backed form makes it ideal for green initiatives as it guarantees a clear connection between the funding and actual economic activity.

Several examples of green sukuk that have been successfully issued in the market are Tadau Green Sukuk (Securities Commission Malaysia, 2017) which is one example of solar energy infrastructure, sovereign Green Sukuk (Ministry of Finance Indonesia, 2022) which finance initiatives related to climate adaptation and mitigation, and Quantum Solar Park (Semenanjung) Sdn Bhd, and PNB Merdeka

Ventures Sdn Bhd (Securities Commission Malaysia, 2017) which aligned with SDG goals to achieve environmental objectives.

Islamic ESG Funds

Shariah-compliant investing and ESG-based investment screening are two morally compatible investment concepts that have come together to form Islamic ESG funds. These funds are made to satisfy sustainability and religious requirements, providing investors with portfolios devoid of items that are prohibited by Islamic law while also encouraging social responsibility, environmental care, and good governance (IFSB, 2020).

Fundamentally, prohibited businesses including those engaged in alcohol production, gambling, traditional banking and insurance, weapons manufacturing, pornography, and tobacco are not included in Islamic ESG funds. They also eliminate companies that have detrimental environmental externalities, such as those engaged in high-carbon industries, coal mining, fossil fuel extraction, and deforestation (GSIA, 2021; IFSB, 2020). By improving the moral and ethical integrity of investment portfolios, this dual-screening procedure positions Islamic ESG funds as a viable option for investors who are concerned about their financial objectives and want to match them with both Shariah values and sustainable development principles.

Notable efforts have been made by Malaysia and the Gulf Cooperation Council (GCC) nations to expand this specialised market. ESG-linked funds and instruments have grown thanks to regulatory frameworks implemented by the Securities Commission of Malaysia under the Sustainable and Responsible Investment (SRI) Sukuk Framework and SRI Roadmap for the Capital Market (Securities Commission Malaysia, 2017). Shariah screening and ESG performance indicators are combined in a number of Islamic ESG equities funds and exchange-traded funds (ETFs) that Malaysia has introduced, including the Principal Islamic ESG Fund and TradePlus Shariah Gold Tracker.

Similar to this, fund managers in Bahrain, the United Arab Emirates, and Saudi Arabia have launched Shariah-compliant ESG funds aimed at both institutional and individual investors in the GCC. One example is the Emirates NBD Asset Management Islamic Global ESG Equity Fund, which filters stocks using both worldwide ESG benchmarks like the MSCI ESG Ratings and Shariah principles that are compliant with the AAOIFI (IFSB, 2020).

Islamic ESG funds represent an important frontier in the ethical investment landscape, bringing together the moral imperatives of Islam with the global sustainability agenda. While the market is still nascent and faces definition and structural challenges, the integration of Shariah and ESG principles offers a robust framework for promoting inclusive, responsible, and environmentally sustainable finance. With proper regulatory support, institutional innovation, and scholarly engagement, Islamic ESG funds can play a transformative role in the transition toward a more just and sustainable global financial system.

Green Waqf (Endowment Funds)

Waqf has long been a cornerstone of Islamic social welfare, sustaining infrastructure, schools, hospitals, and mosques. It is typically characterised as a charitable endowment in perpetuity (*abs al-mal*) (Kahf, 2003). The modern term "green *waqf*" describes how this traditional organisation has been redesigned to support sustainability and environmental objectives, bringing Islamic social financing into line with the Sustainable Development Goals (SDGs) of the UN.

Devoting land, money, or assets that provide income to ecologically beneficial endeavours such as reforestation, climate-smart agriculture, waste management, clean water supply, and the development of renewable energy is known as green waqf (Shaikh, 2020; Hassan et al., 2022). The ethical precepts of *khilāfah* (stewardship), *amānah* (trust), and *ma la ah* (public interest), which are central to Islamic economic theory, are reflected in this contemporary application.

Although they are still in the experimental or pilot stages in many jurisdictions, workable models of green *waqf* have started to appear. *Waqf* property designated for urban farming and renewable energy projects are noteworthy instances. Pilot projects have converted underutilised *waqf* land into profitable, climate-resilient assets in nations like Malaysia and Indonesia by installing solar panels, vertical farming, and agroforestry (Yaacob et al., 2021).

Another contemporary kind of *waqf* is the cash *waqf* associated with green investment instruments, which pools endowments into sukuk or green funds and uses the investment profits to fund conservation initiatives, eco-education initiatives, or environmental non-governmental organisations. For instance, SRI-compliant sukuk can be purchased using green cash *waqf*, and the proceeds can be utilised to support the preservation of biodiversity hotspots or water filtration systems in rural regions (Hassan et al., 2022). These developments show how *waqf* has changed from a static philanthropy model to a dynamic, impact-driven financial tool that combines intergenerational equity, sustainability principles, and Shariah compliance.

Islamic Microfinance for Environmental Objectives

As part of their dual purpose to advance social justice and financial inclusion, Islamic microfinance institutions (IMFIs) are progressively adopting environmental sustainability. IMFIs have historically worked to reduce poverty by giving underprivileged groups small-scale, Shariah-compliant loans. However, they are now changing to include green goals, providing financial products that help low-income and rural communities lead environmentally sustainable lives (Obaidullah & Khan, 2008; UNESCAP, 2020a).

Green microfinance products have been introduced by several IMFIs to assist customers in implementing environmentally friendly practices and technology. In off-grid rural areas, these include funding for solar home systems that will replace diesel generators and kerosene lamps; sustainable farming inputs like drip irrigation, organic fertilisers, and drought-resistant seeds; and environmentally friendly equipment like clean cookstoves, composting toilets, and energy-efficient machinery for small-scale producers. These kinds of initiatives empower disadvantaged communities via economic resilience while also immediately advancing SDGs 7 (Affordable and Clean Energy), 12 (Responsible Consumption and Production), and 13 (Climate Action).

Contracts like *murāba ah* (cost-plus financing), *ijarah* (lease), and *qard al- asan* (benevolent loan) are commonly used in green Islamic microfinance because they may be modified for environmentally friendly usage. The following real-world examples highlight the increasing importance of green IMFIs:

- Baitul Maal wa Tamwil (BMT) cooperatives in Indonesia have funded biogas digesters and solar-powered irrigation systems for smallholder farmers (UNESCAP, 2020b).
- Islami Bank Bangladesh Limited's (IBBL) Islamic microfinance division has assisted rural households in Bangladesh with the switch to clean water and solar energy technology.
- In Sudan, *qard al- asan* and *zakat* monies have been utilised in conjunction with Islamic microfinance to promote climate-resilient agriculture in regions that are prone to drought (Obaidullah & Khan, 2008).

These initiatives not only show that green aims and Islamic finance can coexist, but they also highlight the importance of IMFIs in advancing *maqā id al-sharī ah*, particularly the protection of wealth (*if al-māl*), life (*if al-nafs*), and the environment (*if al-bi ah*).

Green Takaful (Islamic Insurance)

Although still in its infancy, green takaful holds considerable promise in supporting climate adaptation and resilience, particularly in vulnerable Muslim-majority countries. Takaful, rooted in the principles of *ta'āwun* (mutual assistance) and *tabarru'* (donation), offers a Shariah-compliant alternative to conventional insurance.

Several products can be offered under green takaful initiatives as stated in Figure 2.

Figure 2. Green takaful products

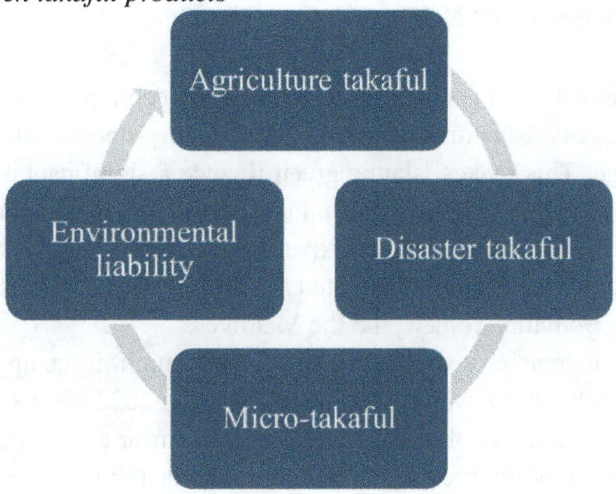

Agricultural takaful can be offered to smallholder farmers and provide protection against crop loss due to droughts, floods, or pest outbreaks. These are among crucial risks that are intensifying due to climate change. The proposed agricultural takaful is particularly relevant for countries like Sudan, Pakistan, and Bangladesh, where agriculture is highly climate-sensitive (IFSB, 2020).

In addition, disaster takaful schemes can also be introduced by takaful operators. Disaster takaful could provide payouts to communities who are affected by natural catastrophes, such as cyclones or landslides. The disaster takaful initiative would facilitate faster recovery and reducing dependency of affected communities on government aid.

Micro-takaful that is linked to renewable energy technologies (e.g., solar panel installations or biogas units) can offer protection against asset damage or technical failure. Takaful coverage on renewable energy technologies would encourage wider adoption of clean technologies in rural or underserved areas (Obaidullah, 2021).

Lastly is the takaful for environmental liability. This type of takaful coverage may cover firms or projects involved in green infrastructure or industrial transitions by offering protection for compliance failures, environmental accidents, or pollution clean-up. This proposed coverage is aligned with rising ESG expectations and regulatory scrutiny.

Such offerings not only provide climate resilience but also embody the *maqā id al-Sharī'ah*, particularly in preservation of life (*if al-nafs*), preservation of wealth (*if al-māl*), and the preservation of environment (*if al-bi'ah*).

OPPORTUNITIES AND BENEFITS OF ISLAMIC GREEN FINANCE

Due to a combination of geographic exposure, socioeconomic fragility, and limited adaptive capacity, Muslim-majority nations are disproportionately vulnerable to climate change. This makes Islamic green finance a significant opportunity to mobilise capital for environmentally sustainable development. Serious challenges include rising sea levels, harsh weather, expanded droughts, water scarcity, and ecosystem degradation for nations that affected Muslim countries such as Bangladesh, Pakistan, Sudan, Somalia, Yemen, and the Maldives.

For example, increasing sea levels in Bangladesh might force up to 30 million people to relocate by 2050, while floods in Pakistan in 2022 displaced 33 million people and caused damages of over USD 30 billion (Ansar et al., 2022).

The economic stability, food security, and public health of these countries are all significantly impacted by these climatic risks. Their ability to adjust to climatic stress is further hampered by the political unrest and violence that many of these nations face, take for example, Somalia and Yemen. To promote social welfare and environmental sustainability, it is becoming increasingly important to integrate climate resilience into development and financial systems, especially through Islamic finance mechanisms, since most of these populations are highly dependent on climate-sensitive industries like agriculture and fisheries.

In addition to providing a religious and ethical justification for green finance, the intersection of Islamic finance principles with sustainability objectives presents a calculated approach to funding climate mitigation, adaptation, and the Sustainable Development Goals (SDGs).

Mobilising Ethical Capital for Climate Action

Over the last 20 years, the Islamic finance sector has experienced significant expansion, with its estimated worldwide assets of USD 4.5 trillion as of 2023 and anticipated to reach USD 6.7 trillion by 2027 (ICD - LSEG, 2023). This scale has enormous possibilities for mobilising green financing, especially through Islamic social finance (e.g., *zakat* and *waqf*), takaful, Islamic banks, and sukuk.

However, there is still a substantial climate funding deficit. By 2030, developing nations would require around USD 340 billion yearly for adaptation, according to the United Nations Environment Programme (UNEP). Unfortunately, present adaptation financing flows only amount to USD 21 billion annually (UNEP, 2023). By providing tools in line with religious principles, Islamic green finance can bridge this divide, particularly in OIC (Organisation of Islamic Cooperation) member nations.

This potential is demonstrated by the green sukuk market. As of the end of 2023, the total amount of green and sustainability-linked sukuk issued globally since the initial issue in 2017 was USD 30.6 billion, with the UAE, Saudi Arabia, Indonesia, and Malaysia leading the market (ICMA, 2024;). This suggests that investors are becoming more interested in financial products that satisfy sustainability and Shariah requirements.

Financial Inclusion and Support for Climate-Vulnerable Communities

According to World Bank estimates, around 1.7 billion people worldwide do not have access to banking services. Majority of these groups of people live in Muslim-majority areas of South and Southeast Asia, the Middle East, and Sub-Saharan Africa (Ansar et al., 2022). Islamic finance may improve climate resilience and financial inclusion that affecting this low-income group of people through Islamic social financing tools which nomally offered by Islamic microfinance institutions (IMFIs).

When IMFIs incorporate green goals, they can offer people access to environmentally friendly technology like clean cookstoves and solar lights. This would encourage livelihood of low-income group of people in response to climate-related shocks such as floods or drought. In addition, IMFIs could also provide funding for climate-resilient agriculture, which includes drought-resistant crops and sustainable irrigation systems. One example of this initiative has been taken by Islami Bank in Bangladesh, which has introduced green *qard al-hasan* goods for solar irrigation pumps, cutting carbon emissions and reliance on diesel (Afroz, 2017).

Enhancing Islamic Social Finance for Sustainable Development

Islamic social finance, which includes *sadaqah*, *waqf*, and *zakat*, is a relatively unexplored tool for tackling poverty. In addition to tackling poverty, these tools can be used to achieve the sustainability agenda. The OIC nations' yearly zakat potential is projected to be between $200 and $300 billion, but less than 20% of that amount is collected and used (IsDB, 2021). Such an immense potential but left unexplored.

Green *waqf* projects can allocate funds to several development of renewable infrastructure such as solar panel and hydroelectric, and preservation of enviroment. For instance, pilot projects in Indonesia have explored *waqf* models for reforestation and carbon offsetting, while Malaysia's Yayasan Waqaf Malaysia has collaborated with regional organisations to create solar-powered *waqf* properties (BWI, 2022).

Supporting the Transition to a Circular and Green Economy

Islamic finance has significant role to support the transition to circular and green economy. This is in line with both environmental sustainability and Islamic teachings. A circular economy refers to economic system which aimed at minimizing waste and maximizing the efficient utilization of resources. This can be observed through the principles of reuse, recycling, regeneration and responsible consumption. Green start-ups in waste management and production of compostable and sustainable packaging are among business lines that Islamic finance could finance.

KEY CHALLENGES IN ISLAMIC GREEN FINANCE

Despite its immense potential, several interrelated problems are impeding the expansion of Islamic green financing. These problems are both structural and operational in nature, and they include conceptual ambiguities, legislative fragmentation, institutional capacity limitations, and market-related restraints. Understanding these challenges is essential to creating targeted strategies to boost Islamic green finance's effectiveness in advancing sustainable development.

Conceptual and Theological Challenges

Lack of a Unified Shariah Perspective on Environmental Sustainability

The lack of a thorough and cohesive Shariah framework that specifically incorporates environmental preservation into financial decisions is one of the most basic issues facing Islamic green finance. Although Islamic law offers moral underpinnings for trust (*amanah*), stewardship (*khalifah*), and the prohibition of damage (*la darara wa la dirar*), their actual implementation in green finance is still in its infancy and varies from jurisdiction to jurisdiction (Kamali, 2010; Laldin & Furqani, 2013). According to a joint report issued by UNDP and ISRA, inconsistent fatwas and interpretations of what constitutes “green” or “sustainable” under Shariah are the consequence of many Shariah boards' ignorance of sustainability principles or lack of access to environmental experts, knowledge and exposure. (2021), Islamic Finance and the S

Insufficient Fiqh Discourse on Environmental Jurisprudence

The topic of Islamic environmental jurisprudence, or *fiqh al-bi'ah*, is still in its infancy within the larger context of Islamic legal studies. Islamic teachings on stewardship (*khilāfah*), trust (*amānah*), and the prohibition of harm (*lā arar wa lā irār*) are rich, but they have not been formally formalised into codified standards, structured legal opinions (*fatāwā*), or applied jurisprudence for contemporary environmental and climate-related issues (Hasan & Ebrahim, 2020b; Dinar, 2019). The proactive involvement of Islamic financial institutions in green sectors, especially in areas involving innovative instruments like carbon trading, climate-linked sukuk, renewable energy investment, and biodiversity credits, is hampered by the substantial jurisprudential gap created by this underdevelopment.

Although Islamic economics and Shariah scholars are becoming more conscious of the importance of environmental ethics, institutional frameworks for *ijtihād*, or independent legal reasoning, in environmental issues are still lacking or disjointed. Regarding the permissibility of climate financing instruments, there is no agreement or defined framework, in contrast to more established fields of Islamic finance like *murāba ah* or *takāful*. Carbon credits, for example, have generated discussions on whether trading them is against the ban on *bay' al-mā'dūm* (selling what is not yet in existence) or if it is an example of *gharar* (extreme ambiguity) (Asutay & Harningtyas, 2015). Likewise, concerns regarding asset-backing, Shariah screening, or the social impact standards necessary for compliance may be brought up by green bonds or SRI sukuk.

Regulatory hesitancy and reputational risk aversion among Islamic finance actors, particularly Shariah boards, who serve as crucial gatekeepers, are exacerbated by this jurisprudential uncertainty. Institutions frequently adopt a conservative approach, avoiding green innovation that lacks established jurisprudential precedent, when there are no authoritative fatwa collections or unified institutional positions from organisations like the AAOIFI, IFSB, or national Shariah councils (Hasan & Ebrahim, 2020a; Laldin & Furqani, 2013).

Additionally, environmental issues are marginalised in applied finance because they are frequently seen in Islamic legal discourse as subsidiary (*tābi'*) rather than main (*a lī*) concerns. Although the preservation of wealth (*if al-māl*) and life (*if al-nafs*) are recognised even within the framework of *maqā id al-Sharī'ah*, the preservation of the environment (*if al-bi'ah*) has not yet been formalised as an explicit legal goal in many Shariah governance documents or fatwa collections. The extent of *ijtihād* and the creation of practical instruments to assist Islamic financing have been constrained by this omission (Kamla, 2009).

Cross-disciplinary research that combines environmental science, financial innovation, *usul al-fiqh*, and *fiqh* is required to close this gap. To give practitioners more precise advice, Islamic legal and financial institutions must also make investments in fatwa harmonisation, capacity-building, and the creation of Shariah-based environmental standards. The Value-Based Intermediation (VBI) Framework in Malaysia, the SRI Sukuk Framework, the Maqasid al-Shariah Guidance Islamic Capital Market Malaysia, Bursa Carbon Exchange and early attempts by organisations like ISRA and the Islamic Development Bank to promote environmental jurisprudence through teaching and research are examples of promising projects in this field.

Operational and Technical Challenges

Lack of Standardised Green Taxonomies

Product development is hampered by the lack of an internationally accepted green taxonomy that complies with Islamic and environmental norms. While Bank Negara Malaysia's Climate Change and Principle-Based Taxonomy (CCPT) serves as a paradigm, other countries lack comparable frameworks (Bank Negara Malaysia, 2021a). As a result, it becomes more difficult to gauge effect, confirm compliance, and maintain investor trust. Although it is difficult to standardize green taxonomies, regulators and standard setting bodies could refer to Shariah principles as a guidance in harmonising taxonomies.

Inadequate Capacity and Expertise

The technical know-how to analyse climate risks, appraise green projects, and incorporate ESG considerations into credit evaluations and investment choices is lacking in many Islamic financial institutions (IFIs). Fewer Islamic financial institutions had the internal capability to use environmental screening criteria during project evaluation, and only small number of them had specialised sustainability teams. Furthermore, the majority of Shariah Board members have training in classical jurisprudence rather than environmental science or climate policy. This could hinder the creation of sophisticated fatwas and novel products.

Market and Awareness Challenges

Limited Demand and Public Awareness

Islamic green financial products continue to be a niche market within the larger Islamic finance sector, despite rising regional and worldwide awareness of sustainability and environmental stewardship. In areas with most Muslims, the adoption of products like sustainability-linked Islamic finance, ESG-compliant Islamic equities funds, and green sukuk remains low, particularly among small institutional players and retail investors.

A combination of market-driven, educational, and structural constraints has generated this low level of demand. To foster knowledge of green finance concepts within a Shariah-compliant framework, Islamic financial institutions and authorities have not consistently launched public awareness programs. The integration of environmental, social, and governance (ESG) criteria with Islamic principles like *maslahah* (public interest), *amanah* (trust), and *istislah* (public welfare) is therefore yet unknown to many Muslim investors.

Second, there are still few products available. A small number of nations, including Malaysia, Indonesia, and the Gulf Cooperation Council (GCC), are home to the majority of Islamic green finance services. Even in these marketplaces, Islamic green products like Islamic ESG ETFs, green takaful, and SRI sukuk are frequently only available to institutions or are sold in modest quantities. The Securities Commission's SRI Sukuk Framework, for instance, has made Malaysia a leader in SRI sukuk since 2015.

Third, green and ESG investment products are seen by many retail investors as complicated, having unpredictable returns, or being hard to get. It is made more difficult to communicate the value of these instruments by the absence of established ESG criteria in the Islamic finance system. Confusion or indifference may result from retail clients' failure to distinguish between generic Islamic financial solutions and those that are specifically green or sustainability-focused (Elasrag, 2020).

Additionally, there is a clear discrepancy between product design and investor values. While many Muslim investors show concern for sustainable development and environmental ethics, values that are deeply ingrained in Islamic teachings, they are presented with goods that prioritise financial success above adequate explanation of their effects on the environment or society. This imbalance restricts long-term capital mobilisation towards sustainability-oriented initiatives and deters wider market involvement.

Underdeveloped Green Investment Pipeline

A recurring operational constraint is the scarcity of bankable green projects that meet both Shariah and sustainability requirements. For instance, many Islamic banks have reported challenges in sourcing green infrastructure projects that are Shariah-compliant (e.g., free from interest-based financing), ESG-certified, and creditworthy for sukuk issuance or *murabahah* structuring. Demand for ESG-compliant investments is rising on a global scale. According to the Global Sustainable Investment Alliance, ESG assets surpassed USD 35 trillion in 2020 and are expected to reach USD 50 trillion by 2025 (GSIA, 2021). Even while Islamic ESG funds only make up a small share of this industry at the moment, they have a lot of potential, especially in nations that are members of the Organisation of Islamic Cooperation (OIC), where a sizable population finds ethical and faith-based financing appealing.

Despite growing interest, several structural and methodological challenges persist. One major issue is the lack of harmonised ESG metrics and reporting standards tailored for Islamic finance. While global ESG frameworks such as the Sustainability Accounting Standards Board (SASB), Global Reporting Initiative (GRI), and Task Force on Climate-related Financial Disclosures (TCFD) offer guidance, they are largely designed for conventional institutions and may not fully capture the *maqā id al-Sharī ah* (objectives of Shariah), such as justice ('adl), welfare (ma la ah), and environmental stewardship (*if al-bi'ah*) (Laldin & Furqani, 2013).

Moreover, current Shariah screening methodologies primarily focus on financial ratios (e.g., interest-based income thresholds, debt ratios) and sectoral exclusions, but do not systematically incorporate environmental or social criteria. There is a pressing need for the development of integrated Shariah–ESG screening tools, supported by bodies such as the Accounting and Auditing Organization for Islamic Financial Institutions (AAOIFI), the Islamic Financial Services Board (IFSB), and national Shariah advisory councils (AAOIFI, 2021).

To advance the Islamic ESG investment, stakeholders, including regulators, asset managers, and Shariah scholars, must collaborate to establish standardised guidelines, promote data transparency, and encourage capacity building among investors and financial institutions. Initiatives such as the Islamic Reporting Initiative (IRI) and Malaysia's Value-Based Intermediation (VBI) framework offer promising starting points for aligning Shariah compliance with ESG objectives (Securities Commission Malaysia, 2022a).

Furthermore, fintech innovations, such as blockchain-based ESG reporting tools and robo-advisory platforms with ethical filters, could help democratise access to Islamic ESG funds, particularly among millennial and Gen-Z investors who show increasing preference for values-driven finance.

IMPORTANT ACHIEVEMENTS IN ISLAMIC GREEN FINANCE

Despite the challenges outlined in the previous section, several countries and institutions have taken significant steps to operationalise Islamic green finance through policy initiatives, product innovation, and institutional collaboration. These case studies demonstrate how Islamic finance can be effectively mobilised to support environmental sustainability and the Sustainable Development Goals (SDGs), offering valuable lessons for broader replication across the Muslim world.

Malaysia: A Pioneer in Islamic Green Finance

Malaysia is widely recognised as a global leader in Islamic finance and has also positioned itself at the forefront of Islamic green finance. The country's regulatory, institutional, and market-based initiatives have enabled the successful integration of green initiatives and Islamic finance.

Among initiatives of Malaysia in developing green finance are through development of relevant framework and tax incentives, issuance of green sukuk, and issuance of climate change taxonomy. To facilitate and encourages issuance of sukuk for green initiatives, Malaysia through Securities Commission issued Sustainable and Responsible Investment (SRI) Sukuk Framework in 2014 (later on revised in 2022). Following the issuance of SRI Sukuk Framework, Malaysia successfully issued the world's first green sukuk through Tadau Energy in 2017. This sukuk issuance has successfully raised RM 250 million for the purpose of financing solar photovoltaic power plants. In addition, Malaysia introduced tax deduction on issuance costs for green sukuk until 2025 (Securities Commission Malaysia, 2022b).

Following the initiative by the Securities Commission of Malaysia, the Bank Negara Malaysia has issued Climate Change and Principle-Based Taxonomy (CCPT) in 2021. Among the aim of CCPT is to offers guidance to financial institutions on classification and reporting of climate-related exposures to support risk assessments at the institutions and systemic levels, strengthen accountability and market transparency, and encourage financial flows towards supporting climate objectives.

Indonesia: Advancing Sovereign and Retail Green Sukuk

Indonesia has also established itself as a global reference for sovereign green sukuk issuance. Since 2018, the government of Indonesia has actively utilized Islamic finance to support its national climate goals under the Nationally Determined Contributions (NDCs). This can be evidenced by its effort to be the first country to issue a Sovereign Green Sukuk (SDG Bonds) in 2018 and have successfully raised USD 1.25 billion for climate mitigation and adaptation. By the end of 2023, the total issuance of green sukuk exceeded USD 5 billion across multiple tranches (Ministry of Finance Indonesia, 2023).

In addition, Indonesian government have issued its first retail green sukuk, named Sukuk Tabungan. This is indeed a good initiative by Indonesian government to promote citizen participation in climate finance with the objective of overcoming climate change. According to the information released by Indonesian Ministry of Finance, the funds raised form Sukuk Tabungan will be utilized for environmentally friendly projects in two sectors, namely sustainable transportation and resilience to climate change. This is expected to mitigate the impact of climate change and adaptation to climate change effect.

United Arab Emirates: Institutionalising ESG in Islamic Finance

The UAE has embraced sustainability as part of its national economic vision and has begun mainstreaming ESG principles in Islamic finance. The UAE's experience highlights the importance of private sector leadership and corporate governance in scaling Islamic ESG-aligned investments.

Majid Al Futtaim Holding, the leading shopping mall, communities, retail and leisure pioneer across Middle East, Africa and Asia, is among the regional private sector leader in responsible financing. The company has successfully issued its first green sukuk in May 2019 valued amounting USD 600 million to finance green projects such as developing green buildings and reducing operational carbon emissions (Nasdaq Dubai, 2019). Since then, the company has successfully issued four green sukuk showing its leadership in ESG initiatives.

POLICY RECOMMENDATIONS AND STRATEGIC WAY FORWARD

To ensure the meaningful contribution of Islamic finance to sustainability and the global climate agenda, a set of comprehensive, multi-stakeholder strategies is required. These strategies must address structural constraints while leveraging the inherent values of Islamic finance, particularly its emphasis on ethics, justice, and stewardship (*khalifah*). The following recommendations are vital to the successfulness of Islamic green finance.

Harmonising Shariah and Sustainability Standards

There is an urgent need for standard-setting bodies such as AAOIFI and IFSB to issue comprehensive Shariah guidance notes or standards on environmental protection, climate risk, and sustainability-linked contracts. Such efforts should define what constitutes "green" from both Shariah and environmental perspectives. In addition, the guidance should integrate *maqasid al-Shariah* with the Sustainable Development Goals (SDGs). This is important to avoid activities which seem to contribute to SDGs but at the same time is not in compliance to the *maqasid al-Shariah.* Furthermore, a guideline that evaluating the permissibility of carbon trading, renewable energy financing, and environmental impact assessment tools should also be developed.

Enhancing Regulatory and Institutional Frameworks

Countries with Islamic finance sectors should formulate dedicated national roadmaps that align green finance objectives with Shariah principles. Malaysia's Value-based Intermediation (VBI) and Indonesia's Green Sukuk Framework offer exemplary templates. Among important elements that should be considered in the national roadmaps are target of penetration for green initiatives, green tax incentives, sustainable banking guidelines which are tailored to the requirements of IFI, and direction for public-private partnerships in green initiatives.

In addition, the climate risk should be considered as mainstream risk in prudential regulations. To achieve this, the central banks and relevant financial regulators should require IFIs to integrate climate-related financial disclosures in their annual integrated reporting or specific annual sustainable reporting. Furthermore, central banks should require IFIs to conduct climate stress tests and ESD due diligence processes in any investment initiative undertaken by the IFI. This is important so that the IFI does not channel or limit their investment in projects which are prone to climate change.

Building Market Capacity and Green Product Innovation

As the urgency of climate change and environmental degradation intensifies, Islamic finance must evolve beyond conventional offerings and play a proactive role in facilitating green transformation across sectors. This involves both the development of innovative Islamic financial products that integrate environmental, social, and governance (ESG) criteria, and the institutional capacity to originate, structure, and scale green projects. Strengthening market capacity requires collaboration between financial institutions, regulators, governments, and multilateral development banks to create a robust ecosystem for Islamic green finance.

Expand Islamic Green Product Offerings

Islamic financial institutions (IFIs) must diversify and innovate their product portfolios to meet the growing demand for sustainability-aligned investments. Beyond green sukuk, which remains the flagship Islamic green product, there is scope to develop a broad spectrum of instruments that combine Shariah principles with environmental and social impact objectives.

(a) Green Mudarabah and Musharakah Venture Capital Funds

These equity-based contracts can be structured to finance startups and SMEs engaged in circular economy, renewable energy, clean tech, and sustainable agriculture. In a green *mudarabah* arrangement, the investor (*rabb al-mal*) provides capital while the entrepreneur (mudarib) manages a project with defined environmental goals. In *musharakah*, both parties share capital and managerial responsibility, making it ideal for joint ventures in low-carbon technologies. These funds can be guided by impact performance metrics such as CO_2 emissions avoided, water saved, or biodiversity preserved.

(b) Sustainability-Linked Sukuk and Islamic ESG Exchange-Traded Funds (ETFs)

Sustainability-linked sukuk (SLS) tie the financial or structural characteristics of the sukuk to the achievement of predefined sustainability performance targets (SPTs), such as reducing greenhouse gas emissions or achieving LEED-certified construction. Unlike green sukuk, SLS proceeds can be used for general corporate purposes, making them flexible and scalable. Islamic ESG ETFs, meanwhile, offer retail and institutional investors exposure to Shariah-screened, ESG-compliant portfolios, enabling broader market participation in sustainable investing. These products must be benchmarked against both Shariah compliance filters and environmental performance indicators.

(c) Takaful for Climate Risk, Including Weather-Indexed Micro-Takaful

To protect vulnerable populations against climate-induced losses, takaful operators can design micro-takaful schemes linked to weather indices, such as rainfall, temperature, or drought duration. These products offer parametric payouts, which are quicker and more efficient than conventional indemnity-based insurance. Weather-indexed takaful is particularly relevant for smallholder farmers and rural communities in countries such as Sudan, Pakistan, and Bangladesh, where climate shocks threaten livelihoods. Green takaful also opens avenues for protecting renewable energy assets, climate-resilient housing, and eco-tourism infrastructure.

To ensure credibility and effectiveness, all Islamic green products must undergo rigorous Shariah screening, supported by frameworks such as AAOIFI's Shariah standards and the Climate Change and Principle-Based Taxonomy (CCPT) issued by Bank Negara Malaysia. Additionally, impact monitoring and reporting should follow established sustainability standards such as ICMA's Green Bond Principles or SASB/GRI guidelines, adapted to Islamic ethical considerations.

Establish Green Project Development Facilities

One of the key bottlenecks in scaling Islamic green finance is the shortage of bankable, Shariah-compliant green projects. To address this, governments and multilateral development institutions should establish Green Project Preparation Facilities (GPPFs) that support the early-stage development of high-impact, climate-aligned investments.

(a) Structuring Bankable and Shariah-Compliant Green Infrastructure Projects

These facilities can provide technical expertise, feasibility studies, legal structuring, and Shariah advisory to help developers design projects—such as solar parks, waste-to-energy plants, or water reuse systems—that meet both investor expectations and Islamic legal requirements. The IsDB and Islamic finance infrastructure institutions such as the International Islamic Trade Finance Corporation (ITFC) and Islamic Corporation for the Development of the Private Sector (ICD) could play catalytic roles in supporting these efforts across OIC member countries.

(b) Providing Blended Finance and De-risking Mechanisms

Many green projects in developing Muslim-majority countries face high upfront costs, long payback periods, or technology risks. GPPFs can offer blended finance solutions, combining concessional funds from public sources (e.g., climate funds, zakat, *waqf*) with commercial Islamic finance to de-risk projects and crowd in private capital. Instruments such as first-loss guarantees, profit rate subsidies, or Shariah-compliant risk-sharing arrangements can enhance the bankability of green ventures.

(c) Facilitating Technical Assistance and Capacity Building

Beyond financing, GPPFs should invest in capacity building for developers, financial institutions, and Shariah scholars on green finance literacy, climate risk analysis, and Islamic project finance. This may include training modules, toolkits, and regional workshops. Building a skilled workforce and ecosystem is essential to mainstream Islamic green finance and ensure long-term institutional resilience.

Strengthening Human Capital and Awareness

It is vital for relevant parties in Islamic financial system to invest in interdisciplinary capacity building. There is a need to equip Shariah scholars, Islamic bankers, and sustainability professionals with cross-functional training in both Islamic jurisprudence and ESG finance. Among initiatives that could be explored to embed cross-functional training include joint certification programmes by training institutions.

In addition, initiative to integrate ESG curriculum in Islamic finance and law faculties is imperative action that need to be taken by the public and private higher education institutions. This could assist companies who will be the future employer of Islamic finance and law graduates from these universities. Graduates with knowledge and awareness on the importance of green initiatives could facilitate the direction of companies towards sustainability agenda. Furthermore, Association of Shariah Advisors (ASAS) and Asian Institute of Chartered Bankers (AICB) could offer training for Shariah boards on climate science and green taxonomies.

Besides strengthening human capital knowledge on Islamic green finance initiatives, the sustainability agenda would not be successful in deficiency of public awareness and demand for Islamic green financial products. Hence, greater public engagement is necessary. Therefore, it is necessary to get print media, radio and television to make environmental preservation part of their agenda. For Muslim society, integration of Islamic green finance can be introduced during the Friday sermons. In addition, engagement with mosque can also be done to promote eco-Islamic values through lessons and religious lecture. Nationwide campaigns should be conducted to promote sustainable blended finance which incorporate *waqf*, *zakat*, and *sadaqah*.

Other than that, initiatives to introduce Islamic green finance can also be done to national school syllabus and civil society at all. It is necessary to incalcute the idea of conservation and preservation of the environment to young generations.

CONCLUSION

The convergence between Islamic finance and sustainable development offers a unique opportunity to align faith-driven values with global environmental imperatives. This chapter has examined the conceptual foundations, evolving landscape, practical challenges, and strategic policy directions for Islamic green finance.

Islamic finance, with its intrinsic principles of prohibition of harm (*arar*), promotion of public interest (*ma la ah*), and environmental stewardship (*khalīfah*), is inherently well-positioned to support the United Nations Sustainable Development Goals (SDGs), especially those related to climate action, clean energy, and sustainable infrastructure. As demonstrated, Islamic green finance has progressed significantly, especially in jurisdictions like Malaysia and Indonesia, through the development of green sukuk, ESG frameworks, and principle-based taxonomies. However, its expansion remains constrained by fragmented regulatory environments, a lack of standardized green taxonomies, limited Shariah discourse on environmental jurisprudence, and inadequate institutional capacity.

To overcome these challenges, the chapter has proposed four key strategic way forward for Islamic green finance. These include harmonising Shari'ah and sustainability standards, enhancing regulatory and institutional framework, building market capacity and green product innovation, and strengthening human capital and awareness. Empirical evidence from regulatory reports and academic research supports the urgency and feasibility of these recommendations. As Islamic financial institutions deepen their environmental engagement, it is imperative that they move beyond compliance toward value-based intermediation that actively contributes to environmental regeneration and social well-being.

In summary, Islamic green finance is not merely a financial innovation but a moral imperative and a transformative opportunity. Bridging faith and sustainability requires a holistic ecosystem, rooted in Shariah, guided by sustainability, and mobilized through strategic policy and cross-sector collaboration. As climate risks intensify, the Islamic finance industry must rise to the occasion, not only to ensure its own resilience but to serve as a catalyst for an equitable and sustainable global future.

REFERENCES

AAOIFI. (2021). *Governance Standards for Islamic Financial Institutions*. AAOIFI.

Abu-Sway, M. (1998). Towards an Islamic Jurisprudence of the Environment. In Foltz, R. C., Denny, F. M., & Baharuddin, A. (Eds.), *Islam and Ecology*. Harvard University Press.

Adewale, A. A. (2022, December). *Islamic Infrastructure Financing: Imperatives, Prospects, and Challenges* (IFSB Working Paper Series WP-25/12/2022). https://www.ifsb.org/wp-content/uploads/2023/10/WP-25_En.pdf

Afroz, N. N. (2017). Green Banking Initiatives of Islamic Bank Bangladesh Limited. *Global Journal of Management and Business Research.* https://journalofbusiness.org/index.php/GJMBR/article/view/2224/1-Green-Banking-Initiatives_JATS_NLM_xml#info

Ansar, S., Demirguc-Kunt, A., Klapper, L., & Singer, D. (2022). *The Global Findex Database 2021: Financial Inclusion, Digital Payments, and Resilience in the Age of COVID-19 (English).* World Bank Group. https://documents.worldbank.org/curated/en/099818107072234182

Asutay, M. (2012). Conceptualising and Locating the Social Failure of Islamic Finance: Aspirations of Islamic Moral Economy vs. the Realities of Islamic Finance. *Asian and African Area Studies*, *11*(2), 93–113.

Asutay, M., & Harningtyas, A. F. (2015). Developing Maqasid al-Shari'ah index to evaluate social performance of Islamic banks: A conceptual and empirical attempt. *International Journal of Islamic and Middle Eastern Finance and Management*, *8*(1), 25–49.

Auda, J. (2008). *Maqasid al-Shariah as Philosophy of Islamic Law: A Systems Approach*. International Institute of Islamic Thought. DOI: 10.2307/j.ctvkc67tg

Ayub, M. (2007). *Understanding Islamic Finance*. Wiley.

Bank Negara Malaysia. (2021a). *Climate Change and Principle-Based Taxonomy (CCPT).* Bank Negara Malaysia. https://www.bnm.gov.my/-/climate-change-principle-based-taxonomy

BWI. (2022). *Green Waqf Framework.* Badan Wakaf Indonesia. https://www.bwi.go.id/wp-content/uploads/2022/09/INS-20SEP-GREEN-WAQF-FRAMEWORK.pdf

Chapra, M. U. (2008). *The Islamic Vision of Development in the Light of Maqasid al-Shariah*. International Institute of Islamic Thought.

Dinar, A. (2019). Islam and the Environment: Towards Fiqh al-Bi'ah al-Mu'asirah. *Islamic Economic Studies, 27*(2), 1–19.

Dusuki, A. W., & Abdullah, N. I. (2007). Maqasid al-Shariah, Maslahah, and Corporate Social Responsibility. *The American Journal of Islamic Social Sciences, 24*(1), 25–45. DOI: 10.35632/ajiss.v24i1.415

Dusuki, A. W., & Abozaid, A. (2007). A Critical Appraisal of the Challenges of Realizing Maqasid al-Shariah in Islamic Banking and Finance. *International Journal of Economics, Management and Accounting, 15*(2), 143–165.

El-Gamal, M. A. (2006). *Islamic Finance: Law, Economics, and Practice.* Cambridge University Press. DOI: 10.1017/CBO9780511753756

Elasrag, H. (2020). *Green Finance in the Framework of Islamic Finance: Principles and Instruments.* Munich Personal RePEc Archive (MPRA Paper No. 101327). https://mpra.ub.uni-muenchen.de/101327

GSIA. (2021). *Global Sustainable Investment Review* 2020. Global Sustainable Investment Alliance. https://www.gsi-alliance.org/wp-content/uploads/2021/08/GSIR-20201.pdf

Hasan, Z., & Ebrahim, M. S. (2020a). Islamic Finance and the Sustainable Development Goals: A Review of the Linkages and the Role of Fiqh. *Journal of Islamic Accounting and Business Research, 11*(6), 1271–1285.

Hasan, Z., & Ebrahim, M. S. (2020b). Islamic finance and the Shari'ah-compliant approach to climate change: A critical review. *Review of Islamic Economics, 24*(1), 27–53. DOI: 10.1108/RIE-03-2019-0041

Hassan, M. K., Sarea, A., & Aliyu, S. (2022). Green Waqf: A Sustainable Mechanism for Climate Action in Muslim Societies. *Journal of Islamic Accounting and Business Research, 13*(4), 627–646. DOI: 10.1108/JIABR-06-2021-0179

ICD – LSEG. (2023). *ICD – LSEG Islamic Finance Development Report 2023.* London Stock Exchange Group. https://solutions.lseg.com/IslamicFinance_ICD_LSEG

ICMA. (2024). *Sustainable Bond Market Data.* International Capital Market Association. https://www.icmagroup.org/sustainable-finance/sustainable-bonds-database/

IFSB. (2020). *Environmental, Social and Governance (ESG) Issues in Islamic Finance.* Islamic Financial Services Board.

IsDB. (2021). *Islamic Social Finance Report.* Islamic Development Bank.

Kahf, M. (2003). *The Role of Waqf in Improving the Ummah Welfare* [Paper presentation]. International Seminar on Waqf as a Private Legal Body, Kuala Lumpur, Malaysia.

Kamali, M. H. (2010). *Environment in Islam* [Paper presentation]. *International Conference on Environment in Islam*, Amman, Jordan.

Kamla, R. (2009). Critical insights into contemporary Islamic accounting. *Critical Perspectives on Accounting*, *20*(8), 921–932. DOI: 10.1016/j.cpa.2009.01.002

Laldin, M. A., & Furqani, H. (2013). Developing Islamic Finance in the Framework of Maqasid al-Shariah: Understanding the Ends (Maqasid) and the Means (Wasa'il). *International Journal of Islamic and Middle Eastern Finance and Management*, *6*(4), 278–289. DOI: 10.1108/IMEFM-05-2013-0057

Ministry of Finance Indonesia. (2022). *Green Sukuk Allocation and Impact Report.* Ministry of Finance of the Republic of Indonesia.

Nasdaq Dubai. (2019). Majid Al Futtaim lists world's first benchmark corporate Green Sukuk on Nasdaq Dubai. https://www.nasdaqdubai.com/exchange/media/press-releases/majid-al-futtaim-lists-worlds-first-

Obaidullah, M. (2021). *Islamic Social Finance for Climate Resilience: A Framework for Action*. Islamic Development Bank Institute.

Obaidullah, M., & Khan, T. (2008). *Islamic Microfinance Development: Challenges and Initiatives*. Islamic Research and Training Institute.

OECD. (2020). *Developing Sustainable Finance Definitions and Taxonomies, Green Finance and Investment.* OECD Publishing.

Securities Commission Malaysia. (2017). Malaysia'a Green Sukuk Under the SC's Sustainable and Responsible Investment Sukuk Framework. *Malaysian ICM*, 12(2), 5-6. https://www.sc.com.my/api/documentms/download.ashx?id=1316fd32-1993-44cb-9669-5d5687adda35

Securities Commission Malaysia. (2022a). *SRI Roadmap for the Malaysian Capital Market: Mid-Term Review*. Securities Commission Malaysia.

Securities Commission Malaysia. (2022b). *SRI Sukuk and Tax Incentives Framework.* Securities Commission Malaysia.

Shaikh, S. A. (2020). Waqf and Sustainable Development: A Critical Appraisal of the Potentials and Governance Challenges. *Islamic Economic Studies*, *28*(1), 57–77. DOI: 10.1108/IES-09-2020-0052

UNDP & IsDB. (2019). *Islamic Finance for the Sustainable Development Goals*. United Nations Development Programme and Islamic Development Bank.

UNEP. (2023). *Adaptation Gap Report 2023*. United Nations Environment Program. https://www.unep.org/resources/adaptation-gap-report-2023

UNESCAP. (2020a). *Green Microfinance: Trends, Challenges, and Opportunities in Asia-Pacific*. United Nations Economic and Social Commission for Asia and the Pacific.

UNESCAP. (2020b). *Leveraging Islamic Finance for Climate-Smart Agriculture*. United Nations Economic and Social Commission for Asia and the Pacific. https://www.unescap.org

Yaacob, N. M., Abu Bakar, N., & Alias, M. (2021). Reviving Waqf for Environmental Sustainability: Issues, Challenges, and Prospects in Malaysia. *Journal of Fatwa Management and Research*, *26*(1), 87–104.

Chapter 2

Bridging Waqf and Technology for TVET Innovation: The Role of E-wallet in Research and Design (R&D) Funding

Mohd Asyraf bin Yusof
http://orcid.org/0009-0007-3116-2837
Universiti Teknologi Mara, Malaysia

Norshahira Kamarzaman
http://orcid.org/0009-0005-9045-4149
UKM, Malaysia

Nurul Asikin Abdul Razak
http://orcid.org/0009-0004-2789-6377
UKM, Malaysia

ABSTRACT

This chapter examines the innovative integration of waqf (Islamic endowment) with digital technology, specifically e-wallets, as an alternative funding mechanism for research and development (R&D) in Technical and Vocational Education and Training (TVET) institutions. TVET plays a crucial role in developing skilled human capital for Malaysia's economic advancement, yet these institutions face significant funding constraints that limit their research capabilities and innovation potential. The study synthesizes data from diverse sources, including literature reviews, government reports, and statistical analyses, to evaluate how technology-enabled waqf systems can address this funding gap. The analysis reveals that Malaysian

DOI: 10.4018/979-8-3373-1842-4.ch002

TVET institutions allocate only 4.7% of their operational budgets to R&D activities, significantly below international benchmarks, resulting in outdated infrastructure, limited research capacity, and weak industry collaboration. The research examines the theoretical foundations of waqf in Islamic finance, the evolution from traditional to contemporary applications, and the potential of fintech innovations to enhance waqf collection and distribution efficiency. Key findings demonstrate that e-wallet-based waqf systems can democratize charitable giving through micro-contributions, enhance transparency through blockchain technology, and create sustainable funding streams through strategic asset management. However, implementation faces multiple challenges, including regulatory fragmentation across Malaysia's state-based waqf governance, cybersecurity concerns, digital literacy limitations, and Shariah compliance requirements. The study proposes a comprehensive implementation framework encompassing regulatory harmonization, technological infrastructure development, public education initiatives, and strategic industry partnerships. The findings suggest that while technology-enabled waqf offers substantial potential for addressing TVET funding challenges, successful implementation requires multidisciplinary approaches integrating technological, theological, and educational perspectives. This research contributes to a theoretical understanding of Islamic social finance in the digital era and practical applications for educational funding in Muslim-majority contexts, offering a model for enhancing TVET innovation while maintaining alignment with Islamic principles.

1. INTRODUCTION

The term waqf originates from the Arabic root verb “waqafa,” which signifies the act of causing something to halt and remain stationary. It additionally encompasses the interpretations of ‘detention’, ‘holding’, or maintaining. Waqf, referred to as Boniyad in Iran and Habs in North and West Africa. Nevertheless, by contemplating its various interpretations, waqf can be utilized for non-perishable assets from which benefits are derived without depleting the asset itself (Yusof & Ab. Aziz, 2015).

While the term waqf does not appear explicitly in the Holy Quran, the principle of wealth distribution is profoundly underscored within its verses (Aziz & Yusof, 2014). The Quran contains numerous verses that address the importance of charity and encourage Muslims to engage in acts of giving. Notable references can be found in Surah al-Baqarah (2: 261, 2: 271), Ali Imran (3: 92, 3: 134), al-Lail (92:18-21), and al-Hadid (57: 18).

The allocation of wealth represents a fundamental concern within the contemporary economic landscape, essential for fostering a more dynamic, equitable, and entrepreneurial environment (Yusof et al., 2013). Nonetheless, a hadith transmitted by Abu Hurairah is regarded as the foundational source of this institution within the realm of Islam. "Abu Hurairah conveyed that the Prophet Mohammad (PBUH) stated: "Upon a man's death, all his deeds cease, except for three: ongoing charity (sadaqah jariyah), beneficial knowledge, or a righteous child who prays for him" (Reported by Muslim, No. 4223).

On the other hand, one notable feature of Islam is its capacity to adjust to an evolving and expanding context. The technological dimension is regarded as one of the most swiftly evolving and advancing aspects of our era and environment. The perspective within Islamic thought regarding this technology is unequivocal; it serves as a tool or conduit through which individuals fulfill their needs and desires (Mat et al., 2022).

Malaysia's TVET ecosystem has evolved significantly since the country's independence, developing into a complex network of institutions under various ministries and private entities. According to the Ministry of Human Resources (2023), Malaysia's TVET landscape currently comprises 1,344 institutions across both public and private sectors. These include polytechnics, community colleges, vocational colleges, and industry-based training institutes. The Department of Skills Development (2023) reports that these institutions collectively produced 189,450 TVET graduates in 2022, yet this number falls short of the projected demand of 250,000 skilled workers annually required to support Malaysia's industrial transformation goals.

The 12th Malaysia Plan (2021-2025) has positioned TVET as a critical enabler for the country's economic transformation, particularly in driving high-value industries and supporting the Fourth Industrial Revolution (4IR). The plan allocates RM6.6 billion specifically for TVET development, representing a 15% increase from the previous Malaysia Plan (Economic Planning Unit, 2021). However, a significant portion of this funding (approximately 72%) is directed toward operational expenditures, leaving limited resources for research and development initiatives that could drive innovation in technical education.

Malaysia's TVET institutions are governed by seven different ministries, creating a fragmented ecosystem that often results in duplication of resources and inconsistent quality standards. The Ministry of Higher Education oversees polytechnics and community colleges, while the Ministry of Education manages vocational colleges. Other key stakeholders include the Ministry of Human Resources, the Ministry of Youth and Sports, and the Ministry of Rural Development, each operating their own TVET institutions with varying governance structures and funding mechanisms (Malaysian Qualifications Agency, 2022).

Research and development are increasingly recognized as vital components of TVET excellence, yet statistical evidence reveals significant shortfalls in Malaysia's current investment. While the National Survey of Research and Development in Malaysia indicates that the country's overall R&D expenditure remains relatively modest, the available indicators do not show a strong investment focus in TVET-related research. Compared to advanced economies such as Singapore and Germany which consistently record higher national R&D intensity, Malaysia's limited allocation towards strategic and skills-driven research areas raises concerns about the capacity of technical education to keep pace with industry demands (Malaysian Science and Technology Information Centre, 2025).

In terms of research output, Malaysian TVET institutions produced 845 research publications in 2022, representing just 3.6% of the country's total academic output (Malaysian Science and Technology Information Centre, 2025). While data from the Intellectual Property Corporation of Malaysia indicate that the country recorded 7,542 patent applications and 6,205 granted patents in 2022, the publicly available statistics do not provide disaggregated information on patent filings by institutional category, including TVET institutions (Intellectual Property Corporation of Malaysia, 2024). In contrast, vocational education and training systems in advanced economies such as Germany characterised by a strong dual-system model that integrates school-based learning with enterprise-based training are widely recognised for producing industry-relevant competencies, although reliable national-level data on their specific contribution to research publications remain limited (OECD, 2025). The absence of transparent, TVET-specific indicators on research output and intellectual property generation in Malaysia therefore restricts any robust assessment of the innovation capacity within the national TVET ecosystem.

The Department of Polytechnic and Community College Education reports that only 17% of TVET lecturers are actively involved in research activities, with the majority citing insufficient funding and heavy teaching loads as primary barriers to research engagement (Department of Polytechnic Education, 2023). Several analyses of the Malaysian TVET ecosystem report persistent deficiencies in infrastructure and training facilities at many public TVET centres, which can hinder efforts to deliver industry-relevant training and impede collaboration with industrial partners (Penang Institute, 2023).

Industry collaboration statistics further highlight the research and development challenges. The Industry-Academia Collaboration Report (2023) by TalentCorp Malaysia shows that only an estimated 14% of TVET research projects include significant industry involvement, compared to 35% in universities. This limited engagement reduces both the relevance of research activities and the potential for commercialization of research outcomes. The same report indicates that just 8.5% of TVET research projects successfully transition to commercial applications, highlighting a critical gap in the research-to-market pipeline.

The funding landscape for TVET research and development in Malaysia reveals a persistent gap between institutional needs and available resources. Several studies and policy analyses highlight persistent funding and infrastructure constraints in

Malaysia's TVET institutions, with inadequate access to equipment, workshops, and training resources undermining the system's capacity for industry-relevant training and research (Penang Institute, 2023;Kamarzaman et al., 2025).

A significant portion of existing literature highlights persistent equipment shortages across Malaysian polytechnics and community colleges, affecting both teaching quality and research capability. Studies consistently show that many laboratories and workshops lack updated tools, modern training technologies, and sufficient resource sharing mechanisms, resulting in a widening gap between institutional capacity and current industry standards (Kamarzaman et al., 2025).

Second, human capital development for research excellence faces significant financial constraints. The Malaysian TVET Lecturer Development Report (2023) highlights that only 23% of TVET educators have received specialized research training, compared to 58% in universities. Furthermore, just 17% of TVET institutions have dedicated research units with full-time staff, limiting their capacity to develop and manage complex research projects. The report estimates that closing this capability gap would require an additional investment of RM78 million annually for specialized training, research leave provisions, and industry attachment programs.

Third, the commercialization pathway for TVET innovations suffers from severe underinvestment. An analysis by the Malaysian Technology Development Corporation (2023) reveals that while TVET institutions generate numerous practical innovations with immediate industrial applications, less than 5% receive adequate funding for prototyping, testing, and market development. The study estimates a funding gap of approximately RM150 million annually for effectively translating TVET research into marketable products and services.

The consequences of this funding gap extend beyond the institutions themselves. Industry partnerships, which could potentially supplement government funding, remain underdeveloped partly due to perceived limitations in research capabilities. The Federation of Malaysian Manufacturers' Education Survey (2023) indicates that only 22% of industry respondents consider Malaysian TVET institutions as viable research partners, citing concerns about technological capabilities, research management expertise, and project completion timelines. This perception creates a self-reinforcing cycle where limited funding constrains research capacity, which in turn reduces industry engagement and private sector investment.

Current government funding mechanisms further exacerbate these challenges through structural limitations. The Malaysia Education Blueprint 2015–2025 (Higher Education) and subsequent policy analyses indicate that research and innovation funding frameworks have been largely designed around university-based institutions, leaving TVET providers at a structural disadvantage despite their distinct applied research orientation and mandate for industry-relevant training (Ministry of Education Malaysia, 2015; The Asia Foundation, 2022; Wan, 2025).

Islam embraces technology and recognizes that it does not contravene its principles in any way. Technology has been employed across various domains, including Islamic finance and business. The majority of products or services derived from this technology have found application within the financial and banking sectors. This study centres on a particular product or service known as an e-wallet. It enhances electronic payment systems within the realm of e-business through the utilization of electronic currency (Mat et al., 2022).

This research delves into the nuances of Shariah compliance in the context of e-wallet implementation, emphasizing the necessity of scrutinizing contracts through the lens of their conditions and implications. Furthermore, the implementation of this system diverges significantly from Islamic banking and its associated financial products and services, particularly regarding mode, content, revenue, benefits, and risks. This necessitates a dedicated examination to elucidate the uncertainties pertaining to Shariah compliance within this e-wallet framework (Mat et al., 2022).

Fintech represents a transformative service within the financial sector, leveraging advancements from the technology industry. The evolution of fintech significantly influences a multitude of industrial sectors within financial services institutions. This offers a comprehensive overview of the current landscape in financial services, encompassing banks, insurance institutions, capital markets, and Islamic philanthropy (Asyraf, 2025).

Data from Bank Indonesia indicates that the total transactions involving electronic money have shown a remarkable year-on-year increase. Within the domain of Islamic economics, the contemporary application of fintech, including e-wallets, extends beyond the financial and banking services sector; it is also employed in Islamic philanthropic initiatives, particularly in the realm of cash waqf (Ramdhani et al., 2022).

In various nations, waqf has evolved into a mechanism for social security, encompassing diverse sectors including education, social welfare, economic development, and cultural initiatives, particularly in the realm of cash waqf. Indonesia, home to the largest Muslim population globally, possesses significant potential to enhance the optimization of cash waqf. The prospective value of cash waqf in 2020 is estimated at IDR 100 trillion (Ramdhani et al., 2022).

However, the actual amount collected stands at merely Rp 500 billion. This indicates that the funds obtainable from cash waqf are minimal, representing only 0.5% of the current potential for cash waqf (Ramdhani et al., 2022). Conversely, in Malaysia, cash waqf presents considerable promise as a mechanism for socio-economic advancement. Research indicates that should every adult Malaysian Muslim contribute a minimum of RM1 daily (or RM30 monthly) to cash waqf funds, the total annual collection could approximate RM4.3 billion (Yusof et al., 2013).

Waqf, an enduring endowment regulated by Sharia principles, has historically been acknowledged as a significant financial mechanism for fostering diverse social and educational initiatives. Technical and Vocational Education and Training (TVET) represents an essential element of the educational framework, promoting the cultivation of a skilled workforce and addressing the swiftly evolving demands of various industries. Nonetheless, TVET institutions frequently encounter obstacles in securing funding, especially concerning research and innovation initiatives (Kamarzaman et al., 2024).

The constraints imposed by this funding limitation impede not only the progress of technological advancement and innovation but also detrimentally impact the quality of education delivered. Within the framework of Islamic economic development, the function of waqf is perceived as a solution to the financial limitations encountered in research and innovation, particularly in the TVET sector (Kamarzaman et al., 2024).

This study seeks to enhance comprehension of the concept of waqf within Islamic finance by synthesizing data from diverse sources, including literature reviews, reports, and statistical analyses. It will explore the role of fintech innovations, such as e-wallets, in waqf financing and assess the potential of waqf as a viable alternative financing mechanism to bolster research and innovation initiatives in TVET institutions. The findings underscore the significance of waqf as a potent financing mechanism in overcoming the challenges associated with research and innovation funding in TVET, thus facilitating the cultivation of quality human capital and propelling the Islamic economy towards a more sustainable and inclusive trajectory.

2. THE CONCEPT OF WAQF IN ISLAMIC FINANCE

Islamic finance has witnessed remarkable developments in recent decades, with waqf emerging as a vital instrument for educational funding. While traditional perspectives viewed waqf primarily through the lens of real estate endowments, contemporary applications have expanded significantly (Ismail Abdel Mohsin, 2013). This transformation reflects broader changes in financial mechanisms and social needs. Modern waqf structures encompass various asset classes, extending beyond conventional property-based endowments. Research by Rashid (2018) demonstrates how waqf instruments now incorporate movable assets, including cash endowments, securities, and intellectual property rights. These adaptations maintain fundamental Shariah principles while addressing contemporary funding requirements.

The International Islamic University Malaysia's experience offers valuable insights into practical waqf implementation. Their pioneering digital waqf collection system, launched in 2021, exemplifies how traditional Islamic financing principles can adapt to modern technological frameworks. The program's success in funding scholarships and infrastructure development demonstrates the viability of modernized waqf structures (IIUM, 2021).

Intellectual property waqf represents a particularly innovative development in Islamic finance. Turkish educational institutions have successfully utilized patent royalties to fund research initiatives, creating sustainable funding streams for academic advancement (Saduman & Aysun, 2009). However, Malaysian institutions face regulatory challenges in implementing similar programs, particularly regarding Shariah compliance in intellectual property management (Mahamood & Ab Rahman, 2015).

Recent data from Yayasan Wakaf Malaysia (2023) reveals encouraging trends in waqf adoption. The 25% increase in cash waqf contributions over five years suggests growing public acceptance of modernized waqf instruments. In 2022, Malaysian institutions allocated RM50 million in waqf funds toward educational development, marking significant progress in alternative funding mechanisms.

The theoretical foundations of educational waqf continue to evolve within contemporary Islamic finance discourse. Al-Attas and Ibrahim (2021) propose a comprehensive framework for educational waqf governance that addresses both Shariah compliance and operational efficiency. Their research emphasizes the importance of transparent management structures that balance traditional religious principles with modern accountability standards. This integration of classical Islamic jurisprudence with contemporary governance models provides a roadmap for institutions seeking to establish sustainable waqf programs.

Corporate waqf represents another significant development in this field. Hassan and Abdullah (2018) document how Malaysian corporations have contributed to educational funding through structured waqf programs. The Johor Corporation's Waqf An-Nur initiative demonstrates how corporate entities can participate in educational philanthropy while maintaining commercial objectives. Their model has funded vocational training programs that directly address skills gaps in technical industries, providing both economic and social returns (Johor Corporation, 2020).

Digital transformation has further revolutionized waqf collection and management. Ahmad et al. (2022) examine how blockchain technology enhances transparency and reduces administrative costs in waqf management. Their findings indicate that technology-enabled waqf platforms can increase donor confidence through immutable transaction records and automated compliance verification. The Bank Negara Malaysia's regulatory sandbox for Islamic fintech has facilitated experimentation with such innovative approaches to waqf management (Bank Negara Malaysia, 2022).

The globalization of waqf practices presents both opportunities and challenges. Comparative analysis by Rahman and Haneef (2020) of waqf implementations across Malaysia, Indonesia, and the Gulf states reveals important contextual variations. While sharing common Shariah foundations, each region has developed distinctive regulatory frameworks that reflect local cultural and economic conditions. These differences highlight the adaptability of waqf as an institution while emphasizing the need for context-specific implementation strategies.

Looking forward, integration of waqf with other Islamic financial instruments offers promising possibilities for educational funding. Sulaiman et al. (2019) explore synergistic models combining waqf with sukuk (Islamic bonds) to finance large-scale educational infrastructure projects. This hybrid approach leverages market mechanisms while preserving the perpetual nature of waqf assets. The World Bank's 2021 report on Islamic finance notes that such innovative structures could significantly expand the capital available for educational development in Muslim-majority countries (World Bank, 2021).

3. CHALLENGES AND SOLUTIONS FOR R&D FUNDING IN TVET INSTITUTIONS

The funding landscape for Technical and Vocational Education and Training presents complex challenges across developing economies. Malaysian TVET institutions, despite their strategic importance, face substantial resource constraints. Government allocations, while significant, often prove insufficient for comprehensive research and development initiatives (International Labour Organization, 2023). This limitation particularly affects research infrastructure development and talent retention.

Research infrastructure deficiencies manifest through outdated laboratory equipment and insufficient technological resources. Analysis by Yun, Tun, and Cheng (2021) reveals how funding constraints impede Malaysian TVET institutions from maintaining competitive research facilities. The resultant technology gap affects both research output quality and industry collaboration potential.

Industry-academia partnerships present additional complexities. Malaysian TVET institutions struggle to establish sustainable collaboration frameworks with industrial partners, partly due to perceived misalignment between institutional capabilities and market requirements (Rusli, 2024a). This misalignment creates a self-perpetuating cycle where limited industry engagement further restricts funding opportunities.

International comparisons provide instructive examples of alternative funding models. German TVET institutions demonstrate remarkable success through their dual system approach. The Fraunhofer Institutes exemplify effective industry-academia collaboration, generating substantial research funding through commercial partnerships (Ziderman, 2018). Similarly, Singapore's SkillsFuture initiative showcases successful government-industry funding coordination, employing matching grants to stimulate private-sector investment (Varaprasad, 2021).

Statistical evidence underscores the funding disparity between Malaysian TVET institutions and their international counterparts. While Malaysia's 15% increase in

TVET funding represents progress, Singapore's SGD 1.2 billion allocation through SkillsFuture and Germany's €3 billion investment via Fraunhofer Institutes demonstrate significantly higher commitment levels (UNESCO, 2022).

The implementation of digital technologies offers promising solutions for funding challenges. Blockchain applications enhance transparency in fund management, while e-wallet integration facilitates micro-contributions from broader donor bases (Razali et al., 2021). These technological solutions, when properly implemented, create efficient channels for resource mobilization and allocation.

The integration of traditional and contemporary funding mechanisms requires careful consideration of local contexts and institutional capabilities. Successful implementation demands robust digital infrastructure, clear regulatory frameworks, and strong stakeholder engagement. Evidence suggests that institutions adopting comprehensive funding approaches, incorporating both traditional and innovative elements, demonstrate greater resilience and sustainability in their research initiatives.

Talent retention represents another critical dimension of TVET funding challenges. Hassan and Ibrahim (2023) document how funding limitations contribute to researcher attrition, with 32% of surveyed TVET lecturers citing inadequate research support as a primary factor in seeking alternative employment. This brain drain undermines institutional capacity-building efforts and threatens long-term research sustainability. Effective retention strategies require not only competitive compensation but also adequate research infrastructure and professional development opportunities. According to Ahmad and Lim (2024), institutions implementing comprehensive researcher support programs report 45% lower turnover rates compared to those focusing solely on salary adjustments.

Regional disparities in funding allocation further complicate the Malaysian TVET landscape. Wong et al. (2022) identify significant variations in research funding accessibility between urban and rural institutions. Their longitudinal study reveals that urban TVET institutions receive approximately 2.7 times more research funding per researcher than rural counterparts, despite facing comparable industry needs. This geographical inequality reinforces existing advantages of established institutions while limiting the development potential of emerging ones. Decentralized funding mechanisms and targeted allocation formulas offer potential solutions to this structural imbalance.

Intellectual property commercialization presents both a challenge and an opportunity for TVET funding diversification. TVET institutions typically generate practical innovations with immediate industrial applications, yet they often lack the infrastructure to effectively commercialize these outputs (Rahman & Abdullah, 2023). The establishment of technology transfer offices within Malaysian polytechnics has yielded promising early results, with a 23% increase in patent applications between 2019 and 2023. However, substantial barriers remain in translating patents into revenue streams. Successful models from South Korea demonstrate how specialized commercialization units within TVET institutions can bridge this gap by providing legal expertise, market analysis, and business development support (Kang & Park, 2022).

Public-private partnership models offer promising pathways for sustainable TVET funding. Effective examples include Malaysia's Collaborative Research in Engineering, Science and Technology (CREST) program, which demonstrates how structured engagement mechanisms can align academic research with industrial priorities (Mohd Noor, 2021). The program's matching fund approach has generated RM45 million for applied research in participating TVET institutions. Similarly, the Industry Centres of Excellence (ICoE) initiative provides a framework for shared governance and resource contribution. Expanding and refining these models could substantially enhance the funding landscape for Malaysian TVET institutions.

Policy coherence represents a fundamental prerequisite for effective TVET funding reform. Abdullah and Lee (2022) identify significant fragmentation in Malaysia's TVET funding policies, with overlapping mandates across seven ministries creating administrative inefficiencies and coordination challenges. Their analysis suggests that streamlining governance structures and establishing centralized funding coordination could increase effective resource utilization by 18-24%. International best practices, such as Australia's unified TVET funding framework, provide valuable models for policy integration while maintaining sectoral diversity (Cameron & O'Hanlon-Rose, 2023).

4. THE ROLE OF TECHNOLOGY IN MODERN WAQF MANAGEMENT

Technology integration in modern waqf management has changed how Islamic waqf is managed, monitored, and used. Historically, waqf management depended on the manual process, often exposed to inefficacy, poor management, and a lack of transparency (Kasdi et al., 2022). However, the emergence of digital tools and platforms enables more efficient collection, distribution, and monitoring of the waqf fund. Technologies such as blockchain, artificial intelligence (AI), and cloud computing have played a significant role in enhancing accountability and ensuring that funds are distributed according to Islamic principles (Wildana et al., 2022). As an example, blockchain technology provides a ledger that cannot be altered, records all the transactions, simultaneously reduces the risks of fraud, and ensures transparency (Luntajo & Hasan, 2023).

Apart from that, technology has facilitated the democratization of waqf's contributions, giving way to more layers of society to be part of this noble practice. Online platforms and portable applications have facilitated individuals to contribute to the waqf fund, without accounting for their geographical locations (Ardiyansyah & Kasdi, 2021). This has widened the basis of donors tremendously, which increases the funding for a variety of social projects, education, and the economy. The use of technology also allows for the monitoring of the waqf fund in real-time, enabling donors to see how their contributions are expended (Aldeen, 2021). This level of transparency instills trust and encourages more people to be involved in this waqf initiative.

In the context of Technical and Vocational Education and Training (TVET), waqf management based on technology can play a significant role in funding research and development initiatives (R&D). By benefiting from the digital platform, the waqf fund can be channeled efficaciously to innovative projects seeking to increase the quality of the TVET program. For instance, the fund can be allocated for sophisticated training module development, the latest equipment acquisition, and the establishment of cooperation with industry players. This not only enhances the education quality but also ensures that TVET graduates are equipped well to fulfill the demand for modern labor (Riyanda et al., 2022).

Nonetheless, technology integration in waqf management is not without any challenges. One primary concern is the digital gap that may exempt certain segments of society from taking the digital waqf initiative. Other than that, there is a need to lay out strong cyber security steps to protect sensitive donors' information and ensure the integrity of the fund (Ismail, 2021). Despite these challenges, the potential benefit of technology in modern waqf management is far greater than the risks, making the tool integral to efficacious and transparent Islamic waqf management.

All in all, technology has changed the waqf management landscape, making it more transparent, efficacious, and easy to access. By taking advantage of digital tools and platforms, waqf institutions can give better services to their community, especially in the TVET innovation field. Thus, waqf management needs to continue to follow the latest technological developments and integrate them into their operations (Ismail et al., 2021). This not only enhances the effectiveness of waqf management, but it also ensures that the waqf fund is used in a way that maximizes the social and economic impacts.

5. E-WALLET AS WAQF FUND MANAGEMENT TOOL

E-wallet has emerged as a powerful tool to manage the waqf fund, offering an easy and efficacious way to collect, distribute, and monitor donations or contributions (Zakariyah et al., 2022). Generally, an e-wallet, or electronic wallet, refers to a digital payment system that allows users to store money in electronic form and conduct transactions without the need for cash or physical cards. This technology enables transactions to be carried out more quickly, securely, and efficiently, in line with the development of the global digital economy. In the context of Islamic finance, e-wallets play a crucial role in ensuring that transactions are free from riba (usury) and *gharar* (uncertainty), making them a valuable instrument for managing waqf funds. With the digital payment system that is expanding, e-wallet has provided an interrupted platform for donors to contribute to the waqf fund with just a few clicks. The ease of use has reduced the obstacles for potential donors to take part, encouraging more and more people to engage in waqf initiatives. Other than that, e-wallets have offered a level of transparency and accountability often scarce in traditional waqf management (Ambrose & Asuhami, 2021). Donors can easily track their contributions and see how their funds are used, at the same time building their trust and confidence in the system.

One of the main advantages of using e-wallet for waqf fund management is the capability to automate various processes, such as fund collection and distribution. This not only reduces the administrative load on the waqf institution but also minimizes the risk of human error (Salman et al., 2021). For example, e-wallets can be programmed to distribute funds automatically to certain projects or recipients, ensuring that the contributions are used following donors' intentions. Other than that, e-wallets can produce real-time reports, give invaluable opinions to the waqf management about the fund flow, and enable them to make data-based decisions (Aldeen, 2021).

In the context of TVET innovation, e-wallets can play an important role in funding the research and development (R&D) initiative. A safe and efficacious platform is essential to collect the waqf donation, and an e-wallet can aid in the fund collection to lend support to innovative projects in the TVET sector. For example, the funds collected through e-wallet can be used to develop new training programs, obtain sophisticated equipment, and form cooperation with industry leaders. This not only enhances TVET education but also ensures that the graduates are well-prepared and equipped to cater to the demands of modern labor (Mohamad et al., 2023). In addition, digital waqf management opens opportunities for strategic collaboration between TVET institutions and industry. Through this model, companies can contribute to the waqf funds as part of their corporate social responsibility (CSR), where the funds are used to finance industrial training, skills certification programs, as well as research and development in industry-related technologies. This approach not only enhances the competitiveness of TVET students but also ensures that they are well-prepared to meet the demands of the modern labor market.

However, the use of e-wallets in modern waqf management also carries some main concerns. The main concern lies in the cyber security issue, because e-wallets have always become the target of hackers and cybercriminals (Ahmed et al., 2021).

To mitigate this risk, waqf organizations have to implement strong security measures, such as confidentiality and two-factor validation measures. Other than that, there is a need to lay out clear rules and guidance to monitor the use of e-wallets in waqf management, to verify that it is used consistently with the Islamic stances (Ambrose & Asuhami, 2021).

Overall, e-wallet offers an easy, efficient, and transparent way to manage the waqf fund, making it a very valuable tool for modern waqf institutions. By making good use of e-wallets, waqf managers can facilitate operations, enhance accountability, and collect funds to support innovative projects in the TVET sector. Nonetheless, addressing challenges such as cyber security and rule compliance is vital so that the use of e-wallets is effective and does not stray from the principles of Islam (Ramli, 2021). In tandem with the development of the digital payment system, e-wallet is expected to play a much greater role in the management of waqf funds.

6. SHARIA GOVERNANCE FRAMEWORK FOR E-WALLET IN WAQF MANAGEMENT

The e-wallet integration in the waqf management necessitates a formidable Sharia Governance framework to ensure good compliance with Islamic principles. The framework establishes a set of guidelines and standards that regulate the use of e-wallets in waqf management, ensuring that all transactions are Sharia-compliant (Zakariyah et al., 2022). The framework is also important to maintain the integrity of the waqf fund and to ensure that it is used for the intended purposes. Sharia Governance can be defined as a system that regulates, supervises, ang ensures that all financial operations and transactions within Islamic financial institutions or related sectors comply with Sharia principles. According to international Sharia governance standards set by bodies such as the Accounting and Auditing Organization for Islamic Financial Institutions (AAOIFI, 2018) and the Islamic Financial Services Board (IFSB), Shariah governance involves a framework that encompasses structural aspects, processes, regulatory controls, and strict monitoring mechanisms to ensure adherence to Islamic law in all aspects of Islamic financial management.

Along with these international standards, Muslim countries have also introduced their own Sharia governance standards. For example, in Malaysia, Shariah governance in the Islamic financial sector is controlled by Bank Negara Malaysia (BNM) through the framework Shariah Governance Policy Document (SGPD) which outlines the strict requirements for Islamic financial institutions to establish Shariah committees, implement Shariah audits, as well as provide dispute resolution mechanisms related to Shariah compliance. While in Saudi Arabia, Saudi Central Bank (SAMA) obligate Islamic financial institutions to comply with Sharia regulation overseen by Shariah Committee of Islamic Banking. In addition, countries like Indonesia has introduced National Sharia Council - Indonesian Ulema Council (DSN-MUI) as the main body responsible for controlling Sharia compliance in the Islamic financial sector. This system stipulates that every Islamic financial product, including e-wallets used for waqf, needs to get approval from DSN-MUI before it can be used by the community.

One of the major components in the Sharia governance framework for e-wallets is the establishment of the Sharia Consultation Board (Abd Aziz et al., 2021). This Board is responsible for monitoring the use of e-wallets in waqf management and ensuring that all the transactions comply with Islamic principles. The board must comprise scholars and experts in Islamic finance, who can guide on issues such as the applicability of certain transactions, fund allocation, and the use of technology in waqf management. With this supervision, the Sharia consultation board helps to ensure that the use of e-wallets does not deviate from Islamic values.

Another important aspect of the Sharia governance framework is the clear guidance development for the use of e-wallet in waqf management. This guideline should encompass the permitted use of e-wallets, the permitted transaction types, and the procedure that ensures that the fund is allocated according to Islamic principles. For instance, the guideline should dictate that e-wallet can only be used to collect and distribute the waqf fund for purposes that are in line with the laws of Islam, such as education, healthcare, and social welfare (Ayub, 2022). It should also be clarified in the guideline that there is to be a procedure to ensure that the fund is distributed fairly and without prejudice, with the priority given to those who are most in need.

In the context of the TVET innovation, the Sharia governance framework plays an integral role in making sure that the fund collected e-wallet is used to support projects that are consistent with Islamic principles. As an example, this framework should ensure that the fund is used to develop training programs that are in line with Islamic values, such as programs that promote ethical behavior, social responsibilities, and community development (Abd Aziz et al., 2021). Other than that, this framework should ensure that the fund is used to obtain the necessary equipment and resources for high-quality TVET program development while ascertaining that the resources comply with Islamic principles.

That said, challenges are unavoidable when it comes to the development and implementation of the Sharia governance framework for e-wallets in waqf management. One of the main challenges is the need for ongoing monitoring and evaluation to ensure that this framework is followed, and that the e-wallet is used in a way that is in line with Islamic principles (Zakariyah et al., 2022). This requires a strong monitoring and evaluation system that can track the fund flow, identify any potential issues, and take corrective actions, if necessary. Also, there is a need for continuous training and education to ensure that waqf managers and stakeholders understand the guidelines and standards outlined in the Sharia governance framework (Wahid et al., 2023).

Overall, the development of the Sharia governance framework is important to ensure that e-wallet is used in a way that stays in tandem with the Islamic principles in waqf management. By setting a clear guideline and standards, establishing a Sharia consultation board, and implementing a strong monitoring and evaluation system, the waqf institution can ensure that e-wallet is used to support projects that are consistent with Islamic values, especially in the context of TVET innovation (Zakariyah et al., 2022). Although there are challenges related to the development and implementation of the framework, potential benefits outperform the risks, rendering the component very important in the management of modern waqf. Summary of Sharia Governance Framework shows below:

Figure 1. Sharia Governance Framework for E-wallet in Waqf Management

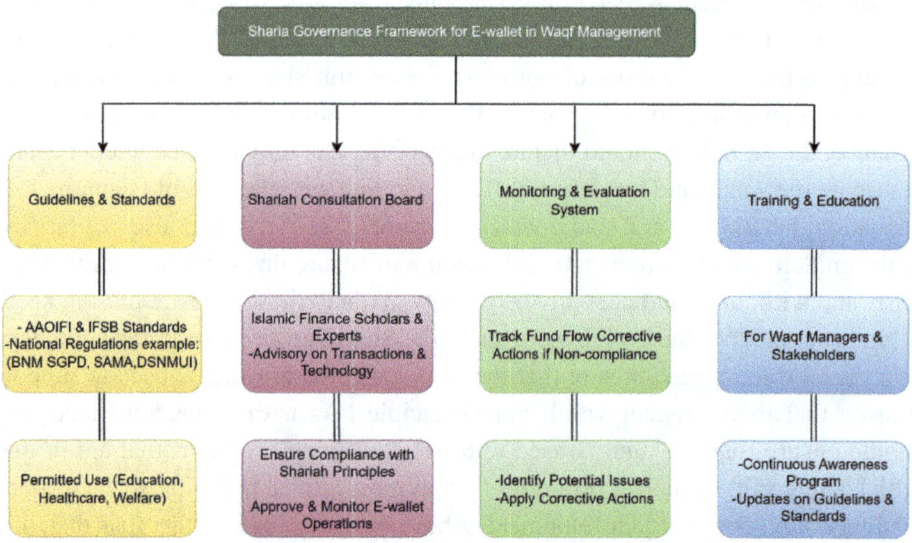

Source: Author's compilation

7. BRIDGING WAQF AND TECHNOLOGY FOR TVET R&D FUNDING

TVET institutions play a vital role in human capital development and industrial innovation, yet insufficient funding for R&D remains a major challenge. In Malaysia, TVET institutions rely heavily on government development allocations as their primary sources of funding. However, budget constraints and competing development priorities, such as basic education and healthcare, often limit the funds allocated for R&D (Dung, Consultant, Christine, Gonçalves, & Lan, 2019). This lack of funding not only hinders TVET institutions from investing in advanced research infrastructure but also makes it difficult for them to retain skilled researchers and undertake large-scale R&D projects that could lead to groundbreaking innovations (Mohd Zain, Aspah, Abdullah, & Ebrahimi, 2017). Additionally, the gap in collaboration between TVET institutions and industries poses another challenge. Studies indicate that a lack of alignment between industry needs and TVET capabilities often prevents the formation of effective partnerships, thereby limiting opportunities for joint funding and technology transfer (Rusli, 2024b).

To address these challenges, integrating waqf (Islamic endowment) and technology offers innovative solutions that can help TVET institutions secure alternative funding for their R&D activities. One promising approach is the use of e-wallets as a tool for collecting cash waqf. E-wallets provide a digital platform that is easily accessible for individuals to contribute cash waqf, enabling TVET institutions to expand their donor base and leverage the growing trend of digital philanthropy (Madani & Thomafy, 2024). However, implementing e-wallets requires robust digital infrastructure, collaboration with Islamic financial institutions, and compliance with personal data protection regulations. Additionally, blockchain technology can be utilized to enhance transparency and accountability in waqf management. By using smart contracts, the distribution of waqf funds can be automated based on predefined criteria ensuring that funds are allocated to intended R&D projects promptly and transparently (Elasrag, 2019). This technology not only streamlines the waqf management process but also builds donor trust as they can track the use of funds in real time.

Beyond e-wallets and blockchain, crowdfunding platforms also hold significant potential for TVET R&D funding. These platforms allow TVET institutions to showcase their R&D initiatives to a global network of donors, attracting funding from diverse sources and building a community of supporters who believe in the impact of their research (Mohd Thas Thaker, Mohd Thas Thaker, & Allah Pitchay, 2018). For example, platforms like Global Sadaqah in Malaysia and Waqf Chain in Indonesia have successfully utilized digital technology to raise waqf funds for various educational and welfare projects (Madani & Thomafy, 2024; Mutmainah, Nurwahidin & Huda, 2021). While the development and maintenance costs of these technologies may be high, the long-term benefits, such as increased funding transparency and cost-effectiveness make them worthwhile investments for TVET institutions. By implementing measures such as digital infrastructure development, industry collaboration, and the use of smart contracts, TVET institutions can tap into new funding sources, enhance their research impact, and contribute to human capital development and industrial innovation. The integration of artificial intelligence (AI) into waqf management represents another frontier for enhancing TVET R&D funding efficiency. Suhaimy and Hassan (2023) demonstrate how AI-powered analytics can optimize waqf asset allocation by analyzing historical performance data and predicting future returns. Their study of 15 Malaysian waqf institutions found that AI-optimized portfolios yielded 12.4% higher returns than traditionally managed funds. For TVET institutions, this translates to more sustainable funding streams for long-term research initiatives. Furthermore, AI can enhance donor matching by identifying potential contributors based on their giving patterns and aligning them with specific TVET research projects that match their interests (Aziz & Rahman, 2022).

Corporate waqf partnerships offer substantial potential for TVET funding diversification. Ismail et al. (2024) document how Malaysia's corporate sector has increasingly engaged with educational waqf, creating dedicated endowments for technological research and development. Their analysis of 25 corporate waqf initiatives reveals that structured partnerships between corporations and TVET institutions resulted in RM67 million of dedicated R&D funding between 2019-2023. The Axiata Digital Innovation Fund exemplifies this approach, establishing a waqf-based venture capital mechanism that provides both funding and mentorship for technology innovation in TVET institutions (Kadir & Ibrahim, 2023). This model combines commercial expertise with philanthropic objectives, creating sustainable funding ecosystems for applied research.

Cross-border waqf mobilization through fintech platforms presents an untapped opportunity for TVET institutions. Abdullah and Mohammad (2022) explore how digital platforms can facilitate international waqf contributions, enabling Malaysian TVET institutions to access global funding sources. Their research highlights successful implementations in Qatar and the UAE, where dedicated international waqf platforms have mobilized over USD 150 million for educational initiatives. However, regulatory harmonization remains a significant challenge, as cross-border waqf transactions must navigate varying interpretations of Shariah compliance and financial regulations (Noordin et al., 2022). The development of standardized protocols for international waqf transactions could substantially expand the funding base for Malaysian TVET institutions.

Hybrid waqf-sukuk structures represent an innovative funding model particularly suitable for large-scale TVET infrastructure projects. Rahman and Ahmad (2023) analyze how these combined instruments can mobilize market capital while preserving the perpetual nature of waqf assets. Their case study of Indonesia's Waqf-Linked Sukuk demonstrates how this approach raised IDR 15 trillion for educational infrastructure while generating sustainable returns for both investors and beneficiary institutions. For Malaysian TVET institutions, such hybrid models could finance substantial research facilities while creating recurring income streams for operational expenses.

Data interoperability across waqf platforms remains a critical challenge for effective implementation. Hassan and Wong (2023) identify how fragmented data systems impede comprehensive analysis of waqf performance and prevent the creation of unified donor experiences. Their technical analysis suggests that adopting standardized data protocols and API frameworks could enhance system integration, reducing administrative costs by approximately 35% while improving donor engagement through unified tracking interfaces. For TVET institutions managing multiple technology-enabled waqf streams, data standardization represents a crucial enabler for scaling these funding approaches.

The psychological dimensions of digital waqf participation merit careful consideration in platform design. Azman and Jaafar (2022) reveal how interface elements and user experience significantly impact donation behaviors in digital waqf platforms. Their experimental study involving 320 participants found that transparency features showing real-time fund utilization increased average contribution amounts by 28%. Additionally, gamification elements that recognized donor milestones increased recurring contribution rates by 42%. These insights suggest that TVET institutions should invest in user-centered design approaches when developing their digital waqf platforms to maximize donor engagement and contribution levels.

In conclusion, integrating waqf and technology such as e-wallets, blockchain, crowdfunding, AI-powered analytics, corporate partnerships, international platforms, hybrid financial structures, and optimized user experiences offers sustainable solutions to address the funding challenges faced by TVET institutions in their R&D efforts. While there are technical and legal challenges to overcome, these approaches can help TVET institutions reduce their reliance on government funding, increase donor trust, and strengthen their role in driving innovation and economic competitiveness.

8. BENEFITS AND OPPORTUNITIES

The integration of waqf and technology presents avenues for financial support to TVET and fosters innovation. The application of fintech innovations, such as e-wallets, to facilitate cash waqf contributions for the advancement of research and development presents a multitude of opportunities and advantages. In terms of increased inclusiveness, including e-wallets into waqf-based R&D funding has a clear benefit (Mat et al., 2022).

Utilizing digital payment methods, those from various financial backgrounds are enabled to participate in micro-waqf contributions, therefore enabling little and consistent payments to accumulate major waqf funds. Especially in TVET growth, this approach revitalizes the waqf system and harmonizes with the digital revolution of financial instruments, therefore enabling donations to cash waqf by communities and institutions (Kamarzaman et al., 2024).

Acceptance of e-wallets for waqf donations also lowers processing times and administrative costs, therefore enhancing monetary collecting and distribution efficiency. Digital transactions quicken processing, unlike conventional banking systems, ensuring that money is promptly provided to TVET institutions (Kamarzaman et al., 2024). Research and development initiatives targeted at sustaining continuous investigation efforts especially obtained from this efficiency depend on quick funding. The reduction of bureaucratic obstacles helps TVET institutions to concentrate on the development of technologies including artificial intelligence-driven learning tools, renewable energy innovations, and improved procurement processes for vocational training equipment (Yapilami et al., 2024).

TVET institutions and politicians have indeed great opportunities to adopt this approach. Working jointly among TVET institutions, fintech enterprises, and Islamic financial organizations can help to enhance the perfect integration of e-wallet waqf systems (Shafie et al., n.d.). By managing and rewarding digital waqf donations, that is, matching contributions to increase the efficacy of waqf funds or tax benefits for benefactors— governments can have a significant impact. Blockchain-based waqf endowments guarantee that donations are only used for programs connected to national educational goals, therefore ensuring that research and development activities align with national priorities and greatly lower money misuse risks.

More generally, including waqf-based e-wallet funding into national TVET development plans, can help the industry to be much enhanced. Covering digital change, skills essential for the halal sector, and developments in green technologies, this method may improve many specialized training courses in vocational education. By smartly investing waqf money into these growing areas, TVET colleges could educate students with the necessary skills to satisfy the changing needs of a dynamic work environment. This structure emphasizes the need for waqf as a basic tool for reducing poverty and advancing sustainable development since it interacts with the ideas of Islamic social finance (Kassim et al., 2024).

Eventually, e-wallets paired with waqf and technology offer a new approach to support technical and vocational education as well as research and development. This approach guarantees that waqf contributions are sufficiently used in promoting educational innovation using improved accessibility, openness, and efficiency of money collecting and management (Asyraf, 2025). TVET institutions may provide sustainable funding sources, lower reliance on government support, and encourage long-term economic development through skill upgrading by adopting digital waqf models. Depending on whether appropriate legislative frameworks, strategic alliances, and comprehensive public awareness campaigns support e-wallet waqf funding, the path of innovation in TVET could be considerably changed (Kamarzaman et al., 2024).

9. CHALLENGES AND RISK

Although combining waqf with technology via e-wallets has several advantages for TVET R&D funding, some dangers and issues should be closely addressed. Technical, legal, financial, and social factors all contribute to generating these difficulties that can affect the sustainable operation of the project. One of the primary challenges in using e-wallet-based waqf funding is the lack of clear policies among many nations (Kamarzaman et al., 2024). In Malaysia, state religious authorities oversee waqf, therefore influencing various waqf governance and administration. The absence of a centralized control system for digital waqf transactions could cause differences in money gathering, handling, and distribution. One also has to guarantee adherence to data protection guidelines, anti-money laundering (AML) legislation, and financial policies to stop abuse and fraud (Ahmad Tarmizi et al., 2023).

The digital character of e-wallet-based waqf contributions reveals the system to cybersecurity issues including hacking, data breaches, and identity theft. Unauthorized access to waqf cash or donor data could undermine public trust and discourage participation (Asyraf, 2025; Kasmon et al., 2024; Mat et al., 2022; Ramdhani et al., 2022). Crucially, data privacy and security compliance with Shariah-compliant financial technology laws and the Personal Data Protection Act (PDPA) is assured. If inadequate protection is given, sensitive donor information could be used to cause financial losses as well as damage to the reputation (Alibeigi et al., 2016).

Society still is not aware of digital waqf systems even if daily transactions with e-wallets are happening more and more. E-wallet waqf is not familiar to many possible contributors, which might deter digital fund contributing behavior. Moreover, some people would reject fintech sites for religious donations since they worry that money would be utilized against Shariah rules or misused. Establishing openness, good government, and educational programs helps one inspire adoption and develop confidence (Asyraf, 2025; Eldersevi & Muhammad, 2021; Kasmon et al., 2024; Mat et al., 2022; Ningrat & Nurzaman, 2019; Ramdhani et al., 2022).

Digital literacy of donors, as well as waqf managers, will define how efficient e-wallet waqf money is for TVET R&D. Particularly in rural areas and elderly donors less familiar with mobile payment methods, limited availability to digital infrastructure and poor internet penetration in some places may inhibit cooperation. Furthermore, lacking technological understanding to combine e-wallets with blockchain-based waqf management systems, TVET institutions, and waqf management bodies could cause operational interruptions and inefficiencies (Akmal et al., 2021; Alam et al., 2021; Mat et al., 2022; Tahiri Jouti, 2019; Yapilami & Adamu Z Balami, 2024).

Although e-wallet transactions increase openness, without suitable monitoring tools funds could still be subject to misbehavior, corruption, or poor allocation. Should TVET institutions or the waqf authorities ignore unambiguous evidence of money use, donors would start to doubt the system. Moreover, the lack of a performance-tracking system for R&D projects funded by waqf grants begs issues about the impact and effectiveness of such funds (Mat et al., 2022; Yapilami & Adamu Z Balami, 2024).

The long-term sustainability of donations is one of the key issues of e-wallet waqf funding. Although micro-waqf contributions are outstanding, over time donor weariness might lead to irregular or declining gifts. Unlike conventional waqf assets—like land or buildings—which generate continuous income—cash waqf using e-wallets requires ongoing participation to sustain funding levels. Maintaining a constant flow of funds could prove challenging without suitable marketing plans, participation projects, and rewards (BNM, 2022; Eldersevi & Muhammad, 2021).

Ensuring e-wallet waqf monies fit TVET R&D priorities presents yet another challenge. The kind of research projects funded by waqf would not fit the actual demand of TVET institutions. TVET institutions would need money for developing innovations, artificial intelligence-driven technologies, and sustainable energy solutions even while some sponsors could want to help halal industry-related research or Islamic financing. A lack of precise alignment could prohibit money from being used most strategically and effectively (Kamarzaman et al., 2024).

Although e-wallet-based waqf funding can affect TVET R&D funding, effective deployment of this technology depends on overcoming these issues and hazards. The four areas that need development are public education, cybersecurity policy, regulatory consistency, and continuous donor involvement. Overcoming these challenges, e-wallet waqf projects can be a useful and fast tool for ensuring financial sustainability, driving TVET innovation, and advancing technology improvements in vocational education.

10. RECOMMENDATIONS FOR IMPLEMENTATION

The beneficial use of e-wallet-based waqf funding for TVET R&D depends on some strategic activities. To guarantee the viability and long-term profitability of the project, these activities center on legal frameworks, technology innovations, public participation, and sustainable finance models. Dealing with these issues will help waqf-based digital funding to become a transforming tool for TVET college support of research and innovation.

First and most important is building a consistent legislative framework for digital waqf. In Malaysia, state religious institutions mostly regulate waqf; however, their management presents contradictions. Successful collection, management, and distribution of digital waqf money calls for a nationally coordinated regulatory framework. E-wallet waqf transactions should also meet Shariah compliance, and financial rules including anti-money laundering (AML) and data security procedures. By giving tax benefits to people and businesses utilizing e-wallets, the government can help waqf and thereby promote more public engagement.

Furthermore, using digital technologies will help to boost confidence and openness. Real-time tracking and reporting features included in e-wallet transactions will enable contributors to monitor gift usage. Tamper-proof records of waqf transactions offered by blockchain technology would ensure that money is spent only for its intended use, therefore reducing cash waste. Smart contracts also let TVET colleges automatically get money, depending on specified project criteria, therefore lowering their risk of mismanagement. The development of publicly accessible dashboards letting donors review information on waqf fund allocation and impact will particularly help to build further system confidence.

Since digital waqf refers to online transactions, cybersecurity, and data protection have to be given top importance. Donor data will be safeguarded and cyberattacks will be blocked by taking together end-to-end data protection, multi-factor authentication (MFA), and high-security encryption. Following international cybersecurity standards including ISO 27001 and Malaysia's Personal Data Protection Act (PDPA) allows one to keep the security of e-wallet waqf systems. Building public confidence mostly depends on addressing issues concerning data breaches or financial crime since they could deter individuals from using technology.

Increasing involvement in e-wallet waqf finance also primarily depends on public knowledge and digital literacy initiatives. Many people, especially those in rural areas and older generations, might not know about digital gift options. Public knowledge of the advantages and security of e-wallet waqf contributions should be enlightened by social media campaigns, seminars, and educational activities. Gamification tool digital certificates, reward-based donations, or donor recognition—could potentially motivate constant engagement. To further the Islamic relevance of digital waqf and its implications on education, TVET institutions should also cooperate with religious leaders and local authorities.

Effective implementation also depends quite much on cooperation among TVET institutions, fintech startups, and Islamic banks. Major e-wallet providers could be worked with by TVET institutions like Touch "n Go, Boost, and GrabPay help to establish smooth channels of donation. Investing waqf money into Shariah-compliant products like Sukuk (Islamic bonds) helps Islamic financial institutions to also create ongoing profits for TVET R&D. Corporate alliances can also be established in which case companies match employee waqf contributions, therefore promoting more corporate social responsibility (CSR) in the development of vocational education.

We should accept many unique funding ideas if we wish to guarantee long-term profitability. With a subscription-based micro-waqf model, one approach users of e-wallets might set recurring monthly payments. This method guarantees consistent income flow, thus less reliance on one-time gifts is needed. Using the waqf-linked crowdfunding model is another way TVET institutions could start digital fundraising activities to gather community-based donations for certain R&D initiatives. Moreover, hybrid waqf models that which integrate monetary waqf with revenue-generating waqf assets such as rental income from waqf properties can give TVET innovators greater continuous support.

Crucially also, with regard to economic development, is matching national TVET targets with e-wallet waqf funding. Including this project within Malaysia's more comprehensive TVET reform agenda will help to raise the financial viability of vocational schools. Moreover, strategically targeted should be waqf donations to priority R&D domains such as halal industry skill development, artificial intelligence-driven educational tools, and sustainable energy solutions. Including matching funds will help the government boost the impact of waqf-based TVET funding even more by matching every RM1 received via e-wallet with an equivalent amount of government money.

At last, the effective use of e-wallet-based waqf for TVET R&D asks for a varied approach combining governmental assistance, technology integration, cybersecurity precautions, public education, and strategic alliances. These suggestions will help TVET institutions find a clear and sustainable source of funding, therefore enabling them to support technical innovation, skills development, and economic progress. Good implementation of this project could update waqf financing, boosting its accessibility, and impactfulness, and fit with Malaysia's goal for TVET excellence and digital transformation.

11. FINDINGS AND DISCUSSION

The integration of waqf with modern technology, particularly e-wallets, represents a promising approach to addressing the persistent funding challenges in TVET institutions.Through comprehensive analysis of the existing literature, policy documents, and empirical studies, several significant patterns, contradictions, and implications have emerged that warrant detailed discussion.

A consistent pattern observed across multiple studies is the significant gap between waqf's theoretical potential and its practical implementation in educational funding. Research by Ismail Abdel Mohsin (2013), Yusof et al. (2013), and Kamarzaman et al. (2024) consistently highlights the substantial theoretical capacity of waqf to generate educational funding.Yusof et al. (2013) estimate that Malaysian Muslims contributing just RM30 monthly could generate approximately RM4.3 billion annually through cash waqf. Similarly, Ramdhani et al. (2022) identify a potential value of IDR 100 trillion for cash waqf in Indonesia. However, actual collection rates remain drastically lower - approximately 0.5% of potential in Indonesia according to Ramdhani et al. (2022) and similarly modest figures in Malaysia as reported by Yayasan Wakaf Malaysia (2023).

This implementation gap appears consistently across geographical contexts and is particularly pronounced in the application of technoloav-enabled waqf systems. Studies by Zakariyah et al. (2022), Mat et al. (2022), and Madani & Thomafy (2024) all identify similar barriers to effective implementation, including regulatory fragmentation, technological infrastructure limitations, and public awareness deficits. The persistence of these patterns across different research contexts suggests fundamental structural challenges rather than context-specific issues.

Traditional interpretations focusing exclusively on immovable property have consistently given way to broader understandings that include cash, intellectual property, and digital assets. This evolution is documented by Rashid (2018), Mahamood & Ab Rahman (2015), and Ahmad et al. (2022), illustrating a progressive adaptation of classical Islamic jurisprudence to contemporary economic contexts. This reconceptualization appears most advanced in countries with established Islamic finance frameworks, notably Malaysia and Indonesia

Several notable contradictions emerge when comparing research findings across studies. One significant divergence concerns the appropriate governance model for technology-enabled waqf systems. Abd Aziz et al. (2021) advocate for centralized governance mechanisms with strong regulatory oversight, while Ahmad et al. (2022) propose decentralized blockchain-based governance that minimizes institutional control. This fundamental tension between centralized and decentralized abroaches reflects broader debates within Islamic finance regarding the opriate balance between traditional authority structures and technological innovauun.

Another apparent contradiction relates to the primary barriers to e-wallet waqf adoption. Ambrose & Asuhami (2021) identify technical literacy and access as the principal constraints, suggesting digital inclusion interventions as the priority solution. Conversely, Zakariyah et al.

(2022) emphasize religious and theological concerns as the primary barrier, recommending enhanced Shariah governance frameworks as the key intervention. These differing perspectives highlight the multidimensional challenges facing e-wallet wagf implementation and suggest the need for comprehensive approaches addressing both technical and theological dimensions.

Despite these contradictions, significant agreement exists regarding the transformative potential of technology in waqf management. Studies by Wildana et al. (2022), Luntajo & Hasan (2023), and Salman et al. (2021) consistently highlight how technologies like blockchain and artificial intelligence can enhance transparency, reduce administrative costs, and increase donor confidence. This consensus spans geographical contexts and methodological approaches, suggesting robust evidence for technology's positive impact on waqf management efficiency.

There is also strong agreement regarding the need for regulatory harmonization. Abdullah and Mohammad (2022), Noordin et al. (2022), and Zakariyah et al. (2022) all emphasize regulatory fragmentation as a critical barrier to effective implementation, particularly for cross-border waaf initiatives. This consensus extends to recommendations, with most studies advocating for unified regulatory frameworks that maintain Shariah compliance while facilitating technological innovation. The findings have significant implications for policy, practice, and theoretical understanding of Islamic social finance. First, the persistent gap between wag's potential and implementation suggests that technical solutions alone may be insufficient without addressing underlying structural and cultural factors. The development of e-wallet platforms must therefore be accompanied by broader ecosystem interventions, including regulatory reform, public education, and institutional capacity building.

Second, the emerging consensus on technology's positive impact suggests that digital transformation should be a strategic priority for wagf institutions. However, the contradictory perspectives on governance models imply that implementation approaches must be contextually tailored rather than universally applied. Malaysian TVET institutions may require governance models that reflect the country's specific regulatory environment. cultural factors, and technological infrastructure.

Third, the findings reveal a critical need for multidisciplinary approaches that integrate technological, theological, and educational perspectives. The tension between technical and religious barriers highlighted in contradictory studies suggests that effective implementation requires collaboration across disciplines. TVET institutions seeking to implement e wallet waqf systems must engage not only technical experts but also Shariah scholars, educational specialists, and community representatives.

Although direct quantitative data on TVET research funding gaps are limited, several academic studies highlight persistent funding shortages and research gaps within Malaysia's TVET ecosystem. Qualitative research underscores that funding constraints significantly hinder research innovation in TVET institutions (Kamarzaman et.al, 2025). Additionally, although the Malaysian government has invested substantially in TVET development, a major gap remains between Malaysian TVET and the systems of more developed countries, including in terms of research capacity and industry alignment (Amin et al., 2023). Furthermore, governance analyses reveal that research on TVET policy and funding remains underdeveloped, pointing to a need for more targeted, evidence-based funding mechanisms (Syed Chear, 2023).

In conclusion, the findings reveal a complex but promising landscape for e-wallet waqf implementation in TVET institutions. While significant challenges exist at regulatory, technological, and cultural levels, the consensus on technology's transformative potential suggests that well-designed implementation approaches could substantially address TVET funding gaps. Successful implementation will require multidisciplinary collaboration, contextually tailored governance models, and strategic targeting of high-priority R&D needs.

12. CONCLUSION

Combining waqf with technology via e-wallet-based finance is one novel strategy for TVET R&D support. Including digital financial technology will enable this method to provide open, reasonably priced, and effective waqf contributions, therefore promoting the growth of vocational education and research. If e-wallet waqf is to be long-term successful, it must thus be correctly used inside a full legislative framework, strong public participation, sustainable financial schemes and enough cybersecurity measures.

E-wallet waqf for TVET R&D wins the most from its ability to democratize money utilizing micro-waqf contributions from numerous sources. Reducing many of the difficulties related to traditional waqf models enables the digital platform to let individuals routinely contribute small amounts combined to have a major impact. Using increased openness and lowering the danger of financial manipulation, smart contracts, and blockchain technologies guarantee the effective use of donations for research and development.

Notwithstanding its benefits, the concept generates great risks and challenges including cybersecurity problems, public mistrust, unfair legislation, and technology limitations. Policymakers have to guarantee financial security in digital transactions and blend waqf criteria across several countries to solve these issues and Shariah compliance. Especially significant initiatives in public awareness campaigns and digital literacy also motivate more participation and confidence in e-wallet waqf contributions.

Well-developed financial planning will help to ensure the long-term availability of this income source. Three ways TVET institutions assure a continuous finance flow include hybrid waqf models, waqf-linked crowdsourcing, and subscription-based micro-waqf. Matching government finance with corporate backing with CSR projects permits e-wallet money to be even more efficient.

At last, the implementation of e-wallet waqf for TVET R&D depends only on cooperation among TVET institutions, fintech startups, Islamic banks, and government agencies. Combining Islamic social funding with digital technologies allows Malaysia to lead a creative and sustainable waqf ecosystem supporting vocational education sector technical innovation, skill acquisition, and economic development by means of digital tools. Appropriate laws, infrastructure, and community involvement help e-wallet-based waqf funding to greatly improve TVET quality and future-ready workforce development.

REFERENCES

AAOIFI. (2018), available at: www.aaoifi.com (accessed June 2018).

Abd Aziz, H., & Abd Ghadas, Z. A. (2021, December). Corporate governance framework for Shariah compliant corporation. In *International Joint Conference on Arts and Humanities 2021 (IJCAH 2021)* (pp. 528-532). Atlantis Press. (ICMR), I. for C. M. R. M. (2024). *Market-based financing for SMEs in Malaysia: Enhancing access and affordability.*

Abdullah, M., & Mohammad, S. (2022). Cross-border waqf mobilization through digital platforms: Opportunities and challenges for educational funding. *Journal of Islamic Finance, 11*(1), 78–94.

Abdullah, S., & Lee, K. H. (2022). Fragmentation and integration in TVET policy governance: A comparative analysis of Southeast Asian approaches. *Journal of Vocational Education and Training, 74*(3), 412–429.

Ahmad, F., & Lim, J. (2024). Beyond compensation: Comprehensive strategies for researcher retention in Malaysian TVET institutions. *Asian Journal of Technical Education, 16*(1), 78–93.

Ahmad, K., Hassan, M. K., & Siraj, S. A. (2022). Blockchain-based waqf management: Enhancing transparency and efficiency. *International Journal of Islamic and Middle Eastern Finance and Management, 15*(1), 78–96.

Ahmad Tarmizi, M., Zolkaflil, S., Omar, N., Hasnan, S., & Syed Mustapha Nazri, S. N. F. (2023). Compliance determinants of anti-money laundering regime among professional accountants in Malaysia. *Journal of Money Laundering Control, 26*(2), 361–387. DOI: 10.1108/JMLC-01-2022-0003

Ahmed, W., Rasool, A., Javed, A. R., Kumar, N., Gadekallu, T. R., Jalil, Z., & Kryvinska, N. (2021). Security in next generation mobile payment systems: A comprehensive survey. *IEEE Access : Practical Innovations, Open Solutions, 9*, 115932–115950. DOI: 10.1109/ACCESS.2021.3105450

Akmal, A., Izzat, A., Marzuki, A., Atiqah, S., Amin, M., Haroming, N. A., Mohideen, R. S., Ilyas, I. Y., Universiti, K., & Melaka, I. (2021). THE AWARENESS TOWARDS THE IMPORTANCE OF HEALTH IN MALAYSIA. *E-Journal of Media & Society, 7*, 1–18.

Al-Attas, S. M. N., & Ibrahim, M. F. (2021). Governance models for educational waqf institutions: Balancing tradition and innovation. *Journal of Islamic Finance, 10*(2), 34–49.

Alam, M. M., Awawdeh, A. E., & Muhamad, A. I. (2021). Using e-wallet for business process development: Challenges and prospects in Malaysia. *Business Process Management Journal, 27*(4), 1142–1162. DOI: 10.1108/BPMJ-11-2020-0528

Aldeen, K. N. (2021). 40-year bibliometric analysis of waqf: Its current status and development, and paths for future research. *Journal of Islamic Monetary Economics and Finance, 7*(1), 181–200. DOI: 10.21098/jimf.v7i1.1308

Alibeigi, A., Munir, A. B., & Asemi, A. (2016). Compliance with Malaysian Personal Data Protection Act 2010 by Banking and Financial Institutions, a Legal Survey on Privacy Policies. *Taylor & Francis in the International Review of Law. Computing Techniques*, (April), 247–269.

Amin, S. M., Suhaimi, S. A., & Nazuri, N. S. (2023). The present and future of Malaysian technical and vocational education and training (TVET). *International Journal of Academic Research in Business & Social Sciences, 13*(18). Advance online publication. DOI: 10.6007/IJARBSS/v13-i18/19952

Ardiyansyah, R., & Kasdi, A. (2021). Strategies and Optimizing the Role of Productive Waqf in Economic Empowerment of the Ummah. *Ziswaf: Jurnal Zakat Dan Wakaf, 8*(1), 61. DOI: 10.21043/ziswaf.v8i1.9871

Asyraf, M. (2025). *Waqf- Driven Inclusive Prosperity Exploring the Intersection of Islamic Finance*. Fintech, and Sustainable Development Goals., DOI: 10.4018/979-8-3693-5653-1.ch012

Ayub, M. (2022). Promoting the Institution of Waqf for Socio-economic Development in Islamic Societies. *Journal of Islamic Business and Management, 12*(02).

Aziz, M. R. A., & Yusof, M. A. (2014). Examining the Relationship between Level of Income and Appointment of Agent in Collecting Waqf Fund. *International Journal of Trade. Economics and Finance, 5*(2), 167–169. DOI: 10.7763/IJTEF.2014.V5.363

Aziz, N. A., & Rahman, A. A. (2022). Artificial intelligence in philanthropic matching: Optimizing donor-cause alignment for educational waqf. *International Journal of Islamic Economics and Finance, 5*(2), 145–163.

Azman, F., & Jaafar, N. I. (2022). The psychology of digital giving: User experience design for waqf platforms. *Journal of Islamic Marketing, 13*(3), 512–531.

BNM. (2022). *Financial Sector Blurprint 2022-2026.*

Cameron, R., & O'Hanlon-Rose, T. (2023). Australia's unified funding framework for technical education: Lessons for developing economies. *International Journal of Training Research, 21*(1), 45–62.

Department of Polytechnic Education. (2023). *Malaysian TVET Lecturer Development Report 2023*. Ministry of Higher Education Malaysia.

Department of Skills Development. (2023). *Annual Report 2022: Skills Development in Malaysia*. Ministry of Human Resources.

Economic Planning Unit. (2021). *Twelfth Malaysia Plan, 2021-2025: A prosperous, inclusive, sustainable Malaysia* [PDF]. https://pulse.icdm.com.my/wp-content/uploads/2021/09/Twelfth-Plan-Document_compressed-1.pdf

Elasrag, H. (2019). *Blockchains for Islamic finance: Obstacles & Challenges. Munich Personal RePEc Archive*. Retrieved from https://mpra.ub.uni-muenchen.de/92676/

Eldersevi, S., & Muhammad, M. (2021). "Asnaf Care: A Case Study of the Malaysian-based Charity Crowdfunding Platform to Combat the Impact of COVID-19." *5th International Conference of Zakat,* 2020, 615–626.

Hassan, A., & Abdullah, A. (2018). Corporate waqf models and their distinctive features: The future of Islamic philanthropy. Journal of Islamic Economics. *Banking and Finance*, *14*(3), 147–165.

Hassan, N., & Ibrahim, M. (2023). Factors influencing researcher retention in Malaysian TVET institutions: A mixed-methods study. *Technical and Vocational Education Journal*, *15*(2), 189–206.

Hassan, R., & Wong, B. (2023). Data interoperability challenges in digital waqf ecosystems: Technical requirements and implementation frameworks. *International Journal of Islamic Finance*, *15*(2), 201–219.

Intellectual Property Corporation of Malaysia. (2024). *Statistical booklet 2024: Applications and registrations/grants by intellectual property components.* MyIPO. https://www.myipo.gov.my/statistic-application-registration/

International Labour Organization. (2023). *Skills shortages and the green transition in Asia and the Pacific*. International Labour Office. https://labordoc.ilo.org/discovery/fulldisplay/alma995320392002676/41ILO_INST:41ILO_V2

Ismail Abdel Mohsin, M. (2013). Financing through cash-waqf: a revitalization to finance different needs. International journal of Islamic and Middle Eastern finance and management, 6(4), 304-321.

Ismail, A., Yusof, M. Y., Mohamed, S., & Ibrahim, Z. (2024). Corporate waqf and TVET innovation: Institutional partnerships for sustainable development. *Waqf Studies Review*, *7*(1), 112–130.

Ismail, W. M. B. W., Rasool, B. A., Saladin, M., & Noor, A. H. B. M. (2021). Technology Acceptance and Technology Usage: Importance to Cash Waqf Contribution. *International Journal of Academic Research in Business & Social Sciences, 11*(9), 942–953. DOI: 10.6007/IJARBSS/v11-i9/11082

Ismail, W. M. W. (2021). Significance of technology to cash waqf collection: Application of unified theory acceptance and use of technology (UTAUT). *International Journal of Academic Research in Business & Social Sciences, 11*(1), 777–788.

Kadir, M. A., & Ibrahim, S. (2023). The Axiata Digital Innovation Fund: A case study in corporate waqf for technological development. *Journal of Islamic Business and Management, 13*(1), 67–83.

Kamarzaman, N., Ahmad, A. A., Zain, M. N. M., & Muda, M. Z. (2024). Peranan Wakaf dalam Penggerak Ekonomi Islam bagi Menangani Keterbatasan Dana dalam Penyelidikan dan Inovasi di Sektor Pendidikan TVET [The Role of Waqf in Driving Islamic Economics to Address Funding Limitations in Research and Innovation Within The TVET. *BITARA International Journal of Civilizational Studies and Human Sciences (e-ISSN: 2600-9080), 7*(2), 290–308.

Kamarzaman, N., Mat Zain, M. N., & Azlin Alisa, A. (2025). Funding shortages impact on research and innovation in TVET institutions: A qualitative analysis. *Online Journal for TVET Practitioners, 10*(1), 1–11. DOI: 10.30880/ojtp.2025.10.01.001

Kang, J., & Park, S. (2022). Commercialization of TVET innovations: The South Korean model for intellectual property management. *The Journal of Technology Transfer, 47*(3), 582–601.

Kasdi, A., Karim, A., Farida, U., & Huda, M. (2022). Development of Waqf in the Middle East and its Role in Pioneering Contemporary Islamic Civilization: A Historical Approach. *Journal of Islamic Thought and Civilization, 12*(1), 140–153. DOI: 10.32350/jitc.121.10

Kasmon, B., Ibrahim, S. S., Daud, D., Raja Hisham, R. R. I., & Ratnasari, R. T. (2024). Future behavior in waqf digitalization: Integrating UTAUT and DIT theories. *Journal of Islamic Marketing*. Advance online publication. DOI: 10.1108/JIMA-03-2024-0111

Kassim, S., Redzuan, N. H., & Zakariyah, H. (2024). *IMPORTANCE OF FINANCIAL LITERACY AND AWARENESS IN MICROTAKAFUL : IMPLICATIONS FOR INDUSTRY. 2024.*

Luntajo, M. M. R., & Hasan, F. (2023). Optimalisasi Potensi Pengelolaan Zakat di Indonesia melalui Integrasi Teknologi. *Al-'Aqdu. Journal of Islamic Economics Law*, *3*(1), 14–28.

Madani, R. I., Nurhidayati, N., & Thomafy, K. (2024). Examining The Potential of Cash Waqf and Development Model. *Munazzama: Journal of Islamic Management and Pilgrimage*, *4*(2), 83–103.

Malaysia., G. of. (2021). *Twelfth Malaysia Plan, 2021-2025: Sustainable growth for Malaysia's future.*

Malaysian Qualifications Agency. (2022). *TVET Quality Assurance Framework*. MQA.

Malaysian Science and Technology Information Centre. (2025). *Research and development (R&D) indicators*. Ministry of Science, Technology and Innovation. https://mastic.mosti.gov.my/statistic/research-and-development-rd-indicators/

Malaysian Technology Development Corporation. (2023). *Commercialization Pathways for Technical Innovation in Malaysia*. MTDC.

Mat, M., Shamsuddin, J., Sitiris, M., Yunus, S. M., Abu, A. H., & Kulliyyah, S. (2022). E-Wallet in Malaysia: A Proposed Structure of Contracts According to The Juristic Adaptation (Takyif Fiqhi). *Malaysian Journal Of Islamic Studies (MJIS)*, *6*(2), 15–37. https://journal.unisza.edu.my/mjis/index.php/mjis/article/view/203

Ministry of Education Malaysia. (2015). *Malaysia Education Blueprint 2015–2025 (Higher Education)*. Ministry of Education Malaysia. https://www.kooperation-international.de/uploads/media/3._Malaysia_Education_Blueprint_2015-2025__Higher_Education__.pdf

Ministry of Higher Education. (2023). *Research Grant Distribution Report 2022*. MOHE.

Ministry of Human Resources. (2023). *Technical and Vocational Education and Training Report 2023*. MOHR.

Mohamad, N., Affandi, H. M., Sohimi, N. E., Kamal, M. F. M., Herrera, L. M., Zulkifli, R. M., & Abas, N. H. (2023). Exploring TVET Institution Directors' Barriers in Managing Malaysian TVET Institutions-Industry Partnership. *Journal of Technical Education and Training*, *15*(1), 277–287. DOI: 10.30880/jtet.2023.15.01.024

Mohd Noor, A. (2021). Industry-academia collaboration through CREST: Impacts on TVET research funding in Malaysia. *Malaysian Journal of Technical Studies*, *8*(2), 112–129.

Mutmainah, L. L., Nurwahidin, N., & Huda, N. (2025). Optimizing productive waqf for halal tourism development. *Journal of Islamic Accounting and Business Research.*

Ningrat, R. G., & Nurzaman, M. S. (2019). Developing Fintech and Islamic Finance Products in Agricultural Value Chain. *Journal of Islamic Monetary Economics and Finance*, *5*(3), 491–516. DOI: 10.21098/jimf.v5i3.1077

Noordin, K. A., Ahmad, S., Ismail, Z., & Wahid, H. (2022). Regulatory challenges in international waqf transactions: A comparative analysis. *International Journal of Islamic and Middle Eastern Finance and Management*, *15*(3), 356–371.

OECD. (2025). Vocational education and training systems in nine countries: Germany. OECD Publishing. https://www.oecd.org/en/publications/vocational-education-and-training-systems-in-nine-countries_1a86eb6c-en/full-report/vocational-education-and-training-in-germany_dae78944.html

Penang Institute. (2023). *TVET in Malaysia: Current situation, challenges and recommendations*. Penang Institute. https://penanginstitute.org/publications/issues/tvet-in-malaysia-current-situation-challenges-and-recommendations/

Rahman, Z. A., & Abdullah, A. (2023). From innovation to commercialization: Challenges and opportunities for Malaysian TVET institutions. *International Journal of Technology and Vocational Education*, *12*(1), 34–52.

Rahman, Z. A., & Ahmad, S. (2023). Waqf-linked sukuk for TVET infrastructure development: Structural analysis and performance metrics. *Journal of Islamic Monetary Economics and Finance*, *9*(1), 123–142.

Rahman, Z. A., & Haneef, M. A. (2020). Comparative analysis of waqf regulations: A study of Malaysia, Indonesia and GCC countries. *Islamic Economic Studies*, *28*(1), 55–74.

Ramdhani, A. F., Mulyana, R., & Afendi, F. M. (2022). Analysis Of Factors Influencing The Cash Waqf Receiving: Electronic Money Transaction. *Journal of Islamic Economics. Finance and Accounting Studies*, *1*(1), 1–17.

Ramli, F. A. A. (2021). Mobile payment and e-wallet adoption in emerging economies: A systematic literature review. *Journal of Emerging Economies and Islamic Research*, *9*(2), 1–39.

Razali, M., Mohd, N., Hadigunawan, N., & Saidon, R. (2021). Maqasid shariah hifz mal in e-wallet application. *Islamiyyat. International Journal of Islamic Studies*, *43*(1).

Riyanda, A. R., Jalinus, N., Abdullah, R., Ranuharja, F., Islami, S., Adi, N. H., & Aminuddin, F. H. (2022). The New Paradigm of Technical and Vocational Education and Training (TVET). EDUKATIF: jurnal ilmu pendidikan, 4(1), 364-371.

Rusli, N. A. (2024a). A Comparative Analysis of Technical and Vocational Education and Training (TVET) for Special Needs Students in Malaysia and Hungary. *Online Journal for TVET Practitioners*, *9*(1), 14–23. DOI: 10.30880/ojtp.2024.09.01.002

Salman, M. J., Mohamad, N. A., & Sadique, M. A. (2021). E-WAQF IMPLEMENTATION: A PARADIGM SHIFT IN NIGERIA WAQF SYSTEM. *Journal of Asian and African Social Science and Humanities*, *7*(4), 41–53. DOI: 10.55327/jaash.v7i4.255

Shafie, Z. B., Premier, U. O., Karamah, Z., Baharul, A., Technology, I., & Premier, U. O. (n.d.). *Chapter 7 : ANALYSIS OF LECTURERS ' INVOLVEMENT IN FOR POLYTECHNIC*. 147–166.

Suhaimy, K. A., & Hassan, M. K. (2023). Artificial intelligence in waqf portfolio optimization: Empirical evidence from Malaysian institutions. *Journal of Islamic Finance*, *12*(2), 178–194.

Sulaiman, S., Hasan, R., & Mohammad, M. T. S. (2019). Integration of waqf and sukuk for educational infrastructure financing: A proposed model. *International Journal of Islamic Economics and Finance Research*, *2*(2), 1–15.

Syed Chear, S. L. (2023). *Governance of TVET in Malaysia: Gaps and opportunities for researchers*. TVET-Online Journal.

Tahiri Jouti, A. (2019). An integrated approach for building sustainable Islamic social finance ecosystems. *ISRA International Journal of Islamic Finance*, *11*(2), 246–266. DOI: 10.1108/IJIF-10-2018-0118

TalentCorp Malaysia. (2023). *Industry-Academia Collaboration Report: Bridging the Gap in Malaysia's Talent Development*. TalentCorp.

The Asia Foundation. (2022). *Recommendations towards improving technical and vocational education and training in Malaysia*. The Asia Foundation. https://asiafoundation.org/wp-content/uploads/2024/08/Recommendations-Towards-Improving-Technical-and-Vocational-Education-and-Training-in-Malaysia.pdf

Varaprasad, N. (2021). Technical and Vocational Education Trends and Issues in Singapore. In Trends and Issues in International Technical and Vocational Education in the Indo-Pacific Region (p. 287).

Wahid, F. N., Rosli, M. S. D. A., Afandi, M., Rani, M., & Arif, M. I. A. M. (2023). Catalysing National Health Security by The Islamic Micro Endowment Mechanism Through Financial Technology Platform. *International Journal of Academic Research in Business & Social Sciences, 13*(7), 39–46. DOI: 10.6007/IJARBSS/v13-i7/17672

Wan, C. D. (2025). *TVET in Malaysia's human resource development plans: Realities and "game changers"* (ISEAS Perspective No. 2025/5). ISEAS–Yusof Ishak Institute. https://www.iseas.edu.sg/articles-commentaries/iseas-perspective/2025-5-tvet-in-malaysias-human-resource-development-plans-realities-and-game-changers-by-wan-chang-da/

Wildana, M. D. A., & Imamia, T. L. (2022, April). Waqf in the 21st Century: The Implementation of Blockchain and Smart Contract Technology. *Journal of International Conference Proceedings, 5*(1), 456–466. DOI: 10.32535/jicp.v5i1.1774

Wong, K. T., Lim, S. Y., & Hassan, F. (2022). Geographical disparities in TVET research funding: A longitudinal analysis of Malaysian institutions. *Education Sciences, 12*(3), 235–251.

Yapilami, A., & Adamu, Z. Balami. (2024). *ISSN : 2204-012X African Journal of Innovative Research and Advanced studies ISSN : 2204-012X African Journal of Innovative Research and Advanced studies. 14*(4), 9–20.

Yayasan Wakaf Malaysia. (2023). Cash Waqf Collection and Distribution Report 2018-2023. Kuala Lumpur: YWM.

Yusof, M. A., & Ab. Aziz, M. R. (2015). Scrutinizing the Method of Contribution for Islamic Waqf Bank Fund. *Journal of Islamic Economics Banking and Finance, 11*(1), 181–192. DOI: 10.12816/0026024

Yusof, M. A., Ridhwan, M., Aziz, A., & Ramli, Y. (2013). Exploring New Opportunity and Mechanism for Islamic Waqf Bank Model. *2nd Applied International Business Conference (AIBC2013)*, 805–816.

Zain, N. M., Aspah, V., Abdullah, N., & Ebrahimi, M. (2017). Challenges and evolution of higher education in Malaysia. *UMRAN-Journal of Islamic and Civilizational Studies, 4*, 1–1.

Zakariyah, H., Salaudeen, A. O., Othman, A. H. A., & Rosman, R. (2022). Enhancing waqf management through fintech in Malaysia. *Journal of Emerging Economies and Islamic Research, 10*(2), 62–73.

Ziderman, A. (2018). *Funding Mechanisms for Financing Vocational Training: An Analytical Framework.* DOI: 10.1007/978-3-319-90388-0_8

Chapter 3
Development and Validation of the Islamic Financial Literacy Construct

Farah Amalina Md Nawi
https://orcid.org/0009-0001-9204-6182
Universiti Sultan Zainal Abidin, Malaysia

Muhammad Ridhwan Ab. Aziz
https://orcid.org/0000-0003-0177-7869
Universiti Sains Islam Malaysia, Malaysia

Syahidawati Hj Shahwan
Universiti Sains Islam Malaysia, Malaysia

ABSTRACT

This study addresses the need for a contextually relevant assessment of financial literacy within the Islamic framework by developing and validating a comprehensive measurement instrument. Islamic Financial Literacy (IFL) is conceptualized through three dimensions: Islamic financial knowledge, Islamic financial attitudes, and Islamic financial behaviours, along with the role of religious orientation. A two-phase approach was employed. Phase one involved a pilot study using a self-administered questionnaire with 150 randomly selected AKPK clients in Kuala Lumpur. Exploratory Factor Analysis (EFA) refined the instrument, leading to item removals and reassignments for better conceptual alignment. Phase two involved a survey of 400 systematically sampled AKPK clients across Malaysia. Confirmatory Factor Analysis (CFA) supported the model's unidimensionality, validity, and reli-

DOI: 10.4018/979-8-3373-1842-4.ch003

ability. The resulting tool is both psychometrically sound and practically valuable. This study offers a novel, empirically grounded instrument tailored to the Malaysian Islamic finance context.

1.0 INTRODUCTION

Islamic financial literacy (IFL) is essential for Muslims not only to achieve financial well-being, but also to ensure all financial conducts align with Islamic principles. More than just financial competence, IFL incorporates religious awareness, ethical conduct, and moral accountability, distinguishing it from conventional financial literacy. Its importance has become increasingly pronounced in today's financial environment, where Muslim financial consumers are navigating a complex and rapidly evolving financial landscape that demands a higher degree of financial knowledge, ethical judgment, and religious compliance.

In Malaysia, the urgency to enhance financial literacy among the population has become more pressing. According to the report by the Ministry of Finance (Ministry of Finance, 2025), nearly 1.4 million individuals have sought financial advisory services from the Credit Counselling and Debt management Agency (AKPK), showing the reliance on eternal support for financial decision-making. In the same report, approximately 495,000 individuals are currently enrolled in it the Debt Management Program (DMP) administered by AKPK, reflecting the magnitude of financial vulnerability among Malaysian consumers.

Moreover, it is particular alarming that more than 53,000 Malaysians below the age of 30 are burden with debt, amounted nearing RM1.9 billion (Ministry of Finance, 2024). Several factors contributed including the rising cost of living, easy credit assesses, and further compounded by the limited financial preparedness. Thus, the need to strengthen IFL among this demographic is increasingly urgent as a means to enhance their financial resilience.

Additionally, the rapid transformation of financial technology reshapes the way financial services are accessed and utilized, particularly the younger and digitally savvy consumers. Various innovations including digital banking, robo-advisors, and mobile payments have enhanced financial accessibility, but also come with new risks such as exposure to unethical products, privacy violations, and online fraud (Alsaghir, 2023). For Muslim customers, these risks are magnified by the obligation to ensure Shariah compliance. Without a holistic framework that integrates ethical, digital, and religious literacy, Muslim customers may inadvertently engage in non-compliant financial arrangements, hence resulting in both financial harm and distress (Al-Hammadi et al., 2024).

Nevertheless, despite its importance, studies in IFL remains limited. In fact, there is ongoing debate among scholars on the conceptualization and measurement of financial literacy in general (Koskelainen et al, 2023; Ouachani et al., 2021; Huston, 2010), as well as Islamic financial literacy in particular (Lahsasna, 2016). This lack of consensus resulted in inconsistencies pertaining to how IFL is understood and assessed across different studies.

Due to its importance, there is a need for a validated instrument designed to measure IFL among the Muslim population. The availability of such tool will facilitate the identification of the current state of IFL and the necessary steps required to reach an adequate level. However, studies on the conceptualization and measurement of IFL is still limited, with several IFL studies adopted conventional financial literacy instrument without appropriate modification (see: Er & Mutlu, 2017; Rahman et al., 2018), hence abandoning religious and moral values uphold in Islamic finance. Meanwhile, several instruments were only focusing on specific areas such as Islamic banking (Albaity & Rahman, 2019), Takaful (Maduku & Mbeya, 2024), and investment behaviour (Dinc et al., 2021), which hinders the development of a comprehensive IFL instrument. Only few instruments are noticeably holistic in measuring IFL, such as those by Antara et al. (2017).

Therefore, this study seeks to develop and validate a multidimensional construct of IFL. By focusing on Muslim emerging adults who are among the clients of Credit Counselling and Debt management Agency (AKPK), this study targets an important yet under-research population, that are those who not only experiencing financial challenges but also actively seeking financial knowledge, all within the context of Islamic values and obligations. Through this study, we aim to provide a rigorous and practical instrument that can be used for educational, policy and research purpose in advancing IFL.

2.0 LITERATURE REVIEW

2.1 Overview of Financial Literacy: Evolution and Measurement

Financial literacy is a critical determinant of individual and household financial well-being. The 2008 global financial crisis served as a wake-up call, exposing the societal costs of inadequate financial knowledge and prompting a renewed emphasis on financial education as a foundation for economic stability (Atkinson & Messy, 2012). More recently, the economic fallout from the COVID-19 pandemic recently has reaffirmed the importance of financial resilience, particularly among vulnerable and low-income populations (OECD, 2021).

The need to make independent and complex financial decisions within volatile and uncertain economic environment demands adequate financial knowledge. However, studies acknowledged that knowledge alone does not necessarily translate into sound financial behaviours (Nunez et al., 2025; Xiao & Porto, 2017; Lusardi, 2015). Therefore, Huston (2010) proposed financial literacy as a combination of financial knowledge and the ability to apply that knowledge. Building on this definition, OECD (2011) introduced a more comprehensive framework that is, "a combination of awareness, knowledge, skill, attitude and behaviour necessary to make sound financial decisions and ultimately achieve individual financial well-being." This multidimensional and behavioural-oriented perspective has shaped many of the widely adopted financial literacy frameworks, including those proposed by Atkinson and Messy (2012), Lusardi and Mitchell (2014), and Credit Counselling and Debt Management Agency (AKPK, 2019), all of which highlight the interplay between knowledge, attitude, and behaviour.

The contemporary financial literacy assessment typically covers three interrelated domains namely financial knowledge (understanding of financial concepts), financial attitudes (psychological predisposition toward financial management), and financial behaviours (financial practices including saving, investing, and financial products adoption). Even though there is growing consensus on this tripartite framework, some limitations exist. For instance, Huston (2010) noted that many studies not only failed to clearly define financial literacy but also to operationalize its components, which probably can hinder comparability and validity in research. Similarly, Koskelainen et al. (2023) highlighted a lack of consistency in measurement tools and definitions, which impedes the comparability of findings across studies and limits the utility of meta-analyses. The absence of standardized constructs has led to methodological fragmentation, limiting the overall impact and scalability of financial education interventions.

Although the widely used tools such as those by Lusardi and Mitchell (2011) have gained widespread adoption, it only captures cognitive knowledge. Critics argue that this narrow approach overlooks the behavioural and attitudinal dimensions of financial literacy, which may be stronger predictors of real-world financial decision-making (Potrich et al., 2016). Furthermore, it would provide an incomplete picture of a person's financial capability.

Additionally, the limitation also pertains to the insufficient of religious and cultural contextualization of mainstream financial literacy models. Since most of the frameworks have been developed in secular context, they may not be applicable in settings where religious values strongly influence financial behaviours. For Muslims, financial arrangements are shaped by Shariah principles which guide every single conduct including the prohibition of *riba* (interest), obligation of zakat payment, and the importance of Shariah-compliant investment. These religious norms make financial practices not only an economic act but also a religious obligation. Applying conventional frameworks without accounting for these factors may result in inaccurate assessments of IFL and misinformed interventions.

2.2 Islamic Financial Literacy: Conceptualization and Gaps

The conceptualization of Islamic financial literacy is crucial for distinguishing it from the conventional counterpart, as well as for capturing the distinct religious, ethical and socio-economic dimensions. However, there is no universally agreed definition of financial literacy from conventional perspective (Huston, 2010) as well as from Islamic standpoint (Lahsasna, 2016). This conceptual ambiguity has led to fragmented interpretation, which resulted in adoption of conventional financial literacy model without proper modifications, hence risking the dilution of the distinctive features embedded in Islamic financial literacy (Rahman, et al., 2018).

2.2.1 Conventional vs. Islamic Financial Literacy

Conventional financial literacy revolves mainly maximizing individual well-being through wealth accumulation, high-return investments, and effective financial management. It is rooted in secular and empiric paradigms that are directed towards material outcomes, rational choice, and value-neutral financial strategies. Consequently, conventional financial literacy may permit involvement in interest-bearing financial products, speculative investments, or non-Shariah compliant business, provided they maximize returns. The overall aim is worldly financial success (*dunyawi*) with minimal consideration for religious or ethical boundaries (Abdullah & Majid, 2003).

Meanwhile, IFL grounded in divine revelation and religious accountability. It integrates financial knowledge and behaviour with Islamic principles, treating financial arrangements as part of one's religious obligation and an act of worship (*'ibadah*). Three theological foundations guide IFL includes: *tawhid* (oneness of Allah), *nubuwwah* (prophethood), and *ma'aad* (accountability in the hereafter) (Iqbal & Mirakhor, 2011). These principles elevate financial behaviour beyond rational calculation to include ethical and eschatological dimensions. Additionally, IFL emphasizes Shariah compliance, such as the prohibition of *riba* (interest), *gharar* (excessive uncertainty), *maysir* (gambling), and investment in unethical sectors, while promoting justice, transparency, halal business activities, and social solidarity (ISRA, 2023).

2.2.2 Early Definition and Foundational works

Early studies predominantly adopted conventional financial literacy framework without appropriate contextual adaptation. As a result, they often overlooking the socio-cultural and religious nuances relevant for the population under the study. For instance, Abdullah and Anderson (2015) and Abdullah et al. (2017) adopted Huston's (2010) model, where IFL was defined as financial knowledge acquired through learning and experience about the core principles and products of finance. Similarly, Rahim et al. (2016) followed the OECD (2011) in their definition, highlighting the ability to apply knowledge, skills, and attitudes in managing resources. Although these frameworks provide a point of departure, they have a tendency to neglect broader aspects such as personal financial management and religious orientation.

Over time, researchers apparently introduced broader and more integrative elements of IFL. For instance, Abdullah and Razak (2016) include the components of personal financial management such as Takaful, retirement savings, and Islamic investment, as well as acknowledging obligations like zakat, *waqf*, and *sadaqah*. Lahsasna (2016) expanded further with the addition of Shariah principles in transactions, debt management, and zakat calculation. These advances point to increasing recognition that IFL is not just financial literacy in an Islamic "wrapper," but a multidimensional phenomenon that demands its own theoretical basis.

2.2.3 Evolving and Recent Conceptualizations

Current studies continue to refine and extend the conceptualization of IFL. For instance, Abdullah et al. (2021) expressed IFL as the ability to comprehend Islamic financial concepts and products, which enables individuals to make decisions that are both financially and religiously sound. Meanwhile, Antara et al. (2017) defined IFL as a progressive integration of knowledge, awareness, and skills that directs financial decision-making according to Islamic norms. Masrizal et al. (2024) added an affective component by conceptualizing IFL as a combination of knowledge, skills, and beliefs that cultivate positive financial attitudes and behaviours. Similarly, Hidajat and Hamdani (2017) emphasized the importance of aligning financial behaviours with ethical and religious values, thus diverting focus from theoretical knowledge to behavioural practice.

This shift reflects a broader interpretation of IFL as a process that is values-guided and behaviour-oriented, requiring compliance with Islamic ethical imperatives. Sari et al. (2021), for example, defined IFL as the application of Islamic financial knowledge in daily financial decisions, highlighting the role of faith in determining financial behaviours.

2.2.4 Proposed Operational Definition

In order to address the above gaps, this study conceptualizes IFL as a developmental process, suggesting the following working definition: "Islamic financial literacy is a process through which individuals acquire adequate Islamic financial knowledge, cultivate Islamic financial attitudes, and ultimately apply that knowledge in real-life situations reflected in Shariah-compliant financial behaviours". This definition highlights the dynamic interrelationship between knowledge (input), attitudes (throughput), and behaviours (output), mirroring both cognitive development and spiritual commitment. It concurs with the *maqasid al-Shariah* as it encourages ethical decision-making, financial justice, and socio-economic empowerment. It also harmonizes with modern demands for value-based intermediation and inclusive financial wellness, placing IFL not only as an individual skillset, but rather as a means to collective prosperity and responsibility. As reiterated in the Qur'an: "The reward of Allah SWT is better for he who believes and does righteousness." (Al-Qasas, 28:80), Islamic financial decisions are not simply economic choices but acts of faith and ethical responsibility. As such, IFL plays both material and moral functions in the financial lives of Muslims.

2.2.5 Critical gaps in the Literature

Despite growing scholarly and institutional interest, considerable conceptual gaps persist in the development of IFL models. Many definitions are descriptive in nature, lacking a robust grounding in either the principles of Islamic finance or behavioural theory. Moreover, integration of *maqasid al-Shariah* is also limited, with only a few models linking IFL to objectives like justice, equitable wealth distribution, and the protection of faith and intellect. In addition, most frameworks prioritize cognitive knowledge at the expense of affective (values, ethics) and behavioural (habits, decision-making) dimensions, thus sacrificing theoretical breadth. Methodologically, many instruments lack psychometric validation across diverse settings, circumscribing their generalizability (Koskelainen et al., 2023). The literature tends to treat Muslims as homogeneous, ignoring contextual differences such as religious education, financial systems, and socio-economic heterogeneity. For instance, studies in Indonesia point to moderate levels of IFL among youth (Firdausi & Kasri, 2022), whereas those in Malaysia report relatively higher levels (Shafik & Ahmad, 2020). Such differences highlight the influence of institutional and cultural contexts. While multidimensional tools such as Dinc et al.'s (2021) four-dimensional scale show promise, their application and validation across diverse populations are still lacking. Furthermore, the rapid development of digital finance makes continuous refinement of IFL concepts and tools necessary. These challenges highlight the need for a comprehensive, theory-driven, and context-sensitive IFL framework that integrates Islamic ethical foundations with empirical soundness.

2.3 Components of Islamic Financial Literacy

IFL is increasingly being acknowledged as a dynamic process instead of a static trait, shaped by interrelated cognitive, attitudinal, and behavioural facets (OECD, 2023; Barbic et al., 2019; Potrich et al., 2016). Underpinned by the Family Resource Management Theory (FRMT), this study conceptualizes IFL as a continuum whereby Islamic financial knowledge is the requisite input, Islamic financial attitude is the mediating throughput, and Islamic financial behaviours is the ultimate output. FRMT, developed by Deacon and Firebaugh (1988), delineates management as "the process of using resources to achieve goals" (Goldsmith, 2005). This view aligns with how people utilize Islamic financial knowledge to allocate resources and make value based, informed financial decisions. This section discusses the pertinent literature to gain a clear picture of each IFL components and to guide the construction of a strong and contextually relevant measurement framework.

2.3.1 Islamic Financial Knowledge: Domains and Measurement Considerations

Islamic financial knowledge encompasses the understanding gained through education and experience related to key Islamic finance principles and products (Abdullah & Anderson, 2015). Studies consistently affirms that financial knowledge is the basis of financial literacy (Lin & Bates, 2022; Warmath & Zimmerman, 2019; Huston, 2010). This comprises theoretical and practical understanding of financial matters, which, in turn, influence financial attitudes and behaviours (Yong et al., 2018). In Islamic finance, such knowledge is a guiding principle that allows individuals to conduct financial transactions in a way that conforms to Shariah, which adhere to religious considerations (Hidajat & Hamdani, 2017).

Islamic financial knowledge goes beyond familiarity with financial instruments to include an in-depth grasp of the principles, contracts, and instruments of Islamic finance. Literature has explored the breadth of this knowledge, spanning the basics in areas like Islamic banking, Takaful, and capital markets (Gunawan et al., 2021; Setiawati et al., 2018). In addition, knowledge about basic contracts like *murabahah, ijarah, wakalah,* and *mudarabah* is also essential in measuring IFL (see: Ahmad et al., 2020; Bley & Kuehn, 2003) to capture whether individuals can make informed decisions in real financial settings.

Beyond contracts and financial products, IFL also includes critical aspects of personal financial management such as saving, spending, financing, investing, and retirement planning (Mokhtar et al., 2018). Another significant facet is Islamic philanthropy, e.g., zakat, *waqf*, and *sadaqah,* embodies the socio-economic and redistributive goals of the Islamic economic system (Shafik & Ahmad, 2019). A sophisticated grasp of financial terms such as assets, liabilities, and returns (Dinc et al., 2021), and numerical skills such as profit margin calculation, financing repayment and zakat calculation (Setyowati et al., 2018) is also vital to facilitate informed decision-making.

In the contemporary digital context, IFL needs to include digital and FinTech literacy. The emergence of Islamic FinTech has reconfigured the ways in which Shariah-compliant products are accessed, understood, and used (Scott, 2024). Such innovations not only promote financial inclusion but also require new levels of digital and financial literacy among Muslim users (Mohamed & Otake, 2025). Grasping fintech tools and their Shariah compliance mechanisms is therefore now imperative, since low digital literacy could prevent users from assessing their adherence to Islamic principles.

Given the multifaceted nature of Islamic financial knowledge, it can be systematically categorized into several key domains including foundational Islamic finance concepts and principles; Shariah-compliant contracts; Islamic financial products; personal financial management; and Islamic philanthropy, as shown in **Table 1**. These domains are synthesized and thoroughly assessed in this study.

Table 1. Aspects Evaluated in Measuring Islamic Financial Knowledge

No.	Authors	Islamic finance principles	Islamic finance contracts	Islamic financial products	Numerical questions	Financial concepts & terms	Financial management	Islamic philanthropy
1.	**Dinc et al. (2021)**							
2.	Gunawan et al. (2021)	✓		✓			✓	
3.	Ahmad et al. (2020)	✓	✓					
4.	Albaity & Rahman (2019)	✓		✓				
5.	Shafik & Ahmad (2019)					✓		✓
6.	Setyowati et al. (2018)	✓	✓	✓	✓			

continued on following page

Table 1. Continued

No.	Authors	Islamic finance principles	Islamic finance contracts	Islamic financial products	Numerical questions	Financial concepts & terms	Financial manage-ment	Islamic philan-thropy
1.	**Dinc et al. (2021)**							
7.	Mokhtar et al. (2018)			✓			✓	
8.	Setiawati et al. (2018)	✓	✓	✓				
9.	Er and Mutlu (2017)			✓				
10.	Antara et al. (2017)	✓	✓					
11.	Taofik et al. (2017)		✓					
12.	Rahim et al. (2016)	✓		✓			✓	
13.	Abdullah & Anderson (2015)			✓			✓	
14.	Bley and Kuehn (2003)		✓	✓				
15.	Hamid & Nordin (2001)		✓	✓				

2.3.2 Measurement of Islamic Financial Knowledge

IFL can be measured using a well-structured framework that not only evaluates consolidates existing knowledge but also determines gaps that are inhibiting Shariah-compliant financial decision-making. This research follows Krathwohl's (2002) taxonomy, which defines knowledge in four dimensions: factual (basic terminologies), conceptual (underlying theories and principles), procedural (steps and procedures), and metacognitive (self-awareness and critical thinking). This categorization serves as a foundational structure for constructing a comprehensive and methodologically sound Islamic financial knowledge measurement instrument. However, most developed instruments have frequently not been empirically validated across varied demographics. Most studies use convenience sampling and self-report questionnaires without in-depth psychometric testing, which limits the generalizability and reliability of findings (e.g., Koskelainen et al., 2023; Antara & Musa, 2020). In order to enhance future evaluations, researchers must include more sophisticated methods like item response theory (IRT), structural equation modelling (SEM), and longitudinal designs.

2.4 Islamic Financial Attitudes and the Measurement Framework

As a psychological construct, attitude has been extensively theorized by the scholars. Thurstone (1928) defined attitude as an individual's inclinations, emotions, prejudices, and beliefs regarding a particular subject. Campbell (1950) conceptualized attitude as a consistent pattern of responses toward social entities, while Altmann (2008) emphasized the role of attitude in shaping behaviour through beliefs, emotions, and values. Ajzen and Fishbein (1980) defined attitude as an individual's favourable or unfavourable evaluation of particular behaviours. Structurally, attitudes are formed through cognitive (beliefs), affective (emotions), and conative (intentions) components (Ajzen, 2005).

In financial contexts, attitudes influence how individuals perceive, interpret and manage financial decisions. Positive financial attitudes that are marked by trust, responsibility, and future orientation are often linked with sound financial behaviours (Adiputra & Patricia, 2020). In contrast, negative attitudes can lead to avoidance, impulsivity, and poor financial choices (Fenton & Furnham, 2020). Idris (2002) underscored attitude as multifaceted and not always predictive of behaviour, proposing dimensions like general, positive, conditional, and technical attitudes to reflect this complexity.

According to Shrigley et al. (1988), attitudes evolve over time through personal experience, social norms, and education, which suggest that individual financial attitudes can be reshaped through effective interventions (Bhushan & Medury, 2014). Therefore, financial literacy programs must address not just knowledge, but also attitudes, to achieve meaningful behavioural change (OECD, 2022). In the Islamic context, attitudes hold an even more significant role, as it is not only a reflection of rational financial judgement but also integrate religious values and ethical commitments which shape individual financial behaviour that align with Shariah (Shah et al., 2023). In short, Islamic financial attitude is perceived as the "throughput" that links Islamic financial knowledge (input) with Islamic financial behaviours (output). This multidimensionality of Islamic financial attitudes comprises of four domains:

1. General attitudes toward Islamic finance: Encompassing trust and acceptance of Islamic financial systems. Positive financial attitudes are linked to higher usage intentions and product uptake (Rahman et al., 2018).

2. Attitudes toward specific Islamic financial products: Including perceptions of Islamic banking products, Takaful, and Shariah-compliant investments. Positive product-specific attitudes lead to product adoption (Gunawan et al., 2021).
3. Attitudes toward Islamic philanthropy instruments: Covering zakat, *waqf*, and *sadaqah*, which are essential for wealth redistribution and social justice. Positive attitudes of these instruments foster active participation in charitable giving (Shafik & Ahmad, 2019).
4. Attitudes toward personal financial management: Reflecting financial discipline in terms of budgeting, debt management, and saving behaviours within an Islamic ethical framework. Positive attitudes towards personal financial management support sound financial management (Mokhtar et al., 2018).

All these four domains are crucial particularly for this study, and for IFL studies in general in order to design more effective financial literacy interventions that not only emphasizing on knowledge but also nurture value-driven attitudes that can foster Shariah-compliant financial behaviours.

2.5 Islamic Financial Behaviours and the Measurement Framework

Financial behaviour refers to activities of managing money including saving, spending, borrowing, and investing (Xiao, 2008). These financial behaviours are key pointers to financial well-being and long-term economic resilience. From Islamic perspective, financial behaviour is more than economic rationality. It involves religious commitment, moral obligation, and spiritual accountability. Wealth management in Islam is both an act of worship (*'ibadah*) and a trust (*amanah*). As such, Muslims are obligated to earn, spend, and share wealth in manners that demonstrate their adherence to divine principles and accountability to God.

To Muslim, the Qur'an is an important source of financial guidance. All financial activities are subject to moral responsibility (As-Sabaa' 34:31). The prohibition of *riba* (usury) (Al-Baqarah 2:275–279) promotes fair dealing and discourages exploitative tendencies. The principles of *wasatiyyah* (moderation) and *amanah* (trustworthiness) guide Muslims toward responsible financial behaviour, such as avoiding extravagance (Al-A'raf 7:31), fulfilling obligations to dependents (Al-Baqarah 2:233–234), and upholding the rights of others in one's wealth (Al-Baqarah 2:254). These principles demonstrate that, in Islam, financial conduct extends beyond the management of money to include the compliance of financial decisions with social justice, moral commitments, and spiritual values.

Elaborating on this basis, existing literature classifies financial behaviours into areas like saving, borrowing, investing, and financial planning (Dinc et al., 2021;

Er & Mutlu, 2017). These areas are further delineated by Shariah, like avoiding haram income, participating in halal investments, being responsible with debt, and discharging religious obligations like *zakat* and *sadaqah* (Biplob & Abdullah, 2019). Saving, investing, and financial protection are the fundamental dimensions identified by Huston (2010), which, for IFL, must incorporate ethical and religious aspects.

In spite of this robust conceptual basis, empirical evidence on Islamic financial behaviour is inconclusive. Although most Muslims support Islamic financial ideals, actual behavioural participation is inconsistent. For instance, Nasira et al. (2021) revealed that among Malaysian Muslims, Takaful knowledge did not significantly predict purchase intention. Likewise, Jiang and Shimizu (2024) noted that increasing financial literacy may not directly boost engagement in financial investments or retirement planning in Japan. Mansori et al (2020) contend that financial behaviour is influenced not only by religiosity or financial knowledge, but also by structural conditions such as socio-economic circumstances and the credibility of Islamic financial institutions.

2.6 Integrating Religious Values into Financial Literacy Framework

Despite the fact that over 80% of the world's population finds religion central to their lives (Sedikides, 2010), financial literacy research has been oblivious to religious influences. Religion affects one's values, behaviours, and lifestyle, which are mirrored in financial decisions (Graafland, 2017; Sham & Yusof, 2015; Alam et al., 2011). It not only delineates the moral landscape of life but also prescribes social behaviours and consumption patterns (Hirschman, 1983). For Muslims, religious teachings directly prescribe personal financial management such as prohibiting interest-based transactions, denouncing extravagance (*israaf*), prescribing halal consumption, repayment of debt, zakat, savings, and charitable giving.

Notably, the impact of religion on financial attitude among Muslims is different compared to non-Muslims. Sabri and Falahati (2014) find that Muslims are more motivated by religion, while non-Muslims are relatively more affected by secondary agents such as peers and media. With this differentiation, the current research introduces religion to further explain the financial literacy among Muslims. This study adheres to Hassan's (2005) operationalisation of Muslim religiosity, based on Glock's (1972) five-dimensional model: ideological, ritualistic, devotional, experiential, and consequential.

1. Ideological (ID): Pertains to fundamental religious beliefs, e.g., belief in Allah, Prophet, and divine will. In Islamic finance, this means strict compliance with Shariah principles, such as preferring Islamic banking to interest-based systems.

2. Ritualistic (RT): Entails religious duties like prayer and zakat. Financially, it comprises meeting duties like *zakat, sadaqah*, and *waqf*, which signify adherence to Islamic financial ethics.
3. Devotional (DV): Transcends public rituals to faithful, private actions motivated by religion. In terms of finance, this involves utilizing resources to satisfy Allah SWT, e.g., giving *sadaqah* with pure intention.
4. Experiential (EX): Refers to spiritual and emotional experiences of the divine. In finance, this includes the peace and contentment that result from aligning financial choices with Islamic values.
5. Consequential (CO): Represents the outcomes of religious adherence in secular and spiritual terms. Islamic finance promotes justice, fairness, and social welfare, delivering both spiritual rewards and worldly societal benefits, such as wealth redistribution and ethical economic practices.

3.0 RESEARCH METHODOLOGY

3.1 Scale Design

The scale was developed based on Churchill's (1979) multi-step scale development process, beginning with the specification of the construct domain through conceptual definitions. Survey items were formulated based on an extensive review of pertinent academic literature, primarily IFL and related constructs. This process ensure that critical dimensions are adequately addressed and connected with the study objectives.

Prior to actual data collection, a pre-test was conducted to identify the precision, pertinence, and overall appropriateness of the items in the questionnaire. To begin with, the questionnaire was previewed and pre-tested with a small group of postgraduate students and lecturers to ensure there were no ambiguities and item clarity (face validity). The bilingual version of the questionnaire was then subjected to a panel of experts to confirm face, content, and measurement validity. The professional critique was intended to assess the overall content, language, question design, appropriateness of terminologies and concepts, and measurement scale employed.

3.2 Sample Selection and Data Collection

The population for the study included Muslim clients of Agensi Kaunseling dan Pengurusan Kredit (AKPK) in Malaysia aged between 18 and 40 years old. Systematic sampling was employed such that every third client among the visiting clients in eight AKPK branches nationwide was selected. This ensured a still more systematic and representative sample from diverse geographic locations.

According to Hair et al. (2019), sample size for Structural Equation Modeling (SEM) would be a function of several factors including model complexity, number of constructs, number of indicators for each construct, and communality levels. In the case of models with seven or fewer constructs, low communalities (below 0.45), or less than three items per construct, a minimum of 300 cases would be appropriate. For more complex models that involve several constructs, low communalities, or few indicators for each factor, a sample of 500 is required. Based on these standards and to ensure viable statistical analysis, 550 questionnaires were distributed.

There were two data collection phases. In the first phase, 150 participants participated in a pilot study to try out the instrument's clarity, structure, and reliability. On the basis of pilot results, refinements were done as and when required. The second phase consisted of the main survey, which duly provided 400 complete and valid responses for final analysis. During the process of data collection, strict ethical standards were followed, and respondent anonymity and confidentiality were ensured. Data collected were analysed through SPSS and AMOS using both exploratory factor analysis and confirmatory factor analysis.

Table 2 provides a summary of the demographic and socio-economic profile of the 400

respondents. 52.5% of the sample consisted of male respondents, with 47.5% of the respondents being female, highly representative of the national gender composition of the country as reported by the Department of Statistics Malaysia (DOSM, 2023). The group aged between 36 to 40 years was the largest (35.0%), and they were predominantly were in the private sector (44.3%). Results are in accordance with Malaysian Department of Insolvency statistics (2023), which report that the most affected population in the event of bankruptcy are Malay males aged 35–44 who work in the private sector. Because they were clients of AKPK, participants visited the agency for various reasons involving money and are a suitable sample for this research.

Table 2. Demographic Characteristics of the Respondents

Demographic	Characteristics	n	%
Gender	Male	210	52.5
	Female	190	47.5
Age	18 – 20	37	9.3
	21 – 25	61	15.3
	26 – 30	83	20.8
	31 – 35	79	19.8
	36 – 40	140	35
Occupational sector	Government	73	18.3
	Semi-government	32	8.0
	Private	177	44.3
	Self-employed	82	20.5
	Housewife	14	3.5
	Student	13	3.3
	Others	9	2.3
Total household income	Less than RM2,500	143	35.8
	RM2,500 – RM4,849	141	35.3
	RM4,850 – RM7,099	82	20.5
	RM7,100 – RM10, 959	19	4.8
	RM10, 960 – RM15,039	10	2.5
	More than RM15,039	5	1.3
Educational background	Finance	113	28.2
	Non-Finance	287	71.8

Interestingly, AKPK (2019) also found that females are more likely to make financial planning for how they spend their money, while 40- to 49-year-olds, as well as private sector respondents, claim to have lower financial planning. This breakdown by population increases the representativeness of the study and allows analysis by targeted segments of population.

A large majority of respondents (71.1%) fall in the B40 income group, with household incomes below RM4,850 per month. Moreover, 71.8% of them did not have any formal financial education. The statistics above reiterate the previous results of AKPK (2018) and Mansor et al. (2022), showing that individuals within the B40 group, especially those earning less than RM4,000 monthly, are most likely to be in financial hardship when they do not have adequate financial knowledge. Hence, conducting IFL research on this group is relevant and timely since it is addressing an economically exposed segment with limited access to financial education.

3.3 Exploratory Factor analysis

Exploratory Factor Analysis (EFA) is conducted in order to refine measurement items, and attain construct validity before Confirmatory Factor Analysis (CFA). The process is significant since it identifies latent structures without assuming a known factor structure, and hence significant in theory-building for multi-factorial constructs (MacCallum et al., 1999). By investigating inter-item relationships, EFA reduces redundancy and increases construct interpretability.

For best factor structure, variance reduction is achieved with Principal Component Analysis (PCA) maximizing variance extraction (Bentler & Kano, 1990). Strong indicators only are retained with a factor loading of 0.50 to enhance model reliability (Hair et al., 2019). Low and cross-loading items are excluded to ensure conceptual consistence. The exercise maximizes the theoretical foundation, giving the established measurement model that will be validated by CFA subsequently.

3.4 Confirmatory Factor Analysis

Once EFA has been conducted, the CFA is done to validate the measurement model such that every construct accurately reflects the theoretical concept. This step refines the model by verifying whether observed variables measure the related latent constructs effectively.

CFA tests three facets of validity: construct validity, convergent validity, and discriminant validity. Construct validity is evaluated using fit indices like parsimonious, absolute, and incremental fit measures (Awang et al., 2018). Strong model fit increases confidence in the theory. Convergent validity is confirmed using factor loadings, Average Variance Extracted (AVE), and Composite Reliability (CR), with high internal correlations. Discriminant validity guarantees each construct is conceptually distinct, not redundant, and enhances interpretability.

Reliability is quantified with CR, where values greater than 0.70 indicate internal consistency and no significant measurement error (Hair et al., 2019). Establishing validity and reliability gives the measurement model stability that is a good foundation for Structural Equation Modeling (SEM) and enables proper hypothesis testing.

4.0 RESULTS

4.1 Exploratory Factor analysis

EFA was separately applied to the four constructs, i.e., (1) Islamic Financial Knowledge, (2) Islamic Financial Attitudes, (3) Islamic Financial Behaviours, and

(4) Religious Orientation. The results of EFA of all the constructs are shown in Table 3. The KMO of each of the constructs was more than 0.80, implying that the data were perfectly suitable for factor analysis (Chua, 2014). In addition, Bartlett's Test of Sphericity was significant ($p < 0.05$), further validating the appropriateness of the data for forthcoming analysis.

Table 3. KMO and Barlett's Test Score

Statistical Criteria		**Constructs**			
		IFK	**IFA**	**IFB**	**RO**
KMO (>.080)		**.888**	**.946**	**.855**	**.838**
Bartlett's Test of Sphericity	**Approx. Chi-Square**	3129.056	3542.085	1972.088	1154.869
	df	325	210	190	55
	Sig. (p<.05)	.000	.000	.000	.000

The next step involved verifying extraction communalities, eigenvalues, TVE, and factor loadings for all constructs. Items that had communalities below 0.50 were omitted as they explained less than half of the variance in measuring the latent construct (Hair et al., 2006). The eigenvalues should be higher than 1.0, and TVE should be greater than 0.60, such that at least 60% of the construct was explained by its items (Awang et al., 2018). TVE reflects the degree to which the measurement items adequately represent the construct. The summary of the changes made is presented in Table 4.

Table 4. Summary of Item Modifications After EFA

Constructs	Factors	Changes (Relocated/Deleted Items)
Islamic Financial Knowledge (26 items)	1. Basic principles of Islamic finance (6 items) 2. Islamic financial contracts (9 items) 3. Islamic philanthropy (6 items) 4. Personal financial management (5 items)	• **Relocated:** K22 (Islamic Philanthropy) falls under Personal Financial Management factor. • **Deleted:** K14 (low factor loading). • **No. of remaining items:** 25
Islamic Financial Attitudes (21 items)	1. Attitudes towards Islamic finance (7 items) 2. Attitudes towards Islamic philanthropy (5 items) 3. Attitudes towards personal financial management (9 items)	• **Relocated item:** A8 (Attitudes towards Islamic Philanthropy) falls under Attitudes towards Personal Financial Management. • **Deleted item:** A10 (low factor loading). • **No. of remaining items:** 20
Islamic Financial Behaviours (21 items)	1. Adoption of Islamic financial products (4 items) 2. Islamic philanthropy engagement (4 items) 3. Financial planning (7 items) 4. Debt and financing (5 items)	• **Relocated item:** B10 relocated to Financial Planning factor. • **Deleted item:** B4 (low value of extraction communalities); B7 (low factor loading). • **No. of remaining items:** 19 items
Religious Orientation (11 items)	1. Islamic financial products adoption (4 items) 2. Wealth management & distribution (7 items)	• **Relocated items:** RO10 is relocated to wealth management & distribution. • **No. of items:** Remain.

Following the EFA, 75 of 79 items measuring the IFL constructs were retained. One item was eliminated due to a low extraction communality value, that is, the item lacked sufficient variation with the remaining items and was not strongly correlated with the underlying factors, thus contributing little to the being measured construct (Hair et al., 2019). Three items were also removed due to low factor loadings, which meant that they represented poor fit to any of the factors extracted and contributed little to the overall factor structure (Hair et al., 2019). Removing these items or items resulted in a more reliable, interpretable, and statistically robust factor model.

4.2 Confirmatory Factor Analysis

Based on the EFA findings, CFA is conducted under the premise of Structural Equation Modeling (SEM) for the purpose of validating the measurement model. SEM consists of two interconnected models, the measurement model, which is tested under CFA in order to determine the factor structure, and the structural model, which examines causal relationships between constructs. CFA plays a crucial role in establishing construct validity through refining measurement indicators and overall general reliability and validity of the model.

In the initial CFA, the model's fitness indices did not meet recommended thresholds (RMSEA=0.085; Chis/df=3.893; CFI=0.816), indicating a poor model fit. Consequently, items with factor loadings below 0.5 were identified and removed, as such items weaken construct representation and negatively affect model fit. Following the guidelines by Awang et al. (2018), item removal was limited to no more than 20% of the total items, resulting in the deletion of 15 items: B10, B15, B16, B18, B21, K4, K5, K6, K7, K8, K9, K15, K22, A8, and RO11.

Despite these adjustments, the model's fit remained inadequate. Therefore, Modification Indices (MI) were examined to detect redundant items. High MI values suggest substantial shared variance between measurement errors, indicating overlapping item content. MI indicates the expected decrease in Chi-Square value if a fixed parameter is allowed to vary. To improve the model, three correlated measurement errors were freed, which contributed to a better model fit. Table 5 summarises the final fit indices for the measurement model.

The revised CFA model (see Figure 1) demonstrated acceptable fit indices (RMSEA=0.08, ChiSq/df=3.54, CFI=0.88) as shown in Table 5, confirming that 60 items reliably represent the intended constructs.

Table 5. Fitness Index for Measurement Model

Name of category	Name of index	Index value	Comments
1. Absolute fit	RMSEA	0.08	The required level is achieved
2. Incremental fit	CFI	0.88	The required level is achieved
3. Parsimonious fit	ChiSq/df	3.54	The required level is achieved

Figure 1. The Measurement Model after Modification Process

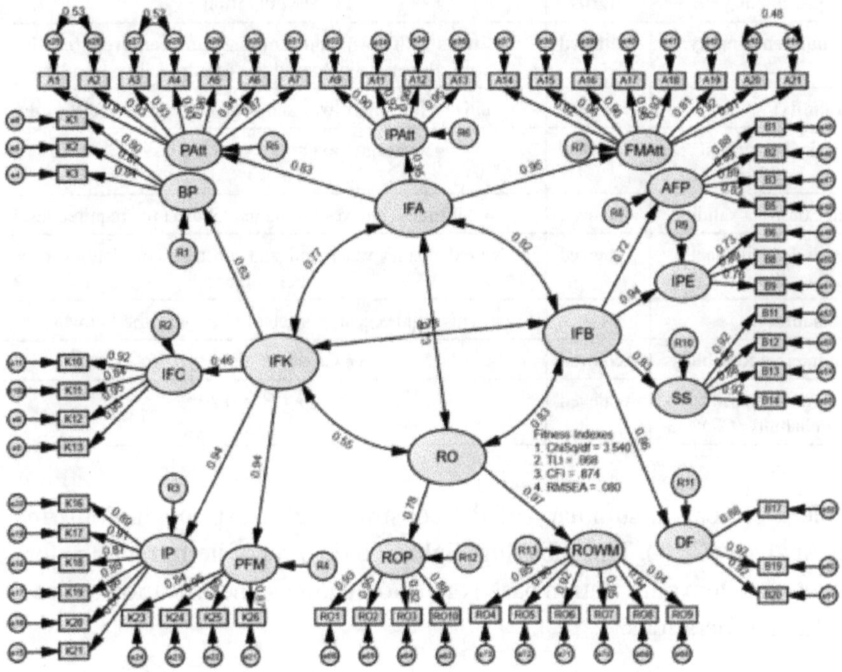

4.2.1 Assessment of Unidimentionality, Validity and Reliability of the Measurement Model

After completing the CFA for each measurement model, it is essential to evaluate unidimensionality, validity, and reliability to ensure the robustness of the constructs before proceeding to the structural model. All assessment criteria were satisfactorily met, as detailed in Table 6 below:

Table 6. Results for Unidimensionality, Validity and Reliability Assessment

Assessment	Status	Explanation
1. Unidimensionality:	**Achieved**	**• Items with low factor loadings were removed iteratively until the model achieved the required fitness indices.**
2. Validity:		**This requirement was achieved through the following:**
i. Convergent validity:	**Achieved**	**• Average Variance Extracted (AVE) ≥ 0.50**
ii. Construct validity:	Achieved	• All fitness indexes for the model meet the required level.
iii. Discriminant validity:	Achieved	• No redundancy was found, and construct correlations remained below 0.85.
3. Reliability:		This requirement was achieved through the following:
i. Internal Reliability:	Achieved	• Cronbach alpha ≥ 0.70
ii. Composite Reliability (CR):	Achieved	• CR ≥ 0.70

Table 7 presents a summary of the constructs refined through Confirmatory Factor Analysis (CFA). This table highlights the final set of items retained for each construct after item purification based on factor loadings, modification indices, and model fit considerations.

Table 7. Confirmatory Factor Analysis (CFA) Summary for All Constructs

Construct	Item	Factor loading	Cronbach Alpha	CR (>0.7)	AVE (>0.6)
Islamic Financial Knowledge	K1 (Riba)	0.80	0.882	0.983	0.774
	K2 (Gharar)	0.87			
	K3 (Maysir)	0.84			
	K10 (AITAB)	0.92			
	K11 (Musharakah)	0.84			
	K12 (Mudarabah)	0.95			
	K13 (Qard)	0.95			
	K16 (Zakat obligation)	0.89			
	K17 (Zakat al-fitr)	0.91			
	K18 (Nisab)	0.87			
	K19 (Zakat on income)	0.89			
	K20 (Sadaqah)	0.86			
	K21 (Waqf)	0.84			
	K23 (Credit card)	0.84			
	K24 (Spending)	0.95			
	K25 (Investing)	0.85			
	K26 (Debt repayment)	0.87			

continued on following page

Table 7. Continued

Construct	Item	Factor loading	Cronbach Alpha	CR (>0.7)	AVE (>0.6)
Islamic Financial Attitude	A1 (Islamic values)	0.91	0.970	0.990	0.733
	A2 (Islamic financial system)	0.93			
	A3 (Islamic banking)	0.93			
	A4 (Islamic financing)	0.93			
	A5 (Islamic financial products)	0.96			
	A6 (Islamic investment)	0.94			
	A7 (Takaful)	0.87			
	A9 (Zakat as social support)	0.90			
	A11 (Waqf as community welfare)	0.92			
	A12 (Sadaqah as spiritual purification)	0.96			
	A13 (Return on sadaqah)	0.95			
	A14 (Budgeting)	0.92			
	A15 (Modest spending)	0.96			
	A16 (Saving for future)	0.96			
	A17 (Repayment ability)	0.96			
	A18 (Debt repayment)	0.92			
	A19 (Needs-based borrowing)	0.81			
	A20 (Retirement saving)	0.92			
	A21 (Regular saving habit)	0.91			

continued on following page

Table 7. Continued

Construct	Item	Factor loading	Cronbach Alpha	CR (>0.7)	AVE (>0.6)
Islamic Financial Behaviours	B1 (Deposit)	0.88	0.899	0.977	0.710
	B2 (Financing)	0.89			
	B3 (Investment)	0.89			
	B5 (Product selection)	0.83			
	B6 (Zakat al-fitr payment)	0.73			
	B8 (Nafaqah)	0.89			
	B9 (Donate income for sadaqah)	0.76			
	B11 (Spending plan)	0.92			
	B12 (Budget adherence)	0.95			
	B13 (Avoiding israaf)	0.88			
	B14 (Spending prioritization)	0.92			
	B17 (Timely debt payment)	0.88			
	B19 (Debt affordability assessment)	0.92			
	B20 (Debt repayment)	0.92			
Religious Orientation	RO1 (Refuse conventional financing)	0.93	0.886	0.977	0.808
	RO2 (Use Islamic banking)	0.95			
	RO3 (Takaful contribution)	0.82			
	RO4 (Pay zakat)	0.88			
	RO5 (Provide nafaqah)	0.85			
	RO6 (Give sadaqah)	0.90			
	RO7 (Make waqf)	0.92			
	RO8 (Prudent spending)	0.85			
	RO9 (Saving money)	0.94			
	RO10 (Refuse conventional investment0	0.94			

Table 8 also shows square root of Average Variance Extracted (AVE) on the diagonal in bold, and off-diagonal values that are correlations between the constructs. Discriminant validity is confirmed if the bold diagonal value is larger than all other values in the same row and column (Awang et al., 2018). Based on this requirement, the model strongly satisfies the discriminant validity requirement.

Table 8. Summary of Discriminant Validity Index

	IFK	IFA	IFB	RO
IFK	**0.88**			
IFA	0.77	**0.86**		
IFB	0.78	0.82	**0.84**	
RO	0.55	0.73	0.83	**0.90**

Overall, both Confirmatory Factor Analysis (CFA) and Exploratory Factor Analysis (EFA) were conducted systematically to ensure the strength and accuracy of the measurement model. EFA determined the underlying factor structure and aided in initial item refinement, while CFA validated the model through fit indices as well as item diagnostics. Given unidimensionality, convergent validity, discriminant validity, and reliability being established, the measurement model is considered sufficient for proceeding to structural model analysis.

5.0 DISCUSSION

5.1 Summary of Key Findings

The study makes a notable contribution to the literature on IFL by developing and validating a large-scale measurement model that captures Islamic financial knowledge, attitudes, and behaviours, as well as the role of religious orientation. Applying Exploratory Factor Analysis (EFA), the study methodically arrives at the latent factors of the IFL construct in a manner whereby elements are conceptually sound and empirically significant. The Confirmatory Factor Analysis (CFA) also corroborates the model's validity by testing its reliability, validity, and structural soundness.

5.2 Theoretical and Conceptual Contributions

This research fills an enduring gap in the literature by offering a standardized, Shariah-aligned measurement framework for financial literacy. In contrast to conventional models that adopt a mainly secular framework, the established IFL model incorporates Islamic ethical and religious needs, thus returning an all-inclusive, faith-based construct of financial decision-making. It further contributes the theoretical advancement of financial literacy along the lines of the input-throughput-output paradigm (Fessler et al., 2020), whereby knowledge leads to attitudes, and these in turn lead to behaviour. The addition of religious orientation is a further explanatory ability, namely in the prediction of compliance with Shariah-compliant financial practices.

5.3 Practical Implications

From a policy and institutional perspective, the validated IFL instrument offers a timely and culturally relevant tool for:

i. Islamic financial institutions, to assess client literacy levels and design Shariah-compliant outreach and advisory services
ii. Educators and curriculum developers, to build Islamic finance education modules that reflect both technical knowledge and ethical values
iii. Policymakers and regulators, to support national financial inclusion strategies that integrate Islamic values, particularly among underserved Muslim populations.

In a digital and increasingly complex financial environment, this model can also inform Islamic FinTech education by helping users assess the Shariah-compliance and ethical alignment of digital financial tools. The model supports the creation of targeted awareness campaigns and financial education interventions that address both literacy gaps and behavioural inconsistencies.

The model also serves as a foundation for developing educational tools, training modules, and public awareness campaigns that are tailored to the religious and cultural context of Muslim societies. Institutions such as zakat agencies, Islamic banks, and regulatory bodies can use this framework to align their strategies with ethical finance objectives. Its integration into higher education curricula and community-based programs can enhance the relevance and impact of Islamic financial education initiatives.

5.4 Limitations and Direction for Future Research

While the EFA and CFA processes ensured a rigorous validation of the construct, the study acknowledges some limitations. The EFA, although effective in identifying underlying dimensions, inherently involves subjective interpretative judgments that may influence the resulting factor structure. Furthermore, the sample was limited to Muslim clients of a specific financial advisory body, which may constrain the generalizability of the findings to broader Muslim populations across different socioeconomic and cultural contexts.

To advance this area of research, future studies should undertake cross-regional and cross-cultural validations of the measurement instrument to ensure its applicability and relevance in diverse settings. Employing longitudinal research designs would also provide insights into how IFL evolves over time and responds to shifting economic conditions and technological advancements. Collaborative efforts with Islamic FinTech platforms could further strengthen digital financial literacy initiatives by integrating Shariah-compliant technological solutions, thereby enhancing financial inclusion and ethical financial engagement among Muslim users.

6.0 CONCLUSION

This study establishes a robust, empirically validated model for measuring Islamic financial literacy. By integrating Islamic financial knowledge, attitudes, behaviours, and religious orientation, the model provides a comprehensive and adaptable tool for academic, policy, and practical applications. It supports broader efforts to promote financial well-being, ethical decision-making, and Shariah-compliant financial practices across diverse Muslim communities. Ultimately, the model aligns financial literacy with *maqasid al-Shariah* by fostering responsibility, justice, and social welfare through informed and ethical financial conduct.

REFERENCES

Abdullah, A., Salleh, M. Z. M., Zakaria, M. N., Din, N. M., Aziz, M. I., & Muhammad, M. Z. (2021, November). Achieving Islamic financial literacy in Malaysia: Issues and challenges. In *International Conference on Business and Technology* (pp. 889-896). Cham: Springer International Publishing.

Abdullah, M. A., & Anderson, A. (2015). Islamic Financial Literacy among bankers in Kuala Lumpur. *Journal of Emerging Economies and Islamic Research, 3*(2), 1–14. DOI: 10.24191/jeeir.v3i2.6408

Abdullah, M. A., Wahab, S. N. A., Sabar, S., & Abu, F. (2017). Factors determining Islamic financial literacy among undergraduates. *Journal of Emerging Economies & Islamic Research*. DOI: 10.1088/0953-8984/15/4/201

Abdullah, N., & Majid, M. S. A. (2003). The influence of religiosity, income and consumption on saving behavior: The case of International Islamic University Malaysia. *Journal of Islamic Economics*, *4*(1), 37–55. DOI: 10.20885/iqtisad.vol4.iss1.art3\

Adiputra, I. G., & Patricia, E. (2020, May). The effect of financial attitude, financial knowledge, and income on financial management behavior. In *Tarumanagara International Conference on the Applications of Social Sciences and Humanities (TICASH 2019)* (pp. 107-112). Atlantis Press. DOI: 10.2991/assehr.k.200515.019

Agensi Kaunseling dan Pengurusan Kredit (AKPK). (2019). *Annual report 2019.* https://www.akpk.org.my/annual-report-2019

Ahmad, G. N., Widyastuti, U., Susanti, S., & Mukhibad, H. (2020). Determinants of the Islamic financial literacy. *Accounting*, *6*, 961–966. DOI: 10.5267/j.ac.2020.7.024

Ajzen, I. (2005). *Attitudes, personality and behaviour*. McGraw-hill Education.

Ajzen, I., & Fishbein, M. (1980). *Understanding attitudes and predicting social behavior*. Prentice-Hall.

Al-Hammadi, M., Jimber-Del Río, J. A., Ochoa-Rico, M. S., Montero, O. A., & Vergara-Romero, A. (2024). Risk Management in Islamic Banking: The Impact of Financial Technologies through Empirical Insights from the UAE. *Risks*, *12*(2), 17. DOI: 10.3390/risks12020017

Alam, S. S., Mohd, R., & Hisham, B. (2011). Is religiosity an important determinant on Muslim consumer behaviour in Malaysia? *Journal of Islamic Marketing*, *2*(1), 83–96. DOI: 10.1108/17590831111115268

Albaity, M., & Rahman, M. (2019). The intention to use Islamic banking: An exploratory study to measure Islamic financial literacy. *International Journal of Emerging Markets, 14*(5), 988–1012. DOI: 10.1108/IJOEM-05-2018-0218

Alsaghir, M. (2023). Digital risks and Islamic FinTech: A road map to social justice and financial inclusion. *Journal of Islamic Accounting and Business Research.* Advance online publication. DOI: 10.1108/JIABR-10-2022-02

Altmann, T. K. (2008, July). Attitude: A concept analysis. [). Malden, USA: Blackwell Publishing Inc.]. *Nursing Forum, 43*(3), 144–150. DOI: 10.1111/j.1744-6198.2008.00106.x

Antara, P. M., & Musa, R. (2020). Validating Islamic financial literacy instruments among mum generation: Rasch analysis approach. *International Journal of Business and Society, 21*(3), 1113–1121. DOI: 10.33736/ijbs.3315.2020

Antara, P. M., Musa, R., & Hassan, F. (2017). Conceptualisation and operationalisation of Islamic financial literacy scale. *Pertanika Journal of Social Science & Humanities, 25*, 251–260. http://www.pertanika.upm.edu.my

Atkinson, A., & Messy, F.-A. (2012). Measuring financial literacy: Results of the OECD/ International Network on Financial Education (INFE) pilot study. In *OECD Working Papers on Finance, Insurance and Private Pensions*. https://doi.org/https://doi.org/10.1787/bb2cd70c-en

Awang, Z., Hui, L. S., & Nur Zainudin, N. F. S. (2018). *Pendekatan mudah SEM: structural equation modelling* (1st ed.). MPWS Rich Resources.

Barbic, D., Lucic, A., & Chen, J. M. (2019). Measuring responsible financial consumption behaviour. *International Journal of Consumer Studies, 43*(1), 102–112. DOI: 10.1111/ijcs.12489

Bentler, P. M., & Kano, Y. (1990). On the equivalence of factors and components. *Multivariate Behavioral Research, 25*(1), 67–74. DOI: 10.1207/s15327906mbr2501_8

Bhushan, P., & Medury, Y. (2014). An empirical analysis of inter linkages between financial attitudes, financial behaviour and financial knowledge of salaried individuals. *Indian Journal of Commerce and Management Studies, 5*(3), 58–64. https://www.ijcms.in/index.php/ijcms/article/view/380/357

Biplob, H., & Abdullah, M. F. (2019). The importance of Islamic financial literacy for Muslims: A general review. *Islam and Civilisational Renewal*, 106–117.

Bley, J., & Kuehn, K. (2003). Conventional versus Islamic finance: Student knowledge and perception in the United Arab Emirates. *International Journal of Islamic Financial Services, 5*(4). http://e-moghavemat.com/files/34.pdf

Campbell, D. T. (1950). The indirect assessment of social attitudes. *Psychological Bulletin, 47*(1), 15–38. DOI: 10.1037/h0054114

Chua, Y. P. (2014). *Regression and Factor Analysis* (5th ed.). McGraw-Hill.

Churchill, G. A.Jr. (1979). A paradigm for developing better measures of marketing constructs. *JMR, Journal of Marketing Research, 16*(1), 64–73. DOI: 10.1177/002224377901600110

Deacon, R. E., & Firebaugh, F. M. (1988). *Family resource management: Principles and applications.* (2nd ed.). DOI: 10.1016/B978-1-4160-3344-8.50090-1

Dinc, Y., Çetin, M., Bulut, M., & Jahangir, R. (2021). Islamic financial literacy scale: An amendment in the sphere of contemporary financial literacy. *ISRA International Journal of Islamic Finance, 13*(2), 251–263. DOI: 10.1108/IJIF-07-2020-0156

Er, B., & Mutlu, M. (2017). Financial inclusion and Islamic finance: A survey of Islamic financial literacy index. *International Journal of Islamic Economics and Finance Studies, 3*(2). Advance online publication. DOI: 10.25272/j.2149-8407.2017.3.2.02

Fenton-O'Creevy, M., & Furnham, A. (2020). Personality, ideology, and money attitudes as correlates of financial literacy and competence. *Financial Planning Review, 3*(1), e1070. DOI: 10.1002/cfp2.1070

Fessler, P., Silgoner, M., & Weber, R. (2020). Financial knowledge, attitude and behavior: Evidence from the Austrian Survey of Financial Literacy. *Empirica, 47*(4), 929–947. DOI: 10.1007/s10663-019-09465-2

Firdausi, M. R. A., & Kasri, R. A. (2022). Islamic financial literacy amongst Muslim students in Indonesia: A multidimensional approach. *Al-Muzara'ah*, 77-94.

Graafland, J. (2017). Religiosity, attitude, and the demand for socially responsible products. *Journal of Business Ethics, 144*(1), 121–138. DOI: 10.1007/s10551-015-2796-9

Gunawan, A., Asmuni, A., & Siregar, S. (2021). Islamic financial literacy and financial behavior: The case of Muhammadiyah community in Medan City. *Journal of Accounting and Investment, 22*(3), 500–516. DOI: 10.18196/jai.v22i3.10043

Hair, J. F., Black, W. C., Babin, B. J., & Anderson, R. E. (2019). *Multivariate data analysis* (8th ed.). Cengage Learning.

Hamid, A. H. A., & Nordin, N. A. M. (2001). A study on Islamic banking education and strategy for the new millennium-Malaysian experience. *International Journal of Islamic Financial Services*, *2*(4), 3–11. https://www.iiibf.org/journals/journal8/abdulhalim.pdf

Hidajat, T., & Hamdani, M. (2017). Measuring Islamic financial literacy. *Advanced Science Letters*, *23*(8), 7173–7176. DOI: 10.1166/asl.2017.9321

Hirschman, E. C. (1983). Religious affiliation and consumption processes: An initial paradigm. *Research in Marketing*, *6*(1), 131–170.

Huston, S. J. (2010). Measuring financial literacy. *The Journal of Consumer Affairs*, *44*(2), 296–316. DOI: 10.1111/j.1745-6606.2010.01170.x

Idris, K. M. (2002). *Gelagat Kepatuhan zakat pendapatan gaji di kalangan kakitangan awam persekutuan negeri Kedah* [Unpublished PhD thesis]. Universiti Utara Malaysia.

Iqbal, Z., & Mirakhor, A. (2011). *An introduction to Islamic finance: Theory and practice* (2nd ed.). John Wiley & Sons (Asia) Pte. Ltd.

ISRA. (2023). *Islamic financial system: Principles and operations* (3rd ed.). International Shariah Research Academy for Islamic Finance (ISRA).

Jiang, Y., & Shimizu, S. (2024). Does Financial Literacy Impact Investment Participation and Retirement Planning in Japan? *arXiv preprint arXiv:2405.01078.*

Koskelainen, T., Kalmi, P., Scornavacca, E., & Vartiainen, T. (2023). Financial literacy in the digital age - A research agenda. *The Journal of Consumer Affairs*, *57*(1), 507–528. DOI: 10.1111/joca.12510

Krathwohl, D. R. (2002). A revision of Bloom's taxonomy: An overview. *Theory into Practice*, *41*(4), 212–218. DOI: 10.1207/s15430421tip4104_2

Lahsasna, A. (2016). Framework of Islamic financial education and literacy. *Journal of Wealth Management and Financial Planning*, *3*(6), 1–14.

Lin, C. A., & Bates, T. C. (2022). Smart people know how the economy works: Cognitive ability, economic knowledge and financial literacy. *Intelligence*, *93*, 101667. DOI: 10.1016/j.intell.2022.101667

Lusardi, A. (2015). Financial literacy: Do people know the ABCs of finance? *Public Understanding of Science (Bristol, England)*, *24*(3), 260–271. DOI: 10.1177/0963662514564516

Lusardi, A., & Mitchell, O. S. (2011). Financial literacy around the world: An overview. *Journal of Pension Economics and Finance*, *10*(4), 497–508. DOI: 10.1017/S1474747211000448

Lusardi, A., & Mitchell, O. S. (2014). The economic importance of financial literacy: Theory and evidence. American Economic Journal. *Journal of Economic Literature*, *52*(1), 5–44. DOI: 10.1257/jel.52.1.5

MacCallum, R. C., Widaman, K. F., Zhang, S., & Hong, S. (1999). Sample size in factor analysis. *Psychological Methods*, *4*(1), 84–99. DOI: 10.1037/1082-989X.4.1.84

Maduku, D. K., & Mbeya, S. (2024). Understanding family takaful purchase behaviour: The roles of religious obligation and gender. *Journal of Financial Services Marketing*, *29*(2), 440–458. DOI: 10.1057/s41264-023-00213-z

Mansor, M., Sabri, M. F., Mansur, M., Ithnin, M., Magli, A. S., Husniyah, A. R., Mahdzan, N. S., Othman, M. A., Zakaria, R. H., Satar, N. M., & Janor, H. (2022). Analysing the predictors of financial stress and financial well-being among the bottom 40 percent (B40) households in Malaysia. *International Journal of Environmental Research and Public Health*, *19*(19), 12490. Advance online publication. DOI: 10.3390/ijerph191912490

Mansori, S., Safari, M., & Mohd Ismail, Z. M. (2020). An analysis of the religious, social factors and income's influence on the decision making in Islamic microfinance schemes. *Journal of Islamic Accounting and Business Research*, *11*(2), 361–376. DOI: 10.1108/JIABR-03-2016-0035

Masrizal, S., Sukmana, R., & Trianto, B. (2024). The effect of Islamic financial literacy on business performance with emphasis on the role of Islamic financial inclusion: Case study in Indonesia. *Journal of Islamic Marketing*, *16*(1), 166–192. DOI: 10.1108/JIMA-07-2022-0197

Ministry of Finance Malaysia. (2024, October 26). *AKPK reports 53,000 under-30s owe RM1.9 billion – Amir Hamzah*. https://www.mof.gov.my/portal/en/news/press-citations/akpk-reports-53-000-under-30s-owe-rm1-9-bln-amir-hamzah

Ministry of Finance Malaysia. (2025, January 8). *AKPK benefits 1.4 million individuals as at December 2024: MoF*. https://www.mof.gov.my/portal/en/news/press-citations/akpk-benefits-1-4-million-individuals-as-at-december-2024-mof

Mohamed, H. A., & Otake, T. (2025). The role of Islamic FinTech in digital financial inclusion and sustainable development post covid-19: Cross-country analysis. *International Journal of Islamic and Middle Eastern Finance and Management*, *18*(3), 649–671. DOI: 10.1108/IMEFM-02-2024-0100

Mokhtar, N., Sabri, M. F., Ho, C. S. F., & Dass, T. A. M. (2018). Profile and differences in financial literacy: Empirical evidence. *Malaysian Journal of Consumer and Family Economics*, *21*, 164–185. http://psasir.upm.edu.my/id/eprint/73653/

Nasira, N. F., Roslin, R. M., Nasir, M. N. F., Nasir, M. F., Nasir, M. A., & Mohamed, N. A. (2021). Investigating Knowledge as a Possible Predictor of Purchase Intention among Muslims in Malaysia for Life Insurance and Takaful. *International Journal of Academic Research in Business & Social Sciences*, *11*(2), 727–740. DOI: 10.6007/IJARBSS/v11-i2/8880

OECD. (2011). *Measuring financial literacy: Questionnaire and guidance notes for conducting an internationally comparable survey of financial literacy*. International Network on Financial Education.

OECD/INFE. (2021). *Supporting the financial resilience of citizens throughout the COVID-19 crisis*. Organisation for Economic Co-operation and Development. https://www.oecd.org/financial /education/ supporting-the-financial-resilience-of-citizens-throughout-the-covid-19-crisis-38a2ffd5-en.htm

Ouachani, S., Belhassine, O., & Kammoun, A. (2021). Measuring financial literacy: A literature review. *Managerial Finance*, *47*(2), 266–281. DOI: 10.1108/MF-04-2019-0175

Potrich, A. C. G., Viera, K. M., & Silva, W. M. D. (2016). Development of a financial literacy model for university students. *Management Research Review*, *39*(3), 356–376. DOI: 10.1108/MRR-06-2014-0143

Rahim, S. H. A., Rashid, R. A., & Hamed, A. B. (2016). Islamic financial literacy and its determinants among university students: An exploratory factor analysis. *International Journal of Economics and Financial Issues*, *6*(7), 32–35. DOI: 10.15405/epsbs.2016.08.58

Rahman, S. A., Tajudin, A., & Tajuddin, A. F. A. (2018). The significance of Islamic financial literacy among youth in Malaysia. *International Journal of Business and Management Invention*, *7*(10), 27–31.

Sabri, M. F., & Falahati, L. (2014). Toward a framework of financial wellness determinants: Investigating the moderating effect of religion. *Australian Journal of Basic and Applied Sciences*, *8*(9), 275–281. https://api.semanticscholar.org/CorpusID:154287518

Sari, R. C., Fatimah, P. R., Ilyana, S., & Hermawan, H. D. (2021). Augmented reality (AR)-based sharia financial literacy system (AR-SFLS): A new approach to virtual Sharia financial socialization for young learners. *International Journal of Islamic and Middle Eastern Finance and Management*, *15*(1), 48–65. DOI: 10.1108/IMEFM-11-2019-0484

Sedikides, C. (2010). Why does religiosity persist? *Personality and Social Psychology Review*, *14*(1), 3–6. DOI: 10.1177/1088868309352323

Setiawati, R., Nidar, S. R., Anwar, M., & Masyita, D. (2018). Islamic financial literacy: Construct process and validity. *Academy of Strategic Management Journal*, *17*(4), 1–12. https://www.proquest.com/scholarly-journals/islamic-financial-literacy-construct-process/docview/2124080881/se-2

Setyowati, A., Harmadi, H., & Sunarjanto, S. (2018). *Islamic financial literacy and personal financial planning: A socio-demographic study.* *22*(1), 63–72. DOI: 10.26905/jkdp.v22i1.1625

Shafik, A. S. M., & Ahmad, W. M. W. (2019). Financial literacy among Malaysian Muslim undergraduates. *Journal of Islamic Accounting and Business Research*, *11*(8), 1515–1529. DOI: 10.1108/JIABR-10-2017-0149

Sham, F. M., & Yusof, S. (2015). Religiosity of Muslim adolescents from single parent families living in government-subsidised settlement. *Global Journal Al-Thaqafah*, *5*(2), 31–42. DOI: 10.7187/GJAT882015.05.02

Shrigley, R. L., Koballa, T. R.Jr, & Simpson, R. D. (1988). Defining attitude for science educators. *Journal of Research in Science Teaching*, *25*(8), 659–678. DOI: 10.1002/tea.3660250805

Thurstone, L. L. (1928). Attitudes can be measured. *American Journal of Sociology*, *33*(4), 529–554. https://www.journals.uchicago.edu/doi/epdf/10.1086/214483. DOI: 10.1086/214483

Warmath, D., & Zimmerman, D. (2019). Financial literacy as more than knowledge: The development of a formative scale through the lens of Bloom's domains of knowledge. *The Journal of Consumer Affairs*, *53*(4), 1602–1629. DOI: 10.1111/joca.12286

Xiao, J. J. (2008). Applying behavior theories to financial behavior. In *Handbook of Consumer Finance Research* (pp. 69–81). Springer., DOI: 10.1007/978-0-387-75734-6_5

Xiao, J. J., & Porto, N. (2017). Financial education and financial satisfaction: Financial literacy, behavior, and capability as mediators. *International Journal of Bank Marketing*, *35*(5), 805–817. DOI: 10.1108/IJBM-01-2016-0009

Yong, C., Yew, S., & Wee, C. (2018). Financial knowledge, attitude and behaviour of young working adults in Malaysia. *Institutions and Economies, 10*(4), 21–48. https://ijie.um.edu.my/article/view/13444

Chapter 4
Implementation of Defence Waqf in Islamic History

Nur Amni Syafiqah Binti Saufe
https://orcid.org/0009-0003-8932-1600
National Defence University of Malaysia, Malaysia

Rais Yasin
National Defence University of Malaysia, Malaysia

Sayuti Ab Ghani
National Defence University of Malaysia, Malaysia

Mohd Mahzan Awang
National University of Malaysia, Malaysia

Redwan Yasin
https://orcid.org/0009-0004-5687-2809
National Defence University of Malaysia, Malaysia

Mohd Daud Awang
Universiti Putra Malaysia, Malaysia

ABSTRACT

Other than political, economic, and social factors, the element of defence waqf was highly significant in the strengthening, strengthening, and stability of a government throughout the time of the Prophet, the companions, the Uthmaniyah government, and the Abbasiyyah government. This research will look at how defence waqf was implemented during the time of the Prophet, his companions, the Uthmaniyah government, and the Abbasiyyah government. This article's technique is qualitative, involving secondary investigation with academic references to describe the defence waqf during the war. The data was then analysed to determine the Prophet's and companions' contributions to armaments and welfare. The findings reveal that the weapons used by Allah's Messenger, his companions, the Uthmaniyah adminis-

DOI: 10.4018/979-8-3373-1842-4.ch004

tration, and the Abbasiyyah government are powerful and sophisticated, capable of defeating the enemy. In terms of welfare, Islamic history demonstrates that the Muslim community has the potential to practise welfare.

1. INTRODUCTION

Military waqf aspects are important to Muslims since they help to enhance Islam's administration throughout the time of the Prophet, his companions, the Uthmaniyah government, and the Abbasiyyah government. The employment of effective warfare equipment and administration is essential for military strength. At all times, the Prophet was concerned about the military's war preparation. This preparation takes into account the weapon's strength as well as the skill knowledge earned through training. The Messenger of Allah and Islamic warriors were able to successfully combat the enemy with just regular equipment that was not constituted of chemical or high-tech weapons, such as swords, horses, and spears, during the war during his time. Thus, the purpose of Allah's Messenger's (may peace be upon him) war was not to fight or kill his adversaries, but to prevent the invasion of him and those who desired to freely practise their separate faiths.

In addition, to preserve and defend the welfare of Islamic society, waqf welfare at the time of the Prophet and his companions in battle should be emphasised. Welfare practise, as mentioned in the Islamic brochure, is a highly valued component that should be strengthened and quantified, according to the Islamic booklet's assertion. "*And whatever good they perform, they will never be rejected (or barred from receiving his recompense"*)," says Allah SWT. (Surah Ali Imran, verse 115.) This demonstrates that welfare practises are built on the concept of social responsibility among caring individuals.

"*When the death of Adam's son is cut off by all his activities, but three things: Jariah's charity, useful knowledge, and the virtuous son who prayed for him," says the hadith* (Hadith of Sahih Muslims). As a result, the Messenger of Allah (peace be upon him) was noted for his excellent command of the military field. The administration of the Military Sector is deeply worried about the nation's interests in protecting the lives of future generations of allies and Muslims in order to raise living standards and push superb human civilisation. The writer of this essay will look at the Prophet, his companions, the Uthmaniyah administration, and the Abbasiyyah government's contributions to the state's defence based on weaponry and welfare.

2. LITERATUR REVIEWS

2.1 Weapons and Welfare Contributions During the Prophet SAW Period

Hamid (2014) explains the contribution of Rasulullah SAW in providing weapons of war. He tried his best to provide various armaments to the Muslim army. Among the types of weapons available are: first, (a) protective weapons such as (i) armour used in warfare, such as *Sabighah, al-Bitra, al-Maghfar*, and *al-Baydoh*; (ii) hand shield, which is a type of shield made of iron used on the hand to repel the slings of the enemy's weapons; among its names are *al-Majn* and *al-Daroqoh* and (iii) the chained metal shirt used to protect the back of the body from the enemy's weapons; the second, (b) Weapons of attack such as (i) Swords for example: Sword of *al-Yamaniah* which is attributed to its place of manufacture and greatness, (ii) Spear named as *al-Qonat* because of its shape made of long wood with at the end there is a tool a sharp stab for the purpose of stabbing the enemy, (iii) An arrow bow used for firing arrows where the arrow is made of hard wood with at the end there is a sharp iron and is named *al-Nabal* and *al-Nasyab*, (iv) *Manjanik* is Cannons or Artillery and (v) *Al-Dabbabah* is Armored Cars.

The military system experienced a scarcity of weapons equipment throughout the reign of the kingdom of Madinah during the time of the Prophet SAW. The Prophet SAW was concerned about the situation, therefore prior to the Battle of Badr, he went in search of some horses. He gave the horse to Sa'd ibn As'ad ibn Zuraral Al-Khazraji to care for and train. Rasulullah SAW and the Muslim army won the first war soon after, and they were able to collect the spoils of war (*maghanim*) and distribute them among the Muslim soldiers. Camels, leather jackets, and weaponry such as swords (*suyuf*), armour (*duru*), helmets (*biz*), and spears (*rimah*) were among the items confiscated during the conflict (W.Ahmad, nd).

Furthermore, Al-Waqidi (1989) indicated that, in addition to the current armaments utilised by the Islamic army, firearms are routinely obtained through war confiscation. After being besieged for 15 days, the Bani Qainuqad surrendered, leaving behind many weaponry, including 400 pieces of armour. Among the huge spoils of war were 1,500 swords, 300 shirts, 2,000 spears, and 1,500 shields taken from the Bani Qurayzah. The above statements are only a portion of what was obtained and used as a source for the Islamic army's arsenal. This demonstrates the Prophet SAW's contribution to the spoils of war.

According to Terzi (2017), Prophet Muhammad SAW defended himself with weapons and battle equipment such swords, daggers, spears, and arrows. He also donned a leather shield tanned throughout the conflict. A description of the personal things utilised by the Prophet SAW during the war may be found in the book *Zad al-Ma'ad* (1994). There are nine swords, seven armour pieces, and six bows. The names of the swords used by the Prophet are *Ma'sur, Adb, Zulfiqar, Qali, Battar, Khatf, Rasob, Mehzam, Qadib. Dhat al Fudul, Dhat al-Wishah, Dhat al-Hawashi, Sadiyyah, Fidda, Batra,* and *Hirneq* are the names of His armor. His bows are *Zawra, Rawha, Bayda, Ketoom*, and *Sadad.*

Rasulullah SAW has openly and secretly introduced da'wah as one of his charitable contributions. The Prophet SAW chose Al-Arqam bin Abi Al-residence Arqam's as the most strategic site for a place to move activities and execute community obligations and activities by establishing Al-Rufaidah Al-Islamiyah, a medical service (Ibn Hisyam, 1995). Aside from that, the Prophet SAW has the intelligence and prowess to organise a variety of good plans, from membership selection to attack launch. There are three marhalah (levels) in His Majesty's military series: the first is *Marhalah ad-Difa* (Defense), the second is *Marhalah al-hujum* (Launching an attack), and the third is *at-Takamul* (Perfection) (Azmi & Zaighu, 2020).

2.2 Weapons and Welfare Contributions During the Companions Period

The military contribution made by the Companions, for example, was among the Companions of His Majesty the Caliph Usman bin Affan, who contributed 950 horses to the Muslim troops for use during the Battle of Tabuk (Nasution, 2002). Abu Nu'aim recounts Abdul Rahman bin Auf's contribution in the book *Al-Hilyah of Az-Zuhry*. "Abdul Rahman bin Auf offered charity during the time of the Prophet SAW, then he sacrificed 40,000 dirhams, 500 horses, and 1500 camels for *jihad*, and the majority of his riches came from his business," he explained. So the contribution of Abdul Rahman bin Auf to the Muslim forces, which is 500 horses and 1500 camels for *jihad* in Allah's cause, is obvious from the above account.

In addition, Commander Khalid ibn Walid provided Muslim forces with armour, weaponry, and agricultural tools (Alauddin, n.d.). Salman al-Farisi, one of the Prophet SAW's companions, advocated for the employment of stone-throwing weaponry because, based on his own experience in Persia, it had long been the army's habit to besiege and attack fortifications with stone-throwing (Ghoffar & Kusumo, n.d.).

The *manjanik* (a heavy weapon that may also be used as a missile launcher) was utilised by the Muslim army in the early days of Islam, particularly during futuhat (the opening and expansion of land) against the Persian army in the War of *al-Mada'in*. Apart from that, in the year 73H/692M, the Umawi army led by al-Hajjaj ibn Yusuf al-Thaqafi utilised *manjanik* to shell the Kaaba region, which was 'Abd Allah ibn al-defense Zubayr's base. *Manjanik* attacks are usually undertaken as a "introduction" to a big fight including siege tactics and defence systems behind fortifications (Ashari et al., 2020).

In this way, charitable contributions during the period of the Companions were analogous to Saidina Umar Al-meeting Khattab's with the first caliph, Saidina Abu Bakr As-Siddiq, to propose the bookkeeping of the Al-Quran in order to indicate care for the Muslims' future. He was also a Quran memorizer, but he still sees the necessity to match or adapt the other Companions' memorising or notes, which were witnessed by two witnesses, in the sake of the Quran, which is extremely important to Muslims (Firdaus & Shukor, 2019).

2.3 Weapons and Welfare Contributions During the Uthmaniyah Period

The Uthmaniyah Empire was a significant Islamic state in Islamic history. It flourished for 643 years, from the 13th century to the 20th century, around 1281-1924M (680-1342H). Various events and advancements have benefited Muslims and non-Muslims from the past to the present during the Uthmaniyah government's comparatively long tenure. Uthman bin Ertoghrul, who ruled between 680H/1281M and 726H/1326M, is regarded as the founder of the Uthmaniyah Empire. Starting with Uthman, he and his family gradually invaded the Saljuk region of Rome until, by the end of the fourteenth century, the Uthmaniyah administration had absorbed all other kingdoms (Sulong, 2013).

When Sultan Muhammad Al-Fateh was appointed to the throne in 1451, the Uthmaniyah authority made a military commitment. Among his achievements during the struggle to seize Constantinople, he managed to bring down Constantinople's defence walls using the weapon technology of the Shahi Bronze Cannon, which can be heard from a distance of 25 kilometres. The Shahi Bronze Cannon fires a 500 kg stone projectile capable of bursting through defensive walls and destroying the morale of opposing armies (Ridzuan et al., 2018).

Sultan Muhammad Al-Fateh, according to Ismail et al. (2019), was a wise battle strategist. He provided 140 battleships, cutting-edge weapons equipment like cannons, and a training programme for 200,000 men. The Fief Army was one of the Uthmaniyah Turkish government warriors supplied to defend the Uthmaniyah government, with spears, swords, arrows, and shields among their weaponry (Said & MD Jumri, 2017).

According to Haris (2020), the Uthmaniyah Turkish government managed to develop technology in terms of weaponry, namely explosive powder as well as some modern weapons such as large cannons and modern rifles. In addition, the Ottoman government also had a very strong naval force at that time. They use more modern and sophisticated weapons namely galleys (small warships) that allow them to dominate around the Black Sea.

Among the other contributions made by Sultan Mahmud II at the start of his reign were the repair of the defence fort along the national border and the formation of a new line corps on the frontier against the enemy. He also went to Europe and bought a new cannon, a smaller rifle, and smaller armour, storing them in the palace and elsewhere in preparation for use as a cover for the Sultan (Mustapha & Hasbullah, 2021).

Mustapha and Hasbullah (2020) also stated that the Uthmaniyah administration provided sophisticated artillery from Germany in 1885, in response to the Sultan's request. A large calibre rifle developed for fixed positions in the Dardanelles beachside defence, as well as vehicle and mortar artilleries for military purposes, make up the artillery. The growth of Ottoman authority in the 16th century was successful, according to Said and MD Jumri (2017), since they had acquired armed expertise and bronze cannons..

The Uthmaniyah government also greatly contributes to showing Islamic teachings that organise the Islamic government to protect the rights and welfare of all its people, regardless of race or religion. The legal system known as "*Kanunname*" or "*Suleyman* Code," the Code of Law, was established by Suleyman I in 1520 and continued until 1566, when he was known as Suleyman "*Al-Qanuni*" (Haris, 2020).

Furthermore, there is a welfare contribution from the Uthmaniyah era's medical component, which includes Fatih Hospital, Suleyman Hospital, Bayezid II Hospital, and Haseki Hospital, which gave free service to the population at the time (Alias & Rozali, 2017). In addition, according to Ali and Nor (2018), Sultan Abdul Hamid II provided transportation and communication to the Uthmaniyah government, including telegraphic communication networks and railway construction systems.

2.4 Weapons and Welfare Contributions During the Abbasiyyah Period

During the Abbasiyyah period (636M–644M), the magnitude and sophistication of combat weaponry increased dramatically. Among the battle weaponry is the ability to convert manjanic bullets from solid rock lumps to the more fragile substance. Then he invented a fireproof clothing, which allowed Muslim warriors wearing it to enter enemy territory even while the fire was still burning. He also built an archer machine that shot a large number of arrows at once and employed firearms to fire at a defence stronghold (Said & MD Jumri, 2017).

Abu Jaafar Abdullah bin Muhammad bin Ali Al-Abbas, the second Abbasiyyah caliphate after Abu Al-Abbas al-Saffah, was among those who contributed to welfare throughout the Abbasiyyah period. He has built a palace called *al-Khuldi* on the banks of the *Dajlah* River. The palace's design is stunning, and its strategic location inspired him to name it "*Qasr al-Khuldi*," which translates to "Abadi Palace." He has also constructed the *Jami 'al-Mansur* mosque in front of the Al-Zahab Palace, which is Baghdad's oldest mosque (Mahayudin, 2004).

Furthermore, further welfare contributions are in the form of philosophical areas organised by the government of Abbasiyyah, particularly during the reign of Caliph *al-Ma'mum*. This is accomplished through translating Greek intellectual works. *Al-Ma'mum* has developed a library to gather scientific publications translated into Arabic as a means of future support. "*Bait Al Hikmah*" was the name given to the library. In reality, he has spent a significant amount of money to fund the translation of scientific publications into Arabic, particularly in the subject of philosophy (al-Khalidi, 1985).

3. METHODOLOGY

This article's methodology is qualitative, and it employs a variety of focal methods, including the use of naturalistic (naturalistic) ways to investigate issues (Ospina, 2004). This research uses secondary analysis with references to academic materials from a variety of sources, including journals, papers, websites, and books, to explain Waqf Defense in Islamic history. The collected data was analysed to demonstrate the Prophet's and his companions' contributions. The contribution of the Uthmaniyah regime and Abbasiyyah are also mentioned. The goal of this qualitative study is to explore, investigate, and examine more systematic investigations in order to find solutions to research difficulties. The study's findings concluded the aspects of battle during the Prophet's period, the companions' time, the Uthmaniyah government's time, and the Abbasiyyah government's time.

4. FINDING

As is well known, the elements of defence in terms of armament and welfare in the days of the Prophet SAW, his companions, the Uthmaniyah Empire, and the Abbasiyyah government were very vital to Muslim forces in order to demonstrate the greatness of him and his companions against the adversary. According to the findings of the previous study, the Prophet suffered a shortage of war weapons during his reign, yet he worked as hard as he could to provide varied armoury equipment for the Muslim army for as long as he could. When battling, the Prophet SAW employed protective weapons such as iron shirts, hand shields, and chain metal shirts, as well as attack weapons such as spear swords, arrow bows, *manjanik*, cannon or artillery, and *al-Dabbabah*, that is, the armoured automobile.

Furthermore, the Messenger of Allah and Islamic warriors were able to collect and divide the war seizure (*Maghanim*) into Islamic troops. A camel, leather shirts, and weapons such as swords (*suyuf*), iron shirts (*Duru*), iron caps (*biz*), spears (*Rimah*), and others were among the items seized during the fight. As a result, it is apparent that the Prophet had the power of modern warfare technology in his day, referring to the equipment. When Allah's Messenger (peace be upon him) was ruling the Islamic empire at the time, he had a powerful personality. There have never been any complaints or concerns concerning his embezzlement from Muslims or non-Muslims. They all agree and follow his recommendations based on the notion of justice, especially when it comes to dividing rights for the advantage of Muslims. As a result, the Prophet's (peace and blessings of Allah be upon him) contribution to welfare is in putting in place numerous stable preparations from the standpoint of membership to launch an attack.

Furthermore, the contribution of weaponry in the age of friends can be defined as most of his companions, such as Panglima Khalifah Khalid al-Walid, contributing military equipment, horses, and camels. Friends like Saidina Usman bin Affan, Abdul Rahman bin Auf, and others have also donated horses and camels. This demonstrates that the companions' weapons of war were very methodical and powerful at the time, and they played an essential role in the success of a military leader designing a battle strategy and defence. In addition, the companions make a virtue contribution, such as Saidina Umar al-proposal Khattab's for the bookkeeping of the Qur'an, which expresses her love for the Qur'an and concern for Muslims' future.

During the 17th century, the Uthmaniyah Empire, recognised as a strong and long-lasting Islamic state, began to encounter threats from the West. The Uthmaniyah Empire had sophisticated and high-tech fighting equipment at the period. They have Shahi's bronze cannon, which can be heard from 25 kilometres away, as well as modern cannons. Meanwhile, during Sultan Muhammad al-rule, Fateh's he outfitted 140 warships with cutting-edge weaponry like as cannons, spears, swords, arrows, and shields. Furthermore, the Uthmaniyah administration has a powerful naval force that employs more contemporary and advanced weapons, such as galleys (small warships). As a result, the magnificence and sophistication of the Uthmaniyah government's weapons may have contributed to its ability to strengthen its military force through scientific and weaponry technology expertise.

The Uthmaniyah government is one of the few Muslim kingdoms to have succeeded in establishing a wide empire, and it is a government that connects Muslims all over the world. The Uthmaniyah government has made significant contributions to the Islamic world in a variety of areas. Contributions in the disciplines of legislation, economics, social sciences, education, architecture, and medical are among them, and they all contribute to the people's togetherness. Thus, over the first two centuries after the creation of the government, notably between the early 14th century and the end of the 16th century, the Uthmaniyah government rose to prominence and made significant contributions in a variety of sectors.

Previous studies on complex combat equipment like as *manjanik, dabbah, baruud*, and warships have clarified the role of arms in the Abbasiyyah government. It has risen significantly. They've tinkered with battle gear like *manjanik* ammo and created a fireproof clothing. He's also developed an archery machine that can fire and use firearms to attack enemy defence strongholds. As a result, we can observe that the Abbasiyyah era's combat equipment is quite large and high-tech, and capable of successfully resisting the enemy.

Furthermore, welfare contributions in the abbasid period, such as in economics, education, medicine, and other sectors, had a significant impact on empowerment and the ability to practise welfare. During the Abbasiyyah period, we may witness examples of welfare contributions, such as Abu Jaafar Abdullah bin Muhammad bin Ali, who built the Jami al-Mansur mosque in Baghdad and established the al-Khuldi palace. This demonstrates a highly esteemed practise in the community, as well as Allah SWT's approval. As a result, it is apparent that the well-being of Muslims is always ensured when the Abbasiyyah period is methodical and has a useful system plan.

5. CONCLUSION

The contribution of Waqf Defense throughout the Prophet's time, the Salahat, the Uthmaniyah Empire, and the Abbasiyyah government demonstrated the sophistication of methodical and high-tech combat equipment. This demonstrates that the potency of the Prophet's and companions' equipment, rather than the abundance of military weaponry, determines combat victory. Even so, it is more determined by the spiritual strength and the accuracy of the internal spirit of every member of the Islamic army. The weaponry technology that was at that time, coupled with political stability, economic integrity, and armed skills, succeeded in giving the Messenger of Allah, the companions, the Uthmaniyah government, and the Abbasiyyah government at that time the ability to make and produce their own equipment and armaments, thus strengthening the military. The use of sophisticated and high-tech military equipment in any war can indirectly increase the spirit of military personnel to fight hard to beat the enemy.

APPRECIATION

Appreciation to the National Defense University of Malaysia and the Ministry of Higher Education for the cooperation of this study as well as the research grant support which is study code: FRGS/1/2021/SSO/UPNM/02/6.

REFERENCES

W. Ahmad, W.Y. (n.d). Sistem Ketenteraan Kerajaan Madinah Pada Zaman Nabi Muhammad SAW, *Jurnal Usuluddin*, 134-145.

Al Khalidi, M. (1985). *alAqidahWa Ilmal Kalam*. Amman:Maktabah al Risalah al Hadithah

Al-Waqidi, Muhammad bin Umar bin Waqid al-Sahmiyy al-Aslamiyy. (1989). Al-Maghazi. *Tahqiq*. Jil. 1 & 2. Beyrut: Dar al- Aclamiyy.

Ali, N.Z.Y., & Nor, M.R.M. (2018). Ketokohan dan Sumbangan Sultan Abdul Hamid II Sebagai Khalifah Terakhir Dawlah Uthmaniyyah Berlandaskan Prinsip al-Quran dan al-Sunnah, *Journal of Ma'alim Al-Quran wa Al-Sunnah*, 14(1), 91-98.

Alias, N.A.B., & Rozali, E.A. (2017). Pembinaan Institusi Waqf Kesihatan di Istanbul pada Tahun 1470 M (Hospital Fatih), 39(2), 153-164.

Ashari, M. Z. A. H., Jamsari, E. A., Safian, H. L., & Safiai, M. H. (2020). Sejarah Pembangunan Teknologi Ketenteraan Kerajaan Banu Marin di Al-Maghrib. *Journal of Al-Tamaddun*, *15*(2), 147–161. DOI: 10.22452/JAT.vol15no2.11

Azmi, A. G. I., & Zaighu, A. A. G. (2020). Kepimpinan Strategik Rasulullah SAW: Kajian Perlaksanaanya oleh Kagat. *Journal of Islamic Management and Finance*, *1*(1), 32–47.

Firdaus, A. M. N., & Shukor, K. A. (2019). Kurikulum Pendidikan Islam Para Sahabat: Satu Sorotan. *Jurnal Al-Munzir*, *12*(2), 209.

Hamid, Y. B. (2014). *Perancangan Ketenteraan dalam al-Sunnah, Terj. Jabatan Arah Kor Agama Angkatan Tentera*. Penerbit Markas Angkatan Tentera Malaysia.

Haris, A. H. (2020). Sejarah Kerajaan Turki Uthmaniyah dan Sumbangannya Dalam Bidang Sosiopolitik Abad ke-14 hingga Abad ke-20. *Journal of Al-Tamaddun*, *15*(1), 85–107. DOI: 10.22452/JAT.vol15no1.6

Ibnu Hisyam (1995). *Sirah an-Nabawiyyah.* Al-Halabi Waauladihi Bimsr: Maktabah Mustapha, h. 258.

Ismail, N. A., Wahid, N. A., Wahab, N. A., & Majid, N. A. (2019), Tokoh Tamadun Islam Sultan Muhammad Al-Fateh dipandang Dari Sudut Personaliti, *Proceedings of the International Conference on Islamic Civilization and Technology Management pada 23*-24 November 2019.

Mahayudin, Y. (2004). *Tamadun Islam.* Penerbit Fajar Bakti Sdn.Bhd.

Mustapha, F., & Hasbullah, M. (2021). Kemasukkan Sains dan Teknologi dari Barat ke dalam Kerajaan Uthmaniyah pada Abad ke-18 dan Abad ke-19: Satu Penilaian Sejarah. *Journal of History Department, 30*(1), 20–42.

Nasution, S. (2002). *Sejarah Peradaban Islam*, Yayasan Pustaka Riau: Riau, h.h. 102.

Ridzuan, A.A., Zainol, M.N.A., Hai Liaw, J.O., Mohaiyadin. N.M., & Yaacob, S. (2018). Dimensi-dimensi Kejayaan Sultan Muhammad Al-Fateh Arkitek Penaklukan Kota Konstantinopel, e-Prosiding Persidangan Antarabangsa Sains Sosial dan Kemanusian pada 23-24 April 2018.

MD Said, M.H., & Jumri, M.F. (2017). *Tamadun Islam*: Politeknik Port Dickson, Negeri Sembilan. h.h. 60.

Sulong, A.R. (2013). Pemikiran Turki Uthmaniyah Menurut Syeikh Wan Ahmad bin Muhammad Zain Al-Fatani dalam bukunya Hadiqat Al-Azhar Wa Al-Rayahin, Tesis yang diserahkan untuk memenuhi keperluan bagi ijazah Doktor Falsafah yang diambil pada Jun 2013.

Terzi, M. Z. Hz. (2017) *Peygamber ve Hulefâ-yi Râşidîn Döneminde Askeri Teşkilat.* Istanbul: Siyer Yayınları.

Chapter 5
Integrating Islamic Financial Literacy, Social Entrepreneurship, and Social Finance:
Innovative Pathways to Inclusive and Sustainable Development

Wahyu Wibowo
https://orcid.org/0009-0000-5176-7103
Sunan Kalijaga State Islamic University, Yogyakarta, Indonesia

Nofriansyah Nofriansyah
https://orcid.org/0009-0001-5150-6082
Universitas Pendidikan Indonesia, Indonesia

Nasrudin Nasrudin
https://orcid.org/0009-0008-2215-6192
Universitas Islam Kalimantan Muhammad Arsyad Al-Banjari, Banjarmasin, Indonesia

Aminuddin Aminuddin
https://orcid.org/0009-0002-0798-3479
Sunan Kalijaga State Islamic University, Yogyakarta, Indonesia

ABSTRACT

The integration of Islamic Financial Literacy, social entrepreneurship, and social finance is positioned as an innovative path to inclusive and sustainable development. Islamic Financial Literacy provides an ethical basis and understanding in accordance

DOI: 10.4018/979-8-3373-1842-4.ch005

with Sharia principles in financial management. So that economic decisions follow religious values. Social entrepreneurship emphasizes business models based on the combined impact of economic sustainability through the creation of social values. Social finance, including zakat, waqf and investment, has a sharia effect and serves as a means of mobilizing resources to strengthen our communities. The integration of these three pillars provides an integrated Islamic economic framework that not only expands financial capacity and inclusion, but also contributes to reducing socioeconomic inequalities. The findings of this study show the need to strengthen Islamic digital financial literacy and guidelines that support investment in impact on sharia. The Zakat Institute recommends expanding the productive zakat program to transform Mustahik with Muzakki, but entrepreneurs are expected to use social effects for business models. New research fields are open to academic aspects, such as the development of Islamic index development indexes, Islamic digital financial literacy, and a hybrid model between zakat and investment income. This integration is in line with the Sustainable Development Goals (SDGs) and Maqā id al-Sharī ah and can become a new paradigm of just and more sustainable global development.

INTRODUCTION

Sustainable development now faces substantial financing constraints with recent estimates showing that investment is needed to achieve the Sustainable Development Goals (SDGs) with financing of around $4 trillion per year in developing countries (UNCTAD, 2024). Fiscal pressures and debt servicing burdens narrow fiscal space for social and infrastructure investments, thus presenting alternative solutions and new business models (George, 2024). To bridge this gap, the Seville Commitment, which has more than 70 heads of state, has mobilized a large number to address poverty and accelerate the performance of the SDGs (Wilson & Lederer, 2025).

In the midst of limited sources of conventional funds, Islamic financial instruments, especially Islamic philanthropy (zakat, infaq, alms, waqf/ZISWAF), are not only positioned as a redistribution mechanism, but also as a strategic component for social capital mobilization. In developing countries such as Indonesia, this instrument has been implemented in the form of green sukuk to support renewable energy projects. Now Indonesia is the largest pioneer worth USD 3.526 billion, even though the value of global green sukuk reaches USD 15.2 billion, of course this shows the real contribution of Islamic finance to the SDGs (IAEI, 2025). This is an important proof that the role of Islamic finance in sustainable development is not only practically relevant, but also requires a strong normative foundation, namely the perspective of Maqa hid al-Shariʿah.

The concept of Maqa hid al-Shariʿah formulated by Al-Ghazali (1997) in *al-Mustasfa min Ilm al-Usul*, emphasizes the fundamental objectives of sharia which consist of the protection of religion (hifz al-dīn), soul (hifz al-nafs), reason (hifz al-'aql), heredity (hifz al-nasl), and property (hifz al-māl). Maqa hid al-Shariʿah as a normative framework that makes the study of financial instruments based on technical compliance with contracts, contribution to public welfare and loss prevention (mafsadah), as affirmed by Auda (2013), Chapra (2016), and Kamali (2019). Perspektif ini mengarahkan tujuan sosial-ekonomi dan spiritual saling mengokohkan. Drawing on contemporary literature, it is emphasized the need to operationalize these principles into governance, accountability, and impact measurement indicators (Napitupulu et al., 2024).

Cutting-edge empirical research confirms the relevance of Islamic financial integration with the development agenda. Harahap et al. (2023) in his research describes the significant contribution of Islamic finance to the SDGs, especially related to humanity, justice, and poverty alleviation. In line with that, Wahyudi et al. (2025) report 86% of ISF indicators in line with the achievement of the SDGs, which have the greatest impact on poverty alleviation (SDG 1) and hunger reduction (SDG 2). In addition, the emphasis on digital transformation can increase program efficiency by up to 85%.

Meanwhile, according to Maulina et al. (2023) the integration of ISF and Islamic commercial finance is able to strengthen financial inclusion through technology and multi-stakeholder collaboration. OECD (2023) also highlighted blended finance which is able to mobilize USD 70 billion of private funds, although the effectiveness of this model is still debated. On the other hand, Jan et al. (2023) introduced the Islamic Corporate Sustainability Practices Index which has an impact on improving the performance of Islamic financial institutions in Malaysia and Indonesia. So it is known that sharia-based practices are able to provide financial and ethical value.

Behind the great potential that exists, there are critical challenges in implementing Islamic social finance. The governance of zakat and waqf is quite vulnerable to transparency and accountability issues, and has the potential to be subject to political interference. The digital divide limits inclusion because vulnerable groups are often unable to access technology-based services. There is also the potential for conflict with social and commercial goals in impactful investment that can also trigger mission drift, which is a shift in orientation from social goals to profits. Another obstacle can arise in the measurement of social impact that is limited to the methodology and suitability of SDGs indicators. Recognizing the limitations that exist is very important if the ISF integration framework can be positioned in a more realistic and academic perspective.

ISLAMIC FINANCIAL LITERACY IN AN INCLUSIVE PERSPECTIVE

Modern economic empowerment requires financial literacy to be present according to the context. For the Muslim community, Islamic financial literacy (IFL) is the key that bridges spiritual values with practical skills. IFL has an impact on product knowledge, risk attitudes, and choice of Islamic financial services, thus influencing financial inclusion and MSME performance. A study revealed that increasing IFL drives inclusion and local economic output, especially when supported by effective marketing communication and digital access (Mujiatun et al., 2023).

The growth of Islamic fintech makes IFL integration even more important. Perceptions of sharia compliance, trust, and digital skills are proven to influence the adoption of Islamic fintech services (Maniam, 2024). The combination of Islamic literacy and digital literacy in the use of e-payment can increase access and benefits of formal financial services and strengthen people's economic resilience. IFL's literature from 2016 on is rapidly evolving with four main themes: measurement, adoption of Islamic banking services, determinants, and community-based educational interventions (Kaweesa et al., 2024). These findings are the basis for the design of sharia and digital financial education programs, such as community modules, mosque-based training, and integration of sharia fintech content.

1. Definition and Characteristics of Islamic Financial Literacy

IFL includes understanding, evaluating, and using financial instruments in accordance with sharia principles, with the internalization of Islamic ethical values such as justice, integrity, and sustainability (Antara et al., 2016). IFL combines the cognitive aspect of proficiency in financial instruments with a normative dimension that leads to compliance with Maqā id al-Sharīʿah. Thus, not only related to technical skills, but IFL also adds moral and spiritual aspects to daily practice regarding finance.

IFL has an important role in increasing Sharia financial inclusion, supporting business performance, especially MSMEs and the halal tourism sector, and strengthening individual financial management through a combination of religiosity and literacy (Mujiatun et al., 2023; Wijaya et al., 2024; Masrizal et al., 2025). IFL is very relevant in the context of sustainability through Islamic sustainable finance that is able to support the achievement of the SDGs while reducing financial risks, including the introduction of the Islamic capital market in the community (Raimi et al., 2024; Yusfiarto et al., 2023).

IFL's main foundation leads to Sharia compliance. Instruments such as murāba ah, mu ārabah, and qar asan serve as financial means and represent Islamic ethical values by rejecting the practices of usury, gharar, and maysir (Dinc et al., 2021).

However, the low level of Islamic financial literacy in many countries, including Indonesia, is still a major obstacle to the adoption of Islamic financial products. Survey by OJK (2022) shows that Islamic financial literacy only reaches 9%, far below general financial literacy. This condition has implications for low Islamic financial inclusion, weak penetration of Islamic products, and limited access to capital for MSMEs. So that the development of IFL normatively is very crucial, besides that it is also a practical strategy to expand the reach of Islamic finance and support inclusive development.

2. Digital-Sharia Literacy: Opportunities and Risks

The recent development of sharia fintech has opened up great opportunities for sharia-compliant financial inclusion. Sharia-based peer-to-peer lending services, waqf crowdfunding, and online zakat applications are able to reduce transaction costs and are able to reach widely by Islamic financial institutions. Most studies state that groups with basic digital literacy and understanding of sharia products have the highest adoption rates, especially in empowering MSMEs and women through access to non-bank capital (Al-Mustofa et al., 2025; Saro et al., 2023). However, other evidence suggests that expanding access to digital credit without adequate literacy actually increases the risk of debt accumulation, especially for vulnerable groups (Khan et al., 2024; Lahnech & Chami, 2025). Recent literature shows a pattern that is not always consistent: there is great potential for inclusion, but also serious risks for groups with low literacy capacity.

In this context, digital-sharia literacy serves a dual function: first, as a normative filter to distinguish halal-haram products and assess their sustainability; Second, as a managerial tool to avoid exploitative practices. Understanding non-interest contracts such as murāba ah, mu ārabah, musyārakah, and qar asan is key for consumers to be able to distinguish halal financing from high-interest loans (Wijaya et al., 2024). Conversely, low literacy has the potential to fall into debt traps (over-indebtedness) or online fraud, something that is also identified by Choung et al. (2023).

In addition to literacy risks, governance risks also arise in the sharia fintech sector. Many platforms charge relatively high service fees, thus reducing the benefits of sharia financing compared to the initial claim. Access is also still uneven, especially rural communities, women, and the elderly often have difficulty using digital-based applications due to limited infrastructure and skills. Furthermore, the absence of transparency standards in the explanation of contracts poses a risk of information asymmetry that can weaken the principles of sharia justice.

Effective practical interventions include community financial education, sharia-based guidance, and the provision of alternative non-usury financing through the qar asan scheme. A number of studies have encouraged hybrid models that combine literacy, micro-savings, and social protection, such as turning interest subsidies into profit-sharing mechanisms or qar as an additional layer of protection (Khoshakhlagh et al., 2024; Yumna et al., 2025).

In terms of policy, regulations need to emphasize the obligations of platform transparency, contract information, and consumer protection so that digital innovation does not actually deepen financial vulnerability. The combination of literacy, regulation, and innovation needs to be positioned not only as a technical strategy, but also as an instrument of consumer protection and fair governance, so that digital transformation in Islamic finance remains in line with Maqa hid al-Shariʿah and contributes to sustainable collective well-being.

3. Literacy as a Community Empowerment Tool

IFL plays a role in improving individual capabilities as well as being a collective empowerment tool that fosters local economic resilience. Cutting-edge empirical evidence shows that literacy initiatives combined with community-based financing structures such as Baitul Maal wa Tamwil (BMT), sharia cooperatives, and sharia ta'awun cooperatives encourage increased productive savings, equitable access to capital, and more sustainable business management practices (Fawaid, 2024; Wijaya et al., 2024). The program also strengthens social capital so that communities are able to withstand economic shocks and reduce their dependence on exploitative informal loans.

The community-based financial literacy approach will be effective when it combines technical education such as budgeting, business risk management, understanding of sharia contracts, the formation of savings and loan groups, access to qar asan, and productive waqf management. Program evaluations in Indonesia and Southeast Asia in 2023–2025 show that the combination of collective education and trust-based financing mechanisms can increase women's involvement, MSME capital absorption, and business sustainability (Barus et al., 2025; Raimi et al., 2024). Community literacy also encourages more transparent and accountable governance, which is important to convert social funds (zakat/waqf) into productive capital.

Digital transformation requires the community to include digital literacy modules so that members understand sharia fintech and its risks. Recent research shows that the success of empowerment depends on education, local institutions, and supportive policies (Harrieti et al., 2024). So that community-based IFL that integrates digital literacy is able to build a resilient local economy and is in harmony with Maqā id al-Sharīʿah.

4. Financial Resilience for Poor Households

Poor households build financial resilience through financial literacy, access to the right instruments, and the ability to manage liquidity to deal with economic shocks. Cross-country research shows financial literacy, including cash flow management, emergency savings, and debt, increases household recovery capacity (Bertola & Lo Prete, 2025; Liu et al., 2024). In Muslim-majority countries, the combination of religiosity and IFL improves household financial management behaviors, such as budgeting, debt management, and halal product selection, so that low-income households can avoid usury and remain resilient in the face of economic shocks (Wijaya et al., 2024).

The integration of financial literacy with Islamic Social Finance (zakat, waqf, qar asan) and sharia fintech accelerates access to productive financing and emergency assistance, provided that good governance, transparent management, and adequate digital literacy are provided. This integrative model is also proposed in cutting-edge conceptual research that suggests the use of socio-Islamic instruments in emergency response mechanisms to strengthen the resilience of vulnerable communities (Al-Daihani et al., 2025).

SOCIAL ENTREPRENEURSHIP: DRIVING THE ECONOMY OF THE UMMAH

Islamic social entrepreneurship is now evolving from a normative discourse to a measurable economic practice. Waqf assets, student base, and pesantren leadership are social capital that is able to drive sharia business units that are oriented towards benefit. Research conducted in West Java showed an increase in the income of Islamic boarding school business units and the creation of local jobs, while the evaluation of the Micro Waqf Bank confirmed the improvement of access to financing for MSMEs even though they still faced governance challenges (Safei, 2021; Nugraha & Sudrajad, 2025).

Similar models are also seen outside Indonesia. Micro waqf banks in Malaysia integrate sharia financing with women's training, while zakat cooperatives in Pakistan expand financial inclusion of vulnerable groups (Alom et al., 2025; Aziz et al., 2025). This fact shows that pesantrenpreneurs are part of the global trend of social entrepreneurship based on religious values that are able to increase economic inclusion.

Despite its great potential, there is a critical question: can this model be replicated outside of Islamic boarding schools? Success determinants such as credible leadership, social capital, and market access can indeed be found in other communities, but local adaptation is absolutely necessary. In addition, the risk of exclusivity arises when economic benefits only revolve in the inner circle of the pesantren, as well as the risk of mission drift when the business orientation shifts from social to profit. Therefore, transparent governance and social impact evaluation need to be upheld so that pesantrenpreneurs remain inclusive and in line with Maqā id al-Sharīʿah.

SOCIAL FINANCE: AN INNOVATIVE INSTRUMENT FOR SUSTAINABILITY

Islamic social finance through ZISWAF plays an important role in inclusive and sustainable development, which is not only a redistribution of wealth but also economic empowerment and social solidarity. Innovations such as zakat-impact investment, productive waqf, as well as blockchain technology and smart contracts increase transparency, efficiency, and accountability in fund management (Kunhibava et al., 2024; Setiawan & Nurzaman, 2022).

1. Islamic Social Finance (ISF) Concept

ISF as an umbrella for religious instruments such as zakat, infaq, alms, and waqf. Unlike commercial financial instruments, the ISF has a focus on redistributing justice, solidarity, and social development. According to Obaidullah (2015) ZISWAF touches on the aspects of redistribution, risk sharing, and collective empowerment, making it key to inclusive growth and ensuring that the benefits of development are felt globally. Zakat as the most important pillar of Islamic social finance is aimed at eight groups of recipients (asnaf), including the poor, the poor, and people in debt, as stated in the Qur'an (Surah At-Taubah). This mechanism promotes fairness and bridges economic disparities. Infak and alms are voluntary, commonly used for humanitarian and emergency needs, while waqf provides the potential for sustainable investment, for example productive waqf for education or health.

The ISF reflects a vision of development that balances economic justice and spiritual values, based on Maqā id al-Sharīʿah which emphasizes the protection of religion, soul, intellect, lineage, and property. ISF is not just a solution to a crisis, but a form of the collective commitment of the ummah to common prosperity through inclusive, ethical, and Islamic development. Marwah et al. (2025) recommends the systemic integration of Maqā id al-Sharīʿah into economic policy and the design of institutions such as Islamic financial institutions and cooperatives, not as a crisis response alone, but as a spiritually conscious approach to development.

2. The Role of Islamic Social Finance in MSMEs and Social Projects

ISF through the ZISWAF instrument plays an important role in sustainable economic and social development. Productive zakat provides access to alternative working capital for MSMEs, especially women and vulnerable groups, thereby increasing business independence and reducing poverty. The integration of zakat institutions with Islamic financial institutions has been proven to strengthen the economic resilience of small communities (Maulina et al., 2023).

Productive waqf is rapidly developing as a development instrument, used for social facilities such as schools, clinics, and green energy projects, making passive assets more productive and sustainable. The concept of green waqf, for example, finances solar power plants to support green infrastructure and emission reductions (BWI, 2025). Research in Saudi Arabia shows positive impacts on income, access to health services, and education (Elmahgop et al., 2025). In addition, digital innovation through waqf crowdfunding also expands the scope of ISF. A more detailed discussion of the hybrid model that integrates zakat, waqf, and impact investment will be explained in the next section.

3. Hybrid Model: Integration of Zakat with Impact Investment

The hybrid model in Islamic social finance combines zakat instruments with an impact investing approach to create sustainable social impact. This model allows social funds to grow and be reused, so they don't run out after they're disbursed. For example, Bank Islam Malaysia Berhad developed the Sakeena Home Ownership Programme (SakeenaHOPe), which integrates personal financing with zakat funds to help low-income people own homes. This program shows how zakat funds can be redirected to achieve broader social goals (Asia Property Awards, 2021).

Further, the research by Ibrahim et al. (2023) developing the Waqf Integrated Income Generating Model (WIIGM), which integrates collaborative investment, technology, and governance to empower the community's economy through productive waqf. This model shows that the integration between zakat and impact investing can generate sustainable income that supports infrastructure development and economic empowerment. In addition, a study by Raimi et al. (2024) highlighting the role of zakat in achieving sustainable development goals and reducing economic disparities. This research shows that zakat can be used as an instrument to fund social projects that support the achievement of sustainable development goals.

Despite its great potential, this hybrid model is not free from challenges. The microfinance literature highlights the risk of mission drift, which is the shift of institutional orientation from social goals to profit orientation (Armendariz & Szafarz, 2011; Jia & Sun, 2023). The complexity of governance is also increasing, as institutions must balance the interests of investors, regulators, and beneficiaries. If transparency and accountability are not maintained, the risk of conflict of interest could undermine the legitimacy of the ISF. Therefore, the development of hybrid models needs to be accompanied by a clear regulatory framework, standardized social impact measurement (Zain et al., 2023), and commitment to maintain Maqā id al-Sharīʿah so that the integration of zakat-impact investing truly supports social justice and sustainable development."

4. Productive Waqf for SDGs

Productive waqf is now developing as a strategic instrument in supporting the achievement of the SDGs. According to Judijanto et al. (2025) Productive waqf through investment in the real estate and social enterprises sectors greatly contributes to poverty alleviation, education, health, to economic empowerment and environmental sustainability. In addition, the study by Sa'adah et al. (2025) show various productive waqf models that can be important literature for waqf institutions (nadzir), focusing on optimizing waqf assets for SDGs goals.

Furthermore, the green waqf approach shows the transformation of passive waqf into an active environmental financing tool. Hasan & Syahruddin (2022) propose the concept of green waqf for carbonization technology (waste management into renewable energy), which is in line with SDGs 7 (clean energy), SDGs 11 (sustainable cities and communities), and SDGs 13 (climate action). In addition, a study by Shahmi et al. (2025) Examine the potential of energy waqf in expanding access to renewable energy and generating positive socio-economic impacts. This study highlights that although the concept and application of energy waqf is still limited, there is great potential to utilize waqf as a sustainable renewable energy financing instrument. Junarti et al. (2024) Through a systematic review, it was found that social business principles in waqf management are important to ensure financial sustainability, social impact, governance, and multi-stakeholder partnerships. This indicates that productive waqf can function as a proactive instrument of social change, combining spiritual values with real economic benefits that are in line with the spirit of inclusive and sustainable development.

5. Blockchain and Smart Contracts for Transparency and Efficiency

Blockchain technology and smart contracts offer significant opportunities for transparency, efficiency, and accountability in Islamic social finance. As a decentralized ledger, blockchain allows for the recording of zakat and waqf transactions that are secure and immutable, thereby increasing public trust (Omar & Khairi, 2021; Zulfikri et al., 2022; Rahayu et al., 2025). The implementation of smart contracts allows automatic zakat distribution according to nisab and musta iq criteria, which has implications for reducing operational costs and accelerating services (Fatmawati et al., 2024). Research by Kunhibava et al. (2024) regarding the project Finterra and Blossom Finance affirmed the potential of blockchain in the post-pandemic revitalization of ISF with three main impacts: automation of distribution, immutability of data for audits, and higher public accountability. From the perspective of fiqh, Kunhibava et al. (2024) and Zamroni et al. (2023) affirmed that the use of smart contracts can be justified if it is in accordance with Maqā id al-Sharīʿah and the principles of maslahah, justice, and openness.

Despite its great potential, the adoption of blockchain and smart contracts still faces serious obstacles. Immature regulations and differences in legal frameworks between countries create uncertainty in implementation, while technological infrastructure, adoption costs, and human resource capacity in small-scale zakat and waqf institutions are still limited (Farezy et al., 2025). If these challenges are not addressed immediately, the adoption of technology risks adding complexity and digital divides, instead of strengthening inclusion. Therefore, the successful integration of blockchain in the ISF requires a combination of technical innovation, clear regulatory standards, and the translation of sharia principles into operational parameters that can be audited and accepted by the public.

INTEGRATION OF THE THREE PILLARS IN AN INCLUSIVE AND SUSTAINABLE FRAMEWORK

Literacy, entrepreneurship, and social finance are 3 pillars that complement each other in creating an inclusive and sustainable Islamic financial ecosystem. First, literacy provides capabilities and awareness to the public to understand Islamic Social Finance instruments such as zakat, waqf, and sharia microfinance. Study by Rantaprasaja (2025) shows that campuses and higher education institutions play a strategic role in improving Islamic financial literacy through collaboration with financial institutions, applied research, and mentoring MSMEs.

Second, entrepreneurship is an important mechanism to create innovative solutions that are productive and inclusive. Sharia-based entrepreneurship can expand the reach of equitable economic development, especially for marginalized groups, with the support of access to capital and social value-based assistance. Third, social finance through sustainability instruments such as productive zakat, productive waqf, and impact-driven funding, plays a role in providing sustainable capital for inclusive businesses. Islamic financial instruments, if properly integrated, can play an important role in achieving the SDGs, such as poverty alleviation, quality education, and social empowerment.

1. Literacy, Entrepreneurship, and Social Finance as One Ecosystem

IFL, entrepreneurship, and social finance are not three separate entities, but complement each other in building an inclusive Islamic economic ecosystem. Literacy provides cognitive capabilities and normative understanding so that people can manage resources according to sharia principles. Entrepreneurship is an applicative channel that transforms knowledge into productive, innovative, and value-added activities. Meanwhile, social finance such as zakat, waqf, and community-based financial initiatives function as a social safety net as well as initial capital in reducing access inequality (Ascarya et al., 2022). This means that the integration of these three pillars creates an Islamic economic development cycle that not only relies on growth, but also on welfare, distributive justice, and sustainability (Dusuki & Bouheraoua, 2023), and operates as a space for the actualization of Maqā id al-Sharī́ah in contemporary development.

2. Framework Konseptual

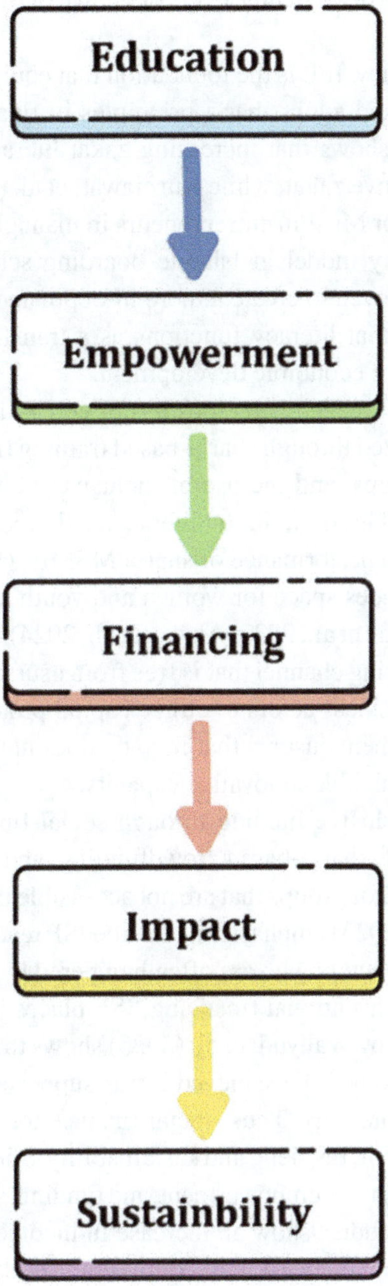

The conceptual framework offered views the integration of literacy, empowerment, funding, impact, and sustainability as progressive stages that strengthen each other in forming an inclusive and sustainable Islamic finance ecosystem. These flows do not run in isolation, but form a dynamic cycle of knowledge towards socio-economic transformation.

The first stage is literacy. IFL is the foundation that equips individuals and communities to understand and adopt sharia principles in financial decision-making. Fatmawati et al. (2024) shows that increasing zakat literacy strengthens people's understanding of productive zakat, while Kurniawati et al. (2024) affirming its role as an important capital for Muslim entrepreneurs in managing non-cash zakat. The community-based literacy model in Islamic boarding schools, BMTs, or sharia cooperatives has been proven to create a more in-depth and sustainable contextual learning ecosystem. So that literacy functions as a transformative cognitive and social capital for inclusive economic development.

Next is empowerment, which is the process of converting knowledge into real capabilities. This is realized through sharia-based training (mu ārakah, mu ārabah), incubation of halal startups, and the use of inclusive digital markets. A study in Aceh found that financial literacy, digital literacy, and access to micro capital have a significant effect on the performance of sharia MSMEs (Wediawati et al., 2025). Empowerment also provides space for women and youth to innovate according to their social context (Azizah et al., 2022; Aisyah et al., 2024). Islamic fintech plays an important role as a financing channel that is free from usury, while Islamic business ethics training equips business actors to utilize capital productively (Latifah et al., 2025). So that empowerment ensures that literacy does not stop at knowledge, but also develops into a sustainable innovative capacity.

The third stage is inclusive funding through social finance. Productive zakat instruments, money waqf, sharia-based crowdfunding, and micro-schemes are important sources of capital for groups that are not accessible by conventional banking services. Harahap et al. (2023) emphasizing that the ISF reaches low-income households and small business actors who are often hampered by guarantees and service charges. In contrast to conventional financing, ISF places justice and solidarity as the main goals. Research by Wahyudi et al. (2025) shows that the integration of ISF with the SDGs is very likely to be achieved if it is supported by transparency, risk management, and accountability. Thus, social finance not only provides access to capital, but also fosters a fair, resilient, and sustainability-oriented economic culture.

From the synergy of literacy, empowerment, and funding, socio-economic impacts are born. Cross-context studies show an increase in income, labor absorption, and strengthening social capital in the form of community solidarity and trust networks (Adbi et al., 2024). Digital literacy has been proven to increase household financial resilience (Verma & Chatterjee, 2025), while the adoption of fintech reduces MSME liquidity constraints and improves business performance (Mohapatra et al., 2025; Sun & Zhang, 2024). This impact is not only felt by individuals, but also extends to communities through co-created value that strengthens entrepreneurial networks and cross-stakeholder collaboration. Thus, the socio-economic impact serves as tangible evidence of the success of the three-pillar integration.

The last stage is sustainability. In this phase, the entire system is geared towards aligning with Maqā id al-Sharīʿah and the goals of the SDGs, especially poverty alleviation, gender equality, decent work, and the reduction of inequality. According to Anwar et al (2025) Islamic economic planning based on Maqā id al-Sharīʿah provides moral legitimacy as well as strategic direction of development. Study by Prasojo et al. (2024) In practice, Bank Syariah Indonesia shows that the integration of Maqā id with the SDGs is able to create governance that supports sustainability and social legitimacy. Thus, sustainability is not the end point, but rather the foundation for a new cycle of inclusive development that is resilient to the challenges of the future.

3. Inclusive Islamic Finance Ecosystem (IIFE)

The Inclusive Islamic Finance Ecosystem (IIFE) is an integrative conceptual framework designed to bring together Islamic financial literacy, entrepreneurship, and Islamic social financial instruments (such as zakat, infaq, alms, and waqf) into one inclusive system based on Maqā id al-Sharīʿah and the goals of the SDGs. This model rejects fragmentation between subsystems, such as financial literacy that runs without access to funding, or unsupported productive social financing entrepreneurship, and instead emphasizes the importance of synergy among all actors: governments, social institutions, the Islamic financial sector, and grassroots communities (Harahap et al., 2023; Hotman & Luthfi, 2025).

An inclusive ecosystem of Islamic social finance is formed through multi-stakeholder collaboration. The government plays an important role by issuing regulations and incentives, such as productive zakat, to expand financial inclusion and encourage entrepreneurship, as well as the practice of Value-Based Intermediation (VBI) in Malaysia which is in line with Maqā id al-Sharīʿah and the goals of the SDGs (Conventus Law, 2024). Zakat and waqf institutions manage Islamic social funds professionally and channel them to the productive sector, including initiatives such as environmental waqf that support social justice and sustainable development. On the other hand, the Islamic finance industry provides financial products and services that are relevant to the needs of society and digitally integrated. Islamic fintech, for example, opens up broad access for the unbanked population and MSMEs, while accelerating the achievement of the SDGs. Civil society and communities also have a central role, not only as beneficiaries, but also as drivers of the solidarity and locality-based economy, so that this inclusive ecosystem becomes more sustainable and firmly rooted at the community level.

INNOVATIVE PATHWAY TO INCLUSIVE DEVELOPMENT

Sustainable inclusive development requires a holistic approach that brings together IFLs, social entrepreneurship, and Islamic social finance instruments in a mutually reinforcing ecosystem. IFL has a fundamental role in expanding public understanding of Islamic finance products and principles, so as to be able to encourage financial inclusion and strengthen the basis of economic empowerment. Research shows that the increase in IFL has a direct impact on improving the performance of MSMEs, for example in the halal tourism sector in Indonesia (Mujiatun et al., 2023). Effective literacy not only introduces the concept of Islamic finance, but also emphasizes its application in the practical context of daily life.

Within this framework, Islamic social entrepreneurship is present as an important catalyst that translates literacy into real action, creating jobs while reducing poverty. Maqā id al-Sharīʿah-based social entrepreneurship incubators, for example, provide not only technical training, but also ongoing mentoring and relevant market access. Incubators like this have proven to be able to answer the classic limitations that micro business actors often face, ranging from limited capital, weak business management, to difficulty in market penetration. Multi-stakeholder collaboration is a prerequisite for success: the government creates regulations and incentives, Islamic non-governmental organizations and philanthropy flow productive social funds, while the Islamic finance industry provides fair and sharia-compliant financing instrumentsh (Alom et al., 2025; Aziz et al., 2025).

A broader policy strategy is also needed to realize the Islamic Inclusive Financial Ecosystem (IIFE). The integration of IFL in formal and non-formal education is a crucial foundation, not only introducing zakat, waqf, alms, or sharia financing products, but also emphasizing their use in daily economic activities. Literacy combined with digital skills has been proven to strengthen women's and youth groups' access to Islamic financial services in a safe and sustainable manner (Harahap et al., 2023; Mishra et al., 2024). Furthermore, cross-sector collaboration accelerates the spread of Islamic financial technology and expands the reach of productive zakat programs and MSME financing (Raimi et al., 2024). Thus, literacy, incubation, regulation, and multi-stakeholder collaboration together create an inclusive and long-term viable ecosystem.

Economic incubation and empowerment become a real bridge to turn financial knowledge into practical skills. The incubation programs not only provide access to capital, but also instill the values of Islamic business ethics and social responsibility, which ensure that businesses grow in line with Maqā id al-Sharī'ah (Aziz et al., 2025). Collaboration For vulnerable groups such as women, youth, and small MSMEs, empowerment based on entrepreneurship training, integration with digital markets, and connections with Islamic fintech presents more equal economic transformation opportunities (Alom et al., 2025; Mishra et al., 2024). Digitalization strengthens this process by opening up real-time access to market information and expanding consumer networks, so that micro enterprises are able to compete in a digitalized global economic landscape.

Digitalization and sharia fintech are also major accelerators in expanding financial inclusion. Digital platforms allow people to access Islamic financial services faster, safer, and more transparently. Services such as waqf crowdfunding, sharia peer-to-peer lending, mobile zakat, and financial education applications present financial participation opportunities that were previously difficult to reach (Alom et al., 2025). However, digital literacy is absolutely an important requirement for people to use this technology effectively. Those who have a better understanding of fintech applications, data security, and sharia principles are proven to be able to access digital services more optimally, reducing the risk of misuse and misinterpretation (Mishra et al., 2024).

Although this innovative path has great potential, a number of obstacles still loom over its implementation. The main obstacle is low digital literacy for rural and low-income communities, which has an impact on the loss of opportunities to utilize sharia fintech services to the fullest. On the other hand, the capacity of entrepreneurial incubators has not been fully developed as many programs stop at the short training stage without continuous assistance so that micro businesses are vulnerable to failure in the first two years. The governance of social funds such as zakat and waqf also often faces problems of transparency and accountability, even though the sustainability of the program is highly determined by this factor (Harahap et al., 2023).

Regulations that are not yet uniform in the field of sharia fintech can cause uncertainty for investors and users, especially related to consumer protection and sharia compliance mechanisms. In addition, multi-stakeholder coordination is often partial, so the integration of literacy, empowerment, and financing programs has not reached optimal scale. If these constraints are ignored, then various innovations risk only becoming short-term projects without transforming into sustainable ecosystems. Therefore, adaptive governance, proactive policies, and collaborative commitment are needed for innovative pathways to truly realize inclusive development that is just, sustainable, and in line with Maqā id al-Sharī'ah.

GLOBAL AND REGIONAL ISLAMIC SOCIAL FINANCE INITIATIVES

The Islamic Development Bank (IsDB) consistently supports sustainable development financing through Islamic social finance that integrates zakat, waqf, and sharia microfinance. The IsDB disburses funds for projects that are in line with the SDGs' goals, with a focus on social inclusion, poverty alleviation, and green development. The IsDB Sustainable Finance Framework regulates financing for green, social, and sustainable projects that are managed in a transparent and responsible manner (IsDB, 2025).

In Dubai, the Islamic economic ecosystem is growing rapidly with the development of a strategy based on regulations, the promotion of the halal industry, sharia fintech, and the strengthening of international sharia finance. The Dubai Islamic Economic Development Centre (DIEDC) is implementing a roadmap to make Dubai a global Islamic economic hub with a foundation of innovation, standardisation and poverty, as well as supporting the contribution of the Islamic economy to the UAE's GDP in line with the SDGs (Ahmed, 2024).

At the Southeast Asian regional level, community-based Islamic finance initiatives are developing in Indonesia and Malaysia. Micro Waqf Banks in Indonesia provide waqf-based capital for micro business actors with a mentoring and financing approach without usury, strengthening economic empowerment and reducing social inequality (Ascarya et al., 2022). Pesantrenpreneur as a model for the development of pesantren education that combines entrepreneurial literacy and market access to strengthen the economic capacity of students(Assayyidi & Farhan, 2024).

In Malaysia, an innovative approach is in the form of the BangKIT Microfinance product from Bank Islam Malaysia Berhad, which offers adaqah-based microfinance for micro entrepreneurs, especially those who are unbanked or underbanked along with entrepreneurship training to ensure the sustainability of their businesses (Wahab et al., 2023). This model shows the integration of sharia principles, financial literacy, and social finance in creating an inclusive and sustainable economic impact.

In Africa, Islamic zakat and social finance instruments have proven to be effective in alleviating poverty through the empowerment of micro-enterprises, education, and health services. Productive zakat funds are managed through the involvement of local communities to improve accountability and poverty programs, thereby supporting Maqā id al-Sharīʿah and sustainable development goals. Empirical studies show that the development of Islamic finance in Africa plays a significant role in poverty reduction in an inclusive and sustainable manner (Jimoh et al., 2024; Wudil et al., 2025).

CRITICAL CHALLENGES OF IMPLEMENTATION

Although the integration between Islamic Social Finance (ISF), Islamic Fintech, and social entrepreneurship instruments promises many benefits for efforts to achieve the SDGs, there are some implementation challenges that should not be overlooked. First, governance and regulation are still the main obstacles because the latest literature shows that zakat/waqf institutions and Islamic fintech operate within a fragmented regulatory framework between jurisdictions, without clear international standards in terms of accountability, transparency, and sharia compliance (Napitupulu et al., 2024; Wahyudi et al., 2025). Second, there is the problem of mission drift based on research in developing countries reporting that with the growth of Islamic financial institutions, some Micro-Finance Institutions (MFIs) have started targeting clients who have financially profitable prospects as a result of competition and profit targets so that the poorest groups may be overlooked (Pati, 2021).

The third challenge is the digital divide and financial/technology literacy, where the adoption of fintech or digital platforms does increase access, but access is uneven, especially for rural communities, lack of adequate internet infrastructure, and lack of knowledge about modern Islamic finance technology and concepts (Haris & Manangin, 2024; Alfian et al., 2025; Fatimah et al., 2025). Fourth, there are obstacles in measuring social impact and sustainability, so it is necessary to objectively and consistently measure social outcomes (in the form of poverty alleviation, inclusion) resulting from the combination of ISF, fintech, and social entrepreneurship. Many studies show that the indicators used are still heterogeneous, longitudinal data are limited, and there is often no independent evaluation mechanism.

CONCLUSION AND IMPLICATIONS

The integration of Islamic financial literacy (IFL), social entrepreneurship, and social finance offers an innovative approach towards inclusive and sustainable development. IFL provides an ethical and cognitive foundation in financial management in accordance with sharia principles. Social entrepreneurship supports the transformation of value into productive activities that benefit society, while social finance provides a fair and solidaristic funding instrument. The three, when synergized, form an Islamic economic development framework that not only focuses on growth, but also on social justice and sustainability.

Academically, the integration of these three pillars offers a new research space. For example, the development of the Islamic Inclusive Development Index as a multidimensional measure of Islamic development. Digital financial literacy is also an important agenda in the era of technological transformation, while a hybrid model between zakat and impact investment has the potential to be further developed both in theoretical frameworks and empirical testing. However, this study still has limitations. The complexity of governance, the limitations of cross-border empirical data, and the variation in implementation at the local level are indicators that further research is needed to strengthen the validity and deepen understanding of the effectiveness of the three-pillar integration.

The practical implications of this integration are layered. For regulators, literacy guidelines and innovative governance frameworks are needed that are able to accommodate digital developments while complying with sharia. For zakat and waqf institutions, the main priority is to strengthen productive programs so that musta iq can transform into muzakki. For entrepreneurs, the impact-based entrepreneurship model provides strategic opportunities to align profit orientation with social and ecological contributions.

In general, an inclusive Islamic economy has the potential to become a new development paradigm, in line with the Sustainable Development Goals and Maqā id al-Sharīʿah. However, the implementation of this potential is highly dependent on institutional capacity, the sustainability of multi-stakeholder collaboration, and the adaptation of regulations that are responsive to social and technological dynamics.

REFERENCES

Adbi, A., Lee, M., & Singh, J. (2024). Community Influence on Microfinance Loan Defaults Under Crisis Conditions: Evidence from Indian Demonetization. *Strategic Management Journal*, *45*(3), 535–563. DOI: 10.1002/smj.3558

Ahmed, H. M. (2024). *DIEDC Outlines Future Plans for Islamic Economy*. The Halal Times. https://www.halaltimes.com/diedc-outlines-future-plans-islamic-economy/

Aisyah, E. N., Pratikto, H., Wardoyo, C., & Restuningdiah, N. (2024). The Right Literacy on the Right Performance: Does Islamic Financial Literacy Affect Business Performance Through Islamic Financial Inclusion? *Journal of Social Economics Research*, *11*(3), 275–289. DOI: 10.18488/35.v11i3.3766

Al-Daihani, M., Dirie, K. A., Muneem, A., Abdul Lateb, N., & Bouteraa, M. (2025). Islamic Social Finance and Its Potential in Addressing Natural Disaster Emergencies and Advancing Sustainable Development Goals: A Proposed Model. *International Journal of Ethics and Systems*. https://doi.org/DOI: 10.1108/IJOES-05-2024-0138/1250881/ISLAMIC-SOCIAL-FINANCE-AND-ITS-POTENTIAL-IN

Al-Ghazali. (1997). *Mustasfa Min Ilm al-Usul, Vol. I*. https://archive.org/details/GAZALIMustasfaMinIlmUsulI/page/n15/mode/2up

Al Mustofa, M. U., Shophia, S. P., Muhibbin, Z., Ardiantono, D. S., Mawardi, I., Widiastuti, T., Fahmi, A., & Windiani, W. (2025). Risk Perception on Intention to Pay Zakat Via Financial Technology (Fintech). *Journal of Islamic Marketing*, *16*(12), 3559–3590. Advance online publication. DOI: 10.1108/JIMA-03-2024-0110

Alfian, I., & Majid, M. S. A. (2025). The Role of Sharia Fintech in Enhancing Financial Inclusion in the Digital Era. *Journal of Finance and Islamic Banking*, *8*(1), 79–94. DOI: 10.22515/jfib.v8i1.11798

Alom, K., Rahman, M. Z., Khan, A. I., Akbar, D., Hossain, M. M., Ali, M. A., & Mallick, A. (2025). Digital Finance Leads Women Entrepreneurship and Poverty Mitigation for Sustainable Development in Bangladesh. *Journal of Innovation and Entrepreneurship*, *14*(1), 1–18. DOI: 10.1186/s13731-025-00471-2

Antara, P. M., Musa, R., & Hassan, F. (2016). Bridging Islamic Financial Literacy and Halal Literacy: The Way Forward in Halal Ecosystem. *Procedia Economics and Finance*, *37*, 196–202. DOI: 10.1016/S2212-5671(16)30113-7

Anwar, D. R., Wahab, A., & Waris, W. (2025). Maqasid Syariah and Sustainable Development: Integrating Islamic Objectives into Economic Planning. *Formosa Journal of Multidisciplinary Research*, *4*(6), 2601–2618. DOI: 10.55927/fjmr.v4i6.269

Armendariz, B., & Szafarz, A. (2011). *On Mission Drift in Microfinance Institutions.* https://papers.ssrn.com/abstract=1918096

Ascarya, A., Hosen, M. N., & Rahmawati, S. (2022). Designing Simple Productive Waqf Models for Indonesia. *International Journal of Ethics and Systems, 38*(3), 380–401. DOI: 10.1108/IJOES-07-2020-0101

Asia Property Awards. (2021). *Bank Islam pioneers housing scheme to help those in need.* https://www.asiapropertyawards.com/en/bank-islam-pioneers-housing-scheme-to-help-those-in-need/

Assayyidi, N., & Farhan, M. (2024). Pesantrenpreneurship dalam Perspektif Pendidikan Islam. *TA'DIBUNA: Jurnal Pendidikan Agama Islam, 6*(2), 162–171. DOI: 10.30659/jpai.6.2.162-171

Auda, J. (2013). Al-Maqashid untuk Pemula. In *Filsafat Hukum Islam.* Suka Press.

Aziz, Y., Mansor, F., Waqar, S., & Zada, N. (2025). Zakat and Sustainable Development Goals (SDGs). Assessing the Ripple Effect of Obligatory-Alms Spending on Education. Empirical Evidence From Pakistan. *Asian Social Work and Policy Review, 19*(1), e70006. DOI: 10.1111/aswp.70006

Azizah, S. N., Saleh, S., & Sulistyaningrum, E. (2022). The Effect of Working Mother Status on Children's Education Attainment: Evidence from Longitudinal Data. *Economies 2022, Vol. 10, Page 54, 10*(2), 54. DOI: 10.3390/economies10020054

Barus, E. E., Al Mujadid, N. S., Umar, M. R., Dores, E., & Zahra, N. R. (2025). The Role of Sharia Cooperatives in Supporting the Sustainable Development Goals (SDGs) 2030 in Medan City. [AKSY]. *Jurnal Ilmu Akuntansi Dan Bisnis Syariah, 7*(2), 264–285. DOI: 10.15575/aksy.v7i2.46230

Bertola, G., & Lo Prete, A. (2025). Financial Literacy and Risk Protection During the Covid-19 Pandemic. *Italian Economic Journal, 11*(2), 645–666. DOI: 10.1007/s40797-024-00286-2

BWI. (2025). *BWI, MOSAIC Dan Yayasan Hutan Wakaf Kolaborasi Strategis Hutan Wakaf untuk Pengembangan Green Wakaf dan Green Energy.* https://www.bwi.go.id/11081/2025/02/25/bwi-mosaic-dan-yayasan-hutan-wakaf-kolaborasi-strategis-hutan-wakaf-untuk-pengembangan-green-wakaf-dan-green-energy/

Chapra, M. U. (2016). *The Future of Economics: An Islamic Perspective.* https://books.google.co.id/books?hl=id&lr=&id=0NGpDAAAQBAJ&oi=fnd&pg=PR11&ots=295lYLxRLB&sig=amDQAY8JHYGpjoZA4lmxKN_IprY&redir_esc=y#v=onepage&q&f=false

Choung, Y., Chatterjee, S., & Pak, T. Y. (2023). Digital Financial Literacy and Financial Well-Being. *Finance Research Letters, 58*, 104438. DOI: 10.1016/j.frl.2023.104438

Dinc, Y., Çetin, M., Bulut, M., & Jahangir, R. (2021). Islamic Financial Literacy Scale: An Amendment in the Sphere of Contemporary Financial Literacy. *ISRA International Journal of Islamic Finance, 13*(2), 251–263. DOI: 10.1108/IJIF-07-2020-0156

Elmahgop, F., Alsulami, F., Mohammed, M. G. A., Abdel-Gadir, S., & Elhassan, T. (2025). The Socio-Economic Impacts of Waqf Investment Funds as a Model for Sustainable Financing in Saudi Arabia. *Sustainability 2025, Vol. 17, Page 3805, 17*(9), 3805. DOI: 10.3390/su17093805

Farezy, I., Ariani, Z., Hidayanti, N. F., Agustina, A., & Hulaimi, A. (2025). *Integration of Blockchain Technology in Islamic Finance: Opportunities and Challenges Towards Transparency and Sharia Compliance*. https://journal.ummat.ac.id/index.php/iicece/article/view/31325

Fatimah, S., Wibowo, W., Irfaniah, N. R., Harahap, R. A., & Panggabean, N. A. (2025). Local Digital Ecosystem: Peran Komunitas Digital dalam Mendorong Bisnis Kreatif Daerah. *JUMINTAL: Jurnal Manajemen Informatika Dan Bisnis Digital, 4*(1), 127–136. DOI: 10.55123/jumintal.v4i1.5479

Fatmawati, F., Kahfi, N. S., Aisyah, N. H., & Asyifa, L. N. (2024). Application of Blockchain and Smart Contracts in Zakat Management: Perspective of SWOT Analysis and Islamic Law. *Indonesian Conference of Zakat - Proceedings*, 240–250. https://doi.org/DOI: 10.37706/ICONZ.2024.977

Fawaid, F. (2024). Beyond Profit: How BMT NU Jambesari Empowers MSMEs Through Sharia Financing. *Tadayun: Jurnal Hukum Ekonomi Syariah, 5*(2), 185–210. DOI: 10.24239/tadayun.v5i2.345

George, L. (2024). *Debt Burden Threatens Poor Countries' Development Goals, UN Official Says*. https://www.reuters.com/world/debt-service-burden-forcing-poor-make-tough-choices-un-official-says-2024-10-07/

Harahap, B., Risfandy, T., & Futri, I. N. (2023). Islamic Law, Islamic Finance, and Sustainable Development Goals: A Systematic Literature Review. *Sustainability 2023, Vol. 15, Page 6626, 15*(8), 6626. DOI: 10.3390/su15086626

Haris, C., & Manangin, S. (2024). The Digital Revolution in Exploring the Impact of Fintech on Islamic Financial Services. *Kunuz: Journal of Islamic Banking and Finance, 4*(2), 171–187. DOI: 10.30984/kunuz.v4i2.1267

Harrieti, N., Ikhwansyah, I., & Alisa Ahmad, A. (2024). The Role of Sharia Banking in Strengthening the Assets of Village-Owned Enterprises in Indonesia. *Cogent Social Sciences, 10*(1), 2350557. DOI: 10.1080/23311886.2024.2350557

Hasan, N. F., & Syahruddin, S. (2022). Enhancing Green Waqf For Carbonization Technology: Opportunities for Sustainable Development Goals (SDGs) in Indonesia. *El Barka*, *5*(2), 235–251. DOI: 10.21154/elbarka.v5i2.4739

Hotman, & Luthfi, M. (2025). The Influence of Maqasid Al-Shariah on Sustainable Investment Decisions in Islamic Finance. *Economics Studies and Banking Journal (DEMAND), 2*(1), 295–309. https://doi.org/DOI: 10.62207/E0HM4677

IAEI. (2025). *Indonesia Joins the List of the Largest Issuers in the ESG Sukuk Market*. https://iaei.or.id/en/news-and-articles/news/indonesia-joins-the-list-of-the-largest-issuers-in-the-esg-sukuk-market

Ibrahim, S. S., Daud, D., Hidayah, K., Shaharuddin, A., & Al-Amin, A. A. M. (2023). Waqf Integrated Income Generating Model (WIIGM) for Enhancing Sustainable Development Goals (SDGS) in Malaysia: An Evaluation of Behavioural Intention. *International Journal of Ethics and Systems*, *39*(4), 841–858. DOI: 10.1108/IJOES-02-2022-0030

IsDB. (2025). *IsDB Sustainable Finance Framework (July 2025)*. Islamic Development Bank. https://www.isdb.org/publications/isdb-sustainable-finance-framework-july-2025

Jan, A., Rahman, H. U., Zahid, M., Salameh, A. A., Khan, P. A., Al-Faryan, M. A. S., Che Aziz, R. B., & Ali, H. E. (2023). Islamic Corporate Sustainability Practices Index Aligned with SDGs Towards Better Financial Performance: Evidence from the Malaysian and Indonesian Islamic Banking Industry. *Journal of Cleaner Production*, *405*, 136860. DOI: 10.1016/j.jclepro.2023.136860

Jia, P., & Sun, S. L. (2023). Mission Drift or Mission Fulfillment? Examining Microfinance's Financial and Social Performance with Growth Curve Modeling and Variance Decomposition. *Cross Cultural & Strategic Management*, *30*(3), 467–487. DOI: 10.1108/CCSM-07-2021-0125

Jimoh, A. T., David Kolawole, K., & Bamigbade, D. (2024). Islamic Microfinance as a Panacea for Poverty Alleviation. *European Journal of Islamic Finance*, *11*(1), 17–30. DOI: 10.13135/2421-2172/9414

Judijanto, L., Sarif, A., & Ariyanti, R. (2025). Productive Waqf as a Sustainable Financial Instrument in the Perspective of Islamic SDGs. *West Science Islamic Studies*, *3*(02), 106–110. DOI: 10.58812/wsiss.v3i02.1833

Junarti, A. S. M., Amirsyah, & Mardika, I. H. (2024). Integrating Social Business for Sustainable Impact: A Systematic Literature Review in the Context of Waqf. *Journal of Islamic Finance, 13*(2), 149–159. https://journals.iium.edu.my/iiibf-journal/index.php/jif/article/view/931

Kamali, M. H. (2019). Maqasid Al-Shariah Made Simple. In *Maqasid Al-Shariah Made Simple*. DOI: 10.2307/j.ctvkc67vz

Kaweesa, Y., Rosman, R., Syahira, S., & Yusoff, M. (2024). Examining the Trend of the Research on Islamic Financial Literacy from 2016-2023: A Bibliometric Review. *Journal of Islamic Finance, 13*(1), 70–90. https://journals.iium.edu.my/iiibf-journal/index.php/jif/article/view/886

Khan, M. S., Azad, I., Moosa, S., & Javed, M. Y. (2024). Do we really need financial literacy to access the behavioral dynamics of generation Z? A case of Oman. *Heliyon, 10*(13), e32739. DOI: 10.1016/j.heliyon.2024.e32739

Khoshakhlagh, M., Amini Milani, M., & Abolhasani Hastiani, A. (2024). Investigating the Impact of Qard al-Hasna (Interest-Free Loan) Facilities on the Misery Index in Iran: An ARDL Approach. *Iranian Journal of Economic Studies, 12*(2), 531–550. DOI: 10.22099/IJES.2025.52171.1991

Kunhibava, S., Muneeza, A., Mustapha, Z., Khalid, M., & Kiran, G. (2024). Blockchain Use Case in Islamic Social Finance. *ISRA International Journal of Islamic Finance, 16*(1), 93-110–193 – 110. DOI: 10.55188/ijif.v16i1.659

Kurniawati, Y., Alfin, A., Suseno, F., Hanifa Seftiani, F., Islam Negeri Sjech Djamil Djambek Bukittinggi, U. M., Gurun Aua, J., Putiah, K., Banuhampu, K., Bukittinggi, K., Barat, S., Djambek Bukittinggi, D., & Author, C. (2024). The Role of Ziswaf in Improving Financial Literacy and Reducing Unemployment for Economic Growth. *ICEFS Proceeding, 2*, 102–107. https://doi.org/DOI: 10.30983/iciefs.v2.763

Lahnech, A., & Chami, M. (2025). Exploring the Synergy Between Microfinance and Poverty: A Bibliometric and Comprehensive Systematic Literature Review. *SAGE Open, 15*(2), 21582440251340771. Advance online publication. DOI: 10.1177/21582440251340771

Latifah, L., Rodoni, A., & Aziz, R. M. (2025). The Empowerment of MSMEs through Islamic P2P Financing: A Value-Based Social Entrepreneurship Framework. [IJIEF]. *International Journal of Islamic Economics and Finance*, *8*(2), 246–267. DOI: 10.18196/IJIEF.V8I2.27985

Law, C. (2024). *Maqasid Al-Shariah And The Sustainable Development Goals In The Practice Of Takaful: An Analysis.* https://conventuslaw.com/report/malaysia-maqasid-al-shariah-and-the-sustainable-development-goals-in-the-practice-of-takaful-an-analysis/

Liu, T., Fan, M., Li, Y., & Yue, P. (2024). Financial Literacy and Household Financial Resilience. *Finance Research Letters*, *63*, 105378. DOI: 10.1016/j.frl.2024.105378

Maniam, S. (2024). Determinants of Islamic Fintech Adoption: A Systematic Literature Review. *Journal of Islamic Marketing*, *15*(11), 2916–2936. DOI: 10.1108/JIMA-11-2023-0373

Marwah, A., Sapa, N. bin, & Syatar, A. (2025). Integrating Maqashid al-Shariah into Islamic Economic Practices: A Contemporary Analytical Framework and Its Applications. *El-Kahfi | Journal of Islamic Economics, 6*(01), 36–44. https://doi.org/DOI: 10.58958/ELKAHFI.V6I01.456

Masrizal, S., Sukmana, R., & Trianto, B. (2025). The Effect of Islamic Financial Literacy on Business Performance With Emphasis on The Role of Islamic Financial Inclusion: Case Study in Indonesia. *Journal of Islamic Marketing*, *16*(1), 166–192. DOI: 10.1108/JIMA-07-2022-0197

Maulina, R., Dhewanto, W., & Faturohman, T. (2023). The Integration of Islamic Social and Commercial Finance (IISCF): Systematic Literature Review, Bibliometric Analysis, Conceptual Framework, and Future Research Opportunities. *Heliyon*, *9*(11), e21612. DOI: 10.1016/j.heliyon.2023.e21612

Mishra, D., Kandpal, V., Agarwal, N., & Kumar, R. singh, R., Priyadarshi, N., & Twala, B. (2024). Digital and Financial Literacy for Uplifting Women and Achieving Sustainable Development Goals. *F1000Research 2024 13:1364, 13*, 1364. DOI: 10.12688/f1000research.156744.1

Mohapatra, N., Das, M., Shekhar, S., Singh, R., Khan, S., Tewari, L. M., Félix, M. J., & Santos, G. (2025). Assessing the Role of Financial Literacy in FinTech Adoption by MSEs: Ensuring Sustainability Through a Fuzzy AHP Approach. *Sustainability 2025, Vol. 17, Page 4340, 17*(10), 4340. DOI: 10.3390/su17104340

Mujiatun, S., Trianto, B., Cahyono, E. F., & Rahmayati. (2023). The Impact of Marketing Communication and Islamic Financial Literacy on Islamic Financial Inclusion and MSMEs Performance: Evidence from Halal Tourism in Indonesia. *Sustainability 2023, Vol. 15, Page 9868, 15*(13), 9868. DOI: 10.3390/su15139868

Napitupulu, R. M., Sukmana, R., & Rusydiana, A. S. (2024). Governance of Islamic Social Finance: Learnings from Existing Literature. *International Journal of Islamic and Middle Eastern Finance and Management, 17*(3), 552–571. DOI: 10.1108/IMEFM-06-2023-0222

Nugraha, A. L., & Sudrajad, O. Y. (2025). *Pesantrenpreneur: The Fusion of Piety, Profit and Progress*. Islamic Bussiness Review. https://islamicbr.com/read_article/pesantrenpreneur-the-fusion-of-piety-profit-and-progress

Obaidullah, M. (2015). Enhancing Food Security with Islamic Microfinance: Insights from Some Recent Experiments. *Agricultural Finance Review, 75*(2), 142–168. DOI: 10.1108/AFR-11-2014-0033

OECD. (2023). *Increasing Development Finance Efforts to Scale Private Finance Mobilised and Its Impact*. https://www.oecd.org/en/publications/increasing-development-finance-efforts-to-scale-private-finance-mobilised-and-its-impact_345b768b-en/full-report/component-2.html

OJK. (2022). *Survei Nasional Literasi dan Inklusi Keuangan Tahun 2022*. https://ojk.go.id/id/berita-dan-kegiatan/siaran-pers/Pages/Survei-Nasional-Literasi-dan-Inklusi-Keuangan-Tahun-2022.aspx

Omar, N., & Khairi, K. F. (2021). Zakat and Blockchain: A Review. *International Journal of Islamic Economics and Finance Research, 4*(2 December), 60–66. DOI: 10.53840/ijiefer53

Pati, A. P. (2021). Structural Transformation, Profit and Cost: What Drive(s) Mission Drift in Indian Microfinance? *International Journal of Rural Management, 17*(1), 75–92. DOI: 10.1177/0973005220967223

Prasojo, S. L., & Muhfiatun. (2024). Harmonizing Sustainable Development Goals and Maqasid Shariah: A Strategic Framework for Indonesian Islamic Banks (Case Study on Bank Syariah Indonesia). *Journal of Islamic Finance, 13*(2), 106–117. https://journals.iium.edu.my/iiibf-journal/index.php/jif/article/view/928

Rahayu, N. W. I., Rahayu, N. W. I., Al Ahsani, N., Suroyya, D., & Yudiawan, A. (2025). A Bibliometric Analysis of Blockchain-Based Zakat System Design: Solutions for Transparency and Oversight of Zakat Funds in the Digital Era. *Academic Journal of Interdisciplinary Studies, 14*(1), 346. DOI: 10.36941/ajis-2025-0023

Raimi, L., Abdur-Rauf, I. A., & Ashafa, S. A. (2024). Does Islamic Sustainable Finance Support Sustainable Development Goals to Avert Financial Risk in the Management of Islamic Finance Products? A Critical Literature Review. *Journal of Risk and Financial Management 2024, Vol. 17, Page 236, 17*(6), 236. DOI: 10.3390/jrfm17060236

Rantaprasaja, L. (2025). Economic Empowerment Through Islamic Financial Inclusion: The Strategic Role of Universities in Synergy with Islamic Financial Institutions. *Diversity: Jurnal Ilmiah Pascasarjana, 5*(1), 73–83. DOI: 10.32832/diversityjournal.v5i1.19304

Sa'adah, T. P., Ritonga, I., Latifah, F. N., & Mugiyati, M. (2025). Systematic Literatur Review of Productive Waqf in Indonesia and Their Contribution to SDGs. *Perisai : Islamic Banking and Finance Journal, 9*(1), 27–48. DOI: 10.21070/perisai.v9i1.1802

Safei, A. A. (2021). The Formula of Islamic Community Development in Indonesia Through the Social Entrepreneurship Approach. *Religious: Jurnal Studi Agama-Agama Dan Lintas Budaya, 5*(1), 47–58. DOI: 10.15575/rjsalb.v5i1.9685

Saro, N., Bhari, A., Rani, M. A. M., & Yusof, M. F. M. (2023). *Analysis of Digital Zakat Payment Implementation: A Comparison in Southeast Asia.* https://www.researchgate.net/publication/371039191_Analysis_of_Digital_Zakat_Payment_Implementation_A_Comparison_in_Southeast_Asia

Setiawan, A., & Nurzaman, M. S. (2022). Application of Blockchain and Smart-Contract on Waqf Asset Management: Is It Necessary? *EL DINAR: Jurnal Keuangan Dan Perbankan Syariah, 10*(2), 85–101. DOI: 10.18860/ed.v10i2.15529

Shahmi, M. A., Putra, M. D., Fahlefi, R., Arifah, L., & Mansur, M. (2025). Energy Waqf and the Environmental Crisis: Advancing Islamic Philanthropy for Sustainability. *Economica: Jurnal Ekonomi Islam, 16*(1), 1–17. DOI: 10.21580/economica.2025.16.1.23549

Sun, J., & Zhang, J. (2024). Digital Financial Inclusion and Innovation of MSMEs. *Sustainability 2024, Vol. 16, Page 1404, 16*(4), 1404. DOI: 10.3390/su16041404

UNCTAD. (2024). *Financing for Sustainable Development Report 2024: Financing for Development at a Crossroads.* https://unctad.org/publication/financing-sustainable-development-report-2024

Verma, R., & Chatterjee, D. (2025). Relative Impact of Digital and Traditional Financial Inclusion on Financial Resilience: Evidence from 13 Emerging Countries. *Journal of Economics and Business, 133*, 106233. DOI: 10.1016/j.jeconbus.2025.106233

Wahab, N. A., Bin-Nashwan, S. A., Chik, M. N., & Hussin, M. Y. M. (2023). Islamic Social Finance Initiatives: An Insight into Bank Islam Malaysia Berhad's Innovative BangKIT Microfinance Product. *ISRA International Journal of Islamic Finance, 15*(1), 22–35. DOI: 10.55188/ijif.v15i1.483

Wahyudi, I., Yama, I., & Said, M. (2025). Islamic Social Finance as a Catalyst for SDGs: A Systematic Analysis of Implementation Models and Digital Innovation. *Falah: Jurnal Ekonomi Syariah, 10*(1), 54–70. DOI: 10.22219/jes.v10i1.37591

Wediawati, B., Adriani, Z., Setiawati, R., Ratnawati, R. T. S., & Dewi, E. (2025). The Impact of Entrepreneurial, Financial, and Digital Literacy on MSME Performance. *Jurnal Ilmiah Manajemen Kesatuan, 13*(4), 2643–2658. DOI: 10.37641/jimkes.v13i4.3411

Wijaya, H. R., Hati, S. R. H., Ekaputra, I. A., & Kassim, S. (2024). The Impact of Religiosity and Financial Literacy on Financial Management Behavior and Well-Being Among Indonesian Muslims. *Humanities & Social Sciences Communications, 11*(1), 1–13. DOI: 10.1057/s41599-024-03309-6

Wilson, J., & Lederer, E. M. (2025). *US Skips Global UN Meeting Aimed at Raising Trillions to Combat Poverty.* https://apnews.com/article/poverty-inequality-development-financing-un-spain-e7b965e2a160b7c51f7da6fcf58edc29

Wudil, A. A., Saad, N. M., Omercic, J., Zakaria, L., & Muhammad, R. (2025). Islamic Finance and Poverty Reduction in African Countries: An Empirical Analysis. *International Journal of Economics, Management and Accounting, 33*(1), 77–97. DOI: 10.31436/ijema.v33i1.1299

Yumna, A., Marta, J., & Yanuarta RE, R. (2025). The Impact of Financial and Social Inclusion on Well-Being: Evidence from a Waqf-Based Microfinance Institution in Indonesia. *International Journal of Ethics and Systems.* https://doi.org/DOI: 10.1108/IJOES-08-2024-0243/1253232/THE-IMPACT-OF-FINANCIAL-AND-SOCIAL-INCLUSION-ON

Yusfiarto, R., Nugraha, S. S., Mutmainah, L., Berakon, I., Sunarsih, S., & Nurdany, A. (2023). Islamic Capital Market Adoption from a Socio-Psychological Perspective and Islamic Financial Literacy. *Journal of Islamic Accounting and Business Research, 14*(4), 574–594. DOI: 10.1108/JIABR-02-2022-0037

Zain, N. S., Hassan, R., & Marwan, S. (2023). Social Impact Measurement as a Tool of Governance and Accountability for Waqf Organisations. *International Journal of Islamic Economics and Finance Research, 1*(1), 132–148. DOI: 10.53840/ijiefer122

Zamroni, M. A., Toha, M., Zuana, M. M. M., & Isbahi, M. B. (2023). Exploring Zakat Distribution Via Blockchain in Indonesia Perspective of Maslahah Mursalah Wahbah Zuhaili. [IIJSE]. *Indonesian Interdisciplinary Journal of Sharia Economics*, *6*(3), 3544–3555. DOI: 10.31538/IIJSE.V7I3.5821

Zulfikri, Z., Adam, A., Kassim, S., & Hassan, A. (2022). Trust Enhancement in Zakat Institutions using Blockchain Technology: A Qualitative Approach. *European Journal of Islamic Finance*, *9*(1), 31–36. DOI: 10.13135/2421-2172/6312

Chapter 6
Islamic Digital Financial Literacy in Navigating Wealth Ethics and Sustainability in the 21st Century

Nofriansyah Nofriansyah
https://orcid.org/0009-0001-5150-6082
Universitas Pendidikan Indonesia, Indonesia

Rendika Vhalery
https://orcid.org/0000-0001-7244-1620
Universitas Indraprasta PGRI, Indonesia

Wahyu Wibowo
https://orcid.org/0009-0000-5176-7103
UIN Sunan Kalijaga Yogyakarta, Indonesia

Endang Supardi
https://orcid.org/0000-0002-0946-9644
Universitas Pendidikan Indonesia, Indonesia

ABSTRACT

This chapter discusses the integration of financial literacy with Islamic ethical principles in the context of digital financial tools. The rise of fintech, mobile banking, blockchain, and AI has revolutionized financial management, offering both opportunities for inclusion and risks such as impulsive consumption, debt dependency, and cybersecurity threats. From an Islamic perspective, financial literacy goes beyond

DOI: 10.4018/979-8-3373-1842-4.ch006

technical knowledge, emphasizing moral responsibility, with wealth considered an amanah (trust) from Allah. The chapter explores how digital financial platforms can adhere to Islamic principles, focusing on moderation, wealth purification through zakat and waqf, and the importance of Shariah compliance. Key themes include the foundation of financial literacy, the role of fintech in inclusion, building ethical financial habits, and aligning financial practices with sustainability and social justice, contributing to the collective good and ethical stewardship in the digital economy.

INTRODUCTION

In the twenty-first century, mastering financial literacy has become indispensable. The rise of digital platforms such as mobile banking, e-wallets, peer-to-peer lending, blockchain, and artificial intelligence has fundamentally reshaped the ways individuals, households, and institutions manage wealth. These innovations promise efficiency and broadened access, yet they also bring systemic risks, including impulsive consumption, debt dependency, cybersecurity breaches, and widening inequalities. In secular research, financial literacy is often defined as the cognitive and behavioral capacity to make sound financial decisions (Huston, 2010; Lusardi & Mitchell, 2017; Kaiser et al., 2022). However, evidence shows that education alone rarely shifts behavior, as social pressures, impulsivity, and market manipulation frequently override rational calculation (Fernandes et al., 2014; Isaia et al., 2024).

Islamic thought reframes this landscape by embedding financial literacy within ethics, spirituality, and accountability. Wealth (*al-māl*) is considered an *amanah*, or trust from God, not merely a private asset but a resource to be managed responsibly for personal welfare and social good (Qur'an 33:72). The Qur'an prohibits *riba* (2:275), forbids unjust enrichment (4:29), warns against *isrāf* and *tabdhīr* (17:26–27), and calls for moderation (*wasatiyyah*) (25:67). Hadith literature further emphasizes the moral burden of debt, such as the narration in Sunan Ibn Mājah (no. 2413), which states that the soul of the believer is held hostage by debt until it is repaid. Classical scholars reinforced this ethos: al-Ghazālī in *I yā' 'Ulūm al-Dīn* argued that economic activity is inseparable from justice and piety, while Ibn Khaldūn in *al-Muqaddimah* described wealth circulation as the foundation of social cohesion and prosperity. Modern thinkers such as Chapra (2000), Siddiqi (2004), and Kahf (2007) warn that financial systems divorced from ethical principles inevitably breed inequality and instability.

This book chapter situates financial literacy within this dual context of digital transformation and Islamic ethical imperatives. The first theme, *The Foundation of Financial Literacy in the Digital Age: An Islamic and Sustainable Perspective*, establishes conceptual pillars by contrasting conventional approaches that emphasize numeracy, skills, and behavior with an Islamic paradigm where literacy entails compliance with divine law, moral consciousness, and wealth purification through zakat and waqf. The second theme, *Digital Financial Tools, and Platforms: Between Innovation, Inclusion, and Ethical Boundaries*, examines how fintech, blockchain, and cashless systems expand access but also risk exclusion, exploitation, and uncertainty when regulation and Shariah governance are weak (Daniele et al., 2020; Hudaefi, 2020; Kaur et al., 2021). The third theme, *Building Smart and Shariah-Compliant Financial Habits in the Digital Era*, focuses on everyday practices such as budgeting, saving, and investing, showing how digital tools aligned with Qur'anic principles of moderation and obligations like zakat can transform routine financial choices into acts of stewardship. The final theme, *Towards Financial Independence and Sustainability*, links literacy to resilience, green finance, and intergenerational equity through instruments such as sukuk, takaful, and AI-driven financial education (World Bank, 2022; Sun et al., 2024).

Through these themes, financial literacy is presented not only as a technical skill for navigating digital finance but also as a moral compass rooted in the higher objectives of Shariah (*maqā id al-sharī ah*). These objectives include the preservation of faith, life, intellect, lineage, and wealth, ensuring that financial behavior contributes to justice, sustainability, and the collective good. By uniting classical Islamic insights, contemporary scholarship, and emerging digital innovations, this chapter advances a framework in which literacy becomes both a survival skill in the digital economy and a form of worshipful stewardship in an age of profound transformation.

THE FOUNDATION OF FINANCIAL LITERACY IN THE DIGITAL AGE: AN ISLAMIC AND SUSTAINABLE PERSPECTIVE

In Islamic thought, wealth (*al-māl*) is not mere material accumulation but an amanah entrusted by Allah to be managed responsibly, circulated justly, and preserved for future generations. The Qur'an commands moderation (w*asatiyyah*) condemns *isrāf* and *tabdhīr*, and frames finance within a moral economy (Qur'an 2:261–280). This contrasts with secular models of financial literacy, which emphasize numeracy and retirement security (Huston, 2010; Lusardi & Mitchell, 2017) or multidimensional skills and behaviors (Kaiser et al., 2022) yet often treat decisions as value-neutral, with limited behavioral impact (Fernandes et al., 2014). An Islamic perspective reframes literacy as both technical capacity and moral consciousness, guided by the maqā id al-sharī'ah to preserve wealth, life, intellect, lineage, and faith. Classical scholars such as al-Ghazālī, who emphasized justice and the avoidance of exploitation, and Ibn Khaldūn, who viewed economic activity as sustaining social cohesion, anticipated critiques of riba-based systems. Modern thinkers like Chapra (2016), Siddiqi (2005), and Kahf (2007) reinforce those financial systems devoid of ethics breed inequality and instability, affirming Islamic financial literacy as a distinct paradigm that integrates competence with accountability.

1. Basic Concepts and Main Components of Financial Literacy

Financial literacy is most defined in functional terms: the knowledge and skills required to make sound financial decisions. Huston (2010) popularized this definition, and it remains widely adopted by policymakers, framing financial literacy as a technical toolkit. Lusardi and Mitchell (2017) extend this argument by showing its positive long-term impact on household welfare, particularly in retirement planning. Kaiser et al. (2022) further refine the concept into four interdependent pillars knowledge, skills, attitudes, and behavior marking an important step toward a multidimensional understanding.

Yet even this enriched framework reveals notable limitations. Fernandes et al. (2014) demonstrate that programs narrowly focused on knowledge transfer have limited impact on real-world financial behavior. Overconfidence bias, impulsive consumption, and cultural norms frequently override rational calculation (Isaia et al., 2024). This has produced an unresolved debate in the literature: is financial literacy primarily a cognitive competence, or does it require a deeper ethical and behavioral foundation?

Islamic economics provides a sharper resolution to this impasse by insisting that literacy is never value neutral. From an Islamic perspective, al-thaqāfah al-māliyah al-Islāmiyyah (Islamic financial literacy) entails both technical proficiency and moral orientation. Within this framework, the four pillars identified in the mainstream literature acquire distinct Shariah dimensions:

- Knowledge must extend beyond concepts such as inflation, diversification, or compound interest to encompass the prohibitions of riba (usury), gharar (excessive uncertainty), and maysir (gambling). It also requires an understanding of contracts (*akad*) such as *mudarabah* and *musharakah*, as well as obligations like zakat and waqf which serve as mechanisms of wealth purification and redistribution.
- Skills are not confined to budgeting or the use of financial applications but also involve the ability to calculate zakat, to evaluate halal-compliant financial products, and to engage with Shariah governance standards such as those issued by AAOIFI or the IFSB.

• Attitudes are shaped by taqwā (God-consciousness), abr (patience), and wara' (prudence), cultivating moderation in consumption, caution in risk-taking, and a sense of stewardship over wealth.
• Behavior then becomes the ultimate evidence of literacy, reflected in practices such as saving through Shariah-compliant accounts, investing in sukuk, avoiding prohibited industries, and implementing cybersecurity as part of if al-māl (the protection of wealth).

This reframing underscores a central divergence from secular approaches: while conventional models treat behavior as the endpoint of literacy, Islamic thought views behavior without ethical compliance as incomplete. A person adept at financial techniques but engaged in prohibited assets may appear literate in secular terms yet remains illiterate in Islamic terms. Classical scholars such as al-Ghazālī, who stressed justice and the avoidance of exploitation, and Ibn Khaldūn, who defined money as a medium of exchange rather than a tradable commodity, laid the groundwork for modern critiques of interest-based finance.

2. Financial Evolution: From Traditional to Digital

The financial system has undergone a dramatic transformation over the past few decades, moving from traditional, bank-centric arrangements into a highly digitalized ecosystem of fintech, blockchain, and cashless payment infrastructures. Conventional accounts of this shift often celebrate its efficiency, speed, and accessibility (Daniele et al., 2020; Miroshnychenko et al., 2024). Yet when examined through both ethical and Islamic lenses, the narrative reveals persistent exclusions and new risks that demand critical scrutiny.

Traditional banking was organized around physical cash, branch offices, and passbook accounts. These systems established reputational trust and offered stability, but they were expensive, slow, and geographically limited. Rural households frequently remained underbanked, while interest-based products left Muslim communities in tension between financial necessity and religious obligation (Chapra, 2016). The reliance on riba not only contradicted Islamic law but also entrenched structural inequalities by privileging creditors over debtors, an imbalance that Islamic economics has consistently sought to redress.

The digital transformation appeared to offer a corrective. Mobile wallets, peer-to-peer lending, and robo-advisors have expanded access and lowered transaction costs. Cross-country evidence shows that fintech adoption is correlated with gains in financial inclusion and micro-investment (Daniele et al., 2020). Yet these benefits are uneven. Urban and digitally literate users can leverage new platforms, while vulnerable groups such as the rural poor, women, and the elderly are often left further behind (Ozili, 2023). Islamic fintech has emerged as a response to this dual challenge of access and compliance. Innovations such as *qard al-hasan* microloans, zakat distribution platforms, and Shariah-compliant robo-advisory services (Hudaefi, 2020) illustrate how digital tools can be re-engineered to promote both inclusion and faithfulness to Islamic law.

Blockchain and tokenization introduce another layer of both promise and complexity. By enabling near real-time settlement, fractional ownership, and tamper-resistant records, they carry the potential to revolutionize capital markets. The issuance of tokenized sukuk and blockchain-based waqf projects demonstrates how Islamic finance can strategically harness these technologies (Kaur et al., 2021). Yet without strong Shariah governance and regulatory safeguards, blockchain risks becoming a vehicle for speculation and gharar, undermining its legitimacy and exposing communities to systemic vulnerabilities.

The push toward cashless societies similarly embodies both opportunity and danger. Digital payments reduce transaction costs, increase transparency, and facilitate broader participation in the formal economy. At the same time, they risk excluding those without access to smartphones, stable internet, or digital literacy. From an Islamic standpoint, this exclusion represents not merely a logistical shortcoming but a violation of justice (*'adl*), as equity and inclusion are central to the Maqasid al-Shariah. Furthermore, manipulative digital design so-called "dark patterns" that nudge users into over-borrowing or compulsive spending contradicts the principle of amanah (trustworthiness) and echoes the Qur'anic prohibition against isrāf and tabdhīr.

3. The Role of Financial Literacy in Everyday Life

The significance of financial literacy emerges most clearly not in abstract definitions but in the everyday decisions that households and individuals must make. Choices about whether to consume or save, to borrow or defer, or to invest prudently rather than speculate recklessly, are all deeply shaped by levels of financial literacy. Empirical evidence from randomized controlled trials indicates that context-specific and interactive financial education interventions can improve saving behavior and reduce reliance on harmful forms of credit (Kaiser et al., 2022). Yet, as Fernandes et al. (2014) argue, knowledge transmission alone rarely produces lasting behavioral change. The persistence of behavioral biases, including overconfidence, impulsivity, and present bias, continues to undermine rational financial decision-making (Isaia et al., 2024). This unresolved debate—between cognitive sufficiency and behavioral limitation—remains central to the financial literacy discourse.

For Muslim communities, the stakes of these debates are magnified by the ethical and spiritual framing of financial acts. Everyday financial decisions are not merely technical choices but are evaluated within the moral economy of Islam. The Qur'an condemns *isrāf* (wasteful consumption) and *tabdhīr* (squandering), while advocating *wasatiyyah* (moderation) as the guiding principle of economic life. From this perspective, budgeting, saving, and investment are not only economic behaviors but also moral acts of worship (*'ibadah*), subject to accountability before Allah. This creates a distinctive Islamic conception of financial literacy: one that integrates numeracy, behavioral discipline, and ethical consciousness.

The rise of digital financial literacy (DFL) adds further layers of responsibility. A digitally literate Muslim must evaluate not only the technical safety of platforms but also their Shariah compliance. This involves the ability to read terms and conditions critically, identify gharar in opaque contracts, and avoid manipulative "dark patterns" that encourage debt dependence. Cybersecurity practices such as two-factor authentication, strong password management, and responsible data sharing are no longer merely technical best practices; they become extensions of *if al-māl*, the Shariah imperative to protect wealth.

However, gaps in financial literacy remain profound across socio-demographic lines. Women, youth, rural populations, and gig-economy workers often experience systematic exclusion from both traditional and digital finance (Salleh et al., 2023). While mainstream scholars highlight these inequalities as barriers to financial inclusion, Islamic economics reframes them as violations of *'adl* (justice) and failures to uphold the collective obligation of ensuring equitable access. Addressing these disparities requires curricula that combine digital competencies with Shariah-specific content: calculating zakat, evaluating halal investments, and understanding ethical consumption. In this way, financial literacy becomes both a twenty-first-century survival skill and a means of fulfilling divine trust (*amanah*).

4. Challenges and Opportunities in the Digital Era

The digital age presents a paradox for financial literacy. On the one hand, technology lowers barriers, accelerates inclusion, and creates new avenues for sustainable finance. On the other hand, it introduces systemic risks that, if left unaddressed, may deepen inequality and conflict with Shariah principles. This duality calls for a careful balance between innovation, ethics, and governance.

One of the most pressing risks lies in consumer overconfidence and the consumption traps enabled by digital credit products such as Buy Now, Pay Later schemes and one-click lending. While these tools promise convenience, empirical studies show that they often encourage impulsive spending and household debt accumulation a pattern the Qur'an condemns as *isrāf* and *tabdhīr* (Djamhari et al., 2024; Isaia et al., 2024). Fraudulent investment applications and phishing attacks compound these dangers, eroding *if al-māl* by exposing vulnerable users to financial loss (Afzal et al., 2025; Alam et al., 2023; Swandaru & Muneeza, 2022). Cybersecurity and privacy breaches further illustrate the ethical dilemmas of digital finance, where manipulative "dark patterns" and data misuse compromise consumer autonomy (Zetzsche et al., 2020). Equally critical is the problem of digital exclusion: elderly populations, rural communities, and low-income groups are often left behind due to limited access to devices, skills, or connectivity (Demirgüç-Kunt et al., 2018; Ozili, 2023). From an Islamic perspective, such exclusion violates the principle of *'adl* and undermines the collective welfare envisioned in the *maqā id al-Sharī'ah.*

At the same time, digitalization offers remarkable opportunities that align closely with Islamic finance and sustainability. Platforms for zakat and waqf crowdfunding have demonstrated how technology can enhance transparency and public trust, enabling resources to reach education, healthcare, and poverty alleviation more efficiently (Hudaefi, 2020). Similarly, green sukuk represent a milestone in mobilizing Shariah-compliant finance for environmental objectives: Indonesia's sovereign green sukuk has successfully raised funds for renewable energy and climate adaptation, earning international recognition (World Bank, 2022). Advances in artificial intelligence also hold promise, from robo-advisors that screen halal portfolios to fraud-detection algorithms and bias-free credit-scoring systems, as seen in pilot initiatives by leading Islamic banks (Sun et al., 2024).

The decisive factor in navigating these risks and opportunities is governance. Without strong regulation, inclusive infrastructure, and Shariah-compliant product design, digital finance may become a vehicle for exploitation rather than empowerment. However, when innovation is guided by Islamic principles transparency, fairness, risk-sharing, and social justice it can advance the higher objectives of the Shariah by preserving wealth, protecting the vulnerable, and promoting sustainability (Chapra, 2016; Siddiqi, 2005; Kahf, 2007).

DIGITAL FINANCIAL TOOLS AND PLATFORMS: BETWEEN INNOVATION, INCLUSION, AND ETHICAL BOUNDARIES

The digitalization of finance represents not merely a technological shift but a paradigmatic transformation in the way individuals, households, and firms interact with money. Mobile banking, e-wallets, peer-to-peer lending, and crypto-based assets are reshaping the contours of inclusion, risk, and governance. In much of the Global South, these innovations are framed as instruments of empowerment: bringing millions into the financial system, lowering transaction costs, and offering new modes of investment.

Yet, the academic literature and policy debate remind us that digitalization is profoundly ambivalent. For every narrative of democratized access, there are counternarratives of exploitation, exclusion, and fragility. Scholars debate whether e-wallets cultivate saving discipline or encourage impulsive spending (Khando et al., 2023; Rahardja et al., 2023), whether fintech lending alleviates credit gaps or reproduces debt traps (Frost et al., 2022; Shupe et al., 2023), and whether cryptocurrencies democratize finance or amplify systemic volatility (Wang et al., 2022).

In Muslim-majority contexts, these questions are further complicated by Shariah imperatives. Finance must avoid riba (usury), gharar (excessive uncertainty), and maysir (gambling), while positively realizing the objectives of the Shariah (*maqasid al-shariah*) protecting wealth (*hifz al-mal*), ensuring justice, and supporting sustainability. Classical scholars such as Ibn Khaldun and Al-Ghazali located commerce at the intersection of morality and prosperity, while modern thinkers like Chapra (2016), Kahf (2007), and Siddiqi (2005) insist that markets without ethics are inherently unstable. Thus, digital finance cannot be evaluated only in terms of efficiency; it must also be examined through the lenses of equity, spirituality, and governance.

1. E-Wallets, Mobile Banking, and E-Payments

The rise of e-wallets and mobile banking reflects a structural transformation in financial intermediation, where payments have shifted from stand-alone transactions to embedded features within lifestyle ecosystems. In Indonesia, platforms such as GoPay, OVO, DANA, and ShopeePay are not merely utilities but gateways linking transport, food delivery, e-commerce, and social media. This mirrors global patterns where financial services are increasingly integrated into daily consumption, blurring the line between finance, technology, and culture (Rahardja et al., 2023).

Empirical evidence highlights both opportunities and risks. On one side, e-wallets reduce barriers to financial access by lowering documentation requirements and transaction costs, thereby enabling women, youth, and rural households to join the formal financial system (Daniele et al., 2020). They also support remittances, micro-investments, and bill payments, enhancing financial inclusion. On the other side, platform design strategies such as cashback, gamification, and voucher promotions—encourage impulsive spending and may weaken household budgeting discipline (Khando et al., 2023). Such practices create dependency loops that serve commercial interests but undermine financial resilience in vulnerable groups.

Mobile banking has undergone a similar evolution. Initially designed as remote account access, it has become a comprehensive platform for payments, microcredit, investment, and financial management. Studies identify perceived usefulness, ease of use, and trust in security as the strongest predictors of adoption (Gomber et al., 2018). However, adoption patterns remain uneven: younger, urban, and educated users dominate uptake, while the elderly and rural poor remain disadvantaged, reinforcing digital divides (Zavolokina et al., 2017). This inequality shows that digital inclusion is not automatic; without targeted literacy programs and regulation, the very tools designed to expand access can deepen exclusion.

From the perspective of Islamic finance, digital payment platforms carry both promise and dilemmas. They can facilitate automated zakat contributions, waqf crowdfunding, and halal-certified marketplaces, strengthening the infrastructure for faith-based inclusion. Yet unresolved questions remain. Should cashback and gamification schemes be considered forms of *gharar*? Are e-wallet providers that invest float funds in interest-bearing instruments Shariah-compliant? Such debates demonstrate that digitalization does not diminish the importance of ethical deliberation—it amplifies it. Embedding Shariah governance and consumer protection into digital payment ecosystems is therefore essential to ensure that innovation contributes not only to efficiency but also to justice, accountability, and sustainability.

2. Digital Investment: Between Democratization and Speculation

Digital investment platforms ranging from robo-advisors and mutual fund apps to cryptocurrency exchanges are often hailed as drivers of financial democratization. By offering fractional ownership, low or zero commission trading, and simplified KYC procedures, they lower barriers that historically restricted access to blue-chip stocks, ETFs, and diversified portfolios (Lu et al., 2024). For middle-class households in emerging markets, these platforms have broadened participation in wealth accumulation.

Yet, inclusion often masks overexposure. During the COVID-19 pandemic, retail investors relying on such platforms suffered disproportionate losses, lacking diversification, and succumbing to herd behavior during volatile market swings (Havakhor et al., 2025). Gamified interfaces rewards, badges, and instant notifications encourage speculative trading, reinforcing biases such as overconfidence and loss aversion (Isaia et al., 2024). In this sense, democratization risks being conflated with gamification.

Cryptocurrencies crystallize these contradictions. Advocates point to blockchain-based waqf management and tokenized sukuk as instruments of transparency and inclusion, while critics highlight liquidity gaps, susceptibility to manipulation, and speculative bubbles (Almeida & Gonçalves, 2022; Wang et al., 2022). Islamic scholars remain divided: blockchain as a technology is widely welcomed, but many cryptocurrencies fall under the prohibitions of *gharar* and *maysir*. The Indonesian Ulema Council's 2021 fatwa banning crypto as a currency, while permitting blockchain for sukuk issuance, illustrates this tension.

Case studies reveal the stakes. Indonesia's pioneering Green Sukuk, issued partly through digital platforms, demonstrates how technology can advance sustainability and Shariah compliance simultaneously. Conversely, waves of retail speculation in meme-coins show how unregulated access can replicate casino-like behavior. Ibn Khaldun long ago observed that when wealth is disconnected from productive activity, it fosters instability rather than cohesion. Modern voices like Chapra (2016) and Kahf (2007) reiterate that financial innovation must serve justice, not exploitation.

Practical implications vary across stakeholders. For investors, disciplined risk management clear horizons, diversification, and limits on speculative exposure remains essential. For platforms, embedding nudges, default caps on leverage, and transparent fee disclosures can reduce behavioral traps (Back et al., 2023). For regulators, ensuring disclosure integrity, supervising crypto exchanges, and mandating Shariah oversight are indispensable. Ultimately, whether digital investment becomes democratization or speculation depends on the integration of governance, education, and ethics.

3. Online Loans and Fintech Lending: Between Access and Entrapment

Fintech lending, including peer-to-peer platforms and buy-now-pay-later (BNPL) schemes, epitomizes the paradox of digital credit. On one hand, instant onboarding, alternative data, and automated disbursement expand liquidity for unbanked households and micro-enterprises excluded from conservative banks (Frost et al., 2022). On the other, the very features that enhance access ease, speed, and minimal checks also generate risks of impulsive borrowing and debt spirals (Shupe et al., 2023).

Evidence remains contested. Barkley and Schweitzer (2021) find that flexible repayment structures can reduce bankruptcies, while Ali and Marisetty (2023) report that easy digital loans accelerate defaults among financially illiterate borrowers. Field evidence from Indonesia confirms both sides: while P2P lending has financed thousands of small traders, waves of defaults between 2019–2022 exposed systemic weaknesses in consumer protection and lender due diligence.

For Islamic finance, the stakes are even higher. Conventional BNPL schemes often embed hidden interest charges, raising questions of compliance. Classical alternatives such as *qard al-hasan* (benevolent loans), *murabahah* (cost-plus sales), and *ijarah* (leasing) provide ethical credit models, yet remain marginal in mainstream fintech platforms. Embedding these contracts digitally could transform fintech lending from a driver of over-indebtedness into a mechanism for justice and resilience. As Chapra (2016) argued, debt in Islam is permissible only when it preserves dignity and avoids exploitation.

Demographic dimensions matter. Studies show that youth, women, and gig workers are disproportionately targeted by aggressive BNPL marketing. Meanwhile, elderly populations remain excluded due to digital barriers, producing both over-inclusion and under-inclusion risks. Regulation must therefore address not only transparency of costs and reasonable caps on penalties (Croux et al., 2020) but also data privacy, algorithmic bias, and exploitative targeting. In Muslim contexts, Shariah boards must scrutinize whether "profit-sharing" schemes genuinely embody justice and disclosure, rather than rebranding interest with Islamic terminology.

The lesson is clear: fintech lending is neither a universal solution nor a universal trap. Outcomes depend on regulation, education, and the ethical contracts embedded in platforms. Without these safeguards, promises of access risk collapsing into cycles of exploitation.

4. Fintech Security and User Education: Governance at the Edge

As finance digitalizes, exposure to cybercrime grows exponentially. Phishing, malware, account takeovers, and mass data breaches threaten not only individual users but systemic trust in financial platforms (Javaheri et al., 2024). Technical vulnerabilities are compounded by human ones: weak authentication, negligence, and manipulation through social engineering.

Recent case studies highlight these vulnerabilities. Fraudulent loan apps and OTP scams in Indonesia caused widespread losses, with users often unaware of regulatory recourse (Brogi & Lagasio, 2024; Carè & Fatima, 2025). While technical measures—end-to-end encryption, AI-driven anomaly detection, third-party audits—are critical, they cannot substitute for governance. Regulatory accountability requires mandatory breach reporting, penalties for negligence, and enforceable consumer protection frameworks.

Education represents the final and most indispensable layer of defense. Empirical studies show that strong password management, phishing-resistant multi-factor authentication, and device hygiene substantially reduce risks (Datta & Krancher, 2024). Yet literacy programs must extend beyond technical advice. They must confront manipulative design practices dark patterns, predatory nudges that exploit cognitive biases and undermine informed consent.

Here governance intersects with morality. In Islamic ethics, safeguarding wealth (*hifz al-mal*) and protecting trust (*amanah*) are not optional but foundational. Protecting user data and preventing exploitation are simultaneously regulatory duties and moral obligations. As Kahf (2007) notes, the legitimacy of finance rests on its ability to uphold justice and accountability. For fintech, this means embedding security and literacy not as afterthoughts but as central pillars of sustainable design.

BUILDING SMART AND SHARIAH-COMPLIANT FINANCIAL HABITS IN THE DIGITAL ERA

The cultivation of smart financial habits has become both more urgent and more complex in today's digital economy. On one hand, digital tools budgeting apps, e-wallets, robo-advisors, and pay-later services promise unprecedented efficiency and inclusion. On the other hand, they also create fertile ground for impulsive spending, speculative investing, and predatory lending. Conventional financial literacy frameworks emphasize budgeting, saving, and investing as technical skills (Yoganandham, 2025; Hilgert et al., 2023; Lusardi & Mitchell, 2017). Yet, from the perspective of Islamic economics, financial habits are not merely technical competencies, but moral practices embedded in divine accountability. Wealth is understood as *amanah* (trust), spending without reflection risks *isrāf* (waste), and debt laden with *riba* (usury) contradicts Shariah. As Chapra (2016) and Kahf (2007) argue, financial well-being in Islam is inseparable from justice, stewardship, and sustainability.

1. Income, Savings, and Expense Management

Personal finance mismanagement frequently arises from the absence of clear goals and weak self-control in prioritizing needs (Hilgert et al., 2023; Hermawan & Wahyudi, 2025). In the digital era, these vulnerabilities are magnified as cashless transactions reduce the "pain of paying," thereby encouraging impulsive consumption (Faraz & Anjum, 2025). This condition highlights the urgent need for structured approaches that discipline financial behavior while remaining adaptive to digital lifestyles.

One of the most widely recognized frameworks is the 50/30/20 budgeting rule, introduced by Warren and Tyagi and increasingly applied in digital contexts (Cabannes & Lipietz, 2018). By allocating 50% of post-tax income to essentials, 30% to discretionary spending, and 20% to savings or debt repayment, the rule provides a simple yet effective mechanism to balance immediate needs with long-term goals. Empirical evidence confirms its value in countering overspending in cashless environments where digital payments obscure the psychological cost of money (Faraz & Anjum, 2025). This model becomes more powerful when supported by digital finance applications such as Mint, YNAB, and regional fintech platforms, which offer real-time monitoring, personalized alerts, and behavioral nudges (Tang, 2019; Panos & Wilson, 2020). Studies further show that app users improve budgeting discipline, increase micro-savings, and participate more actively in investment opportunities (Prabhakaran & Mynavathi, 2025).

Nevertheless, the benefits of these tools are not evenly distributed. Women, rural communities, and low-income households often remain excluded due to limited smartphone access, digital literacy gaps, and irregular income flows (Demirgüç-Kunt et al., 2018). This digital divide reveals that financial inclusion is not merely a technological issue but also a matter of distributive justice. In Islamic thought, justice (*'adl*) and equity are foundational principles, requiring that financial systems empower vulnerable groups rather than deepen inequality (Chapra, 2016; Kahf, 2007).

From an Islamic perspective, financial management cannot be reduced to efficiency alone but must embody moral accountability. The Qur'an emphasizes moderation: *"And those who, when they spend, are neither extravagant nor miserly, but hold a just balance between those extremes"* (Qur'an 25:67). The Prophet Muhammad (peace be upon him) reinforced this by saying: *"Eat, drink, give charity, and wear [good clothes] without extravagance or arrogance"* (Sunan Ibn Majah, no. 3605). These teachings establish that wealth management must avoid *isrāf* (extravagance), uphold *wasatiyyah* (moderation), and ensure the fulfillment of obligatory redistributions such as zakat. Ibn Khaldun (1377/2019) also observed that zakat is not simply a fiscal tool but a pillar of social cohesion and justice, preventing concentration of wealth in the hands of a few.

This ethical foundation has direct implications for digital innovation. A household cannot be considered financially literate if it excels in budgeting but neglects zakat obligations or persists in riba-based consumption. Recent Shariah-compliant financial applications attempt to bridge this gap by automating zakat calculation, monitoring halal and haram expenditures, and channeling surplus income toward waqf contributions. Yet unresolved questions remain: do cashback incentives or gamified rewards constitute *gharar* (excessive uncertainty)? Can e-wallet providers that place customer float funds into interest-bearing deposits be considered compliant? These debates illustrate that digitalization intensifies rather than eliminates the need for ethical and jurisprudential deliberation.

2. Short-Term and Long-Term Financial Planning

Financial planning is indispensable for ensuring resilience and sustainability in an increasingly volatile global economy. While short-term strategies provide liquidity and immediate protection, long-term approaches focus on wealth accumulation, intergenerational justice, and sustainable development. Empirical evidence confirms that households with structured financial planning enjoy greater security during crises (Fox & Bartholomae, 2020; Lusardi & Mitchell, 2017). Yet in Muslim societies, financial planning is not merely a technical arrangement but an ethical and spiritual responsibility, requiring alignment with Shariah principles that frame wealth as a trust (*amanah*).

A critical foundation of short-term planning lies in maintaining emergency funds and securing insurance. Research shows that households with liquid savings covering three to six months of expenses are significantly better prepared to withstand shocks such as illness, job loss, or disasters (Tiwari, 2024). The digital era facilitates this through mobile savings accounts and e-wallets, which make emergency reserves more accessible. Insurtech platforms extend coverage further by providing micro-insurance at low premiums to populations underserved by traditional providers (Boj et al., 2022). However, conventional insurance often raises Shariah concerns due to elements of *gharar* (excessive uncertainty) and *maisir* (speculation). In response, takaful based on mutual cooperation offers a Shariah-compliant alternative that fulfills the objectives of Shariah (*maqasid al-shariah*), particularly the protection of life (*hifz al-nafs*) and wealth (*hifz al-mal*). The Qur'an underscores this protective ethos: *"And cooperate in righteousness and piety, but do not cooperate in sin and aggression"* (QS. Al-Maidah [5]:2), a principle that underpins the ethical basis of takaful.

Long-term financial planning extends from individual security to intergenerational equity. Pension digitalization allows contributors to monitor balances, simulate retirement needs, and adjust portfolios with greater ease, significantly improving long-term security for younger generations (Yadav et al., 2025). Yet in an Islamic framework, retirement planning must also integrate redistributive and ethical elements. Zakat obligations ensure wealth circulation to the needy, while inheritance distribution (*faraid*) is divinely mandated in the Qur'an: *"Allah commands you regarding your children: to the male, a portion equal to that of two females"* (QS. An-Nisa [4]:11). These provisions safeguard justice across generations, while investment screening prevents engagement with prohibited industries. The Prophet Muhammad (peace be upon him) emphasized that providing for one's dependents is itself an act of worship: *"It is sufficient sin for a man to neglect those whom he maintains"* (HR. Abu Dawud, no. 1692). Hence, retirement and estate planning in Islam transcends financial efficiency to embody accountability before God.

Beyond individual households, financial planning must also align with broader sustainability goals. The rise of ESG funds and green sukuk demonstrates how finance can be mobilized for ethical and environmental outcomes (Broadstock et al., 2020). Younger generations, particularly Gen Z and millennials, already express strong preferences for socially responsible investments (Prabhakaran & Mynavathi, 2025). Yet Islamic finance anticipated these movements centuries ago by embedding sustainability within *maqasid al-shariah*, which encompass not only the preservation of wealth but also the safeguarding of life and the environment. The Qur'an affirms this vision: *"The example of those who spend their wealth in the way of Allah is like a seed of grain which grows seven ears; in every ear a hundred grains"* (QS. Al-Baqarah [2]:261), highlighting the multiplier effect of ethical and sustainable investment. Green sukuk, financing renewable energy and sustainable infrastructure, exemplify how Islamic instruments not only comply with Shariah but also lead in advancing global sustainability agendas.

3. Digital Lifestyle, Consumer Behavior, and Financial Protection

The digitalization of everyday life has transformed how consumers engage with markets, reshaping purchasing patterns through e-commerce platforms, social media marketing, and seamless payment systems (Liu et al., 2024). While these innovations increase efficiency, they also facilitate impulsive consumption. Flash sales, limited time offers, and gamified vouchers amplify *fear of missing out* (FOMO), especially among Gen Z consumers who, due to lower financial literacy and heightened peer influence, are particularly vulnerable (Afzal et al., 2025; Pokharel & Maharjan, 2024).

Countering such tendencies requires cultivating mindful spending the deliberate evaluation of wants versus needs, and the conscious alignment of expenditures with long-term goals (Iborra et al., 2024). Islamic teachings reinforce this practice through the prohibition of *isrāf* (extravagance) and encouragement of *wasatiyyah* (moderation). The Qur'an states: *"Indeed, the wasteful are brothers of the devils"* (QS. Al-Isra [17]:27), underscoring that unrestrained consumption is not merely imprudent but spiritually detrimental. Redirecting discretionary spending toward *sadaqah* or savings reflects both financial prudence and spiritual accountability, turning lifestyle choices into acts of stewardship (*khalifah*).

Debt traps represent another major risk of digital lifestyles. The expansion of online lending and buy-now-pay-later (BNPL) schemes provide short-term liquidity but frequently results in over-indebtedness when coupled with weak literacy and overconfidence (Hamid, 2025; Ameh et al., 2022). Warning signs include reliance on credit for everyday expenses, chronic delays in repayment, and using new loans to service existing ones. Islamic tradition treats habitual indebtedness with great seriousness. The Prophet Muhammad (peace be upon him) refused to perform funeral prayers for those who died with unpaid debts until they were settled (HR. Muslim, no. 1619), highlighting that financial imprudence can extend into one's accountability in the hereafter.

The digital economy also multiplies risks of fraud and exploitation. Ponzi schemes, phishing, identity theft, and social engineering exploit not only technical weaknesses but also human psychology (Kaur et al., 2021). While cybersecurity measures such as two-factor authentication and data encryption are vital, lasting protection requires literacy and ethical vigilance. Within the Islamic framework, safeguarding wealth (*if al-māl*) is one of the higher objectives of Shariah, making financial protection both a pragmatic necessity and a moral obligation. Integrating awareness campaigns with Shariah-based ethics can ensure that financial resilience is underpinned by both technical competence and spiritual responsibility.

4. Strategies to Avoid Debt Traps and Financial Fraud

Debt traps occur when individuals repeatedly roll over loans to repay existing obligations, locking households in a cycle of repayment that erodes long-term financial stability (Li et al., 2021). The most common warning signs include using credit to finance daily consumption, recurring delays in installments, and taking out new loans to refinance old ones (Chen et al., 2024). Preventive strategies require a multi-layered approach: (1) financial education that clarifies the dangers of compound debt, (2) prudent budgeting to ensure expenses remain within sustainable limits, and (3) behavioral safeguards such as paying cash for discretionary purchases. These strategies transform financial literacy into practical resilience.

Equally urgent is the rise of scams and fraud in digital finance. Fraudulent investment schemes promising guaranteed high returns, unlicensed platforms, and manipulative social engineering constitute systemic risks (Chen et al., 2024). Effective anti-scam literacy combines technical measures secure passwords, phishing-resistant multi-factor authentication, regular device updates with moral discernment. Many fraudulent schemes succeed because they exploit greed and haste, qualities that Islamic teachings explicitly warn against. The Qur'an cautions: *"Do not consume one another's wealth unjustly, but only [in lawful] business by mutual consent"* (QS. An-Nisa [4]:29). This verse frames fraud not simply as a financial crime but as a violation of divine trust.

From an Islamic perspective, avoiding riba, fraud, and exploitation is not optional but obligatory. Just as riba corrodes justice, financial fraud undermines *amanah.* Embedding Shariah boards within fintech regulation, mandating transparency in digital contracts, and promoting literacy programs that integrate financial skills with ethical teachings can prevent exploitation. Hadith literature reinforces this integration: *"The truthful and trustworthy merchant will be with the Prophets, the truthful, and the martyrs"* (HR. Tirmidhi, no. 1209). Thus, financial integrity is not only a technical safeguard but a path to moral excellence.

In the digital era, strategies to avoid debt traps and fraud must therefore go beyond reactive measures. They must be embedded in systemic governance, institutional accountability, and a cultural ethos of responsibility. When households, regulators, and financial institutions integrate technical competence with Islamic ethics, financial systems can shift from cycles of vulnerability to frameworks of justice, resilience, and sustainability.

TOWARDS FINANCIAL INDEPENDENCE AND SUSTAINABILITY

The aspiration for financial independence and sustainability is universal, yet its interpretation varies across traditions. In secular discourse, independence is often defined as freedom from debt and the capacity to pursue consumption or investment goals, while sustainability emphasizes aligning financial choices with environmental and social priorities. In Islamic thought, however, independence and sustainability are inseparable from ethics, spirituality, and accountability. Wealth is regarded as an *amānah* (trust) from God, to be used responsibly for both personal welfare and societal good (Qur'an 33:72). The Qur'an explicitly prohibits *riba* (2:275), warns against *isrāf* or wastefulness (17:26–27), and forbids unjust enrichment (4:29). Prophet Muhammad (peace be upon him) also sought refuge from overpowering debt, underscoring its moral and spiritual burden (a ī al-Bukhārī; Jāmiʿ al-Tirmidhī).

1. Financial Literacy for the Younger Generation

The younger generation faces unprecedented financial pressures in the digital era. Aggressive online marketing, frictionless e-payments, and social commerce blur the boundary between genuine needs and impulsive wants. Research consistently shows that low levels of financial literacy among youth are associated with overspending, poor saving habits, and vulnerability to debt traps (Mancone et al., 2024; Raza et al., 2024). Early interventions, however, can alter this trajectory. Experiential learning—such as gamified budgeting, market simulations, and micro-projects—helps children and adolescents internalize prudent behaviors, cultivating habits that endure into adulthood (Khalil, 2020). At the university level, students who regularly use personal finance applications demonstrate stronger planning awareness and improved expenditure control (Cedeño et al., 2021). Accordingly, higher education institutions can institutionalize financial labs, entrepreneurship clinics, and fintech partnerships, ensuring that theoretical knowledge is consistently translated into practical skills (Garg et al., 2024).

Family remains the first school of financial responsibility. Evidence shows that children who practice simple budgeting of allowances, save part of their pocket money, or assist in household planning develop stronger financial competencies as adults (De Beckker et al., 2021). Collaborative efforts between schools and families—such as joint workshops, financial clubs, and parent–child education programs—magnify these effects and ensure inclusivity across socioeconomic groups (Damane & Ho, 2025). Such integration also reduces the digital divide, particularly for children from rural or low-income households who may otherwise lack exposure to structured financial education.

Islamic teachings reinforce and elevate these imperatives. The Qur'an explicitly warns against extravagance (*isrāf*) and commands moderation (*wasatiyyah*) in spending (17:26–27). It also prohibits unjust enrichment and exploitation (4:29), underscoring the moral dimension of financial conduct. Hadith literature highlights the dangers of excessive debt, with Prophet Muhammad (peace be upon him) teaching that "the soul of the believer is held hostage by his debt until it is paid off" (Sunan Ibn Mājah, no. 2413). Within this framework, financial literacy for youth is not merely technical competence but also a moral ethos: income must be *alāl*, *zakāt* is a mandatory obligation, and spending should avoid *isrāf*.

Digital innovation can support this ethical framework. Applications that categorize transactions as *halal* or *haram*, automate *zakāt* calculations and payments, and facilitate micro-waqf contributions integrate modern convenience with spiritual accountability.

2. Financial Independence in the Digital Era

Financial independence in the digital era encompasses two dimensions: resilience, or the ability to withstand financial shocks, and agency, the capacity to pursue long-term goals with confidence. Both dimensions demand layered protections, productive accumulation, and ethical governance that aligns with Shariah principles.

Resilience begins with the establishment of liquidity buffers equivalent to three to six months of household expenses (Tiwari, 2024). In Muslim contexts, these reserves must be safeguarded in Shariah-compliant savings instruments or money-market funds to avoid riba. Protection against risk requires similar ethical vigilance. While conventional insurance is often criticized for elements of gharar, *takaful* grounded in mutual solidarity and cooperation fulfills the maqā id al-sharī'ah by protecting both life and wealth. Digital platforms further enhance accessibility by automating contributions and simplifying participation, ensuring that resilience is not only an ideal but a practical reality.

Beyond resilience, independence requires ethical accumulation. Households can diversify portfolios through *sukūk*, Shariah-screened equities, or *mudarabah* and *mushārakah* funds. Ibn Khaldun (1377/2019) emphasized that productive capital circulation sustains prosperity, while modern scholars such as Chapra (2016), Siddiqi (2005), and Kahf (2007) argue that risk-sharing models mitigate exploitation and distribute wealth more justly. These principles resonate strongly in the digital era, where online platforms extend access to investment markets. Yet behavioral risks persist: gamified trading applications can trigger overconfidence, herding, and speculative churn (Isaia et al., 2024). Therefore, literacy must combine Shariah-compliant screening with robust risk management education to balance opportunity with prudence.

Income diversification through digital entrepreneurship represents another pathway to independence. The rise of e-commerce, gig work, and content creation expands earning opportunities but also externalizes risks to workers. Studies show that SMEs managed by financially literate youth who possess strong social capital and emotional intelligence are more resilient in the face of competition (Maravilla & Flores, 2025; Worokinasih et al., 2023; Boohene et al., 2020). Policymakers must reinforce these efforts by ensuring fair platform practices, transparent fee structures, and access to *takaful* schemes that provide a safety net for gig workers and digital entrepreneurs.

However, independence cannot be sustained without ethical governance. Algorithmic credit scoring must be audited to prevent bias and discrimination, while buy-now-pay-later schemes must operate transparently. In Muslim markets, such schemes should be restructured through *murāba ah* or *ijārah* contracts rather than interest-based models, ensuring compliance with Islamic principles. Here, systemic design becomes as critical as individual choices. True independence emerges not from isolated ingenuity but from collective alignment among households, regulators, technology providers, and Shariah governance. Only when these actors work in concert can financial independence be both resilient and just.

3. Financial Literacy and Economic Sustainability

Sustainability and financial literacy must be understood as mutually reinforcing. Financial literacy equips households to allocate resources wisely, while sustainability directs those resources toward outcomes that protect society and the environment. This interplay is visible through three dimensions: what is financed (screening), how it is financed (instruments), and who is included (distribution).

Screening defines the ethical limits of investment. ESG investing popularizes non-financial criteria, yet it is often criticized for inconsistency and greenwashing (Broadstock et al., 2020). Islamic finance offers a stronger foundation by excluding haram industries and embedding stewardship (*khalifah*) as a religious duty. Classical thinkers such as Al-Mawardi emphasized trade serving the public good (*maslahah*), while Ibn Taymiyyah cautioned against speculation and exploitation. When combined with ESG metrics, Shariah screening yields both ethical coherence and measurable impact (Prabhakaran & Mynavathi, 2025). The Qur'an (6:141) explicitly links economic activity with restraint and accountability, underscoring that literacy is not just about returns but about aligning investment with justice.

Instruments operationalize these values. Indonesia's sovereign green sukūk, which finances renewable energy and climate resilience, illustrates how Islamic finance can lead global sustainability (World Bank, 2022). Waqf-linked sukūk and digital zakāt platforms further channel resources into education, healthcare, and poverty alleviation. These mechanisms fulfill *maqā id al-sharī ah* by protecting wealth, life, and environment, while echoing the Prophetic teaching: *"If the Final Hour comes while you have a sapling in your hand, plant it"* (Musnad Ahmad, no. 12902). For literate households, knowledge of such tools enables them to deploy savings toward projects that deliver both private security and communal resilience.

Distribution ensures that sustainability is not monopolized by the privileged. Gender gaps, rural connectivity barriers, and generational divides still exclude many from green finance (Demirgüç-Kunt et al., 2018). Without inclusive access, sustainability remains an elite agenda. Policy responses include assisted-digital channels, capped fees for small investors, and vernacular literacy programs. In Muslim societies, integrating zakāt, waqf, and takaful into state programs creates layered safety nets that stabilize household finances while funding public goods.

4. The Future of Digital Financial Literacy: AI and Big Data with Ethical Guardrails

If sustainability represents the *purpose* of financial literacy, digital technology constitutes its *frontier*. Artificial intelligence (AI) and big data are rapidly reshaping personal finance, from robo-advisors that align portfolios with risk profiles to anomaly-detection systems that flag suspicious transactions and predictive analytics that encourage saving and investment (Sun et al., 2024; Zavolokina et al., 2017). Properly governed, these innovations can democratize financial advice, reduce transaction costs, and extend financial inclusion to underserved communities.

Yet automation without ethical guardrails risks reproducing old harms at greater scale. Algorithmic opacity may conceal riba-like interest structures, embed discriminatory biases in credit scoring, or default users into exploitative contracts. Persuasive design techniques, so-called "dark patterns" can lure individuals into compulsive trading or over-borrowing, undermining self-control. Meanwhile, unchecked data aggregation threatens privacy, raising concerns of surveillance capitalism and unjust enrichment. These dangers underscore that digital literacy alone is insufficient; it must evolve into *algorithmic literacy*, enabling individuals not only to use financial tools but also to interrogate their assumptions, outputs, and compliance with ethical and Shariah standards.

Four pillars of governance are essential to embed ethics into this frontier. First, Shariah-by-design product development integrates Shariah scholars alongside data scientists, ensuring contracts such as *murāba ah*, *mushārakah*, and *ijārah* are free from gharar and aligned with maqā id al-sharīʿah. Second, fairness audits and explainability protocols subject algorithms to independent testing, making biases visible and disclosing model limitations (Zetzsche et al., 2020). Third, privacy and security baselines, including data minimization, encryption, breach reporting, and phishing-resistant multi-factor authentication are non-negotiable safeguards for protecting wealth (Datta & Krancher, 2024). Fourth, human-in-the-loop literacy reframes users as active decision-makers: AI should assist, not replace, human judgment, and education programs must equip individuals to critically evaluate recommendations rather than follow them passively.

Global and regional initiatives illustrate how these principles can be operationalized. In Malaysia, AI-powered zakāt distribution platforms enhance targeting accuracy while preserving transparency, demonstrating how automation can strengthen equity. In Indonesia, the OJK's regulatory sandbox tests fintech innovations under controlled oversight, ensuring compliance with both financial stability goals and Shariah principles. These cases show that technology is never value-neutral; it becomes a tool of justice or exploitation depending on governance, design, and intent.

From an Islamic perspective, these guardrails are not optional but integral to fulfilling if al-māl (the preservation of wealth) and the duty of amānah (trust). The Qur'an prohibits unjust enrichment: *"Do not consume one another's wealth unjustly"* (Qur'an 4:29), while a hadith teaches: *"Render back the trust to the one to whom it is due"* (Sunan al-Tirmidhi, no. 1264). In the digital age, this obligation extends beyond individual transactions to the architecture of algorithms and data infrastructures. Thus, the future of financial literacy lies not in the proliferation of ever more digital tools, but in embedding ethical governance, accountability, and spiritual responsibility into every layer of the financial ecosystem. In this way, digital innovation can serve not only as a driver of efficiency, but as a vehicle for justice, inclusion, and sustainable prosperity.

REFERENCES

Afzal, M., Meraj, M., Kaur, M., & Shamim Ansari, M. (2025). How does cybersecurity awareness help in achieving digital financial inclusion in rural India under escalating cyber fraud scenario? *Journal of Cyber Security Technology*, *9*(2), 88–126. DOI: 10.1080/23742917.2024.2347674

Al-Ghazālī. (n.d.). *I yā' 'Ulūm al-Dīn* [The revival of religious sciences]. (Original work published ca. 11th century).

Al-Tirmidhī, M. (n.d.). *Sunan al-Tirmidhī*, Hadith no. 1209 & no. 1264.

Alam, A., Herianingrum, S., Ryandono, M. N. H., & Rohmawati, N. P. (2023). The role of Islamic investment ethics in preventing fraudulent investments. *Perbanas Journal of Islamic Economics and Business*, *3*(1), 37–46. DOI: 10.56174/pjieb.v3i1.81

Ali, A., & Marisetty, V. B. (2023). Are FinTech lending apps harmful? Evidence from user experience in the Indian market. *The British Accounting Review*, *101269*, 101269. Advance online publication. DOI: 10.1016/j.bar.2023.101269

Almeida, J., & Gonçalves, T. C. (2022). A Systematic Literature Review of Volatility and Risk Management on Cryptocurrency Investment: A Methodological Point of View. *Risks*, *10*(5), 107. Advance online publication. DOI: 10.3390/risks10050107

Ameh, J. K., Atiase, V. Y., & Dzansi, D. Y. (2022). Does Microcredit Increase Household Wellbeing ? Empirical Evidence from Ghana. *ISBE 2022: New Approaches to Raising Entrepreneurial Opportunity: Reshaping Inclusive Enterprise, Policy, and Practice Post-PandemicAt: York, October*.

Back, C., Morana, S., & Spann, M. (2023). When do robo-advisors make us better investors? The impact of social design elements on investor behavior. *Journal of Behavioral and Experimental Economics*, *103*(November 2022), 101984. DOI: 10.1016/j.socec.2023.101984

Barkley, B., & Schweitzer, M. (2021). The rise of fintech lending to small businesses: Businesses' perspectives on borrowing. *International Journal of Central Banking*, *17*(1), 35–65.

Boj, E., Claramunt, M. M., & Varea, X. (2022). Reverse Mortgage and Financial Sustainability. *Technological and Economic Development of Economy*, *28*(4), 872–892. DOI: 10.3846/tede.2022.16617

Boohene, R., Gyimah, R. A., & Osei, M. B. (2020). Social capital and SME performance: The moderating role of emotional intelligence. *Journal of Entrepreneurship in Emerging Economies*, *12*(1), 79–99. DOI: 10.1108/JEEE-10-2018-0103

Broadstock, D. C., Chan, K., Cheng, L. T. W., & Wang, X. (2020). Since January 2020 Elsevier has created a COVID-19 resource centre with free information in English and Mandarin on the novel coronavirus COVID- 19. The COVID-19 resource centre is hosted on Elsevier Connect, the company ' s public news and information. *Finance Research Letters*, *38*(January), 101716. PMID: 32837385

Brogi, M., & Lagasio, V. (2024). New but naughty. The evolution of misconduct in FinTech. *International Review of Financial Analysis, 95*(PB), 103489. DOI: 10.1016/j.irfa.2024.103489

Cabannes, Y., & Lipietz, B. (2018). Revisiting the democratic promise of participatory budgeting in light of competing political, good governance and technocratic logics. *Environment and Urbanization*, *30*(1), 67–84. DOI: 10.1177/0956247817746279

Carè, R., & Fatima, R. (2025). Financial Market Misconduct: A Bibliometric Perspective. *European Financial Management*, *31*(3), 1042–1071. DOI: 10.1111/eufm.12525

Cedeño, D., Lannin, D. G., Russell, L., Yazedjian, A., Kanter, J. B., & Mimnaugh, S. (2021). The effectiveness of a financial literacy and job-readiness curriculum for youth from low-income households. *Citizenship. Social and Economics Education*, *20*(3), 197–215. DOI: 10.1177/20471734211051770

Chapra, M. U. (2016). *The future of economics: An Islamic perspective* (Vol. 21). Kube Publishing Ltd.

Chen, Y., Ye, J., & Shi, Q. (2024). Does managerial myopia promote enterprises over-financialization? Evidence from listed firms in China. *PLoS One*, *19*(9), e0309140. DOI: 10.1371/journal.pone.0309140 PMID: 39236054

Croux, C., Jagtiani, J., Korivi, T., & Vulanovic, M. (2020). Important factors determining Fintech loan default: Evidence from a lendingclub consumer platform. *Journal of Economic Behavior & Organization*, *173*, 270–296. DOI: 10.1016/j.jebo.2020.03.016

Damane, M., & Ho, S. Y. (2025). Effects of financial inclusion of small and medium-sized enterprises on financial stability: Evidence from selected sub-Saharan African countries. *Journal of Innovation and Entrepreneurship*, *14*(1), 81. Advance online publication. DOI: 10.1186/s13731-025-00526-4

Daniele, M., Pelucco, V., & Quarato, F. (2020). *Since January 2020 Elsevier has created a COVID-19 resource centre with free information in English and Mandarin on the novel coronavirus COVID- 19 . The COVID-19 resource centre is hosted on Elsevier Connect, the company ' s public news and information . January.*

Datta, P. M., & Krancher, O. (2024). Cybersecurity end-user compliance: Password management versus update compliance. *Information & Management, 61*(8), 104060. DOI: 10.1016/j.im.2024.104060

De Beckker, K., De Witte, K., & Van Campenhout, G. (2021). The effect of financial education on students' consumer choices: Evidence from a randomized experiment. *Journal of Economic Behavior & Organization, 188*, 962–976. DOI: 10.1016/j.jebo.2021.06.022

Demirgüç-Kunt, A., Klapper, L., & Singer, D. (2018). Household finance and economic development. In *Handbook of finance and development* (pp. 534–549). Edward Elgar Publishing. DOI: 10.4337/9781785360510.00029

Djamhari, S. I., Mustika, M. D., Sjabadhyni, B., & Ndaru, A. R. P. (2024). Impulsive buying in the digital age: Investigating the dynamics of sales promotion, FOMO, and digital payment methods. *Cogent Business & Management, 11*(1), 2419484. Advance online publication. DOI: 10.1080/23311975.2024.2419484

Faraz, N., & Anjum, A. (2025). Spendception: The Psychological Impact of Digital Payments on Consumer Purchase Behavior and Impulse Buying. *Behavioral Sciences (Basel, Switzerland), 15*(3), 1–20. DOI: 10.3390/bs15030387 PMID: 40150281

Fernandes, D., Lynch, J. G.Jr, & Netemeyer, R. G. (2014). Financial literacy, financial education, and downstream financial behaviors. *Management Science, 60*(8), 1861–1883. DOI: 10.1287/mnsc.2013.1849

Fox, J., & Bartholomae, S. (2020). Household finances, financial planning, and COVID-19. *Financial Planning Review, 3*(4), e1103. DOI: 10.1002/cfp2.1103

Frost, J., Gambacorta, L., & Jagtiani, J. (2022). *Working Papers Giulio Cornelli Bank for International Settlements Bank for International Settlements The Impact of Fintech Lending on Credit Access for U.S. Small Businesses The Impact of Fintech Lending on Credit Access for U.S. Small Businesses Giulio C.* DOI: 10.21799/frbp.wp

Garg, N., Priyadarshi, P., & Malik, A. (2024). Financial well-being: An integrated framework, operationalization, and future research agenda. *Journal of Consumer Behaviour, 23*(6), 3194–3212. DOI: 10.1002/cb.2372

Gomber, P., Kauffman, R. J., Parker, C., & Weber, B. W. (2018). On the Fintech Revolution: Interpreting the Forces of Innovation, Disruption, and Transformation in Financial Services. *Journal of Management Information Systems, 35*(1), 220–265. DOI: 10.1080/07421222.2018.1440766

Hamid, F. S. (2025). Behavioral biases and over-indebtedness in consumer credit: Evidence from Malaysia. *Cogent Economics & Finance, 13*(1), 2449191. Advance online publication. DOI: 10.1080/23322039.2024.2449191

Havakhor, T., Rahman, M. S., Zhang, T., & Zhu, C. (2025). Tech-Enabled Financial Data Access, Retail Investors, and Gambling-Like Behavior in the Stock Market. *Management Science, 71*(2), 1646–1670. DOI: 10.1287/mnsc.2021.01379

Hermawan, B., & Wahyudi, D. (2025). Analysis of the Influence of Financial Literacy on Personal Financial Management Behavior in the Millennial Generation. [INJOLE]. *International Journal of Economic Literature, 3*(4), 101–116.

Hilgert, R. K., & Luttrell, M. (2023). Investigating the Impact of Financial Literacy and Income on Financial Behaviors Among Millennials. *Indonesia Accounting Research Journal, 11*(1), 37–50. DOI: 10.35335/iacrj.v11i1.211

Hudaefi, F. A. (2020). How does Islamic fintech promote the SDGs? Qualitative evidence from Indonesia. *Qualitative Research in Financial Markets, 12*(4), 353–366. DOI: 10.1108/QRFM-05-2019-0058

Huston, S. J. (2010). Measuring financial literacy. *The Journal of Consumer Affairs, 44*(2), 296–316. DOI: 10.1111/j.1745-6606.2010.01170.x

Ibn Khaldūn. (2019). *Al-Muqaddimah* [The introduction]. (Original work published 1377).

Ibn Mājah, M. (n.d.). *Sunan Ibn Mājah*, Hadith no. 2413 & no. 3605.

Iborra, M., López-Muñoz, J. F., & Safón, V. (2024). Lack of resilience after COVID-19: The role of family firm heterogeneity and behavior. fsQCA versus regression. *European Journal of Management and Business Economics*, (August). Advance online publication. DOI: 10.1108/EJMBE-05-2023-0140

Indonesian Ulema Council (Majelis Ulama Indonesia). (2021). *Fatwa on the prohibition of using cryptocurrency as a currency*. MUI.

Isaia, E., Oggero, N., & Sandretto, D. (2024). Is financial literacy a protection tool from online fraud in the digital era? *Journal of Behavioral and Experimental Finance, 44*, 100977. DOI: 10.1016/j.jbef.2024.100977

Javaheri, D., Fahmideh, M., Chizari, H., Lalbakhsh, P., & Hur, J. (2024). Cybersecurity threats in FinTech: A systematic review. *Expert Systems with Applications, 241*, 1–42. DOI: 10.1016/j.eswa.2023.122697

Kahf, M. (2007). Islamic banks and economic development. In *Handbook of Islamic banking*. Edward Elgar Publishing. DOI: 10.4337/9781847205414.00028

Kaiser, T., Lusardi, A., Menkhoff, L., & Urban, C. (2022). Financial education affects financial knowledge and downstream behaviors. *Journal of Financial Economics, 145*(2), 255–272. DOI: 10.1016/j.jfineco.2021.09.022

Kaur, P., Dhir, A., Tandon, A., Alzeiby, E. A., & Abohassan, A. A. (2021). A systematic literature review on cyberstalking. An analysis of past achievements and future promises. *Technological Forecasting and Social Change, 163*(June 2020), 120426. DOI: 10.1016/j.techfore.2020.120426

Khalil, M. (2020). Financial citizenship as a broader democratic context of financial literacy. *Citizenship. Social and Economics Education, 20*(1), 3–16. DOI: 10.1177/2047173420948411

Khando, K., Islam, M. S., & Gao, S. (2023). The Emerging Technologies of Digital Payments and Associated Challenges: A Systematic Literature Review. *Future Internet, 15*(1), 21. Advance online publication. DOI: 10.3390/fi15010021

Liu, J., Chen, Y., Chen, X., & Chen, B. (2024). Digital financial inclusion and household financial vulnerability: An empirical analysis of rural and urban disparities in China. *Heliyon, 10*(15), e35540. DOI: 10.1016/j.heliyon.2024.e35540 PMID: 39170403

Lu, Z., Wu, J., Li, H., & Galloway, B. (2024). Digital finance and stock market participation: The case of internet wealth management products in China. *Economic Systems, 48*(1), 101148. DOI: 10.1016/j.ecosys.2023.101148

Lusardi, A., & Mitchell, O. S. (2017). How Ordinary Consumers Make Complex Economic Decisions: Financial Literacy and Retirement Readiness. *The Quarterly Journal of Finance, 7*(3), 1750008. Advance online publication. DOI: 10.1142/S2010139217500082

Mancone, S., Tosti, B., Corrado, S., Spica, G., Zanon, A., & Diotaiuti, P. (2024). Youth, money, and behavior: the impact of financial literacy programs. *Frontiers in Education, 9*(2014). DOI: 10.3389/feduc.2024.1397060

Maravilla, V. S.Jr, & Flores, G. (2025). Entrepreneurial competency, resilience, and financial literacy: Drivers of sustainable performance in SMEs for societal welfare. *Journal of Sustainability, Society, and Eco-Welfare*, *2*(2), 159–176. DOI: 10.61511/jssew.v2i2.2025.1374

Miroshnychenko, I., Torres de Oliveira, R., De Massis, A., & Überbacher, R. (2024). Family Involvement and Firm Performance: A Worldwide Study Unveiling Key Mechanisms. *Family Business Review*, *37*(4), 449–475. DOI: 10.1177/08944865241290856

Muslim ibn al- ajjāj. (n.d.). *a ī Muslim*, Hadith no. 1619.

Ozili, P. K. (2023). Impact of Monetary Policy on Financial Inclusion in Emerging Markets. *Journal of Risk and Financial Management*, *16*(7), 303. Advance online publication. DOI: 10.3390/jrfm16070303

Panos, G. A., & Wilson, J. O. S. (2020). Financial literacy and responsible finance in the FinTech era: Capabilities and challenges. *European Journal of Finance*, *26*(4–5), 297–301. DOI: 10.1080/1351847X.2020.1717569

Pokharel, J., & Maharjan, I. (2024). Financial Behavior of Generation Z and Millennials. *Journal of Emerging Management Studies*, *1*(2), 148–170. DOI: 10.3126/jems.v1i2.71522

Prabhakaran, S., & Mynavathi, L. (2025). Does Fintech Usage Alter the Relationships Between Financial Literacy, Behaviour and Well-Being? Evidence from India. *Organizations and Markets in Emerging Economies*, *16*(1(32)), 133–154. DOI: 10.15388/omee.2025.16.6

Qur'an. (n.d.).. . *Surah Al-A zāb*, (33), 72.

Qur'an. (n.d.).. . *Surah Al-Baqarah*, (2), 261.

Qur'an. (n.d.).. . *Surah Al-Baqarah*, (2), 261–280.

Qur'an. (n.d.).. . *Surah Al-Baqarah*, (2), 275.

Qur'an. (n.d.).. . *Surah Al-Furqān*, (25), 67.

Qur'an. (n.d.).. . *Surah Al-Isrā*, (17), 26–27.

Qur'an. (n.d.).. . *Surah Al-Mā'idah*, (5), 2.

Qur'an. (n.d.).. . *Surah An-Nisā*, (4), 11.

Qur'an. (n.d.).. . *Surah An-Nisā*, (4), 29.

Rahardja, U., Sigalingging, C. T., Putra, P. O. H., Nizar Hidayanto, A., & Phusavat, K. (2023). The Impact of Mobile Payment Application Design and Performance Attributes on Consumer Emotions and Continuance Intention. *SAGE Open, 13*(1), 1–18. DOI: 10.1177/21582440231151919

Raza, A., Rehmat, S., Ishaq, M. I., Haj-Salem, N., & Talpur, Q. (2024). Gamification in financial service apps to enhance customer experience and engagement. *Journal of Consumer Behaviour, 23*(4), 1653–1670. DOI: 10.1002/cb.2294

Salleh, N. M., Shukry, S. N. M., Maylyn, V., & Jokinol, C. (2023). Analyzing the challenges, effects, and motivations of gig economy workers. *International Journal of Academic Research in Business & Social Sciences, 13*(6), 2125–2142. DOI: 10.6007/IJARBSS/v13-i6/17514

Shupe, C., Li, G., & Fulford, S. (2023). Consumer Use of Buy Now, Pay Later Insights from the CFPB Making Ends Meet Survey. *Consumer Financial Protection Bureau ....* https://papers.ssrn.com/sol3/papers.cfm?abstract_id=4399626

Siddiqi, M. N. (2005). *Teaching Islamic Economics.* Islamic Economics Research Centre, King Abdul Aziz University.

Sun, Y., Liu, L., Xu, Y., Zeng, X., Shi, Y., Hu, H., Jiang, J., & Abraham, A. (2024). Alternative data in finance and business: Emerging applications and theory analysis [review]. *Financial Innovation, 10*(1), 127. Advance online publication. DOI: 10.1186/s40854-024-00652-0

Swandaru, R., & Muneeza, A. (2022). Can fraud in Islamic financial institutions be prevented using high standards of Shariah governance?. *International journal of law and management, 64*(6), 469-485. https://doi.org/DOI: 10.1108/IJLMA-07-2022-0162

Tang, A. K. Y. (2019). A systematic literature review and analysis on mobile apps in m-commerce: Implications for future research. *Electronic Commerce Research and Applications, 37*(August), 100885. DOI: 10.1016/j.elerap.2019.100885

Tiwari, S. K.Sujeet Kumar Tiwari. (2024). The Future of Digital Retirement Solutions: A Study of Sustainability and Scalability in Financial Planning Tools. *Journal of Computer Science and Technology Studies, 6*(5), 229–245. DOI: 10.32996/jcsts.2024.6.5.19

Wang, J., Bouri, E., & Ma, F. (2022). Which Factors Drive Bitcoin Volatility: Macroeconomic, Technical, or Both? SSRN *Electronic Journal*, 1–38. DOI: 10.2139/ssrn.4080107

Worokinasih, S., Nuzula, N. F., Damayanti, C. R., & Sirivanh, T. (2023). The resilience of youth entrepreneur: The role of social capital, financial literacy, and emotional intelligence on SMEs' performance in Indonesia. [Bisnis Dan Manajemen]. *BISMA*, *16*(1), 1–27. DOI: 10.26740/bisma.v16n1.p1-27

Yadav, M., Banerji, P., & Garg, A. (2025). Digital financial literacy and retirement planning with mediating effect of saving behaviour. *American Journal of Business*, *40*(June), 127–143. Advance online publication. DOI: 10.1108/AJB-12-2023-0221

Yoganandham, G. (2025). Mastering Economic And Financial Sources With Reference To Budgeting, Savings, Early Investing, Debt Management And The Power Of Financial Planning-A Comprehensive Analysis. *Degres Journal, 10*(1), 19-33. Retrieved from https://degres.eu/wp-content/uploads/2-DEJ1457.pdf

Zavolokina, L., Dolata, M., & Schwabe, G. (2017). FinTech transformation: How IT-enabled innovations shape the financial sector. *Lecture Notes in Business Information Processing*, *276*, 75–88. DOI: 10.1007/978-3-319-52764-2_6

Zetzsche, D. A., Arner, D. W., & Buckley, R. P. (2020). Decentralized finance. *Journal of Financial Regulation*, *6*(2), 172–203. DOI: 10.1093/jfr/fjaa010

Chapter 7

Islamic Retirement Planning Strategies for Special Needs Families and Their Unique Financial Challenges

Hafizah Mat Nawi
https://orcid.org/0000-0003-2232-9547
Faculty of Defence Studies and Management, National Defence University of Malaysia, Malaysia

Asma' Rashidah Idris
https://orcid.org/0009-0007-2027-9191
Universiti Teknologi MARA, Malaysia

Zarina Kassim
https://orcid.org/0000-0002-3953-1250
National Defence University of Malaysia, Malaysia

Hasan Al Banna Mohamed
https://orcid.org/0000-0001-6096-0052
National Defence University of Malaysia, Malaysia

Shafinar Ismail
https://orcid.org/0000-0002-0339-0003
Universiti Teknologi MARA, Malaysia

Salwa Muda
https://orcid.org/0009-0001-5753-5132
Universiti Teknologi MARA, Malaysia

Mohd Abdullah Jusoh
https://orcid.org/0009-0000-9656-6583
National Defence University of Malaysia, Malaysia

ABSTRACT

Governments are encountering substantial difficulties in funding essential care for disabled individuals. These challenges are compounded by pervasive social concerns associated with the reliance of those needing supplementary assistance, especially

DOI: 10.4018/979-8-3373-1842-4.ch007

following the loss of their elderly carers. The ageing process of carers presents significant issues for parents with special needs children. This issue intensifies when the child's lifestyle and continuous care are closely connected to the income earned by their parents over time. This phenomenon is particularly common among larger Muslim families globally, where familial dynamics and financial strategies significantly influence the care of dependents. A proactive strategy is crucial during critical stages of a family's development, ensuring comprehensive estate planning is executed to meet future lifetime care needs.

1. INTRODUCTION

Retirement planning is important for everyone but is especially critical for families with special needs members. For *Muslim* families, financial planning is deeply connected to Islamic societal and ethical values, emphasizing justice, stewardship, and care for dependants. It is essential that these arrangements align with *Shari'ah* principles (Ahmed, 2011).

Islamic teachings emphasize on providing emotional support, spiritual guidance, and setting boundaries for dependants. For children with special needs, long-term planning must address medical care, education, housing, and daily expenses while following Islamic principles like *faraid* (inheritance laws), *zakat* (charity), *waqf* (endowment), and ethical investments such as sukuk or *Shari'ah*-compliant funds.

Modern *Muslim* families face challenges in cross-border retirement planning due to differences in national laws, financial systems, and legal interpretations. While Islamic financial services like *Takaful* and savings plans offer tailored solutions, many families struggle to integrate them into a long-term strategy (Dusuki & Abdullah, 2007). Additionally, the lack of coordination between Islamic and civil legal systems can cause delays and conflicts in estate distribution and caregiving responsibilities (Laldin & Furqani, 2013).

In Malaysia, families with special needs face unique retirement planning challenges that require customized solutions (Abd Karim et al., 2025; Nawi et al., 2024). These solutions should combine Islamic principles with ethical financial practices that encourage community involvement and shared accountability (Obaidullah et al., 2014).

Providing families with the right resources and information helps parents/ caregivers make better decisions to secure their children's futures. Careful planning not only addresses financial needs but also improves caregivers' quality of life and offers peace of mind. The goal is to create a structured yet compassionate system that respects the special needs and dignity of every individual (Abd Karim et al., 2025; Abdullah et al., 2024; Yusoff, 2024; Saleh & Hassan, 2022; Chelliah et al., 2022).

Governments worldwide are facing increasing costs to support individuals with disabilities, especially as ageing parents struggle to sustain care for their dependants. In larger *Muslim* families, cultural and religious caregiving responsibilities often fall within the household, highlighting the need for long-term strategies that ensure no dependant is neglected. Families, particularly affluent ones, must adopt proactive estate planning to address lifetime care needs. Islamic principles of familial support and *Shari'ah*-compliant legal structures offer effective solutions for special needs planning.

Yet, the question remains: has this potential been fully realized? Or have obstacles related to special needs planning, as well as suggested solutions within the broader global framework of *Shari'ah* compliance, failed to take into account particular resources that are embedded within the Islamic paradigms of human, social, and economic capital? The advent of Financial Technology, or FinTech, has played a significant role in facilitating and unlocking tailored solutions that fit within the Islamic model. However, the existing body of literature appears to be lacking when it comes to analyzing the outcomes stemming from family planning specific to certain *Shari'ah*-compliant products. An example of this is the design of a family *Takaful* plan, which begins with considerations rooted in GINI data that reflect patterns of inequality in wealth distribution.

Retirement planning in *Muslim* societies goes beyond finances, incorporating caregiving aligned with *Shari'ah* regulations. However, there is a need for better financial solutions tailored to families with dependants who have disabilities. This chapter focuses on retirement planning for children with disabilities through an Islamic perspective, highlighting Islamic finance principles, addressing legal, financial, and cultural challenges, and recommending policy and community initiatives. It emphasizes long-term strategies to ensure both material and spiritual well-being for the child across generations.

2. UNDERSTANDING SPECIAL NEEDS AND THE LIFELONG CARE CONTINUUM

Special needs include a range of physical, developmental, behavioural, and emotional disabilities that require extended care. These may include, but are not limited to, autism spectrum disorders, Down syndrome, cerebral palsy, intellectual disabilities, and rare genetic or neurological conditions. Families with special needs members often face prolonged financial obligations, as these individuals may never achieve full independence. Financial planning for such families must extend well beyond the caregivers' retirement and life expectancy (Nawi et al., 2024).

The demand for sustainable funding, housing, medical care, and emotional support creates a complex financial ecosystem that is uniquely challenging for *Muslim* families striving to meet both worldly needs and religious obligations. As Islamic teachings place great importance on the protection and provision for the weak and vulnerable, special needs dependants become a moral priority, making effective planning an act of religious duty and spiritual merit (Chapra, 2016).

2.1 Dependency Beyond Retirement

Children with special needs often remain dependent on their parents or primary caregivers for their entire lives. In *Muslim* communities, this dependency influences retirement decisions significantly. Many parents delay or forgo retirement entirely, driven by fear of abandoning their child without adequate care and financial support. This creates a scenario where financial stress and emotional burden coexist, often leading to burnout and mental health struggles for caregivers (Abd Karim et al., 2025).

In cases where the special needs individual cannot work or qualify for public assistance due to procedural, legal, or religious limitations, the need for a long-term care strategy becomes even more critical. This strategy must include sustainable income generation, risk protection through *Takaful*, and the establishment of a legally and religiously sound estate plan.

2.2 Cultural Expectations and Family Dynamics

In Islamic cultures, family plays a central role in caregiving. The concept of *'birr al-walidayn'* (dutifulness to parents) and *'silatur rahim'* (maintaining family ties) emphasizes interdependence among family members. Traditionally, siblings, cousins, and extended kin were expected to step in to support care responsibilities.

However, with increasing urbanization, smaller family sizes, women's entry into the workforce, and geographic dispersion due to migration, these traditional safety nets are weakening. As a result, the nuclear family — often a single parent or elderly couple — bears the full responsibility of long-term care, sometimes without a clear succession plan (Habibullah et al., 2023).

These cultural dynamics can result in unrealistic expectations or planning paralysis, especially when caregivers assume that other family members will "figure it out" after their death. It is therefore essential to engage the entire family early in the planning process, ensuring alignment of expectations and legal clarity in matters of guardianship, financial delegation, and end-of-life wishes.

In this context, financial and retirement planning must incorporate both the religious framework and practical realities of contemporary *Muslim* families. Islamic tools such as *hibah* and *waqf* can be used to empower selected family members legally and financially to conduct the care mandate but must be implemented with careful legal and *Shari'ah* oversight.

3. ISLAMIC FINANCIAL PRINCIPLES IN RETIREMENT AND ESTATE PLANNING

Islamic financial principles form a holistic framework for ethical, equitable, and sustainable wealth management. For families with special needs dependants, these principles furnish both spiritual and moral guidance, as well as practical resources to guarantee lifelong financial stability and inter-generational support. The principles of *Shari'ah* conformity, social justice, and familial obligation are fundamental to Islamic financial planning. This section details the principal mechanisms and legal frameworks accessible to *Muslim* families.

3.1 *Shari'ah* Compliance in Financial Planning

Islamic financial planning must adhere to fundamental prohibitions, including the avoidance of *riba* (interest), *gharar* (excessive uncertainty), and *haram* (forbidden) activities like as alcohol, gambling, and immoral activities. Consequently, traditional interest-bearing savings accounts, standard insurance, and speculative investments are inappropriate for *Muslims* pursuing *Shari'ah* compliance (Usmani, 2002).

Basically, *Muslim* households are advised to utilise halal financial instruments, including:

i. ***Sukuk* (Islamic bonds)**: These are asset-backed securities that avoid interest by sharing profits from underlying ventures (Ahmed, 2011).
ii. ***Halal* mutual funds**: These funds invest in companies that comply with *Shari'ah* screening standards.
iii. ***Takaful* (Islamic insurance)**: A cooperative risk-sharing model based on mutual assistance (Billah, 2019; Rapi et al., 2022).
iv. **Islamic savings plans**: Offered by Islamic banks with profit-sharing mechanism (*mudarabah* or *wakalah* models).

3.2 *Zakat* and *Sadaqah* as Tools for Support

Zakat is the forth pillar of *Islam* and it is an obligatory act of worship. *Muslims* have to pay 2.5% of their earnings every year to eligible recipients. Eligible recipients are classified into eight categories; as per Quranic injunctions (9:60)[1] . They are "*fuqara*" (the poor), "*masakin*" (needy), *zakat* administrators, "muallaf" (new *Muslim*), slave seeking freedom, "*gharimin*" (debt-ridden), traveler in need, and "*fi sabilillah*" (in the path of Allah) if they are financially dependent (Khamis et al., 2024; Haris, 2020; Obaidullah, 2019).

Further, families with dependants with special needs may consider the following:

- Designate a portion of their *zakat/sadaqah* requirement to institutional programs that provide disability care.
- Request *zakat* assistance from state *Baitulmal* offices to subsidise medical and educational expenses.
- Channel *sadaqah* (voluntary charity) to specific causes such as equipment purchase or therapy.

Recent models in Malaysia and Indonesia show effective *zakat* mobilization for special needs communities through structured outreach and needs-based assessment tools (Ali et al., 2019).

3.3 The Role of *waqf* (Endowment)

Waqf is a perpetual charitable endowment where the principal asset is preserved, and the benefits (usufruct) are used for public or targeted goods. In the context of special needs care, families can establish:

i. **Cash *waqf*** for monthly caregiving costs.
ii. **Property *waqf*** for housing needs or therapy centers.
iii. **Investment *waqf*** to grow capital via halal channels like *Sukuk* or Islamic REITs.

Such *waqf* structures ensure continuity of care beyond the life of the caregiver. Moreover, state institutions in Malaysia (e.g., JAWHAR and MAIS) and international entities like Awqaf SA in South Africa and *waqf* World Foundation in Turkey provide templates and oversight to manage these endowments efficiently (Cizakca, 2011; Mohsin, 2013).

Waqf offers several key benefits, which include:

- Legal separation of endowment from estate.

- Tax exemptions in many jurisdictions.
- Continuous spiritual reward (*sadaqah jariyah*).

However, families must ensure compliance with local *waqf* laws and appoint a qualified *mutawalli* (trustee) for administration and transparency.

3.4 Islamic Inheritance Laws (*Faraid*)

Faraid dictates the mandatory distribution of a *Muslim*'s estate to specified heirs, as per Quranic injunctions (4*: 11-12*)[2]. While this ensures fairness, it can limit financial flexibility, especially for families with special needs dependant. The special needs child may receive a small share compared to other heirs, jeopardizing long-term support.

To address this, families should integrate:

i. ***Wasiyyah*** (wills): A maximum of one-third of the estate may be designated for non-heirs or specific purposes, such as the preservation of a special needs child (Kamali, 2008).
ii. ***Hibah*** (gifts): Inter vivos transfers enable parents to bestow assets during their lifetime to offer instant assistance.
iii. **Trusts**: In some jurisdictions, Islamic-compliant trusts may be created alongside *wasiyyah* to adhere with both *Shari'ah* and civil law.

When developing these instruments, it is important to seek guidance from both a *Shari'ah* scholar and a legal professional. This dual consultation helps ensure that the arrangements comply with Islamic inheritance laws (*faraid*) while also meeting the requirements of civil law. Proper alignment between religious and legal frameworks is key to ensuring that such plans are valid and enforceable.

3.5 Integrated Estate Planning Strategy

An effective Islamic retirement plan for special needs families generally integrates:

i. ***Takaful* policies** with disability riders for immediate financial protection,
ii. ***Halal* investments** for wealth accumulation,
iii. ***Zakat* and *waqf*** to ease caregiving burdens, and
iv. ***Wasiyyah* and *hibah*** to ensure tailored asset distribution.

Islamic financial advisors and estate planners play an essential role in guiding families through this integrated process, ensuring that spiritual obligations correspond with practical needs.

4. RETIREMENT PLANNING STAGES FOR SPECIAL NEEDS FAMILIES

4.1 Early Planning: While the Parents Are Young

This phase typically occurs when parents are in their late twenties to late-30s, and the child is newly diagnosed. Financial and emotional readiness is low, making it essential to build a strong foundation. Figure 1 proposes steps to be taken at early planning for retirement.

Figure 1. Proposed Steps for Early Retirement Planning

1. • **Establish emergency funds** of 6–12 months' expenses to buffer against job loss, health emergencies, or unplanned caregiving costs
2. • **Begin long-term investments** in *halal* mutual funds or *Sukuk* to build a diversified retirement portfolio that avoids *riba* and *haram* sectors. Compounding returns over a longer horizon is critical.
3. • **Consider *Takaful* plans** with long-term disability riders. These Islamic insurance products provide coverage for income replacement and healthcare needs should the parents become disabled.
4. • **Engage with Islamic financial advisors** to create a family financial portfolio, integrating *Shariah*-compliant products and aligning them with short-, mid-, and long-term goals.
5. • **Draft initial versions of wills and guardianship plans.** While legal activation may not be immediate, early documentation ensures clarity about future intentions and guardianship of the dependant child.

4.2 Mid-life Planning: Strengthening Financial Base

Typically occurring between ages 40 to 55, this stage is marked by peak earning years and higher caregiving demands. Figure 2 portrays proposed steps to be taken at mid-life planning for retirement.

Figure 2. Proposed Steps for Mid-life Retirement Planning

1

- **Increase monthly contributions** to retirement and disability savings as household income stabilizes. This is also a time to evaluate the adequacy of projected care costs post-retirement.

2

- **Reassess *Takaful* coverage,** especially to include enhanced medical protection, long-term care, and hospitalization benefits. Costs for special needs children often escalate during adolescence.

3

- **Purchase or invest in real assets** (e.g., property, commercial spaces) suitable for *waqf*. These assets may be designated for future endowment, providing rental income or capital gains for care.

4

- **Begin involving adult siblings** or trusted family members in planning discussions to ensure continuity of care. Their awareness and buy-in are crucial to avoid future disputes.

5

- **Consult legal advisors** to finalize *wasiyyah* and *hibah* structures. This ensures that one-third of the estate is allocated appropriately for the special needs child while balancing faraid obligations.

4.3 Pre-Retirement Planning: Structuring Transition

Between the ages of 56–65, parents enter retirement readiness. Focus shifts from accumulation to preservation and distribution. Figure 3 shows steps to be taken at pre-retirement planning.

Figure 3. Proposed Steps for Pre-Retirement Planning

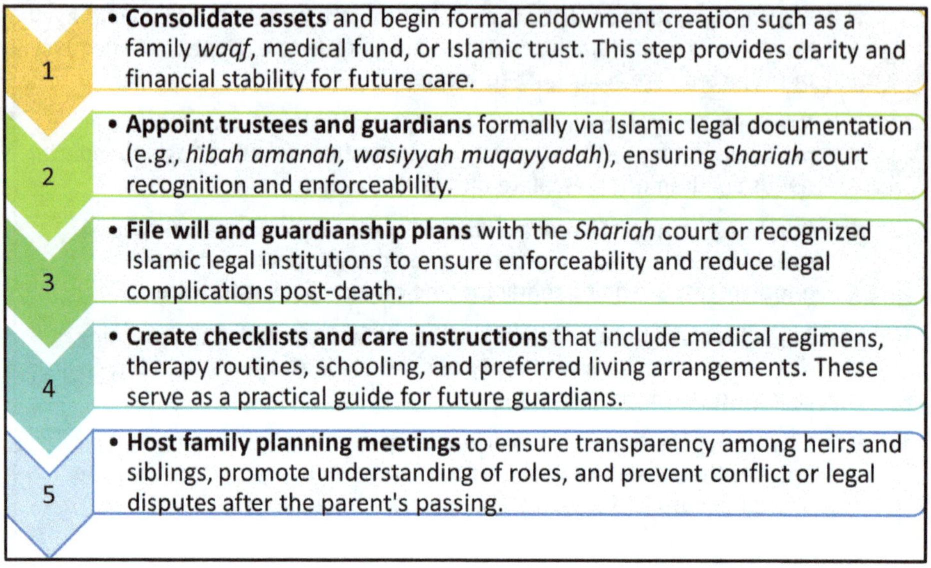

Table 1 presents a sample of a projected retirement care fund. The planning is categorised into three stages (age-based). The sample presumes a monthly allocation that increases by RM500 at each successive step. The projection assumes a steady 5% yearly return throughout.

Table 1. Sample Retirement Care Fund Projection (in MYR)

Planning Stage	Monthly Allocation	Annual Return (5%)	Years Accumulated	Projected Total
Early (age 30-40)	500	5%	10	77,640
Mid-life (age 41-55)	1,000	5%	15	267,289
Pre-retirement (56-60)	1,500	5%	5	102,009
Total				**446,939**

Note: The **Projected Total** for each stage was calculated using the **Future Value of an Ordinary Annuity** formula.

FV=P×((1+r)n−1r)FV = P \times \left(\frac{(1 + r)^n - 1}{r} \right)
Where:

- *FVFV = future value of the investment*
- *PP = monthly contribution*

- *rr = monthly interest rate (annual rate ÷ 12)*
- *nn = total number of months (years × 12)*

Example: Early Stage (RM500/month for 10 years at 5% annual return)

- P=500P = 500
- r=5%12=0.0041667r = \frac{5\%}{12} = 0.0041667
- n=10×12=120n = 10 \times 12 = 120

FV =500×((1+0.0041667)120−10.0041667)≈RM77,641

FV = 500 \times \left(\frac{(1 + 0.0041667)^{120} - 1}{0.0041667} \right) \
approx \text{RM77,641}

5. ISLAMIC ETHICAL PERSPECTIVES ON INTER-GENERATIONAL JUSTICE

Islamic financial planning emphasizes inter-generational justice, a principle from *maqasid al-Shari'ah* that promotes fairness and sustainability across generations. For families with special needs, this means the caregivers should focus on:

a. Avoiding impulsive financial decisions or spending on uncertain therapies.
b. Focusing on stable income and assets to support long-term needs.
c. Establishing *waqf* or structured endowments to ensure ongoing care and support.

This approach also reframes *zakat* and *sadaqah*—not as voluntary gestures of charity, but as instruments of economic justice. In this light, the care and dignity of individuals with disabilities become a shared duty of the *ummah*, not merely a personal or private concern.

6. GENDER ROLES AND FEMALE CAREGIVERS

In most *Muslim* families, caregiving for children with special needs is predominantly undertaken by women—especially mothers. This deeply embedded role is shaped by cultural expectations, religious values of *rahmah* (compassion), and the maternal instinct to nurture and protect. Nonetheless, the substantial emotional and physical responsibilities of caregiving can entail considerable financial sacrifice.

In fact, a significant number of mothers either leave the workforce or reduce their working hours to take care of their special needs children. The decision would lead to reducing the household income and would indirectly reduce the financial independence and limit the access to retirement savings. The study by Habibullah et al. (2023) reveals that majority female caregivers in Malaysia lack direct access to essential retirement planning instruments, bank accounts, *Takaful* insurance, and critical legal documents such as guardianship papers and wills. As a result, they find themselves economically marginalised and are excluded from the decision-making processes regarding family estates and long-term financial planning.

Islamic financial planning must proactively address and mitigate these gender-based inequalities. A variety of instruments within the Islamic finance framework can be strategically utilized to mitigate the issue of gender inequality.

i. ***Hibah* Allocations:** *Hibah* is a type of "inter vivos gifts", by which male guardians may allocate money or assets to the female carers during their lives. *Hibah* is particularly important in circumstances where the child may survive longer than the parents and need third-party caregiving.
ii. ***Wasiyyah* and Guardianship Designation:** Explicit inclusion in the *wasiyyah* can confer legal status of the mother as a guardian of the special needs children, therefore mitigating future challenges and uncertainty.
iii. ***Waqf* Provisions in Their Name:** A mother may create a *waqf* intended for the perpetual support of her kid, regardless of its modest size. Advocating for "cash *waqf*" alternatives renders this accessible to middle-income mothers.

In unravelling the above-mentioned gender inequality issue, there is a need to offer financial and legal literacy trainings or programs or workshops. The projects should focus on *Islamic* inheritance, *wasiyyah*'s procedures, *hibah* entitlements, *Takaful* for female caregivers, investment products tailored for stay-at-home caregivers, and estate planning from female perspective. To promote participation whenever feasible, the programs should be tailored to accommodate majority participants. For instance offering it in local languages and suit literacy levels, and providing childcare support.

Furthermore, Islamic scholars and policymakers ought to promote the official integration of female carers in the formulation of policies and advisory capacities within *Baitulmal* and religious institutions. Their lived experiences provide essential insights for developing inclusive, compassionate, and effective retirement planning models.

Acknowledging and appreciating the unpaid labour of mothers and sisters in special needs caregiving constitutes both a moral imperative and an adherence to the

Maqasid al-Shari'ah objectives of safeguarding life, lineage, and dignity. Financial inclusion and the empowerment of women should be a fundamental component of Islamic retirement planning for families with special needs children.

7. INNOVATIONS IN ISLAMIC SOCIAL FINANCE

Recent advancements in Islamic social finance are creating new avenues for inclusive and sustainable retirement planning for families with special needs (Akhter et al., 2025). These innovations merge ethical financial principles with contemporary tools, harmonising *Maqasid al-Shari'ah* with tangible outcomes. They possess significant capability in connecting spiritual goals with financial circumstances. The following Figure 4 summarizes types of Islamic social finance; which include Green *Sukuk* & Environmental, Social, and Governance (ESG) Funds, Impact *Waqf*, Digital *Takaful* Platform, and Integrated Training Potential.

Figure 4. Islamic Social Finance

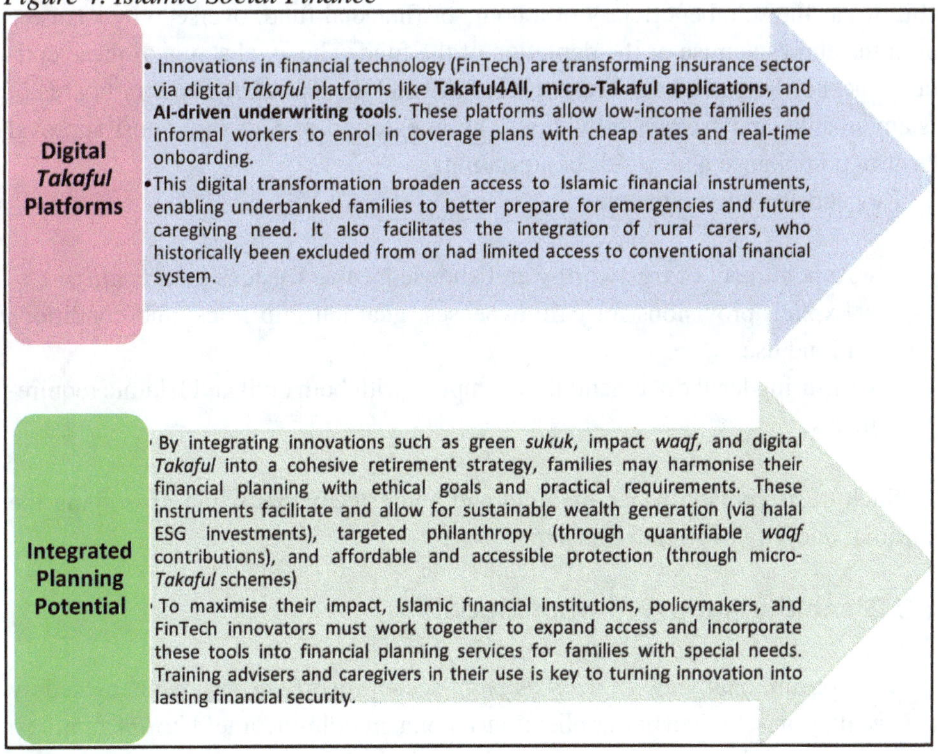

8. SPECIAL PERCEPTIONS TO BE CONSIDERED FOR FUTURE ISLAMIC RETIREMENT PLANNING FOR SPECIAL NEEDS FAMILIES

8.1 *Shari'ah*-Compliant Trusts for Special Needs (*Wakalah Amanah & Hibah Amanah*)

Shari'ah-compliant trusts, including *wakalah amanah* and *hibah amanah*, are vital instruments for guaranteeing ongoing support for special needs dependants after the passing of their primary carers. These structures blend Islamic principles with conventional legal mechanisms to protect assets and clearly assign custodial responsibilities. Unlike conventional trusts, which may involve interest-bearing elements, *Shari'ah*-compliant trusts avoid *riba* and *gharar* by utilising Islamic contracts like *wakalah* (agency) and *hibah* (gifting).

In Malaysia, *hibah amanah* has become increasingly popular, especially among families seeking to allocate assets to vulnerable children without violating *faraid* laws. For instance, parents can set up a *hibah amanah* designating a child with disabilities as the sole beneficiary of a home or financial fund, overseen by a trustee until the child's demise or the depletion of the fund. The legal status of these entities is acknowledged by the Trustee Act 1949 and the *Shari'ah* advisory boards of Islamic banks and *Takaful* providers. The integration of *Shari'ah* court approval ensures compliance and avoids contestation.

Key considerations include:

- Appointment of trustworthy and knowledgeable trustees (*mutawalli*).
- Explicit provisions for care expenses, guardianship roles, and conditions for fund use.
- Ensuring legal documentation complies with both civil and Islamic requirements.

Such trusts provide peace of mind and legal safeguards while preserving the spiritual integrity of wealth transfer.

8.2 Disability-Inclusive *waqf* Models

The conventional view of *waqf* as large-scale property endowments owned by the wealthy has limited its application among middle-income *Muslim* families. However, recent innovations in '*disability-inclusive waqf*' models are shifting this narrative. By allowing small monthly contributions (*cash waqf*), even low- and middle-income families can participate in the creation of sustainable care resources for their dependants.

Examples include:

i. ***Waqf* for therapy centers**: In Penang, a local NGO collaborated with the State Religious Council to establish a community *waqf* that funds early intervention therapy for children with autism. The *waqf* accepts monthly donations as low as RM10.
ii. ***Waqf* homes**: A project in Turkey converted *waqf*-funded housing into safe living spaces for intellectually disabled adults, supervised by certified care workers.
iii. **Vocational *waqf***: In Indonesia, vocational training programs for young adults with Down syndrome have been funded through *waqf* contributions.

These *waqf* models are guided by *maqasid al-Shari'ah*, particularly the objectives of preserving life (*nafs*) and lineage (*nasl*). Transparency in administration, community governance, and digital donation platforms have made *waqf* accessible and impactful.

8.3 Islamic Microfinance for Special Needs Families

Islamic microfinance presents a powerful means of economic empowerment for caregivers (Ali, 2024), particularly mothers of special needs children who are often unable to participate in the formal workforce. Microfinance supports financial independence for women, reduced long-term dependence on welfare, and higher quality of care for dependants.

Instruments such as *Qard al-Hasan* (benevolent loans), *Musharakah* (joint ventures), and *Murabahah* (cost-plus financing) can be tailored to fund home-based businesses, therapy costs, or assistive device purchases.

Several models are emerging:

i. **Lembaga Zakat Negeri Selangor** provides *Qard al-Hasan* to caregivers seeking to establish home daycare or therapy services.
ii. **Amanah Ikhtiar Malaysia (AIM)** has piloted micro-entrepreneur schemes for mothers of special needs children, offering *Shari'ah*-compliant loans and business mentoring.

Additionally, integrating *Takaful* protection into these schemes ensures that participants are safeguarded against loss of income due to unforeseen events.

8.4 Legal Guardianship and Disability Law in Malaysia

In Malaysia, the intersection between Islamic family law and civil law complicates guardianship planning for children with disabilities. Under civil law, guardianship is usually formalized through court orders under the Guardianship of Infants Act 1961. In *Shari'ah* law, guardianship (*wilayah* and *hadanah*) follows different rules, with priority given to the closest male relatives unless otherwise ruled by the court.

Challenges include:

- Lack of standardized processes for special needs guardianship.
- Limited awareness among *Muslim* parents regarding the importance of formal guardianship documentation.
- Bureaucratic delays in registering wills or *wasiyyah* in *Shari'ah* courts.

Therefore, Islamic estate planning must ensure:

- Guardianship appointments are clearly named in *wasiyyah* or via *hibah amanah* structures.
- Alternative guardians (siblings, uncles, community members) are pre-identified and briefed.
- Civil and *Shari'ah* legal advisors work together to align the documentation.

Such planning can avoid future disputes, ensure continuity of care, and protect the legal rights of special needs children.

8.5 Role of Mosques as Retirement Planning Hubs

Mosques, as central institutions in *Muslim* communities, have the potential to be more than places of worship—they can serve as retirement planning hubs for *Muslim* families with special needs dependants. Several pioneering mosques in Kuala Lumpur, Selangor, and Penang have piloted initiatives offering:

- Weekend legal clinics for drafting *wasiyyah*, *hibah*, and guardianship documents.
- Financial literacy classes on *halal* investing and *Takaful*.
- Parent support groups facilitated by Islamic counsellors and psychologists.

Benefits of mosque-based models include:

- High trust and familiarity within the community.

• Spiritual reinforcement of the need for planning.

• Accessibility for caregivers who may face transportation or childcare challenges.

With partnerships between mosques and institutions like *Tabung Haji* or *zakat* offices, these initiatives can be scaled nationwide.

9. THEORETICAL FRAMEWORK

This chapter is anchored in the foundational framework of *Maqasid al-Shari'ah*—the higher objectives of Islamic law. These principles, which guide ethical and just living, emphasize five core areas of protection (refer to Figure 5).

Figure 5. Five Core Areas of Protection

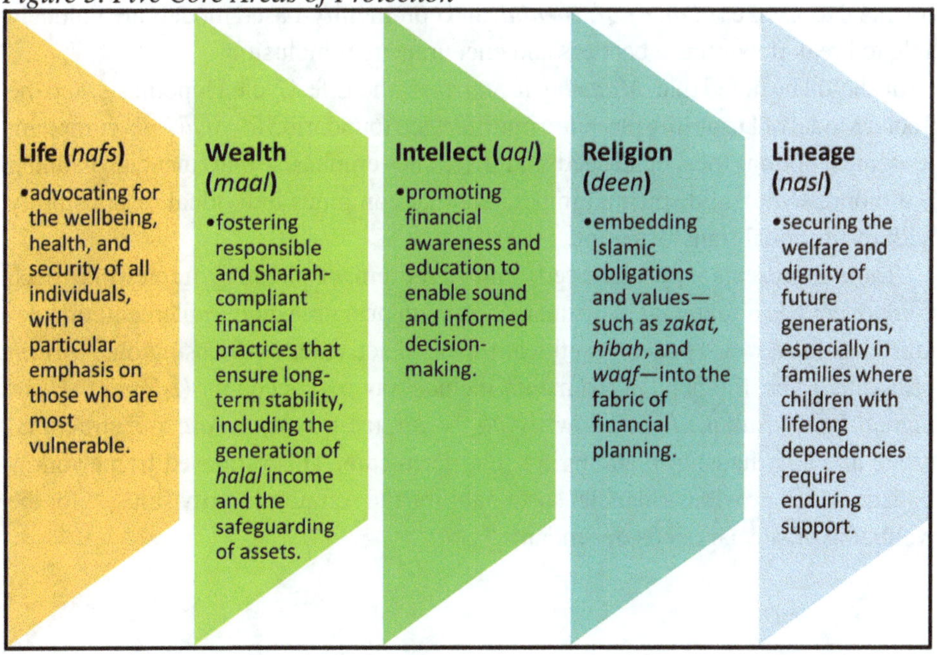

Remarkably, retirement planning for special needs families should concern financial and non-financial (i.e. spiritual and social) areas. For instance, ensuring lifelong care and guardianship upholds the sanctity of life and lineage. Ethical management of wealth through *halal* means contributes to both economic stability and spiritual well-being. The strategic use of instruments like *zakat* and *waqf* underscores a collective responsibility—merging individual planning with broader communal values.

The Life-Cycle Hypothesis (Modigliani & Brumberg, 1954) looks at how people save and spend money at different points in their lives from a macroeconomic point of view. It claims that people save money while they work and spend it when they retire. However, for families with special needs dependants, this life cycle lasts much longer. Parents need to not only plan for their own retirement, but also set up a lasting financial foundation that will help their child even after they die. This shows how important it is to save early, how compounding (or *halal* alternatives like returns from *sukuk*) can help, and how income smoothing can help families meet their long-term financial obligations for lifelong care.

The "Social Model of Disability" takes a different approach than the economic view. Instead of focussing on individual disabilities, it focusses on the societal and structural barriers that keep people from being able to work. Islamic ethics are very similar to this point of view, which is based on dignity, shared responsibility, and social justice. The social model says that poverty, lack of access, and not being financially ready should be seen as systemic problems, not personal failures. Islamic financial tools like *zakat, waqf*, *Takaful*, and community-based models are uniquely able to break down these barriers and encourage real inclusion.

It should be noted that, *Maqasid al-Shari'ah*, the Life-Cycle Hypothesis, and the Social Model of Disability provide a multifaceted foundation for *Shari'ah*-compliant retirement options for special needs families. They emphasise that financial planning is a moral, social, and spiritual imperative that combines individual responsibility with institutional transformation.

Table 2 presents a special-needs family retirement planning framework. Each component has a financial instrument, *Shari'ah* principle, and implementation details. The framework promotes ethical financial activities by focusing on *Shari'ah* principles. The financial instruments include savings accounts (*Islamic*), *Halal* mutual funds/ Sukuk, *Takaful*, *wasiyyah, hibah*, trust, *waqf, zakat*, and structured estate and guardianship planning for long-term care. This proposed framework is holistic which provides financial sustainability and religious clarity suitable for the wellbeing of special needs dependants.

Table 2. Elements, Tools, and Shari'ah Principles of Shari'ah-Compliant Retirement Planning

Element	Instruments	*Shari'ah* Principle	Notes
Emergency Fund	Islamic savings account	No *riba*	6–12 months' expenses
Long-term Investment	*Halal* mutual funds / *Sukuk*	No gharar, no riba	Diversify risk
Risk Protection	*Takaful*	Cooperative, risk-sharing	Include disability riders
Estate Planning	*Wasiyyah* + *Hibah* + Trust	*Faraid*-compliant	Allocate up to one-third to special needs care
Charitable Provision	Cash *waqf* + *zakat*	*Sadaqah jariyah*	Endowment for long-term care
Guardianship	Legal guardianship form + fatwa endorsement	Legal/Islamic harmony	File with *Shari'ah* court

10. COMMON CHALLENGES AND BARRIERS

10.1 Financial Illiteracy and Misinformation

Misunderstandings about which financial products are permissible can lead families to delay or avoid important financial decisions (Mahdzan et al., 2024), resulting in insufficient savings and unclear succession plans that jeopardize the long-term security of special needs dependants. Additionally, many guardians lack knowledge about the use and legal restrictions of tools like *hibah* and *wasiyyah*, especially within Malaysian or other national legal systems (Rasul & Awang, 2024).

10.2 Legal Complexities

Navigating between civil law and *Shari'ah* inheritance law can be challenging, as their coexistence often leads to inconsistent interpretations and implementations. In Malaysia and other countries, this overlap creates uncertainty, particularly in cases involving guardianship, mental incapacity, or disputes over estates. Families may also face bureaucratic delays when filing *wasiyyah* documents or appointing guardians through the *Shari'ah* court. The absence of standardised legal templates tailored to Islamic and national contexts further complicates retirement planning for families (Laldin & Furqani, 2013).

10.3 Social Stigma and Denial

Despite rising awareness, some families still struggle with accepting a child's lifelong dependency. Cultural shame, fear of judgment, or belief that "Allah will provide" without initiative-taking effort may hinder planning. Such stigma leads to denial of the child's condition, resulting in poor documentation, lack of engagement with financial institutions, and refusal to appoint alternative caregivers. As a result, families delay creating wills or trusts, leaving children vulnerable when parents pass away. This emotional barrier is especially prevalent in rural communities where awareness programs have not yet penetrated (Yusof et al., 2024; Chu et al., 2023; Chu et al., 2020).

10.4 Other challenges and barriers

Other challenges or barriers could be related to *Takaful* illiteracy, *zakat* bureaucracy and myths about *waqf*.

***Takaful* Illiteracy:** Many *Muslim* families still hold misconceptions about *Takaful*, viewing it as either too expensive or irrelevant, especially if they are not primary income earners. This misperception often stems from a lack of awareness about the differences between conventional insurance and Islamic *Takaful*, which is based on mutual assistance (*tabarru'*) and risk-sharing rather than profit-driven premiums. Moreover, many *Takaful* providers lack transparent communication regarding fees, benefits, and claims procedures, making it difficult for families to assess product suitability. A significant challenge is the limited availability of disability-specific riders in existing *Takaful* products. As a result, special needs families often find themselves unprotected against scenarios such as the parent's sudden disability or death. Greater education efforts and product innovation are needed, particularly the development of specialized family *Takaful* plans that include long-term care provisions, income replacement, and caregiving expenses (Abd Wahab et al., 2024).

Zakat Bureaucracy: While *zakat* is intended as a mechanism to support the needy, including those with disabilities, the current administrative processes often present significant hurdles. Families have reported inconsistent eligibility criteria between different state *Baitulmal* offices, prolonged waiting periods, insufficient public communication on required documentation, and a lack of digital application channels. These challenges discourage many eligible families from applying, or they abandon the process midway due to frustration. To address these issues, a national-level unified database of verified special needs applicants, integrated with medical records and disability status, can streamline assessment. Digital platforms for application, real-time status updates, and e-disbursement could enhance accessibility, especially for rural families. Moreover, training *Baitulmal* officers to recognize the unique, lifelong financial needs of these families is essential for empathetic and effective service delivery.

Myths About *waqf*: *Waqf*, though deeply rooted in Islamic tradition, is often misunderstood as something reserved for the wealthy—those who can afford to donate land, buildings, or large sums of money. This misconception tends to discourage middle- and lower-income families from taking part in one of Islam's most enduring forms of charity. The myth continues largely because of limited public education and the lack of awareness about modern *waqf* models. In truth, *cash waqf*—which allows individuals to contribute small, regular amounts—has gained traction worldwide, including in Malaysia. With proper pooling and professional oversight, even modest monthly donations (as little as RM10–50) can fund meaningful initiatives like therapy, education, or housing for people with special needs. Digital *waqf* platforms have made the process even more accessible, allowing users to donate quickly and monitor where their contributions go. Promoting these inclusive models through mosques, community centres, and Islamic financial institutions can help dispel myths and encourage wider participation in sustainable care efforts.

11. POLICY RECOMMENDATIONS AND COMMUNITY INITIATIVES

11.1 Developing Islamic Financial Literacy Programs

Islamic financial planning is a new field that combines religious beliefs with the facts of today's economy. Dusuki and Abdullah (2007) say that Islamic finance is naturally moral because it promotes justice and welfare through *Maqasid al-Shari'ah*. Chapra (2016) states that it is important to protect your money, your intelligence, and your family history. These things are all important when planning for dependants with special needs.

According to Saleh and Hassan (2022), a lot of *Muslim* families are unaware of structured Islamic financial tools like *Takaful* or *hibah*. Chelliah et al. (2022) found that a lot of *Muslim* parents are ignorant about the *halal* options that are out there for them, even though they know they have to plan for their kids' futures.

There is scarcity of research that looks into financial perspective of families with special needs children. We should make a hybrid model that uses both Islamic financial tools and civil legal structures. This would fix issues with guardianship and inheritance while still respecting differences in culture and religion. Abdullah et al. (2024) who carried out studies in Southeast Asia found that *zakat* and *waqf,* which are social finance tools, are still not being used enough to help with long-term care. An inclusive financial literacy programs is needed and include everyone, as well as specific policy interventions.

Therefore, governments, non-governmental organisations (NGOs), and Islamic financial institutions should all work together to make financial literacy programs that are easy to understand and aimed at *Muslim* families with special needs dependants. These programs need to be tailored to the local culture and have the backing of well-known financial planning councils and Islamic organisations in guaranteeing their acceptance. They should include lesson on *halal* investing, estate planning (with *wasiyyah, hibah,* and *waqf*), and how to be a guardian. Some ways to get the information are through workshops at mosques, mobile apps, and online webinars.

11.2 Institutional Collaboration

Islamic banks, *Takaful* providers, charitable organizations, and *zakat* boards should create collaborative packages tailored to families with special needs. These can include bundled savings plans, subsidized *Takaful* coverage, and simplified *waqf* setup services. Formal agreements (e.g., Memorandum of Understanding- MOU) between religious councils and financial institutions can encourage the creation of resolute units to serve such families with compassion and confidentiality (Nor et al., 2024).

11.3 Incentivizing *waqf* and zakat Allocation

Governments should introduce tax incentives or *zakat*-matching grants to encourage charitable endowments and financial sustainability for long-term care. This could involve allowing *waqf* funds to be partially matched with *zakat* disbursements or government top-ups. For instance, a *waqf* created for a special needs child's medical expenses could qualify for matching *zakat* under healthcare categories, easing the financial burden on families.

11.4 Establishing Dedicated Retirement Planning Clinics

Mosques and Islamic centers can be transformed into resource hubs by hosting regular retirement planning clinics. These clinics should involve a multidisciplinary team including Islamic legal experts, financial planners, and special needs advocates. Topics can include guardianship documentation, halal investing, end-of-life care planning, and family mediation. Weekend workshops or clinic days after Friday prayers can help improve attendance and awareness, particularly among older caregivers (Salleh & Hassan, 2022).

11.5 Developing FinTech-Enabled Tools

Mobile-friendly Islamic retirement planning apps could transform financial literacy and access for special needs families. *Zakat* calculators for real estate, savings, and investments can be included in these computerised applications. *Hibah* form generators can also help customers arrange *Shari'ah*-compliant of gifts during their lifetime. Besides, estate trackers help with secure, centralise asset allocations, guardianship appointments, and *waqf* pledges for families. Integrated *zakat, Takaful* policy, and wasiyyah updates can help in ensuring compliance. To promote confidence, these apps should be bilingual, secure, and *Shari'ah*-endorsed. FinTech can also bridge rural and urban gaps, making Islamic financial planning accessible to families with logistical and knowledge limitations (Hasan et al., 2020).

11.6 Conducting Specialized Training

Given the complex and lifelong financial needs of families with special needs, Islamic financial advisors must go beyond standard training to provide effective, tailored guidance. Islamic universities, *zakat* groups, and groups that fight for the rights of people with disabilities should all work together to make certification programs. The modules should cover not only Islamic retirement planning, Islamic estate planning, Islamic investment planning, wealth management, and *zakat*, but also other important parts of financial planning. It should also have *Takaful* products that people with disabilities can use, rules about guardianship, ways to figure out what people need, and emotional intelligence in client advice. Training should also include learning about the difficulties that people with special needs have to deal with in legal and financial situations, as well as how to be sensitive and keep things private. Certified consultants can help people in the community by giving advice at mosques, Islamic centres, and banks. This makes it easier for everyone to plan for retirement.

11.7 Convening Multi-Stakeholder Forums

To fix systemic fragmentation, there should be annual forums that bring together a wide range of stakeholders, such as *Baitulmal* officers, *Shari'ah* scholars, NGO representatives, Islamic financial professionals, caregivers, and academics. These forums can be used for multiple purposes, such as proposing new policies, training people, and raising public awareness. Key themes may include updates on *waqf* law, new ways to pay digital *zakat*, new case law in guardianship, and new Islamic finance products. The forums will be meaningful by including families with special needs as their main participants. The suggestions made at these meetings can help in setting national policy, standardising best practices, and encouraging people to collaborate to find long-term solutions for financial planning problems.

11.8 Youth Engagement

To instill a culture of long-term care planning and financial literacy in young *Muslims*, universities, student associations, and community organizations should offer workshops, webinars, and service-learning activities. Interactive exercises like *zakat* budgeting and mock estate planning can make learning engaging. Islamic financial ethics and social responsibility should be integrated into relevant courses, helping young adults see financial planning as both worship and community care, preparing them to be ethical professionals and caregivers.

12. COMPARATIVE GLOBAL FRAMEWORKS, LEGAL HARMONIZATION, AND FINTECH SCALABILITY

To enhance the utility and completeness of Islamic retirement planning for families with special needs, it is crucial to examine global comparative models and emerging technological enablers. This broader lens supports policy harmonization, cross-jurisdictional planning, and scalable solutions through Financial Technology (FinTech).

12.1 Cross-Cultural and Global Trends

Global case studies offer instructive models that harmonize care, legal rights, and sustainable funding:

i. **United States**: The *Achieving a Better Life Experience (ABLE) Act* allows tax-advantaged savings accounts for individuals with disabilities without affecting their Medicaid eligibility. The *Special Needs Trust* (SNT) is structured to bypass income limits while ensuring long-term financial care (Peterson, 2018).
ii. **United Kingdom**: Disability-related *Discretionary Trusts* operate within civil law to protect benefits access and enable caregiver discretion. Legal guardianship is streamlined under the *Mental Capacity Act 2005*, offering clarity absent in many Muslim-majority jurisdictions (Kanter, 2014).
iii. **Indonesia and Turkey**: Productive waqf and blended social finance initiatives—like digital zakat and inclusive housing projects—demonstrate how Islamic instruments can serve state-led disability welfare agendas. These models bridge classical fiqh with modern governance and civil rights.

Such comparative analysis reveals the need for Malaysian or Gulf Cooperation Council (GCC) Islamic frameworks to integrate tax incentives, asset protection trusts, and national disability savings mechanisms within Shari'ah-compliant structures.

12.2 FinTech as a Catalyst for Islamic Inclusion

The scalability of Shari'ah-compliant retirement and estate planning is greatly enhanced through FinTech innovations. Mobile *zakat* apps, online hibah generators, and AI-based guardianship planners are already gaining traction in Southeast Asia and the MENA (Middle East and North Africa) region. These platforms:

- Increase reach among low-literacy users via multilingual interfaces.
- Enable real-time guidance from Shari'ah advisors and financial planners.
- Digitize compliance by aligning Takaful, wasiyyah, and waqf documents with national and religious registration systems.

According to Hasan et al. (2020), FinTech platforms can be powerful equalizers in communities where physical access to Islamic financial advisory services is limited. Their integration with *Baitulmal*, Islamic banks, and disability registries enhances planning accuracy and participation.

12.3 Harmonizing Shari'ah and Civil Law Globally

Countries with dual-legal frameworks often face interpretational conflicts in estate distribution, guardianship rights, and trust enforcement. Harmonization strategies should include:

- **Unified model laws** for Islamic estate instruments that are enforceable under civil statutes (e.g., hybrid hibah-wasiyyah codifications).
- **Transnational Islamic legal councils** to issue fatwas on cross-border estate issues.
- **Mutual recognition agreements** (MRAs) across OIC countries for retirement documents, disability trusts, and guardian designations.

These legal pathways ensure that Shari'ah-based family plans are not undermined in civil courts due to technical non-alignment.

13. CAREGIVERS' MENTAL HEALTH AND PSYCHOLOGICAL INCLUSION

While the financial and legal challenges in planning for special needs dependants are well-documented, the psychological burden on caregivers—especially women—requires equal attention. Islamic retirement planning must incorporate mental wellness frameworks grounded in both empirical research and Quranic values of patience, perseverance, and divine reliance.

13.1 Empirical Burnout and Mental Health Data

Caregivers of children with disabilities are highly vulnerable to burnout, depression, and anxiety due to chronic stress, financial strain, and social isolation. Recent studies reveal:

- **60–70% of mothers** of special needs children in Malaysia report symptoms of emotional fatigue and anxiety disorders (Chu et al., 2020; Habibullah et al., 2023).
- Over **45% reduce or leave employment**, impacting their mental well-being, financial independence, and access to retirement savings (Abd Karim et al., 2025).
- Caregiver strain directly correlates with poorer outcomes in dependent children, emphasizing the need for comprehensive family-centric planning (Demirpençe Seçinti et al., 2024).

13.3 Inclusive Planning and Support

Islamic retirement planning frameworks should include:

i. **Mental health waqf funds** to provide therapy, respite services, and psychosocial training.
ii. **Community peer groups** in mosques facilitated by Islamic psychologists or trained khatibs.
iii. **Gender-sensitive advisory clinics** to address the compounded burdens of female caregivers.

Recognizing caregiver resilience as an *Islamic virtue*—not just a private responsibility—ensures alignment with Maqasid al-Shari'ah principles of dignity (*karamah*), life preservation (*nafs*), and mental well-being (*'aql*).

13.4 Islamic Psychological Resilience and Caregiver Well-being

Caregiving for special needs children entails profound emotional, spiritual, and physical demands. Yet the psychological dimension of caregivers—particularly mothers—is underexamined in policy and retirement planning literature.

Islamic teachings offer rich guidance on emotional resilience and coping. Quranic narratives such as the trials of Prophet Ayyub (AS) reflect profound endurance in the face of personal loss and physical suffering, illustrating the Islamic concept of *sabr* (patience), *du'a* and *dhikir* (supplication and remebrance), and *tawakkul* (trust in Allah) as core pillars of psychological strength.

- **Tawakkul (trust in Allah)** as a cognitive anchor against uncertainty (Qur'an 3:159)[3].
- **Sabr (patience)** as a transformative state praised in 90+ verses (e.g., Qur'an 2:153)[4].
- **Du'a and dhikr (supplication and remembrance)** as stress-relieving practices supported by empirical neuroscience.

According to Almajri et al. (2025), Islamic mental health interventions integrate *dhikr* (remembrance), *shukr* (gratitude), and social support as therapy components. Integrating these frameworks into caregiver support programs can elevate mental health from a clinical issue to a spiritual and communal concern. In addition, Daulay et al. (2025) found that mothers of autistic children showed reduced burnout symptoms when supported with spiritual counseling and Quranic reflection practices.

14. EMPIRICAL EMBEDDING IN POLICY PROPOSALS

To move from theoretical prescriptions to actionable policy, retirement and estate frameworks must be grounded in quantifiable outcomes. This is particularly important for convincing institutional stakeholders, including zakat councils, Islamic financial regulators, and family welfare ministries.

Table 3. Comparative Performance of Cash Waqf Models for Special Needs Support

Country	Waqf Type	Avg. Annual ROI (%)	Sustainability Period (Years)	Target Beneficiaries	Outcome
Malaysia	Community-based cash waqf	3.5%	10	120 autistic children	Funded therapy, equipment
Turkey	Residential waqf homes	4.2%	15	60 intellectually disabled adults	Independent assisted living
Indonesia	Vocational waqf program	2.8%	7	75 Down syndrome youth	45% employment placement
South Africa	Health-focused waqf	5.0%	12	200+ disabled individuals	Mobile clinics, home visits

Sources: Awqaf SA (2021), Hassan et al. (2021), Indonesian Waqf Board (2022)

These data points allow policymakers to assess cost-benefit effectiveness, replication viability, and long-term returns of waqf-based disability care models.

14.1 Evolving from Gendered to Sibling-Inclusive Planning

While the chapter rightly centers on *female caregivers*—especially mothers—as primary planners, future-ready models must incorporate *sibling-inclusive structures*. As parents age or pass away, siblings (particularly eldest daughters or sons) often become de facto caregivers. However, legal recognition and financial empowerment of these siblings are often missing in retirement documents.

Strategies for Sibling Inclusion via Hibah Amanah

i. **Named Successor Trustees**: Embed clauses in *hibah amanah* appointing elder siblings as co-trustees or successor trustees for special needs dependants upon the demise of the mother.

ii. **Staggered Asset Access**: Structure hibah allocations to siblings in stages—an initial portion for transitional care, and future disbursements conditional upon continuous support and compliance with care agreements.

iii. **Training-Inclusive Hibah**: Attach *conditional clauses* requiring siblings to attend guardianship or financial planning workshops (organized by *Baitulmal* or Islamic banks) before fully assuming their roles.

iv. **Sibling waqf incentives**: Establish a family waqf that distributes part of its annual returns to the sibling-caretaker to compensate for opportunity costs and emotional labor.

By evolving from a mother-centric paradigm to a holistic sibling-based approach, the plan ensures generational continuity in care and asset stewardship—aligned with the maqasid of *hifz al-nasl* (protection of lineage) and *hifz al-mal* (protection of wealth).

15. CONCLUSION

Islamic retirement planning for special needs families goes beyond finances; it focuses on ensuring dignity, continuity, and lifelong care. These families face unique challenges that require early planning, legal preparation, and community support.

Instruments like *waqf, Takaful*, and *wasiyyah* offer both spiritual and practical solutions to secure care after caregivers pass away. Examples from several countries show how Islamic traditions and local laws can work together. However, issues like financial illiteracy, legal hurdles, and social stigma still create barriers, highlighting the need for better education, partnerships, and charitable efforts.

Importantly, families are not solely responsible. Governments, scholars, financial institutions, and religious leaders may promote readiness and compassion. With appropriate preparation and a strong Islamic financial ecology, the *ummah* can protect all vulnerable people, regardless of age, ability, or circumstance.

Islamic retirement planning goes beyond finances. It is a moral obligation to bring justice and care. *Waqf, Takaful, wasiyyah*, and *zakat* can assist families build sustainable support systems for special needs children. To close gaps, fintech innovation, institutional collaboration, and grassroots education must be integrated. Malaysia can set worldwide faith-based inclusive planning norms as a pioneer in Islamic finance. The future of Islamic retirement planning resides in policies and principles that boost the *ummah* with purpose and compassion, not just products.

Further, to support the systematic approach to retirement planning for families with special needs, the authors have developed the following tables:

- **Table 4** presents a continuity financial planning model for families with special needs children. The framework is categorised into two primary tracks: (i) special needs children with surviving parents, and (ii) special needs children without parents (orphans).
- **Table 5** offers a structured approach tailored to such families, emphasizing financial, legal, and caregiving aspects. The template is intended to serve as a guide for *Muslim* families facing the dual challenge of fulfilling Islamic obligations while preparing for the lifelong needs of dependants. It is advisable to consult with Islamic financial experts, *Shari'ah* scholars, and legal professionals when applying this template in practice.

Table 4. Proposed Framework of Special Needs Continuity Financial Planning

TRACK A: Special Needs Children WITH Parents		
Focus	**Inter-generational planning, guardianship, and asset continuity.**	**Remarks**
Key Components	**Islamic Financial Planning:** i. ***Hibah Amanah* / Wills (*Wasiyyah*):** Allocate assets to the child in a *Shari'ah*-compliant way. ii. ***Takaful* (with disability riders):** Ensure replacement income if parents become disabled/die. iii. ***Halal* Investment Portfolios / *Sukuk* / Retirement Funds.** **Guardianship & Care Delegation:** ■ Legally appoint alternate guardians. ■ Define roles in the will (Islamic and civil). ***Waqf* for Long-Term Needs:** ■ Create a **personal or community *waqf*** to fund therapy, housing, and caregivers. ■ Monthly "cash *waqf*" models for middle-income families.	
Digital Tools & Checklists	Estate planning apps, medical records, guardianship letters, *zakat* eligibility calculators.	
Government Support Needed	■ Offer **subsidized *Takaful* plans** for parents of special needs children. ■ Provide **legal aid** for preparing *wasiyyah*, guardianship, or *waqf* deeds. ■ Integrate *waqf* and *zakat* tools into public Islamic finance literacy campaigns. ■ Tax deductions for setting up child-specific *waqf* or *Takaful*.	
TRACK B: Special Needs Children WITHOUT Parents		
Focus	**Community-based safety nets and state-managed financial protection.**	**Remarks**
Key Components	**State-Managed Islamic Trust (*Wakalah Amanah Awam*):** ■ *Baitulmal* or Department of *waqf, zakat* and *Hajj* (JAWHAR) acts as trustee of funds for orphaned special needs children. ■ Guardians or social workers appointed via *Shari'ah* court or welfare department. **Orphaned Child *Zakat* Registry:** ■ Maintain **digital database** to automate *zakat* disbursement. ■ Monthly payments for therapy, education, food, and housing. **Institutional W*aqf* Projects:** ■ Endowments for **inclusive residential homes**, day centers, and therapy services. ***Takaful*4All / Micro-*Takaful*:** ■ *Baitulmal* or NGOs pay group *Takaful* plans covering medical costs and daily needs. **Social Protection Stipends:** ■ Monthly **Disability Living Allowance (DLA)** from the Department of Social Welfare, Malaysia (*Jabatan Kebajikan Masyarakat*-JKM). ■ Prioritize this group in welfare budgeting.	
Government Support Needed	■ Create **Special Needs waqf & Trust Authority** under *Baitulmal* to manage collective funds. ■ Offer **housing grants and caregiving subsidies** via JKM or Selangor Islamic Religious Council (MAIS). ■ Fund Islamic NGOs to provide community care and guardianship supervision. ■ Expand **sheltered employment programs** for high-functioning individuals.	

Table 5. Sample Comprehensive Shari'ah-Compliant Retirement Planning

	Remarks:
1. Personal Profile **Dependants' Information:** Name, age, diagnosis, and care requirements of the special needs individual. Names and contact details of other dependants (e.g., spouse, children, elderly parents). **Caregivers' Information:** Primary caregiver(s), their relationship to the dependants, and their current employment/income status. Secondary caregivers or support network (siblings, relatives, and hired caregivers).	
2. Current Financial Standing **Income:** Monthly/annual income from employment, pensions, business, or passive sources. **Assets:** Movable and immovable assets (property, gold, vehicles, investments). *Shari'ah*-compliant investments (sukuk, Islamic mutual funds, Islamic savings accounts). **Debts:** Outstanding loans, credit obligations, and *zakat* due. Debt repayment plan. **Savings:** Emergency fund status (recommendation: 6–12 months of expenses). Special needs care reserve fund.	
3. Future Needs Estimation **Medical Needs:** Projected costs for therapy, assistive devices, medications, and hospitalizations. **Educational Needs:** Tuition, specialized learning programs, vocational training. **Housing Needs:** Current and future accommodation requirements. Potential costs for modifications or assisted living. **Lifestyle Needs:** Transportation, dietary, recreational, and spiritual well-being expenses.	
4. Islamic Financial Instruments and Strategies ***Zakat* Eligibility and Distribution Plan:** Determine if the dependants qualifies for *zakat.* Identify potential *zakat* contributors (family, community). Coordinate with local *Baitulmal* or *zakat* institutions. ***Waqf* Plan:** Establishment of a family *waqf* for ongoing care (property, cash, or investment *waqf*). Appointment of trustee (*mutawalli*). Periodic reporting to a *Shari'ah* committee or court. ***Hibah* (Lifetime Gifts):** Assets reserved for the dependants during the caregiver's lifetime. Documentation and legal transfer in accordance with local laws.	

continued on following page

Table 5. Continued

	Remarks:
5. Guardianship Plan **Legal Guardians:** Appointed person(s) to act in loco parentis posthumously. Certification through civil and *Shari'ah* courts. **Trustee (*Amin*):** Responsible for administering the estate, *waqf*, or trust. Should be financially literate and *Shari'ah*-aware. **Oversight Mechanism:** Appointment of a family advisory committee or Islamic financial advisor.	
6. Will and *Wasiyyah* Drafting Guide ***Wasiyyah:*** Up to one-third of the estate is directed to the special needs dependants. Executed with witness signatures and legal registration. **Civil Will (if applicable):** Alignment with national legal requirements (e.g., probate laws). Instructions for funeral rites, debt settlement, and bequests.	
7. Contingency Fund Strategy **Emergency Funds:** Demarcated reserve for unexpected costs (medical, legal, housing). ***Takaful* Coverage:** Comprehensive *Takaful* plan with long-term disability and death benefits. **Investment Diversification:** A mix of low-risk *halal* investments to maintain liquidity and sustainability.	
8. Documentation Checklist ✓ Identity documents of all parties. ✓ Property titles and investment certificates. ✓ Legal documentation (wills, guardianship letters, trust deeds). ✓ Medical and educational assessments of the dependants. ✓ *Zakat, waqf*, and *hibah* paperwork.	
9. Annual Review and Family Meeting Protocol ✓ Conduct yearly reviews with guardians, trustees, and advisors. ✓ Update financial status, legal documents, and care plans. ✓ Encourage the involvement of siblings and family members in caregiving and financial education.	

ACKNOWLEDGEMENT

The National Defence University of Malaysia partially funded this work. The funders had no role in the study design, data collection and analysis, decision to publish, or preparation of the manuscript.

REFERENCES

Abd Karim, A. H., Kassim, S. K., Ismail, N. A. H., & Rais, H. (2025). Challenges Faced by Low-Income Muslim Malaysian Parents in Caring for Children with Disabilities. Asian Journal of Research in Education and Social Sciences e-ISSN: 2682-8502 | Vol. 7, No. 3, 77-90

Abd Wahab, N., Isa, M. Y., Yusof, R. M., & Lotfi, W. A. N. W. A. (2024). Protecting the Well-Being of Households: Delineating a Social Takāful Fund Initiative for Positive Social Impact. *International Journal of Islamic Finance and Sustainable Development, 16*(4), 117–135. DOI: 10.55188/ijifsd.v16i4.909

Abdullah, A., Salleh, M. Z. M., Ismail, W. A. A. Z. W., Anuar, T. F. T. M., Simpong, D. B. B., Rahman, N. A., & Rasdi, S. A. B. M. (2024). Retirement Financial Planning: Strategies and Challenges in Avoiding the Incidence of Poverty. In *Artificial Intelligence (AI) and Customer Social Responsibility (CSR)* (pp. 101–109). Springer Nature Switzerland. DOI: 10.1007/978-3-031-50939-1_8

Ahmed, H. (2011). *Product Development in Islamic Banks*. Edinburgh University Press. DOI: 10.1515/9780748644889

Akhter, A., Javed, M. Y., & Akhter, J. (2025). Research trends in the field of Islamic social finance: A bibliometric analysis from 1914 to 2022. *International Journal of Ethics and Systems, 41*(2), 455–483. DOI: 10.1108/IJOES-03-2023-0044

Ali, A. F. M., Ibrahim, M. F., & Ab Aziz, M. R. (2019). Missing items in zakat distribution: A case in Kelantan, Malaysia. *International Journal of zakat, 4*(1), 1-24.

Ali, H. (2024). *Islamic microfinance: landscape, models and future prospects*. Walter de Gruyter GmbH & Co KG.

Almajri, S., Baroud, N., Alouzi, K. M., & Kasheem, A. (2025). Islamic psychology: An integrative approach to human behavior and mental well-being. *Bulletin of Islamic Research, 3*(4), 687–704. DOI: 10.69526/bir.v3i4.353

Awqaf, S. A. (2021). *Annual Financial Statements for the year ended 28 February 2021*. Audited by Deloitte. Awqaf South Africa. Retrieved from https://awqafsa.org.za/annual-financial-statements/

Billah, M. M. S. (2019). Sukuk *Takaful* Plan. *Islamic Insurance Products: Exploring Takaful Principles, Instruments and Structures*, 221-226.

Chapra, M. U. (2016). *The future of economics: An Islamic perspective* (Vol. 21). Kube Publishing Ltd.

Chelliah, P., Shanmugam, A., & Sin, T. S. (2022). A study on the factors impacting retirement planning among low-income workers in the Northern Region, Malaysia. *Journal of Entrepreneurship and Business*, *10*(2), 69–84. DOI: 10.17687/jeb.v10i2.928

Chu, S. Y., Park, H., Lee, J., Shaharuddin, K. K. B., & Gan, C. H. (2020). Self-stigma and its associations with stress and quality of life among Malaysian parents of children with autism. *Child: Care, Health and Development*, *46*(4), 485–494. DOI: 10.1111/cch.12771 PMID: 32396218

Chu, S. Y., Rafi, A. B. M., Lee, J., Fierro, V., Gan, C. H., Joginder Singh, S., Hersh, D., & Lin, L. Y. (2023). The relationship between affiliate stigma, stress, and quality of life for parents of individuals with cerebral palsy in Malaysia. *Disability and Rehabilitation*, *45*(24), 4035–4047. DOI: 10.1080/09638288.2022.2153304 PMID: 36541160

Cizakca, M. (2011). *Islamic Capitalism and Finance: Origins, Evolution and the Future*. Edward Elgar Publishing. DOI: 10.4337/9780857931481

Daulay, N., Daulay, H., & Rohman, F. (2025). Religious coping of Muslim mothers of children with autism spectrum disorder in Indonesia. *Journal of Disability & Religion*, *29*(1), 33–50. DOI: 10.1080/23312521.2024.2372021

Demirpençe Seçinti, D., Diş, D., Albayrak, Z. S., & Şen, E. (2024). Depression and parental distress among caregivers of autistic children: A serial mediator analysis in caregivers of autistic children. *BMC Psychology*, *12*(1), 339. DOI: 10.1186/s40359-024-01704-x PMID: 38858797

Dusuki, A. W., & Abdullah, N. I. (2007). Maqasid al-Shari'ah, Maslahah, and Corporate Social Responsibility. *The American Journal of Islamic Social Sciences*, *24*(1), 25–45. DOI: 10.35632/ajiss.v24i1.415

Habibullah, M., Hassan, R., & Zain, N. R. M. (2023). Women's Empowerment and Participation in Islamic Financial Planning Diversity, Equity and Inclusion: Evidence from Maqasid al-*Shari'ah. Al-Burhān. Journal Of Qur Ān And Sunnah Studies*, *7*(2), 152–161.

Haris, G. (2020). The application of dynamic zakat percentage by Yusuf al-qaradawy on the professional zakat in Indonesian BAZNAS. *Asy-Syir'ah: Jurnal Ilmu Syari'ah dan Hukum, 54*(2), 299-317.

Hasan, R., Hassan, M. K., & Aliyu, S. (2020). Fintech and Islamic finance: Literature review and research agenda. [IJIEF]. *International Journal of Islamic Economics and Finance*, *3*(1), 75–94. DOI: 10.18196/ijief.2122

Hassan, M. A. M., Alias, A., Mahamood, S. M., & De Costa, F. (2021). Waqf land development approaches and practices in the state islamic religious councils. *Planning Malaysia, 19*(17).

Kamali, M. H. (2008). *Shari'ah law: An introduction*. Simon and Schuster.

Kanter, A. S. (2014). *The development of disability rights under international law: From charity to human rights*. Routledge. DOI: 10.4324/9780203711712

Khamis, M. R., Jameelah Hashim, M., & Ab Rahman, A. (2024). Effectiveness Role of zakat in Reducing Income Inequality Among Muslim Society. *Ulum Islamiyyah*, *36*(03), 26–37. DOI: 10.33102/uij.vol36no03.604

Laldin, M. A., & Furqani, H. (2013). Developing Islamic Finance in the Framework of Maqasid al-Shari'ah: Understanding the Ends (Maqasid) and the Means (Wasa'il). *International Journal of Islamic and Middle Eastern Finance and Management*, *6*(4), 278–289. DOI: 10.1108/IMEFM-05-2013-0057

Mahdzan, N. S., Zainudin, R., Wan Ahmad, W. M., & Hanifa, M. H. (2024). Does Islamic financial literacy and motives influence the holdings of Islamic financial products? A study on bank customers in Klang Valley, Malaysia. *Journal of Islamic Marketing*, *15*(9), 2286–2309. DOI: 10.1108/JIMA-05-2022-0158

Modigliani, F., & Brumberg, R. (1954). Utility analysis and the consumption function: An interpretation of cross-section data. *Franco Modigliani*, *1*(1), 388–436.

Mohsin, M. I. A. (2013). Financing through cash-waqf: a revitalization to finance different needs. *International Journal of Islamic and Middle Eastern finance and management, 6*(4), 304-321.

Nawi, H. M., Siong, O. H., Tanaraj, K., Sapiai, N. S., Nee, C. Y., & Jusoh, M. A. (2024). Visualising the research landscape on financial issues among special needs children: A bibliometric analysis from 1992 to 2024. *Edelweiss Applied Science and Technology*, *8*(6), 5214–5235. DOI: 10.55214/25768484.v8i6.3146

Nor, S. M., Yaacob, S. E., Rahman, A. A., & Zainal, H. (2024). Digitizing zakat Distribution in Malaysia: A Case Study on Application Process at Kedah State zakat Board. *Samarah: Jurnal Hukum Keluarga dan Hukum Islam, 8*(3), 1901-1927.

Obaidullah, M. (2019). *Islamic Social Finance Report 2019: Current Trends and Future Pathways*. Islamic Research and Training Institute (IRTI), IDB Group.

Obaidullah, M., Shirazi, N. S., Muljawan, D. S., & Izhar, H. (2014). Islamic Social Finance Report 2014.

Peterson, T. L. (2018). Future care planning by older grandparents raising adolescent grandchildren. *Families in Society*, *99*(1), 67–77. DOI: 10.1177/1044389418756615

Rapi, M. Z. H., Salaudeen, A. O., Ravi, M. I. R., Wongsangiam, R., & Redzuan, N. H. (2022). Micro *Takaful* programs for the poor: The Malaysian experience. *The International Journal of Accounting*, *7*(45), 65–81.

Rasul, N. M., & Awang, M. S. (2024, December). Faraid And Hibah as Islamic Estate Planning Tools Among Muslim Society in Malaysia, The Concept, Importance and Issues. In *Salam Digest: Syariah and Law Undergraduate Symposium* (Vol. 2, No. 1, pp. 104-122).

Saleh, M. N. A. H., & Hassan, H. H. (2022). Determinants of Secured Post-Retirement Lifestyle in Klang Valley. *International Journal of Early Childhood Special Education, 14*(3).

Usmani, M. T. (2002). An introduction to Islamic finance. *Language, 17*(397p), 22cm.

Yusoff, N. D., Ismail, S., Abd Razak, N., Rafien, N. S. M., & Yaakub, W. (2024). Retirement Preparedness among Malaysia's Low-Income Private Sector Employees: A Conceptual Model. *Information Management and Business Review*, *16*(3(I)S, 3 (S)), 613–627. DOI: 10.22610/imbr.v16i3(I)S.4088

ENDNOTES

1 Alms-tax is only for the poor and the needy, for those employed to administer it, for those whose hearts are attracted to the faith , for freeing slaves, for those in debt, for Allah's cause, and for needy travelers. This is an obligation from Allah. And Allah is All-Knowing, All-Wise." [al-Tawbah 9:60]

2 Allah commands you regarding your children: the share of the male will be twice that of the female.1 If you leave only two or more females, their share is two-thirds of the estate. But if there is only one female, her share will be one-half. Each parent is entitled to one-sixth if you leave offspring.2 But if you are childless and your parents are the only heirs, then your mother will receive one-third.3 But if you leave siblings, then your mother will receive one-sixth4—after the fulfilment of bequests and debts.5 Be fair to your parents and children, as you do not fully know who is more beneficial to you.6 This is an obligation from Allah. Surely Allah is All-Knowing, All-Wise. (Surah An-Nisa: 11-12)

3 "... And when you have decided, then rely upon Allah . Indeed, Allah loves those who rely [upon Him]." (Surah Al-Imran: 159)

4 *"O you who believe, seek help through patience and prayer. Indeed, Allah is with the patient." (Surah Al-Baqarah: 153).*

Chapter 8
Personal Saving for Retirement From an Islamic Perspective

Asma' Rashidah Idris
https://orcid.org/0009-0007-2027-9191
Universiti Teknologi MARA, Malaysia

Hafizah Mat Nawi
https://orcid.org/0000-0003-2232-9547
National Defense University of Malaysia, Malaysia

Salwa Muda
https://orcid.org/0009-0001-5753-5132
Universiti Teknologi MARA, Malaysia

Noor Azila Mohd Zaid
https://orcid.org/0009-0009-9830-9957
Universiti Teknologi MARA, Malaysia

Dalila Abu Bakar
Tuanku Abdul Rahman University of Management and Technology, Malaysia

ABSTRACT

Personal retirement saving is crucial to ensure financial security during old age. Saving is viewed as a holistic approach from the perspective of Islam, which is shaped by religious and ethical values as well as socioeconomic factors. Thus, this conceptual paper emerges to examine the four determinants of choosing Islamic personal saving for retirement which are religious obligation, Islamic financial literacy, motivation and financial inclusion. Additionally, this paper highlights the

DOI: 10.4018/979-8-3373-1842-4.ch008

role of Maqasid al-Shariah in fostering responsible saving behavior and enhancing financial well-being. This contributes to the significance of structured personal saving for retirees. Hence, it is essential to integrate the Islamic perspectives in any financial education programs, financial products promotions and financial planning initiatives. Such shariah-compliant and faith-based Islamic values can empower individuals to achieve both material security and spiritual fulfillment in retirement. Ultimately, a more sustainable and inclusive financial ecosystem will be achieved.

1.0 INTRODUCTION

Saving for retirement holds importance for Muslims primarily within the framework of Islamic financial literacy (IFL) and the broader religious obligation to manage one's financial affairs according to Islamic principles. IFL is a Religious Obligation for True Success (Al-Falah) and it is a religious obligation for every Muslim to realise true success in this world and the hereafter (Al-Falah) (Kasmon et al., 2025; Wijaya et al., 2019). Sound financial planning and management like saving for future needs for retirement, is part of fulfilling this religious duty.

Islamic financial management aims to achieve the higher objectives of Islamic law (Maqasid al-Shariah), which include safeguarding Muslims' wealth (mal) and realizing well-being (falah) and a fulfilling life (hayat tayyibah)(Hati et al., 2021). Saving for retirement means of safeguarding wealth to ensure future well-being and contribute to a fulfilling life, aligning with these objectives. Maqasid al-Shariah also aims to facilitate the normal functioning of society and enhance the public good.

A core principle emphasized is the strict prohibition of interest (riba) in Islam (Mahdzan et al., 2024; Sen et al., 2020). It must be done in a manner that is Sharia-compliant and avoids interest-based transactions (Burhanudin, 2022; Masrizal et al., 2025; Sen et al., 2020). Islamic banks are established to fulfill banking transaction needs by not violate the Islamic principles. This action reflects a commitment to abiding by religious teachings and avoiding forbidden acts that could cause regret among Muslims later (Candra Sari et al., 2022; Hati et al., 2022; Muflih et al., 2024; Widyastuti et al., 2022). Being financially savvy in Islam is vital as it help achieve a balanced existence and they may worry less about money, allowing them to focus on other things (Osman et al., 2024; Shirazi et al., 2022). This contributes to personal well-being, which is a desired outcome in Islamic teachings (Hati et al., 2021).

The role of *Maqasid al-Shariah* in shaping responsible saving behavior is very important in the context of retirement savings. Principles such as property protection (*hifz al-mal*) and social welfare does not only encourage systematic financial planning but also benefit the society. However, despite the availability of Sharīʿah-compliant financial instruments, many Malaysians, especially Muslims, still lack sufficient personal savings for retirement. This issue is often linked to influencing factors include religious obligation, Islamic financial literacy, motivation, financial inclusion, perceived risk, and past financial behavior, all of which shape an individual's decision-making process regarding Islamic personal retirement savings. *Maqasid al-Shariah* can serve as a moderating framework that strengthens the impact of these factors by aligning individual financial choices with ethical and spiritual objectives rooted in Islam. By providing a values-based lens, *Maqasid al-Shariah* enhances the effectiveness of these determinants in encouraging disciplined and purposeful retirement savings. Therefore, by analyzing the connection between religious convictions and financial behavior in retirement planning, this paper will add to the body of knowledge on Islamic finance and factors that influence retirees' decisions to choose Islamic personal savings for their retirement.

1.1 Current Scenario on Pension Scheme and Retirees' Challenges After Retirement in Malaysia

In Malaysia, retirement schemes are offered by few financial institutions. However the most prominent one is Employees Provident Fund (EPF).The EPF is the national provident fund designed to ensure financial security for members during retirement. It is a compulsory savings scheme managed by a social security organization for private sector employees and non-pensionable public servants. In contrast, government servants have been covered under the government pension scheme since 1968 through the Pensions Act 1980 (Lee, 1997). The EPF, a statutory body under the Ministry of Finance, oversees retirement planning and compulsory savings for private sector employees.

Malaysia's current pension system faces challenges in ensuring financial security for its growing elderly population (Azhar and Omar, 2025). With limited coverage through public pensions for civil servants, EPF for the private sector, SOCSO, many retirees are left vulnerable (Zin, 2012). Rising life expectancy and living costs further strain the system, and more than 50 percent of older adults are often proves insufficient (EPF,2024), and increasing the risk of old-age poverty (Zainalaludin et al., 2021). As of October 2024, only 36% of active members meet the Basic Savings target of RM240,000 by age 55 which below the updated benchmark of RM290,000 needed for 20 years of retirement (EPF, 2024). While, the average global life expectancies are expected to rise to above 77 by 2050 (United Nations, 2022). Based on this, an average Malaysian would be at risk of having depleted retirement savings 20 years before death. This sizeable gap between the median longevity of retirement savings and life expectancy after retirement highlights the urgent need to rebuild savings buffers.

Despite having retirement schemes, savings inequality remains a major concern among different groups in Malaysia. Savings disparities are evident, with younger workers, low-income earners, informal sector workers, and women saving less due to income gaps, career breaks, and longer life expectancy (Krishnaveni et al., 2024). Rising healthcare costs and increasing longevity further worsen the situation. Without proper planning, many retirees face financial insecurity, underscoring the need for early, consistent, and informed retirement preparation (Batizani, 2024).

1.2 Islamic Personal Saving for Retirement in Malaysia

The introduction of *Simpanan Shariah* which the first Shariah-compliant retirement savings fund by the Employees Provident Fund (EPF) of Malaysia has marked a significant milestone in the development of Islamic retirement planning in the country. As a global leader in Islamic banking and finance, Malaysia has witnessed a growing demand for Shariah-compliant financial products, particularly in the area of retirement planning.

The launch of *Simpanan Shariah* on 8 August 2016 signified a transformative shift in the retirement savings landscape. This initiative provides EPF members, including non-Muslims, the option to have their retirement savings managed and invested in accordance with Shariah principles. The fund operates based on the *akad wakalah* (agency contract), and a Shariah Advisory Committee (SAC) has been appointed to ensure that all investment decisions and fund management activities remain in full compliance with Islamic principles. In line with Islamic teachings, which emphasize the importance of avoiding *riba* (interest), *Simpanan Shariah* offers Muslim workers a retirement savings option free from concerns related to non-compliant investment strategies, asset selection, or fund governance. As a result, retirees can be assured that their post-retirement income is ethically and religiously aligned, allowing them to fully benefit from their savings in achieving their retirement goals.

Malaysia is experiencing a demographic shift due to longer life expectancy and smaller family sizes, leading to a rapidly ageing population. By 2030, 15.3% of the population (about 5.8 million) will be aged 60 and above, rising to 8.2 million by 2040 (Abdullah et al., 2024) This trend highlights the urgent need to address retirees' financial security and healthcare needs. In response to these challenges, Chowdhury (2021) proposed the Islamic Health Protection Retirement Plan (i-HPRP), as an innovative Islamic retirement product which integrates medical benefits with retirement income. The plan is structured based on an exchange mechanism, where contributors make regular payments throughout their working life under the principle of commitment to donation (*iltizām bi al-tabarru*) (Johari et al., 2014). In order to benefit from this scheme, individuals are encouraged to begin contributing to a *takaful* or annuity-based plan from a young age. For example, the proposed model suggests a 30-year contribution period, with retirement benefits accessible at the age of 60.

The i-HPRP offers two key benefits which consists of a monthly retirement income and health protection coverage, making it a valuable complement to existing retirement schemes such as the Employees Provident Fund (EPF). This is particularly beneficial for retirees who may encounter insufficient savings in their EPF accounts. A distinguishing feature of this plan is the inclusion of health protection, which is not covered under the conventional EPF scheme. Importantly, the i-HPRP adheres strictly to Islamic principles, as all contributions are invested in Sharīʿah-compliant instruments, under the supervision of the Shariah Advisory Council of Bank Negara Malaysia, ensuring the ethical and religious integrity of the fund (Salleh et al., 2023).

According to the Financial Planning Association of Malaysia (FPAM, 2009), the foundation of Islamic finance is rooted in Sharīʿah, which serves as a comprehensive guide for Muslims in managing their worldly affairs and striving for success in the hereafter. This principle extends to personal financial planning, including savings for retirement, which is not only a financial responsibility but also a religious obligation in Islam. Islamic personal retirement planning emphasizes ethical saving and investment practices that align with Sharīʿah principles, such as avoiding *riba* (interest), *gharar* (uncertainty), and *haram* (prohibited) activities.

1.3 Private Retirement Scheme in Malaysia

The Private Retirement Scheme (PRS) in Malaysia was introduced on July 18, 2012, and is regulated primarily by the Capital Markets and Services Act (CMSA) 2007. CMSA defines PRS as a trust-governed retirement plan offered or made available to the public with the sole intent of or with the effect of enabling participants to accumulate long-term savings for retirement. This is a complementary scheme to the existing pension systems whereby the focus is to enhance retirement savings for both employed and self-employed individuals (Mohd Ali et. al, 2016). This retirement plan is being created to address the issue of retirees' inadequate retirement needs due to increased living standards and longer life expectancies.

In the revised guideline of Oct 1, 2014, CMSA stated that the PRS Providers shall be guided by the following three (3) principles. Firstly, PRS Providers must act in the interest of members as a whole with the aim of providing cost-effective voluntary Schemes and ensure that the Schemes are operated in a proper and efficient manner. Secondly, the PRS Providers must ensure that the Schemes are accessible to a wide cross-section of the population. Unreasonable exclusions from participation in a Scheme should be avoided, for example, the imposition of a high minimum contribution amount or not accepting contributions from employers who make contributions on behalf of their employees. Lastly, PRS Providers are required to make sure that the investment policies for the funds under the Schemes must be consistent with the objective of building savings for retirement and ensure that there is a prudent spread of risk.

PRS involvement and knowledge are still quite low despite its launch years ago. A study conducted by Zabri (2016) found that, among private sector employees in Malacca, awareness of PRS is still not widespread, with only 77% of those aware showing interest in investing. Factors influencing retirement planning practices include social, marketing, and personal aspects, as well as demographic factors like government support, age, and income.

As of 2025, there are nine (9) available PRS offered by PRS Providers who are approved by the Securities Commission Malaysia, namely AHAM Asset Management Berhad, AIA Pension and Asset Management Sdn. Bhd., AmFunds Manangement Berhad, Hong Leong Asset Management Bhd, Kenanga Investors Berhad, Manulife Investment Management (M) Berhda, Principal Asset Management Berhad, Public Mutual Berhad, RHB Asset Management Sdn. Bhd.

The PRS is designed to complement the Employee Provident Fund (EPF), which is a compulsory savings scheme for workers in Malaysia. Both schemes aim to provide financial security for retirees, but they operate differently. The EPF is a defined contribution scheme, while the PRS offers more flexibility and is voluntary (Shah et al., 2023).

The PRS account is considered affordable, as it only requires a minimum contribution of RM100 to open the account. This is a flexible scheme when investors can choose from a total of nine (9) PRS Providers and various funds (Conventional or Shariah-compliant) to match any unique investment profile and risks. The PRS also provides various tax incentives to encourage participation; for example, investors can enjoy up to RM3,000 personal tax relief annually. Private Pension Administrator (PPA) also provides one-stop account management and ongoing member service to protect the investors. Furthermore, PRS is a safe investment because it's regulated by the Securities Commission Malaysia, and the schemes are safeguarded by the Scheme Trustees.

2.0 LITERATURE REVIEW

2.1 Theoretical Background

This paper integrates both conventional and Islamic theoretical frameworks. The Theory of Planned Behavior (TPB) and the Life-Cycle Model of Consumption and Savings represent the conventional approach, while *Maqasid al-Shariah*, as the fundamental objective of shariah, is emphasized from the Islamic perspective.

Previous studies utilize and extend established behavioral theories to understand muslims' financial decisions, including saving intentions.

2.1.1 Theory of Planned Behavior

Initially, the Theory of Planned Behaviour (TPB) is proposed by Azjen (1985), It is the superior model theory to understand human behavior. It is said that most human behaviour results from an individual's intention to take on specific behaviour and the capability of an individual to make a precise decision about it. According to TPB, intentions are strong predictors of actual behavior. TPB thus suggests that motivation, subjective norm and perceived control lead to one's intention to perform a behavior (Ajzen, 1985). This theory is extended by incorporating Islamic financial literacy and perceived moral obligation to predict financial management behavioral intentions, which encompass saving (Osman et al., 2024; Widyastuti et al., 2022).

The core components of TPB are attitude toward the behavior, subjective norms and perceived behavioral control (Osman et al., 2024; Widyastuti et al., 2022). Attitude toward the behavior refers to an individual's evaluation of performing the specific behavior. It can be assessing through harmful or beneficial or enjoyable or unenjoyable. The optimistic attitude towards a certain action would amplify their intention to act. Subjective norms represent the perceived social pressure to perform or not perform the behavior. It reflects an individual's belief about whether important referent individuals or groups approve or disapprove of them performing the behavior. Perceived behavioral control (PBC) relates to the perceived ease or difficulty in performing a behavior. It reflects a person's confidence in their ability to perform the behavior and their perception of the availability of necessary resources and opportunities, as well as potential obstacles or barriers. Concepts like self-efficacy are often used to describe PBC.

With regard to TPB and the context of personal saving for retirement, She et al. (2023) further described that individuals with strong intentions to prepare for retirement are more likely to engage in behaviors such as saving, investing, and making informed financial decisions that contribute to retirement plan. Hence, an individual's level of knowledge or financial literacy, and motivation can be prerequisite factors for effective behaviour related to retirement.

2.1.2 Life Cycle Theory

Another theory is Life Cycle Theory (LCT) which was found in Penrose (1952). This theory introduced the life-cycle model of asset allocation and accumulation. The model differentiates between the propensity to consume and save at various stages of an individual's life. Basically, the Life-cycle theory states that household consumption is a function of long-term income. It further proposes that consumption and savings are determined by an individual's position in life. This is evident in Nawi and Hussin (2020) study which reported that an individual's level of financial literacy was found to change significantly with the objective (the income) and the subjective factors (the age and the marital status) during the various stages of individual's life. Additionally, the levels of financial literacy among the participants also depend on their intentions to behave and they will act following their beliefs.

From an Islamic perspective, *Maqasid al-Shariah* represents the core objectives that Islamic law seeks to achieve in order to ensure the well-being of individuals and society. Chapra (2008) has stated five objective goals of *Maqasid al-Shariah* identified by Islamic scholars like Imam al-Ghazali and Imam al-Shatibi. They are the safeguarding faith (*al-Din*), self (*al-Nafs*), intellect (*al-'Aql*), lineage (*al-Nasl*), and wealth (*al-Maal*). These have become the foundation of Islamic rulings as a guide for Muslims toward a balanced, meaningful, and secure way of life. Saladin (2020) added that this also helps to improve quality of life and motivate people to achieve optimal well-being.

According to Ifwat Ishak and Mohammad Nasir (2021), the principles can be directly related to retirement savings. *Maqasid al-Shariah* (objectives of Islamic law) provides a comprehensive framework that guides financial behavior, including personal saving for retirement. This ensures both material well-being and spiritual fulfillment. Güney (2024) emphasized that *Maqasid al-Shariah* (objectives of Islamic law) ensures financial planning is in line with ethical and religious values. This promotes responsible wealth management (*hifz al-maal*), the prohibition of *riba* (interest), and social contributions through *zakat, sadaqah*, and *waqf*. This faith-based approach encourages financial discipline while integrating social responsibility into retirement planning.

This paper integrates both conventional and Islamic perspectives on retirement savings. TPB explains how attitudes and motivation influence saving intentions, while the Life-Cycle Model highlights financial decision-making across life stages. *Maqasid al-Shariah* ensures ethical financial planning, emphasizing responsible wealth management, *riba* avoidance, and social contributions. As income, age, and responsibilities change, so does the approach to saving and spending. By combining these perspectives, this paper provides a well-rounded view of retirement planning. Understanding *Maqasid al-Shariah*, behavior and financial habits over time can help create better support systems, financial education programs, and strategies to help old-age retirees secure their future.

2.2 Philosophy of Saving in Islam

Retirement savings in Islam are grounded by fundamental Sharia principles, which markedly differ from those governing conventional financial systems. These principles emphasize the ethical earning, management, and distribution of wealth, ensuring financial conduct aligns with Islamic moral values. To underscore the significance of selecting an Islamic personal savings scheme, this paper explores key determinants influencing such choices, namely religious obligation, Islamic financial literacy, financial inclusion, and individual motivation.

2.2.1 Religious obligation

Religious obligation refers to duties or responsibilities that individuals are required to fulfill as part of their faith. These obligations are typically prescribed by religious teachings, scriptures, or laws and are considered acts of worship, devotion, or ethical conduct (Asutay, 2012). In Islam, religious obligations (*fard*) are essential acts that Muslims must perform to maintain their spiritual and moral responsibilities. These include *Salah* (daily prayers), *Zakat* (obligatory charity), fasting in Ramadan, *Hajj* (pilgrimage to Mecca), *sadaqah, waqf,* avoiding *riba* (interest) in financial dealings, financial responsibility and debt avoidance and seeking knowledge, both religious and worldly, to make informed and ethical decisions (Naqvi, 2016).

Religious obligations play a crucial role in shaping personal saving for future old-age life to ensure both financial security and spiritual well-being (Mansour and Jlassi, 2014). *Zakat* (obligatory charity) requires Muslims to donate 2.5% of their eligible wealth to the poor, fostering social responsibility and necessitating structured financial management to continue fulfilling this duty in old age (Zailani et. al, 2022). *Sadaqah* (voluntary charity) encourages ongoing generosity, which highlights the importance of disciplined saving habits to sustain charitable giving post-retirement. Similarly, *waqf* (endowment for social benefit) allows individuals to dedicate assets such as property, land, or money to religious or social causes, ensuring their wealth benefits others even after their passing (Maulida, and Ali, 2023). The first *waqf* established by the Prophet was a mosque in Madinah. Early *waqf* were created for the benefit of the public, and over time, their scope expanded to include various fields such as public utilities, education, research, and healthcare (Dusuki and Abdullah, 2007). *Waqf* benefits will be assigned to the beneficiaries. For example, *waqf* allocation can be benefited to the specified group of people (pensioners), humanitarian objective to the public (covid-19 research), or charitable (needy people).

Islam also mandates the avoidance of *riba* (interest). This requires retirement savings to be placed in *shariah*-compliant financial instruments like Islamic savings accounts, *sukuk*, *takaful* (Islamic insurance), and retirement funds that do not involve interest-based transactions (Rusydiana and Ali, 2022). Additionally, Islam promotes financial responsibility and debt avoidance, discouraging wastefulness (*israf*) and financial dependency. This makes a proper personal saving for retirement essential for self-sufficiency and dignity in old age (Kholisha et al., 2020). Incorporating these obligations into saving decision enables individuals to achieve a balance between material stability and religious fulfillment throughout their retirement years.

2.2.2 Islamic Financial Literacy

Islamic financial literacy has been identified as one of the most important determinants of choice, and it is essential when selecting Islamic financial solutions (Widityani et al., 2020). Islamic financial literacy can be described as an individual skill and knowledge that shapes a person's attitude and intention towards Islamic financial services (Khan and Arif, 2022). Customers with a high degree of Islamic financial literacy can differentiate between traditional and Islamic financial products, guaranteeing that their choices are compliant with *Shariah*. Ahmad (2010) and Antara et al. (2016) agreed that a person's financial behavior is expected to be able to differentiate products and services in banking, conventional and *Sharia* financing, Islamic and non-Islamic capital markets, as well as conventional and *Sharia* insurance products.

Furthermore, a high Islamic financial literacy will boost trust in Islamic financial institutions, lowers financial risk, and boost confidence while making financial decisions. Greater awareness also encourages responsible financial behavior, including *Shariah-compliant* savings and investment practices. Previous research supports that a high level of Islamic financial literacy leads to higher Islamic financial product-holding practices. Albaity and Rahman (2019) discovered that Islamic financial literacy significantly influences the propensity to adopt Islamic banking in the United Arab Emirates.

Islamic financial literacy is crucial for economic empowerment in Muslim-majority nations because it empowers people to make more informed financial decisions. Md Husin and Ab Rahman (2013) found a significant relationship between financial literacy and Takaful participation. Widityani et al. (2020) reported that Islamic financial literacy significantly predicted the probability of holding Islamic financial products in Indonesia. Hence, increasing Islamic financial literacy is essential for financial inclusion and long-term economic prosperity, given the Islamic financial sector's explosive global expansion.

2.2.3 Financial Inclusion

Financial inclusion refers to individuals and businesses which have access to and utilize financial services such as banking, credit, insurance, and pensions (Demirguc-Kunt et al., 2018). This accessibility enables individuals to manage their finances effectively, accumulate savings, invest in education and healthcare, expand businesses, and secure their retirement. Financial inclusion is widely recognized as a key driver of economic growth and poverty reduction. This ensures that all segments of society, especially the underserved and low-income populations, can participate in and benefit from financial opportunities.

In Malaysia, Bank Negara Malaysia (BNM) defines financial inclusion as ensuring the availability of suitable, affordable, and high-quality financial services for all levels of society. BNM highlights that financial inclusion contributes to balanced and sustainable economic growth, particularly by providing access to essential financial services for low-income groups and marginalized communities (Bank Negara Malaysia, 2022). To strengthen financial inclusion, Malaysia has developed a comprehensive Islamic financial ecosystem. *Shariah-compliant* alternatives have been introduced through institutions such as Islamic banks, Takaful operators, and Islamic investment firms.

Islam places a strong emphasis on financial inclusion, but its approach differs from the conventional financial model through two key principles; risk-sharing and wealth distribution. Islamic finance promotes equity-based financing such as *Mudharabah* (profit-sharing) and *Musharakah* (joint partnership), ensuring that risks and returns are fairly distributed between financial institutions and individuals (Kalifah et al., 2024). For wealth redistribution, Islamic financial systems incorporate social finance instruments such as *Zakat* (mandatory almsgiving), *Sadaqah* (voluntary charity), and *Waqf* (Islamic endowment) to support financial inclusion and economic equity. Consequently, this ensures that wealth is not concentrated among the elite but is circulated to benefit society (Hassan and Aliyu, 2018).

Malaysia's Islamic retirement planning landscape reflects its commitment to financial inclusion by ensuring that Muslims have access to ethical savings and investment options for old age security. Nayan and Othman (2019) stated that Employees Provident Fund (EPF) *Shariah-Compliant* Option was launched in August 2016. It offers contributors a fully *Shariah-compliant* retirement savings plan. The fund provides *Halal* investment options for and avoiding investments in sectors involving *Riba* (interest), *Gharar* (uncertainty), and *Haram* (prohibited activities). The EPF *Shariah* fund is managed by a *Shariah* Advisory Council, ensuring that investments align with Islamic ethical values (BNM, 2022).

Besides the EPF, Islamic takaful operators also offer retirement savings and investment-linked Takaful products that help individuals secure their financial future while complying with *Shariah* guidelines. For instance, they provide *Takaful Hibah* (Islamic inheritance planning), allowing individuals to distribute retirement savings to their heirs without legal complications. On top of that, Islamic social finance instruments such as *Zakat* and *Waqf* play an essential role in ensuring financial inclusion for retirees, particularly those without sufficient retirement savings. Zakat Institutions in Malaysia allocate funds to assist elderly individuals from low-income backgrounds, ensuring they receive basic financial support.

2.2.4 Motivation

The responsibility to care for one's family and ensure financial security serves as a strong motivation for retirement savings. The need to maintain dignity, achieve financial independence, and provide for loved ones encourages individuals to plan and build a stable future. It is important to acknowledge how individuals perceive retirement to encourage both higher savings and a stronger motivation to save. According to Othman et al. (2024), there were studies which found that older individuals tend to have clearer retirement goals compared to younger ones. In Islamic society, family support has traditionally played a crucial role, with parents relying on their children for both financial and emotional care in their later years. However, as societies evolve with urbanization, smaller family units, longer life expectancy, and increasing living costs, more people are motivated to secure their own financial independence rather than depending entirely on family. Islam strongly encourages self-sufficiency, as reflected in the *Hadith* where the Prophet Muhammad (PBUH) emphasized that it is better for a person to work and provide for themselves than to rely on others. This principle underscores the importance of planning for retirement, allowing individuals to maintain their dignity and avoid becoming a financial burden on their children or extended family.

Additionally, the act of saving for many individuals does not only for their own retirement but also to secure the financial well-being of their spouses, children, and even aging parents. Individuals with a strong future time perspective are more likely to prioritize retirement planning, set financial goals, and actively save for the future (Rabinovich et al., 2010). This is particularly relevant in Islamic teachings, which stress the importance of caring for one's family and leaving behind a financial legacy. Parents are motivated to accumulate savings to support their children's education, marriage, and future needs. This is to minimize or avoid any financial struggles that might appear later. This sense of responsibility as a form of motivation to provide for their families and ease their burdens are rooted in Islamic values.

2.2.5 Perceived Risk

Perceived Risk plays a significant role in the larger context of intention to save. According to Hati et al. (2021) perceived risk is defined as the potential for negative consequences from using a product or service. Income is seen as a gift from Allah, so it should be managed with care and responsibility. Islam does not support keeping too much wealth without purpose, but it encourages saving for future needs and financial protection. This includes having emergency savings to help with unexpected problems like sickness, losing a job, or other urgent expenses. This follows the Islamic idea that people should prepare for the future while also trusting in Allah.

At the same time, Islam warns against being too focused on collecting wealth. There should be a balance between saving for security and avoiding pride, greed, or wasting money. In the context of banking, financial risk is a main focus for consumers because the core products are financial. However, perceived risk not only encompass financial loss, it also including discrepancies from expected utility, physical damage, unhappiness, and negative social image. Perceived financial risk can be measured using items related to the chance of something going wrong or the chance of losing money. High perceived risk decreases saving intention (Mahdzan et al., 2024)

Early research suggests that the intention to save is generally greater in individuals who are more risk-tolerant. However, one study focusing on withdrawal intention from Sharia mutual funds found no significant contribution of financial risk tolerance to this intention, a result consistent with other findings suggesting risk tolerance has less contribution in determining saving intention (Widyastuti et al., 2022). Religious individuals are noted as being somewhat more risk-averse.

2.2.6 Past Behavior.

Islamic financial principles also play a significant role in shaping individual saving behavior. Teachings in Islam emphasize responsible financial management, including the timely repayment of debts, avoidance of interest-based transactions, and careful planning of financial matters. Borrowing is only encouraged when truly necessary, and restraint in spending is promoted. These values are often reinforced through family and community influence, contributing to habit formation and long-term financial discipline (Nugraheni & Widyani, 2021). Practical advice such as limiting credit card use and preferring debit transactions reflects a broader cultural expectation of financial prudence. Furthermore, Islamic estate planning (Faraid) provides a structured approach to wealth distribution, which not only ensures justice but may also influence saving behavior with a long-term perspective on financial responsibility and legacy.

These teachings align with the behavioral mechanisms that are influenced by past saving experiences and social recommendations. These recommendations are impactful because they are often based on the parents' own knowledge and experience in saving and shape an individual's current intention. Ahmad et al. (2023) studies whether individuals have engaged in prior Islamic formal savings as a variable influencing their subsequent behavior. They found and highlights that past saving experience can modulate the impact of interventions designed to encourage further saving. Habit formation also a potential behavioral mechanism that could explain the long-run effects of temporary savings subsidies on increasing savings. Habits are patterns of behavior established through repetition in the past, implying that past saving frequency could influence future saving behavior through this mechanism.

The emphasis on moderation, responsibility, and ethical conduct in Islam serves not only as a moral guide but also as a behavioral framework that encourages consistent saving practices. Religious values, therefore, may strengthen the formation of positive financial habits over time, supporting individuals in their efforts to maintain regular saving behavior.

3.0 DISCUSSION

3.1 Role of *Maqasid al-Shariah* in Personal Saving for Retirement

Chapra (2008) stated that one of the objectives of *Maqasid al-Shariah* is the protection and responsible management of wealth (*hifz al-maal*). This plays a significant role in encouraging personal saving for retirement. In Islam, wealth is seen as a trust (*amanah*) from Allah that must be managed responsibly. Implementing this principle in retirement planning begins with the intention (*niyyah*) to save not just for personal comfort, but to avoid becoming a burden on others and to maintain dignity in old age. According to Zailani et. al, (2022), personal saving for retirement ensures financial independence in old age, reducing dependency on others and securing a dignified life in accordance with Islamic principles. Starting early and budgeting wisely helps prevent extravagance (*israf*), which is strongly discouraged in the Qur'an. According to the Quranic guidance: *"Do not spend wastefully. Verily, the spendthrifts are brothers of the devils."* (*Surah Al-Isra*, 17:26-27). This role of Maqasid al-Shariah is aligned with saving for retirement to ensure financial stability in old age, reducing dependence on others and preventing financial hardship. Saladin

(2020) emphasized that wealth management (*hifz al-maal*) encourages responsible financial management, ethical investment, and structured personal saving.

Islamic financial planning prohibits *riba*, uncertainty (*gharar*), and unethical investments (Kholisha et al., 2020). Muslims retirement savings should be placed in *shariah*-compliant financial products, such as Islamic savings accounts, Islamic unit trusts, *takaful* (Islamic insurance), and *shariah*-compliant retirement funds (*Tabung Haji*, *EPF-i*, or *Sukuk* investments). This ensures that savings or their wealths grow in a permissible and ethical manner which avoiding *riba* (interest), *gharar* (uncertainty) and unethical sectors (Che Mohd Salleh, 2023).

The second objective of *Maqasid al-Shariah* is known as preservation of faith (Hifz al-Din). While saving for retirement is crucial, *Maqasid al-Shariah* also emphasizes social responsibility. Rahman et al., (2024) described that participating in takaful schemes promotes mutual protection and aligns with the Islamic value of cooperation (*ta'awun*). Responsible retirement planning also includes preparing for the distribution of wealth through *hibah* (gifts), *waqf* (endowment), or a proper Islamic will (*wasiat*), ensuring wealth continues to benefit others after one's death (Mahmud et. al, 2021). It is equally important to minimize debt in retirement, as Islam strongly discourages debt unless necessary. Avoiding debt in old age is essential, as consistent saving throughout one's working life helps reduce the need for loans or borrowing during retirement. Islam strongly discourages unnecessary debt, as it can lead to stress, dependence, and potential injustice (Hossain et. al, 2024). The Prophet Muhammad frequently sought refuge in his *du'a* from the burden of debt, highlighting its serious spiritual and social consequences (Salik, 2024). By planning ahead and saving responsibly, Muslim retirees can maintain financial independence and uphold the Islamic principle of living within one's means.

Additionally, Islam requires one's to pay *zakat* (mandatory charity) on savings and investments as it purifies wealth and supports the community, while *sadaqah* (voluntary charity) ensures that wealth is used for good and *waqf* (endowment) to support those in need (Hamzah, 2024). Altogether, saving for retirement in this manner not only secures one's financial future but also fulfills the higher goals of *Shariah*. This makes it both a practical and spiritually rewarding act (Shahariman et al., 2024). Muslim retirees who have sufficient retirement savings allows them to continue fulfilling religious obligations, not only *zakat*, charity (*sadaqah*), but even performing Hajj or Umrah if financially able (Saladin, 2020). This preservation of faith (Hifz al-Din) prevents situations where financial desperation could lead to actions that contradict Islamic values, such as borrowing with interest or engaging in unethical work. This ensures wealth circulation and helps retirees maintain spiritual well-being while securing their financial future (Habibullah et al., 2023).

The third objective of *Maqasid al-Shariah* is preservation of life (*Hifz al-Nafs*). This can be practically implemented in saving for retirement. This is to ensure that a Muslim retiree has sufficient savings to meet basic needs such as food, shelter, and healthcare during old age. As the physical ability to work decreases with age, having financial security becomes crucial to maintain one's health, independence, and overall well-being (Asari, 2024). Islam emphasizes the importance of protecting human dignity, and part of that dignity lies in being able to live comfortably and respectfully without dependence on others. By saving consistently during their working years, Muslim retirees can plan for future medical expenses, daily living costs, and emergencies, thus upholding the quality of life in their future retirement years (Mahmud et al., 2021). This proactive approach does not only reflect responsible financial behavior but also supports the Islamic principle that every individual deserves to live with dignity, safety, and peace of mind, regardless of age (Ali et al., 2024). Moreover, savings for retirement prevents situations where one might be forced to beg, borrow, or fall into desperation, which Islam seeks to avoid in order to preserve a person's honor and integrity (Hossain et al., 2024).

The fourth objective of *Maqasid al-Shariah* is preservation of lineage (*Hifz al-Nasl*). This focuses on protecting the family structure and ensuring the well-being of future generations. In the context of retirement saving, this objective can be implemented by planning ahead to ensure financially independent in old age to avoid burdening children and grandchildren. It also allows for proper planning of intergenerational wealth transfer through *hibah*, *waqf*, or Islamic inheritance (*faraid*) as mentioned by Mahmud et al., 2021). Early savings for retirement protect Muslim family harmony, supports future generations, and ensures a fair wealth distribution in accordance to *Shariah*.

Last but not least is the role of preserving intellect (Hifz al-Aql). This is related to future old-age life of retirees for a stable and stress-free life in old age. Without adequate personal savings, individuals may experience financial difficulties, leading to anxiety, depression, and cognitive decline due to ongoing concerns about basic needs (Guan et al., 2022). Zailani et al. (2022) added that a well-planned retirement enables individuals to focus on personal growth, fulfill religious duties, and contribute to society without financial burdens. It also fosters financial literacy and responsible money management from a young age, promoting informed decisions based on Islamic principles. Chopra emphasized the need for practicing ethical spending, and ensuring long-term financial stability. By embracing these values, retirees can maintain mental well-being while upholding Islamic financial ethics.

In Islam, preparing for retirement through personal saving is not merely a practical step but a way to fulfill the objectives of *Shariah*. It upholds an individual's dignity, prevents financial hardship, supports independence in old age, and demonstrates responsible management of wealth as a trust from Allah.

4.0 PROPOSED CONCEPTUAL FRAMEWORK OF PERSONAL SAVING FOR RETIREMENT FROM AN ISLAMIC PERSPECTIVE

This conceptual paper proposes a framework to examine the determinants influencing Muslim retirees' decisions to engage in Islamic personal retirement savings. It focuses on six independent variables include religious obligation (Mansour and Jlassi, 2014), Islamic financial literacy (Albaity and Rahman, 2019; Md Husin and Ab Rahman, 2013), motivation (Othman et al., 2024; Rabinovich et al., 2010), financial inclusion (Hassan & Aliyu, 2018), perceived risk (Mahdzan et al., 2024), and past financial behavior (Nugraheni & Widyani, 2021). These variables are posited to directly influence the dependent variable, which is the intention or behavior towards Islamic personal retirement saving. By looking at these factors together, the framework aims to offer a clearer understanding of why and how individuals make retirement-saving decisions within the context of Islamic finance.

Crucially, this proposed framework is supported by previous scholar that highlights the role of Maqasid al-Shariah in guiding solution within Islamic finance which act as moderating variable that influences the strength and direction of the relationship between the identified determinants and personal retirement saving behavior. Dusuki and Bouheraoua (2011) emphasize that applying the principles of *Maqasid al-Shariah* or the higher objectives of Islamic law such as the safeguarding faith (*al-Din*), self (*al-Nafs*), intellect (*al-'Aql*), lineage (*al-Nasl*), and protection of wealth (*al-Maal*) will be serving as guiding principles which strengthen the purpose to financial decisions of Muslim retirees especially in the context of personal saving for retirement.

Similarly, other scholar have emphasized the important role of *Maqasid al-Shariah* in today's financial landscape by explaining its main principles, the study shows how Islamic ethical values can be connected with modern wealth management practices (Tarique et al., 2021). It highlights how *Maqasid al-Shariah* is not just a theoretical concept, but can be practically applied to promote more responsible, ethical, and socially conscious financial behavior. This supports the proposed framework by showing how *Maqasid al-Shariah* can strengthen personal retirement saving decisions for Muslim retirees in a meaningful and financially sound (Mahmud et al., 2021).

Figure 1. Proposed conceptual framework of personal saving for retirement from an Islamic perspective.

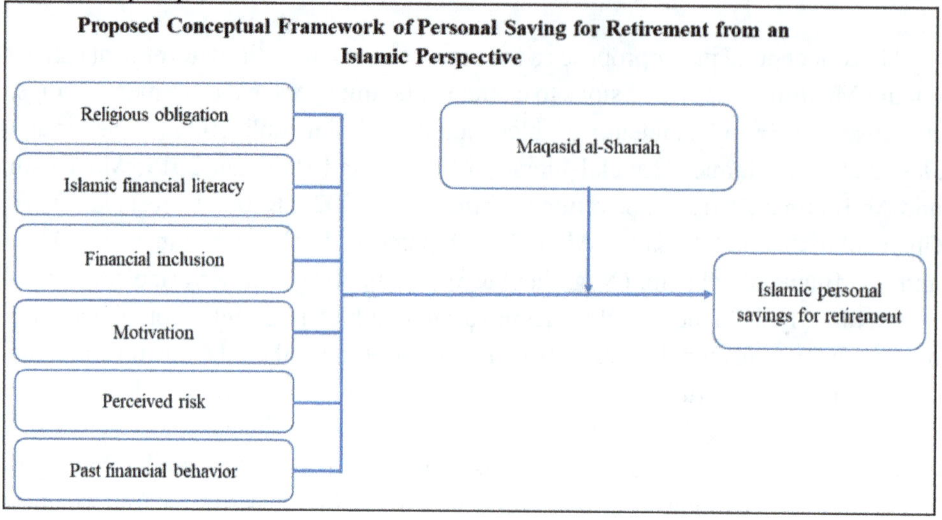

5.0 CONCLUSION

To conclude, personal saving for retirement is essential for financial stability and independence in old age, especially within an Islamic framework that emphasizes ethical financial management and spiritual well-being. This paper has explored key determinants influencing the choice of Islamic personal saving for retirement, including religious obligations (zakat, sadaqah, and waqf), Islamic financial literacy, motivation, and financial inclusion. The role of *Maqasid al-Shariah* guided by the five objectives of *Maqasid al-Shariah*; preservation of faith (*al-Din*), safeguards life (al-*Nafs*), supports the mind (*al-'Aql*) and preserves lineage (*al-Nasl*) and ensures wealth *(al-Maal*) further reinforces the importance of responsible saving behavior. By incorporating Islamic teachings into financial planning, individuals can cultivate disciplined personal saving habits to ensure financial security in the future and also contribute to social welfare and economic sustainability.

6.0 RECOMMENDATION

It is recommended that in order to enhance Islamic personal saving for retirement, appropriate measures and initiatives be undertaken, recognizing the crucial importance of this issue in ensuring long-term financial security in accordance with Islamic values. To begin with, financial literacy programs should integrate Islamic perspectives, educating individuals on *zakat, sadaqah, waqf,* and *shariah*-compliant financial products. The Islamic financial literacy programs should be designed to incorporate core principles of Islamic wealth management, highlighting the importance of retirement planning from a faith-based perspective. These programs should bring values such as *amanah* (trust), *mas'uliyyah* (accountability), and *tawakkul* reliance on Allah coupled with personal effort and taking necessary actions. Key topics should cover the role of *zakat* and *sadaqah* in wealth purification and social duty, the potential of *waqf* as a long-term charitable mechanism for retirement support, and the use of Shariah-compliant financial tools like *takaful* (Islamic insurance), *mudharabah* (profit-sharing), and *sukuk* (Islamic bonds). To enhance reach and impact, especially among rural and underserved populations, delivery methods such as interactive workshops, digital learning platforms, and mosque-based sessions should be utilized.

Secondly, it is crucial for financial institutions to design and offer accessible and inclusive Islamic savings plans that cater to the diverse financial capacities of the population. These plans should be affordable, transparent, and flexible, allowing individuals from various socio-economic backgrounds especially those with lower incomes to participate meaningfully in long-term financial planning. Accessibility also involves simplifying the processes for opening accounts, making contributions, and understanding the financial products offered, all within the framework of Shariah compliance.

The successful adoption of such plans can be achieved through strategic collaboration between government agencies, Islamic financial institutions, and religious organizations is essential. Government agencies can provide policy support, regulatory frameworks, and incentives for example financial institutions can develop and manage innovative, Shariah-compliant financial products. Meanwhile, religious organizations can help promote awareness and trust among the Muslim community through faith-based advocacy and education. Such collaboration ensures that retirement planning is not only financially sound but also spiritually meaningful.

Furthermore, efforts must be made to expand the reach of Islamic banking and financial services, particularly in under served and rural communities, where access remains limited. This can be achieved through digital banking solutions, mobile banking units, and partnerships with local community centers and mosques. By doing so, financial institutions can help bridge the gap in financial inclusion, ensuring that all segments of society regardless of location or income level have the opportunity to participate in ethical, faith-aligned retirement savings schemes. Ultimately, these initiatives will contribute to a more equitable financial system and enhance the overall well-being of the Muslim population.

Lastly, aligning savings policies with Maqasid al-Shariah, the higher objectives of Islamic law, serves as a fundamental approach to ensure that financial planning and retirement savings function effectively and promote ethical, equitable, and sustainable financial practices that benefit both individuals and society.

Further research can highlight the impact of *Maqasid al-Shariah* on long term financial stability. An investigation on how aligning savings policies with *Maqasid al-Shariah* could contribute to sustainable financial well-being is highly proposed. This could provide deeper insights into improving Islamic personal savings framework and fostering security for old-age retirees in accordance with Islamic principles.

An in-depth investigation could explore how financial decisions influenced by *Maqasid al-Shariah* principles promote responsible, balanced, and sustainable wealth accumulation which avoiding excess (*israf*), encouraging moderation (*wasatiyyah*), and fulfilling obligations such as zakat and family support. These principles can serve as a moral compass that strengthens discipline in saving and investment decisions, especially in the preparation for retirement when income typically declines.

Ultimately, this research direction has the potential to offer comprehensive models or frameworks that are both faith-compliant and practically beneficial for Muslims planning for retirement. It can guide policymakers, financial institutions, and individuals in designing systems that promote ethical, inclusive, and sustainable financial well-being rooted in Islamic values.

Note

Hafizah Mat Nawi was the corresponding author for this chapter.

REFERENCES

Abdullah, J. M., Ismail, A., & Yusoff, M. S. B. (2024). Healthy ageing in Malaysia by 2030: Needs, challenges and future directions. *The Malaysian Journal of Medical Sciences : MJMS, 31*(4), 1–13. DOI: 10.21315/mjms2024.31.4.1

Ahmad, M. (2010). Why Islamic Financial Literacy Is Important. Personal Finance, 46.

Ahmad, S., Lensink, R., & Mueller, A. (2023). Uptake, use, and impact of Islamic savings: Evidence from a field experiment in Pakistan. *Journal of Development Economics, 163*, 103098. DOI: 10.1016/j.jdeveco.2023.103098

Ajzen, I. (1985). *From intentions to actions: A theory of planned behavior*. Springer.

Albaity, M., & Rahman, M. (2019). The intention to use Islamic banking: An exploratory study to measure Islamic financial literacy. *International Journal of Emerging Markets, 14*(5), 988–1012. DOI: 10.1108/IJOEM-05-2018-0218

Ali, Z., Anjum, G. M., Iqbal, J., & Ahmad, I. (2024). The Role of Islamic Values in Promoting Social Justice and Community Welfare. *International Research Journal of Management and Social Sciences, 5*(1), 575–585.

Antara, P. M., Musa, R., & Hassan, F. (2016). Bridging Islamic Financial Literacy and Halal Literacy: The Way Forward in Halal Ecosystem. *Procedia Economics and Finance*, 37, 5671(16)30113-7.

Asari, N. A. M. (2024). Empowering Individuals: Islamic Education And Personal Financial Planning. *Available at SSRN,* 4854923. DOI: 10.2139/ssrn.4854923

Asutay, M. (2012). Conceptualising and locating the social failure of islamic finance: Aspirations of islamic moral economy vs. the realities of islamic finance. *Asian and African Area Studies, 11*(2), 93–113.

Azhar, N., & Omar, A. (2025). Aging workforce in Malaysia: Navigating challenges and shaping policies. *Quantum Journal of Social Sciences and Humanities, 6*(2), 226–236. DOI: 10.55197/qjssh.v6i2.615

Bank Negara Malaysia. (2022). *Financial Sector Blueprint 2022–2026*. Bank Negara Malaysia.

Batizani, D. (2024). Navigating retirement: Emerging and challenging smart financial strategies for the aging adults. *International Journal of Entrepreneurial Knowledge, 12*(1), 70–85. DOI: 10.37335/ijek.v12i1.215

Burhanudin, B. (2022). The effect of Muslims' tendency to regret being customers of conventional banks on their intention to save money in Islamic banks. *Journal of Islamic Marketing, 13*(5), 1050–1068. DOI: 10.1108/JIMA-03-2020-0074

Candra Sari, R., Rika Fatimah, P. L., Ilyana, S., & Dwi Hermawan, H. (2022). Augmented reality (AR)-based sharia financial literacy system (AR-SFLS): A new approach to virtual sharia financial socialization for young learners. *International Journal of Islamic and Middle Eastern Finance and Management, 15*(1), 48–65. DOI: 10.1108/IMEFM-11-2019-0484

Capital Markets and Services Act 2007 (CMSA) (Act 671).

Chapra, M. U. (2008). The Islamic vision of development in the light of the Maqasid al-Shari'ah (Research Paper), *Occasional Papers 235*, The Islamic Research and Teaching Institute (IRTI).

Che Mohd Salleh, M., Abdullah, N. I., Chowdhury, M. A. M., Che Embi, N. A., & Kassim, S. (2023). Viability of Islamic Health Protection Retirement Plan (i-HPRP) Among Malaysian Public and Private Employees. *ISRA International Journal of Islamic Finance, 15*(1), 73–90. DOI: 10.55188/ijif.v15i1.486

Chowdhury, M. A. M. (2021). *Islamic health protection retirement plan for Malaysian employees:an investigation from a behavioural approach.* International Islamic University Malaysia.

Demirguc-Kunt, A., Klapper, L., Singer, D., Ansar, S., & Hess, J. (2018). *The Global Findex Database 2017: Measuring financial inclusion and the fintech revolution.* The World Bank. DOI: 10.1596/978-1-4648-1259-0

Dusuki, A. W., & Abdullah, N. I. (2007). Maqasid al-Shariah, maslahah, and corporate social responsibility. *The American Journal of Islamic Social Sciences, 24*(1), 25–45. DOI: 10.35632/ajiss.v24i1.415

Dusuki, A. W., & Bouheraoua, S. (2011). The framework of Maqasid al-Shari'ah and its implication for Islamic finance. *ICR Journal, 2*(2), 316–336. DOI: 10.52282/icr.v2i2.651

EPF. (2024). EPF Releases Belanjawanku 2024/2025 And Retirement Income Adequacy Framework. Editorial and Media Relations Unit, Corporate Affairs Department. https://www.kwsp.gov.my/en/w/epf-releases-belanjawanku-2024/2025-and-retirement-income-adequacy-framework

Financial Planning Association of Malaysia & Islamic Banking and Finance Malaysia. (2009). Islamic Financial Planning: A Brief Introduction. Kuala Lumpur: Financial Planning Association of Malaysia (FPAM)

Guan, N., Guariglia, A., Moore, P., Xu, F., & Al-Janabi, H. (2022). Financial stress and depression in adults: A systematic review. *PLoS One*, *17*(2), e0264041. DOI: 10.1371/journal.pone.0264041

Güney, N. (2024). Maqāsid al-Sharī'a in islamic finance: A critical analysis of modern discourses. *Religions*, *15*(1), 114. DOI: 10.3390/rel15010114

Habibullah, M., & Abdullah Al Faruque, M. (2023). Islamic economic framework for the exercise of Islamic financial activities: Its conformity with Maqasid Shari'ah. *Al-Burhān: Journal Of Qur Ān And Sunnah Studies*, *7*(1), 81–92. DOI: 10.31436/alburhn.v7i1.300

Hamzah, M. (2024). The role and legal aspects of infaq, sadaqah, and waqf in realizing economic equality and people's welfare. *Al-Iqtishadiyah: Ekonomi Syariah dan Hukum Ekonomi Syariah*, 10(1), 107-124.

Hati, S. R. H., Putri, N. I. S., Daryanti, S., Wibowo, S. S., Safira, A., & Setyowardhani, H. (2022). Brand familiarity vs profit-sharing rate: Which has a stronger impact on Muslim customers' intention to invest in an Islamic bank? *Journal of Islamic Marketing*, *13*(8), 1703–1727. DOI: 10.1108/JIMA-08-2020-0247

Hati, S. R. H., Wibowo, S. S., & Safira, A. (2021). The antecedents of Muslim customers' intention to invest in an Islamic bank's term deposits: Evidence from a Muslim majority country. *Journal of Islamic Marketing*, *12*(7), 1363–1384. DOI: 10.1108/JIMA-01-2020-0007

Hossain, B., Hossain, A., Hossain, G. M. S., & Likhon, T. S. (2024). Islamic perspective of household debt management: An in-depth study. *International Journal of Science and Business*, *31*(1), 103–114. DOI: 10.58970/IJSB.2279

Ifwat Ishak, M. S., & Mohammad Nasir, N. S. (2021). Maqasid al-Shari'ah in Islamic finance: Harmonizing theory and reality. *The Journal Of Muamalat And Islamic Finance Research*, *18*(1), 108–119. DOI: 10.33102/jmifr.v18i1.334

Johari, A. H., Zai, F. H., Hussain, L., & Ali, M. M. (2014). Exploring a Shari'ah-compliant model for retirement annuity plans' *I-FIKR*. Available at: https://ifikr.isra.my/library/pub/4912/exploring-a-shariah-compliant-model-for-retirement-annuity-plans (accessed 8 September 2022).

Kalifah, M. H., Aslan, H., & Abdullah, A. B. (2024). Challenges in the implementation of Mudharabah financing in the Islamic banking industry. *Equinox Journal of Economics, Business & Political Studies*, 11(1), 01-23.

Kasmon, B., Ibrahim, S. S., Daud, D., Raja Hisham, R. R. I., & Dian Wisika Prajanti, S. (2025). FinTech application in Islamic social finance in Asia region: A systematic literature review. *International Journal of Ethics and Systems*, *41*(1), 213–237. DOI: 10.1108/IJOES-07-2023-0155

Khan, L., & Arif, I. (2022). Islamic financial literacy and intention to use Islamic banking: A role of financial considerations. *Journal of Finance and Economics Research*, *7*(1), 47–59. DOI: 10.20547/jfer2207104

Kholisha, N., Purwantob, M. R., Muhammad, S., Mukharromd, T., & Marazi, H. (2020). The significance of Maqasid Syariah principles in improving Islamic economics and finance. *International Journal of Innovation, Creativity and Change*, 13(3).

Krishnaveni, V., Jusoh, Z. M., Othman, M. A., & Zainudin, N. (2024). Financial security in retirement: The importance of savings vs earnings in Malaysia. *International Journal of Academic Research in Business & Social Sciences*, *14*(10), 1671–1683. DOI: 10.6007/IJARBSS/v14-i10/23273

Lee, K. C. (1997). The Malaysian government pension scheme. Whither its future direction? *Jurnal Ekonomi Malaysia*, *31*, 87–106.

Mahdzan, N. S., Zainudin, R., Ahmad, W. M. W., & Hanifa, M. H. (2024). Does Islamic financial literacy and motives influence the holdings of Islamic financial products? a study on bank customers in Klang Valley, Malaysia. *Journal of Islamic Marketing*, *15*(9), 2286–2309. DOI: 10.1108/JIMA-05-2022-0158

Mahdzan, N. S., Zainudin, R., Wan Ahmad, W. M., & Hanifa, M. H. (2024). Does Islamic financial literacy and motives influence the holdings of Islamic financial products? A study on bank customers in Klang Valley, Malaysia. *Journal of Islamic Marketing*, *15*(9), 2286–2309. DOI: 10.1108/JIMA-05-2022-0158

Mahmud, M. S., Foziah, N. H. M., Abdul Kareem, I. A., Jamal, A., & Nasir, M. (2021). Retirement planning in perspective of Islamic wealth management. *Journal of Islamic Banking & Finance*, *38*(1).

Mansour, W., & Jlassi, M. (2014). The effect of religion on financial and investing decisions investor behavior. *The Psychology Of Financial Planning And Investing*, 135-151.

Masrizal, S., Sukmana, R., & Trianto, B. (2025). The effect of Islamic financial literacy on business performance with emphasis on the role of Islamic financial inclusion: Case study in Indonesia. *Journal of Islamic Marketing*, *16*(1), 166–192. DOI: 10.1108/JIMA-07-2022-0197

Maulida, S., & Ali, M. M. (2023). Maqasid shariah index: A literature review. *Maqasid al-Shariah Review*, 2(1).

Md Husin, M., & Ab Rahman, A. (2013). What drives consumers to participate into family Takaful schemes? A literature review. *Journal of Islamic Marketing*, *4*(3), 264–280. DOI: 10.1108/JIMA-04-2012-0019

Mohd Ali, A.N., Yeon, A.L., & Hussain, M.A. (2016), Private retirement scheme in Malaysia: Legal analysis. *International Journal of Economics and Financial Issues,* 6(7) Special Issue, 290–295.

Muflih, M., Iswanto, B., & Purbayati, R. (2024). Green loyalty of Islamic banking customers: Combined effect of green practices, green trust, green perceived value, and green satisfaction. *International Journal of Ethics and Systems*, *40*(3), 477–494. DOI: 10.1108/IJOES-03-2023-0062

Nawi, H. M., & Hussin, H. S. (2020). A good cop is never cold or hungry: Antecedents and consequences of financial literacy among members of the royal Malaysia police, International *Journal of Academic Research in Accounting. Finance and Management Sciences*, *10*(1), 270–289.

Nayan, M.A., and Othman, Y.H. (2019). The Important of Islamic Retirement Planning in Malaysia. Unishams-INTERNATIONAL CONFERENCE 2019/ E-PROCEEDINGS

Nugraheni, P., & Widyani, F. N. (2021). A study of intention to save in Islamic banks: The perspective of Muslim students. *Journal of Islamic Marketing*, *12*(8), 1446–1460. DOI: 10.1108/JIMA-11-2019-0233

Osman, I., Syed Alwi, S. F., Rehman, M. A., Muda, R., Hassan, F., Hassan, R., & Abdullah, H. (2024). The dilemma of millennial Muslims towards financial management: An Islamic financial literacy perspective. *Journal of Islamic Marketing*, *15*(1), 59–78. DOI: 10.1108/JIMA-09-2021-0283

Othman, M. N. A., Rashid, M. A. A., Maura, A. A., & Seman, S. A. (2024). Factors influencing the retirement planning among private sector workers in Malaysia. *Journal of Ecohumanism*, *3*(7), 1141–1153I. DOI: 10.62754/joe.v3i7.4283

Penrose, E. T. (1952). Biological analogies in the theory of the firm. *The American Economic Review*, *42*(5), 804–819.

Private Pension Administrator Malaysia. (2025, June 14). *PPA.my*. https://www.ppa.my

Rabinovich, A., Morton, T., & Postmes, T. (2010). Time perspective and attitude-behaviour consistency in future-oriented behaviors. *British Journal of Social Psychology*, *49*(1), 69–89. DOI: 10.1348/014466608X401875

Rahman, M. H., Abdullah, M. F., Osmani, N. M., & Aziz, N. S. Z. (2024). Application of tàawun (mutual assistance) in cross-subsidisation of surplus among different takaful operators: An exploratory study in Malaysia. *International Journal of Islamic and Middle Eastern Finance and Management*, *17*(6), 1136–1154. DOI: 10.1108/IMEFM-12-2023-0479

Rusydiana, A. S., & Ali, M. M. (2022). The application of Maqasid Shariah on banking industry. *Maqasid al-Shariah Review*, 1(1).

Saladin, M., Azmil, M., & Ali, S. M. (2020). Well-being of the society: A Maqasid Shariah approach. *Afkar*, *1*(Special Issue), 25–46.

Salik, I. (2024). *The Islamic Guide to Depression: 10 Spiritual Reflections*. Goodly Word Books.

Sen, S., Antara, N., & Sen, S. (2020). The determinants of opening account with Islamic banks. *Journal of Islamic Marketing*, *12*(9), 1709–1733. DOI: 10.1108/JIMA-04-2020-0110

Shah, N. A. M. A., Nasrul, M. A. D., Rahman, S. F. A., & Seviyana, D. (2023). Comparative analysis of Malaysian and Indonesian retirement plan. *Lex Scientia Law Review*, *7*(2), 659–708. DOI: 10.15294/lesrev.v7i2.69847

Shahariman, A. A. B., Asari, N. A. M. B., Sulaiman, N. A. A. B., & Marzuki, N. A. A. B. (2024). Islamic principles and their application in personal financial decision making. *Accessed*, (Dec), 15.

She, L., Rasiah, R., Weissmann, M.A. & Kaur, H. (2023). Using the theory of planned behaviour to explore predictors of financial behaviour among working adults in Malaysia. *FIIB Business Review*, 1–18

Shirazi, N. S., Kuanova, L. A., Ryskulov, A., & Mukusheva, A. G. (2022). The experience and the prospects of Islamic finance in Kazakhstan. *Qualitative Research in Financial Markets*, *14*(3), 461–482. DOI: 10.1108/QRFM-03-2020-0023

Tarique, K. M., Islam, R., & Mohammed, M. O. (2021). Developing and validating the components of Maqasid al-Shari'ah-based performance measurement model for Islamic banks. *International Journal of Islamic and Middle Eastern Finance and Management*, *14*(2), 366–390. DOI: 10.1108/IMEFM-12-2018-0432

Widityani, S. F., Faturohman, T., Rahadi, R. A., & Yulianti, Y. (2020). Do socio-demographic characteristics and financial literacy matter for selecting Islamic financial products? *Journal of Islamic Monetary Economics and Finance*, *6*(1), 51–76. DOI: 10.21098/jimf.v6i1.1057

Widyastuti, U., Febrian, E., Sutisna, S., & Fitrijanti, T. (2022). Market discipline in the behavioral finance perspective: A case of Sharia mutual funds in Indonesia. *Journal of Islamic Accounting and Business Research*, *13*(1), 114–140. DOI: 10.1108/JIABR-06-2020-0194

Wijaya, I. F., Hakim, A. R., Saputro, N., & Mulyadi, M. (2019). Religiosity level and saving decisions in Baitul Maal wat Tamwil: The case of Indonesia. *Journal of Islamic Marketing*, *11*(6), 1465–1483. DOI: 10.1108/JIMA-09-2018-0160

Zailani, M. N., Mohd Satar, N., & Zakaria, R. H. (2022). A Review of indicators for the preservation of wealth (hifz al-mal) based on maqasid al-shariah. *Journal of Islamic Philanthropy & Social Finance*, *4*(1), 23–29. DOI: 10.24191/jipsf.v4i1.3429

Zailani, M. N., Satar, N. H. M., & Zakaria, R. H. (2022). Maqasid Al-Shariah based index of socio-economic development: A literature review. *The Journal of Muamalat and Islamic Finance Research,* 47-62.

Zainalaludin, Z., Saidi, N., Foong, H. F., & Abdullah, S. F. Z. (2021). Relationship between poverty levels and age categories among male and female consumers in Malaysia. *Jurnal Pengguna Malaysia*, *37*, 90–110.

Zin, R. H. M. (2012). Malaysia: Towards a social protection system in an advanced equitable society. *ASEAN Economic Bulletin*, •••, 197–217.

Chapter 9
Sustainable Digital Finances:
E-Wallets, Detrimental Consumption Behavior, and Financial Well-Being Through Maqasid Al-Shariah

Ahmad Azwan bin Meor Hashim
https://orcid.org/0009-0008-2738-8427
Universiti Sains Islam Malaysia, Malaysia

Muhammad Ridhwan Ab. Aziz
https://orcid.org/0000-0003-0177-7869
Universiti Sains Islam Malaysia, Malaysia

Junaidah Abu Seman
Universiti Sains Islam Malaysia, Malaysia

ABSTRACT

As a leading Southeast Asian digital finance market, Malaysia sees high e-wallet adoption among young adults, raising concerns despite benefits like convenience and inclusivity. This study examines how impulsive, self-expressive, and conspicuous spending mediate the relationship between e-wallet utilisation and financial well-being, considering potential conflicts with Maqasid al-Shariah principles. Data from 315 young professionals in Klang Valley were analysed using PLS-SEM. Results confirmed impulsive spending and conspicuous spending significantly mediate the relationship: higher e-wallet use increases these behaviours, undermining financial

DOI: 10.4018/979-8-3373-1842-4.ch009

well-being. Self-expressive spending mediation was not supported. The findings highlight risks to prudent spending aligned with Maqasid al-Shariah and the need for mitigating strategies.

INTRODUCTION

Digital technologies are evolving rapidly, reshaping the financial landscape and emphasising the role of electronic wallets as a cornerstone of modern payment systems. Electronic wallets (e-wallets) have become an integral part of daily life (Goyal & Kumar, 2021), serving as secure digital platforms for storing and transferring funds and receiving payments. The economic significance of digital wallets is underscored by projections that global transaction values will exceed $25 trillion by 2027 (Worldpay, 2025). In transition economies, e-wallets stand out as powerful tools for financial inclusion, allowing unbanked or underbanked individuals—traditionally lacking access to conventional banking—to participate in the digital financial services ecosystem (Thomas et al., 2024). This advancement highlights the evolution of technology while emphasising the vital, human-centred impact of making finance more accessible and empowering for all.

The growth of digital finance in Malaysia aligns with broader global trends but is uniquely influenced by robust regulations and Islamic financial principles. National initiatives, including the National e-Payment Blueprint and the Financial Sector Blueprint 2022–2026 (Bank Negara Malaysia, 2022), have promoted this sector significantly. In 2023, there was an impressive 300% increase in e-wallet usage among Malaysians, with a remarkable 87% adoption rate. A critical factor in this surge was the government's e-Tunai Rakyat program, which allocated RM500 million through platforms like Touch 'n Go e-wallet, Boost, and GrabPay (Ministry of Finance Malaysia, 2024), encouraging digital payments, particularly within unbanked communities. Bank Negara Malaysia (BNM) recently reported a 25% increase in electronic money (e-money) transaction volume for 2024, with 64% of these transactions conducted via e-wallets and the remaining 36% through card-based e-money transactions (BNM, 2025).

E-wallets are increasingly relied upon for their convenience and ability to promote financial inclusion, yet concerns remain about their impact on users' financial health. In 2024, 63% of Malaysians reported using mobile wallets, drawn by their ease of use, security features, and integration with funding sources like credit cards and BNPL services (Farid, 2024). While such technology expands access, it also heightens the risks of negative spending behaviours which can undermine financial well-being.

As with general fintech, adopting fintech based on Islamic values exhibits variations among consumers and countries. Thus, especially in Malaysia, adopting Islamic values in financial technology (fintech) presents a high level of complexity. Nevertheless, there seems to be some misalignment between the usefulness of Islamic fintech and moral considerations, as pointed out in some research (Maniam, 2024). Additionally, financial literacy is an important determinant of user behaviour and perceptions of Islamic fintech. Complementing financial literacy and Islamic business ethics is important in formulating investment choices. Thus, developing appropriate or new forms of financial guidelines that infuse digital finance with a sense of ethics is required (Dharma et al., 2024). Activating such measures is even more urgent given that millennials in Malaysia are showing behavioural trends in their adoption of fintech, which are unique to the extent that it calls for a more integrated personal mélange of religion and technology (Rahim et al., 2023).

This chapter explores how these behaviours mediate the relationship between e-wallet usage and financial well-being, using the ethical framework of the higher objectives of the *Shariah* (Islamic law) or *Maqasid al-Shariah.*

E-Wallets, Multi-Source Funding, and Consumption Dynamics

Malaysian e-wallets are increasingly linked to several funding sources, blurring liquidity and debt. Buy Now Pay Later (BNPL) platforms have grown in popularity, with 77.3 million transactions in 2023 spending RM 6.2 billion, mostly by under-30s (Abdullah, 2025). Credit card integrations, personal loan augmentations, and "frictionless" credit access create an "illusion of liquidity," giving users the impression they have more financial freedom than they do (Aji & Adawiyah, 2022). E-wallets reduce the psychological anguish of giving up cash, encouraging impulsive buying, while perceived enjoyment and user-friendliness strongly impact impulsive spending among Generations Y and Z (Lee et al., 2023). Digital transactions may encourage inappropriate consumption due to their convenience.

E-wallet transactions reduce the need for real fiat money, reducing psychological resistance to buying and encouraging impulsive spending (Underdown & Tamara, 2025). Conspicuous spending, motivated by the need to show wealth or social status, may be discreetly encouraged by the digital world, where transactions are less obvious but social signalling remains important (Klucarova & He, 2023). Self-expression may seem harmless, but it can be disastrous when it leads to financial debt and the satisfaction of one's identity or ideal through consumerism (Yousef, 2024). The cumulative consequence of such activities might leave a young person with less savings, increased debt, and lower financial health, causing instability.

Maqasid al-Shariah presents a framework for improving individual and societal social, political, and economic well-being. In this ideology, protecting religion, life, mind, lineage, and riches is most important (Nouman et al., 2021). *Maqasid al-Shariah* encourages ethical investment and consumption, resources, and society, and follows the hadith "not to waste" and "not to be extravagant" (Pusparini, 2023). E-wallets' ethical perspective helps us grasp their contribution to financial well-being, even in Islamic finance. In this study, *Maqasid al-Shariah* examines the relationship between long-term e-wallet use, impulsive, conspicuous, and self-expressive spending, and financial well-being.

Problem Statement

Despite the growing literature on e-wallet uptake and use, little is known about how e-wallets mediate harmful spending habits and financial well-being. Recent research typically ignores consumption's ethical and moral aspects, especially from an Islamic perspective, which values responsible financial conduct and wealth preservation (Hajar et al., 2020; Sholihin & Shalihin, 2023). This shortcoming limits the intricacy of financial literacy and consumer behaviour models, especially where Islamic beliefs strongly impact economic behaviour. Thus, it is crucial to examine how e-wallets may unintentionally encourage harmful spending habits and affect financial well-being and how *Maqasid al-Shariah* principles may mitigate these effects.

Research Questions

The present study seeks to address the following research questions:

- How do expectation confirmation and perceived usefulness affect users' satisfaction with e-wallets?
- How do perceived usefulness and satisfaction influence individuals' intentions to continue use e-wallets?
- What is the direct relationship between the sustained use of e-wallets and users' financial well-being?
- To what degree does continued engagement with e-wallets shape impulsive, conspicuous, and self-expressive spending behaviours?
- How do these specific consumption patterns—impulsive, conspicuous, and self-expressive spending—mediate the link between continued e-wallet usage and user's financial well-being?
- What role does the framework of *Maqasid al-Shariah* play in mediating harmful consumption behaviours and promoting financial well-being within the context of e-wallet adoption?

Through these questions, the research aims to unravel the psychological mechanisms that drive digital financial behaviour and how ethical and cultural frameworks can shape healthier, more sustainable financial practices.

Significance of the Study

This study adds detrimental consumption behaviours as mediators between e-wallet use and financial well-being to the Expectation-Confirmation Model (ECM). This expansion clarifies how psychological and behavioural aspects affect consumer financial outcomes with digital payment systems. *Maqasid al-Shariah* offers a novel interdisciplinary approach combining consumer behaviour studies with Islamic ethics. This integration improves theoretical discussions on sustainable consumption and financial well-being, especially within different cultures and religions.

The findings of this study will be useful for a variety of stakeholders. To promote a better design of responsible and ethically aligned digital payment platforms, financial service providers, and e-wallet companies can better understand the drivers behind the detrimental consumption behaviours. These could include the addition of applications that promote mindful spending, offer financial education materials, or utilise *Shariah*-compliant financial advice. The study will inform policymakers and regulators about where they may need to intervene to preserve consumer financial welfare in the digital world. This could involve draughting laws that restrict overspending facilitated by e-wallets or promoting education on responsible digital financial habits. Related to this, the study will, on one hand, create better understanding and awareness about the negative effects associated with using e-wallets among consumers, which will further empower consumers to make sustainable financial decisions and change their consumption behaviour towards practices that are in parallel with principles of long-term financial well-being as prescribed by the philosophy of *Maqasid al-Shariah*.

LITERATURE REVIEW

E-Wallets and Digital Finance

With the advent of the digital age, digital finance is an integral component of all financial arrangements today, and e-wallets have now been established as an essential part of modern payment transactions. E-wallets are "digital applications that store digital identifiers (or keys) in a secure interface for a payment instrument issued to an individual" (Tripathi, 2023, p. 74). The widespread use of mobile payments is often attributed to the convenience, swiftness, and efficiency offered in being able to facilitate transactions without the reliance on cash and traditional banking (Daragmeh et al., 2022). E-wallets are developing rapidly worldwide due to smartphone usage, internet connectivity, and the desire to move away from cash-based transactions, especially in emerging nations (Abdul-Halim et al., 2022). Digital payments affect consumer spending, money management, and economic activity.

Understanding why individuals continue to use a particular system is crucial, especially considering the resources invested in its development and implementation (Windasari & Lin, 2021). Research in e-wallets continued use has frequently adopted the Expectation Confirmation Model (ECM), the Technology Continuance Theory (TCT), the Task-Technology Fit (TTF), Technology Acceptance Model (TAM), and Unified Theory of Acceptance and Use of Technology (UTAUT) as emerging dominant paradigms. Perceived utility, ease of use, and social influence are significant (Ariffin et al., 2021; Tripathi, 2023), while trust and security are important in financial contexts (Adiani et al., 2023).

It is important to assess the longer-term acceptance and impact of using e-wallets. The likelihood that consumers will continue to use a technology post-adoption is strongly correlated with user satisfaction and post-adoption experience (Bhattacherjee, 2001). People may also spend more frequently using e-wallets, as there is no friction in spending in a digital transaction—people may even be less "mindful" of their expenditure.

Expectation-Confirmation Model (ECM)

Oliver's 1980 Expectation-Confirmation Theory (ECT), revised by Bhattacerjee's 2001 Expectation Confirmation Model (ECM) for information systems, is widely utilized in this regard to explain technology continuance use. Influenced by the degree to which expectations derived on initial exposure are confirmed by actual experience with the technology and the TAM views enjoyment and perceived usefulness as the base influences on the intention to continue access to a system. When the user's expectations are exceeded or at least satisfied, they feel empowered and valued. Negative confirmation, on the other hand, has the opposite effect. These are the four main elements of the ECM:

- **Expectation**: Pre-use beliefs of system performance.
- **Confirmation**: Comparison of expectation and perceived performance outcome.
- **Perceived Usefulness**: Users' perception of the system's benefits, such as transaction speed or security.
- **Satisfaction**: Emotional response from the expectation-confirmation process.
- **Continuance Use**: Perceived usefulness and enjoyment drive system use.

In order to predict users' post-adoption behaviours, ECM has also been applied to e-commerce, online education, and mobile services. When considering ethical concerns, including, for example, *Maqasid al-Shariah*, ECM presents a promising avenue to explore the impact of e-wallet adoption on consumer purchasing and their financial well-being.

Maqasid al-Shariah and Sustainable Consumption

Grounded by Quran and *Sunnah* (saying and teachings of Prophet Muhammad), *Maqasid Al-Shariah* offers a thorough ethical framework for financial and economic conduct, intending to ensure benefit or interest (*maslahah*) and mitigate harm (*mafsadah*) at both individual and social levels (Hajar et al., 2020). Prominent *Maqasid* scholars (e.g. Al-Ghazali, Al-Raysuni, and Al-Shatibi) have delineated five primary objectives:

- ***Hifz al-Din*** (Preservation of Religion): Safeguarding faith and religious practice.
- ***Hifz al-Nafs*** (Preservation of Life): Protecting human life and well-being.
- ***Hifz al-Aql*** (Preservation of Intellect): Promoting knowledge and sound reasoning.
- ***Hifz al-Nasl*** (Preservation of Progeny): Ensuring lineage and family integrity.
- ***Hifz al-Mal*** (Preservation of Wealth): Managing and safeguarding wealth responsibly.

Within consumption, *Maqasid al-Shariah* emphasises moderation, responsible stewardship, and gratitude, while opposing wasteful (*tabdhir*) or extravagance spending (*israf*) (Abdullah, 2025; Hajar et al., 2020; Sholihin & Shalihin, 2023). *Hifz al-Mal* particularly underlines prudent financial practices to maintain individual and communal stability. The ethical use of wealth, viewed as a trust from Allah, calls for accountability and eschews extravagance. Applying *Maqasid al-Shariah* to digital finance offers a normative basis for curbing unsustainable consumption, such as excessive or self-expressive spending. Those internalising these values are less likely to engage in financially detrimental behaviours, enhancing overall financial well-being.

In this study, *Maqasid al-Shariah* is positioned not only as a theoretical lens but as a practical guide to promoting sustainable and *Shariah*-compliant digital financial behaviour, mitigating the negative impacts of e-wallet use.

Detrimental Consumption Behaviours

Although e-wallets provide several advantages, their fundamental traits may also promote purchasing patterns that adversely affect an individual's financial well-being. This study explores three types of detrimental spending: impulsive, conspicuous, and self-expressive.

Impulsive Spending (IS)

Impulsive buying is characterised by unplanned, spontaneous, and often emotionally based purchases made with little deliberation (Rook, 1987). Environmental discomfort associated with payment is reduced in e-wallet payment by the elimination of physical transfer of cash, which decreases the psychological discomfort of encountering the cost to purchase, leading to an increase in products' impulsive buying (Lee et al., 2023; Underdown & Tamara, 2025). The ease and flexibility of one-click payments, credit-based source of funding, and instant gratification offered by e-wallets could lead to consumers not making rational financial decisions, which leads to over-consumption, according to the study. Gupta et al. (2024) demonstrate that the increased accessibility of mobile shopping platforms intensifies impulsiveness among younger consumers. Their findings indicate that extended browsing significantly raises the likelihood of unplanned purchases, highlighting a robust positive relationship between web browsing and the tendency to buy impulsively.

The psychological concept referred to as the "pain of paying" suggests that individuals with lower self-control tend to accumulate debt, particularly when experiencing financial stress (Gladstone & Masters-Waage, 2024). Research indicates a substantial positive correlation between the convenience of digital payment systems and impulsive spending (Ghaith et al., 2024). This behaviour adversely affects financial stability by depleting savings, increasing debt, and complicating long-term financial planning. These findings underscore the prevalence of impulsive spending as a significant self-regulatory challenge in today's consumer landscape.

Conspicuous Spending (CS)

Conspicuous consumption, or Veblenian consumption, entails the procurement and exhibition of goods and services to signify wealth, status, or social hierarchy (Veblen, 2017). In the digital era, although the tangible demonstration of affluence may be less obvious, the catalyst for conspicuous consumption persists robustly. By making those purchases for luxury items, high-end services, or visually shareable experiences on social platforms, simple transactions become a medium for indirect encouragement of conspicuous spending habits via the e-commerce transaction facilitated with e-wallets. This detachment from real money might make large expenditures via cashless feel less memorable, making people willing to spend more for positional goods (Schomburgk et al., 2024). Literature shows that digital payment systems can increase the ease of luxury consumption—particularly among certain groups of individuals (Pusparini, 2023; Salivio et al., 2024). Though satisfying a social need, this kind of spending has the potential of compromising financial health when money is stretched thin, prioritising external validation instead of internal financial well-being. This social reward system fosters an environment where spending is not merely transactional but laden with social implications, thereby heightening the potential for violations of the *Maqasid* related to wealth preservation, protection of progeny, and responsible consumption.

Self-Expressive Spending (SS)

Self-expressive spending refers to spending that serves as an affirmation of self-identities, values, beliefs, or personal style (Belk, 1988). While self-expression through consumption is part of being human, it becomes destructive when it leads to spending that threatens financial well-being. By driving the availability of highly specific goods and services customised to taste and special interests, e-wallets may inadvertently encourage overconsumption in the name of self-expression. Instantly buying stuff that represents how someone views oneself without the mental cost of tangible currency can lead to an infinite purchasing loop (Yousef, 2024; Yuan et al., 2021). This spending behaviour can include buying unneeded clothes, gadgets, or events to fit a self-image, frequently at the expense of finances or essential requirements. Self-expression as the primary motivator of consumption can lead to financial stress and lower financial well-being. This trend raises ethical concerns about modern consumer behaviour and its effects on *Maqasid* violations related to wealth preservation and social welfare.

Table 1 explains the archetypes of detrimental consumption behaviours that are harmful to individuals and society. To change these harmful spending habits, we must examine the psychological and social factors that cause them. Thus, future regulations and initiatives could promote responsible financial management and conscious consumption to align consumer behaviour with *Maqasid al-Shariah*.

Table 1. Frameworks of Detrimental Consumption and Their Associated Breaches of Maqasid al-Shariah.

Type of Detrimental Consumption	*Maqasid* Violation
Impulsive Spending	*Israf* (extravagance), eroding *hifz al-mal* (wealth preservation) and responsible consumption.
Conspicuous Spending	*Tabdhir* (wasteful), undermining *hifz al-mal, hifz al-nasl* (protection of progeny), social justice, and modesty.
Self-Expressive Spending	*Gharar* (self-deceptive wants), impairing *hifz al-mal* and responsible behaviour.

Financial Well-being (FWB)

Financial well-being includes an individual's ability to meet current and future financial responsibilities and their sense of economic stability and freedom (Netemeyer et al., 2018). It is about financial comfort, not simply wealth. Financial stability, independence, satisfaction, and literacy affect financial well-being (Bashir & Qureshi, 2023; Nanda & Banerjee, 2021). Financial well-being also refers to managing monthly and daily budgets, dealing with unexpected financial emergencies, and achieving financial objectives.

The connection between e-wallets and financial well-being is not straightforward. E-wallets help in enhancing financial well-being by increasing financial inclusion, aiding in easy budgeting through digital documentation of one's financial life, and providing benefits and rewards such as payback benefits (Abdul-Halim et al., 2022). The convenience of e-wallets may promote behaviours that are harmful to financial well-being. The current study finds that the direct effect of e-wallet uses on financial well-being while exploring indirect effect via detrimental consumption behaviour. Understanding these types of mediation processes is particularly important in developing successful programs in support of sustainable digital finance and consumer financial well-being.

Theoretical Framework and Hypotheses Development

This study integrates the ECM with negative consumption behaviour and *Maqasid al-Shariah* to develop an integrated research model that will provide a holistic theoretical explanation of sustainable digital finance using the e-wallet option. The ECM helps to account for the ongoing long-term use of e-wallets. At the same time, detrimental consumption behaviours (impulsive, conspicuous, self-expressive spending) are proposed as mediators of the relationship between e-wallet continuation and financial well-being. Also, we introduce *Maqasid al-Shariah* to interpret them from an ethical and normative context to assess these ties.

Continuance Use in E-Wallet Context

According to the ECM, a user's continued intention to use a system is contingent on their user satisfaction and perceived usefulness, which are dependent on expectations confirmed by pre-usage experiences (Bhattacherjee, 2001). Convenience, speed and security are dimensions that users already have expectations about concerning e-wallets. Having interacted with the e-wallet, they evaluate this experience based on their expectations, confirming or disconfirming it.

Confirmation (Cf) and Perceived Usefulness (PU)

When consumers' experiences with e-wallets meet or surpass their initial expectations, they are more inclined to view the e-wallet as beneficial. Confirmation reinforces the belief that the e-wallet effectively facilitates transactions and provides the anticipated advantages (Bhattacherjee, 2001). Consistent with prior studies ad theoretical rationale, the following hypothesis is suggested:

- **H1: Confirmation has a positive influence on the perceived usefulness of e-wallets.**

Confirmation (Cf) and Satisfaction (St)

Confirmation of expectations is a direct precursor to user satisfaction. Should the e-wallet function as anticipated or exceed expectations, consumers will derive satisfaction from their experience (Oliver, 1980). This satisfaction is essential for promoting ongoing engagement with the service. Building upon the preceding arguments, the study articulates the subsequent hypothesis:

- **H2: Confirmation has a positive impact on satisfaction with e-wallets.**

Perceived Usefulness (PU) and Satisfaction (St)

Perceived usefulness is essential in shaping user pleasure. Users typically exhibit greater satisfaction with an e-wallet service when they perceive it as advantageous for streamlining financial transactions and facilitating the attainment of their objectives (Bhattacherjee, 2001). An effectively designed e-wallet can markedly improve the overall user experience. In light of the theoretical underpinnings discussed, the following hypothesis is formulated:

- **H3: Perceived usefulness positively affects satisfaction with e-wallets.**

Perceived Usefulness (PU) and Continuance Use (CU)

Users are more likely to persist in using an e-wallet if they perceive it as advantageous for their routine financial transactions. The enduring utility and benefits of the e-wallet encourage the objective of sustaining its utilisation (Bhattacherjee, 2001). Based on this concept, this research advances the following hypothesis:

- **H4: Perceived usefulness positively influences continued use of e-wallets.**

Satisfaction (St) and Continuance Use (CU)

Satisfaction is crucial in influencing the desire to persist in utilising a service. Satisfied users are more inclined to maintain their participation with an e-wallet, as their favourable experiences reinforce their decision to continue utilising it (Bhattacherjee, 2001; Oliver, 1980). This relationship is well recorded in the literature on information systems continuity. Drawing from the empirical context, the following hypothesis is proposed:

- **H5: Satisfaction has a positive effect on the continued use of e-wallets.**

E-Wallet Continuance Use, Detrimental Consumption, and Financial Well-being

The continued use of e-wallets, while offering convenience, may influence consumer buying behaviours, potentially negatively affecting financial well-being. The fluidity of digital payments may reduce the psychological weight of spending, encouraging impulsive, conspicuous, and self-expressive purchases.

Continuance Use (CU) and Financial Well-being (FWB)

The correlation between sustained e-wallet utilisation and financial well-being can be intricate. Although e-wallets provide advantages such as enhanced expense tracking and budgeting, their convenience may result in overspending, adversely affecting consumer finances. The effect may be direct yet very weak, necessitating more examination. Accordingly, the study posits the following hypothesis

- **H6: Continuance Use of e-wallet influences Financial Well-being.**

Continuance Use (CU) and Impulsive Spending (IS)

The ease and promptness of e-wallet transactions reduce the obstacles to impulsive buying. The lack of genuine cash conversion and the ease of one-click payments can reduce the cognitive effort involved in purchasing, increasing the likelihood of impulsive acquisitions (Lee et al., 2023; Underdown & Tamara, 2025). Thus, this study puts forward the following hypothesis:

- **H7: Continuance Use of e-wallet positively influences Impulsive Spending.**

Continuance Use (CU) and Conspicuous Spending (CS)

E-wallets enable convenient purchases for products and services that may be linked to status or social signals. The disconnection from tangible currency may facilitate conspicuous consumption, as the financial repercussions may seem less imminent (Schomburgk et al., 2024). The hypothesis proposed is as follows:

- **H8: Continuance Use of e-wallet positively influences Conspicuous Spending.**

Continuance Use (CU) and Self-Expressive Spending (SS)

The availability of various products and services via e-wallets can promote self-expressive expenditure, wherein consumers acquire items to validate their identity or principles. The convenience of transactions may result in excessive consumption in the quest for self-expression (Yousef, 2024). The research suggests the following hypothesis:

- **H9: Continuance Use of e-wallet positively influences Self-Expressive Spending.**

Mediating Role of Detrimental Consumption Behaviours

This study asserts that impulsive, conspicuous, and self-expressive expenditure mediates the connection between the continued use of e-wallets and financial well-being. The persistent utilisation of e-wallets fosters unfavourable spending patterns, which subsequently adversely affect financial well-being.

Impulsive Spending (IS) and Financial Well-being (FWB)

Impulsive spending inherently results in the acquisition of superfluous products, diminishing savings and even incurring debt, so adversely impacting an individual's financial health. The research puts forth this hypothesis:

- **H10: Impulsive spending negatively influences financial well-being.**

Conspicuous Spending (CS) and Financial Well-being (FWB)

Excessive spending, motivated by a quest for prestige, frequently entails expenditures that exceed one's financial capacity, resulting in economic distress and diminished financial health. Thus, the following hypothesis is introduced:

- **H11: Conspicuous spending negatively influences financial well-being.**

Self-Expressive Spending (SS) and Financial Well-being (FWB)

Although self-expression is significant, excessive expenditure on self-expression can result in overconsumption and financial distress, ultimately undermining financial well-being. The study proposes this hypothesis:

- **H12: Self-Expressive Spending negatively influences Financial Well-being.**

Combining these, the research hypothesises the following mediating effects:

- **H13: Impulsive spending mediates the relationship between continued use of e-wallets and financial well-being.**
- **H14: Conspicuous spending mediates the relationship between continued use of e-wallets and financial well-being.**
- **H15: Self-expressive spending mediates the relationship between continued use of e-wallets and financial well-being.**

This detailed framework, illustrated in Figure 1, delineates the proposed links among the constructs, serving as a guide for the empirical inquiry.

Figure 1. Research Framework

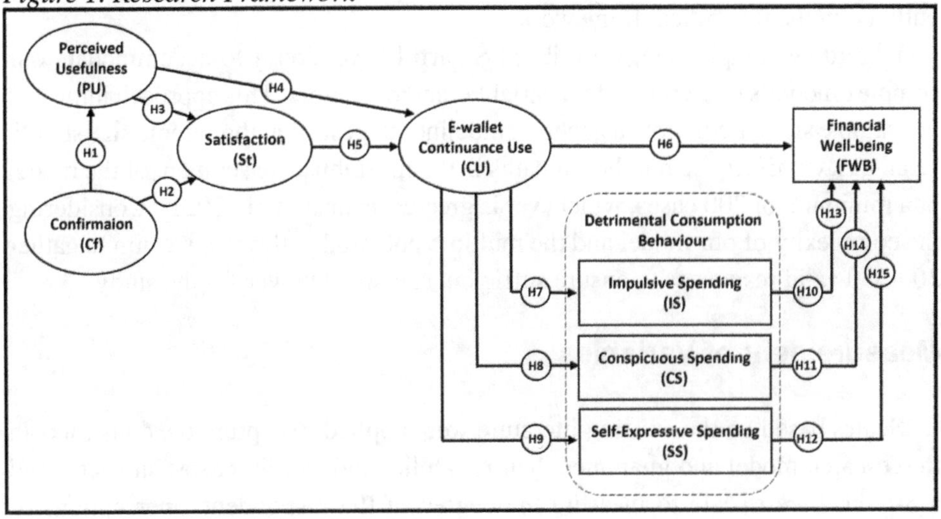

RESEARCH METHODOLOGY

This study utilises a quantitative research methodology to examine the correlations between e-wallet continuing usage, adverse consumption habits, financial well-being, and the impact of *Maqasid al-Shariah*. A quantitative methodology is appropriate for this study since it enables the systematic gathering of numerical data, permitting statistical analysis to evaluate the claimed associations and generalise findings to a broader population (Creswell & Creswell, 2018). The cross-sectional data collection will offer a glimpse of current perceptions and behaviours among e-wallet users.

Research Design

This research employed a descriptive and explanatory quantitative survey methodology. A descriptive design delineates the attributes of a population or phenomenon under investigation, whereas an explanatory design aims to elucidate the relationships among variables (Saunders et al., 2019). An online survey will gather data on active e-wallet users' impressions of e-wallet utilisation, consumption patterns, financial well-being, and compliance with *Maqasid al-Shariah* principles.

This method enables examining direct and indirect effects among the constructs outlined in the theoretical framework.

Regarding sample size, we utilised SmartPLS version 4 to accommodate our complex model's numerous latent variables and mediators. This approach informed our sample size calculation: a general guideline suggests that the sample size should be at least ten times the number of paths in the most intricate segment of the model or a minimum of 300 cases, whichever is greater (Hair Jr et al., 2021). Considering the complexity of our model and the multiple potential pathways, we aim to gather 300-350 valid responses to ensure sufficient statistical power for the study.

Measurement of Variables

Scales based on the existing literature were applied to capture the constructs in the research model and guarantee their reliability and validity. Most subjects used a 5-point Likert scale to measure the degree of the respondents' perceptions or attitudes; "1 = strongly disagree" and "5 = strongly agree".

Confirmation (Cf)

Confirmation was evaluated using items sourced from (Bhattacherjee, 2001) and several ECM-related studies, including Ooi and Tan (2016), Tam et al. (2020), and Zhou (2014). The quantifiable items are presented in Table 2.

Table 2. Items formulated for Confirmation (Cf)

Dimensions	Questions
Expectation-Performance Gap	My experience with this e-wallet has been better than what I initially expected.
Performance Surpass	E-wallet functionality exceeds what I anticipated before adoption.
Expectation Fulfilment	Most features of e-wallet perform as well as I expected.
Service Quality Confirmation	The reliability of e-wallets is higher than what I envisioned.
Overall Confirmation	My initial expectations about this e-wallet's capabilities have been met or exceeded.

Perceived Usefulness (PU)

The assessment of perceived usefulness utilized a scale adapted from (Davis, 1989) and subsequent ECM applications, including those by Alalwan et al. (2018), Talwar et al. (2020), and Zhou (2014). These elements are presented in Table 3.

Table 3. Items construct for Perceived Usefulness (PU)

Dimensions	Questions
Functional Utility	Using this e-wallet improves my efficiency in daily transactions.
Time Efficiency	E-wallet enables me to accomplish payments more quickly.
Financial Management	I find this e-wallet useful for managing my finances.
Productivity Enhancement	Using this e-wallet increases my productivity in financial activities.
Relative Advantage	Overall, e-wallets provide significant advantages over other payment methods.

Satisfaction (St)

Customer satisfaction with the e-wallet was assessed using items derived from the works of Bhattacherjee (2001), Oliver (1980), Talwar et al. (2020), Tam et al. (2020), and Zhou (2014). Elements are shown in Table 4.

Table 4. Items construct for Satisfaction (St)

Dimensions	Questions
Decision Satisfaction	I am satisfied with the overall performance of e-wallets.
Affective Response	My experience with e-wallet has been enjoyable.
Feature Content	I am content with the overall functionality of e-wallets.
Cognitive Evaluation	Choosing e-wallets was a wise decision.
Transactional Delight	I feel pleased with how this e-wallet supports my financial needs.

Continuance Use (CU)

The measurement of use intention was conducted utilising a scale developed from Bhattacherjee (2001) and other pertinent studies, including Ooi and Tan (2016), Talwar et al. (2020), Tam et al. (2020), and Venkatesh et al. (2003). Items measured are provided in Table 5.

Table 5. Items construct for Continuance Use (CU)

Dimensions	Questions
Usage Persistence	I intend to continue using this e-wallet regularly in the future.
Primary Method Commitment	I will keep using this e-wallet as my main payment solution.
Usage Expansion	I plan to increase my usage frequency of this e-wallet over time.
Loyalty	I would not switch to alternatives as long as this e-wallet remains available.
Advocacy Intention	I will actively recommend e-wallet to others.

Maqasid al-Shariah

The evaluation of *Maqasid al-Shariah* involved analysing respondents' compliance with principles concerning responsible consumption and wealth preservation. Items were derived from Islamic finance and ethics literature, emphasising moderation, waste avoidance, and ethical financial practices, in accordance with the five principles of *Maqasid al-Shariah*. These items were incorporated to assess detrimental consumption behaviour and financial well-being.

Impulsive Spending (IS)

Impulsive spending was assessed using items modified from established consumer behaviour literature on impulse purchasing (e.g., Badgaiyan et al., 2016; Rook & Fisher, 1995; Verplanken & Herabadi, 2001). Items are listed in Table 6.

Table 6. Components for Impulsive Spending (IS)

Dimensions	Questions
Cue Reactivity	Limited-time promotions trigger unplanned purchases.
Self-Regulation Failure	I buy items instantly without consulting my budget.
Post-Purchase Regret	I often regret impulsive purchases later.
Preservation of wealth (*mal*)	I frequently spend money on the latest trends, which can lead to excessive spending.
Preservation of wealth (*mal*)	I must control my impulses to overspend to achieve the wealth preservation (savings, investment, etc.) goal.

Conspicuous Spending (CS)

Conspicuous consumption was measured with items taken from scales of the constructs of luxury consumption and status-seeking behaviours (e.g., Eastman et al., 1999; Thoumrungroje, 2018. These are presented in Table 7.

Table 7. Items construct for Conspicuous Spending (CS)

Dimensions	Questions
Status Signaling / Wealth Display	I purchase luxury items to display social status.
Social Comparison	I buy items to match my peers' lifestyles.
Preservation of intellect (*'aql*)	The tendency to flaunt luxury purchases mainly to impress others is not a sign of being full of oneself and showing off.
Preservation of life (*nafs*)	Extravagant spending solely to outdo my peers does not contradict the moderation in lifestyle
Preservation of intellect (*'aql*)	Purchasing the latest smartphones mainly for gaining social status rather than utility does not go against ethics on moral consumption.

Self-Expressive Spending (SS)

Self-expressive spending was assessed using items created from the concept of consumption for identity affirmation (e.g., Ekici et al., 2018; Sirgy et al., 2016). The items are displayed in Table 8.

Table 8. Items construct for Self-Expressive Spending (SS)

Dimensions	Questions
Identity Projection	I buy brands that reflect my core personality traits.
Values Demonstration	I choose ethical/sustainable brands to express my beliefs.
Preservation of life (*nafs*)	I feel that purchasing expensive items to construct an ideal self-image does not contradict selflessness values.
Preservation of life (*nafs*)	Spending significant money to stand out by wearing extravagant clothing does not go against the principles of avoiding social harm.
Preservation of life (*nafs*)	My spending behaviour must balance self-expression with exhibiting the virtues of wisdom, patience, and righteousness.

Financial Well-being (FWB)

Financial well-being was assessed using a multi-dimensional scale incorporating objective and subjective elements, adapted from recognised financial well-being frameworks (e.g., Netemeyer et al., 2018; Strömbäck et al., 2017. Table 9 presents the quantifiable components.

Data Analysis

The generated data was compiled and analysed using the following software tools: SPSS (Statistical Package for the Social Sciences) and SmartPLS. Descriptive statistics and demographic data will be inputted, analysed, and compared using SPSS. This encapsulates the check for null values, detection of outliers and normality of data distribution. Internal consistency of the measurement scales will also be analysed using Cronbach's Alpha by SPSS.

Table 9. Items construct for Financial Well-being (FWB)

Dimensions	Questions
Basic Needs Security	I feel my financial position is steady enough to cover my daily needs.
Debt Control	My current debt level is manageable
Savings	I have extra money at the end of the month.
Goal Progression	I am confident of achieving my long-term financial goals.
Emergency Resilience	My financial position is steady enough to cover an emergency expenditure of RM1,000.
Preservation of wealth (*mal*)	Protecting my wealth and assets is important for my financial well-being.
Preservation of life (*nafs*)	I try to avoid financial practices that could be harmful or exploitative according to my belief.
Preservation of religion (*din*)	When making financial decisions, I consider how it will impact my faith and spiritual well-being.
Preservation of intellect (*'aql*)	I feel confident in my ability to manage financial matters according to my belief.
Preservation of progeny (*nasl*)	Having legal sources of income is important for fulfilling my duties to family and society.

This study benefits from using PLS-SEM, which manages complex models where multiple latent variables with formative and reflective paths are present and works appropriately with non-normal, or even ordinal, data distribution (Hair Jr et al., 2021). The analysis was carried out using SmartPLS in two main stages; namely measurement model (examine the reliability and validity of constructs) and structural model evaluation (testing hypothesis of relationships between latent variables. Such a rigorous analysis will help to examine and assess the different links and best test the proposed research model predicting the direct and indirect effects of e-wallet usage on financial well-being, the mediating influence through negative consumption behaviours, and support of the *Maqasid al-Shariah* perceived support function.

RESULTS AND FINDINGS

Demographic characteristics

The demographic study of the 315 questionnaire responses indicates a balanced gender distribution, comprising 51.1% male and 48.9% female individuals. A substantial majority are married (57.5%), with the primary age groups being 26-30 years (25.1%) and 31-35 years (27.3%). The majority of respondents hold a bachelor's degree (54.9%), with Malays representing the predominant racial group at 67.9%. Household income is diverse, with 41% earning between RM4,001 and RM8,000. E-wallet utilisation is prevalent, with 63.8% engaging in its use more than once weekly. Monthly expenditures primarily remain around RM300 (69.5%), while QRPay is utilised uniformly (100%). Additional significant services encompass Buy Now, Pay Later (38.7%) and online payment (33.3%). Table 10 illustrated the demographic findings.

Measurement scale reliability and validity

The measuring model exhibits sufficient reliability and validity for all constructs after item purification. The internal consistency reliability, measured by Cronbach's alpha (CA), surpassed the suggested minimum of 0.70 (Hair Jr et al., 2021) for all constructs, with values ranging from 0.77 (Self-Expressive Spending) to 0.93 (Financial Well-being). Composite reliability (CR), quantified by rho_c, exceeded 0.70 (Hair et al., 2024), with values ranging from 0.84 (Self-Expressive Spending) to 0.94 (Satisfaction, Financial Well-being). The convergent validity, assessed using the Average Variance Extracted (AVE), was deemed adequate with all variables satisfied the minimum 0.50 criterion (Fornell & Larcker, 1981). To guarantee indicator reliability and convergent validity, five items with loadings markedly below 0.70 were eliminated (PU_2; FWB_1, FWB_4, FWB_7; SS_2; CS_3). Following purification, all retained indicator loadings surpassed 0.70, thereby validating a robust measurement model. Table 11 displays the reliability scores for this study in a tabular style.

Table 10. Demographic Characteristics

	N	%		*N*	%
Gender			**Marital status**		
• Male	161	51.1	• Single	131	41.6
• Female	154	48.9	• Married	181	57.5
			• Divorced / Widowed	3	0.9
Age group			**Highest education**		
• 18–20	21	6.7	• SPM	15	4.8
• 21–25	60	19.0	• Diploma / Technical certs	92	29.2
• 26–30	79	25.1	• Bachelor's degree		
• 31–35	86	27.3	• Master's degree	173	54.9
• 36–40	69	21.9	• Doctoral degree	31	9.8
				4	1.3
Race			**Household income**		
• Malay	214	67.9	• Below RM2,500		
• Chinese	65	20.6	• RM2,501 – RM4,000		
• Indian	32	10.2	• RM4,001 – RM8,000		
• Others	4	1.3	• RM8,001 – RM12,000		
E-wallet usage frequency			• More than RM12,000		
• Almost everyday	66	21.0			
• More than once a week	201	63.8	34		
			91		
• At least once a week	48	15.2	129		
			56		
			5		
			10.8		
			28.9		
			41.0		
			17.8		
			1.5		
			Services and functions used (multiple answers)		
Monthly spending using e-wallet			• Online payment	105	33.3
• Less than RM100	106	33.6	• QRPay	315	100.0
• RM100 or RM300	113	35.9	• Buy Now, Pay Later (BNPL)	122	38.7
• RM301 to RM500	66	21.0	• Investment		
• RM501 to RM750	24	7.6	• Personal loan	41	13.0
• RM751 to RM1,000	6	1.9	• Charity, including *waqf*, *infaq*, and	49	15.6
• More than RM1,000	0	0	*zakat*	98	31.1

Furthermore, a thorough collinearity assessment revealed that all Variance Inflation Factors (VIFs) were below 3.3 (Kock, 2015). The predominant single factor explained merely 0.32 of the variances, as indicated by Harman's single-factor test, much below the 0.5 threshold (Podsakoff et al., 2003). Consequently, it can be inferred that the model is unaffected by common method bias.

Discriminant validity was assessed using the Heterotrait-Monotrait (HTMT) ratio of correlations. All HTMT values were below the suggested threshold of 0.90 (Henseler et al., 2015), ranging from 0.27 to 0.89. The highest value observed was between Cf and St, with an HTMT of 0.89, which still falls within the acceptable range. This finding indicates the empirical uniqueness of all constructs within the measurement model.

Table 11. Reliability, Validity, and Measurement Statistics of Construct Scales

Constructs	CA	CR (rhoa_a)	CR (rho_c)	AVE	Indicator Loadings, IL – post-purify (min – max)	Number of items discarded (IL < 0.7)
Confirmation (Cf)	0.91	0.91	0.93	0.74	0.84–0.87	Nil
Satisfaction (St)	0.92	0.92	0.94	0.75	0.84–0.89	Nil
Perceived Usefulness (PU)	0.84	0.85	0.89	0.61	0.82 – 0.85	1 PU_2 (0.60)
Continuance use (CU)	0.9	0.9	0.92	0.71	0.82 – 0.85	Nil
Financial well-being (FWB)	0.93	0.94	0.94	0.62	0.82 – 0.87	3 FWB_1 (0.63) FWB_4 (0.60) FWB_7 (0.67)
Impulsive Spending (IS)	0.77	0.80	0.84	0.53	0.75–0.80	1 IS_2 (0.52)
Self-Expressive Spending (SS)	0.81	0.81	0.87	0.57	0.72 – 0.80	Nil
Conspicuous Spending (CS)	0.78	0.81	0.85	0.53	0.74 – 0.80	1 CS_3 (0.51)

Note. CR=composite reliability; CA=Cronbach's Alpha; AVE=average

The findings presented in Table 12 show that the loading of all indicators is stronger on their respective constructs than on any other constructs in the path model. As a result, all assessments of most components and indicators in the path model demonstrate discriminant validity. The researchers concluded that the constructs evaluated in the study are reliable and valid. However, some indicators were excluded due to their low loadings. This modification suggests that the measurement models for these constructs are robust and suitable for further investigation.

Table 12. Heterotrait-Monotrait (HTMT) Correlation Matrix

	CS	CU	Cf	FWB	IS	PU	SS	St
CS	-							
CU	0.56	-						
Cf	0.42	0.79	-					
FWB	0.40	0.54	0.73	-				
IS	0.33	0.43	0.37	0.35	-			

	CS	CU	Cf	FWB	IS	PU	SS	St
CS	-							
PU	0.42	0.82	0.77	0.50	0.39	-		
SS	0.33	0.73	0.53	0.38	0.28	0.50	-	
St	0.50	0.85	0.89	0.65	0.39	0.78	0.53	-

Note. Cf-confirmation; St-satisfaction; PU-perceived usefulness; CU-continuance use; FWB-financial well-being; IS-impulsive spending; CS-conspicuous spending; SS-self-expressive spending.

Structural model assessment

Path coefficients and significance testing

Significance of path coefficients was determined using 5,000 resamples in a bootstrapping procedure. The complete list of tested interactions is displayed in Table 13 – including all path coefficients, t-values, p-values and significance levels (Hair Jr et al., 2014). Best models' quality is assessed by the standardized path coefficients and significance in the internal models presented in Hair et al. (2019). The results provide much support for the theorized relationships.

The effect of Cf on St was very large ($\beta = 0.63$, $p < 0.01$), confirming H1. This result is in fact similar to what the ECM suggests, since this model theorizes that confirmation or disconfirmation of expectations has a strong influence on satisfaction. PU was found to greatly affect satisfaction ($\beta = 0.68$, $p < 0.01$) corroborating H2 and consistent with previous studies that have associated perceived usefulness with acceptance of technology and satisfaction with technology use (e.g., Venkatesh et al. (2003)).

Similarly, the effect of St was also significant for CU ($\beta = .65$, $p < .001$), supporting H3. This finding is in line with ECM and previous research on e-wallet usage (Abdul-Halim et al., 2022), which have consistently highlighted the importance of satisfaction in intention to continued used such services. The continuous variable for time used reinforced the impact of the situations on the three forms of adverse consumption, with the strongest attenuation of the effect on IS ($\beta = -0.36$, $p <.001$), followed by CS ($\beta = -0.47$, $p <.001$) and SS ($\beta = -0.63$, $p <.001$). These latter three findings confirm the hypotheses H7, H8, and H9 and thus emphasize the impact of continuous use of e-wallets in the development of different types of detrimental consumption behaviour.

Table 13. Path Coefficients and Significance Testing Results

Hypothesis #		Path coefficient	*t*-value	p-value	Significance/Decision
H1	**Cf → PU (+)**	**0.68**	**24.10**	**0.00**	*****Supported**
H2	Cf → St (+)	0.63	16.72	0.00	***Supported
H3	PU → St (+)	0.26	6.28	0.00	***Supported
H4	PU → CU (+)	0.36	7.65	0.00	***Supported
H5	St → CU (+)	0.53	12.36	0.00	***Supported
H6	CU → FWB	0.36	5.93	0.00	***Supported
H7	CU → IS	-0.36	7.52	0.00	***Supported
H8	CU → CS	-0.48	11.65	0.00	***Supported
H9	CU → SS	-0.63	19.34	0.00	***Supported
H10	IS → FWB (-)	-0.13	2.65	0.01	**Supported
H11	CS → FWB (-)	-0.13	2.54	0.01	**Supported
H12	SS → FWB (-)	-0.05	0.82	0.41	Not Supported

Notes: Cf-confirmation; St-satisfaction; PU-perceived usefulness; CU-continuance use; FWB-financial well-being; IS-impulsive spending; CS-conspicuous spending; SS-self-expressive spending. The # symbol within brackets indicates a positive or negative correlation. *$p<0.1$; **$p<0.05$; ***$p<0.01$

In the analysis of the effects of detrimental consumption behaviours on FWB, IS was identified as having the most pronounced negative influence (β = -0.05, p < 0.001), closely followed by conspicuous expenditure (β = -0.13, p < 0.001). The results validate hypotheses H10 and H11. In contrast, the correlation between FWB and SS was minimal, demonstrating insufficient evidence to support hypothesis H12. IS and CS detrimentally impacts FWB, consistent with the principles of *Maqasid al-Shariah* that promote moderation, the avoidance of excess, and the prioritisation of requirements over wants (Kamali, 1999).

E-wallets' continuance use shows a substantial positive direct effect on FWB (β = 0.36, p < 0.001), corroborating hypothesis H6. This research demonstrates that prolonged utilisation of e-wallets improves financial well-being, beyond its indirect influence on spending behaviour.

Mediation Analysis

The mediation analysis (Table 14) clarifies specific routes by which CU affects FWB. Hypothesis H13 illustrates complementary mediation (Zhao et al., 2010): CU has a substantial direct effect on FWB (β = 0.36, p < 0.01) and a notable indirect effect via IS (β = 0.047, p = 0.01), suggesting that IS partially mediates the relationship while additional mechanisms are simultaneously at play. Hypothesis H14 demonstrates indirect-only (complete) mediation: CU's impact on FWB occurs solely through CS (β = 0.062, p = 0.01), with no significant direct effect observed, indicating that CS is the primary conduit. In contrast, Hypothesis H15 is non-significant ($\beta = 0.032$, $p = 0.42$), suggesting that SS does not influence the link between CU and FWB. The results, derived from bootstrapping (5,000 samples; Preacher & Hayes (2008), emphasise the essential mediating functions of particular spending behaviours (IS and CS) in translating technological continuity into financial results, while highlighting the uniqueness of SS in this setting.

Table 14. Mediation Analysis Results

Mediation Path (Hypotheses)		Indirect Effect	Direct Effect	Total Effect	t-value	p-value	Significance
H13	CU → IS → FWB	0.047	0.36	0.407	2.47	0.01	**Significant
H14	CU → CS → FWB	0.062		0.422	2.44	0.01	**Significant
H15	CU → SS → FWB	0.032		0.392	0.81	0.42	Not Significant

Notes:
*$p<0.1$; **$p<0.05$; ***$p<0.01$

DISCUSSION

This study examined the determinants affecting the intention to persist in using e-wallets among Malaysian users aged 18 to 40, employing the Expectation Confirmation Model and *Maqasid al-Shariah* as its theoretical framework. The findings demonstrate that the validation of expectations and the perceived usefulness of several e-wallet embedded financial services considerably influence user satisfaction, which is essential for maintaining usage. These results align with the ECM posited by (Bhattacherjee, 2001) and augment prior studies on the continued use of e-wallets (Abdul-Halim et al., 2022; Puspitasari et al., 2021). Our results support ECM's assertion that confirmation enhances perceived usefulness and satisfaction, leading to continuance use intentions. Nonetheless, they significantly depart from conventional ECM applications by suggesting that high continuous usage is not a conclusive measure of success. Instead, it catalyses detrimental spending behaviour, challenging the model's fundamental assumption that persistence is inherently beneficial.

The mediation analysis confirms and intricately refines emerging data regarding the "dark side" of technology adoption. In accordance with research connecting frictionless payment systems to diminished self-control over spending (Tuan Pham

& Chang, 2010), our findings indicate that compulsive usage of e-wallets significantly promotes impulsive spending and conspicuous spending. These tendencies, exacerbated by the seamless and rapid characteristics of e-wallets, subsequently exert a considerable negative influence on financial well-being. This mediation pathway reflects Hsiao's findings (Hsiao, 2017) about social media usage and compulsive spending while explicitly highlighting the distinctive features of digital wallets (e.g., one-click purchasing, integrated shop links) that diminish psychological barriers to impulsive and status-orientated consumption. This contrasts with research that mainly examines the cognitive precursors of overspending, emphasising the significant influence of technological friction lessness as a behavioural facilitator (Ridgway et al., 2008). Our research reveals a critical limitation in the conventional ECM framework: its inability to consider the potential adverse behavioural spirals (loss of spending control, status competition) that high consumer utility, influenced by established usefulness and satisfaction, may incite within particular contexts such as ubiquitous payment platforms.

The insignificant mediation function of self-expressive spending in the continuance uses and financial well-being connection presents a nuanced differentiation. Although continued use augmented self-expressive spending, similar to research associating digital involvement with identity expression (O'Cass, 2004), self-expressive spending did not substantially detriment financial well-being in this setting. This implies that self-expressive spending motivations may encompass more intentional decisions or expenditures regarded as inherently important for self-identity, maybe reallocating costs differently or missing the immediate financial imprudence linked to impulsive spending and conspicuous spending.

The results of this study highlight practical implications highly relevant to e-wallet providers who will have a potential substantial benefit from integrating these findings into platform design and business strategies. It proves to conduct a large-scale experimental test that if integrated Islamic behavioural nudges to act as boundaries around *Maqasid*-driven spending (e.g. pre-commitment dealing ceilings against *israf*), friction mechanisms driven by good faith (e.g. sustainable spending - inspired purchase confirmations) and prosocial benchmarks, have a comparative advantage in saturated markets. This integration ensures that the providers are not just engaging in a traditional cashback competition but providing a more meaningful, holistic approach to spiritual-financial well-being by addressing the Shariah-conscious segment (the majority in Malaysia and other major Muslim economies). This approach directly enhances user retention by reducing financially detrimental stress and decreasing churn rates. Concurrently, an ethical framework fosters trust, transforming wallets from mere transactional tools into stewards of long-term sustainable financial well-being. Consequently, providers can achieve greater lifetime value, accompanied by loyalty from users who seek to harmonise the convenience of digital solutions with their core values.

This study provides significant insights into the relationship between e-wallet continuance usage, spending behaviour, and financial well-being; however, numerous limitations require consideration. The cross-sectional design obstructs causal inference, and dependence on self-reported data creates possible bias. The emphasis on Malaysian users aged 18–40 constrains generalisability, and the range of e-wallet characteristics and spending patterns analysed was restricted. Furthermore, potential mediators and modifiers, including financial literacy and cultural values, were not examined. Although the concepts of *Maqasid al-Shariah* were integrated, the users' understanding and implementation of these principles were not evaluated. Furthermore, employing PLS-SEM for analysis entails methodological limitations. Future study should employ longitudinal designs, incorporate objective data sources, enhance demographic and contextual diversity, explore other contributing variables, and utilise different analytical tools for more rigorous conclusions.

CONCLUSION

The analysis of findings highlighted the consistency of results with previous research and the Expectation Confirmation Model, while also providing new insights into the relationship between e-wallet usage, spending behaviour, and financial well-being within the context of *Maqasid al-Shariah* principles. This study deepens our understanding of how digital payment technologies influence financial outcomes by shaping spending habits. It emphasises the importance of integrating ethical frameworks such as *Maqasid al-Shariah* when evaluating these relationships. The findings present valuable insights for e-wallet service providers, financial institutions, consumers, and policymakers seeking to harness digital payment technology's benefits while mitigating potential negative impacts on financial well-being.

REFERENCES

Abdul-Halim, N.-A., Vafaei-Zadeh, A., Hanifah, H., Teoh, A. P., & Nawaser, K. (2022). Understanding the determinants of e-wallet continuance usage intention in Malaysia. *Quality & Quantity*, *56*(5), 3413–3439. DOI: 10.1007/s11135-021-01276-7

Abdullah, I. N. (2025, February 17). *Youth Trapped in Debt As They're Hooked with BNPL Addiction.* FintechNews Malaysia. https://fintechnews.my/48212/payments-remittance-malaysia/youth-trapped-in-debt-with-bnpl-addiction/

Adiani, W., Aprianingsih, A., Fachira, I., Debby, T., & Maharatie, A. P. (2023). Social influence, financial benefit, and e-wallet multi-brand loyalty: The mediating impact of commitment. *Cogent Business & Management*, *11*(1), 2290228. Advance online publication. DOI: 10.1080/23311975.2023.2290228

Aji, H. M., & Adawiyah, W. R. (2022). How e-wallets encourage excessive spending behavior among young adult consumers? *Journal of Asia Business Studies*, *16*(6), 868–884. DOI: 10.1108/JABS-01-2021-0025

Alalwan, A. A., Dwivedi, Y. K., Rana, N. P., & Algharabat, R. (2018). Examining factors influencing Jordanian customers' intentions and adoption of internet banking: Extending UTAUT2 with risk. *Journal of Retailing and Consumer Services*, *40*, 125–138. DOI: 10.1016/j.jretconser.2017.08.026

Ariffin, S. K., Abd Rahman, M. F. R., Muhammad, A. M., & Zhang, Q. (2021). Understanding the consumer's intention to use the e-wallet services. *Spanish Journal of Marketing - ESIC*, *25*(3), 446–461. DOI: 10.1108/SJME-07-2021-0138

Badgaiyan, A. J., Verma, A., & Dixit, S. (2016). Impulsive buying tendency: Measuring important relationships with a new perspective and an indigenous scale. *IIMB Management Review*, *28*(4), 186–199. DOI: 10.1016/j.iimb.2016.08.009

Bank Negara Malaysia. (2022). *Financial Sector Blueprint 2022 - 2026.*

Bank Negara Malaysia. B. (2025, March). *BNM Annual Report 2024 - Bank Negara Malaysia.* https://www.bnm.gov.my/documents/20124/17493532/ar2024_en_book.pdf/

Bashir, I., & Qureshi, I. H. (2023). A Systematic Literature Review on Personal Financial Well-Being: The Link to Key Sustainable Development Goals 2030. In *FIIB Business Review* (Vol. 12, Issue 1). DOI: 10.1177/23197145221106862

Belk, R. W. (1988). Possessions and the Extended Self. *The Journal of Consumer Research*, *15*(2), 139–168. DOI: 10.1086/209154

Bhattacherjee, A. (2001). Understanding information systems continuance: An expectation-confirmation model. *Management Information Systems Quarterly, 25*(3), 351–370. DOI: 10.2307/3250921

Creswell, J. W., & Creswell, J. D. (2018). *Research Design: Qualitative, Quantitative, and Mixed Methods Approaches* (5th ed.). SAGE Publications.

Daragmeh, A., Saleem, A., Bárczi, J., & Sági, J. (2022). Drivers of post-adoption of e-wallet among academics in Palestine: An extension of the expectation confirmation model. *Frontiers in Psychology, 13*, 984931. Advance online publication. DOI: 10.3389/fpsyg.2022.984931

Davis, F. D. (1989). Perceived usefulness, perceived ease of use, and user acceptance of information technology. *Management Information Systems Quarterly, 13*(3), 319–340. Advance online publication. DOI: 10.2307/249008

Dharma, Y., Puteh, A., Widodo, R., Alfaqih, L., & Yahya, A. (2024). The Influence of Financial Literacy and Islamic Business Ethics on Investment in Islamic Financial Instruments: The Mediating Role of Risk Attitude and the Moderating Role of Religious Knowledge. *Journal of Ecohumanism, 3*(8), 264–282. DOI: 10.62754/joe.v3i8.4729

Eastman, J. K., Goldsmith, R. E., & Flynn, L. R. (1999). Status Consumption in Consumer Behavior: Scale Development and Validation. *Journal of Marketing Theory and Practice, 7*(3), 41–52. DOI: 10.1080/10696679.1999.11501839

Ekici, A., Joseph Sirgy, M., Lee, D.-J., Yu, G. B., & Bosnjak, M. (2018). The effects of shopping well-being and shopping ill-being on consumer life satisfaction. *Applied Research in Quality of Life, 13*(2), 333–353. DOI: 10.1007/s11482-017-9524-9

Farid, A. (2024, October 17). *E-Wallet App Usage & Demographics Malaysia (2024 Statistics).* https://upstackstudio.com/blog/e-wallet-malaysia/

Fornell, C., & Larcker, D. F. (1981). Evaluating structural equation models with unobservable variables and measurement error. *JMR, Journal of Marketing Research, 18*(1), 39–50. DOI: 10.1177/002224378101800104

Ghaith, M. M., Al-rawashdeh, G. H., Alzuod, M. A., Ghaith, Y. M., Alotoum, F. J., AlSokkar, A. A. M., Al-Gasawneh, J., & Alghizzawi, M. (2024). Examining the Effects of Digital Payment and Impulsive Buying on Purchase Intention. *2024 2nd International Conference on Cyber Resilience (ICCR)*, 1–7. DOI: 10.1109/ICCR61006.2024.10532804

Gladstone, J. J., & Masters-Waage, T. C. (2024). When Paying Is (Even More) Painful: Personality-Based Heterogeneity in Consumption Responses to Economic Hardship. *Social Psychological & Personality Science, 15*(3), 264–274. DOI: 10.1177/19485506231167020

Goyal, K., & Kumar, S. (2021). Financial literacy: A systematic review and bibliometric analysis. *International Journal of Consumer Studies, 45*(1), 80–105. https://doi.org/https://doi.org/10.1111/ijcs.12605. DOI: 10.1111/ijcs.12605

Gupta, P., Prashar, S., & Parsad, C. (2024). Pure and suggestive impulse buying in mobile shopping app: Shopping pattern of young consumers. *Young Consumers, 25*(6), 824–850. DOI: 10.1108/YC-11-2023-1911

Hair, J. F., Risher, J. J., Sarstedt, M., & Ringle, C. M. (2019). When to use and how to report the results of PLS-SEM. *European Business Review, 31*(1), 2–24. DOI: 10.1108/EBR-11-2018-0203

Hair, J. F., Sarstedt, M., Ringle, C. M., & Gudergan, S. (2024). *Advanced issues in partial least squares structural equation modeling*. PLS-SEM.

Hajar, S., Musadik, S. A., Yusuf, N., Aziz, N. A., Abdul, I., & Azmi, G. (2020). Maqasid Syariah in Islamic Consumption. [IJBEC]. *International Journal of Business and Economy, 2*(4).

Henseler, J., Ringle, C. M., & Sarstedt, M. (2015). A new criterion for assessing discriminant validity in variance-based structural equation modeling. *Journal of the Academy of Marketing Science, 43*(1), 115–135. DOI: 10.1007/s11747-014-0403-8

Hsiao, K. L. (2017). Compulsive mobile application usage and technostress: The role of personality traits. *Online Information Review, 41*(2), 272–295. Advance online publication. DOI: 10.1108/OIR-03-2016-0091

Kamali, M. H. (1999). MAQĀ ID AL-SHARĪ'AH": The objectives of Islamic law. *Islamic Studies, 38*(2), 193–208. https://www.jstor.org/stable/20837037. DOI: 10.52541/isiri.v38i2.6127

Klucarova, S., & He, X. (2023). Cash is the king: Conspicuous consumption and preference for cash payment in restaurants. *Journal of Hospitality and Tourism Management, 54*, 357–360. Advance online publication. DOI: 10.1016/j.jhtm.2023.01.010

Kock, N. (2015). Common method bias in PLS-SEM: A full collinearity assessment approach. *International Journal of e-Collaboration, 11*(4), 1–10. DOI: 10.4018/ijec.2015100101

Lee, Y. Y., Gan, C. L., & Liew, T. W. (2023). Do E-wallets trigger impulse purchases? An analysis of Malaysian Gen-Y and Gen-Z consumers. *Journal of Marketing Analytics, 11*(2), 244–261. DOI: 10.1057/s41270-022-00164-9

Maniam, S. (2024). Determinants of Islamic fintech adoption: A systematic literature review. *Journal of Islamic Marketing, 15*(11), 2916–2936. DOI: 10.1108/JIMA-11-2023-0373

Ministry of Finance Malaysia. M. (2024, January 9). *eMADANI | Portal Manfaat.* Ministry of Finance Malaysia. https://manfaat.mof.gov.my/individu/emadani

Nanda, A. P., & Banerjee, R. (2021). Consumer's subjective financial well-being: A systematic review and research agenda. *International Journal of Consumer Studies, 45*(4), 750–776. Advance online publication. DOI: 10.1111/ijcs.12668

Netemeyer, R. G., Warmath, D., Fernandes, D., & Lynch, J. G.Jr. (2018). How Am I Doing? Perceived Financial Well-Being, Its Potential Antecedents, and Its Relation to Overall Well-Being. *The Journal of Consumer Research, 45*(1), 68–89. DOI: 10.1093/jcr/ucx109

Nouman, M., Siddiqi, M. F., Ullah, K., & Jan, S. (2021). Nexus between higher ethical objectives (Maqasid Al Shari'ah) and participatory finance. *Qualitative Research in Financial Markets, 13*(2), 226–251. DOI: 10.1108/QRFM-06-2020-0092

O'Cass, A. (2004). Fashion clothing consumption: Antecedents and consequences of fashion clothing involvement. *European Journal of Marketing, 38*(7), 869–882. DOI: 10.1108/03090560410539294

Oliver, R. L. (1980). A cognitive model of the antecedents and consequences of satisfaction decisions. *JMR, Journal of Marketing Research, 17*(4), 460–469. DOI: 10.1177/002224378001700405

Ooi, K. B., & Tan, G. W. H. (2016). Mobile technology acceptance model: An investigation using mobile users to explore smartphone credit card. *Expert Systems with Applications, 59*, 33–46. Advance online publication. DOI: 10.1016/j.eswa.2016.04.015

Podsakoff, P. M., MacKenzie, S. B., Lee, J.-Y., & Podsakoff, N. P. (2003). Common method biases in behavioral research: A critical review of the literature and recommended remedies. *The Journal of Applied Psychology, 88*(5), 879–903. DOI: 10.1037/0021-9010.88.5.879

Preacher, K. J., & Hayes, A. F. (2008). Asymptotic and resampling strategies for assessing and comparing indirect effects in multiple mediator models. *Behavior Research Methods*, *40*(3), 879–891. Advance online publication. DOI: 10.3758/BRM.40.3.879

Pusparini, M. D. (2023). Maqasid Sharia-Based Financial Plan to Prevent Conspicuous Consumption Among Muslim Household. *Al-Tijary*, *8*(1), 15–30. DOI: 10.21093/at.v8i1.5040

Puspitasari, I., Wiambodo, A. N. R., & Soeparman, P. (2021). The impact of expectation confirmation, technology compatibility, and customer's acceptance on e-wallet continuance intention. *AIP Conference Proceedings*, *2329*, 050012. Advance online publication. DOI: 10.1063/5.0042269

Rahim, N., Bakri, M. H., Fianto, B. A., Zainal, N., & Hussein Al Shami, S. A. (2023). Measurement and structural modelling on factors of Islamic Fintech adoption among millennials in Malaysia. *Journal of Islamic Marketing*, *14*(6), 1463–1487. DOI: 10.1108/JIMA-09-2020-0279

Ridgway, N. M., Kukar-Kinney, M., & Monroe, K. B. (2008). An Expanded Conceptualization and a New Measure of Compulsive Buying. *The Journal of Consumer Research*, *35*(4), 622–639. DOI: 10.1086/591108

Rook, D. W. (1987). The buying impulse. *The Journal of Consumer Research*, *14*(2), 189–199. DOI: 10.1086/209105

Rook, D. W., & Fisher, R. J. (1995). Normative influences on impulsive buying behavior. *The Journal of Consumer Research*, *22*(3), 305–313. DOI: 10.1086/209452

Salivio, M. P., Rillo, A. C., & Rosete, M. A. (2024). Cashless Commerce: A Study on the Interplay between Digital Payments and Luxury Consumption among Private Enterprises' Employees. *Journal of Business and Strategic Management*, *9*(9), 20–48. DOI: 10.47941/jbsm.2398

Saunders, M., Lewis, P., & Thornhill, A. (2019). *Research Methods for Business Students*. Pearson Deutschland. https://elibrary.pearson.de/book/99.150005/9781292208794

Schomburgk, L., Belli, A., & Hoffmann, A. O. I. (2024). Less cash, more splash? A meta-analysis on the cashless effect. *Journal of Retailing*, *100*(3), 382–403. DOI: 10.1016/j.jretai.2024.05.003

Sholihin, M., Shalihin, N., & Addiarrahman, . (2023). The Scale of Muslims' Consumption Intelligence: A Maqā id Insight. *ISRA International Journal of Islamic Finance*, *15*(2), 98–118. DOI: 10.55188/ijif.v15i2.544

Sirgy, M. J., Lee, D.-J., Grace, B. Y., Gurel-Atay, E., Tidwell, J., & Ekici, A. (2016). Self-expressiveness in shopping. *Journal of Retailing and Consumer Services, 30*, 292–299. DOI: 10.1016/j.jretconser.2016.02.008

Strömbäck, C., Lind, T., Skagerlund, K., Västfjäll, D., & Tinghög, G. (2017). Does self-control predict financial behavior and financial well-being? *Journal of Behavioral and Experimental Finance, 14*, 30–38. DOI: 10.1016/j.jbef.2017.04.002

Talwar, S., Dhir, A., Khalil, A., Mohan, G., & Islam, A. K. M. N. (2020). Point of adoption and beyond. Initial trust and mobile-payment continuation intention. *Journal of Retailing and Consumer Services, 55*, 102086. https://doi.org/https://doi.org/10.1016/j.jretconser.2020.102086. DOI: 10.1016/j.jretconser.2020.102086

Tam, C., Santos, D., & Oliveira, T. (2020). Exploring the influential factors of continuance intention to use mobile Apps: Extending the expectation confirmation model. *Information Systems Frontiers, 22*(1), 243–257. DOI: 10.1007/s10796-018-9864-5

Thomas, S. N., Zacharia, A., Thomas, A. C., Mathew, P. C., & Joseph, M. (2024). The Role of Digital Payments in Enhancing Financial Inclusion: Analysing and Visualizing Research Trends. *Library of Progress-Library Science, Information Technology & Computer, 44*(3).

Thoumrungroje, A. (2018). A cross-national study of consumer spending behavior: The impact of social media intensity and materialism. *Journal of International Consumer Marketing, 30*(4), 276–286. DOI: 10.1080/08961530.2018.1462130

Tripathi, S. (2023). Determinants of Continuance Intention to Use Mobile Wallets Technology in the Post Pandemic Era: Moderating Role of Perceived Trust. *Journal of International Technology and Information Management, 31*(3), 128–170. DOI: 10.58729/1941-6679.1570

Tuan Pham, M., & Chang, H. H. (2010). Regulatory Focus, Regulatory Fit, and the Search and Consideration of Choice Alternatives. *The Journal of Consumer Research, 37*(4), 626–640. DOI: 10.1086/655668

Underdown, K., & Tamara, D. (2025). Digital wallets: a study on the influence of consumer perceptions and attitudes on impulsive consumer behaviour. *Frontiers in Human Dynamics, Volume 7-2025*. DOI: 10.3389/fhumd.2025.1545141

Veblen, T. (2017). *The theory of the leisure class*. Routledge. DOI: 10.4324/9781315135373

Venkatesh, V., Morris, M. G., Davis, G. B., & Davis, F. D. (2003). User acceptance of information technology: Toward a unified view. *Management Information Systems Quarterly, 27*(3), 425–478. Advance online publication. DOI: 10.2307/30036540

Verplanken, B., & Herabadi, A. (2001). Individual differences in impulse buying tendency: Feeling and no thinking. *European Journal of Personality*, *15*(1, suppl), S71–S83. DOI: 10.1002/per.423

Windasari, N. A., & Lin, F. (2021). Why Do People Continue Using Fitness Wearables? The Effect of Interactivity and Gamification. *SAGE Open*, *11*(4), 21582440211056606. Advance online publication. DOI: 10.1177/21582440211056606

Worldpay. (2025). *Global Payments Report | Payment Insights | Worldpay*. https://worldpay.com/en/global-payments-report

Yousef, F. (2024). The Impact of E-Wallets on Consumer Spending Behavior and Financial Management. *International Journal of Scientific Research*, *3*(12), 429–456. DOI: 10.59992/IJSR.2024.v3n12p12

Yuan, W., Gong, S., & Gao, J. (2021). How Does House Demolition Affect Family Conspicuous Consumption? *Frontiers in Psychology*, *12*, 741006. Advance online publication. DOI: 10.3389/fpsyg.2021.741006

Zhao, X., Lynch, J. G.Jr, & Chen, Q. (2010). Reconsidering Baron and Kenny: Myths and truths about mediation analysis. *The Journal of Consumer Research*, *37*(2), 197–206. Advance online publication. DOI: 10.1086/651257

Zhou, T. (2014). Understanding the determinants of mobile payment continuance usage. *Industrial Management & Data Systems*, *114*(6), 936–948. DOI: 10.1108/IMDS-02-2014-0068

Chapter 10

Synergizing Islamic Finance and Islamic Social Finance for Sustainability

R. Velmurugan
https://orcid.org/0000-0002-7925-9757
Karpagam Academy of Higher Education, Coimbatore, India

R. Bhuvaneswari
https://orcid.org/0009-0003-9396-6129
Dr. Mahalingam College of Engineering and Technology, Pollachi, India

Maksud A. Madraswale
https://orcid.org/0000-0001-9565-0775
Presidency University, Bangalore, India

Ravi Thirumalaisamy
https://orcid.org/0000-0002-5954-5940
Modern College of Business and Science, Oman

ABSTRACT

Comprehensive Islamic Finance along with Islamic Social Finance is a very keen development approach into ethically and socially responsible financial reforms into sustainable development. Islamic financing is based on the profit and the risk sharing models. Muslim social finance tools like zakat, waqf and sadaqah address social inequalities through redistributing the wealth and assisting the alienated community. These sectors converge for the compliance of the United Nations' SDGs through the investments in social enterprises, green projects and impact driven initiatives.

DOI: 10.4018/979-8-3373-1842-4.ch010

It is overcoming regulatory challenge and collaboration between the stakeholders which is important, and its done using digital technology such as blockchain and fintech that are enhancing efficiency and accessibility.

INTRODUCTION

Islamic social finance and Islamic finance are on the rise; as part and parcel of a broader world movement toward ethical, socially responsible and sustainable financial systems. The two are based on Shariah which preaches that justice, equity, and moral responsibility exist in any financial transaction. Whereas the main principle of Islamic finance is the need to generate profit by applying ethical business models, social opportunities, wealth distribution and poverty reduction are the key concerns of Islamic social finance. Through a combination of such systems, perspectives of sustainable development, financial inclusion, and ethical business practice are all presented. Moreover, as a way to realize their synergetic impact, it is also necessary to ground this argument in a coherent conceptual framework, e.g., the Maqasid al-Shariah or the alignment with the United Nations Sustainable Development Goals (SDGs) to assess how these can help build inclusive and sustainable economies.

The Islamic finance is driven by unique values that makes it not equal to conventional finance especially the ban on riba (interest) which is exploitive. Rather, they derive financial revenues in the form of profit-and-loss sharing contracts including mudarabah and musharakah where profits and risks are shared between the investors and the entrepreneurs (Ayub, 2007). Moreover, Islamic financing forbids investment in industries which are haram including alcohol, gambling and pork, among others, hence ensuring that the world of finance is ethical. Financial instruments such as sukuk (Islamic bonds), ijarah (leasing) and murabaha (cost-plus financing) are arranged in such a way that they stimulate equity-based financing in preference to debt instruments as this helps achieve a more reasonable sharing of wealth (Iqbal & Mirakhor, 2011).

In parallel, Islamic social finance applies the tools of the zakat (obligatory almsgiving), waqf (charitable endowment), and sadaqah (voluntary charity) in order to reallocate wealth and address poverty in an ethical way. One of the five pillars of Islam, Zakat, dictates that Muslims should give a given share of their revenue (usually 2.5 percent) each year to the poor so as to form a social responsibility that enhances the economic integration (Ahmed, 2004). The Al Azhar Zakat Foundation in Egypt is one of the examples of the practical role of the foregoing in healthcare and education. Waqf forms a long-term donation of assets and the returns thereof are spent on the community welfare; a typical arrangement is that of the Sultan Qaboos Waqf in Oman, which provides funds to health and education sectors (Sullivan,

2011). Sadaqah is voluntary and hence allows adaptive responses to social disasters, to which they have been directed during the COVID-19 pandemic, in order to assist in healthcare, food security, and vulnerable populations in the Muslim world (Karim & Hossain, 2020).

Even though the chapter has this solid ethical ground, it is compelled to speak out on the issues that exist critically. It is time to add some limitations and practical challenges to the implementation of Islamic finance to the discussion of its advantages. This involves having regulatory frameworks, the harmonization of practices in the various jurisdictions as well as integrating them with the new fin-tech. Such a critical gaze ought to look on whether Islamic financial institutions indeed live up to their proclaimed social aims or whether they are merely reproductions of conventional models in a slightly different form. Another way of studying Islamic finance as a potentially superior alternative to conventional ESG frameworks is to compare the two.

Real life examples make the clash between financial and social goals clear. Islamic teachings are used in bolstering the notion of the microfinance and the financial inclusion; an example being BRI (Zin & Abidin, 2018). The Islamic Development Bank (IDB) facilitates infrastructure, health, and education in Muslim-majority states and the institutions contribute to the SDGs poverty reduction and quality education (Ghaleb, 2019). In addition, more developments occur in Islamic finance in terms of environmental sustainability such as the green sukuk that finances projects that support sustainable climates and global climate policy (Thomson Reuters, 2017). To capture the fast-changing environment, the chapter will have to integrate more up-to-date literature (2022-2024) of journals like Sustainability, Journal of Islamic Finance, institutional reports by Islamic Development Bank or UNDP, and offer more current-day debates like fintech integration and ESG compliance.

Overall, the Islamic and Islamic social finance are pillars of an emerging movement toward ethical finance and responsible social finance globally. Their joint focus on risk-sharing, ethical governance and poverty alleviation is a blueprint to viable economic growth. In order to give their full potential though, they must overcome the issues of integration, critical scholarship, and embed their practices within a coherent conceptual framework. Better organized, with recent evidence and critical reflection in support, a more distinct articulation will be effective in illustrating how these systems could play an important role in realizing an ethical and sustainable world order of financial systems.

THE ESSENCE OF ISLAMIC FINANCE AND ITS ROLE IN ECONOMIC SUSTAINABILITY

Conceptual Foundations

Islamic finance and Islamic social finance are coming to be understood as complementary systems that are rooted in the Shariah as part of the emerging global movement to develop ethical, socially responsible and sustainable financial systems. The principles do not only help individuals to conduct themselves with justice, equity, and welfare in mind, but they also lay down institutional norms. Islamic finance focuses on ethical method of profit-making that refers to businesses compliant with the Shariah law, whereas Islamic social finance focuses on social justice that aims to restore wealth distribution and eradicate poverty. The two cooperatively enhance the making of a more inclusive and sustainable financial system. This chapter examines their synergies and the difference between the two in promoting responsible financial standards and social inclusion, within Maqasid al-Shariah and in coherence with the United Nations Sustainable Development Goals (SDGs).

Traditional Instruments of Islamic Finance

The Islamic finance stands out among the conventional systems based on some important tenets, including the ban on the concept of riba (interest) as being exploitive. Rather than revenue generation, profit-and-loss sharing scheme is used to generate income thereby encouraging common risks and responsibility. Mudarabah and musharakah are examples of such contracts, whereby the profit is shared on the basis of an agreed ratio and the loss is paid as per the proportion of the capital invested (Ayub, 2007). In addition, Islamic finance does not condone investment in prohibited industries that include gambling, alcohol, and pork-based industries thus instilling ethics into monetary activity. The precepts of these may be seen in sukuk (Islamic bonds), ijarah (leasing) and murabaha (cost-plus) financing. The equity tools package focuses on equity-based funding, ensuring greater equity with regard to wealth as well as realizing socio-economic justice on a long-term basis (Iqbal & Mirakhor, 2011).

Islamic Social Finance and Wealth Redistribution

The Islamic social finance is an Islamic banking subsector that is accentuated on wealth sharing and social welfare. He also includes zakat (power to give obligatory almsgiving), waqf (Khwanjhang investment) and sadaqah (voluntary charity). One of the five pillars of the Islamic religion, namely, Zakat, involves paying a fixed percentage of a person,s wealth yearly, not only as an act of charity but also as a social duty to promote a socio-economic equilibrium in the society (Ahmed, 2004). It has found true-life application in organizations such as the Al Azhar Zakat Foundation in Egypt which sponsors such things as health and education among the needy. In the same regard, waqf can be used to finance community development in the long term since it allows individuals to invest in donations to charitable work; the Sultan Qaboos Waqf in Oman has been used to fund education and public health projects (Sullivan, 2011). Sadaqah is voluntary and flexible and, therefore, an essential component in emergencies responses, e.g., during the COVID-19 pandemic when the efforts of various individuals and organizations all over the Muslim world were focused on healthcare and food security (Karim & Hossain, 2020).

Integration Challenges and the Need for Analytical Depth

Islamic and Islamic social finance are likely to work in silos, creating a disjointed practice even though both focal areas have similar ethical foundations. Much of the discussion is descriptive, which does not provide a critical analysis of the issues of integration, including discrepancies between the regulatory frameworks, a lack of use of digital means, and the insufficient evaluation of the impacts. The chapter needs to transcend enumerating benefits and become involved in the theoretical squabbles, thresholds to knowledge, and challenges to implementation. A more analytical approach can be taken, such as the comparison of Islamic finance and conventional ESG frameworks, that would identify potential current advantages 3 and possible gaps when it comes to delivering on inclusive, sustainable growth.

Technological Innovations and Emerging Trends

The terrain of Islamic finance is shifting with the technology of digitization and new instruments. Green sukuk, in particular, are one of the very important developments aimed at harmonizing the objectives of Islamic finance with environmental sustainability objectives. These products facilitate climate-friendly projects financing in a Shariah-compliant manner, since they combine the economic with the environmental aspect of the products (Thomson Reuters, 2017). Nevertheless, to be relevant, the literature should capture the more recent innovations (2022 2024) including the application of fintech, online platforms dedicated to holding and discharging said zakat, and blockchain-based waqf registries, transforming the current and future landscape of Islamic financial practice. It will be important to be in touch with the latest events in emissions publishing Sustainability and Journal of Islamic Finance journals among others as also in institutional publications of Islamic Development Bank and the UNDP.

Case Studies and Real-World Applications

Integrating Islamic finance and Islamic social finance has proven to be successful in several institutions to reach the social goals and development. Banks such as Bank Rakyat Indonesia (BRI), have engaged the Islamic microfinance models in an attempt to drive financial inclusion as well as poverty alleviation (Zin & Abidin, 2018). In a similar way, the Islamic Development Bank (IDB) has also used Islamic financial instruments to finance infrastructure, education, and health projects in Muslim-heavy states, providing direct help in the achievement of the SDGs related to reducing poverty and ensuring quality education (Ghaleb, 2019). Such examples support the future prospects of a holistic Islamic financial landscape when it comes to providing economic and social returns.

Policy Implications and Future Directions

Islamic finance and Islamic social finance, when coupled in a unified policymaking and conceptual framework present incredibly potent pursuits towards the achievement of a just, inclusive, and sustainable global economy. Their practices foster ethical governance through the ban on exploitative governance models, their transparency and safeguarding people and environment against financial degradation. The increasing interest in the ESG-linked instruments, including the green sukuk, signals the relevance of such instruments to the modern financial language. Still, in order to achieve the potential of these systems, concerted policy action as well as the harmonization of regulatory approaches should be implemented and theoretical insight, as well as empirical constraints, into their bases, should be investigated.

The combination of Islamic finance and Islamic social finance can be viewed as the constituent part of a socially responsible and ethical financial environment. Islamic financial system promotes a more equitable economic system because Islamic financial system lays greater emphasis on risk sharing, transparency and shuns the use of harmful practices. The Islamic social financing, inhabited by preferences committed to distribution and alleviation of poverty, corresponds to a better well-being and fairness in society. With reasonable embedding, these systems open a window to sustainable growth, access to financing, and responsible corporate behavior. This further requires critical thinking, rational organization and embracement of technological advancement as well as keeping in touch with the modern social demands and development agenda.

ISLAMIC SOCIAL FINANCE: THE PILLARS OF ZAKAT, WAQF, AND SADAQAH

Islamic Social Finance: Ethical Redistribution for Inclusive Development

Islamic social finance is a complement to conventional Islamic finance, as it puts an emphasis on redistributing wealth, social welfare, in accordance with the Maqasid al-Shariah--the higher purpose of the Islamic law in order to achieve justice, social welfare, and human dignity. Islamic social finance is an operating system during which financial payments are made within the framework of the Shariah system; this system is aimed at alleviating the socio-economic inequalities, developing the community, and enforcing social justice. The presence of zakat, waqf, and sadaqah instruments contributes specifically to fact that they are helping the needs of the people and that they promote economic inclusion of the marginalized groups. All these tools provide a guideline to ethical wealth-distribution and wealth reversal phenomena and Islamic social finance is thus an important part of sustainable and inclusive development following the UN Sustainable Development Goals (SDGs).

Zakat: A Mandated Instrument of Wealth Redistribution

Islamic finance is based on obligatory annual payment known as Zakat, which is the contribution of 2.5 percent on eligible wealth (Ahmed, 2004). It is beyond charity- it is a systemic device of wealth redistribution to make the rich equal to the poor. Its economic investment on the needy, indebted, orphans and other vulnerable groups integrate with the welfare economics theory and bring about socio-economic harmonization. The Zakat Foundation of America is one institution that implements its zakat to provide such basic amenities like healthcare, education, and food security to people living in underserved societies throughout the globe (Zakat Foundation, 2021). Asutay, (2012) also confirms empirical evidence of the contribution of zakat to macroeconomic stability and balanced development through enhancing consumption and diminishing inequality.

Waqf: A Sustainable Model for Social Infrastructure Financing

Waqf is the asset endowment- whether land, property, or money- to be held for an ongoing charitable cause. Traditionally, waqf has financed religious, educational, and medical establishments and institutions in the middle of Islamic civilization. What makes it inherently sustainable is that in its untarnished revenue stream system that provides a perpetual income platform and makes it as a valid alternative source of a long term financing of social infrastructure. The most prominent ones are the endowment of Al-Azhar University in Egypt and Sultan Qaboos Waqf in Oman, which targets funding educational and healthcare projects (Sullivan, 2011; Zin & Abidin, 2018). In the modern context, nations such as Malaysia are inculcating waqf into national development plans. A case study of one of the agencies that have used waqf to provide schools, clinics, low-income housing into underdeveloped areas is the Perbadanan Wakaf Selangor, Selangor Waqf Corporation (Abdul Rahman & Muhammad, 2013). The incorporation of waqf in Islamic microfinance makes it very scalable and successful in the contemporary social financing challenges.

Sadaqah: Voluntary Charity for Responsive Social Welfare

Sadaqah is voluntary and consists of money but also good deeds whereas zakat is neither optional or a good deed. That is why its versatility is a key to handling the immediate and varied social needs, especially during the emergency periods. The Muslims contributed money during the COVOID 19 pandemic by giving sadaqah to boost healthcare systems, food distribution and relief activities. In Pakistan, the Saylani Welfare Trust channeled sadaqah money on medical relief, food banks and alleviating poverty initiatives (Saylani Welfare, 2020). Sadaqah acts as a supplement to institutionalized social finance as well as forming a culture of giving and building a spirit of civic community interconnectedness as a means of social solidarity.

Toward a Unified Framework for Sustainable Development

Zakat, waqf, and sadaqah are therefore on the one hand, a combination of obligatory and voluntary instruments of social justice meant to foster social and economic equality and on the other hand, a mutually reinforcement between the two. When combined with the profit-and-loss-sharing structures of Islamic finance, the tools have the potential to enhance inclusive growth and financial resilience. To fully realize this potential, however, it is critical to face Islamic social finance in the context of a robust conceptual system- e.g. its compatibility with SDGs- or equivalent concept- and support it with adequate operational framework, technology (e.g. fintech solutions to the delivery of zakat) and scholarly knowledge. Keeping the discourse up to date with sources published in 2022-2024 and institutional reports of Islamic Development Bank or UNDP will make the paper and the discussion purely of academic value. Islamic social finance represents the convergence of ethical spiritual imperatives with encroaching strategic enhancement ambitions, and should, therefore, represent the prototype of sustainable and socially responsible monetary arrangements world-wide.

The Integration of Zakat, Waqf, and Sadaqah in Addressing Social Inequalities

Traditional Instruments and Their Strategic Roles in Islamic Social Finance

The three main tools of Islamic social finance-zakat, waqf and sadaqah are the main pillars in combating social inequality, creating equity and overall development of the society. All three instruments serve a slightly different but related purpose: zakat is mandatory wealth transfer aimed at the immediate funding of the poor; waqf is a perpetual endowment that in effect provides long-term funding toward critical social infrastructure; and sadaqah is volitional and flexible charity that allows the individual person to contribute to social welfare initiatives on a grassroots level.

All these instruments can be used strategically to maximize impact in either a temporal or structural aspect of social welfare. As an illustration, zakat can be used to deliver short-term relief and subsistence aid to the poor and the marginalized, whereas waqf endowment can be utilized to long-term developmental ends, i.e. funding schools, hospitals, and other public infrastructure. In the meantime, sadaqah is inclusive in enlisting the community in participating by allowing them to contribute where they deem their value and generate a culture of empathy and social conscientiousness.

One exemplification of such synergy is the initiatives of the Islamic Development Bank (IDB) which have successfully utilized all the three instruments to fund development projects in Muslim-majority countries. The IDB (2018) confirmed that its Zakat Fund has played a major role in poverty alleviation, supporting education and improving health in the countries of Sudan, Pakistan and many others including Yemen. In Turkey, Waqf Fund has been used in school systems, health and related social services. According to Al Khouri & Bouzi (2019), revenue generated through waqf endowments has been used to put up universities, hospitals, and affordable housing providers- all of which establish long-term social investment systems.

Though traditional in nature, these instruments are being remodeled into more modern financial systems and experiences, more transparent, scaled and impactful with entrances of technological solutions. Such a shift is essential in order to increase outreach to previously under-served groups, and in order to position Islamic social finance alongside modern international development objectives, such as the Sustainable Development Goals (SDGs). Thus, zakat, waqf and sadaqah not only offer means of poverty eradication and economic justice but they are also the drivers of community-driven development, based on Islamic ethical values and more aligned with contemporary standards of policy and digital effectiveness.

MERGING ISLAMIC FINANCE AND ISLAMIC SOCIAL FINANCE: A HOLISTIC APPROACH TO SUSTAINABLE DEVELOPMENT

Integrating Islamic Finance and Islamic Social Finance for Sustainable Development

The inter-mingling of the Islamic finance with the Islamic social finance introduces a wholesome and morally sound framework of attaining sustainable development. This would engage the profit-making apparatus of Islamic finance with the social welfare element of Islamic social finance, thereby creating a more inclusive, fairer, sustainable-based financial system. This synergy creates a new ecosystem of innovation wherein economic growth cannot be pursued in isolation but must rather be deeply connected to social well-being and environmental consciousness.Combining Islamic finance and Islamic social finance would create a sustainable approach to achieving development that is comprehensive, grounded in ethics, and deeply integrated with social well-being and the responsibility toward the environment. This will introduce greater efficiency and inclusiveness in the system of Islamic finance and contribute to a more equitable and sustainability-oriented financial system by merging the profit motive of Islam finance with social protection emphasis of Islamic social finance. Such synergy creates a new innovative system where the economic growth is not sought independently, but interrelation with police, social and environmental balance is inherent.

Merging Profit and Social Responsibility

Islamic finance is based on morally sound principles of investment that apply the risks sharing systems like mudarabah and musharakah to achieve an even distribution of wealth without the use of interest that leads to exploitation (Ayub, 2007). Such profit-sharing contracts will encourage entrepreneurship and inhibit unjust enrichment and following Islamic moral values will encourage investment. In a complementary manner, Islamic financing focuses on wealth redistribution by means of zakat (compulsory almsgiving), waqf (endowment) and sadaqah (voluntary charity) all of which are driven towards euphoric marginalized and underserved communities.

The mutuality of the two spaces can enable Islamic financial institutions to finance socially responsible enterprises, and green projects where investments will bear not only financial returns but also social and environmental returns that can be measured. This bi-fold aim is well within the bracket of the larger Sustainable Development Goals (SDGs) concerning the alleviation of poverty, healthcare provision, and environmental sustainability (Karim & Hossain, 2020).

Financing Green and Social Projects

An interesting demonstration of this combination that happened was when the Dubai Islamic Bank issued a green sukuk in 2017 to finance a key project on a solar power station in the UAE (Thomson Reuters, 2017). This campaign was in line with the denizens of Islamic finance and global climate change action. On the same note, the social finance instruments have played a critical role in financing social businesses and other services whose funds are provided by the Islamic financial instruments. In Pakistan, Saylani Welfare Trust uses the donations of cream to operate food programs, clinics, and schools, and in Malaysia, the Waqf Fund uses it to finance infrastructure to provide cheap housing, education, and healthcare (Zin & Abidin, 2018).

Advancing Financial Inclusion

The incorporation also boosts the financial inclusion significantly to the underserved population. Models of Islamic microfinance can include qard al-hasan (benevolent loans), beyond the reach of conventional finance to small-business persons of low income. As an example, the Islamic Microfinance Network has backed interest-free lending mechanisms to allow people to engage in business ventures and realize better livelihoods (Khan, 2011). Whereas zakat can be used where there are urgent humanitarian needs, waqf can be used in long-term sustainable development initiatives thereby providing a chain of social change: short term, immediate assistance and long-term structural change.

Strategic Alignment with SDGs

Notably, this comprehensive solution has been matched with the SDGs of the United Nations especially goals of ending poverty, limiting quality healthcare, quality education, and sustainable environment, among others. The ethical underpinnings of Islamic finance, as postulated by Iqbal and Mirakhor (2011), are promoting equity, justice and resource management, which means it is highly appropriate to the pursuit of development goals around the globe. A hybrid between Islamic finance and social finance would open the door to an economic model, which does not solely aim at turning a profit but emphasize social justice and environmental awareness as day-to-day effects.

Real-World Implementations

The benefits of such synergy can be clearly evidenced with real life examples. TheBank Rakyat Indonesia has incorporated Islamic finance and the Islamic social finance to develop microfinance and overcome poverty by providing small-scale loans through the Islamic concept of Zakat to support the educational needs of the poor groups and health facilities. On the same note, Islamic Development Bank (IDB) has been at the forefront in the implementation of this integration within its member nations. By means of its Zakat Fund, the IDB finances development initiatives in renewable energy, education and healthcare, retaining poverty reduction and social development in its financial functions (Islamic Development Bank, 2018).

Generally, Islamic finance paired with Islamic social finance will have strong foundation to come up with an ethical, inclusive, and sustainable economy. It allows investment to be directed to the socially responsible business, green infrastructure, and community-based welfare initiatives, and is on a par conceptualizing, such as the Maqasid al-Shariah and the SDGs. Reduced redundancy, enhanced depth of analysis, as well as interaction with present literature and practical applications of the matters make this integrated model more future-ready and dynamic contributor to global development processes.

THE ECONOMIC POTENTIAL OF WAQF AND ZAKAT IN DRIVING DEVELOPMENT

Traditional Instruments of Islamic Social Finance: Waqf and Zakat in Contemporary Development

Conceptual Foundations

Waqf and zawat are the two instruments in social finance with Islamic roots based on the ideas of asset redistribution, socio-economic equality, and societal duty. Deeply rooted in the rich Islamic tradition, these instruments can be used as effective tools of redressing the socio-economic imbalances as they help to finance deserving areas of education, healthcare, housing, and infrastructure. In modern context, waqf and zakat have been used in a modified fashion, as they are mobilised to help fund large-scale development projects, which are based on Sustainable Development Goals (SDGs), or even in the generic framework of Maqasid al-Shariah, which aims at the preservation of life, intellect, property, faith, and lineage.

Waqf: Institutionalizing Long-Term Community Development

Traditionally, waqf may be described as the voluntary and permanent donation of property, and has conventionally been used to construct such institutions as mosques, hospitals, and schools. In contrast to occasional acts of charity, waqf endowment assets are not consumed, whereas its income is used incessantly to support the communal operations. This self sustaining construct makes waqf a perfect medium of long term social investment.

The modern financial tools of engineering have in more recent decades enabled waqf to reach scale in ways never previously possible. Islamic financial institutions are now devising new mechanisms to pool waqf funds in the interests of public and private partnerships, investments in real estate and hybrid funding approaches. As another example, the Turkish Directorate of Religious Affairs has successfully used the waqf money to fund hospitals, schools, and low-income housing, which have produced a long-term social profit (Al-Khouri & Bouzi, 2019).

The Selangor Waqf Corporation in Malaysia has been leading the use of waqf endowments to provide public amenities of any nature including the provision of education, health care, and housing infrastructure in both the rural and urban underprivileged neighborhoods (Abdul Rahman & Muhammad, 2013). These projects demonstrate the potential of waqf to become a component of the national development planning to cover gaps in service delivery and spatial inequalities.

Zakat: From Charity to Empowerment

Zakat, which is a mandatory donation of 2.5 percent of the wealth, does not only reduce poverty but also invests in the economic empowerment of the height of the productive use of capital. Linked to direct service--food, shelter, and medical care--now there is an attempt to restructure zakat to provide microfinancing, job skills, and enterprises as long-term interventions in the poor communities.

In Pakistan, the Saylani Welfare Trust uses the zakat to lend interest-free microloans to small businesses and allows them to start or expand their businesses and become part of the formal economy (Saylani Welfare, 2020). In Indonesia, the Dompet Dhuafa Foundation uses the funds to pay the skills training fees of agriculture, health care, and handicrafts to not only eliminate income poverty but also to end capability deprivation (Dompet Dhuafa, 2020).

Targeted deployment of zakat signals a transition between the consumption-based model and development oriented model in Islamic ethical finance and capability approach of welfare economics.

Strategic Role in Achieving the SDGs

Waqf and zakt when used strategically, are positioned better to achieve SDG1 (No Poverty); 3 (Good Health); 4 (Quality Education); 8 (Decent Work); and SDG11 (Sustainable Cities and Communities). They are true possibilities of Islamic social finance because they are drawn into national financing plans and international development policy.

The moral principles of Islamic finance that includes risk sharing, equity, and stewardship make it considerably well-adapted to structural poverty and income inequality (Iqbal and Mirakhor, 2011). These are not only tools that are charitable but also have the ability to institutionalize justice, intergenerational fairness, and stimulating inclusive economic growth.

Real-Life Case Studies and Policy Implications

Education and Health:As an illustration, the ancient Al-Azhar University in Egypt has survived and thrived on waqf endowments over many centuries, about 250 in a continual line (Sullivan, 2011).

Microfinance Model of BangladeshIn Bangladesh, the model of zakat and taxation has been combined with the microfinance programs, which has offered a chance to millions of people to start micro-enterprises and uplift their socio-economic status in rural environments (Yunus, 2007).

These experiences demonstrate that when the regulation system props up with innovations and transparency, waqf and zakat can assume the status of institutionalized instruments of development finance where moral imperatives can be backed with measurable social results.

Policy and Innovation Frontiers

To fulfill their potential to the fullest, waqf and zakat organizations should be even further combined with Islamic finance infrastructure, such as fintech, green sukuk, and impact measurement systems. The harmonization of regulation, the reforms in governance and the digitization of the payment of Zakat and waqf are critical to enhance efficiency, transparency and scalability.

Furthermore, in the recent research (2022-2024), particular attention is paid to aligning Islamic social finance with ESG standards that can support international cooperation with partners and increase credibility to contribute to global development discourse (e.g., Islamic Development Bank reports; UNDP Islamic Finance Hub initiatives).

Waqf and zakat are more than historical traditions in charity giving- they are the tools of Islamic social finance that has the potential in helping the countries in achieving their national development objectives, alleviating inequality, and integrating people. In cooperation with Islamic finance and current inventions, they are an appealing set of model sustainable and ethical economic systems. The SDGs and Maqasid al-Shariah provide strategic congruence for a better future guided by financial, social justice and an environmentally friendly world.

OVERCOMING OBSTACLES: REGULATORY CHALLENGES AND INSTITUTIONAL DIVISIONS

Integration Challenges between Islamic Finance and Islamic Social Finance

The interface beyond the parallel between Islamic finance and Islamic social finance has the potential transformational changes to concretize sustainable development to enable financial inclusions and reduce poverty. This synergy has, however, been under-realized and this is owing to a number of structural and regulatory entry impediments. These are lack of cohesiveness in governance, institutional misfit as well as the general lacking of coordination among key stakeholders. The absence of structural change on these impediments means that the assimilation of Islamic financial instruments and social finance tools will be limited and therefore, will not achieve their collective consequences on social welfare and development.

Regulatory Challenges and Fragmented Legal Frameworks

The biggest challenge of incorporating Islamic finance, and Islamic social finance, is the lack of integrated framework. Although there are Shariah-compliant commercial norms governing the scope of Islamic finance, most financial policies concerning instruments such as zakat, waqf and sadaqah remain beyond the scope of mainstream financial practices. This duality results in a lack of coordination in the management of funds and avenues where collaboration could be missed (Ayub, 2007). As an example, despite having a well-established Islamic finance industry, the regulatory misalignment between financial institutions on the one hand, and social finance organizations on the other has hampered the work of channelizing waq and zakat to the development of scalable projects (Abdul Rahman & Muhammad, 2013).

It is also complex without common international standards. The lack of harmonized regulation policies hinders the existence of unilateral regulation policies because of various interpretations and implementation of the Shariah principles by various jurisdictions, thereby frustrating the bridge of gap that exists between regulation of Islamic commercial and philanthropic finance.

Institutional Divisions and Conceptual Misalignment

There is also institutional fragmentation which is a major impediment to integration. Companies of Islamic finance are profit-seeking, whereas ones of social finance are motivated in terms of welfare. This incompatibility acts as a deterrent to cooperation and a bar to break the silos in operations (Iqbal & Mirakhor, 2011). Furthermore, social finance tools in the Islamic context are not always correctly understood by the state commercial financial institutions who may consider it as extraneous or not something that pertains to its business mandate. These misconceptions are the reason why such tools cannot be harnessed to achieve wider development.

The lack of institutional systems and incentive structure that would motivate Islamic bank to cooperate with agencies where waqf and zakat would be an important absence. This split hinders access to capital into socially beneficial projects and it contributes towards further inefficiencies in this Islamic financial ecosystem.

Technological Innovations and Digital Synergies

In spite of structural difficulties, digital financial technologies are opening up exciting prospects of breaking the lines of integration. Islamic social finance could be further decentralized through solutions such as blockchain, mobile banking, and Islamic crowdfunding platforms, further increasing the methods of Islamic social finance that are transparent, more efficient and more accessible.

Blockchain, instance, will provide decentralized and immutable database, which will hold tracks on the zakat and waqf funds, and should interfere with the level of fraud, whilst providing transparent usage (Thomson Reuters, 2017). The tokenization of waqf property also allows fractional ownership, and raises the possibilities of mobilizing funds to undertake large projects in infrastructure and education.

Fintech-based investment systems like Wahed Invest are examples of how ethically aware and Shariah-compliant investing systems can be used to solve some of our social problems like poverty and education. In some nations such as Queensland and Pakistan, mobile phone based microfinance and donar platforms are helping Islamic finance services to be more accessible even to rural and underserved populations.

These include the most important innovations in terms of democratization of access to Islamic finance and possibilities of scale in combining commercial and philanthropic capital to invest in development.

Toward a Coherent Integration Strategy: Conceptual and Policy Directions

In order to achieve full potential of Islamic finance and Islamic social finance in sustainable development, this should be anchored on a coherent conceptual framework, and a coherent regulatory framework. The integration in Maqasid al-Shariah - which prioritizes social justice, redistribution of wealth, and social welfare of the population - can be used to ground the integration in an authoritative normative consensus and inform the development of policy. Alignment of these efforts with global frameworks like Sustainable Development Goals (SDGs) can also be used to make Islamic finance an ally in the global sustainability agenda.

There is a need to enhance institutional coordination within the cross-sectoral platforms involving regulators, Islamic financial institutions and social financiers. The need to create guidelines on how mortgages like sukuk, musharakah, waqf, and zakat can be collaboratively designed and developed will be the solution to creating innovative ways of inclusive finance (Karim & Hossain, 2020).

Moreover, governments and international organizations such as the Islamic Development Bank and UNDP should take the lead in leading the efforts that encourage best practices, capacity-building and cross-country regulatory harmonization. Recent studies (2022-2024) attach great significance to the role of adaptive governance and technological agility in the relevance of Islamic financial systems to the global economy as a whole, including the digital and ESG-friendly environment.

Although the harmonization of Islamic finance and Islamic social finance can achieve significant advances concerning sustainable development and financial inclusion, the scope is restrained by regulatory gaps and mismatch, and conceptual barriers. It will take a collective effort to deal with these challenges across the realms of law, technology, and institutions. The dynamic placement of digital financial solutions facilitated with harmonized regulations, administered within the parameters of welfare-oriented principles such as Maqasid al-Shariah can become a source of an effective and integrated Islamic financial system. Subsequently, this can empower the position of Islamic finance in resolving the issues facing societies in the modern world as reflected in the SDGs and changing global sustainability objectives.

THE ROLE OF DIGITAL TECHNOLOGIES IN ENHANCING ISLAMIC SOCIAL FINANCE

Conceptual Foundations: Leveraging Technology through a Maqasid al-Shariah Lens

However, there is a requirement to ensure the accountability and transparency of the Islamic social finance regarding the operationalization of zakat and waqf, which can be realized through digital technologies aiming at the greater financial inclusion. Basing the framework of the combination of technology and Islamic social finance on the principles of Maqasid al-Shariah which focuses on preservation of wealth (hifz al-mal), social wellbeing, and furtherance of justice, the ethical aims are fulfilled because the development needs are satisfied through technology.

Although Islamic finance has proved to be very successful in the commercial sector, to achieve its full potential, the principles involved in the financing have to be aligned with the mechanisms of the Islamic social finance that focus on making wealth more evenly distributed. In that regard, the strategic utilisation of diaspora networks, fintech, and blockchain can be seen as a means by which to realise inclusive and sustainable progress, especially in underserved Muslim populations.

Blockchain: Ensuring Transparency and Restoring Trust

The blockchain technology provides a paradigm-shifting way of guaranteeing transparency and integrity in the collection and distribution of Islamic social financing especially the zakat and waqf. Blockchain, as a decentralized and unchangeable register, allows the tracking the money path - in real-time - between the charity donor and the recipient, making the process more transparent and eliminating potential leakage issues and increase the trust in the charity system.

As an illustration, asset classes such as waqf properties that are supposed to be used in expending benefits on the community can be tokenized using blockchain technologies. This will not only make it easier to document in a secure way, but also makes it possible to do fractional ownership such that it becomes easier to participate in large scale development, such as schools, hospitals, and social infrastructure.

On a more realistic level is the study by Dubai Islamic Economy Development Centre (DIEDC) on blockchain-based management of the zakat. It has manifested that such systems can be used to offer verification and distribution in real-time, which means that money is received by the appropriate parties in a timely and transparent manner (Thomson Reuters, 2017). These are the key features that will lead to the development of donor confidence and propulsion of donor base to the cause of Islamic charity.

In addition, blockchain lowers the administrative burden, limits fraud and creates permanent auditing trail. It relocates zakat and waqf as flexible, efficient and reliable in current financial systems, which is crucial in the context of the SDGs and Islamic finance addressing greater social impacts.

Fintech: Expanding Access and Efficiency in Service Delivery

In addition to being transparent, the use of fintech is transforming access to Islamic financial services not just in Muslim-majority countries but among the Muslim minorities as well. Digital wallets, peer-to-peer lending, mobile applications to pay Zakat and interest-free microfinance platforms are scalable Shariah-compliant alternatives to conventional banks.

Another example is platforms that provide qard al-hasan (interest-free loans), which allows entrepreneurs and others on the margins to develop livelihoods without implementing the unproductive burden of debt. Financial companies such as Wahed Invest and Amanah Finance have already introduced ethically compliant digital investment platforms and give Muslim users across the world the ability to invest in halal portfolios without using the services of conventional banks (Karim & Hossain, 2020).

Digital systems can also make the distribution of zakat computation, collection and distribution of zakat easier. Apps enable the user to estimate his/her contributions and donate anytime plus real-time update on how the contribution is being used. The Zakat Foundation of America is one such example where they employ the use of fintech products to allow accountability of the donations supporting the humanitarian and poverty alleviation initiatives (Zakat Foundation, 2021). Such inventions not only make operations more efficient, but also help Muslims to turnover their religious duties with certainty.

In this way, fintech is a bridge-builder and a magnifier--it can connect the individual piety with the overall development, and enhance service delivery in a cost-efficient and scalable model.

Integration Challenges: Regulatory Fragmentation and Institutional Disparities

Although technological solutions have been availed, integrating Islamic finance and Islamic social finance has remained a big problem. Uppermost is regulatory fragmentation There is a lack of a unified legal and institutional framework which disrupts a smooth combination of commercial Islamic finance institutions and social finance institutions operating waqf, zakat and sadaqah.

Such social tools tend to exist as silos and are controlled by religion or NGOs and thus have minimal regulation or financing. This is a barrier to potential synergies in which profit institutions could be able to invest their surplus or impact driven investment into social development project. As an example, waqf has been underutilized by ambiguous legal status in most of the jurisdictions and a lack of integrated digital asset management capabilities.

Also, wrong beliefs about Islamic social finance, namely that such investments are more of charity than of a long-term strategy, inhibit the inclusion thereof in overall financial planning by participants on the commercial side. It urgently is time to come up with harmonized policies, standardized reporting frameworks and performance measures that are aligned with Maqasid al-Shariah as well as the SDGs to enable the convergence and scale up.

A new study (2022-24) has highlighted that countries such as Indonesia and Malaysia which have started to experiment with regulatory frameworks on combined digital zakat and Islamic fintech platforms can serve as models to emulate. However, more widespread implementation will entail cross-institutional cooperation, capacity building, and expenditure in general awareness.

CONCLUSION

A fusion of Islamic finance and Islamic social finance through the use of digital technologies will transform the financial ecosystem to be more just, inclusive, and sustainable. Whereas the mechanism of Islamic finance introduces responsible, Shariah compliant investments to the devices of sukuk, musharakah and mudarabah, Islamic social finance introduces ethical redistributive investment directly to poverty, inequality, and social marginalization.

Blockarchin and fintech technologies are already proving the capabilities of how these can be harmonized, digitalized and decentralized. Their integrated application will improve the accountability and efficiency of the Islamic social finance and will reach a wider scope of the society that will be financially included who cannot perform the transaction within the formalised financial systems.

The potential of this integrated model can be achieved only through actions in several fronts:

Integration of the Islamic financing space and social financing space;
Institutional convergence to seal the divides amidst the business and charitable sectors;

Alignment of theories of Maqasid al-Shariah and SDGs to bring congruency between the ethical and developmental objectives.

Inventory on the investment on digital infrastructure to facilitate its adoption in both the developed and developing environments.

In the end, a digitized and ethically formatted Islamic financial ecosystem can be an agent of substantial social change and transformation-- not as a substitute system but as a driver of global economic inclusion. The alignment of values, technology, and financial innovation is a welcome opportunity to place Islamic finance on a pedestal in tackling socio-economic challenges that the world faces today.

REFERENCES

Abdul-Rahman, A. R., & Muhammad, N. (2013). Waqf in Malaysia: A case study of waqf fund management. *Journal of Islamic Economics*, *27*(3), 200–215.

Ahmed, H. (2004). Islamic social finance: The case for zakat and its role in sustainable development. *International Journal of Islamic and Middle Eastern Finance and Management*, *1*(2), 35–49.

Al-Khouri, R., & Bouzi, F. (2019). Waqf as a tool for financing social infrastructure: The Turkish experience. *Journal of Islamic Finance and Development*, *5*(2), 57–74.

Ayub, M. (2007). *Understanding Islamic finance*. John Wiley & Sons.

Dhuafa, D. (2020). Annual report on sadaqah contributions during. *COVID*, •••, 19.

Ghaleb, M. (2019). *Islamic finance and sustainable development: The role of Islamic banks and social finance institutions in achieving the SDGs*. Islamic Development Bank.

Iqbal, M., & Mirakhor, A. (2011). *An introduction to Islamic finance: Theory and practice* (2nd ed.). Wiley. DOI: 10.1002/9781118390474

Islamic Development Bank. (2018). *Islamic social finance and sustainable development*.

Karim, R. A. A., & Hossain, M. (2020). The role of sadaqah in community development during crisis: A case study on COVID-19. *Journal of Islamic Finance and Business*, *8*(1), 16–27.

Khan, M. (2011). Islamic microfinance and poverty alleviation: A case study of the Islamic Microfinance Network. *Journal of Islamic Economics*, *28*(2), 95–110.

Sullivan, A. (2011). The role of waqf in Islamic social finance: The impact of endowments on public services. *Journal of Social Finance*, *5*(2), 71–84.

Thomson Reuters. (2017). *The rise of green sukuk: Islamic finance for a sustainable future*. Thomson Reuters Islamic Finance.

Saylani Welfare. (2020). *COVID-19 relief efforts in Pakistan*.

Yunus, M. (2007). *Creating a world without poverty: Social business and the future of capitalism*. Public Affairs.

Zakat Foundation. (2021). *Zakat Foundation of America: Impact report*.

Zin, M. M., & Abidin, A. (2018). Islamic microfinance for poverty alleviation: A case study of Bank Rakyat Indonesia. *Journal of Islamic Finance*, *7*(3), 56–68.

Chapter 11
Synergizing Islamic Finance for Sustainability
Building Strategic Alliances – Accountability and Disclosure Practices in Baitul Maal and Baznas

Rahmawati Rahmawati
https://orcid.org/0000-0003-2874-9091
Universitas Islam Negeri Syarif Hidayatullah Jakarta, Indonesia

Ramadhan Ilham Bening
Universitas Islam Negeri Syarif Hidayatullah Jakarta, Indonesia

ABSTRACT

Strategic alliances are essential for attaining sustainability by promoting collaboration across enterprises to tackle shared difficulties and accomplish mutual objectives of Islamic organization. The evolution of strategic alliance is influenced by the communication with facilitating effective of operation and have good governance and accountability. The accountability helps build trust and commitment by eliminating the like hood of opportunism among partners. Due to lack of fund mobilization, BMT needs support from BAZNAS. On the other hand, BMT are still lack of accountability. This study aims to examine the extent of Zakat, Infak and Sadaqah disclosure-Baitul Maal in Baitul Maal Wat Tamwil Institution (BMTI) located in Indonesia. The results show that the level of disclosure of Baitul Maal in Indonesia is at low level. This study expects BMTI to certify the good governance in Baitul Maal activities that would attract the Baznas who have to support and provide funding to ensure the effectiveness of BMTIs in facing of crisis.

DOI: 10.4018/979-8-3373-1842-4.ch011

1. INTRODUCTION

Most of financial crisis is caused by unbalancing fundamental of micro and macroeconomics (Radelet & Sachs, 1998); spreading of fraud in mortgage securitization industry (Littlefield & Kneiding, 2009). The current Covid-19 pandemic impact to financial crisis is caused by health issue (McKee & Stuckler, 2020). The lockdown in many countries impacts decrease demands from consumers. The global supply chains were disrupted and pushed the company to reduce the cost of production by reducing the number of employees. In particularly to small medium enterprises (SMEs) are struggling to pay their installment (Hidayat et al., 2020). The pandemic crisis by client of Islamic banking and members of Islamic microfinance in Indonesia was caused by inability to pay the loan to Islamic banking and Islamic microfinance. Consequently, a number of Islamic microfinances have either failed or supported by governments in many countries. This situation had brought Islamic social finance into limelight as a possible alternative. However, the global financial crisis in 2008 have been give some lessons such as the role of debt and interest instruments; human factors; financial innovations; risk management; the regulator and supervisory framework and transparency and governance in Islamic financial institutions (Smolo & Mirakhor, 2010).

In several Muslim countries, such as Indonesia, efforts to utilize zakat schemes appear promising. Zakat collection is no longer carried out by individuals but has also been carried out at the institutional level (Adnan & Bakar, 2009). Furthermore, Indonesia has enormous zakat potential, as its population is predominantly Muslim (Rahman, 2015). Indonesia also has the largest number of Islamic financial institutions (both formal and informal) in any single market, but the exact number is unknown due to limited data (BAPPENAS, 2016).

Indonesia has two primary types of institutions responsible for managing zakat, infaq, and sadaqah: the National Zakat Amil Agency (BAZNAS) and the Zakat Amil Institutions (LAZ)(Nasution, 2020). Under Law No. 23 of 2011 on Zakat Management, BAZNAS—both at the central and regional levels—is a non-structural body under the President with explicit authority to collect, distribute, and develop zakat funds (Saidurrahman, 2013). This law also grants BAZNAS supervisory power over LAZ, which are privately managed zakat institutions (Saidurrahman, 2013), including those embedded in Islamic microfinance entities such as Baitul Maal wat Tamwil (BMT) (Kassim & Wulandari, 2016). Within a BMT, the Baitul Maal functions as an affiliated LAZ to manage zakat assets (Hilmiyah et al., 2023; Sari et al., 2013). Consequently, BMTs acting as LAZ are legally required to comply with Law No. 23 of 2011, operate under BAZNAS's coordination, and submit regular performance reports to BAZNAS (Saidurrahman, 2013).

The absence of operational standards that are specifically designed to meet the unique characteristics of Indonesia's Islamic microfinance sector is a persistent challenge. Although a variety of laws have been passed to allow microfinance institutions to establish operational guidelines that are consistent with the relevant regulations, no formal standards have been established (BAPPENAS, 2016; Saidurrahman, 2013). This regulatory vacuum has resulted in inconsistencies in BMT practices across regions and has weakened institutional capacity and governance (BAPPENAS, 2016; Saidurrahman, 2013). The persistent conflict between BAZNAS and LAZ serves as an illustration of a more extensive governance quandary: how to ensure accountability and standardization without impeding community-driven innovation and trust (Saidurrahman, 2013). Despite the fact that LAZ-affiliated BMTs are frequently successful in mobilizing resources and delivering aid effectively, their viability and credibility may be limited by their limited formal recognition (Saidurrahman, 2013). In order to maintain operations, BMTs must navigate a patchwork of general compliance requirements in the absence of specific regulations. For instance, the Baitul Maal division's function is comparable to that of a Zakat Amil Institution, which necessitates comparable legal and operational requirements (Arafat, 2020; Samsi et al., 2024).

In contrast, Septianingsih et al. (2024) underscore that the persistent challenge of limited funding access significantly hampers BMTs (Baitul Maal wat Tamwil) in Indonesia, preventing them from reaching a wider segment of the impoverished population that desperately needs financial services. As cooperatives, BMTs face institutional barriers in fund mobilization; unlike Islamic banks, they cannot direct funds to or from the general public (Wahyudi, 2014, 2015). Their financial resources are largely confined to two main sources. Firstly, they obtain capital from their members through primary, mandatory, and voluntary savings; however, only voluntary savings offer flexibility, while the other two are fixed in accordance with legal stipulations. Secondly, BMTs can secure financing through third-party loans or contributions from entities like Islamic banks, BAZNAS (National Almsgiving Agency), waqf institutions, and other collaborators (Wahyudi, 2015). To overcome these obstacles, it is imperative for BMTs to cultivate strategic partnerships with Islamic banks (Wahyudi, 2015), BAZNAS, and Lembaga Amil Zakat Nasional (LAZ) (Prasetyo et al., 2018). Such alliances will not only enhance their financial capacity but also significantly expand their outreach to those in need within the community.

In today's dynamic landscape of Islamic social finance, strategic alliances are emerging as a cornerstone for institutional resilience and sustained social impact (Wahyudi, 2015). Baitul Maal and Tamwil Institutions (BMTIs) and national zakat bodies, such as Badan Amil Zakat Nasional (BAZNAS), play synergistic roles in mobilizing, managing, and distributing Islamic social funds (Saidurrahman, 2013). Confronted with escalating economic challenges and limited internal resources,

BMTIs are more reliant on external support such as zakat, infaq, and waqf allocations to enhance their social missions and deliver essential aid to members during financial difficulties. (Kassim & Wulandari, 2016).

According to Abdul Rahman & Dean (2013) and Obaidullah & Khan (2008) there are numerous obstacles to implementing collaborations between zakat institutions and Islamic microfinance institutions (IMFIs), such as BMTs. Despite this, these partnerships have great potential. They are initially governed by separate authorities. Religious ministries or national zakat councils oversee zakat institutions, whilst BMTs are regulated by the Ministry of Cooperatives. Secondly, governance and trust difficulties frequently emerge zakat institutions tend to be more state-controlled and bureaucratic, whereas BMTs are typically more dynamic and community-oriented. Divergences in management styles, reporting standards, and accountability expectations may hinder collaboration, while any deficiency in transparency or subpar performance from either party might undermine confidence (Saidurrahman, 2013).

Despite these hurdles, alliances are both possible and beneficial—especially when there is clear shariah guidance for productive zakat, strong mutual commitment to transparency, and shared development goals. Hybrid models, such as using zakat for initial grants and then channeling beneficiaries into BMT financing for business growth, can be particularly effective (Talavera & Sanchis, 2020).

A third challenge comes from tax policy. Under Law No. 23 of 2011, zakat on income paid to officially recognized national or regional amil zakat organizations can be deducted from taxable income (Saidurrahman, 2013). However, Baitul Maal units within BMTs that are not formally registered as such do not offer this tax benefit (Setianingrum et al., 2018). This may dissuade zakat contributors from utilizing their services. Baitul Maal should augment governance and accountability, maintain adherence to national zakat requirements, and obtain legal recognition to reinforce their role in Islamic social finance and comply with BAZNAS standards, thereby sustaining their social objectives.

In Islamic social finance, strategic alliances are increasingly recognized as a vital tool for uniting efforts, optimizing resource mobilization, and tackling social and economic challenges. Baitul Maal wat Tamwil (BMTIs) and BAZNAS share overlapping mandates in the collection and distribution of Islamic social funds—zakat, infaq, and sadaqah (Nopiardo, 2019; Rifansyah & Suradi, 2024). Despite this natural alignment, their collaborative potential remains largely untapped, hindered by operational fragmentation and weak accountability frameworks (BAPPENAS, 2016).

Strategic alliances require a solid basis of mutual accountability, transparency, and sound governance in addition to a willingness to work together (Talavera & Sanchis, 2020). Alliance theory emphasizes that well-defined structures, roles, and procedures that direct collaboration are necessary for successful interorganizational relationships. Robust accountability frameworks are essential—not only to direct institutional conduct, but also to prevent opportunism, foster trust, and strengthen long-term commitment among all stakeholders (Talavera & Sanchis, 2020). In this framework, disclosure procedures represent a concrete manifestation of accountability. The transparent and uniform documentation of Zakat, Infaq, and Sadaqah (ZIS) sources and expenditures is crucial for BMTIs to demonstrate responsible management, foster stakeholder confidence, and secure ongoing support from BAZNAS and other philanthropic entities (Abdul Rahman & Dean, 2013; Ahmed & Khan, 2016). However, both empirical findings and prior studies reveal that many Islamic microfinance institutions continue to struggle with weak transparency and fragmented reporting mechanisms (D Siswantoro & Nurhayati, 2012; Wahyudi, 2015).

This study examines the accountability and disclosure practices of BMTIs in Indonesia, with a particular focus on how Baitul Maal units manage and report ZIS funds. The research evaluates the preparedness and performance of BMTIs in fulfilling their accountability obligations by employing a disclosure index that is derived from national regulation (Law No. 23 of 2011), PSAK No. 409, and the BAZNAS Zakat Transparency Index. The objective of the findings is to enhance strategic alliances between BMTIs and zakat institutions and to inform improvements in governance frameworks. Advancing toward greater transparency and accountability will not only align BMTIs with Islamic social governance principles but also enhance their ability to serve and empower the communities most in need.

In alliances between BMTIs and BAZNAS, disclosure practices are a direct and visible expression of accountability and trust in particularly given the fiduciary responsibility both entities hold in managing public and religious funds. Despite the increasing significance of accountability in Islamic finance discussions, a considerable research vacuum persists on the management and disclosure of zakat-related activities by BMTIs, particularly in their collaboration with institutions such as BAZNAS. Previous research, Abdul Rahman and Dean, (2013) posit that Islamic microfinance still has problems with openness, tracking funds, and reporting performance. BAZNAS has set up the Zakat Management Organization Transparency Index to look at how well information is shared, although it hasn't been looked at enough across BMTIs. Moreover, little is known about how such accountability indicators influence the success and sustainability of strategic alliances in the Islamic social finance ecosystem. This study explores the potential for building stronger BMT-BAZNAS partnerships by measuring and aligning accountability expectations and offers recommendations on the disclosure practices Baitul Maal should adopt to comply with National Amil Zakat standards.

2. LITERATURE REVIEW

2.1 Zakat Institutions

Zakat institutions are entrusted with managing zakat funds in Muslim countries, with the expectation that they contribute meaningfully to socio-economic development (Wahab & Rahman, 2013). Evaluating their efficiency and governance is therefore essential to ensuring the equitable distribution of wealth (Wahab & Rahman, 2011). From an efficient perspective, zakat should not be limited to immediate fund distribution but should also serve as a tool for poverty alleviation by improving the living standards of low-income households ideally enabling beneficiaries to transition into zakat payers over time (Khan, 2015). When it comes to governance, the goal is to set up strong structures and processes that make institutions more accountable (Wahab & Rahman, 2011). To reach these purposes, zakat needs to be managed by an amil who is open, skilled, and trustworthy. This is necessary to meet both its social and economic goals as well as its governance goals.

In Indonesia, zakat management is centrally regulated under the authority of Badan Amil Zakat Nasional (BAZNAS), established through Badan Amil Zakat Nasional (BAZNAS) is in charge of managing zakat in Indonesia. It was set up by Presidential Decree No. 21/2001 and Law No. 38/1999. BAZNAS is the national zakat amil board, and it is responsible for collecting zakat, infaq, and sadaqah (ZIS) and giving them to people who are eligible according to Islamic rules (Ayuniyyah, 2019). According to Law No. 23 of 2011, Zakat institutions must be responsible not just to the government but also to the public and other interested parties. This entails full transparency—ensuring that processes, institutional structures, and financial information are accessible and sufficient for effective monitoring (Wahab & Rahman, 2011). To support BAZNAS, the law permits the establishment of Lembaga Amil Zakat (LAZ), which must periodically report audited records of zakat collection, distribution, and utilization to BAZNAS. Furthermore, BAZNAS is encouraged to foster alliances and synergies with other organizations pursuing similar socio-economic objectives.

Figure 1. Baznas - The Zakat Transparency Index

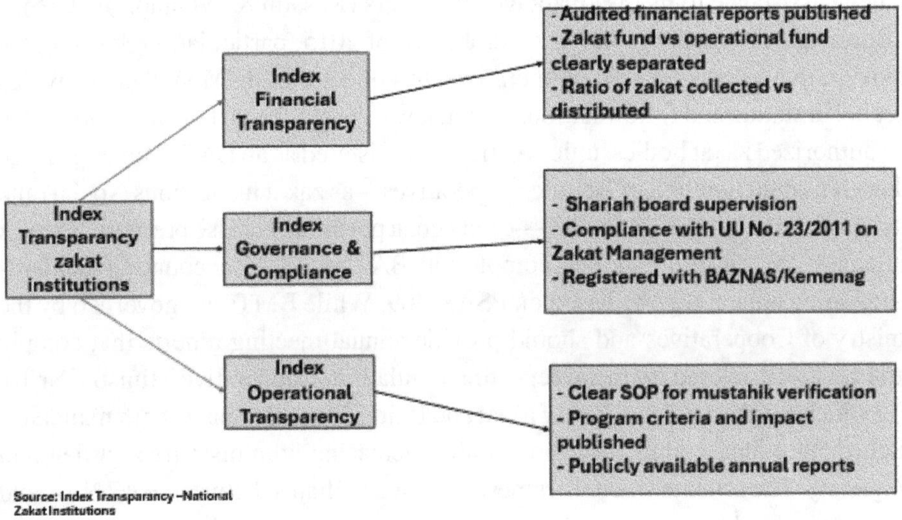

While Indonesia does not yet have a universally standardized national zakat transparency index, various initiatives led by researchers, regulatory bodies such as BAZNAS, and NGOs have sought to develop frameworks for assessing transparency and governance in zakat institutions (Kassim & Wulandari, 2016). Zakat monies has a positive impact on the community when they meet the expectations of stakeholders (Beik et al., 2017). As shown in Figure 1, BAZNAS developed the Zakat Transparency Index (ZTI) to measure performance and accountability. It consists of three primary components: financial transparency, governance and compliance, and operational transparency. These dimensions cover critical aspects of institutional performance, including fund collection, distribution, reporting, and adherence to accounting standards for zakat institutions, such as PSAK 409.

2.2 Baitul Maal Wat Tamwil Institutions (BMTI)

Baitul Mal wat Tamwil (BMT) is a unique institution that carries out two objectives: social and financial missions. The social mission is known as Baitul Maal. Baitul Maal focuses on collecting and distributing charity funds to people experiencing poverty (e.g Zakat, infaq, shodaqah) (Nasution, 2013). While Baitul Tamwil operates based on commercial or economic activities, and the deposits mobilized are placed in productive investments (Holloh, 2001). In line with (Seibel et al., 2006), the mission of BMT is to support the entrepreneurial poor, particularly microentrepreneurs, including food vendors (hawkers). According to the experience of Baitul Maal

Wa Tamwil (BMT) in Indonesia, there are challenges and difficulties in providing financial assistance to its disadvantaged members (Kassim & Wulandari, 2016).

Based on Cooperative Ministry Number 16 of 2015, particularly regarding the provision that allows Islamic cooperatives to collect and distribute zakat, which must be. In statute and follow national zakat law (UU No. 23/2011) and coordinated with authorized zakat bodies, unless officially registered as an LAZ (Lembaga Amil Zakat). The dual function of Islamic cooperatives—as zakat institutions (social) and financing institutions (commercial)—offers great potential, but also presents complex challenges. Zakat institutions must comply with BAZNAS/LAZ accounting standards by providing annual reports based on PSAK 409. While BMTs are governed by the Ministry of Cooperatives and should provide annual meeting reports that comply with PSAK 401 related financial reporting regulation, Cooperative Ministry Nr.16, 2015 which emphasized that Baitul Maal and Baitul Tamwil manage both mandates, which require dual compliance, potentially increasing administrative burden and complexity. The schema (model/framework) for an alliance between BAZNAZ and Baitul Maal should integrate both their respective strengths while maintaining Shariah compliance, accountability, and impact-driven outcomes (Ascarya & Suharto, 2021; Wahyudi, 2014).

When BMT and Zakat institutions form alliances that need strategic, long-term partnerships and gain synergy, they also face greater accountability challenges due to the deeper integration of roles, resources, and responsibilities. Zakat Institution and BMT develop joint zakat-BMT-based programs and must be created in joint committees for program design, fund utilization, governance, compliance, Outcome reporting, and evaluation. Utilize hybrid reporting frameworks (e.g. a unified dashboard that displays zakat distribution and economic performance). Transparency and accountability require Integrated systems or platforms. LAZ and cooperative co-create a *Zakat Productive Unit*, jointly manage funds, share risks, audit, and report under one umbrella. Zakat Productive Unit develops long-term programs, such as *productive zakat funds*, transforming mustahiks into muzaki, or joint fintech platforms.

On the other hand, there are challenges in transparency managing zakat fund in Baitul Maal that lack IT systems for tracking zakat funds separately, Zakat funds may blend with cooperative capital, creating shariah compliance risks, No mandatory reporting of zakat to BAZNAS unless formally partnered, RAT (Rapat Anggota Tahunan) may not discuss zakat specifically (Qutaiba et al., 2024).

According to Suharti (2018) both institutions, Baitul Maal and Baznas, have the same purpose and great potential to alleviate poverty. BAZNAS has a sizeable ZIS fund, which BMT is challenging in funding, and BAZNAS is expected to support the members of BMT who are extremely poor. On the other hand, BMT has challenges in their management, Siswantoro (2013) examine the main constraints in the operations of BMTI are: there is unclear regulation framework for BMT especially in reporting and auditing; the large majority of them reported are dormant or technically bankrupt; the savings of the depositor are at great risk; there is no security for the investors; there is lack of governance framework for BMTI; there is lack of skill of employee; there is no monitoring from government. As a result, Wahyuni (2008) found that the level of accountability of BMTI was low. It implies that the challenges in the connection and the alliance between *Baitul Maal* and BAZNAS are accountability matters, which will be developed in this paper.

2.3 The importance of Strategic Alliance

Based on Bank Indonesia Regulation No. 15/12/PBI/2013, commercial banks are required to allocate at least 20 percent of their credit to micro-businesses as a percentage of total credit(Prasetyo et al., 2018). Based on the regulation, Islamic banks should support BMT as Islamic microfinance. Moreover, Rahman (2007) examines Islamic banks as not well developed and do not provide easy access to financing for the poor, Islamic microfinance has the potential to provide financial services to the poor and impoverished individuals. On the other hand, it is challenging for banks to support Islamic microfinance due to the asymmetric information issue, which contributes to the occurrence of adverse selection (Dalla Pellegrina, 2011). and collateral issues (Agrawal et al., 2002; Sriram, 2012). Moreover, the type of financing that occurred is granular; the quantity of financial resources is high, yet the value of funding for each individual is low (Srinivas, 2005). It implies that the BMTI, as an Islamic microfinance institution, requires support from all Islamic financial elements.

According Milosevic and Kanter (2019) in their study to more than 500 people within 37 companies and their strategies partners to large and small firms covered in manufacturing and services sectors found that there are fundamental characteristic of successful in strategic alliances; alliances that both partners ultimately deem successful involve collaborations (creating new value) rather than mere exchange and alliances cannot controlled by formal system but require developing a connections and internal infrastructures that enhance accountability . The principles to successfully build partnerships and improve collaborative advantage are to acknowledge and manage the human aspects of their alliances effectively. Strategic alliances can take the form of mutual services consortia, which involve a partnership between similar companies in the same industry to gain benefits that are too expensive to develop alone. Eight elements contribute to the success of strategic alliances: sharing information, integration through shared operating procedures, clear responsibilities and processes within institutions, integrity, independence, commitment, long-term and short-term objectives, individual excellence, and trust (Milosevic & Kanter, 2019).

Wohlstetter et al. (2005) examined types of organizations who involved alliances are sector nonprofit such as community-based organizations; faith based organizations (churches, outreach organizations), social service providers; for profit such as education management organizations (EMOs) and local businesses; public such as educational institutions (school districts, community colleges, universities); public health providers (hospitals) and Government/Municipalities (city offices, mayor's office). Wohlstetter et al. (2005) emphasized that the stage of accountability is crucial in strategic alliances; therefore, it is essential to develop methods for tracking performance, financials, and progress, which are significant for transparency, governance, and accountability.

2.3 The Strategic Alliance from Islamic Perspective

From an Islamic perspective, the strategic alliance begins by involving Ulama (Mohamad & Saravanamuttu, 2015). Shariah scholars are engaged in Islamic banking activities to emphasize to the Muslim mind that Islamic banking adheres to Shariah principles. It means Ulama is the first of Alliances in Islamic financial institutions, which relates to human capital (Mohamad & Saravanamuttu, 2015). Shariah scholars have formed a new political alliance, with Shariah members of preparatory committees becoming members of Shariah boards in newly founded banks (Kahf, 2002). Shariah scholars also fostered a new alliance between Islamic bankers and Shariah scholars, developing a mutually rewarding working relationship (Kahf, 2002). Collaboration and synergy between human capital alliances and financial alliances by creating products and services that need to ensure the achievement of the objective and by complying with Shariah principles (Mohamad & Saravanamuttu, 2015). This implies that Islamic financial institutions, such as BMTI, need to communicate and strengthen their engagement to achieve their goal of helping people experiencing poverty, which requires support from other institutions, including Islamic banking and BAZNAS (Mohamad & Saravanamuttu, 2015; Wahyudi, 2014).

Al-Harran (1999) and Wahyudi (2014) examined the benefits of strategic alliances between Ulama and Islamic institutions that create a new power structure in socio–political in Muslim countries, which are:

a. A strategic alliance is effective in the short term for economic and political influence, as well as in the long term for the integration of Islamic finance and banking.
b. A strategic alliance is the best way to reach out to the Muslim masses to convince them to deal with the new Islamic financial institutions.
c. Strategic alliances with Ulama are convinced that Ulama can monitor with the new role, which improves the image of Islamic institutions in Muslim society.

d. Strategic alliance influence the future trends in finance and banking that effect to engineering of financing modes, the expansion of Islamic banks led many profit seekers to enter this new market, the bankers/ulama alliance enhance the shariah research, the alliance contribute to increasing social and economic coherence in the Muslim societies, through schemes that end with the finance beneficiaries become owners of their productive assets such as financing programs addressed to small craftsman.
e. Ulama will encourage the programs.
f. A strategic alliance fosters a new atmosphere of political rapprochement between the Islamic movement and governments in the Muslim world.

2.4 Enhance the Accountability Baitul Maal as strategic alliance with BAZNAS

Since Islamic social finance institutions should comply with critical values, they should consider trust and trustworthiness in the Islamic financial system (Ayub, 2016; Baron & Besanko, 1987). The final purpose of a strategic alliance is synergy, where commitment and trust are essential in achieving financial goals (Wahyudi, 2014).

The challenges in using the profit-loss sharing application are uncertainty in transactions, which results in higher costs. Due to asymmetric information in Islamic microfinance, it results in high transaction costs, which lead to adverse selection. These costs relate to monitoring and investigation expenses, as well as the cost of enforcement, all of which are directly associated with information problems in the remote area (Abdul Rahman & Dean, 2013). The full disclosure of information reduces the adverse selection. The quality of information affects institutional expenditure, which in turn reduces risk (Kazemi & Rahmani, 2013).

When financial statements are incomplete and contain unclear information, it causes uncertainty among stakeholders and enhances risks in the operation of institutions (Kazemi & Rahmani, 2013). Moreover, asymmetrical information and the low quality of accounting information cause the underinvestment (Mohammadi & Esmaeilioghaz, 2017). Preparation of high-quality financial reports reduces asymmetric information and the cost of capital (Lambert et al., 2007). It implies that the institutions should enhance the trust and trustworthiness of strategic alliances by increasing the quality of financial reporting that align with Huang et al. (2023) examine high-quality financial reporting actively reduces risks and makes alliances more effective.

Firms with higher financial reporting quality also are found to deviate less from predicted investment levels and show less sensitivity to macro-economic conditions. Mohammadi & Esmaeilioghaz (2017) suggested one mechanism linking reporting quality and investment efficiency is a reduction of frictions such as moral hazard and adverse selection that hamper efficient investment, inancial reporting quality mitigates the overinvestment.

Figure 2. Conceptual Framework

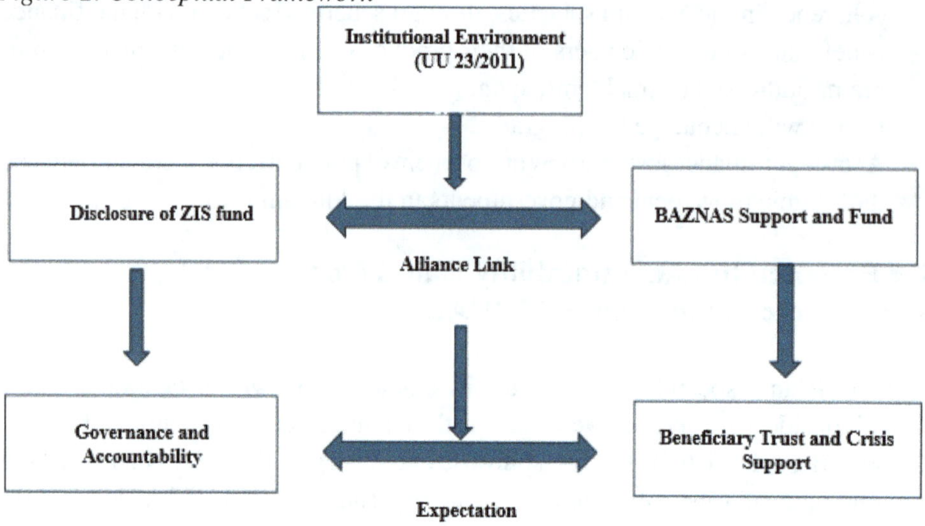

As shown in Figure 2, this study is based on Institutional Act 23, 2011 and accounting standards for zakat institutions and Islamic cooperative regulations to measure accountability of BMTI as Islamic cooperative by alliance approach.

3. METHODOLOGY

To address research objectives one and two, this study used the annual report meeting of BMTIs. The annual reports meeting was collected manually to BMTI in Java Island in Indonesia. Most BMTIs do not publicly publish their annual reports. Data were obtained from the BMTI directly which could obtain BMTIs' annual reports between 2012 and 2023, amounting to 93, albeit 20 are incomplete. Furthermore, the study's data encompassed the annual reports meeting of 73 BMTIs.

3.1 Developing Index for Zakat-Baznas Join Programs.

The researcher designed the transparency index based on three regulations on ZIS fund governance, namely Law No. 23 of 2011 on zakat management, PSAK No. 409 on zakat and infak/sadaqah, and the OPZ transparency index designed by

BAZNAS. Items were validated by 4 researchers, 3 academicians, and 6 experts. The items for the ZIS management disclosure index design can be seen in table 2. Based on the three regulations, the researcher concluded that Baitul Maal in BMT must disclose 48 items of information about ZIS management. The index of Zakat-BMT Join Programs list (appendix)

Accordingly, each BMTI is given a score based on the number of information disclosed to measure the extent of strategic alliances of its disclosure. A score of one is given for each item disclosed. Meanwhile, the disclosure index is calculated by dividing the total number of accounting disclosures presented by the maximum score obtained by a company in the sample. The disclosure index can be mathematically shown as follows:

The following formula will be used to calculate the disclosure level of BMTIs:

$$\text{BMTI} - \text{Join Baznas}_{DI} = \frac{\Sigma X_{i,j}}{\Sigma M_{i,j}}$$

Where:
BMT-Join Baznas DI = BMTIs disclosure index
Mij = Number of items expected to be disclosed by BMTIs.
Xij = Number of disclosure items exhibited by BMTIs.

4. EMPIRICAL RESULTS

4.1 The Descriptive Statistics of BMTIs' Extent of strategic alliance disclosures between BMT and BAZNAS

Concerning the level of disclosure of BMTI, based on the annual report. Based on 73 annual report meetings, the demographic profile of BMTI from 2015 to 2023, by BMT size, indicates 64 medium, 5 small, and 4 micro-sized BMTs. Based on the descriptive statistics in Table 1, we can explain the results of the strategic alliance accountability between BMT (Baitul Maal wat Tamwil) and BAZNAS (Badan Amil Zakat Nasional) by analyzing the three transparency indices: financial, governance, and operational.

The results are summarized in Table 1, which presents the descriptive analysis of 73 BMTIs, indicating that the average level of financial transparency in BMT Join Programs was 33.23%, which is considered low. A high standard deviation (71.05) suggests extensive variation: some BMTs may be very transparent, others barely report at all. While the Index of Governance and Compliance is 59.81%, which indicates the strongest area of alliance performance. The low standard deviation (13.07) shows consistent governance practices across the 73 BMTs.

Meanwhile, the mean disclosure score for Index operational transparency is 13.69%, which indicates a weak level of disclosure. Low variation (Std. Dev. 19.56) indicates inconsistency: some BMTs are making efforts, but the majority lag. In other words, this result suggests that Index Governance and Compliance, as well as Index operational transparency, are at a medium level[1]

The data shows that the strategic alliance between BMT and BAZNAS is moderately strong in governance, but significantly weak in transparency (financial and operational). According to alliance theory, these weaknesses can undermine long-term effectiveness and trust. Targeted improvements in reporting systems, data sharing, and public communication are essential for a more accountable and impactful partnership (Wohlstetter et al., 2005). From a strategic alliance theory perspective, the collaboration between BMT and BAZNAS is strong in governance and operations, but still fragile in financial transparency. Wahyudi (2014) points out that enhancing accountability is based on achieving an alliance.

Table 1. Descriptive Statistics of the Extent of strategic alliance BMTI

Level of Disclosure	N	Min	Max	Mean	Std. Deviation
Index Financial Transparency	73	10.52	71.05	33.23	71.05
Index Governance and Compliance	73	16.67	100.00	59.81	13.07
Index Operational Transparency	73	0.00	75.00	13.69	19.56

4.2 The BMTIs' Extent of strategic alliance disclosures BMT-Join Program

The descriptive statistics of the sample are presented in Table 2; this study explains the extent of strategic alliances disclosure between BMT-Join programs based on dimensions three dimensions are:

a. Dimension Financial Transparency, Table 2 shows a highly uneven pattern of disclosure among BMTs, with clear implications for their accountability and alignment with BAZNAS/LAZ expectations. Certain standard financial statement items, such as cash & cash equivalents, receivables, and fixed assets, score above 90%, reflecting near-universal reporting. These high scores likely stem from mandatory accounting practices in Baitul Tamwil operations, which enforce compliance with basic balance sheet requirements.

In contrast, many critical governance-related disclosures, such as related-party transactions, non-halal fund policies, and detailed distribution reporting, score below 20%, with some indicators at 0%. These low levels highlight significant transparency gaps in areas most relevant to zakat, infaq, and sadaqah (ZIS) fund accountability. While BMTs demonstrate competence in technical financial reporting, especially for items tied to accounting system requirements, these disclosures primarily serve internal financial management rather than public accountability.

In terms of alliances, these kinds of gaps can make it harder for people working together with BAZNAS or LAZ to be held accountable across the board. Partners and stakeholders may lack confidence in the financial management because there is insufficient information available about how funds are used, how they are distributed, and the rules governing control. This pattern shows that the approach is based on compliance and structural reporting rather than a complete transparency framework. As discussed in the agency theory and nonprofit reporting literature (Cordery & Sim, 2018), this type of partial transparency hinders the growth of trust, independent verification, and effective government. The findings indicate an apparent inadequacy in internal control mechanisms in BMT (Wardiwiyono, 2012), which need to maintain spirituality (faith) in fund management and a low adoption of specialized accounting for zakat monies, both of which are critical for ensuring fiduciary accountability (Nuraini, 2022).

Descriptive statistics reveal a stark asymmetry: while basic financial statement elements, such as Cash & Cash Equivalents (100%) and Receivables (98.63%), are almost universally disclosed, governance-oriented disclosures score alarmingly low0% for related-party transactions, 5.48% for fair value policies, and 15.07% for ZIS disbursement details. This pattern shows that BMTs are more likely to meet the bare minimum of accounting standards than to embrace accountability fully. When it comes to strategic partnerships with BAZNAS and LAZ, these differences in disclosure rules pose significant risks. They make it harder for people to trust each other, make it harder for people to work together to keep an eye on things, and make them less sure that ZIS fund management is diminishing public confidence.

b. Dimension Index Governance and Compliance, Table 2 shows that BMTs perform strongly in disclosing strategic direction documents, with most institutions publishing a strategic plan (80.82%), annual budget and work plan (79.45%), and vision and mission statements (78.08%). The result demonstrates an apparent willingness to communicate planned activities and long-term aspirations to stakeholders, reinforcing vertical accountability to regulators and alliance partners such as BAZNAS and LAZ.

However, transparency weakens when it comes to operational processes and leadership. Disclosure of SOPs for zakat collection and distribution stands at 52.05%, while management profile visibility is at 49.32%—both are inconsistent across institutions. More critically, member profile disclosure is extremely low (19.18%), restricting stakeholders' ability to evaluate leadership credibility and decision-making legitimacy. The results show that while BMTs describe a strategic plan with a high score, BMT cannot reveal the accountability mechanism in operational activities, which are disclosed in the annual report meeting. High governance and compliance scores suggest that alliances are more effective when institutional vision and mission are aligned, and when internal accountability mechanisms are robust.

c. Dimension of Operational Transparency: As shown in Table 2, the average disclosure ratings for operational transparency were poor across all metrics, indicating substantial deficiencies in daily accountability and transparency. Merely 15.07% of BMTs disclosed information regarding *muzakki* (donors) and *mustahik* (beneficiaries), whilst only 35.62% offered a public information portal. Mechanisms essential for stakeholder feedback and responsive governance were almost absent: only 4.11% disclosed a complaint-handling system, and none implemented real-time zakat collection and distribution reporting.

These deficiencies severely limit vertical oversight by regulatory and alliance partners such as BAZNAS and LAZ and undermine downward accountability to donors and beneficiaries. The lack of transparent service channels—particularly in beneficiary data, public portals, complaints handling, and real-time reporting—reflects a serious shortfall in stakeholder engagement. From an alliance theory perspective, this weakens the shared information and mutual accountability dimensions that are vital for sustaining inter-organizational trust. BMT should enhance risk management through timely feedback and real-time data sharing in strategic alliances with Islamic social finance to reduce risk and erode public confidence (Wahyudi, 2015).

Table 2. Descriptive Statistics of the Extent of strategic alliance BMTI Join Programs per item

No	Items	
	a. Dimension Financial Transparency	
1	Information the BMT separate the management of *Baitul Maal* and *Baitul Tamwil.*	31.51
2	Information the BMT provide specific reports (management and financial reports) separately for *Baitul Maal* and *Baitul Tamwil*, as well as consolidated.	65.75
3	Information the BMT have a dedicated accounting system for zakat management?	21.92

continued on following page

Table 2. Continued

No	Items	
4	Information the BMT have an internal auditor.	31.51
5	Information the BMT audited by an independent auditor?	30.14
6	Information the BMT publish its financial reports on its website	46,58
7	Information the *Baitul Maal* within the BMT prepare a separate statement of financial position from *Baitul Tamwil*?	68.49
8	Information Cash and Cash Equivalents a required account in *Baitul Maal's* financial statements	100.00
9	Information Financial Instruments a required account in *Baitul Maal's* financial statements	65.75
10	Information Receivables" a required account in *Baitul Maal's* financial statements	98.63
11	Information Fixed Assets" a required account in *Baitul Maal's* financial statements	94.2
12	Information Accrued Expenses" a required account in *Baitul Maal's* financial statements	84.93
13	Information Long-Term Liabilities a required account in *Baitul Maal's* financial statements?	60.27
14	Information the Zakat Fund a required account in *Baitul Maal's* financial statements	43.84
15	Information the "Infaq/Sadaqah Fund a required account in *Baitul Maal's* financial statements	23.29
16	Information the Amil Fund a required account in *Baitul Maal's* financial statements	82.20
17	Information the "Non-halal Fund" a required account in *Baitul Maal's* financial statements	12.33
18	Information the BMT prepare a "Statement of Changes in Funds" to reflect changes in zakat, infaq, and non-halal funds	15.07
19	Information zakat receipts categorized by source (individuals vs institutions)	15.07
20	Information the "Amil's Share of Zakat Receipts" a required account in the statement of changes in funds	16.44
21	Information details of zakat distribution disclosed by recipient group (Fakir, Riqab, Gharim, Muallaf, Sabilillah, Ibn Sabil)	15.07
22	Information the BMT disclose the amount of restricted infaq/sadaqah (muqayyadah)	16.44
23	Information the BMT disclose the amount of unrestricted infaq/sadaqah (mutlaqah)?	19.18
24	Information the BMT disclose the Amil's portion from infaq/sadaqah funds?	9.59
25	Information the BMT disclose returns or income generated from managing infaq/sadaqah funds?	24.66
26	Information the BMT disclose receipts and use of non-halal funds?	6.85
27	Information the BMT report assets managed from infaq/sadaqah funds?	20.55
28	Information the BMT report a mandatory cash flow statement?	52.05
29	Information the BMT prepare Notes to Financial Statements (CaLK) as a required report	46.58
30	Information the BMT disclose policies for determining priority scales for ZIS fund recipients	16.44
31	Information the BMT disclose policies for fair value determination of non-cash donations	5.48
32	Information the BMT disclose detailed disbursement of ZIS funds (including management expenses and direct recipient benefits)	5.48
33	Information the BMT disclose information on related-party relationships between amil and mustahik	0.00
34	Information the BMT disclose assets provided to related-party mustahik	0.00
35	Information the BMT disclose information on the management of infaq/sadaqah funds	27.40

continued on following page

Table 2. Continued

No	Items	
36	Information the BMT disclose policies for handling non-halal funds	00.00
37	Information the BMT explain the rationale behind accepting or disbursing non-halal funds	00.00
38	Information the BMT disclose the percentage of non-halal funds relative to total receipts	63.00
	b. Dimension Governance and Compliance	
39	Information the BMT disclose SOPs for zakat collection and distribution	52.05
40	Information the BMT disclose its strategic plan	80.82
41	Information the BMT disclose its annual budget and work plan	79.45
42	Information the BMT disclose its vision and mission statements	78.08
43	Information the BMT disclose its management profile	49.32
44	Information the BMT disclose member profiles	19.18
	c. Dimension Operational Transparency	
45	Information the BMT disclose data about muzakki and mustahik (e.g. names and addresses)	15.07
46	Information it important for the BMT to have a public information portal	35.62
47	Information it important for the BMT to have a complaint mechanism	4.11
48	Information the BMT operate zakat collection and distribution in real-time	00.00

4.3 Analysis of BMT-Join Programs from five elements

The result in Table 3, demonstrates the matric of strategic alliance BMT Join program based on finding and the action needed to take. Wohlstetter et al. (2005) Alliance theory emphasizes shared goals, shared information, mutual trust, internal structure, and accountability mechanisms.

Table 3. Matrics of strategic alliance with five elements

Dimension	Findings from BMT–BAZNAS Disclosure	Action needed
Shared Goals	High disclosure levels for strategic plans, vision and mission statements, and annual budgets indicate strong alignment in objectives.	Maintain and further strengthen the alignment of strategic plans, vision and mission statements, and work plans to reinforce shared religious, social, and economic goals for ZIS fund distribution.
Shared Information	Very low scores for Items 45–48 show minimal operational and program-related disclosures, with little real-time, public, or granular data shared.	Expand operational and program disclosures, ensuring timely and detailed public reporting of activities and outcomes.
Mutual Trust	Items 33–34 scored 0%, showing no disclosure on related-party transactions, complaint handling systems, or fund allocation rationale—factors that can erode inter-organizational trust.	Disclose related-party transactions, Amil's share, and establish complaint handling mechanisms to build credibility and trust among alliance partners.
Internal Structure	Items 2, 7, and 39–43 score between 50% and 80%, indicating moderate compliance in financial statement preparation, governance reporting, budgeting, and planning.	Strengthen governance through improved SOPs, separate reporting for zakat funds, and more robust strategic planning processes.
Accountability Mechanisms	Items 4, 5, and 20–32 mostly score below 20%, revealing underreporting in audit practices, stakeholder data, and fund disbursement details.	Implement regular internal and external audits, improve transparency in fund disbursement, and establish accessible feedback systems for stakeholders.

5. DISCUSSION

The dataset covers 48 disclosure items measuring the extent of strategic alliance transparency between BMTs (Islamic microfinance cooperatives) and BAZNAS (the national zakat body), expressed as the percentage of BMTs that disclose each item. These findings reveal significant gaps in accountability, transparency, and real-time monitoring elements that are vital for sustaining public trust in Zakat institutions. Drawing on the descriptive statistics of strategic alliance disclosures between BMT and BAZNAS (mean values per item), we can critically examine disclosure patterns, pinpoint key weaknesses, and interpret them through the lenses of alliance theory, Islamic governance principles, and zakat accounting standards. To ensure success, strategic alliances between BMTIs and BAZNAS require enhanced transparency to mitigate information asymmetry and diminish opportunistic behavior. BMTIs show potential in governance compliance; however, their lack of financial and operational transparency hinders the establishment of fully robust alliances. Although

Indonesia's Islamic financial regulations are more comprehensive than those in many other countries, they remain fragmented (BAPPENAS, 2016), making the institutional development of BMTs more challenging (Arafat, 2020). As a result, many BMTs have yet to fully adopt the standards required for managing zakat and infaq/sadaqah funds (Salleh et al., 2022; Samad & Shafii, 2016; Wahyuni, 2008), leading to less-than-optimal compliance with Sharia principles in Islamic financial operations (Salleh et al., 2022).

The information about the strategic alliance between BMT and BAZNAS is very uneven. Much information is shared about simple financial statements, but tiny about ethical government, transparency, and engaging stakeholders. This pattern suggests that most BMTs comply with foundational accounting practices, particularly in preparing financial position statements and strategic governance documents, yet fall short in areas that build deeper accountability. These results align with Austin's (2000) alliance drivers, which highlight four forces essential for cross-sector collaboration: alignment of strategy, mission, and values; personal relationships; value creation and shared vision; and continual learning. Such compliance is likely driven by regulatory requirements (e.g., PMK No. 16/2015 and PSAK 409) and supported by existing internal capacities in personnel and systems.

However, most of these disclosures are structural, focusing on documents and compliance rather than functional or relational aspects, which, in alliance theory, represent only the minimum requirement for cooperation, not the development of strategic trust or relational capital (Gulati, 1998). Furthermore, strategic and social aspect disclosures remain weak, suggesting that BMTs are not consistently fulfilling their public accountability role, particularly in ways that matter to mustahik (beneficiaries), muzakki (donors), and regulators.

In alliance theory terms, this creates relational asymmetry: BAZNAS, as the principal, lacks the complete and transparent information needed to Strengthen alliance by evaluating the performance and integrity of its BMT alliances (agents), focused attention, open communication, robust organizational systems, and mutual accountability, remains critical to improving partnership effectiveness and collaboration between partners (Austin, 2000).

Strategic alliance theory (Dyer & Singh, 1998; Gulati, 1998) posits that effective alliances need four essential elements: trust and commitment, explicit accountability frameworks, reciprocal benefits with proactive information exchange, and congruent objectives underpinned by compatible governance. The findings show that governance compatibility between BMTIs and BAZNAS is relatively strong (moderate-to-high mean scores). However, significant gaps in financial and operational transparency remain a major barrier. These gaps increase transaction costs, erode trust, and heighten perceived risks for institutions like BAZNAS when collaborating with BMTIs.

6. CONCLUSION

Strengthening governance in Islamic social finance is crucial to help Baitul Maal improve its strategic management and institutional effectiveness. A key step is to enhance networking with the national zakat body (BAZNAS) by increasing the level and quality of Baitul Maal's disclosures. Separating the management of Baitul Maal (social functions) and Baitul Maal wat Tamwil (financial functions) can improve operational efficiency, enabling them to support members better and secure assistance from BAZNAS, especially during crises such as the pandemic.

For BMTIs, this separation also reinforces their dual mission: balancing social objectives with financial sustainability in equal measure. However, the long-term sustainability of Baitul Maal is challenged by limited external funding sources—such as government grants, BAZNAS, and LAZ, which cannot be fully addressed without integrating their social and financial roles more effectively. Weak accountability practices further discourage potential funders from contributing. The current disclosure patterns indicate that the BMT–BAZNAS strategic alliance remains weakly institutionalized. While some formal reporting mechanisms exist, they are largely procedural and lack the trust-building, accountability-driven disclosures necessary for a resilient and impactful alliances.

The findings show that disclosure in the BMT joint programs is incomplete and uneven. In contrast, the accountability aspects are weak in terms of ethics and social responsibility. This limits the alliance's ability to build trust, legitimacy, and efficiency in managing Islamic social finance. From an alliance theory perspective, a gap exists between expectations and practice: BMTs do not fully meet their disclosure responsibilities, and BAZNAS lacks vigorous enforcement or incentives to improve transparency.

Strengthening this alliance requires enhancing governance, promoting ethical reporting, and fostering effective stakeholder engagement. Baitul Maal should enhance the quality of disclosure, particularly when collaborating with BAZNAS, and separate the management of Baitul Maal (social functions) from Baitul Maal wat Tamwil (financial functions) to improve effectiveness. This will help them balance social and economic goals while gaining more support from BAZNAS, especially in times of crisis. Sustainability also depends on mobilizing funds from external sources such as government programs, BAZNAS, and LAZ. Without better accountability practices, these external funding opportunities will remain limited, and the full potential of the BMT–BAZNAS alliance will go unrealized.

6. RECOMMENDATIONS FOR BMT

The regulation established by the Ministry of Cooperatives and SMEs aims to enhance the management of Islamic social finance operations, including zakat, infaq, sadaqah (ZIS), and waqf. Moreover, according to Article 27 of Regulation No. 16 of 2015, BMTs must segregate zakat and waqf financial reports from their standard cooperative business reports. This regulation enhances governance, transparency, and accountability, facilitating BMTs in establishing confidence with partners such as BAZNAS, governmental bodies, and benefactors It specifies that the collection, management, and distribution of these monies must adhere to legal standards and Sharia principles, accompanied by distinct reporting for social finance contracts. By applying this regulation effectively, BMTs can enhance their governance and form stronger, more reliable strategic alliances with BAZNAS to achieve broader socio-economic goals.

For Baitul Maal reporting, it is recommended to use a single reporting format (e.g., PSAK 409) for all Baitul Maal entities when reporting zakat, infaq, sadaqah (ZIS), and non-halal funds, in line with PMK No. 16/2015. Moreover, BMT needs to strengthen auditing by applying both internal and independent audits to ensure accuracy and accountability. Furthermore, BMT should increase transparency by disclosing information on amil rights, mustahik profiles, and policies for handling non-halal funds to build public trust. BMT suggests enhancing the use of digitalization by developing real-time dashboards to track ZIS collection and distribution for faster and more transparent reporting. BMT suggests promoting mutual accountability, which includes creating feedback systems, joint performance evaluations, and complaint mechanisms between BAZNAS and BMTs to strengthen trust and reduce information gaps.

REFERENCES

Abdul Rahman, R., & Dean, F. (2013). Challenges and solutions in Islamic microfinance. *Humanomics, 29*(4), 293–306. DOI: 10.1108/H-06-2012-0013

Adnan, M. A., & Bakar, N. B. A. (2009). Accounting Treatment for Corporate Zakat: A Critical Review. *International Journal of Islamic and Middle Eastern Finance and Management*, *2*(1), 32–45. DOI: 10.1108/17538390910946258

Agrawal, R., Raju, K. ., Reddy, K. P., Srinivasan, R., & Sriram, M. . (2002). *Member Funds and Cooperative Performance*.

Al-Harran, S. (1999). New strategic alliances between Islamic financial institutions, international university students and entrepreneurs to implement musharakah financing to meet the challenges of the 21st century. *Arab LQ, 14*(268).

Arafat, F. (2020). Eksistensi BMT sebagai Baitul Maal Wat Tamwil dan Problematika Hukumnya. [JIEB]. *El-Qist: Journal of Islamic Economics and Business*, *10*(1), 89–104. DOI: 10.15642/elqist.2020.10.1.89-104

Ascarya, & Suharto, U. (2021). Integrated Islamic social and commercial finance to achieve SDGs. In *Islamic Wealth and the SDGs: Global Strategies for Socio-economic Impact,* (pp. 105–127).

Austin, J. E. (2000). Strategic collaboration between nonprofits and businesses. *Nonprofit and Voluntary Sector Quarterly*, *29*(1_suppl), 69–97. DOI: 10.1177/0899764000291S004

Ayuniyyah, Q. (2019). Factors Affecting Zakat Payment Through Institution of Amil: Muzakki's Perspectives Analysis (Case Study of Badan Amil Zakat Nasional [Baznas]. *Al-Infaq: Jurnal Ekonomi Islam, 2*(2).

BAPPENAS. (2016). *Masterplan Arsitekstur Keuangan Syariah Indonesia*. https://www.bappenas.go.id/files/publikasi_utama/Masterplan Arsitektur Keuangan Syariah Indonesia.pdf

Beik, I. S., Nurzaman, M. S., Zaenal, M. H., Hendarto, R. G., Annisa, N., & Choirin, M. (2017). *National Zakat Index: Framework and Methodology* (Working Papers-Puskas Baznas, 1).

Dalla Pellegrina, L. (2011). Microfinance and Investment: A Comparison with Bank and Informal Lending. *World Development*, *39*(6), 882–897. DOI: 10.1016/j.worlddev.2011.03.002

Dyer, J. H., & Singh, H. (1998). The relational view: Cooperative strategy and sources of interorganizational competitive advantage. *Academy of Management Review, 23*(4), 660–679. DOI: 10.2307/259056

Gulati, R. (1998). Alliances and networks. *Strategic Management Journal, 19*(4), 293–317. DOI: 10.1002/(SICI)1097-0266(199804)19:4<293::AID-SMJ982>3.0.CO;2-M

Hidayat, S., Farooq, M., & Alim, E. A. (2020). *Impacts of the Covid-19 Outbreak on Islamic Finance in the OIC Countries*. Https://Knks.Go.Id/. https://knks.go.id/storage/upload/1591090473-b71788507b33ad61531b0705ed42b4269a8a994b.pdf

Hilmiyah, N., Izzuddin, M. U., & Waraswasti, P. F. (2023). The Role of Baitulmal as Department of Finance Through Fiscal Policy: Zakat as an Instrument. *N Indonesian Conference of Zakat-Proceedings*, 135–152.

Holloh, D. (2001). *Microfinance Institutions Study*.

Huang, H., Weinbaum, D., & Yehuda, N. (2023). Financial reporting quality and investment efficiency: The role of strategic alliances. *Journal of Contemporary Accounting & Economics, 19*(3), 100377. DOI: 10.1016/j.jcae.2023.100377

Kahf, M. (2002). Strategic trends in the Islamic banking and finance movement. *In Harvard Forum on Islamic Finance and Banking*, 1–31.

Kassim, S., & Wulandari, P. (2016). Issues and challenges in financing the poor: Case of Baitul Maal Wa Tamwil in Indonesia. *International Journal of Bank Marketing, 34*(2), 216–234. DOI: 10.1108/IJBM-01-2015-0007

Kazemi, H., & Rahmani, F. (2013). Relationship between information asymmetry and cost of capital. *Management Science Letters, 3*(1), 321–328. DOI: 10.5267/j.msl.2012.10.026

Lambert, R., Leuz, C., & Verrecchia, R. E. (2007). Accounting information, disclosure, and the cost of capital. *Journal of Accounting Research, 45*(2), 385–420. DOI: 10.1111/j.1475-679X.2007.00238.x

Littlefield, E., & Kneiding, C. (2009). The Global Financial. *Crisis, 52*, 1–8.

McKee, M., & Stuckler, D. (2020). If the world fails to protect the economy, COVID-19 will damage health not just now but also in the future. *Nature Medicine, 26*(5), 640–642. DOI: 10.1038/s41591-020-0863-y PMID: 32273610

Milosevic, D., & Kanter, R. (2019). Collaborative Advantage: The Art of Alliances. *Harvard Business Review, 72*(4), 97–101.

Mohamad, M., & Saravanamuttu, J. (2015). Islamic banking and finance: Sacred alignment, strategic alliances. *Pacific Affairs*, *88*(2), 193–213. DOI: 10.5509/2015882193

Mohammadi, S., & Esmaeilioghaz, H. (2017). A Study of the Impact of Accounting Information Quality and Information Asymmetry on Underinvestment in Iran. *Journal of Industrial Distribution & Business*, *8*(1), 33–39. DOI: 10.13106/ijidb.2017.vol8.no1.33.

Nasution, A. M. (2020). Pengelolaan Zakat Di Indonesia. *Journal of Islamic Social Finance Management*, *1*(2), 293–305. DOI: 10.24952/jisfim.v1i2.3589

Nopiardo, W. (2019). Perkembangan Peraturan Tentang Zakat Di Indonesia. [Jurnal Ilmiah Syariah]. *JURIS*, *18*(1), 65–76. DOI: 10.31958/juris.v18i1.1369

Nuraini, I. (2022). Analysis of Zakat Management Performance Based on The National Zakat Index Approach: A Case Study. *Islamic Social Finance, 2*(2).

Obaidullah, M., & Khan, T. (2008). Islamic Microfinance Development: Challenges and Initiatives. In *Islamic Research & Training institute Policy Dialogue Paper, (2).* (Issue 2).

Prasetyo, A., Effendi, J., & Nursyamsiah, T. (2018). The Effectiveness of Islamic Microfinance Distribution on Microbusiness Owner's Poverty Alleviation (Case Study: BMT Bina Masyarakat Purworejo). *Jurnal AFKARUNA*, *14*(1), 1–26. DOI: 10.18196/AIIJIS.2018.0078.1-26

Qutaiba, M., Owais, M., & Muharam, A. S. (2024). The current issue of reporting zakat in Indonesia: A critical analysis. *Journal of Islamic Economic and Business Research*, *4*(1), 1–25. DOI: 10.18196/jiebr.v4i1.227

Radelet, S., & Sachs, J. (1998). *The onset of the East Asian financial crisis* (No. w6680).

Rifansyah, M., & Suradi, R. (2024). Analysis of the Receipt and Distribution of Zakat, Infaq, and Sadaqah Funds through the National Zakat Amil Agency in Pontianak in 2016-2021. *Journal of Economics. Management and Trade*, *30*(7), 65–79. DOI: 10.9734/jemt/2024/v30i71226

Saidurrahman, S. (2013). The politics of zakat management in Indonesia: The tension between BAZ and LAZ. *Journal of Indonesian Islam*, *7*(2), 366–382. DOI: 10.15642/JIIS.2013.7.2.366-382

Salleh, S., Shafii, Z., Hanefah, M. M., Kamaruddin, M. I. H., Zakaria, N., & Sabri, N. A. M. (2022). Development Of Shariah Governance And Audit In Islamic Cooperative Sector. *Seminar Antarabangsa Islam Dan Sains 2022.*

Samad, R. R., & Shafii, Z. (2016). Adoption of Shari'ah Governance in Cooperative Sector in Cooperative Sector in Malaysia: Case of Cooperative Banks and Credit Unions. *In The Fourth International Tunisian Conference for Islamic Wealth*, 1–21.

Samsi, S., Martomo, Y. P., & Anafih, E. S. (2024). BAZNAS leadership commitment in harnessing zakat potential and strengthening the community economy. *Society, 12*(2), 927–942. DOI: 10.33019/society.v12i2.750

Sari, M. D., Bahari, Z., & Hamat, Z. (2013). Review on Indonesian zakah management and obstacles. *Social Sciences, 2*(2), 76–89. DOI: 10.11648/j.ss.20130202.18

Seibel, H. D., Agung, W. D., Siebel, H., & Agung, D. (2006). Islamic Microfinance in Indonesia. In *Deutsche Gesellschaft für Technische Zusammenarbeit (GTZ) GmbH: Vol. No.2* (Issue February). DOI: 10.1355/sj23-1d

Septianingsih, R., Abdullah, A., & Salleh, M. Z. M. (2024). A Systematic Review: Challenge of Islamic Microfinance Baitul Maal Wat Tamwil in Indonesia. In *Islamic Finance*. New Trends in Law and Regulation. DOI: 10.1007/978-3-031-48770-5_3

Setianingrum, A., Madjid, S., & Asaari, M. (2018). Zakat As Tax Credit for Harmonize Fiscal Setting in Indonesia. *Jurnal Ekonomi Pembangunan (Balai Penelitian dan Pengembangan Ekonomi, Fakultas Ekonomi Universitas Muhammadiyah Surakarta), 16*(1), 57–72.

Siswantoro, D. (2013). Regulatory Compliance and Experiences of Islamic Cooperatives in Competitive Business in Indonesia. *International Journal of Excellence in Islamic Banking and Finance, 3*(1), 1–14. DOI: 10.12816/0001418

Siswantoro, D., & Nurhayati, S. (2012). Factors affecting concern about zakat as a tax deduction in Indonesia. *Int. J. Manag. Bus. Res, 2*(4), 293–312.

Smolo, E., & Mirakhor, A. (2010). The global financial crisis and its implications for the Islamic financial industry. *Journal of Islamic and Middle Eastern Finance and Management, 3*(4), 372–385. DOI: 10.1108/17538391011093306

Srinivas, Y. (2005). Bank finance to the SME sector-Issues and perspectives. Chartered Accountant- New Delhi, 54 (3), 436

Sriram, M. S. (2012). The AP Microfinance Crisis 2010: Discipline or Death? *Vikalpa, 37*(4), 113–128. DOI: 10.1177/0256090920120407

Suharti, F. (2018). Sinergitas Islamic microfinance institution (IMFI): Pemberdayaan dan Peningkatan Usaha Mikro Kecil Menengah (UMKM). *El-Jizya Jurnal Ekonomi Islam, 5*(1), 52–80. DOI: 10.24090/ej.v5i1.1626

Talavera, C., & Sanchis, J. R. (2020). Alliances between for-profit and non-profit organizations as an instrument to implement the economy for the common good. *Sustainability (Basel), 12*(22), 9511. DOI: 10.3390/su12229511

Wahab, N. A., & Rahman, A. R. A. (2011). A framework to analyse the efficiency and governance of zakat institutions. *Journal of Islamic Accounting and Business Research, 2*(1), 43–56. DOI: 10.1108/17590811111129508

Wahab, N. A., & Rahman, A. R. A. (2013). Determinants of efficiency of zakat institutions in Malaysia: A non-parametric approach. *Asian Journal of Business and Accounting, 6*(2).

Wahyudi, I. (2014). Commitment and trust in achieving financial goals of strategic alliance. *International Journal of Islamic and Middle Eastern Finance and Management, 7*(4), 421–442. DOI: 10.1108/IMEFM-10-2013-0113

Wahyudi, I. (2015). Realizing knowledge sharing in strategic alliance: case in Islamic microfinance Realizing knowledge sharing in strategic alliance: case in Islamic microfinance. *Journal of Islamic and Middle Eastern Finance and Management, 31*(4), 260–271.

Wahyuni, E. T. (2008). The Accountability of Islamic Microfinance Institution: Evidence From Indonesia. *The Winners, 9*(1), 22–34. DOI: 10.21512/tw.v9i1.728

Wardiwiyono, S. (2012). Internal control system for Islamic micro financing. *International Journal of Islamic and Middle Eastern Finance and Management, 5*(4), 340–352. https://doi.org/doi:10.1108/17538391211282836. DOI: 10.1108/17538391211282836

Wohlstetter, P., Smith, J., & Malloy, C. (2005). Strategic Alliances in Action: Toward a Theory of Evolution. *Policy Studies Journal: the Journal of the Policy Studies Organization, 33*(3), 419–442. DOI: 10.1111/j.1541-0072.2005.00123.x

ENDNOTE

1 Sarma (2008) examines the level of extent and quality result, which is valued into three categories, viz: $0.5 < IFI \leq 1$ – High financial inclusion, $0.3 \leq IFI < 0.5$ - Medium financial inclusion, and $0 \leq IFI < 0.3$ - Low financial inclusion.

APPENDIX

Table 4. The index of Zakat-BMT Join Programs list

No	Items	Reference
1	Information the BMT separate the management of *Baitul Maal* and *Baitul Tamwil.*	Law No. 23 of 2011
2	Information the BMT provide specific reports (management and financial reports) separately for *Baitul Maal* and *Baitul Tamwil*, as well as consolidated.	Law No. 23 of 2011
3	Information the BMT have a dedicated accounting system for zakat management?	Law No. 23 of 2011
4	Information the BMT have an internal auditor.	OPZ Transparency Index
5	Information the BMT audited by an independent auditor?	OPZ Transparency Index
6	Information the BMT publish its financial reports on its website	OPZ Transparency Index
7	Information the *Baitul Maal* within the BMT prepare a separate statement of financial position from *Baitul Tamwil*?	Law No. 23 of 2011
8	Information Cash and Cash Equivalents a required account in *Baitul Maal's* financial statements	PSAK 409
9	Information Financial Instruments a required account in *Baitul Maal's* financial statements	PSAK 409
10	Information Receivables" a required account in *Baitul Maal's* financial statements	PSAK 409
11	Information Fixed Assets" a required account in *Baitul Maal's* financial statements	PSAK 409
12	Information Accrued Expenses" a required account in *Baitul Maal's* financial statements	PSAK 109
13	Information Long-Term Liabilities a required account in *Baitul Maal's* financial statements?	PSAK 409
14	Information the Zakat Fund a required account in *Baitul Maal's* financial statements	PSAK 409
15	Information the "Infaq/Sadaqah Fund a required account in *Baitul Maal's* financial statements	PSAK 409
16	Information the Amil Fund a required account in *Baitul Maal's* financial statements	PSAK 409
17	Information the "Non-halal Fund" a required account in *Baitul Maal's* financial statements	PSAK 409
18	Information the BMT prepare a "Statement of Changes in Funds" to reflect changes in zakat, infaq, and non-halal funds	PSAK 409
19	Information zakat receipts categorized by source (individuals vs institutions)	PSAK 409
20	Information the "Amil's Share of Zakat Receipts" a required account in the statement of changes in funds	PSAK 409
21	Information details of zakat distribution disclosed by recipient group (Fakir, Riqab, Gharim, Muallaf, Sabilillah, Ibn Sabil)	PSAK 409
22	Information the BMT disclose the amount of restricted infaq/sadaqah (muqayyadah)	PSAK 409
23	Information the BMT disclose the amount of unrestricted infaq/sadaqah (mutlaqah)?	PSAK 409
24	Information the BMT disclose the Amil's portion from infaq/sadaqah funds?	PSAK 409
25	Information the BMT disclose returns or income generated from managing infaq/sadaqah funds?	PSAK 409

continued on following page

Table 4. Continued

No	Items	Reference
26	Information the BMT disclose receipts and use of non-halal funds?	PSAK 409
27	Information the BMT report assets managed from infaq/sadaqah funds?	PSAK 409
28	Information the BMT report a mandatory cash flow statement?	PSAK 409
29	Information the BMT prepare Notes to Financial Statements (CaLK) as a required report	PSAK 409
30	Information the BMT disclose policies for determining priority scales for ZIS fund recipients	PSAK 409
31	Information the BMT disclose policies for fair value determination of non-cash donations	PSAK 409
32	Information the BMT disclose detailed disbursement of ZIS funds (including management expenses and direct recipient benefits)	PSAK 409
33	Information the BMT disclose information on related-party relationships between amil and mustahik	PSAK 409
34	Information the BMT disclose assets provided to related-party mustahik	PSAK 409
35	Information the BMT disclose information on the management of infaq/sadaqah funds	PSAK 409
36	Information the BMT disclose policies for handling non-halal funds	PSAK 409
37	Information the BMT explain the rationale behind accepting or disbursing non-halal funds	PSAK 409
38	Information the BMT disclose the percentage of non-halal funds relative to total receipts	PSAK 409
	Dimension Governance	
39	Information the BMT disclose SOPs for zakat collection and distribution	OPZ Transparency Index
40	Information the BMT disclose its strategic plan	OPZ Transparency Index
41	Information the BMT disclose its annual budget and work plan	OPZ Transparency Index
42	Information the BMT disclose its vision and mission statements	OPZ Transparency Index
43	Information the BMT disclose its management profile	OPZ Transparency Index
44	Information the BMT disclose member profiles	OPZ Transparency Index
	Dimension Program	
45	Information the BMT disclose data about muzakki and mustahik (e.g. names and addresses)	OPZ Transparency Index
46	Information it important for the BMT to have a public information portal	OPZ Transparency Index
47	Information it important for the BMT to have a complaint mechanism	OPZ Transparency Index
48	Information the BMT operate zakat collection and distribution in real-time	OPZ Transparency Index

Chapter 12
Synergizing Islamic Social Finance With Maqasid Al-Shariah

Nazifah Mustaffha
https://orcid.org/0009-0000-8599-6473
Universiti Islam Selangor, Malaysia

Norhanizah Johari
Universiti Islam Selangor, Malaysia

ABSTRACT

Islamic social finance plays a key role in promoting ethical wealth distribution and financial inclusion. Rooted in Maqasid al-Shariah, it aligns with Sustainable Development Goals (SDGs) and Environmental, Social, and Governance (ESG) principles. This study explores how zakat, waqf, sadaqah, qard al-hasan, sukuk sosial, and takaful contribute to poverty reduction, education, and economic growth. Despite its potential, challenges include inefficiencies in fund distribution and regulatory fragmentation. Leveraging fintech innovations, corporate waqf models, and standardized governance can enhance its impact. Case studies from Malaysia, UAE, and Sudan demonstrate successful implementations. Policy recommendations include harmonized regulations, ESG-based sukuk, and fintech integration. This research provides insights for policymakers and financial institutions to strengthen Islamic social finance for sustainable development.

DOI: 10.4018/979-8-3373-1842-4.ch012

1. INTRODUCTION

Islamic social finance (ISF) is now receiving attention from around the world as a potential instrument to address socio-economic inequality and improve the well-being of society. It is rooted in the core tenets of Islam — such as zakat, *waqf*, *sadaqah*, and *qard al-hasan* — and promotes fair wealth distribution and the establishment of a social safety net for underprivileged groups. Major international organizations like the World Bank and the International Monetary Fund (IMF) have recognized ISF's potential and accepted it as a practical means of achieving the Sustainable Development Goals (SDGs), especially the reduction of economic inequality and poverty.

Several Muslim-majority nations, such as Saudi Arabia, Malaysia, and Indonesia, have implemented extensive policy frameworks to institutionalize ISF at the national level. For example, the incorporation of ISF mechanisms into the wider financial ecosystem is emphasized in Malaysia's Islamic Finance Master Plan 2011–2020. Data from *Pusat Pungutan Zakat* of the Federal Territory, Malaysia (one of the zakat collection centres in Malaysia), shows that zakat collection is expected to increase to RM1.035 billion in 2023 (an increase of 12% from 2022) (Pusat Pungutan Zakat - Majlis Agama Islam Wilayah Persekutuan [PPZ - MAIWP], 2023), and data from the Selangor Zakat Board, Malaysia, shows that zakat collection is expected to increase to RM1.12 billion in 2023 (an increase of 4.7% from 2022), reflecting the great potential in using these funds to address poverty and socio-economic gaps. Additionally, Fisol et al. (2021) point out that using *maqasid al-shariah* as the cornerstone of ISF can promote longer-term results that are more significant and sustainable.

These inspiring developments illustrated that ISF can expand further to uphold the virtue of socio-economic justice, especially among the Muslim society. Nevertheless, social finance institutions face various challenges that hinder the effective and efficient implementation of ISF. Among the ongoing debates of ISF is the gap between theory and the real practice of Islamic finance. The discussions include claims that ISF has not yet reached its full potential on the basic goals of *maqa id al-shariah* in growth and social influence (Syed Marwan & Engku Ali, 2019). Conversely, Hassan and Muneeza (2022) found that ISF faces governance failure that leads to mismanagement and corruption. For instance, these organizations are not subject to financial sector regulations, leaving them to regulate the financial matters based on their own discretion, with a lack of coordination mechanisms. Those mentioned issues highlighted the need for better coordination between ISF practices and *maqa id al-shariah*.

Even though *maqasid al-shariah* is important in upholding socio-economic justice and sustainable development, there is still a lack of research examining concrete implementation strategies related to the application or synergy of *maqasid al-shariah* in ISF by Islamic financial institutions to improve the effectiveness and fairness of social fund distribution (Fisol et al., 2021). The literature also finds gaps in understanding and applying *maqasid al-shariah* more systematically and effectively within the existing ISF framework. Hence, this study aims to explore how the synergy between ISF and *maqasid al-shariah* can better address socioeconomic inequality and subsequently proposes a more holistic ISF framework based on an analysis of the synergy between these two paradigms.

This chapter aims to firstly explain the concept of ISF and how *maqasid al-shariah* can be applied systematically within the ISF system; secondly, describe the implementation of ISF across the globe; and thirdly, discuss the synergy between ISF and *maqasid al-shariah*. Fourth, the chapter highlights the limitations in the Islamic financial inclusion approach before suggesting its future directions.

2. OVERVIEW OF ISLAMIC SOCIAL FINANCE AND *MAQASID AL-SHARIAH*

2.1 Islamic Social Finance

Islamic social finance (ISF) is a subset of the Islamic financial system. It was developed in the early days of Islam based on the principles of welfare (*falah*) and justice (*'adl*) to balance wealth in society and curb economic exploitation during that time. Keeping pace with the times, ISF today strives to ensure that financial transactions are conducted ethically and promote economic stability and social cohesion (Chapra, 2016). It emphasizes the prohibition of interest (*riba*), which is exploitative and unjust, and its impact on financial inequality and systemic economic instability. This philosophy contrasts with the conventional financial system, which aims to generate wealth and shareholder value, where *riba*-based transactions are common in practice (Yahya et al., 2013).

Being the most fundamental principle of justice in Islamic finance, the eradication of *riba* ensures that financial transactions foster equitable distribution of wealth and sustainable economic growth (Ahmed, 2023). This stringent ban is grounded in the subsequent Quranic verse:

"Allah has permitted trade and has forbidden riba." (Al-Baqarah, 2:275)

Islam also advocates a risk-sharing system, another principle of justice in Islam. This can be seen through *mudharabah* (profit-loss sharing) and *musharakah* (partnership) contracts, where the parties involved in these contracts share profits and losses based on terms and ratios that have been agreed upon by them (Hassan & Kayed, 2009). In addition, Islam promotes ethical investments to ensure the suitability of investments in shariah-compliant projects while avoiding industries associated with prohibited activities such as uncertainty, gambling, alcohol-related, and unethical labour practices, which violate the principles of justice (Sheikh., 2025).

In general, ISF operates to achieve the *maqasid al-shariah* and contribute to the principles of the Sustainable Development Goals (SDGs) and the Environmental, Social and Governance (ESG) framework simultaneously. Through the various financial instruments available, integrated with the use of fintech and effective internal control, these objectives can be well achieved in a modern economy (Raimi et al., 2024). In particular, the instruments are able to eradicate poverty, unemployment rate, and social inequality, as well as promote ethical financial practices. The instruments like *zakat, sadaqah, waqf, qard al-hasan*, social *sukuk*, and *takaful* are developed and implemented in the Islamic finance industry based on the fundamental belief that wealth is a trust from Allah (SWT) and should be managed and fully utilized to benefit society. Further explanation on these instruments is as follows:

a. *Zakat*

Zakat is one of the five pillars of Islam. It serves as a fundamental mechanism for the redistribution of wealth that aims to eradicate poverty and reduce economic inequality in Muslim society. Zakat is divided into two, zakat on wealth and zakat *fitrah*. Known as a form of worship of wealth, zakat is obligatory for those who have met all the conditions of obligatory zakat, which benefits both zakat payers and beneficiaries. The Holy Qur'an mandates its importance, as in the following verse:

> *"Take [O Muhammad] alms from their wealth, so that they may thereby be cleansed (of sins) and purified (from bad conduct)" (At-Taubah, 9:103).*

Zakat funds are allocated to specific groups of beneficiaries (*asnaf*), which encompass the needy (*fuqara*), the poor (*masakin*), zakat managers (*'aamiliin*), those whose hearts are to be reconciled (*mu'allaf*), slaves (*riqaab*), individuals in debt (*gharimin*), travelers in need (*ibn sabil*), and those engaged in the cause of Allah (*fisabilillah*), as delineated in Surah at-Tawbah, 9:60.

b. *Waqf*

Waqf is a perpetual endowment utilized to finance social welfare initiatives, including mosques, schools, libraries, and hospitals. Historically, *waqf* played a significant role in the Ottoman Empire by financing public services without burdening state resources (Çizakça, 1998).

In contemporary finance, corporate *waqf* models have emerged, in which companies designate a portion of their revenues to endowments. These models are being implemented with innovative structures, focusing on governance, sustainable investment, risk management, and social impact (Kasri & Hilmi, 2020).

c. *Sadaqah*

Sadaqah is a voluntary charitable contribution that exceeds the obligatory zakat. It includes both financial and non-financial contributions to individuals or entities, along with the development of infrastructure, including educational and healthcare institutions.

Sadaqah can be channelled to anyone or party for philanthropic purposes. It can be contributed traditionally or directly to those in need, or through modern applications, including crowdfunding platforms such as GlobalSadaqah, Sadaqa House, and LaunchGood, which leverage financial technology to expand accessibility worldwide (Karakulah & Muneeza, 2024).

d. *Qard al-Hasan*

Qard al-hasan (benevolent loan) is an interest-free loan that aims to help those who are experiencing financial difficulties or pursuing entrepreneurial endeavours. Through ISF, financial institutions offer financial services to those in need and marginalized in conventional finance to empower low-income individuals without charging interest (*riba*). The Quran allows the practice of giving interest-free loans as Allah says:

> *"Who is it that (will) grant Allah a goodly (sincere) loan so He will repay him many times over?" (Al-Baqarah, 2:245).*

Islamic microfinance institutions, particularly those in Bangladesh, Pakistan, and Sudan, have gradually used the idea of *qard al-hasan* to fund SMEs (Ahmed, 2023). This approach protects borrowers from exploitative lending practices while promoting financial inclusion.

e. Social *Sukuk*

Social *sukuk* is a shariah-compliant investment vehicle intended to fund projects that yield immediate social benefits. In contrast to conventional bonds, *sukuk* eschews interest-based transactions and emphasizes asset-backed financing (Mohamad et al., 2017).

Some examples of the latest issuances of social *sukuk* include (i) Indonesia's Green *Sukuk*, which funds renewable energy and climate adaptation projects, and (ii) Malaysia's *Ihsan Sukuk*, aimed at financing educational and health initiatives.

f. *Takaful*

Takaful is an Islamic insurance system founded on the principle of mutual assistance (*ta'awun*). Unlike conventional insurance that integrates interest (*riba*) and uncertainty (*gharar*), *takaful* operates through collective risk and pooled contributions.

The industry provides contemporary *takaful* products, including micro-*takaful* initiatives for low-income individuals, health *takaful* plans that address medical expenses for the underprivileged population, and general *takaful*.

2.2 Comparisons between Islamic and Conventional Social Finance

Islamic social finance (ISF) differs from conventional social finance (CSF) in many dimensions, including principles, mechanisms, objectives, governance, and impact orientation. These differences are explained below.

First, they differ in their underlying principles. ISF is established based on the principles of sharia and *maqasid al-shariah* (the goals of Islamic law), aiming to uphold justice and social welfare for individuals and other entities. This is manifested by the assertion that all transactions must comply with social and ethical responsibilities through the prohibition of interest (*riba*), undue uncertainty (*gharar*), and gambling (*maysir*). In contrast, CSF is based on ethical principles such as human rights, corporate social responsibility (CSR), and sustainability. It supports interest-based finance and speculative ventures within the parameters of the law.

Second, in terms of mechanism, ISF emphasizes faith-based instruments such as *zakat*, *waqf*, *sadaqah*, *qard al-hasan*, and *takaful*, as explained earlier. Additionally, Islamic microfinance operates based on the profit and risk sharing model, such as *musharakah* (partnership), *mudharabah* (profit and loss sharing), or *murabahah* (cost-plus financing) without involving *riba* (interest), *gharar* (excessive uncertainty), and unethical practices, and must be supported by tangible and intangible assets that contribute to the real economy (Tahiri Jouti, 2019). Conversely, the key instruments under CSF include philanthropic grants, social impact bonds (SIBs), microfinance with interest, impact investing, green and social bonds, and crowdfunding platforms. Even though the conventional model promotes inclusivity and social progress like ISF, it often permits financial return expectations on top of social benefits, allowing for interest-bearing instruments and risk transfer strategies (Rexhepi, 2016).

Third, the primary objective of ISF is to achieve *maqasid al-shariah*, while CSF emphasizes social and environmental goals. However, both ISF and CSF are in line with the Sustainable Development Goals (SDGs). To be specific, ISF seeks spiritual and material growth of eligible recipients, especially marginalized groups, which normally focuses on long-term empowerment through zakat and *waqf*-based microfinance. Meanwhile, CSF focuses on improving skills and boosting the economy, along with creating income through social enterprises, grants, and microcredit, targeting a wider group of beneficiaries, which is usually assessed based on their needs, policy objectives, or what donors prefer (Rexhepi, 2016).

2.3 *Maqasid al-Shariah*

Maqasid al-shariah denotes the fundamental objectives and purposes of Islamic law, which are intended to advance human welfare and justice. It is vital in the development of the operational framework and principles of Islamic finance and economics. Furthermore, it establishes a framework for evaluating the effects of financial initiatives, guaranteeing that they are consistent with the fundamental objectives of Islamic law and have a beneficial impact on society.

The concept is based on the view that shariah is not only a legal system but a holistic framework that emphasizes the overall development of Islamic society, integrating economic, social, and environmental dimensions to achieve societal well-being. Five fundamental objectives of *shariah*, as delineated by classical Islamic scholars like Al-Ghazali and Al-Shatibi, encompass the preservation of faith (*hifz al-deen*), life (*al-nafs*), intellect (*al-aql*), lineage (*al-nasl*), and wealth (*al-maal*) (Chapra, 2016). The following describes these objectives:

First, the preservation of faith refers to the safeguarding and protection of individuals' and communities' religious beliefs. Islam prohibits all things that can threaten religion, such as *kufr*, *shirk*, hypocrisy, apostasy, and so on. This important objective also includes the guarantee of autonomy in practicing personal religion, as stated in the Holy Quran:

"There shall be no compulsion in religion (in becoming a Muslim). True guidance (in Islam) is now distinct from error (unbelief)." (Al-Baqarah, 2: 256)

Secondly, the preservation of life underlines the sanctity of human life. This objective highlights the importance of safeguarding life, health, and well-being as well as avoiding anything that could threaten one's self, soul, or life, as outlined in the Quran:

"...whoever kills a human being, except for a punishment for murder or for spreading corruption in the earth, it shall be as though he had killed all mankind." (Al-Maidah, 5: 32).

Third, preservation of intellect. It means protecting the human mind from anything that will damage it. The mind must be preserved and nurtured with noble values and beneficial knowledge. All elements that lead to the loss and damage of the mind and thoughts, such as alcohol, drugs, and destructive films, must be eradicated and prevented immediately.

Fourth, the preservation of lineage. Family structures play a crucial role in maintaining societal stability, demonstrating the importance of protecting one's family and promoting responsible parenting. This is referred to in the Holy Quran:

"And do not kill your children for fear of poverty; We provide sustenance for them and for you. Killing them is truly a great sin." (Al-Isra', 17:31)

And finally, preservation of wealth. In Islam, wealth is considered a means to achieve social welfare. Islam prohibits any act that can harm, destroy, or waste property, such as robbery, wastefulness, or the like. In other words, this objective advocates for just economic practices and prohibits exploitative behaviours, as mentioned in al-Quran:

"And do not consume one another's wealth unjustly or send it [in bribery] to the rulers in order that [they might aid] you [to] consume a portion of the wealth of the people in sin, while you know [it is unlawful]." (Al-Baqarah, 2:188)

Establishing *maqasid al-shariah* as the basis of Islamic economics is essential to safeguard universal *maslahah* (public benefit). This is because it emphasizes economic policies that promote social welfare and reduce inequality (Dusuki & Bouheraoua, 2011). Unlike traditional economic theory that focuses on making the most profit, Islamic economics seeks to create fairness by sharing wealth fairly, sharing risks, and banning unfair practices like *riba* (interest) and *gharar* (excessive uncertainty), all while encouraging the growth of wealth in a way that aligns with ethical values (Alam et al., 2017).

2.4 Significance of Synergizing Islamic Social Finance with *Maqasid al-shariah*

ISF can best achieve the *maqasid al-shariah*, which aims to enhance socioeconomic well-being, justice, and financial inclusion. Increased research over the last ten years has looked at how ISF tools work together with *maqasid al-shariah* to tackle issues like poverty, ethical investing, and financial exclusion. However, most of the existing discussions and research have focused more on legal compliance than on realizing meaningful *maqasid*-driven socio-economic outcomes. The fact has been demonstrated through literature studies that many Islamic financial institutions focus on Shariah compliance and less on a broader mix of Shariah objectives, including poverty eradication, wealth redistribution, and environmental stewardship (El-Gamal, 2006). As a result, shariah-compliant financial products often reflect conventional financial frameworks and fail to acknowledge significant social impacts (Abdullah & Dusuki, 2021). Thus, the incorporation of *maqasid al-shariah* enables ISF to become a more effective means of addressing issues of socio-economic disparity and building a more just and prosperous society.

The synergy between ISF instruments (ISFIs) and *maqasid al-shariah* principles creates a holistic economic framework that also aligns with the Sustainable Development Goals (SDGs). (Awang & Wan Chik, 2023). In other words, this synergy not only ensures that each ISFIs complies with *maqasid al-shariah* but also ensures that the benefits obtained are sustainable for future generations. Table 1 demonstrates the alignment of several ISF instruments with *maqasid al-shariah.*

Table 1. Integration of ISF instruments with maqasid al-shariah

Instrument	***Maqasid* Alignment**
Zakat	Wealth preservation through equitable redistribution
Waqf	Preservation of life (healthcare) and intellect (education)
Sadaqah	Preservation of life through emergency aid
Qard al- hasan	Promotes justice in accessing financial aid
Islamic Microfinance	Promotes justice in accessing financial aid
Takaful	Preservation of lineage through family protection
Social *Sukuk*	Preservation of wealth through ethical investments

The above alignments can reach *maqasid al-shariah* and sustainable development if they are implemented effectively and efficiently with the help of the right enablers. Therefore, this study proposes a comprehensive framework that integrates four important enablers or factors of ISF to achieve *maqasid al-shariah* by improving financial inclusion outcomes, as shown in Figure 1.

Figure 1. Conceptual framework

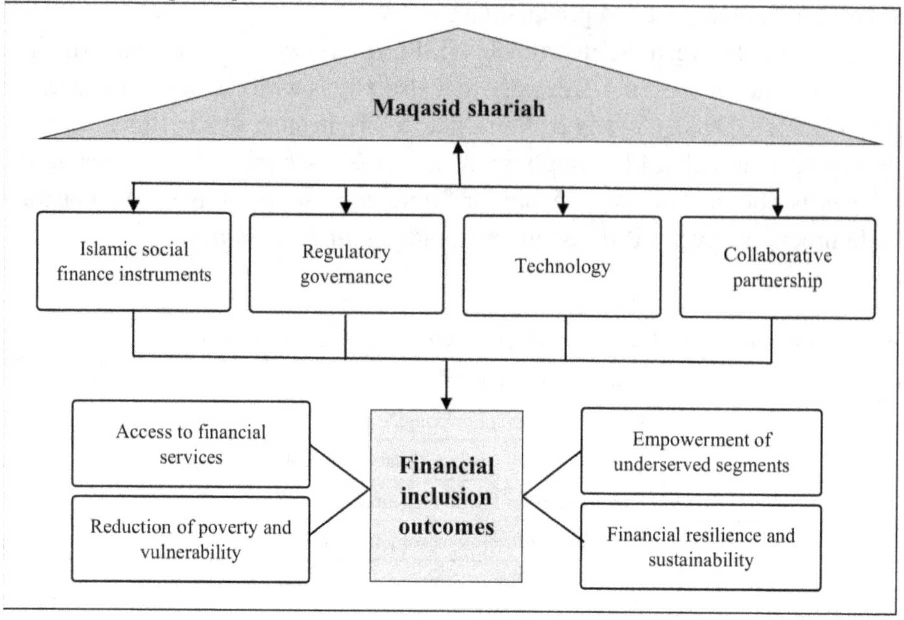

This framework suggests that ISFI is the key strategic factor for achieving *maqasid al-shariah* in Islamic finance. This goal can be achieved through focused financial interventions where financial institutions offer ISFIs to those in need, promoting the inclusion of marginalized and underserved communities in the Islamic financial system. The ISFIs, if utilized efficiently and effectively, can transform the recipients of these instruments to be the contributors of the instruments in the same system, hence illustrating the success of this system in achieving *maqasid al-shariah* and sustainable development simultaneously.

At the same time, regulatory governance also plays an important role in enhancing the functions of ISFs in the local and global economy. A developed governance framework or guidelines enhances transparency, accountability, and compliance with regulations, thereby enabling ISF management to be carried out efficiently and effectively. This effect is exemplified by the MyWakaf Program launched by Bank Negara Malaysia (BNM) in collaboration with the Association of Islamic Banking and Financial Institutions of Malaysia (AIBIM), which demonstrates how structured and transparent governance can make it better to manage and distribute waqf assets (Bank Negara Malaysia, 2017), hence achieving the objectives of the ISF itself.

In addition, fintech applications are the latest developments in Islamic finance, and they are also a contributing factor to the success of ISF. The use of blockchain technology and mobile applications in zakat and waqf management can help increase transparency, reduce fraud, and optimize operational efficiency (Abdullah, 2018), thereby demonstrating accountability in the management of zakat and waqf funds. Finally, strong collaborative partnerships among governments, financial institutions, and non-governmental organizations are essential for the scalability and sustainability of Islamic social finance initiatives (Tahiri Jouti, 2019). This is because each of these entities plays their roles and complements each other in the overall Islamic financial system.

When implemented within the ethical framework of *maqasid al-shariah*, the combination of the four enablers can improve various aspects of financial inclusion, including increasing access to essential financial services (such as savings, credit, and payments), fostering entrepreneurship and businesses, reducing poverty and the wealth gap, and building financial resilience among the marginalized groups, especially women and youth.

This framework contributes to the discourse on the importance of ISF in promoting inclusive development. It highlights the need to incorporate *maqasid al-shariah* into the design, implementation, and evaluation of financial inclusion strategies within the Islamic financial framework, thereby ensuring that these initiatives promote material well-being and spiritual prosperity.

3. GLOBAL TRENDS AND COUNTRY EXPERIENCES

Islamic social finance (ISF) has been accepted and implemented globally through various models and approaches that are appropriate to local socio-economic conditions. The ISF approach has proven to be successful and effective in addressing poverty and economic imbalances in society, thereby promoting financial inclusion. This effect has been demonstrated through case studies of ISF implementation in Southeast Asia, South Asia, the Middle East, and Africa as follows:

3.1 Southeast Asia – Malaysia and Indonesia

ISF practices in Malaysia and Indonesia have evolved due to the incorporation of fintech into the industry. For instance, the use of digital tools, including artificial intelligence (AI), mobile banking, and blockchain in zakat and *waqf* governance in Malaysia, has increased efficiency, transparency, and accessibility for beneficiaries (Rafiki et al., 2024).

ISF practices in Malaysia and Indonesia have evolved due to the integration of fintech into the industry, in line with the fintech revolution in financial systems worldwide. The impacts can be seen through the use of digital tools, including artificial intelligence (AI), mobile banking, and blockchain in the governance of zakat and *waqf* in Malaysia, which has increased efficiency, transparency, and accessibility for beneficiaries (Ahmad & Yahaya, 2023; Rafiki et al., 2024). Customers of the Islamic financial system now have greater ease of dealing with relevant institutions, provided they have internet access.

These developments have facilitated relevant institutions to improve their performance, thereby increasing wealth preservation (*if al-māl*) among zakat and *waqf* donors and beneficiaries, as collected zakat and waqf funds are managed, distributed, and spent in an efficient, effective, and transparent manner. For instance, in 2022, various zakat institutions in Malaysia collected almost RM4 billion in zakat funds (Mydigital Investment Office, 2023). Initiatives such as the National *Waqf* Blueprint 2022 and the *Waqf*-Featured Fund Framework have played a significant role in mobilizing *waqf* assets through Islamic collective investment schemes. As of the end of 2022, the Securities Commission of Malaysia had registered six waqf-based funds, which collectively managed approximately RM47 million in assets ("Malaysia to unlock, 2022).

In Indonesia, fintech applications, including mobile apps and crowdfunding platforms, have transformed waqf fundraising, exemplified by the WakafMu initiative. These tools streamline donation processes, expand donor outreach, and enhance trust, thereby promoting the preservation of wealth (*if al-māl*) and religion (*if al-dīn*) through sustained charitable contributions. Blockchain technology, in particular, presents significant potential for optimizing zakat and waqf management in Indonesia, a nation with a Muslim-majority population exceeding 80%. In 2023, for instance, collections from zakat, *infaq*, *sadaqah*, and waqf amounted to over IDR 34 trillion (Rp34 trillion, 2024).

However, the non-standard regulatory framework in the country emphasizes the need for a robust legal structure to effectively leverage the advantages of fintech without marginalizing Islamic values. Furthermore, blockchain adoption is mostly urban-centric and fragmented, as rural *waqf* institutions often lack the governance capacity and digital infrastructure needed to effectively scale up this innovation (Huda, 2021). With proper oversight, fintech applications enhance the ability of ISF to achieve its objectives by addressing socio-economic inequalities, enhancing institutional integrity, and maximizing the social impact of zakat and *waqf*.

The development of ISFs above aligns with the evolution of conventional social finance mechanisms (CSFs) in Malaysia and Indonesia. This can be seen through the achievement of effective institutions, especially through initiatives such as microfinance, targeted cash programs, and social protection schemes. For example, the iTEKAD initiative introduced by Bank Negara Malaysia, which combines social finance instruments with microfinance and provides structured training to low-income microentrepreneurs, has successfully assisted 9,684 participants with funding assistance of RM63.6 million in 2024 (Bank Negara Malaysia, 2024).

Similarly, in 2023, Indonesia issued sustainability-focused debt instruments totalling IDR 13.6 trillion (approximately USD 868.3 million). Of this, green bonds accounted for IDR 12.9 trillion, while social bonds or *sukuk* totaled IDR 700 billion. This reflects a growing commitment to financing projects with positive environmental and social impacts. These programs, although conventional-based, share the same core objectives of reducing economic inequality and increasing financial inclusion. The integration of fintech in both Islamic and conventional social finance represents a convergence path towards inclusive and sustainable development in both countries.

3.2 South Asia - Bangladesh

ISF instruments have emerged in Bangladesh as significant tools for fostering inclusive and sustainable development. However, the potential of ISF remains underdeveloped due to challenges related to awareness, regulation, and institutions. So far, ISF instruments, particularly Islamic microfinance, have shown significant advantages in the country. For instance, a study conducted in Sunamganj district showed that households involved in microcredit programs experienced significant improvements, where increases were found in total income by 13.57%, total expenditure by 10.39%, and investment by 26.17%. Simultaneously, a 2.39% reduction in household debt was observed, indicating enhanced financial stability (Islam, 2022).

Islamic banks in Bangladesh have significantly contributed to the financial sector. By mid-2022, Islamic banking represented about 28.5% of total industry loans and advances, with deposits reaching BDT 4.21 trillion, which constituted 27% of the overall banking sector deposits ("Islamic finance growing," 2022).

In addition, Hossain et al. (2025) assert that zakat and Islamic microfinance have contributed to sustainable economic growth by improving financial inclusion and facilitating income-generating activities within marginalized communities in Bangladesh. For example, the Jeebika project, managed by the Centre for Zakat Management (CZM), supports livelihood programs, vocational training, and educational opportunities. The Centre has provided healthcare services to 18.3 million patients and facilitated zakat-based literacy programs to 380,038 adults. Additionally, microcredit initiatives have benefited 2,240 recipients throughout the country (Mohiuddin, 2017). Hoque (2023) has also conducted a quantitative analysis, estimating the average annual business zakat fund per enterprise at approximately BDT 144 million (USD 1.7 million). This includes 35% of entrepreneurs utilizing business zakat to fully or partially finance social projects, indicating its great potential for poverty alleviation and social welfare financing.

Notwithstanding these achievements, the integration of fintech with ISF in Bangladesh remains underdeveloped. This was demonstrated by the restricted utilization of digital platforms for *waqf* or zakat administration (Hoque, 2023; Mohiuddin,

2017). The situation is somewhat similar with the fintech acceptance in the rural India (Goswami et al., 2022). The literature inadequately explores consumer perspectives and acceptance of ISF among the unbanked or rural population (Hoque, 2023), indicating a significant research gap in realizing the inclusive scaling of ISF in the Bangladeshi market. In contrast, CSF institutions performed much better than ISF when they successfully achieved broader outreach and significant financial inclusion impact, as exemplified by Grameen Bank, which has reached over 9 million borrowers nationwide, and BRAC, which has served 110 million people globally (Uddin et al., 2020).

From a regulatory perspective, Mohiuddin (2017) emphasizes that Bangladesh suffers from a dearth of a comprehensive legal and institutional framework for Islamic social enterprises and zakat administration. The existing frameworks are voluntary and unregulated, which has led to variations in their governance and practice. A zakat commission was established by the Bangladesh government under the Islamic Foundation in 1982. Nevertheless, its functions are restricted, and the majority of zakat and waqf operations are managed by private institutions, such as Muslim Aid Bangladesh and CZM. These institutions have successfully implemented ISF in many projects, such as the development of the Baitul Mukarram Wakaf Complex, which has provided healthcare services to 18.3 million patients, literacy programs that have reached 380,038 adults, and microcredit that has been distributed to 2,240 beneficiaries. These examples demonstrate the extensive social impacts achievable when Islamic social finance is effectively institutionalized.

3.3 Middle East – United Arab Emirates (UAE)

ISF in the United Arab Emirates (UAE) has developed as a multi-dimensional system, integrating the fundamental principles of traditional Islamic finance with contemporary sustainability goals. ISF instruments have been systematically integrated into the financial framework of the country in line with the national strategic direction of Islamic finance to support the socio-economic development agenda.

Being the manifestation of the implementation of ISF, the UAE has established a zakat management mechanism through authorized institutions such as the Zakat Fund and Sharjah Charity International (SCI). The result of the mechanism is feasible when the Zakat Fund reported a total collection of more than AED 231 million in 2021, indicating a 5 percent increase over the previous year (Zakat Fund, 2022). During the period between 2021 and 2023, SCI allocated AED 207.1 million from its zakat fund, benefiting more than 20,000 recipients, including students facing financial difficulties, individuals involved in financial cases, and those having trouble paying rent ("SCI: 20 thousand," 2024).

To strengthen the participation of the corporate sector in the Islamic social finance ecosystem, the Islamic Affairs, Waqf, and Zakat Authority has launched a digital initiative in 2025 that aims to strengthen zakat compliance among companies. Through the implementation of an innovative corporate zakat calculation tool based on Sharia principles, this initiative is expected to increase the level of transparency and fiscal compliance in the Islamic business sector ("UAE: New initiative," 2025). This approach marks a significant shift towards the institutionalization of corporate zakat as part of ethical and socially impactful corporate governance.

The UAE government has also introduced various support policies for the small and medium-sized enterprise (SME) sector to stimulate economic growth through Islamic microfinance instruments. Specific Islamic financial institutions have been established to offer shariah-compliant financial products tailored to the unique needs of SMEs, supported by educational programs and financial incentives to strengthen Islamic financial literacy among local entrepreneurs. This integrated initiative can increase the level of financial inclusion, thus contributing to the development of a more sustainable and resilient SME ecosystem ("The Role of Islamic Finance," 2023).

Despite the increase in consumer trust and transparency, the development of ISFs in the UAE remains concentrated in urban areas and lacks outreach in rural areas. This is in stark contrast to the level of financial penetration achieved by conventional financial systems (CSFs), which have been widely used to finance education and health initiatives (Al-Okaily, 2025; Al-Qudah et al., 2025). For example, Emirates NBD (one of the initiatives under CSFs) has allocated approximately AED 30 million to community programs in 2023, including financial assistance for students from low-income families, medical expenses, and financial support for individuals with disabilities, and initiatives to empower women (Zakat Fund Issues, 2023).

On a larger scale, First Abu Dhabi Bank (FAB) has offered USD600 million in green bonds, with part of the proceeds being channelled towards infrastructure development such as renewable energy projects and community development in underdeveloped areas (FAB Issues, 2023). This development clearly shows that CSF has moved far ahead in urban development and penetrated rural development in the UAE compared to ISF.

3.4 Africa – Nigeria and Sub-Saharan Africa

Islamic social finance is attracting interest in African nations, especially in Nigeria and Sub-Saharan Africa. Although still new and facing various institutional and structural challenges, there is increasing acceptance of ISF instruments among the population in the region. For example, Nigeria, which has the largest Muslim population in the region, has been at the forefront of ISF initiatives, particularly in the zakat, *waqf*, and Islamic microfinance sectors. This is evidenced by a study by the Islamic Financial Services Board (2022), which showed that over 75% of the Islamic finance market in Sub-Saharan Africa originated in Nigeria. This shows the dominant role played by Nigeria in promoting the development of the ISF sector in the region.

Islamic NGOs and zakat institutions play a very significant role in the implementation of ISF in Nigeria. This role is evidenced by the Zakat and Sadaqat Foundation, who has distributed more than USD 2.3 million in 2021 for health and education purposes to *asnaf* recipients in the northern region of the country (Zakat and Sadaqat Foundation, 2022). Nevertheless, the effectiveness of zakat management is still questionable when over 65% of respondents in Bauchi State (Nigeria) were in doubt about the capability of the formal zakat institutions in managing zakat funds, which leads to collection leakage where many zakat payers choose to channel zakat directly to individuals in need instead of through formal zakat institutions (Muhammad, et al., 2023). The study indicates that aspects of trust and governance still need to be strengthened in the country.

In terms of *waqf*, informal practices still dominate, especially in northern Nigeria. A study by Hamid and Yahya (2021) found that more than 1,500 mosques and religious institutions own *waqf* land that is not systematically recorded. This reflects the great potential of *waqf* in financing social development but also indicates the need for a more robust documentation and legal system to optimize *waqf* assets sustainably.

Islamic microfinance is also actively expanding, especially through institutions such as Jaiz Bank, the only fully Islamic bank in Nigeria (Jaiz Bank, 2022). The bank recorded an impressive increase in customers from 420,000 in 2020 to over 610,000 in 2022. Most of the financing is targeted at small and medium enterprises (SMEs). This financing has successfully increased household income by up to 20% within 12 months among women entrepreneurs who received micro & Shariah financing (Isahi & Muwazir, 2024). In another report, the Islamic Development Bank and EFInA (2021) highlighted that an estimated 1.6 million Muslim households in Nigeria still lack access to conventional financing that has long been established in the country. This indicates that outreach levels remain primarily influenced by conventional microfinance institutions and CSF channels, which receive government backing and operate within a more established legal framework. Thus, there is still an urgent need to strengthen institutions, expand the scope of digitalization, increase the level of shariah-compliance, and raise public awareness of the advantages of ISF systems, subsequently strengthening financial inclusion in the country.

In general, although ISF has demonstrated potential for growth and integration within the global financial industry, its adoption and reach remain constrained compared to CSF. To enhance its effectiveness and global competitiveness, ISF could benefit from adopting CSF strategies, including incorporating impact measurement standards, exploring blended finance structures, and innovating Islamic-compliant outcome-based financing models. Such adaptations would not only strengthen the *maqasid al-shariah* objectives of ISF by ensuring measurable social justice and poverty alleviation outcomes but also improve investor confidence, scalability, and integration with global sustainable finance markets (Habibullah & Hassan, 2023).

4. LIMITATIONS AND SHORTCOMINGS IN ISLAMIC FINANCIAL INCLUSION APPROACHES

It is well known that Islamic social finance (ISF) is increasingly being accepted and recognized worldwide as a potentially transformative tool for ethical financial inclusion, especially in Muslim-majority countries. However, its application remains limited, especially in developing countries, hindering its full impact and scalability. These limitations are classified into three, namely systemic, operational, and perceptual.

4.1 Systemic and Institutional Limitations

A key challenge in the inclusive Islamic finance landscape is the fragmented nature of its institutional governance. For example, in Malaysia, this fragmentation is evident through the lack of integration between Islamic financial instruments such as zakat and *waqf*, which are administered in a decentralized manner by institutions under the State Islamic Religious Councils (Mustaffa et al., 2022), while microfinance, Islamic banking, and takaful are administered in a centralized manner by the Central Bank of Malaysia at the national level. This practice has led to isolated operations, wasted effort, and inefficiency in wealth management. Such governance fragmentation undermines the capacity of ISFs to implement large-scale coordinated initiatives, especially in situations that require rapid and accurate responses, such as financial crises, as well as humanitarian disasters and infectious disease threats.

Furthermore, the emphasis on legalistic shariah compliance overrides the function and substance of financial instruments. Most of the Islamic financial solutions are seen as replicating existing conventional instruments, improved by removing elements prohibited in Islam, like usury (*riba*) and uncertainty (*gharar*). However, inherently, these instruments fail to achieve higher goals (*maqasid*) such as wealth redistribution, poverty eradication, and environmental protection (El-Gamal, 2006). Consequently, ISF risks becoming more symbolic than effective in addressing systemic inequalities and social exclusion.

4.2 Operational and Technological Constraints

Islamic microfinance organizations often face challenges in accessing the poorest demographics. This is due to the need to avoid credit risk, insufficient collateral, low levels of readiness, and limited operational capacity. Despite being mission-oriented, many Islamic microfinance institutions rely on conservative lending practices, thereby rejecting high-risk or undocumented clients who are most in need of assistance (Abdul Rahman, 2010; Habibullah & Hassan, 2023). Furthermore, the administrative procedures of zakat and *waqf* institutions in many countries remain manual and sluggish, thus undermining efficiency, effectiveness, and transparency, which leads to low public confidence (Rosman et al., 2022).

Technology adoption, particularly in fintech, is inconsistent across the Muslim world. While countries such as Malaysia and the UAE are advanced in digitizing zakat and *waqf* systems through blockchain, AI, and crowdfunding platforms, many low-income OIC countries still lack the digital infrastructure and literacy needed to effectively implement the analogue systems (Hossain et al., 2025). The digital divide reduces the scalability of ISFs and exacerbates rural-urban inequalities, leaving marginalized groups with limited access to ethical financial services.

In contrast, CSF models have successfully demonstrated the integration of fintech into instruments such as digital wallets, mobile banking, and outcome-based financing mechanisms such as social impact bonds, particularly in Sub-Saharan Africa and Latin America. This rapid development allows CSF participants to reach a broader demographic, including the rural poor, with scalable and customer-tailored financial solutions (Reeder et al., 2021).

4.3 Perception-Based Barriers and Inclusivity Issues

Public perception also plays an important role in the success of the ISF expansion agenda. However, some people in the community view Islamic finance in a limited context. Typically, Islamic finance is seen as a purely religious or charitable system, involving just the absence of interest, thus closing the door for non-Muslims to participate in this system (Bexley et al., 2000). In fact, this understanding discourages involvement from institutional investors, as well as certain Muslims who doubt the effectiveness or contemporary relevance of the ISF framework in the socio-economic development of society.

In other platforms, the internal discourse in Islamic finance sometimes confuses compliance and the effectiveness of financial instruments. While avoiding interest (*riba*) or uncertainty (*gharar*) is an important foundation in Islamic finance, the need to focus on the effectiveness of financial instruments for the community also needs to be emphasized. For instance, the focus should also be put on instruments that are truly inclusive, adaptable, and specifically designed for marginalized demographics, including women, youth, and micro-entrepreneurs. If industry overlooks how effective these products are, ISF programs might unintentionally mirror the unfair practices found in conventional finance, which would prevent them from meeting their objectives.

Thus, ISF should learn from CSF programs that often prioritize inclusivity and the establishment of measurable outcomes. For example, Grameen Bank, a conventional bank founded in Bangladesh, is a specialized community development bank. It offers collateral-free microfinance along with training, education, and health services to its clients. In the long run, this system fosters comprehensive empowerment and sustainable development (Uddin et al., 2020). Although similar models exist in ISF, the prevalence of such integrated service models in the ISF ecosystem is very limited, as there is often a lack of cross-sector collaboration and ongoing engagement with beneficiaries over time.

5. FUTURE DIRECTIONS AND STRATEGIC PATHWAYS FOR REFORM

Based on the limitations and shortcomings highlighted above, there is a crucial need to reform the existing Islamic social finance (ISF) system. However, the reform plans must comply with Islamic principles in achieving *maqasid al-shariah* and effectively address the actual needs for financial inclusion, accountability, and growth in an increasingly digital and impact-focused development context. The following strategies are proposed to enhance the effectiveness and inclusiveness of ISF in future directions.

5.1 Develop a Standardized ISF Impact Measurement Framework

A key step in making ISF more inclusive is not just to follow shariah rules as a basic requirement, but also to focus on the positive impacts that align with the goals of *maqasid al-shariah*. Various stakeholders, such as Islamic financial institutions, regulators, and international bodies, must cooperate to develop and implement a standardized framework for assessing the social, economic, and environmental impacts of Islamic social finance instruments in society (Abdullah & Dusuki, 2021). Making tools to measure the social impact of ISF, similar to ESG frameworks, would help policymakers and stakeholders see how well ISF initiatives meet their main objectives. This recommendation specifically targets countries like Bangladesh, Nigeria, and the UAE, where formalized and standardized tools for assessing the social and economic impacts of ISF are largely lacking or underdeveloped. This will improve transparency, accountability, and comparability with the CSF model.

5.2 Promote Hybrid Financial Instruments and Blended Finance Models

ISF stakeholders, especially in Malaysia, Indonesia, and the UAE, should investigate innovative hybrid models, including SRI-linked zakat funds, waqf green *sukuk*, and Islamic social impact bonds, which amalgamate performance-based financing with ethical investment strategies (Habibullah & Hassan, 2023). This is due to the existence of advanced capital markets and investor interest in these nations, positioning them favourably to explore hybrid models. The capital markets in Nigeria and Bangladesh are nascent and necessitate foundational advancements, including capacity building, market deepening, and regulatory reforms, prior to the successful and efficient implementation of hybrid models.

5.3 Strengthening Governance and Regulatory Harmonization

Standard-setting bodies, institutions, and governments that formulate standards for Islamic finance should collaborate to align the standards and regulations across different countries. This will help create a system that supports growth, international collaboration, and trust from investors (Dirie et al., 2024; Awang & Wan Chik, 2023). This advice is especially important for countries like Nigeria and Bangladesh, which struggle with inconsistent regulations, weak shariah governance, and limited alignment in Islamic finance rules. This recommendation should focus on countries such as Nigeria and Bangladesh since they face significant regulatory fragmentation, weak shariah governance, and still limited ISF regulatory harmonization.

5.4 Leverage Fintech and Digital Platforms

ISF institutions should accelerate the integration of fintech solutions such as blockchain, digital crowdfunding, and AI-driven impact tracking to improve operational efficiency, inclusiveness, and user trust (Rusydiana et al., 2023). This recommendation is particularly suitable for implementation in Malaysia, Indonesia, UAE as they are leaders in the fintech ecosystem, with vibrant digital payment systems and Islamic fintech startups.

In Bangladesh and Nigeria, this recommendation depends on the context and suitability, as although mobile penetration is high, Islamic fintech still faces challenges such as Shariah governance gaps, digital literacy, and low trust in digital platforms, especially for zakat and waqf. Hence, this requires upfront investment to develop digital infrastructure, increase fintech literacy, and secure regulatory support before scaling up ISF through fintech.

5.5 Expand Public Awareness and Rebrand ISF as Universal and Impact-Driven

Another critical approach is to reshape public perceptions of Islamic finance. To move beyond the common misconception that ISF is exclusive to Muslims or limited to charitable giving, stakeholders should reframe it as a universal ethical finance model that prioritizes justice, sustainability, and human dignity (Kamil et al., 2020). ISF can be positioned as a global approach to addressing socio-economic challenges through the implementation of awareness campaigns, public discourses, inclusive product design, and interfaith social finance dialogue. In line with technological developments, public exposure and awareness can also be instilled through social media and news coverage in mainstream communication channels. Such an approach is particularly important in multicultural or secular societies, where Islamic finance must appeal to a wider audience.

In summary, the ISF strategies that are based on *maqasid al-shariah* and focus on the inclusion of Islamic finance are comprehensive to promote equitable, ethical, and sustainable development. At the same time, ISF needs to adopt digital-friendly and integrated governance. This approach will make Islamic finance a practical universal tool for sustainable development, alongside regulation and technological innovation, thereby fully contributing to the global Sustainable Development Goals (SDGs) and the Environmental, Social, and Governance (ESG) agenda.

6. CONCLUSION

This chapter has described the integration of Islamic Social Finance (ISF) with the *maqasid al-shariah* and its importance in increasing financial inclusion and fostering sustainable development. It emphasizes the potential of ISF in poverty eradication, socio-economic empowerment, and ethical wealth redistribution, based on evidence from countries such as Malaysia, Indonesia, Bangladesh, the UAE, Nigeria, and Sub-Saharan Africa. Regardless of its importance, the case studies reveal that the implementation of ISF is currently constrained by fragmented governance, inadequate impact measurement frameworks, weak integration with fintech and capital markets, and failure to achieve its intended goals.

In contrast, conventional social finance (CSF) models, particularly green bonds and social impact bonds, have demonstrated greater growth potential, effectiveness, and appeal to institutional investors by using clear performance measures, open reporting, and blended financing methods. Without strategic recalibration, ISF risk being marginalized in the rapidly evolving sustainable and impact finance landscape.

Thus, the study underscores the urgent need for ISF to transition from a charity-centric paradigm toward a systemic, data-driven, and investor-inclusive model of social finance. This transformation would help ISF keep its ethical and shariah-compliant values while also making it a strong player in helping achieve Sustainable Development Goals (SDGs) and Environmental, Social, and Governance (ESG) standards. An impact measurement system for ISF can be created by involving all interested parties and combining current methods of Value-Based Intermediation, *maqa id* al-shariah, and Sustainable Development Goals.

REFERENCES

Abdul Rahman, A. R. (2010). Can microfinance alleviate poverty? The case of Bangladesh. *Humanomics, 26*(3), 203–213. DOI: 10.1108/08288661011074962

Abdullah, M. (2018). Blockchain for Islamic Social Finance Governance. International Journal of Islamic Finance.

Abdullah, N. I., & Dusuki, A. W. (2021). Beyond compliance: Operationalizing *Maqasid al-shariah* in Islamic finance. *Journal of Islamic Accounting and Business Research, 12*(2), 175–191. DOI: 10.1108/JIABR-10-2020-0312

Ahmed, A.. (2023). *Islamic Microfinance and Maqasid al-shariah: A New Perspective.* Global Islamic Finance Journal.

Al-Qudah, A. A., Al-Okaily, M., & Yadav, M. P. P. (2025). The growth of FinTech and blockchain technology in developing countries: UAE's evidence. *International Journal of Accounting & Information Management, 33*(2), 383–406. https://doi-org.uitm.idm.oclc.org/10.1108/IJAIM-02-2024-0065. DOI: 10.1108/IJAIM-02-2024-0065

Alam, N., Gupta, L., & Shanmugam, B. (2017). Prohibition of Riba and Gharar in Islamic banking. In *Islamic finance: A practical perspective* (pp. 35–53). Springer International Publishing. DOI: 10.1007/978-3-319-66559-7_3

Awang, M. Z., & Wan Chik, W. M. Y. (2023). Application of Islamic Social Finance in Sustainable Development Goals with Specific Target for Maqasid al-shariah. International Journal of Academic Research in Accounting [HRMARS]. *Finance and Management Sciences, 13*(1), 35–46.

Bank Negara Malaysia. (2017). MyWakaf: A Model for Sustainable Waqf Management.

Bank Negara Malaysia. (2024). *iTEKAD: Empowering low-income microentrepreneurs.* Retrieved from https://www.bnm.gov.my/social-finance

Bexley, J. B., Maniam, B., & James, J. F. (2000). Perception of Islamic Financial System: Its Obstacles in Application, and Its Market. In *Allied Academies International Conference. Academy of Accounting and Financial Studies.* [). Jordan Whitney Enterprises, Inc.]. *Proceedings, 5*(2), 1.

Chapra, M. U. (2016). *The Islamic Vision of Development in Light of Maqasid al-shariah.* Islamic Development Bank.

Dirie, K. A., Alam, M. M., & Maamor, S. (2024). Islamic Social Finance for Achieving Sustainable Development Goals: A Systematic Literature Review and Future Research Agenda. *International Journal of Ethics and Systems*, *40*(4), 676–698. DOI: 10.1108/IJOES-12-2022-0317

Dusuki, A. W., & Bouheraoua, S. (2011). The framework of *Maqasid al-shariah* and its implications for Islamic finance. *Islamic Finance and Maqasid al-shariah*, ISRA Research Paper.

El-Gamal, M. A. (2006). *Islamic finance: Law, economics, and practice*. Cambridge University Press. DOI: 10.1017/CBO9780511753756

"FAB Issues USD 600 million Green Bond." (2023, June 1). *Gulf News*. https://gulfnews.com/business/banking/fab-successfully-prices-600-million-5-year-green-bond-1.96135337

Fisol, W. N. M., & Bakar, M. A., BIN, A. K., & RAHIM, A. (2021). The Scientific of Macro Maqasid in Developing of Social Financing Products. *Journal of Contemporary Issues in Business and Government*, *27*(3), 1–9.

Goswami, S., Sharma, R. B., & Chouhan, V. (2022). Impact of financial technology (Fintech) on financial inclusion (FI) in Rural India. *Universal Journal of Accounting and Finance*, *10*(2), 483–497. DOI: 10.13189/ujaf.2022.100213

Habibullah, M., & Hassan, R. (2023). Developing a Conceptual Shari'ah Framework of Green Sukuk for Bangladesh: Its Implications on Social Welfare by Realizing SDGs. [IIUM Journals]. *Journal of Islamic Finance*, *12*(1), 73–82. DOI: 10.31436/jif.v12i1.748

Hamid, N., & Yahya, F. (2021). Informal Waqf Practice and its Socio-economic Role in Northern Nigeria. *Journal of Islamic Economics and Development*, *6*(1), 45–61.

Hassan, M. K., & Kayed, R. N. (2009). The global financial crisis, risk management and social justice in Islamic finance. *ISRA International Journal of Islamic Finance*, *1*(1), 33–58. DOI: 10.55188/ijif.v1i1.63

Hassan, R., & Muneeza, A. (2022). The need to eliminate mismanagement and corruption in Islamic social finance institutions. *IIUM Law Journal*, *30*(S2), 423–444. DOI: 10.31436/iiumlj.v30iS2.774

Hoque, N. (2023). Promoting business zakah as a product of Islamic finance to fund social causes for well-being of the underprivileged: Evidence from Bangladesh. *Journal of Islamic Marketing*, *14*(4), 966–987. DOI: 10.1108/JIMA-10-2021-0337

Hossain, M. E., Mahadi, N. F. B., Haron, R., Nor, R. M., & Yousuf, M. A. (2025). Islamic Social Finance for Sustainable Economic Growth in Bangladesh. *Journal of Islamic Finance, 14*(1), 85–97.

Huda, N. (2021). Waqf Blockchain in Indonesia. *Al-Awqaf: Jurnal Wakaf Dan Ekonomi Islam, 14*(1), 31–49.

Isahi, A., & Muwazir, M. R. (2024). *Poverty Alleviation in Nigeria: An Insight into Jaiz Bank Islamic Microfinance Scheme.* Online Journal of Islamic Management and Finance (OJIMF), 4(2), 99–114. https://mjlis.um.edu.my/index.php/OJIMF/article/view/56122

Islamic Development Bank & EFInA. (2021). *Financial Inclusion Strategy Report: Nigeria Country Profile.* https://www.efina.org.ng

"Islamic finance growing in Bangladesh despite structural issues." (2022). *The Islamic Economist.* https://theislamiceconomist.org/editorial/islamic-finance-growing-in-bangladesh-despite-structural-issues/

Islamic Financial Services Board. (2022). *Islamic Financial Services Industry Stability Report 2022.* https://www.ifsb.org

Kamil, W. R., Mohd Bakho, S. S., SC, Zhang, W., Aziz, A. A., Reddy, R., & Osman, M. R. (2020, May). Islamic Finance: A Catalyst for Financial Inclusion [pdf]. Kuala Lumpur: Securities Commission Malaysia.

Karakulah, M., & Muneeza, A. (2024). Exploring the Role of Donation-Based Crowdfunding in Islamic Social Finance. *International Journal of Islamic Economics and Finance Research, 7*(1 July), 42-58.

Kasri, N. S., & Hilmi, M. H. (2020). International best practices in existing corporate waqf models: a retrospective–introduction, chapter content, best practices. In *Challenges and Impacts of Religious Endowments on Global Economics and Finance* (pp. 223–253). IGI Global Scientific Publishing. DOI: 10.4018/978-1-7998-1245-6.ch011

"Malaysia to unlock RM1.3 trillion in waqf assets under new blueprint." (2022). *Islamic Finance News.* https://www.islamicfinancenews.com

Mohamad, S., Othman, J., Lehner, O., & Muda, R. (2017). Social sukuk: A new mechanism to fund social services. *Journal of Emerging Economies & Islamic Research, 5*(1), 1–13. DOI: 10.24191/jeeir.v5i1.6252

Mohiuddin, M. (2017). Islamic social enterprises in Bangladesh: Conceptual and institutional challenges. *International Journal of Islamic and Middle Eastern Finance and Management, 10*(2), 246–263. DOI: 10.1108/IMEFM-09-2015-0103

Muhammad, A. A., Shariff, I. A., & Umar, A. (2023). The Impact of Islamic Models of Zakat and Waqf in Reducing Poverty Among Vulnerables During The Pandemic Era in Bauchi State, Nigeria. *AZKA International Journal of Zakat & Social Finance, 4*(1), 69–90. Advance online publication. DOI: 10.51377/azjaf.vol4no1.143

Mustaffa, J., Isa, M. Y. B. M., & Mohammed, Z. (2022). Governance structures: Dependability and efficiency of the waqf institutional system in Malaysia. *Journal of Economics and Business Aseanomics, 7*(2), 058-070.

Mydigital Investment Office. (2023). *Islamic Digital Economy - Driving Investments Through Islamic Digital Economy*. Retrieved from https://mydigitalinvestment.gov.my/islamic-digital-economy

Pusat Pungutan Zakat - Majlis Agama Islam Wilayah Persekutuan. (2023). *Laporan Tahunan 2023.* Pusat Pungutan Zakat Wilayah Persekutuan.

Rafiki, A. Syahrial, H., & Andika, S. (2024). A Review on Digital Zakat Management Research. *Information Management and Business Review*, 16(3)(S): 167-174.

Raimi, L., Abdur-Rauf, I. A., & Ashafa, S. A. (2024). Does Islamic sustainable finance support sustainable development goals to avert financial risk in the management of Islamic finance products? A critical literature review. *Journal of Risk and Financial Management, 17*(6), 236. DOI: 10.3390/jrfm17060236

Reeder, N., Rocyn Jones, G., Loder, J., & Colantonio, A. (2021). *Social impact bonds: The role of outcome-based financing in social innovation*. Routledge.

Rexhepi, G. (2016). The architecture of social finance. In *Routledge handbook of social and sustainable finance* (pp. 35–49). Routledge.

Rosman, R., Redzuan, N. H., Mokhtar, N. Z. N., Engku Ali, E. R. A., & Mohammed, M. O. (2022). Islamic Social Finance and Sustainable Development Goals: Issues and Challenges. *Journal of Islamic Finance, 11*(2), 56–67. DOI: 10.31436/jif.v11i2.690

Rusydiana, A. S., Sukmana, R., & Laila, N. (2023). *Waqf Development Model for SDG-16 (Peace, Justice and Strong Institutions). Islamic Social Finance, 3(2).* SMART Insight.

"SCI: 20 thousand beneficiaries of Zakat aid." (2024, March 12). *Sharjah24*. https://sharjah24.ae/en/articles/2024/03/12/sci-20-thousand-beneficiaries-of-zakat-aid

Sheikh, R. (2025), Developing ethical investment criteria based on Maqasid Shariah. *Qualitative Research in Financial Markets*, Vol. ahead-of-print No. ahead-of-print. https://doi-org.ezaccess.remotexs.co/10.1108/QRFM-04-2025-0103

Syed Azman, S. M. M., & Engku Ali, E. R. A. (2019). Islamic Social Finance and the Imperative for Social Impact Measurement. *Al-Shajarah: Journal of the International Institute Of Islamic Thought & Civilization,* ISSN 1394-6870, pp. 43-68.

Tahiri Jouti, A. (2019). An integrated approach for building sustainable Islamic social finance ecosystems. *ISRA International Journal of Islamic Finance*, *11*(2), 246–266. DOI: 10.1108/IJIF-10-2018-0118

"The role of Islamic finance in supporting small and medium enterprises (SMEs) in the UAE." (2023). *Generis Online*. https://generisonline.com/the-role-of-islamic-finance-in-supporting-small-and-medium-enterprises-smes-in-the-uae/

"UAE: New initiative simplifies Zakat calculation for companies." (2025, February 2). *Gulf News*. https://gulfnews.com/uae/uae-new-initiative-simplifies-zakat-calculation-for-companies-1.500027452

Uddin, S. M., Abedin, M. Z., & Afroz, N. (2020). Islamic Financial Inclusion: An Alternative Approach to Reach the Unbanked of Bangladesh. In Rafay, A. (Ed.), *Growth and Emerging Prospects of International Islamic Banking* (pp. 155–173). IGI Global Scientific Publishing., DOI: 10.4018/978-1-7998-1611-9.ch009

Yahya, M. H., Muhammad, J., Abdullah, A., & Nasir, A. M. (2013). Chinks in the capitalism system-the pertinence of Islamic finance. *Journal of International Business and Cultural Studies*, *7*, 1–16.

Zakat and Sadaqat Foundation. (2022). *Annual Impact Report 2021–2022*. Nigeria.

"Zakat Fund revenue reaches AED231 million in 2021." (2022, February 11). *Emirates News Agency*. https://www.wam.ae/en/details/1395303020056

Chapter 13 The Role of Islamic Microfinance in Promoting Social and Economic Well-Being: Indonesian Cases

Lucky Nugroho
https://orcid.org/0000-0002-9613-1667
Universitas Mercu Buana, Indonesia

ABSTRACT

Islamic micro finance has a high potential in advancing financial inclusion and social inclusion in Indonesia, especially for the poor. While this has potential, there remain obstacles: low levels of Islamic financial literacy, a lack of institutional penetration, and poor systems of Sharia supervision. This book chapter fills the research gap by discussing the four major issues namely the role of MFIs in social welfare, problems in community empowerment, the sustainability of Sharia implementation, and the contribution of MFIs in reducing poverty and inequality. The results underline that MFIs can be used as actuators of social, value-based financing, financial education and the use of social funds. The contribution of this chapter to academia is that it links Islamic economic theory with sustainable development strategies and provides practical suggestions regarding how to strengthen MFIs. It is original in the sense of being written in a post-Covid-19 world and drawing on both normative and empirical considerations in order to evaluate the true social value of Islamic microfinance at the grassroots.

DOI: 10.4018/979-8-3373-1842-4.ch013

1 INTRODUCTION

The COVID-19 pandemic has disrupted the global economic order, albeit Indonesia among others, resulting in rising in number of unemployment, poverty and social inequality (Khambule, 2021; Nugroho et al., 2024). This situation obliges all countries to consider strategic solutions aimed at reversing the economic fortunes of small communities in a sustainable manner. In Indonesia, Micro, Small, and Medium Enterprises (MSMEs) have been regarded as the leading sector to uphold the community economic sustainability (Mightyn et al., 2022; Nugroho et al., 2020; Purwanti et al., 2022). Sadly, these people are usually poor users of formal credit because of lack of financial literacy, scarcity of collaterals and the psychological unavailability of instruments that fit their lifestyle and ethical values. This is also where there is much importance in the existence of Islamic MFIs as an alternative, inclusive, equitable and value-based solution. Islamic microfinance is more than just a source of financing and an instrument of spiritual and social betterment (Usman & Tasmin, 2016; Zalim, 2021; Nugroho, 2014). Financing models such as Mudharabah and Murabahah, as well as Qardhul Hasan, are not only aimed at liquidity of business actors, but they also foster community-based economic system, where ethics is a strategy of value-based approach of fairness, mutual help, and transparency. MFIS also employ empowerment approach, with business training, managerial assistance and social funds management, i.e., zakat, infaq, and waqf, directed to the productive financing (Ayunda et al., 2024; Kosim et al., 2021). And that's the bridge from spiritual value to economic change that's never been there at any financial institution until now. However, the practice on the ground indicates that the performance of Islamic microfinance toward social welfare has not been fully optimal (Ashta et al., 2014; Berger & Humphrey, 1992). There are still various challenges, including low public financial literacy, weak Sharia supervision in operations, limited information technology, and a limited reach of MFIs in remote areas (Ashta et al., 2014; Berger & Nakata, 2013; Nugroho, 2015). Additionally, there is still limited research that reveals in detail how the Sharia financing mechanism can create measurable social and economic impacts. This phenomenon creates an urgent research gap that needs to be answered through a qualitative approach based on Indonesian case studies, considering that each region has different social and economic dynamics.

Islamic microfinance is not only an economic instrument, but also a social instrument. The application of Sharia principles in microfinance presents an approach that prioritizes sustainability, not just profitability (Khan & Badjie, 2020; Nugroho, 2014). In practice, MFI employs various models, including the Grameen model, Village Banking, and the Individual Model, which have been proven effective in increasing the production and income of MSMEs (Hidayat, 2021). However, there has been little research that has critically examined the extent to which Sharia principles are consistently applied in the financing process and how they impact the sustainability of micro-businesses, especially in highly vulnerable socio-economic contexts.

Furthermore, the contribution of MFIs to poverty reduction and economic inequality is a key indicator in assessing the effectiveness of this system. Studies have shown that the existence of MFIs can reach previously marginalized populations. Still, the issues of efficiency, scale, and long-term impact on the structural changes of the community's economy have not been comprehensively studied (Ayunda et al., 2024; Kosim et al., 2021). The latest data shows that more than 25 million Indonesians still live below the poverty line, and inequality of access to finance is still an ongoing structural problem.

Therefore, the writing in this book chapter aims to answer four fundamental questions that have not been fully addressed in previous studies, including (i) what is the role of Islamic microfinance in enhancing the social welfare of low-income individuals? (ii) What are the main challenges that Islamic microfinance institutions face in supporting community economic empowerment? (iii) To what extent are Sharia principles applied in microfinance practices, and how does it impact the sustainability of micro-businesses? (iv) How does Islamic microfinance contribute to reducing poverty and economic inequality at the local level?

This chapter aims to explore the strategic role of Islamic microfinance institutions (MFIs) in enhancing the social and economic well-being of the community, particularly low-income groups and micro-business actors in Indonesia. The primary focus is on understanding how Sharia-based financing, run by MFIs, can help reduce poverty, expand financial inclusion, and strengthen the sustainability of microenterprises, while ensuring the consistent and appropriate application of Sharia principles. Through case studies from various regions in Indonesia, this chapter also aims to identify the main challenges faced by MFIs in financing and community empowerment practices.

In theoretical terms this chapter adds to the literature work on integration of Islamic economic principles and sustainable development theory and argues the significance of value-based approach in the financial system. MFIs are not just perceived as money lenders, but are perceived as agents of change who believe in fair, blessed and inclusive humanity.' The uniqueness of this Book Chapter is that it provides extensive context to the function of post-pandemic MFIs in mitigating the socio-economic challenges at the grass-root level. In this book chapter, an empirical-normative analysis is carried out to address whether Sharia principles can present an answer to constrained access of the masses to formal finance, income discrepancy, and community socio-economic fragility. Not many studies explore the deep relationship of microfinance sharia practices with microeconomic sustainability based on local social complexity as in Indonesia. Therefore, this Book Chapter presents a new outlook in Islamic financial literature which is contextual, applicable and in line with the actual necessity of society.

2 THE ROLE OF ISLAMIC MICROFINANCE IN IMPROVING THE SOCIAL WELFARE OF LOW-INCOME PEOPLE

Social welfare is an essential component of sustainable development, especially with individuals who are economically disadvantaged. In Indonesia, the traditional financial system is not inclusive as millions of people, especially in rural areas, have limited access to the formal financial system as well as low financial literacy, and feel that the conventional banking system is not in line with their values (Hanivan & Nasrudin, 2019; Widyastuti et al., 2023; Rachman & Nugroho, 2024). This makes it very difficult to construct an economic order that is fair and inclusive. In this perspective, Islamic micro-finance is an alternative remedy for them, which not only fulfill the financial needs of masses, but also embody the values of social justice, empowerment and divine blessings rooted in Sharia principles. The issue of financial exclusion for poor people provides an important context behind the strategic role of Islamic microfinance institutions (MFIs). There are not a few who have economic potential through microenterprise but are unable to due to a lack of funds and absence of collateral demanded by the traditional banking system (Tambunan, 2019; Gherhes et al., 2016). Islamic microfinance responds to this need through non-burdensome financing schemes, such as qardhul hasan and mudharabah, and providing business support that targets enhancing the long-term capacity of small business players. The quality of MFIS is not only in their financing but also in the imbibing of responsibility, the transactional blessings and social solidarity among members. In practice, Islamic microfinance has a tangible effect on increasing the social welfare of those who are poor. In addition to being connected to capital, beneficiaries are also provided with business skills training, financial management support, and community-level business networks (Karyanto et al., 2021; Nugroho et al., 2024; Ramdani et al., 2024). This would stimulate the emerging of micro businesses that are less dependent and more competitive. The presence of MFIs also broadens Islamic financial inclusion into the hinterland where formal financial institutions have hitherto been absent (Faizi et al., 2024; Widiastuti et al., 2022). By employing a participatory approach, MFIS has been able to gain trust and create social ties based on Islamic values. Nevertheless, the success of Islamic microfinance is not devoid of some structural obstacles. One challenge, among others, is the low level of literacy on Islamic finance among the beneficiaries (Al-Banna & Nurdany, 2022). Many of them are non-qualified sharia contract savvy – the acquired knowledge is inadequate in this regard, thus leading to lack of comprehension, miscommunication and altercation as regards right in and obligation of the financing contract. Furthermore, MFIS are confronted with drawbacks at the institutional level, such as restricted loan portfolio or working capital, weak HR capacity, and inefficient governance and internal supervision structure. A number of such studies highlight that microfinance institutions (MFIs) possess a huge social potential but still need to improve efficiency and sustainability of their operations in order to be able to compete and survive (Kosim et al., 2021).

This raises serious concerns regarding the potential of Islamic microfinance to really impact on social welfare and the extent to which Shariah principles are being applied in microfinance operations. In this respect, the formulation of the question asked may deserved to be examined. Issues like "how does Islamic micro-finance impact social welfare in the low-income groups." and"What are the key constraints confronted by the MFIs to support the community's economic empowerment? need empirical methods based on field observations of the real-world consequences. Also, not insignificant among the issues, are "How much are Sharia based principles implemented regarding microfinance and how do they affect the sustainability of micro-enterprises?" and "In what ways Islamic microfinance helps to mitigate poverty and unemployment at the bottom?" which suggest the importance for critically reconsidering current policy and practice. The results of several case studies in Indonesia show that the Islamic microfinance institutions (MFIs) can be a trigger of the social movement in various areas, especially when it is integrated with patterns of Sharia financing and social programs using the pattern of zakat, infaq, and shadaqah (ZIS) (Wulandari & Kassim, 2016; Ascarya et al., 2022; Lisa et al., 2023). This approach has proven effective in reducing poverty rates and increasing household income, particularly among women and home-based entrepreneurs (Nugroho & Chowdhury, 2015). By combining philanthropic and commercial aspects in a balanced manner, MFIS demonstrates a uniqueness that other financial institutions lack (Nugroho et al., 2022). However, this success is highly dependent on management commitment, strengthened regulations, and the active participation of the community in maintaining the institution's sustainability (Kosim et al., 2021).

In the future, strengthening the role of Islamic microfinance in enhancing social welfare will require a more integrated approach. The government, financial authorities, and educational institutions must collaborate to establish supportive regulations, enhance institutional infrastructure, and enhance the capacity of human resources in this sector (Ginanjar & Kassim, 2021). Technological innovations must also be adopted to expand the digital reach of Islamic financial services, especially in rural areas (Sudirman et al., 2020; Azizi et al., 2022). At the same time, public literacy about Sharia economics needs to continue improving through contextual and needs-based education that addresses local needs and concerns. With a holistic and long-term oriented approach, Islamic microfinance can be a strategic instrument in realizing inclusive, equitable, and sustainable welfare. Therefore, the discussion in this chapter not only provides a conceptual overview but also highlights the importance of policy reform, institutional innovation, and strengthening Sharia values in all aspects of MFI operations. In this way, it is hoped that the role of Islamic microfinance can be further strengthened in building the social and economic resilience of low-income people in Indonesia.

3 KEY CHALLENGES FACED BY ISLAMIC MICROFINANCE INSTITUTIONS IN SUPPORTING COMMUNITY ECONOMIC EMPOWERMENT

Islamic Microfinance Institutions (MFIs) have long been recognized as key actors in promoting the economic development of small communities, particularly within an economic ecosystem grounded in Islamic values. However, despite its potential and significant contribution, the journey of MFIs is not free of obstacles. Structural and operational challenges remain the primary barriers to optimizing their role in community economic empowerment, particularly for low-income communities (Abdullah et al., 2022). The phenomenon of unequal access to finance is one of the most pressing issues faced by people experiencing poverty in Indonesia (Zia & Prasetyo, 2018). According to data from the Central Statistics Agency (BPS) as of March 2024, it is reported that approximately 25.22 million Indonesians remain living below the poverty line. Under these conditions, conventional financial institutions have been unable to provide inclusive solutions, primarily due to collateral requirements, difficult geographical access, and low public financial literacy. MFIS is an alternative solution offering a financing approach based on the principles of justice, togetherness, and without usury, through products such as mudharabah, murabahah, and qardhul hasan.

However, in its implementation, MFIs face several primary challenges as follows:

- Limited capital and business scale are fundamental obstacles. Many MFIs operate in limited capacity, both in terms of capital, human resources, and technology (Gasmelseid, 2015; Zainal et al., 2020; Muthmainnatun et al., 2022). This has an impact on the service coverage, which remains narrow, especially in rural areas or 3T (Disadvantaged, Frontier, and Outermost) areas, where the need for financial access is high but the infrastructure is inadequate.
- Low financial literacy and public understanding of Islamic financial products and services are equally essential challenges (Mahdzan et al., 2017; Ernawati & Asri, 2020). Most people with low incomes are unfamiliar with the concept of profit sharing or the basic principles of Sharia in financing. This ignorance

leads to low public participation in utilizing MFIS services, despite the service being designed in principle to address their needs.

- From the internal side of the institution, many MFIs face challenges in governance and professionalism (Maîtrot, 2018). Lack of training for managers, a manual administrative system, and limitations in Sharia supervision can pose a risk of deviation from Sharia principles (Azmi & Thaker, 2020). This weakness has an impact on the level of public trust in MFIs, which in turn affects the institution's long-term sustainability.
- Integration with the national financial ecosystem is still weak. MFIs often operate independently without adequate support from fiscal policies, digital infrastructure, or synergy with other financing institutions (Hermes & Hudon, 2018; Ansari et al., 2021). The involvement of MFIs in the national financial system through cooperation with Islamic banks, Islamic cooperatives, and ZISWAF institutions can be a strategic solution to expand reach and strengthen institutional resilience.
- The challenge of regulation and standardization is also an important issue. Although there is already Law No. 1 of 2013 concerning Microfinance Institutions, its implementation and supervision are still weak. Many MFIs are not officially registered or operate without clear supervision, making them vulnerable to practices that are not by Sharia principles or sound financial practices (Kosim et al., 2021).

Conceptually, the existence of MFIS should be viewed not only as a financial service provider but also as an agent of social change. Their holistic approach, which includes productive financing programs accompanied by business mentoring, managerial training, and the utilization of social funds such as zakat and waqf, makes them unique. But if the goal is total emancipation for an entire community, MFIs need help from multiple stakeholders including regulators, academicians and civil society. Strategic partnership is also required to combat the perils encountered by MFIs — digitalization of services, the capacity for human resource development, the role of the community in governance and the existence of the ecosystem conducive to sustainability. Another thing that the government must do is to design a set of incentives to encourage the MFIs to expand and innovate, like low-cost funds, revolving facility to finance, or link programs to the ongoing poverty relief programs. Therefore, the difficulties MFIs face with community economic empowerment are not impossible edges, but rather them a strategic improvements situation that must be tackled with. The achievement of the MFI will not just make life better for millions of poor people; it is also going to be an integral part of the development of a more inclusive, equitable and sustainable national economy.

4 APPLICATION OF SHARIA PRINCIPLES IN MICROFINANCE PRACTICES AND HOW IT IMPACTS THE SUSTAINABILITY OF MICRO ENTERPRISES

Islamic microfinance has evolved into one of the key instruments supporting microbusiness financing in Indonesia. By upholding sharia principles such as justice, transparency, and the prohibition of usury, Islamic microfinance institutions (MFIs) present an alternative model in financing the small and micro business sector. The practice of financing based on sharia contracts such as mudharabah, musyarakah, murabahah, and qardhul hasan is the primary foundation that distinguishes this system from conventional financial institutions (Suprapty et al., 2021; Nugroho et al., 2020). This model prioritizes not only profitability but also social sustainability and economic well-being for low-income communities. According to Nugroho (2022) Islamic institutions, they should implement the Quard P principles, such as Prophet, Profit, People, and Planet.

Interesting phenomena that occur in the field indicate that Islamic microfinance has successfully targeted community groups that were previously difficult to reach by the formal banking system. According to BPS data from 2024, approximately 25.22 million Indonesians live below the poverty line. In this context, MFIS plays a strategic role, which extends beyond providing loans to incorporate financial education and Sharia-based moral values into the lives of its beneficiaries (Ayunda et al., 2024). This approach is considered more humane and holistic because it treats mustahik or micro business actors as empowered partners, not just as credit objects.

However, the application of Sharia principles in microfinance practices faces its challenges. Some studies, such as those conducted by Mightyn et al. (2022), have noted that many MFIs continue to face limitations in risk management and the consistent supervision of Sharia compliance. This has an impact on the incompatibility between the promised contract and the practices applied in the field (Hidayat, 2021). For example, in mudharabah contracts, there is often an information asymmetry between the MFI and business partners, which can lead to injustice in the distribution of business results.

On the other hand, the sustainability of micro-enterprises is highly dependent on the extent to which Sharia principles are implemented in the financing process. When sharia values such as trust, honesty, and cooperation are applied consistently and managed with prudential principles, micro businesses will have a strong foundation to develop sustainably. The partnership-based sharia financing model also provides space for business actors to develop independently, avoiding the high-interest debt cycle that many experience in the conventional lending system. Some of the models that have been proven effective in empowering micro businesses include the Grameen, based on solidarity groups, and Village Banking, which encourages collectivity in fund management. These models have been replicated by various microfinance institutions (MFIs) in Indonesia and have been proven to reduce the default rate and increase the business capacity of the community (Hidayat, 2021).

Nevertheless, the success of Islamic microfinance is not only determined by the contract structure, but also by the quality of the management of the MFI itself. It requires human resources who understand the principles of fiqh muamalah deeply and can integrate them with modern financial practices. In addition, strengthening technology capacity, Islamic financial reporting, and sharia audit systems are essential factors in ensuring system integrity. Classic problems, such as low public financial literacy, pose a significant challenge. Many micro-business actors do not fully understand the difference between Sharia and conventional financing. This leads to potential moral hazards, such as the transfer of funds for personal consumption or use that is not intended for financing purposes. Therefore, the educational process that accompanies financing is inevitable, not just complementary.

Experience in specific areas shows that when sharia principles are applied effectively, micro businesses not only survive but also grow significantly. For example, in the Seberang Ulu I area of Palembang City, the study's results indicate that Islamic Microfinance Institutions have a significant impact on improving MSME performance, making a substantial contribution to financial access and economic inclusion (Kosim et al., 2021). MFIs in this region are giving credit not only in terms of money, but business support too which helps in business survival. This correlation between the application of sharia and the sustainability of micro businesses is proven by the low default rate in the shariabased institutions relative to the conventional ones. This indicates that justice and collective responsibility based on sharia can increase awareness and a sense of responsibility of the micro-business actors. Therefore, they are forced to run business more professional and responsible wise. It can be stated therefore, that the implementation of Sharia principles in micro financing is not only a normative matter but also a business logic. For that to be sufficiently powerful it may need to be accompanied by a stronger regulatory environment, strengthened governance and coordinated efforts between both regulators, MFIs and the community. This is necessary for the development of a fair, sustainable, and inclusive Islamic financial ecosystem to support inclusive economic growth in Indonesia.

5 THE CONTRIBUTION OF ISLAMIC MICROFINANCE IN REDUCING POVERTY AND ECONOMIC INEQUALITY AT THE LOCAL LEVEL

Poverty and economic inequality are still two of the main obstacles of Indonesia's development. As of March 2024, there are 25.22 million Indonesians living under the poverty line (Ayunda et al., 2024), based on Central Statistics Agency (BPS) data. It may be more pronounced because the poor have insufficient access to formal financial services, for reasons of geographic distance, administrative obstacles, or relatively lower education level. This situation highlights the urgent demand for an alternative financial system that is inclusive, fair, and responsive to the social and economic needs of lower-income communities. That is where Islamic Microfinance Institutions (MFIs) come in handy. Contrary to traditional financial organizations, Microfinance Institutions (MFIs) consider Sharia in financing. In addition to by-passing usury and interest payments, this approach prioritizes justice, transparency and social responsibility. Through financing products Qardhul Hasan, Murabahah and Mudharabah, MFIS provides access to capital for excluded micro-business actors from the formal banking services. This support is financial in nature, but it also serves to enable these communities to become self-reliant and walk out of the circle of poverty (Ayunda et al., 2024).

Islamic microfinance model has been successful in serving the underserved population that is unable to access mainstream financial system. We see from Grameen Bank's example of a globally influential model that community-based financial inclusion can lead to sustained micro economic development. In Indonesia, the application of MFIS reflects the spirit of Baitul Mal and Baitul Tamwil is adhered in which under its concept, social and commercial integration could be integrated in balance (Ayunda et al., 2024). This is the biggest benefit of MFIs – they are not only profit-making organizations, but also agents of social change. While the role of MFIs in enhancing poverty economic well-being of poor population is widely acknowledge, there are some issues to be addressed. The lack of public financial literacy for Sharia products and mechanisms could reduce an ideal funding. Apart from that, due to the small scale of operations that MFIs have, their outreach is still inconsistent throughout Indonesia. Hence, institutional strengthening, technological environments and regulatory support are important pre-requisites for future MFIs development. Empirically, some of the works indicated that the existence of MFIs is associated with a better income of micro-entrepreneurs, a decrease in inequality, and an empowerment of rural women in deprived areas (Ayunda et al., 2024; Kosim et al., 2021). It should also allow them to be more productive, scale markets and create new jobs in their communities. Over time, it is envisioned that the dual impact of this Islamic microfinance will contribute to social and economic transformations which make a substantial dent in reducing structural poverty. The problem statements of this chapter raise some important questions such as: What values are laid in Islamic microfinance that is believed to contribute to reducing local poverty and inequality? This contrasts with the reality that low-income people have not been successfully served by the formal financial system. Thus, it is important to explore how MFIs are responding to these different kinds of needs within parameters which are compatible with Sharia principles. In order to resolve the formulation of this problem, the analysis in this chapter adopts a contextual approach based on empirical evidence and an Islamic-based financial inclusion theory. Islamic Microfinance banks (MFIs) are recognized as the key agent in the national poverty alleviation strategy because of their modus operandi in targeting the marginalized groups. More than just a source of financial resources, MFIS have an education role through business support and financial education improvement and are a major actor in community economic development. Therefore, the strategic position of MFIs in the community, neither is it a financial option, but rather a, but instead a lever of social transformation. Its role in promoting economic equality is also critical in relation to the SDGs, particularly SDG 1 (poverty alleviation) and SDG 10 (reduced inequality). The combination of Islamic spiritual value and micro level development strategies, these MFIs represent a new paradigm and should be encouraged as a part of the future governmentâ€(tm) s macroeconomic policy.

REFERENCES

Abdullah, W., Zainudin, W. N. R. A. B., Ismail, S. B., & Zia-ul-haq, H. M. (2022). The impact of microfinance services on Malaysian B40 households' socioeconomic performance: A moderated mediation analysis. *International Journal of Sustainable Development and Planning, 17*(6), 1983–1996. DOI: 10.18280/ijsdp.170634

Al-Banna, H., & Nurdany, A. (2022). Sustainability of Islamic rural banks: A social qardh financing approach. *Global Review of Islamic Economics and Business, 9*(2), 87–95. DOI: 10.14421/grieb.2021.092-08

Ansari, M. A. A., Khan, A. J., Hanif, N., & Ahmed, T. (2021). Factors affecting the acceptability of Islamic micro-finance in emerging economy. *Journal of Business and Social Review in Emerging Economies, 7*(4), 1011–1022. DOI: 10.26710/jbsee.v7i4.2071

Ascarya, A., Sukmana, R., Rahmawati, S., & Masrifah, A. R. (2022). Developing cash waqf models for Baitul Maal Wat Tamwil as integrated Islamic social and commercial microfinance. *Journal of Islamic Accounting and Business Research, 14*(5), 699–717. DOI: 10.1108/JIABR-09-2020-0267

Ashta, A., Couchoro, M. K., & Musa, A. S. M. (2014). Dialectic evolution through the social innovation process: From microcredit to microfinance. *Journal of Innovation and Entrepreneurship, 3*(1), 4. DOI: 10.1186/2192-5372-3-4

Ayunda, A., Ramadhani, I. G., Fahlevy, R., Hayati, F., Islam, U., & Sumatera, N. (2024). Peran lembaga keuangan mikro syariah (LKMS) dalam mendukung ekonomi kerakyatan dan pengentasan kemiskinan umat. *Jurnal Bina Bangsa Ekonomi, 18*(1), 1043–1052.

Azizi, M., Umiyati, H., Nugroho, L., Utami, A. R., Sudirman, A., & Aryani, L. (2022). *Effective digital marketing* (Putri, D. E., & Sari, E. P., Eds.). Widina Media Utama.

Azmi, N. N. I. N. M., & Thaker, M. A. M. T. (2020). Literature survey on Islamic microfinance. *Global Review of Islamic Economics and Business, 8*(1), 23–33. DOI: 10.14421/grieb.2020.081-03

Berger, A. N., & Humphrey, D. B. (1992). Megamergers in banking and the use of cost efficiency as an antitrust defense. *Antitrust Bulletin, 37*(3), 541–600. DOI: 10.1177/0003603X9203700302

Berger, E., & Nakata, C. (2013). Implementing technologies for financial service innovations in base of the pyramid markets. *Journal of Product Innovation Management, 30*(6), 1199–1211. DOI: 10.1111/jpim.12054

. Ernawati, E., & Asri, M. (2020). Knowledge and awareness of Islamic financial in Europe and America countries. *Iqtishadia: Jurnal Kajian Ekonomi dan Bisnis Islam, 13*(1), 23.

Faizi, F., Kusuma, A. S., & Widodo, P. (2024). Islamic green finance: Mapping the climate funding landscape in Indonesia. *International Journal of Ethics and Systems, 40*(4), 711–733. DOI: 10.1108/IJOES-08-2023-0189

Gasmelseid, T. M. (2015). Empowering microfinance processes through hybrid cloud based services. *International Journal of Systems and Service-Oriented Engineering, 5*(3), 1–17. DOI: 10.4018/IJSSOE.2015070101

Gherhes, C., Williams, N., Vorley, T., & Vasconcelos, A. C. (2016). Distinguishing micro-businesses from SMEs: A systematic review of growth constraints. *Journal of Small Business and Enterprise Development, 23*(4), 939–963. DOI: 10.1108/JSBED-05-2016-0075

Ginanjar, A., & Kassim, S. (2021). Roles of Islamic microfinance institutions in improving financial inclusion in Indonesia: Empirical evidence from Baitulmaal Wa Tamwil. *Al-Iqtishad: Jurnal Ilmu Ekonomi Islam, 13*(1), 87–108. DOI: 10.15408/aiq.v13i1.19842

Hanivan, H., & Nasrudin, N. (2019). A financial inclusion index for Indonesia. *Bulletin of Monetary Economics and Banking, 22*(3), 351–366. DOI: 10.21098/bemp.v22i3.1056

Hermes, N., & Hudon, M. (2018). Determinants of the performance of microfinance institutions: A systematic review. *Journal of Economic Surveys, 32*(5), 1483–1513. DOI: 10.1111/joes.12290

. Hidayat, A. (2021). Model praktik lembaga keuangan mikro syariah dalam pemberdayaan UMKM di masa pandemi Covid-19. *Al-Tasyree: Jurnal Bisnis, Keuangan dan Ekonomi Syariah, 13*(1), 21–32.

Karyanto, B., Aziz, L. H., Yusuf, M., Muzayyanah, M., Putra, A. R., & Darussalam, A. Z. (2021). *Pengantar ekonomi syariah* (Fasa, M. I., Ed.). Widina Bhakti Persada Bandung.

Khambule, I. (2021). COVID-19 and the counter-cyclical role of the state in South Africa. *Progress in Development Studies, 21*(4), 380–396. DOI: 10.1177/14649934211030457

Khan, T., & Badjie, F. (2020). Islamic blended finance for circular economy impactful SMEs to achieve SDGs. *The Singapore Economic Review, 67*(1), 219–244. DOI: 10.1142/S0217590820420060

Kosim, B., Safitri, E., & Sindi, S. (2021). Pengaruh inklusi keuangan dan peran lembaga keuangan mikro terhadap kinerja UMKM di Kecamatan Seberang Ulu I Kota Palembang. *Motivasi*, *6*(2), 144. DOI: 10.32502/mti.v6i2.3797

Lisa, O., Nugroho, L., Ildiko, O., Utami, W., & Nugraha, E. (2023). The performance of Islamic microfinance institutions in the COVID-19 pandemic: Is asset quality important? *Sosyoekonomi*, *31*(58), 145–160. DOI: 10.17233/sosyoekonomi.2023.04.07

Mahdzan, N. S., Zainudin, R., & Au, S. F. (2017). The adoption of Islamic banking services in Malaysia. *Journal of Islamic Marketing*, *8*(3), 496–512. DOI: 10.1108/JIMA-08-2015-0064

Maîtrot, M. (2018). Understanding social performance: A 'practice drift' at the frontline of microfinance institutions in Bangladesh. *Development and Change*, *50*(3), 623–654. DOI: 10.1111/dech.12398

Mightyn, A., Nugroho, L., & Hidayah, N. (2022). Kajian usaha pemerintah dalam mempertahankan keberlangsungan UMKM di masa pandemi Covid-19. *Jurnal Cakrawala Ilmiah*, *2*(4), 1553–1564. DOI: 10.53625/jcijurnalcakrawalailmiah.v2i4.4281

Muthmainnatun, A. T., Nugroho, L., & Sugiarti, D. (2022). Analisa prosedur penyaluran pembiayaan murabahah pada lembaga keuangan mikro syariah (Studi kasus pada BMT Syarif Hidayatullah Gunungwungkal). *Jurnal Cakrawala Ilmiah*, *2*(3), 1121–1129. DOI: 10.53625/jcijurnalcakrawalailmiah.v2i3.4111

Nugroho, L. (2014). Challenges sharia microfinance institutions: Evidence from Indonesia. *European Journal of Islamic Finance*, *1*, 1–6. http://www.ojs.unito.it/index.php/EJIF

Nugroho, L. (2014). Challenges sharia microfinance institutions: Evidence from Indonesia. *EJIF – European Journal of Islamic Finance, 3*, 1–6. http://www.ojs.unito.it/index.php/EJIF/article/view/793/766

Nugroho, L. (2015). Islamics principles versus green microfinance. *European Journal of Islamic Finance*, *3*, 1–10. http://www.ojs.unito.it/index.php/EJIF

Nugroho, L. (2022). The relationship between maqasid sharia and profitability ratio in Islamic banking industries performance. *Sosyoekonomi*, *30*(53), 243–259. DOI: 10.17233/sosyoekonomi.2022.03.13

Nugroho, L., Badawi, A., Hidayah, N., & Ahmad, N. (2020). Pancasila (five principles of Indonesia nation) snapshot in customer deposit of Islamic bank (religion, age and gender perspective of Bank Mandiri Syariah). *Journal of Research in Business, 5*(1), 74–95. https://dergipark.org.tr/en/pub/jrb/issue/55478/670229. DOI: 10.35333/JRB.2020.177

. Nugroho, L., Chaniago, N., Firdayetti, F., Pratiwi, F. A., & Aurelia, F. N. (2024). Corporate social responsibility (CSR) in sharia accounting perspective: Challenges and opportunities towards sustainability. *Pelita: Jurnal Penelitian, Terapan dan Aplikasi, 1*(3), 153–167.

Nugroho, L., & Chowdhury, S. L. K. (2015). Mobile banking for empowerment Muslim women entrepreneur: Evidence from Asia (Indonesia and Bangladesh). *Tazkia Islamic Finance and Business Review, 9*(1), 83–100. https://tifbr-tazkia.org/index.php/TIFBR/article/view/79

Nugroho, L., Melzatia, S., & Indriawati, F. Nurhasanah, & Safira. (2022). *Lembaga keuangan syariah dari konsep ke praktik.* Widina Bhakti Persada. https://books.google.co.id/books?id=w4uREAAAQBAJ

Nugroho, L., Mor, S., Iskandar, D., Setiany, E., Asih, D., & Mellin, F. (2024). The urgency of digitalization vis-a-vis business trends (Indonesia case). In *Proceeding International Annual Conference Economics* (pp. 1–13). Management, Business, and Accounting., https://proceeding.inacemba.org/index.php/eproceeding-inacemba/article/view/1

Nugroho, L., Suganda, A. D., Febrianty, F., Hamid, M. A. L., Ihwanudin, N., & Trimulato, T. (2020). *Pengantar perbankan syariah.* Widina Bhakti Persada Bandung. www.penerbitwidina.com

Purwanti, T., Ristiyana, R., Libriantono, B., Widayati, T., Budiman, N. A., & Nugroho, L. (2022). *UMKM membangun ekonomi kreatif.* Global Eksekutif Teknologi. https://books.google.co.id/books?id=IaqmEAAAQBAJ

Rachman, R., & Nugroho, L. (2024). Understanding the drivers of customer interest in Islamic banks in Bali: Challenges and strategic solutions. In *International Seminar Conference of Economics and Business Excellence* (pp. 61–67). DOI: 10.33830/iscebe.v1i1.3604

. Ramdani, M. R., Khosyarina, Q., Hawadinar, P. R., Chaniago, N., & Nugroho, L. (2024). Diskursus optimalisasi pengelolaan wakaf tunai di era digital: Integrasi good corporate governance dan tawhid string relationship di BWUT MUI DIY. *Pelita: Jurnal Penelitian, Terapan dan Aplikasi, 1*(3), 195–203.

Sudirman, A., Alaydrus, S., Rosmayati, S., Syamsuriansyah, S., Nugroho, L., & Arifudin, O. (2020). *Perilaku konsumen dan perkembangannya di era digital*. Widina Bhakti Persada Bandung. www.penerbitwidina.com

. Suprapty, R., Witjaksono, A., Nugroho, L., Badawi, A., Susanti, M., Mardanugraha, E. (2021). *Perbankan hasil pemikiran dari para dosen berbagai perguruan tinggi di Indonesia* (Vol. 1).

Tambunan, T. (2019). Recent evidence of the development of micro, small and medium enterprises in Indonesia. *Journal of Global Entrepreneurship Research, 9*(1), 18. DOI: 10.1186/s40497-018-0140-4

Usman, A. S., & Tasmin, R. (2016). The role of Islamic micro-finance in enhancing human development in Muslim countries. *Journal of Islamic Finance, 5*(1), 53–62. DOI: 10.31436/jif.v5i1.111

Widiastuti, T., Robani, A., Sukmaningrum, P. S., Mawardi, I., Ningsih, S., Herianingrum, S., & Al-Mustofa, M. U. (2022). Integrating sustainable Islamic social finance: An analytical network process using the benefit opportunity cost risk (ANP BOCR) framework: The case of Indonesia. *PLoS One, 17*(5), e0269039. DOI: 10.1371/journal.pone.0269039 PMID: 35617300

Widyastuti, M., Ferdinand, D. Y. Y., & Hermanto, Y. B. (2023). Strengthening formal credit access and performance through financial literacy and credit terms in micro, small and medium businesses. *Journal of Risk and Financial Management, 16*(1), 52. DOI: 10.3390/jrfm16010052

Wulandari, P., & Kassim, S. (2016). Issues and challenges in financing the poor: Case of Baitul Maal Wa Tamwil in Indonesia. *International Journal of Bank Marketing, 34*(2), 216–234. DOI: 10.1108/IJBM-01-2015-0007

Zainal, N., Nassir, A., Kamarudin, F., & Law, S. H. (2020). Does bank regulation and supervision impede the efficiency of microfinance institutions to eradicate poverty? Evidence from ASEAN-5 countries. *Studies in Economics and Finance, 38*(2), 272–302. DOI: 10.1108/SEF-10-2019-0414

Zalim, S. N. A. (2021). Performance measurement in Islamic microfinance institutions: Does it change social norms and values? *Qualitative Research in Financial Markets, 14*(2), 306–323. DOI: 10.1108/QRFM-09-2020-0186

Zia, I. Z., & Prasetyo, P. E. (2018). Analysis of financial inclusion toward poverty and income inequality. *Jurnal Ekonomi Pembangunan (Balai Penelitian dan Pengembangan Ekonomi, Fakultas Ekonomi Universitas Muhammadiyah Surakarta), 19*(1), 114. DOI: 10.23917/jep.v19i1.5879

Compilation of References

Abd Aziz, H., & Abd Ghadas, Z. A. (2021, December). Corporate governance framework for Shariah compliant corporation. In *International Joint Conference on Arts and Humanities 2021 (IJCAH 2021)* (pp. 528-532). Atlantis Press. (ICMR), I. for C. M. R. M. (2024). *Market-based financing for SMEs in Malaysia: Enhancing access and affordability.*

Abd Karim, A. H., Kassim, S. K., Ismail, N. A. H., & Rais, H. (2025). Challenges Faced by Low-Income Muslim Malaysian Parents in Caring for Children with Disabilities. Asian Journal of Research in Education and Social Sciences e-ISSN: 2682-8502 | Vol. 7, No. 3, 77-90

Abd Wahab, N., Isa, M. Y., Yusof, R. M., & Lotfi, W. A. N. W. A. (2024). Protecting the Well-Being of Households: Delineating a Social Takāful Fund Initiative for Positive Social Impact. *International Journal of Islamic Finance and Sustainable Development, 16*(4), 117–135. DOI: 10.55188/ijifsd.v16i4.909

Abdul Rahman, A. R. (2010). Can microfinance alleviate poverty? The case of Bangladesh. *Humanomics, 26*(3), 203–213. DOI: 10.1108/08288661011074962

Abdul Rahman, R., & Dean, F. (2013). Challenges and solutions in Islamic microfinance. *Humanomics, 29*(4), 293–306. DOI: 10.1108/H-06-2012-0013

Abdul-Halim, N.-A., Vafaei-Zadeh, A., Hanifah, H., Teoh, A. P., & Nawaser, K. (2022). Understanding the determinants of e-wallet continuance usage intention in Malaysia. *Quality & Quantity, 56*(5), 3413–3439. DOI: 10.1007/s11135-021-01276-7

Abdullah, I. N. (2025, February 17). *Youth Trapped in Debt As They're Hooked with BNPL Addiction.* FintechNews Malaysia. https://fintechnews.my/48212/payments-remittance-malaysia/youth-trapped-in-debt-with-bnpl-addiction/

Abdullah, M. (2018). Blockchain for Islamic Social Finance Governance. International Journal of Islamic Finance.

Abdullah, M. A., Wahab, S. N. A., Sabar, S., & Abu, F. (2017). Factors determining Islamic financial literacy among undergraduates. *Journal of Emerging Economies & Islamic Research.* DOI: 10.1088/0953-8984/15/4/201

Abdullah, A., Salleh, M. Z. M., Ismail, W. A. A. Z. W., Anuar, T. F. T. M., Simpong, D. B. B., Rahman, N. A., & Rasdi, S. A. B. M. (2024). Retirement Financial Planning: Strategies and Challenges in Avoiding the Incidence of Poverty. In *Artificial Intelligence (AI) and Customer Social Responsibility (CSR)* (pp. 101–109). Springer Nature Switzerland. DOI: 10.1007/978-3-031-50939-1_8

Abdullah, A., Salleh, M. Z. M., Zakaria, M. N., Din, N. M., Aziz, M. I., & Muhammad, M. Z. (2021, November). Achieving Islamic financial literacy in Malaysia: Issues and challenges. In *International Conference on Business and Technology* (pp. 889-896). Cham: Springer International Publishing.

Abdullah, J. M., Ismail, A., & Yusoff, M. S. B. (2024). Healthy ageing in Malaysia by 2030: Needs, challenges and future directions. *The Malaysian Journal of Medical Sciences : MJMS, 31*(4), 1–13. DOI: 10.21315/mjms2024.31.4.1

Abdullah, M. A., & Anderson, A. (2015). Islamic Financial Literacy among bankers in Kuala Lumpur. *Journal of Emerging Economies and Islamic Research, 3*(2), 1–14. DOI: 10.24191/jeeir.v3i2.6408

Abdullah, M., & Mohammad, S. (2022). Cross-border waqf mobilization through digital platforms: Opportunities and challenges for educational funding. *Journal of Islamic Finance, 11*(1), 78–94.

Abdullah, N. I., & Dusuki, A. W. (2021). Beyond compliance: Operationalizing *Maqasid al-shariah* in Islamic finance. *Journal of Islamic Accounting and Business Research, 12*(2), 175–191. DOI: 10.1108/JIABR-10-2020-0312

Abdullah, N., & Majid, M. S. A. (2003). The influence of religiosity, income and consumption on saving behavior: The case of International Islamic University Malaysia. *Journal of Islamic Economics, 4*(1), 37–55. DOI: 10.20885/iqtisad.vol4.iss1.art3\

Abdullah, S., & Lee, K. H. (2022). Fragmentation and integration in TVET policy governance: A comparative analysis of Southeast Asian approaches. *Journal of Vocational Education and Training, 74*(3), 412–429.

Abdullah, W., Zainudin, W. N. R. A. B., Ismail, S. B., & Zia-ul-haq, H. M. (2022). The impact of microfinance services on Malaysian B40 households' socioeconomic performance: A moderated mediation analysis. *International Journal of Sustainable Development and Planning, 17*(6), 1983–1996. DOI: 10.18280/ijsdp.170634

Abdul-Rahman, A. R., & Muhammad, N. (2013). Waqf in Malaysia: A case study of waqf fund management. *Journal of Islamic Economics*, *27*(3), 200–215.

Abu-Sway, M. (1998). Towards an Islamic Jurisprudence of the Environment. In Foltz, R. C., Denny, F. M., & Baharuddin, A. (Eds.), *Islam and Ecology*. Harvard University Press.

Adbi, A., Lee, M., & Singh, J. (2024). Community Influence on Microfinance Loan Defaults Under Crisis Conditions: Evidence from Indian Demonetization. *Strategic Management Journal*, *45*(3), 535–563. DOI: 10.1002/smj.3558

Adewale, A. A. (2022, December). *Islamic Infrastructure Financing: Imperatives, Prospects, and Challenges* (IFSB Working Paper Series WP-25/12/2022). https://www.ifsb.org/wp-content/uploads/2023/10/WP-25_En.pdf

Adiani, W., Aprianingsih, A., Fachira, I., Debby, T., & Maharatie, A. P. (2023). Social influence, financial benefit, and e-wallet multi-brand loyalty: The mediating impact of commitment. *Cogent Business & Management*, *11*(1), 2290228. Advance online publication. DOI: 10.1080/23311975.2023.2290228

Adiputra, I. G., & Patricia, E. (2020, May). The effect of financial attitude, financial knowledge, and income on financial management behavior. In *Tarumanagara International Conference on the Applications of Social Sciences and Humanities (TICASH 2019)* (pp. 107-112). Atlantis Press. DOI: 10.2991/assehr.k.200515.019

Adnan, M. A., & Bakar, N. B. A. (2009). Accounting Treatment for Corporate Zakat: A Critical Review. *International Journal of Islamic and Middle Eastern Finance and Management*, *2*(1), 32–45. DOI: 10.1108/17538390910946258

Afroz, N. N. (2017). Green Banking Initiatives of Islamic Bank Bangladesh Limited. *Global Journal of Management and Business Research*. https://journalofbusiness.org/index.php/GJMBR/article/view/2224/1-Green-Banking-Initiatives_JATS_NLM_xml#info

Afzal, M., Meraj, M., Kaur, M., & Shamim Ansari, M. (2025). How does cybersecurity awareness help in achieving digital financial inclusion in rural India under escalating cyber fraud scenario? *Journal of Cyber Security Technology*, *9*(2), 88–126. DOI: 10.1080/23742917.2024.2347674

Agensi Kaunseling dan Pengurusan Kredit (AKPK). (2019). *Annual report 2019*. https://www.akpk.org.my/annual-report-2019

Agrawal, R., Raju, K. ., Reddy, K. P., Srinivasan, R., & Sriram, M. . (2002). *Member Funds and Cooperative Performance*.

Ahmad Tarmizi, M., Zolkaflil, S., Omar, N., Hasnan, S., & Syed Mustapha Nazri, S. N. F. (2023). Compliance determinants of anti-money laundering regime among professional accountants in Malaysia. *Journal of Money Laundering Control, 26*(2), 361–387. DOI: 10.1108/JMLC-01-2022-0003

Ahmad, M. (2010). Why Islamic Financial Literacy Is Important. Personal Finance, 46.

Ahmad, F., & Lim, J. (2024). Beyond compensation: Comprehensive strategies for researcher retention in Malaysian TVET institutions. *Asian Journal of Technical Education, 16*(1), 78–93.

Ahmad, G. N., Widyastuti, U., Susanti, S., & Mukhibad, H. (2020). Determinants of the Islamic financial literacy. *Accounting, 6*, 961–966. DOI: 10.5267/j.ac.2020.7.024

Ahmad, K., Hassan, M. K., & Siraj, S. A. (2022). Blockchain-based waqf management: Enhancing transparency and efficiency. *International Journal of Islamic and Middle Eastern Finance and Management, 15*(1), 78–96.

Ahmad, S., Lensink, R., & Mueller, A. (2023). Uptake, use, and impact of Islamic savings: Evidence from a field experiment in Pakistan. *Journal of Development Economics, 163*, 103098. DOI: 10.1016/j.jdeveco.2023.103098

Ahmed, H. M. (2024). *DIEDC Outlines Future Plans for Islamic Economy*. The Halal Times. https://www.halaltimes.com/diedc-outlines-future-plans-islamic-economy/

Ahmed, A.. (2023). *Islamic Microfinance and Maqasid al-shariah: A New Perspective*. Global Islamic Finance Journal.

Ahmed, H. (2004). Islamic social finance: The case for zakat and its role in sustainable development. *International Journal of Islamic and Middle Eastern Finance and Management, 1*(2), 35–49.

Ahmed, H. (2011). *Product Development in Islamic Banks*. Edinburgh University Press. DOI: 10.1515/9780748644889

Ahmed, W., Rasool, A., Javed, A. R., Kumar, N., Gadekallu, T. R., Jalil, Z., & Kryvinska, N. (2021). Security in next generation mobile payment systems: A comprehensive survey. *IEEE Access : Practical Innovations, Open Solutions, 9*, 115932–115950. DOI: 10.1109/ACCESS.2021.3105450

Aisyah, E. N., Pratikto, H., Wardoyo, C., & Restuningdiah, N. (2024). The Right Literacy on the Right Performance: Does Islamic Financial Literacy Affect Business Performance Through Islamic Financial Inclusion? *Journal of Social Economics Research, 11*(3), 275–289. DOI: 10.18488/35.v11i3.3766

Aji, H. M., & Adawiyah, W. R. (2022). How e-wallets encourage excessive spending behavior among young adult consumers? *Journal of Asia Business Studies, 16*(6), 868–884. DOI: 10.1108/JABS-01-2021-0025

Ajzen, I. (1985). *From intentions to actions: A theory of planned behavior*. Springer.

Ajzen, I. (2005). *Attitudes, personality and behaviour*. McGraw-hill Education.

Ajzen, I., & Fishbein, M. (1980). *Understanding attitudes and predicting social behavior*. Prentice-Hall.

Akhter, A., Javed, M. Y., & Akhter, J. (2025). Research trends in the field of Islamic social finance: A bibliometric analysis from 1914 to 2022. *International Journal of Ethics and Systems, 41*(2), 455–483. DOI: 10.1108/IJOES-03-2023-0044

Akmal, A., Izzat, A., Marzuki, A., Atiqah, S., Amin, M., Haroming, N. A., Mohideen, R. S., Ilyas, I. Y., Universiti, K., & Melaka, I. (2021). THE AWARENESS TOWARDS THE IMPORTANCE OF HEALTH IN MALAYSIA. *E-Journal of Media & Society, 7*, 1–18.

Al Khalidi, M. (1985). *alAqidahWa Ilmal Kalam*. Amman:Maktabah al Risalah al Hadithah

Al Mustofa, M. U., Shophia, S. P., Muhibbin, Z., Ardiantono, D. S., Mawardi, I., Widiastuti, T., Fahmi, A., & Windiani, W. (2025). Risk Perception on Intention to Pay Zakat Via Financial Technology (Fintech). *Journal of Islamic Marketing, 16*(12), 3559–3590. Advance online publication. DOI: 10.1108/JIMA-03-2024-0110

Alalwan, A. A., Dwivedi, Y. K., Rana, N. P., & Algharabat, R. (2018). Examining factors influencing Jordanian customers' intentions and adoption of internet banking: Extending UTAUT2 with risk. *Journal of Retailing and Consumer Services, 40*, 125–138. DOI: 10.1016/j.jretconser.2017.08.026

Alam, A., Herianingrum, S., Ryandono, M. N. H., & Rohmawati, N. P. (2023). The role of Islamic investment ethics in preventing fraudulent investments. *Perbanas Journal of Islamic Economics and Business, 3*(1), 37–46. DOI: 10.56174/pjieb.v3i1.81

Alam, M. M., Awawdeh, A. E., & Muhamad, A. I. (2021). Using e-wallet for business process development: Challenges and prospects in Malaysia. *Business Process Management Journal, 27*(4), 1142–1162. DOI: 10.1108/BPMJ-11-2020-0528

Alam, N., Gupta, L., & Shanmugam, B. (2017). Prohibition of Riba and Gharar in Islamic banking. In *Islamic finance: A practical perspective* (pp. 35–53). Springer International Publishing. DOI: 10.1007/978-3-319-66559-7_3

Alam, S. S., Mohd, R., & Hisham, B. (2011). Is religiosity an important determinant on Muslim consumer behaviour in Malaysia? *Journal of Islamic Marketing*, *2*(1), 83–96. DOI: 10.1108/17590831111115268

Al-Attas, S. M. N., & Ibrahim, M. F. (2021). Governance models for educational waqf institutions: Balancing tradition and innovation. *Journal of Islamic Finance*, *10*(2), 34–49.

Albaity, M., & Rahman, M. (2019). The intention to use Islamic banking: An exploratory study to measure Islamic financial literacy. *International Journal of Emerging Markets*, *14*(5), 988–1012. DOI: 10.1108/IJOEM-05-2018-0218

Al-Banna, H., & Nurdany, A. (2022). Sustainability of Islamic rural banks: A social qardh financing approach. *Global Review of Islamic Economics and Business*, *9*(2), 87–95. DOI: 10.14421/grieb.2021.092-08

Al-Daihani, M., Dirie, K. A., Muneem, A., Abdul Lateb, N., & Bouteraa, M. (2025). Islamic Social Finance and Its Potential in Addressing Natural Disaster Emergencies and Advancing Sustainable Development Goals: A Proposed Model. *International Journal of Ethics and Systems*. https://doi.org/DOI: 10.1108/IJOES-05-2024-0138/1250881/ISLAMIC-SOCIAL-FINANCE-AND-ITS-POTENTIAL-IN

Aldeen, K. N. (2021). 40-year bibliometric analysis of waqf: Its current status and development, and paths for future research. *Journal of Islamic Monetary Economics and Finance*, *7*(1), 181–200. DOI: 10.21098/jimf.v7i1.1308

Alfian, I., & Majid, M. S. A. (2025). The Role of Sharia Fintech in Enhancing Financial Inclusion in the Digital Era. *Journal of Finance and Islamic Banking*, *8*(1), 79–94. DOI: 10.22515/jfib.v8i1.11798

Al-Ghazali. (1997). *Mustasfa Min Ilm al-Usul, Vol. I.* https://archive.org/details/GAZALIMustasfaMinIlmUsulI/page/n15/mode/2up

Al-Ghazālī. (n.d.). *I yā' 'Ulūm al-Dīn* [The revival of religious sciences]. (Original work published ca. 11th century).

Al-Hammadi, M., Jimber-Del Río, J. A., Ochoa-Rico, M. S., Montero, O. A., & Vergara-Romero, A. (2024). Risk Management in Islamic Banking: The Impact of Financial Technologies through Empirical Insights from the UAE. *Risks*, *12*(2), 17. DOI: 10.3390/risks12020017

Al-Harran, S. (1999). New strategic alliances between Islamic financial institutions, international university students and entrepreneurs to implement musharakah financing to meet the challenges of the 21st century. *Arab LQ, 14*(268).

Ali, A. F. M., Ibrahim, M. F., & Ab Aziz, M. R. (2019). Missing items in zakat distribution: A case in Kelantan, Malaysia. *International Journal of zakat, 4*(1), 1-24.

Ali, N.Z.Y., & Nor, M.R.M. (2018). Ketokohan dan Sumbangan Sultan Abdul Hamid II Sebagai Khalifah Terakhir Dawlah Uthmaniyyah Berlandaskan Prinsip al-Quran dan al-Sunnah, *Journal of Ma'alim Al-Quran wa Al-Sunnah*, 14(1), 91-98.

Ali, A., & Marisetty, V. B. (2023). Are FinTech lending apps harmful? Evidence from user experience in the Indian market. *The British Accounting Review, 101269*, 101269. Advance online publication. DOI: 10.1016/j.bar.2023.101269

Alias, N.A.B., & Rozali, E.A. (2017). Pembinaan Institusi Waqf Kesihatan di Istanbul pada Tahun 1470 M (Hospital Fatih), 39(2), 153-164.

Alibeigi, A., Munir, A. B., & Asemi, A. (2016). Compliance with Malaysian Personal Data Protection Act 2010 by Banking and Financial Institutions, a Legal Survey on Privacy Policies. *Taylor & Francis in the International Review of Law. Computing Techniques*, (April), 247–269.

Ali, H. (2024). *Islamic microfinance: landscape, models and future prospects*. Walter de Gruyter GmbH & Co KG.

Ali, Z., Anjum, G. M., Iqbal, J., & Ahmad, I. (2024). The Role of Islamic Values in Promoting Social Justice and Community Welfare. *International Research Journal of Management and Social Sciences*, *5*(1), 575–585.

Al-Khouri, R., & Bouzi, F. (2019). Waqf as a tool for financing social infrastructure: The Turkish experience. *Journal of Islamic Finance and Development*, *5*(2), 57–74.

Almajri, S., Baroud, N., Alouzi, K. M., & Kasheem, A. (2025). Islamic psychology: An integrative approach to human behavior and mental well-being. *Bulletin of Islamic Research*, *3*(4), 687–704. DOI: 10.69526/bir.v3i4.353

Almeida, J., & Gonçalves, T. C. (2022). A Systematic Literature Review of Volatility and Risk Management on Cryptocurrency Investment: A Methodological Point of View. *Risks*, *10*(5), 107. Advance online publication. DOI: 10.3390/risks10050107

Alom, K., Rahman, M. Z., Khan, A. I., Akbar, D., Hossain, M. M., Ali, M. A., & Mallick, A. (2025). Digital Finance Leads Women Entrepreneurship and Poverty Mitigation for Sustainable Development in Bangladesh. *Journal of Innovation and Entrepreneurship*, *14*(1), 1–18. DOI: 10.1186/s13731-025-00471-2

Al-Qudah, A. A., Al-Okaily, M., & Yadav, M. P. P. (2025). The growth of FinTech and blockchain technology in developing countries: UAE's evidence. *International Journal of Accounting & Information Management, 33*(2), 383–406. https://doi -org.uitm.idm.oclc.org/10.1108/IJAIM-02-2024-0065. DOI: 10.1108/IJAIM-02-2024-0065

Alsaghir, M. (2023). Digital risks and Islamic FinTech: A road map to social justice and financial inclusion. *Journal of Islamic Accounting and Business Research*. Advance online publication. DOI: 10.1108/JIABR-10-2022-02

Al-Tirmidhī, M. (n.d.). *Sunan al-Tirmidhī*, Hadith no. 1209 & no. 1264.

Altmann, T. K. (2008, July). Attitude: A concept analysis. []. Malden, USA: Blackwell Publishing Inc.]. *Nursing Forum, 43*(3), 144–150. DOI: 10.1111/j.1744-6198.2008.00106.x

Al-Waqidi, Muhammad bin Umar bin Waqid al-Sahmiyy al-Aslamiyy. (1989). Al-Maghazi. *Tahqiq*. Jil. 1 & 2. Beyrut: Dar al- Aclamiyy.

Ameh, J. K., Atiase, V. Y., & Dzansi, D. Y. (2022). Does Microcredit Increase Household Wellbeing ? Empirical Evidence from Ghana. *ISBE 2022: New Approaches to Raising Entrepreneurial Opportunity: Reshaping Inclusive Enterprise, Policy, and Practice Post-PandemicAt: York, October.*

Amin, S. M., Suhaimi, S. A., & Nazuri, N. S. (2023). The present and future of Malaysian technical and vocational education and training (TVET). *International Journal of Academic Research in Business & Social Sciences, 13*(18). Advance online publication. DOI: 10.6007/IJARBSS/v13-i18/19952

Ansar, S., Demirguc-Kunt, A., Klapper, L., & Singer, D. (2022). *The Global Findex Database 2021: Financial Inclusion, Digital Payments, and Resilience in the Age of COVID-19(English)*. World Bank Group. https://documents.worldbank.org/curated/en/099818107072234182

Ansari, M. A. A., Khan, A. J., Hanif, N., & Ahmed, T. (2021). Factors affecting the acceptability of Islamic micro-finance in emerging economy. *Journal of Business and Social Review in Emerging Economies, 7*(4), 1011–1022. DOI: 10.26710/jbsee.v7i4.2071

Antara, P. M., Musa, R., & Hassan, F. (2016). Bridging Islamic Financial Literacy and Halal Literacy: The Way Forward in Halal Ecosystem. *Procedia Economics and Finance*, 37, 5671(16)30113-7.

Antara, P. M., & Musa, R. (2020). Validating Islamic financial literacy instruments among mum generation: Rasch analysis approach. *International Journal of Business and Society*, *21*(3), 1113–1121. DOI: 10.33736/ijbs.3315.2020

Antara, P. M., Musa, R., & Hassan, F. (2016). Bridging Islamic Financial Literacy and Halal Literacy: The Way Forward in Halal Ecosystem. *Procedia Economics and Finance*, *37*, 196–202. DOI: 10.1016/S2212-5671(16)30113-7

Antara, P. M., Musa, R., & Hassan, F. (2017). Conceptualisation and operationalisation of Islamic financial literacy scale. *Pertanika Journal of Social Science & Humanities*, *25*, 251–260. http://www.pertanika.upm.edu.my

Anwar, D. R., Wahab, A., & Waris, W. (2025). Maqasid Syariah and Sustainable Development: Integrating Islamic Objectives into Economic Planning. *Formosa Journal of Multidisciplinary Research*, *4*(6), 2601–2618. DOI: 10.55927/fjmr.v4i6.269

Arafat, F. (2020). Eksistensi BMT sebagai Baitul Maal Wat Tamwil dan Problematika Hukumnya. [JIEB]. *El-Qist: Journal of Islamic Economics and Business*, *10*(1), 89–104. DOI: 10.15642/elqist.2020.10.1.89-104

Ardiyansyah, R., & Kasdi, A. (2021). Strategies and Optimizing the Role of Productive Waqf in Economic Empowerment of the Ummah. *Ziswaf: Jurnal Zakat Dan Wakaf*, *8*(1), 61. DOI: 10.21043/ziswaf.v8i1.9871

Ariffin, S. K., Abd Rahman, M. F. R., Muhammad, A. M., & Zhang, Q. (2021). Understanding the consumer's intention to use the e-wallet services. *Spanish Journal of Marketing - ESIC*, *25*(3), 446–461. DOI: 10.1108/SJME-07-2021-0138

Armendariz, B., & Szafarz, A. (2011). *On Mission Drift in Microfinance Institutions*. https://papers.ssrn.com/abstract=1918096

Asari, N. A. M. (2024). Empowering Individuals: Islamic Education And Personal Financial Planning. *Available at SSRN*, 4854923. DOI: 10.2139/ssrn.4854923

Ascarya, & Suharto, U. (2021). Integrated Islamic social and commercial finance to achieve SDGs. In *Islamic Wealth and the SDGs: Global Strategies for Socio-economic Impact*, (pp. 105–127).

Ascarya, A., Hosen, M. N., & Rahmawati, S. (2022). Designing Simple Productive Waqf Models for Indonesia. *International Journal of Ethics and Systems*, *38*(3), 380–401. DOI: 10.1108/IJOES-07-2020-0101

Ascarya, A., Sukmana, R., Rahmawati, S., & Masrifah, A. R. (2022). Developing cash waqf models for Baitul Maal Wat Tamwil as integrated Islamic social and commercial microfinance. *Journal of Islamic Accounting and Business Research, 14*(5), 699–717. DOI: 10.1108/JIABR-09-2020-0267

Ashari, M. Z. A. H., Jamsari, E. A., Safian, H. L., & Safiai, M. H. (2020). Sejarah Pembangunan Teknologi Ketenteraan Kerajaan Banu Marin di Al-Maghrib. *Journal of Al-Tamaddun, 15*(2), 147–161. DOI: 10.22452/JAT.vol15no2.11

Ashta, A., Couchoro, M. K., & Musa, A. S. M. (2014). Dialectic evolution through the social innovation process: From microcredit to microfinance. *Journal of Innovation and Entrepreneurship, 3*(1), 4. DOI: 10.1186/2192-5372-3-4

Asia Property Awards. (2021). *Bank Islam pioneers housing scheme to help those in need.* https://www.asiapropertyawards.com/en/bank-islam-pioneers-housing-scheme-to-help-those-in-need/

Assayyidi, N., & Farhan, M. (2024). Pesantrenpreneurship dalam Perspektif Pendidikan Islam. *TA'DIBUNA: Jurnal Pendidikan Agama Islam, 6*(2), 162–171. DOI: 10.30659/jpai.6.2.162-171

Asutay, M. (2012). Conceptualising and locating the social failure of islamic finance: Aspirations of islamic moral economy vs. the realities of islamic finance. *Asian and African Area Studies, 11*(2), 93–113.

Asutay, M. (2012). Conceptualising and Locating the Social Failure of Islamic Finance: Aspirations of Islamic Moral Economy vs. the Realities of Islamic Finance. *Asian and African Area Studies, 11*(2), 93–113.

Asutay, M., & Harningtyas, A. F. (2015). Developing Maqasid al-Shari'ah index to evaluate social performance of Islamic banks: A conceptual and empirical attempt. *International Journal of Islamic and Middle Eastern Finance and Management, 8*(1), 25–49.

Asyraf, M. (2025). *Waqf- Driven Inclusive Prosperity Exploring the Intersection of Islamic Finance.* Fintech, and Sustainable Development Goals., DOI: 10.4018/979-8-3693-5653-1.ch012

Atkinson, A., & Messy, F.-A. (2012). Measuring financial literacy: Results of the OECD/ International Network on Financial Education (INFE) pilot study. In *OECD Working Papers on Finance, Insurance and Private Pensions.* https://doi.org/https://doi.org/10.1787/bb2cd70c-en

Auda, J. (2008). *Maqasid al-Shariah as Philosophy of Islamic Law: A Systems Approach.* International Institute of Islamic Thought. DOI: 10.2307/j.ctvkc67tg

Auda, J. (2013). Al-Maqashid untuk Pemula. In *Filsafat Hukum Islam*. Suka Press.

Austin, J. E. (2000). Strategic collaboration between nonprofits and businesses. *Nonprofit and Voluntary Sector Quarterly*, *29*(1_suppl), 69–97. DOI: 10.1177/0899764000291S004

Awang, M. Z., & Wan Chik, W. M. Y. (2023). Application of Islamic Social Finance in Sustainable Development Goals with Specific Target for Maqasid al-shariah. International Journal of Academic Research in Accounting [HRMARS]. *Finance and Management Sciences*, *13*(1), 35–46.

Awang, Z., Hui, L. S., & Nur Zainudin, N. F. S. (2018). *Pendekatan mudah SEM: structural equation modelling* (1st ed.). MPWS Rich Resources.

Awqaf, S. A. (2021). *Annual Financial Statements for the year ended 28 February 2021.* Audited by Deloitte. Awqaf South Africa. Retrieved from https://awqafsa.org.za/annual-financial-statements/

Ayub, M. (2007). *Understanding Islamic finance*. John Wiley & Sons.

Ayub, M. (2007). *Understanding Islamic Finance*. Wiley.

Ayub, M. (2022). Promoting the Institution of Waqf for Socio-economic Development in Islamic Societies. *Journal of Islamic Business and Management*, *12*(02).

Ayunda, A., Ramadhani, I. G., Fahlevy, R., Hayati, F., Islam, U., & Sumatera, N. (2024). Peran lembaga keuangan mikro syariah (LKMS) dalam mendukung ekonomi kerakyatan dan pengentasan kemiskinan umat. *Jurnal Bina Bangsa Ekonomi*, *18*(1), 1043–1052.

Ayuniyyah, Q. (2019). Factors Affecting Zakat Payment Through Institution of Amil: Muzakki's Perspectives Analysis (Case Study of Badan Amil Zakat Nasional [Baznas]. *Al-Infaq: Jurnal Ekonomi Islam, 2*(2).

Azhar, N., & Omar, A. (2025). Aging workforce in Malaysia: Navigating challenges and shaping policies. *Quantum Journal of Social Sciences and Humanities*, *6*(2), 226–236. DOI: 10.55197/qjssh.v6i2.615

Azizah, S. N., Saleh, S., & Sulistyaningrum, E. (2022). The Effect of Working Mother Status on Children's Education Attainment: Evidence from Longitudinal Data. *Economies 2022, Vol. 10, Page 54, 10*(2), 54. DOI: 10.3390/economies10020054

Azizi, M., Umiyati, H., Nugroho, L., Utami, A. R., Sudirman, A., & Aryani, L. (2022). *Effective digital marketing* (Putri, D. E., & Sari, E. P., Eds.). Widina Media Utama.

Aziz, M. R. A., & Yusof, M. A. (2014). Examining the Relationship between Level of Income and Appointment of Agent in Collecting Waqf Fund. *International Journal of Trade. Economics and Finance*, *5*(2), 167–169. DOI: 10.7763/IJTEF.2014.V5.363

Aziz, N. A., & Rahman, A. A. (2022). Artificial intelligence in philanthropic matching: Optimizing donor-cause alignment for educational waqf. *International Journal of Islamic Economics and Finance*, *5*(2), 145–163.

Aziz, Y., Mansor, F., Waqar, S., & Zada, N. (2025). Zakat and Sustainable Development Goals (SDGs). Assessing the Ripple Effect of Obligatory-Alms Spending on Education. Empirical Evidence From Pakistan. *Asian Social Work and Policy Review*, *19*(1), e70006. DOI: 10.1111/aswp.70006

Azman, F., & Jaafar, N. I. (2022). The psychology of digital giving: User experience design for waqf platforms. *Journal of Islamic Marketing*, *13*(3), 512–531.

Azmi, A. G. I., & Zaighu, A. A. G. (2020). Kepimpinan Strategik Rasulullah SAW: Kajian Perlaksanaanya oleh Kagat. *Journal of Islamic Management and Finance*, *1*(1), 32–47.

Azmi, N. N. I. N. M., & Thaker, M. A. M. T. (2020). Literature survey on Islamic microfinance. *Global Review of Islamic Economics and Business*, *8*(1), 23–33. DOI: 10.14421/grieb.2020.081-03

Back, C., Morana, S., & Spann, M. (2023). When do robo-advisors make us better investors? The impact of social design elements on investor behavior. *Journal of Behavioral and Experimental Economics*, *103*(November 2022), 101984. DOI: 10.1016/j.socec.2023.101984

Badgaiyan, A. J., Verma, A., & Dixit, S. (2016). Impulsive buying tendency: Measuring important relationships with a new perspective and an indigenous scale. *IIMB Management Review*, *28*(4), 186–199. DOI: 10.1016/j.iimb.2016.08.009

Bank Negara Malaysia. (2017). MyWakaf: A Model for Sustainable Waqf Management.

Bank Negara Malaysia. (2021a). *Climate Change and Principle-Based Taxonomy (CCPT)*. Bank Negara Malaysia. https://www.bnm.gov.my/-/climate-change-principle-based-taxonomy

Bank Negara Malaysia. (2022). *Financial Sector Blueprint 2022 - 2026.*

Bank Negara Malaysia. (2022). *Financial Sector Blueprint 2022–2026*. Bank Negara Malaysia.

Bank Negara Malaysia. (2024). *iTEKAD: Empowering low-income microentrepreneurs*. Retrieved from https://www.bnm.gov.my/social-finance

Bank Negara Malaysia. B. (2025, March). *BNM Annual Report 2024 - Bank Negara Malaysia*. https://www.bnm.gov.my/documents/20124/17493532/ar2024_en_book.pdf/

BAPPENAS. (2016). *Masterplan Arsitekstur Keuangan Syariah Indonesia*. https://www.bappenas.go.id/files/publikasi_utama/Masterplan Arsitektur Keuangan Syariah Indonesia.pdf

Barbic, D., Lucic, A., & Chen, J. M. (2019). Measuring responsible financial consumption behaviour. *International Journal of Consumer Studies*, *43*(1), 102–112. DOI: 10.1111/ijcs.12489

Barkley, B., & Schweitzer, M. (2021). The rise of fintech lending to small businesses: Businesses' perspectives on borrowing. *International Journal of Central Banking*, *17*(1), 35–65.

Barus, E. E., Al Mujadid, N. S., Umar, M. R., Dores, E., & Zahra, N. R. (2025). The Role of Sharia Cooperatives in Supporting the Sustainable Development Goals (SDGs) 2030 in Medan City. [AKSY]. *Jurnal Ilmu Akuntansi Dan Bisnis Syariah*, *7*(2), 264–285. DOI: 10.15575/aksy.v7i2.46230

Bashir, I., & Qureshi, I. H. (2023). A Systematic Literature Review on Personal Financial Well-Being: The Link to Key Sustainable Development Goals 2030. In *FIIB Business Review* (Vol. 12, Issue 1). DOI: 10.1177/23197145221106862

Batizani, D. (2024). Navigating retirement: Emerging and challenging smart financial strategies for the aging adults. *International Journal of Entrepreneurial Knowledge*, *12*(1), 70–85. DOI: 10.37335/ijek.v12i1.215

Beik, I. S., Nurzaman, M. S., Zaenal, M. H., Hendarto, R. G., Annisa, N., & Choirin, M. (2017). *National Zakat Index: Framework and Methodology* (Working Papers-Puskas Baznas, 1).

Belk, R. W. (1988). Possessions and the Extended Self. *The Journal of Consumer Research*, *15*(2), 139–168. DOI: 10.1086/209154

Bentler, P. M., & Kano, Y. (1990). On the equivalence of factors and components. *Multivariate Behavioral Research*, *25*(1), 67–74. DOI: 10.1207/s15327906mbr2501_8

Berger, A. N., & Humphrey, D. B. (1992). Megamergers in banking and the use of cost efficiency as an antitrust defense. *Antitrust Bulletin*, *37*(3), 541–600. DOI: 10.1177/0003603X9203700302

Berger, E., & Nakata, C. (2013). Implementing technologies for financial service innovations in base of the pyramid markets. *Journal of Product Innovation Management, 30*(6), 1199–1211. DOI: 10.1111/jpim.12054

Bertola, G., & Lo Prete, A. (2025). Financial Literacy and Risk Protection During the Covid-19 Pandemic. *Italian Economic Journal, 11*(2), 645–666. DOI: 10.1007/s40797-024-00286-2

Bexley, J. B., Maniam, B., & James, J. F. (2000). Perception of Islamic Financial System: Its Obstacles in Application, and Its Market. In *Allied Academies International Conference. Academy of Accounting and Financial Studies.* [). Jordan Whitney Enterprises, Inc.]. *Proceedings, 5*(2), 1.

Bhattacherjee, A. (2001). Understanding information systems continuance: An expectation-confirmation model. *Management Information Systems Quarterly, 25*(3), 351–370. DOI: 10.2307/3250921

Bhushan, P., & Medury, Y. (2014). An empirical analysis of inter linkages between financial attitudes, financial behaviour and financial knowledge of salaried individuals. *Indian Journal of Commerce and Management Studies, 5*(3), 58–64. https://www.ijcms.in/index.php/ijcms/article/view/380/357

Billah, M. M. S. (2019). Sukuk *Takaful* Plan. *Islamic Insurance Products: Exploring Takaful Principles, Instruments and Structures*, 221-226.

Biplob, H., & Abdullah, M. F. (2019). The importance of Islamic financial literacy for Muslims: A general review. *Islam and Civilisational Renewal*, 106–117.

Bley, J., & Kuehn, K. (2003). Conventional versus Islamic finance: Student knowledge and perception in the United Arab Emirates. *International Journal of Islamic Financial Services, 5*(4). http://e-moghavemat.com/files/34.pdf

BNM. (2022). *Financial Sector Blurprint 2022-2026.*

Boj, E., Claramunt, M. M., & Varea, X. (2022). Reverse Mortgage and Financial Sustainability. *Technological and Economic Development of Economy, 28*(4), 872–892. DOI: 10.3846/tede.2022.16617

Boohene, R., Gyimah, R. A., & Osei, M. B. (2020). Social capital and SME performance: The moderating role of emotional intelligence. *Journal of Entrepreneurship in Emerging Economies, 12*(1), 79–99. DOI: 10.1108/JEEE-10-2018-0103

Broadstock, D. C., Chan, K., Cheng, L. T. W., & Wang, X. (2020). Since January 2020 Elsevier has created a COVID-19 resource centre with free information in English and Mandarin on the novel coronavirus COVID- 19. The COVID-19 resource centre is hosted on Elsevier Connect, the company ' s public news and information. *Finance Research Letters, 38*(January), 101716. PMID: 32837385

Brogi, M., & Lagasio, V. (2024). New but naughty. The evolution of misconduct in FinTech. *International Review of Financial Analysis, 95*(PB), 103489. DOI: 10.1016/j.irfa.2024.103489

Burhanudin, B. (2022). The effect of Muslims' tendency to regret being customers of conventional banks on their intention to save money in Islamic banks. *Journal of Islamic Marketing, 13*(5), 1050–1068. DOI: 10.1108/JIMA-03-2020-0074

BWI. (2022). *Green Waqf Framework.* Badan Wakaf Indonesia. https://www.bwi.go.id/wp-content/uploads/2022/09/INS-20SEP-GREEN-WAQF-FRAMEWORK.pdf

BWI. (2025). *BWI, MOSAIC Dan Yayasan Hutan Wakaf Kolaborasi Strategis Hutan Wakaf untuk Pengembangan Green Wakaf dan Green Energy.* https://www.bwi.go.id/11081/2025/02/25/bwi-mosaic-dan-yayasan-hutan-wakaf-kolaborasi-strategis-hutan-wakaf-untuk-pengembangan-green-wakaf-dan-green-energy/

Cabannes, Y., & Lipietz, B. (2018). Revisiting the democratic promise of participatory budgeting in light of competing political, good governance and technocratic logics. *Environment and Urbanization, 30*(1), 67–84. DOI: 10.1177/0956247817746279

Cameron, R., & O'Hanlon-Rose, T. (2023). Australia's unified funding framework for technical education: Lessons for developing economies. *International Journal of Training Research, 21*(1), 45–62.

Campbell, D. T. (1950). The indirect assessment of social attitudes. *Psychological Bulletin, 47*(1), 15–38. DOI: 10.1037/h0054114

Capital Markets and Services Act 2007 (CMSA) (Act 671).

Carè, R., & Fatima, R. (2025). Financial Market Misconduct: A Bibliometric Perspective. *European Financial Management, 31*(3), 1042–1071. DOI: 10.1111/eufm.12525

Cedeño, D., Lannin, D. G., Russell, L., Yazedjian, A., Kanter, J. B., & Mimnaugh, S. (2021). The effectiveness of a financial literacy and job-readiness curriculum for youth from low-income households. *Citizenship. Social and Economics Education, 20*(3), 197–215. DOI: 10.1177/20471734211051770

Chapra, M. U. (2008). The Islamic vision of development in the light of the Maqasid al-Shari'ah (Research Paper), *Occasional Papers 235*, The Islamic Research and Teaching Institute (IRTI).

Chapra, M. U. (2016). *The Future of Economics: An Islamic Perspective*. https://books.google.co.id/books?hl=id&lr=&id=0NGpDAAAQBAJ&oi=fnd&pg=PR11&ots=295lYLxRLB&sig=amDQAY8JHYGpjoZA4lmxKN_IprY&redir_esc=y#v=onepage&q&f=false

Chapra, M. U. (2008). *The Islamic Vision of Development in the Light of Maqasid al-Shariah*. International Institute of Islamic Thought.

Chapra, M. U. (2016). *The future of economics: An Islamic perspective* (Vol. 21). Kube Publishing Ltd.

Chapra, M. U. (2016). *The Islamic Vision of Development in Light of Maqasid al-shariah*. Islamic Development Bank.

Che Mohd Salleh, M., Abdullah, N. I., Chowdhury, M. A. M., Che Embi, N. A., & Kassim, S. (2023). Viability of Islamic Health Protection Retirement Plan (i-HPRP) Among Malaysian Public and Private Employees. *ISRA International Journal of Islamic Finance*, *15*(1), 73–90. DOI: 10.55188/ijif.v15i1.486

Chelliah, P., Shanmugam, A., & Sin, T. S. (2022). A study on the factors impacting retirement planning among low-income workers in the Northern Region, Malaysia. *Journal of Entrepreneurship and Business*, *10*(2), 69–84. DOI: 10.17687/jeb.v10i2.928

Chen, Y., Ye, J., & Shi, Q. (2024). Does managerial myopia promote enterprises over-financialization? Evidence from listed firms in China. *PLoS One*, *19*(9), e0309140. DOI: 10.1371/journal.pone.0309140 PMID: 39236054

Choung, Y., Chatterjee, S., & Pak, T. Y. (2023). Digital Financial Literacy and Financial Well-Being. *Finance Research Letters*, *58*, 104438. DOI: 10.1016/j.frl.2023.104438

Chowdhury, M. A. M. (2021). *Islamic health protection retirement plan for Malaysian employees: an investigation from a behavioural approach*. International Islamic University Malaysia.

Chua, Y. P. (2014). *Regression and Factor Analysis* (5th ed.). McGraw-Hill.

Churchill, G. A.Jr. (1979). A paradigm for developing better measures of marketing constructs. *JMR, Journal of Marketing Research*, *16*(1), 64–73. DOI: 10.1177/002224377901600110

Chu, S. Y., Park, H., Lee, J., Shaharuddin, K. K. B., & Gan, C. H. (2020). Self-stigma and its associations with stress and quality of life among Malaysian parents of children with autism. *Child: Care, Health and Development*, *46*(4), 485–494. DOI: 10.1111/cch.12771 PMID: 32396218

Chu, S. Y., Rafi, A. B. M., Lee, J., Fierro, V., Gan, C. H., Joginder Singh, S., Hersh, D., & Lin, L. Y. (2023). The relationship between affiliate stigma, stress, and quality of life for parents of individuals with cerebral palsy in Malaysia. *Disability and Rehabilitation*, *45*(24), 4035–4047. DOI: 10.1080/09638288.2022.2153304 PMID: 36541160

Cizakca, M. (2011). *Islamic Capitalism and Finance: Origins, Evolution and the Future*. Edward Elgar Publishing. DOI: 10.4337/9780857931481

Creswell, J. W., & Creswell, J. D. (2018). *Research Design: Qualitative, Quantitative, and Mixed Methods Approaches* (5th ed.). SAGE Publications.

Croux, C., Jagtiani, J., Korivi, T., & Vulanovic, M. (2020). Important factors determining Fintech loan default: Evidence from a lendingclub consumer platform. *Journal of Economic Behavior & Organization*, *173*, 270–296. DOI: 10.1016/j.jebo.2020.03.016

Dalla Pellegrina, L. (2011). Microfinance and Investment: A Comparison with Bank and Informal Lending. *World Development*, *39*(6), 882–897. DOI: 10.1016/j.worlddev.2011.03.002

Damane, M., & Ho, S. Y. (2025). Effects of financial inclusion of small and medium-sized enterprises on financial stability: Evidence from selected sub-Saharan African countries. *Journal of Innovation and Entrepreneurship*, *14*(1), 81. Advance online publication. DOI: 10.1186/s13731-025-00526-4

Daniele, M., Pelucco, V., & Quarato, F. (2020). *Since January 2020 Elsevier has created a COVID-19 resource centre with free information in English and Mandarin on the novel coronavirus COVID- 19 . The COVID-19 resource centre is hosted on Elsevier Connect, the company ' s public news and information . January.*

Daragmeh, A., Saleem, A., Bárczi, J., & Sági, J. (2022). Drivers of post-adoption of e-wallet among academics in Palestine: An extension of the expectation confirmation model. *Frontiers in Psychology*, *13*, 984931. Advance online publication. DOI: 10.3389/fpsyg.2022.984931

Datta, P. M., & Krancher, O. (2024). Cybersecurity end-user compliance: Password management versus update compliance. *Information & Management*, *61*(8), 104060. DOI: 10.1016/j.im.2024.104060

Daulay, N., Daulay, H., & Rohman, F. (2025). Religious coping of Muslim mothers of children with autism spectrum disorder in Indonesia. *Journal of Disability & Religion*, *29*(1), 33–50. DOI: 10.1080/23312521.2024.2372021

Davis, F. D. (1989). Perceived usefulness, perceived ease of use, and user acceptance of information technology. *Management Information Systems Quarterly*, *13*(3), 319–340. Advance online publication. DOI: 10.2307/249008

De Beckker, K., De Witte, K., & Van Campenhout, G. (2021). The effect of financial education on students' consumer choices: Evidence from a randomized experiment. *Journal of Economic Behavior & Organization*, *188*, 962–976. DOI: 10.1016/j.jebo.2021.06.022

Deacon, R. E., & Firebaugh, F. M. (1988). *Family resource management: Principles and applications.* (2nd ed.). DOI: 10.1016/B978-1-4160-3344-8.50090-1

Demirgüç-Kunt, A., Klapper, L., & Singer, D. (2018). Household finance and economic development. In *Handbook of finance and development* (pp. 534–549). Edward Elgar Publishing. DOI: 10.4337/9781785360510.00029

Demirguc-Kunt, A., Klapper, L., Singer, D., Ansar, S., & Hess, J. (2018). *The Global Findex Database 2017: Measuring financial inclusion and the fintech revolution.* The World Bank. DOI: 10.1596/978-1-4648-1259-0

Demirpençe Seçinti, D., Diş, D., Albayrak, Z. S., & Şen, E. (2024). Depression and parental distress among caregivers of autistic children: A serial mediator analysis in caregivers of autistic children. *BMC Psychology*, *12*(1), 339. DOI: 10.1186/s40359-024-01704-x PMID: 38858797

Department of Polytechnic Education. (2023). *Malaysian TVET Lecturer Development Report 2023.* Ministry of Higher Education Malaysia.

Department of Skills Development. (2023). *Annual Report 2022: Skills Development in Malaysia.* Ministry of Human Resources.

Dharma, Y., Puteh, A., Widodo, R., Alfaqih, L., & Yahya, A. (2024). The Influence of Financial Literacy and Islamic Business Ethics on Investment in Islamic Financial Instruments: The Mediating Role of Risk Attitude and the Moderating Role of Religious Knowledge. *Journal of Ecohumanism*, *3*(8), 264–282. DOI: 10.62754/joe.v3i8.4729

Dhuafa, D. (2020). Annual report on sadaqah contributions during. *COVID*, •••, 19.

Dinar, A. (2019). Islam and the Environment: Towards Fiqh al-Bi'ah al-Mu'asirah. *Islamic Economic Studies*, *27*(2), 1–19.

Dinc, Y., Çetin, M., Bulut, M., & Jahangir, R. (2021). Islamic financial literacy scale: An amendment in the sphere of contemporary financial literacy. *ISRA International Journal of Islamic Finance*, *13*(2), 251–263. DOI: 10.1108/IJIF-07-2020-0156

Dirie, K. A., Alam, M. M., & Maamor, S. (2024). Islamic Social Finance for Achieving Sustainable Development Goals: A Systematic Literature Review and Future Research Agenda. *International Journal of Ethics and Systems*, *40*(4), 676–698. DOI: 10.1108/IJOES-12-2022-0317

Djamhari, S. I., Mustika, M. D., Sjabadhyni, B., & Ndaru, A. R. P. (2024). Impulsive buying in the digital age: Investigating the dynamics of sales promotion, FOMO, and digital payment methods. *Cogent Business & Management*, *11*(1), 2419484. Advance online publication. DOI: 10.1080/23311975.2024.2419484

Dusuki, A. W., & Bouheraoua, S. (2011). The framework of *Maqasid al-shariah* and its implications for Islamic finance. *Islamic Finance and Maqasid al-shariah*, ISRA Research Paper.

Dusuki, A. W., & Abdullah, N. I. (2007). Maqasid al-Shariah, Maslahah, and Corporate Social Responsibility. *The American Journal of Islamic Social Sciences*, *24*(1), 25–45. DOI: 10.35632/ajiss.v24i1.415

Dusuki, A. W., & Abozaid, A. (2007). A Critical Appraisal of the Challenges of Realizing Maqasid al-Shariah in Islamic Banking and Finance. *International Journal of Economics, Management and Accounting*, *15*(2), 143–165.

Dusuki, A. W., & Bouheraoua, S. (2011). The framework of Maqasid al-Shari'ah and its implication for Islamic finance. *ICR Journal*, *2*(2), 316–336. DOI: 10.52282/icr.v2i2.651

Dyer, J. H., & Singh, H. (1998). The relational view: Cooperative strategy and sources of interorganizational competitive advantage. *Academy of Management Review*, *23*(4), 660–679. DOI: 10.2307/259056

Eastman, J. K., Goldsmith, R. E., & Flynn, L. R. (1999). Status Consumption in Consumer Behavior: Scale Development and Validation. *Journal of Marketing Theory and Practice*, *7*(3), 41–52. DOI: 10.1080/10696679.1999.11501839

Economic Planning Unit. (2021). *Twelfth Malaysia Plan, 2021-2025: A prosperous, inclusive, sustainable Malaysia* [PDF]. https://pulse.icdm.com.my/wp-content/uploads/2021/09/Twelfth-Plan-Document_compressed-1.pdf

Ekici, A., Joseph Sirgy, M., Lee, D.-J., Yu, G. B., & Bosnjak, M. (2018). The effects of shopping well-being and shopping ill-being on consumer life satisfaction. *Applied Research in Quality of Life*, *13*(2), 333–353. DOI: 10.1007/s11482-017-9524-9

Elasrag, H. (2019). *Blockchains for Islamic finance: Obstacles & Challenges. Munich Personal RePEc Archive*. Retrieved from https://mpra.ub.uni-muenchen.de/92676/

Elasrag, H. (2020). *Green Finance in the Framework of Islamic Finance: Principles and Instruments.* Munich Personal RePEc Archive (MPRA Paper No. 101327). https://mpra.ub.uni-muenchen.de/101327

Eldersevi, S., & Muhammad, M. (2021). "Asnaf Care: A Case Study of the Malaysian-based Charity Crowdfunding Platform to Combat the Impact of COVID-19." *5th International Conference of Zakat,* 2020, 615–626.

El-Gamal, M. A. (2006). *Islamic Finance: Law, Economics, and Practice*. Cambridge University Press. DOI: 10.1017/CBO9780511753756

Elmahgop, F., Alsulami, F., Mohammed, M. G. A., Abdel-Gadir, S., & Elhassan, T. (2025). The Socio-Economic Impacts of Waqf Investment Funds as a Model for Sustainable Financing in Saudi Arabia. *Sustainability 2025, Vol. 17, Page 3805, 17*(9), 3805. DOI: 10.3390/su17093805

EPF. (2024). EPF Releases Belanjawanku 2024/2025 And Retirement Income Adequacy Framework. Editorial and Media Relations Unit, Corporate Affairs Department. https://www.kwsp.gov.my/en/w/epf-releases-belanjawanku-2024/2025-and-retirement-income-adequacy-framework

Er, B., & Mutlu, M. (2017). Financial inclusion and Islamic finance: A survey of Islamic financial literacy index. *International Journal of Islamic Economics and Finance Studies, 3*(2). Advance online publication. DOI: 10.25272/j.2149-8407.2017.3.2.02

Faizi, F., Kusuma, A. S., & Widodo, P. (2024). Islamic green finance: Mapping the climate funding landscape in Indonesia. *International Journal of Ethics and Systems, 40*(4), 711–733. DOI: 10.1108/IJOES-08-2023-0189

Faraz, N., & Anjum, A. (2025). Spendception: The Psychological Impact of Digital Payments on Consumer Purchase Behavior and Impulse Buying. *Behavioral Sciences (Basel, Switzerland), 15*(3), 1–20. DOI: 10.3390/bs15030387 PMID: 40150281

Farezy, I., Ariani, Z., Hidayanti, N. F., Agustina, A., & Hulaimi, A. (2025). *Integration of Blockchain Technology in Islamic Finance: Opportunities and Challenges Towards Transparency and Sharia Compliance*. https://journal.ummat.ac.id/index.php/iicece/article/view/31325

Farid, A. (2024, October 17). *E-Wallet App Usage & Demographics Malaysia (2024 Statistics)*. https://upstackstudio.com/blog/e-wallet-malaysia/

Fatimah, S., Wibowo, W., Irfaniah, N. R., Harahap, R. A., & Panggabean, N. A. (2025). Local Digital Ecosystem: Peran Komunitas Digital dalam Mendorong Bisnis Kreatif Daerah. *JUMINTAL: Jurnal Manajemen Informatika Dan Bisnis Digital*, *4*(1), 127–136. DOI: 10.55123/jumintal.v4i1.5479

Fatmawati, F., Kahfi, N. S., Aisyah, N. H., & Asyifa, L. N. (2024). Application of Blockchain and Smart Contracts in Zakat Management: Perspective of SWOT Analysis and Islamic Law. *Indonesian Conference of Zakat - Proceedings*, 240–250. https://doi.org/DOI: 10.37706/ICONZ.2024.977

Fawaid, F. (2024). Beyond Profit: How BMT NU Jambesari Empowers MSMEs Through Sharia Financing. *Tadayun: Jurnal Hukum Ekonomi Syariah*, *5*(2), 185–210. DOI: 10.24239/tadayun.v5i2.345

Fenton-O'Creevy, M., & Furnham, A. (2020). Personality, ideology, and money attitudes as correlates of financial literacy and competence. *Financial Planning Review*, *3*(1), e1070. DOI: 10.1002/cfp2.1070

Fernandes, D., Lynch, J. G.Jr, & Netemeyer, R. G. (2014). Financial literacy, financial education, and downstream financial behaviors. *Management Science*, *60*(8), 1861–1883. DOI: 10.1287/mnsc.2013.1849

Fessler, P., Silgoner, M., & Weber, R. (2020). Financial knowledge, attitude and behavior: Evidence from the Austrian Survey of Financial Literacy. *Empirica*, *47*(4), 929–947. DOI: 10.1007/s10663-019-09465-2

Financial Planning Association of Malaysia & Islamic Banking and Finance Malaysia. (2009). Islamic Financial Planning: A Brief Introduction. Kuala Lumpur: Financial Planning Association of Malaysia (FPAM)

Firdaus, A. M. N., & Shukor, K. A. (2019). Kurikulum Pendidikan Islam Para Sahabat: Satu Sorotan. *Jurnal Al-Munzir*, *12*(2), 209.

Firdausi, M. R. A., & Kasri, R. A. (2022). Islamic financial literacy amongst Muslim students in Indonesia: A multidimensional approach. *Al-Muzara'ah*, 77-94.

Fisol, W. N. M., & Bakar, M. A., BIN, A. K., & RAHIM, A. (2021). The Scientific of Macro Maqasid in Developing of Social Financing Products. *Journal of Contemporary Issues in Business and Government*, *27*(3), 1–9.

Fornell, C., & Larcker, D. F. (1981). Evaluating structural equation models with unobservable variables and measurement error. *JMR, Journal of Marketing Research*, *18*(1), 39–50. DOI: 10.1177/002224378101800104

Fox, J., & Bartholomae, S. (2020). Household finances, financial planning, and COVID-19. *Financial Planning Review, 3*(4), e1103. DOI: 10.1002/cfp2.1103

Frost, J., Gambacorta, L., & Jagtiani, J. (2022). *Working Papers Giulio Cornelli Bank for International Settlements Bank for International Settlements The Impact of Fintech Lending on Credit Access for U.S. Small Businesses The Impact of Fintech Lending on Credit Access for U.S. Small Businesses Giulio C.* DOI: 10.21799/frbp.wp

Garg, N., Priyadarshi, P., & Malik, A. (2024). Financial well-being: An integrated framework, operationalization, and future research agenda. *Journal of Consumer Behaviour, 23*(6), 3194–3212. DOI: 10.1002/cb.2372

Gasmelseid, T. M. (2015). Empowering microfinance processes through hybrid cloud based services. *International Journal of Systems and Service-Oriented Engineering, 5*(3), 1–17. DOI: 10.4018/IJSSOE.2015070101

George, L. (2024). *Debt Burden Threatens Poor Countries' Development Goals, UN Official Says*. https://www.reuters.com/world/debt-service-burden-forcing-poor-make-tough-choices-un-official-says-2024-10-07/

Ghaith, M. M., Al-rawashdeh, G. H., Alzuod, M. A., Ghaith, Y. M., Alotoum, F. J., AlSokkar, A. A. M., Al-Gasawneh, J., & Alghizzawi, M. (2024). Examining the Effects of Digital Payment and Impulsive Buying on Purchase Intention. *2024 2nd International Conference on Cyber Resilience (ICCR)*, 1–7. DOI: 10.1109/ICCR61006.2024.10532804

Ghaleb, M. (2019). *Islamic finance and sustainable development: The role of Islamic banks and social finance institutions in achieving the SDGs*. Islamic Development Bank.

Gherhes, C., Williams, N., Vorley, T., & Vasconcelos, A. C. (2016). Distinguishing micro-businesses from SMEs: A systematic review of growth constraints. *Journal of Small Business and Enterprise Development, 23*(4), 939–963. DOI: 10.1108/JSBED-05-2016-0075

Ginanjar, A., & Kassim, S. (2021). Roles of Islamic microfinance institutions in improving financial inclusion in Indonesia: Empirical evidence from Baitulmaal Wa Tamwil. *Al-Iqtishad: Jurnal Ilmu Ekonomi Islam, 13*(1), 87–108. DOI: 10.15408/aiq.v13i1.19842

Gladstone, J. J., & Masters-Waage, T. C. (2024). When Paying Is (Even More) Painful: Personality-Based Heterogeneity in Consumption Responses to Economic Hardship. *Social Psychological & Personality Science, 15*(3), 264–274. DOI: 10.1177/19485506231167020

Gomber, P., Kauffman, R. J., Parker, C., & Weber, B. W. (2018). On the Fintech Revolution: Interpreting the Forces of Innovation, Disruption, and Transformation in Financial Services. *Journal of Management Information Systems*, *35*(1), 220–265. DOI: 10.1080/07421222.2018.1440766

Goswami, S., Sharma, R. B., & Chouhan, V. (2022). Impact of financial technology (Fintech) on financial inclusion (FI) in Rural India. *Universal Journal of Accounting and Finance*, *10*(2), 483–497. DOI: 10.13189/ujaf.2022.100213

Goyal, K., & Kumar, S. (2021). Financial literacy: A systematic review and bibliometric analysis. *International Journal of Consumer Studies*, *45*(1), 80–105. https://doi.org/https://doi.org/10.1111/ijcs.12605. DOI: 10.1111/ijcs.12605

Graafland, J. (2017). Religiosity, attitude, and the demand for socially responsible products. *Journal of Business Ethics*, *144*(1), 121–138. DOI: 10.1007/s10551-015-2796-9

GSIA. (2021). *Global Sustainable Investment Review* 2020. Global Sustainable Investment Alliance. https://www.gsi-alliance.org/wp-content/uploads/2021/08/GSIR-20201.pdf

Guan, N., Guariglia, A., Moore, P., Xu, F., & Al-Janabi, H. (2022). Financial stress and depression in adults: A systematic review. *PLoS One*, *17*(2), e0264041. DOI: 10.1371/journal.pone.0264041

Gulati, R. (1998). Alliances and networks. *Strategic Management Journal*, *19*(4), 293–317. DOI: 10.1002/(SICI)1097-0266(199804)19:4<293::AID-SMJ982>3.0.CO;2-M

Gunawan, A., Asmuni, A., & Siregar, S. (2021). Islamic financial literacy and financial behavior: The case of Muhammadiyah community in Medan City. *Journal of Accounting and Investment*, *22*(3), 500–516. DOI: 10.18196/jai.v22i3.10043

Güney, N. (2024). Maqāsid al-Sharī'a in islamic finance: A critical analysis of modern discourses. *Religions*, *15*(1), 114. DOI: 10.3390/rel15010114

Gupta, P., Prashar, S., & Parsad, C. (2024). Pure and suggestive impulse buying in mobile shopping app: Shopping pattern of young consumers. *Young Consumers*, *25*(6), 824–850. DOI: 10.1108/YC-11-2023-1911

Habibullah, M., & Abdullah Al Faruque, M. (2023). Islamic economic framework for the exercise of Islamic financial activities: Its conformity with Maqasid Shari'ah. *Al-Burhān: Journal Of Qur Ān And Sunnah Studies*, *7*(1), 81–92. DOI: 10.31436/alburhn.v7i1.300

Habibullah, M., & Hassan, R. (2023). Developing a Conceptual Shari'ah Framework of Green Sukuk for Bangladesh: Its Implications on Social Welfare by Realizing SDGs. [IIUM Journals]. *Journal of Islamic Finance, 12*(1), 73–82. DOI: 10.31436/jif.v12i1.748

Habibullah, M., Hassan, R., & Zain, N. R. M. (2023). Women's Empowerment and Participation in Islamic Financial Planning Diversity, Equity and Inclusion: Evidence from Maqasid al-*Shari'ah. Al-Burhān. Journal Of Qur Ān And Sunnah Studies, 7*(2), 152–161.

Hair, J. F., Black, W. C., Babin, B. J., & Anderson, R. E. (2019). *Multivariate data analysis* (8th ed.). Cengage Learning.

Hair, J. F., Risher, J. J., Sarstedt, M., & Ringle, C. M. (2019). When to use and how to report the results of PLS-SEM. *European Business Review, 31*(1), 2–24. DOI: 10.1108/EBR-11-2018-0203

Hair, J. F., Sarstedt, M., Ringle, C. M., & Gudergan, S. (2024). *Advanced issues in partial least squares structural equation modeling*. PLS-SEM.

Hajar, S., Musadik, S. A., Yusuf, N., Aziz, N. A., Abdul, I., & Azmi, G. (2020). Maqasid Syariah in Islamic Consumption. [IJBEC]. *International Journal of Business and Economy, 2*(4).

Hamid, A. H. A., & Nordin, N. A. M. (2001). A study on Islamic banking education and strategy for the new millennium-Malaysian experience. *International Journal of Islamic Financial Services, 2*(4), 3–11. https://www.iiibf.org/journals/journal8/abdulhalim.pdf

Hamid, F. S. (2025). Behavioral biases and over-indebtedness in consumer credit: Evidence from Malaysia. *Cogent Economics & Finance, 13*(1), 2449191. Advance online publication. DOI: 10.1080/23322039.2024.2449191

Hamid, N., & Yahya, F. (2021). Informal Waqf Practice and its Socio-economic Role in Northern Nigeria. *Journal of Islamic Economics and Development, 6*(1), 45–61.

Hamid, Y. B. (2014). *Perancangan Ketenteraan dalam al-Sunnah, Terj. Jabatan Arah Kor Agama Angkatan Tentera*. Penerbit Markas Angkatan Tentera Malaysia.

Hamzah, M. (2024). The role and legal aspects of infaq, sadaqah, and waqf in realizing economic equality and people's welfare. *Al-Iqtishadiyah: Ekonomi Syariah dan Hukum Ekonomi Syariah,* 10(1), 107-124.

Hanivan, H., & Nasrudin, N. (2019). A financial inclusion index for Indonesia. *Bulletin of Monetary Economics and Banking, 22*(3), 351–366. DOI: 10.21098/bemp.v22i3.1056

Harahap, B., Risfandy, T., & Futri, I. N. (2023). Islamic Law, Islamic Finance, and Sustainable Development Goals: A Systematic Literature Review. *Sustainability 2023, Vol. 15, Page 6626, 15*(8), 6626. DOI: 10.3390/su15086626

Haris, G. (2020). The application of dynamic zakat percentage by Yusuf al-qaradawy on the professional zakat in Indonesian BAZNAS. *Asy-Syir'ah: Jurnal Ilmu Syari'ah dan Hukum, 54*(2), 299-317.

Haris, A. H. (2020). Sejarah Kerajaan Turki Uthmaniyah dan Sumbangannya Dalam Bidang Sosiopolitik Abad ke-14 hingga Abad ke-20. *Journal of Al-Tamaddun, 15*(1), 85–107. DOI: 10.22452/JAT.vol15no1.6

Haris, C., & Manangin, S. (2024). The Digital Revolution in Exploring the Impact of Fintech on Islamic Financial Services. *Kunuz: Journal of Islamic Banking and Finance, 4*(2), 171–187. DOI: 10.30984/kunuz.v4i2.1267

Harrieti, N., Ikhwansyah, I., & Alisa Ahmad, A. (2024). The Role of Sharia Banking in Strengthening the Assets of Village-Owned Enterprises in Indonesia. *Cogent Social Sciences, 10*(1), 2350557. DOI: 10.1080/23311886.2024.2350557

Hasan, N. F., & Syahruddin, S. (2022). Enhancing Green Waqf For Carbonization Technology: Opportunities for Sustainable Development Goals (SDGs) in Indonesia. *El Barka, 5*(2), 235–251. DOI: 10.21154/elbarka.v5i2.4739

Hasan, R., Hassan, M. K., & Aliyu, S. (2020). Fintech and Islamic finance: Literature review and research agenda. [IJIEF]. *International Journal of Islamic Economics and Finance, 3*(1), 75–94. DOI: 10.18196/ijief.2122

Hasan, Z., & Ebrahim, M. S. (2020a). Islamic Finance and the Sustainable Development Goals: A Review of the Linkages and the Role of Fiqh. *Journal of Islamic Accounting and Business Research, 11*(6), 1271–1285.

Hasan, Z., & Ebrahim, M. S. (2020b). Islamic finance and the Shari'ah-compliant approach to climate change: A critical review. *Review of Islamic Economics, 24*(1), 27–53. DOI: 10.1108/RIE-03-2019-0041

Hassan, M. A. M., Alias, A., Mahamood, S. M., & De Costa, F. (2021). Waqf land development approaches and practices in the state islamic religious councils. *Planning Malaysia, 19*(17).

Hassan, A., & Abdullah, A. (2018). Corporate waqf models and their distinctive features: The future of Islamic philanthropy. Journal of Islamic Economics. *Banking and Finance*, *14*(3), 147–165.

Hassan, M. K., & Kayed, R. N. (2009). The global financial crisis, risk management and social justice in Islamic finance. *ISRA International Journal of Islamic Finance*, *1*(1), 33–58. DOI: 10.55188/ijif.v1i1.63

Hassan, M. K., Sarea, A., & Aliyu, S. (2022). Green Waqf: A Sustainable Mechanism for Climate Action in Muslim Societies. *Journal of Islamic Accounting and Business Research*, *13*(4), 627–646. DOI: 10.1108/JIABR-06-2021-0179

Hassan, N., & Ibrahim, M. (2023). Factors influencing researcher retention in Malaysian TVET institutions: A mixed-methods study. *Technical and Vocational Education Journal*, *15*(2), 189–206.

Hassan, R., & Muneeza, A. (2022). The need to eliminate mismanagement and corruption in Islamic social finance institutions. *IIUM Law Journal*, *30*(S2), 423–444. DOI: 10.31436/iiumlj.v30iS2.774

Hassan, R., & Wong, B. (2023). Data interoperability challenges in digital waqf ecosystems: Technical requirements and implementation frameworks. *International Journal of Islamic Finance*, *15*(2), 201–219.

Hati, S. R. H., Putri, N. I. S., Daryanti, S., Wibowo, S. S., Safira, A., & Setyowardhani, H. (2022). Brand familiarity vs profit-sharing rate: Which has a stronger impact on Muslim customers' intention to invest in an Islamic bank? *Journal of Islamic Marketing*, *13*(8), 1703–1727. DOI: 10.1108/JIMA-08-2020-0247

Hati, S. R. H., Wibowo, S. S., & Safira, A. (2021). The antecedents of Muslim customers' intention to invest in an Islamic bank's term deposits: Evidence from a Muslim majority country. *Journal of Islamic Marketing*, *12*(7), 1363–1384. DOI: 10.1108/JIMA-01-2020-0007

Havakhor, T., Rahman, M. S., Zhang, T., & Zhu, C. (2025). Tech-Enabled Financial Data Access, Retail Investors, and Gambling-Like Behavior in the Stock Market. *Management Science*, *71*(2), 1646–1670. DOI: 10.1287/mnsc.2021.01379

Henseler, J., Ringle, C. M., & Sarstedt, M. (2015). A new criterion for assessing discriminant validity in variance-based structural equation modeling. *Journal of the Academy of Marketing Science*, *43*(1), 115–135. DOI: 10.1007/s11747-014-0403-8

Hermawan, B., & Wahyudi, D. (2025). Analysis of the Influence of Financial Literacy on Personal Financial Management Behavior in the Millennial Generation. [INJOLE]. *International Journal of Economic Literature*, *3*(4), 101–116.

Hermes, N., & Hudon, M. (2018). Determinants of the performance of microfinance institutions: A systematic review. *Journal of Economic Surveys*, *32*(5), 1483–1513. DOI: 10.1111/joes.12290

Hidajat, T., & Hamdani, M. (2017). Measuring Islamic financial literacy. *Advanced Science Letters*, *23*(8), 7173–7176. DOI: 10.1166/asl.2017.9321

Hidayat, S., Farooq, M., & Alim, E. A. (2020). *Impacts of the Covid-19 Outbreak on Islamic Finance in the OIC Countries.* Https://Knks.Go.Id/. https://knks.go.id/storage/upload/1591090473-b71788507b33ad61531b0705ed42b4269a8a994b.pdf

Hilgert, R. K., & Luttrell, M. (2023). Investigating the Impact of Financial Literacy and Income on Financial Behaviors Among Millennials. *Indonesia Accounting Research Journal*, *11*(1), 37–50. DOI: 10.35335/iacrj.v11i1.211

Hilmiyah, N., Izzuddin, M. U., & Waraswasti, P. F. (2023). The Role of Baitulmal as Department of Finance Through Fiscal Policy: Zakat as an Instrument. *N Indonesian Conference of Zakat-Proceedings*, 135–152.

Hirschman, E. C. (1983). Religious affiliation and consumption processes: An initial paradigm. *Research in Marketing*, *6*(1), 131–170.

Holloh, D. (2001). *Microfinance Institutions Study.*

Hoque, N. (2023). Promoting business zakah as a product of Islamic finance to fund social causes for well-being of the underprivileged: Evidence from Bangladesh. *Journal of Islamic Marketing*, *14*(4), 966–987. DOI: 10.1108/JIMA-10-2021-0337

Hossain, B., Hossain, A., Hossain, G. M. S., & Likhon, T. S. (2024). Islamic perspective of household debt management: An in-depth study. *International Journal of Science and Business*, *31*(1), 103–114. DOI: 10.58970/IJSB.2279

Hossain, M. E., Mahadi, N. F. B., Haron, R., Nor, R. M., & Yousuf, M. A. (2025). Islamic Social Finance for Sustainable Economic Growth in Bangladesh. *Journal of Islamic Finance*, *14*(1), 85–97.

Hotman, & Luthfi, M. (2025). The Influence of Maqasid Al-Shariah on Sustainable Investment Decisions in Islamic Finance. *Economics Studies and Banking Journal (DEMAND)*, *2*(1), 295–309. https://doi.org/DOI: 10.62207/E0HM4677

Hsiao, K. L. (2017). Compulsive mobile application usage and technostress: The role of personality traits. *Online Information Review*, *41*(2), 272–295. Advance online publication. DOI: 10.1108/OIR-03-2016-0091

Huang, H., Weinbaum, D., & Yehuda, N. (2023). Financial reporting quality and investment efficiency: The role of strategic alliances. *Journal of Contemporary Accounting & Economics*, *19*(3), 100377. DOI: 10.1016/j.jcae.2023.100377

Hudaefi, F. A. (2020). How does Islamic fintech promote the SDGs? Qualitative evidence from Indonesia. *Qualitative Research in Financial Markets*, *12*(4), 353–366. DOI: 10.1108/QRFM-05-2019-0058

Huda, N. (2021). Waqf Blockchain in Indonesia. *Al-Awqaf: Jurnal Wakaf Dan Ekonomi Islam*, *14*(1), 31–49.

Huston, S. J. (2010). Measuring financial literacy. *The Journal of Consumer Affairs*, *44*(2), 296–316. DOI: 10.1111/j.1745-6606.2010.01170.x

IAEI. (2025). *Indonesia Joins the List of the Largest Issuers in the ESG Sukuk Market*. https://iaei.or.id/en/news-and-articles/news/indonesia-joins-the-list-of-the-largest-issuers-in-the-esg-sukuk-market

Ibn Khaldūn. (2019). *Al-Muqaddimah* [The introduction]. (Original work published 1377).

Ibn Mājah, M. (n.d.). *Sunan Ibn Mājah*, Hadith no. 2413 & no. 3605.

Ibnu Hisyam (1995). *Sirah an-Nabawiyyah*. Al-Halabi Waauladihi Bimsr: Maktabah Mustapha, h. 258.

Iborra, M., López-Muñoz, J. F., & Safón, V. (2024). Lack of resilience after COVID-19: The role of family firm heterogeneity and behavior. fsQCA versus regression. *European Journal of Management and Business Economics*, (August). Advance online publication. DOI: 10.1108/EJMBE-05-2023-0140

Ibrahim, S. S., Daud, D., Hidayah, K., Shaharuddin, A., & Al-Amin, A. A. M. (2023). Waqf Integrated Income Generating Model (WIIGM) for Enhancing Sustainable Development Goals (SDGS) in Malaysia: An Evaluation of Behavioural Intention. *International Journal of Ethics and Systems*, *39*(4), 841–858. DOI: 10.1108/IJOES-02-2022-0030

ICD – LSEG. (2023). *ICD – LSEG Islamic Finance Development Report 2023*. London Stock Exchange Group. https://solutions.lseg.com/IslamicFinance_ICD_LSEG

ICMA. (2024). *Sustainable Bond Market Data*. International Capital Market Association. https://www.icmagroup.org/sustainable-finance/sustainable-bonds-database/

Idris, K. M. (2002). *Gelagat Kepatuhan zakat pendapatan gaji di kalangan kakitangan awam persekutuan negeri Kedah* [Unpublished PhD thesis]. Universiti Utara Malaysia.

IFSB. (2020). *Environmental, Social and Governance (ESG) Issues in Islamic Finance*. Islamic Financial Services Board.

Ifwat Ishak, M. S., & Mohammad Nasir, N. S. (2021). Maqasid al-Shari'ah in Islamic finance: Harmonizing theory and reality. *The Journal Of Muamalat And Islamic Finance Research, 18*(1), 108–119. DOI: 10.33102/jmifr.v18i1.334

Indonesian Ulema Council (Majelis Ulama Indonesia). (2021). *Fatwa on the prohibition of using cryptocurrency as a currency*. MUI.

Intellectual Property Corporation of Malaysia. (2024). *Statistical booklet 2024: Applications and registrations/grants by intellectual property components*. MyIPO. https://www.myipo.gov.my/statistic-application-registration/

International Labour Organization. (2023). *Skills shortages and the green transition in Asia and the Pacific*. International Labour Office. https://labordoc.ilo.org/discovery/fulldisplay/alma995320392002676/41ILO_INST:41ILO_V2

Iqbal, Z., & Mirakhor, A. (2011). *An introduction to Islamic finance: Theory and practice* (2nd ed.). John Wiley & Sons (Asia) Pte. Ltd.

Iqbal, M., & Mirakhor, A. (2011). *An introduction to Islamic finance: Theory and practice* (2nd ed.). Wiley. DOI: 10.1002/9781118390474

Isahi, A., & Muwazir, M. R. (2024). *Poverty Alleviation in Nigeria: An Insight into Jaiz Bank Islamic Microfinance Scheme*. Online Journal of Islamic Management and Finance (OJIMF), 4(2), 99–114. https://mjlis.um.edu.my/index.php/OJIMF/article/view/56122

Isaia, E., Oggero, N., & Sandretto, D. (2024). Is financial literacy a protection tool from online fraud in the digital era? *Journal of Behavioral and Experimental Finance, 44*, 100977. DOI: 10.1016/j.jbef.2024.100977

IsDB. (2021). *Islamic Social Finance Report*. Islamic Development Bank.

IsDB. (2025). *IsDB Sustainable Finance Framework (July 2025)*. Islamic Development Bank. https://www.isdb.org/publications/isdb-sustainable-finance-framework-july-2025

Islamic Development Bank & EFInA. (2021). *Financial Inclusion Strategy Report: Nigeria Country Profile*. https://www.efina.org.ng

Islamic Development Bank. (2018). *Islamic social finance and sustainable development*.

Islamic Financial Services Board. (2022). *Islamic Financial Services Industry Stability Report 2022*. https://www.ifsb.org

Ismail Abdel Mohsin, M. (2013). Financing through cash-waqf: a revitalization to finance different needs. International journal of Islamic and Middle Eastern finance and management, 6(4), 304-321.

Ismail, A., Yusof, M. Y., Mohamed, S., & Ibrahim, Z. (2024). Corporate waqf and TVET innovation: Institutional partnerships for sustainable development. *Waqf Studies Review*, *7*(1), 112–130.

Ismail, N. A., Wahid, N. A., Wahab, N. A., & Majid, N. A. (2019), Tokoh Tamadun Islam Sultan Muhammad Al-Fateh dipandang Dari Sudut Personaliti, *Proceedings of the International Conference on Islamic Civilization and Technology Management pada 23*-24 November 2019.

Ismail, W. M. B. W., Rasool, B. A., Saladin, M., & Noor, A. H. B. M. (2021). Technology Acceptance and Technology Usage: Importance to Cash Waqf Contribution. *International Journal of Academic Research in Business & Social Sciences*, *11*(9), 942–953. DOI: 10.6007/IJARBSS/v11-i9/11082

Ismail, W. M. W. (2021). Significance of technology to cash waqf collection: Application of unified theory acceptance and use of technology (UTAUT). *International Journal of Academic Research in Business & Social Sciences*, *11*(1), 777–788.

ISRA. (2023). *Islamic financial system: Principles and operations* (3rd ed.). International Shariah Research Academy for Islamic Finance (ISRA).

Jan, A., Rahman, H. U., Zahid, M., Salameh, A. A., Khan, P. A., Al-Faryan, M. A. S., Che Aziz, R. B., & Ali, H. E. (2023). Islamic Corporate Sustainability Practices Index Aligned with SDGs Towards Better Financial Performance: Evidence from the Malaysian and Indonesian Islamic Banking Industry. *Journal of Cleaner Production*, *405*, 136860. DOI: 10.1016/j.jclepro.2023.136860

Javaheri, D., Fahmideh, M., Chizari, H., Lalbakhsh, P., & Hur, J. (2024). Cybersecurity threats in FinTech: A systematic review. *Expert Systems with Applications*, *241*, 1–42. DOI: 10.1016/j.eswa.2023.122697

Jiang, Y., & Shimizu, S. (2024). Does Financial Literacy Impact Investment Participation and Retirement Planning in Japan? *arXiv preprint arXiv:2405.01078*.

Jia, P., & Sun, S. L. (2023). Mission Drift or Mission Fulfillment? Examining Microfinance's Financial and Social Performance with Growth Curve Modeling and Variance Decomposition. *Cross Cultural & Strategic Management*, *30*(3), 467–487. DOI: 10.1108/CCSM-07-2021-0125

Jimoh, A. T., David Kolawole, K., & Bamigbade, D. (2024). Islamic Microfinance as a Panacea for Poverty Alleviation. *European Journal of Islamic Finance*, *11*(1), 17–30. DOI: 10.13135/2421-2172/9414

Johari, A. H., Zai, F. H., Hussain, L., & Ali, M. M. (2014). Exploring a Shari'ah-compliant model for retirement annuity plans' *I-FIKR*. Available at: https://ifikr.isra.my/library/pub/4912/exploring-a-shariah-compliant-model-for-retirement-annuity-plans (accessed 8 September 2022).

Judijanto, L., Sarif, A., & Ariyanti, R. (2025). Productive Waqf as a Sustainable Financial Instrument in the Perspective of Islamic SDGs. *West Science Islamic Studies*, *3*(02), 106–110. DOI: 10.58812/wsiss.v3i02.1833

Junarti, A. S. M., Amirsyah, & Mardika, I. H. (2024). Integrating Social Business for Sustainable Impact: A Systematic Literature Review in the Context of Waqf. *Journal of Islamic Finance, 13*(2), 149–159. https://journals.iium.edu.my/iiibf-journal/index.php/jif/article/view/931

Kadir, M. A., & Ibrahim, S. (2023). The Axiata Digital Innovation Fund: A case study in corporate waqf for technological development. *Journal of Islamic Business and Management*, *13*(1), 67–83.

Kahf, M. (2002). Strategic trends in the Islamic banking and finance movement. *In Harvard Forum on Islamic Finance and Banking*, 1–31.

Kahf, M. (2003). *The Role of Waqf in Improving the Ummah Welfare* [Paper presentation]. International Seminar on Waqf as a Private Legal Body, Kuala Lumpur, Malaysia.

Kahf, M. (2007). Islamic banks and economic development. In *Handbook of Islamic banking*. Edward Elgar Publishing. DOI: 10.4337/9781847205414.00028

Kaiser, T., Lusardi, A., Menkhoff, L., & Urban, C. (2022). Financial education affects financial knowledge and downstream behaviors. *Journal of Financial Economics*, *145*(2), 255–272. DOI: 10.1016/j.jfineco.2021.09.022

Kalifah, M. H., Aslan, H., & Abdullah, A. B. (2024). Challenges in the implementation of Mudharabah financing in the Islamic banking industry. *Equinox Journal of Economics, Business & Political Studies*, 11(1), 01-23.

Kamali, M. H. (2019). Maqasid Al-Shariah Made Simple. In *Maqasid Al-Shariah Made Simple*. DOI: 10.2307/j.ctvkc67vz

Kamali, M. H. (1999). MAQĀ ID AL-SHARĪ'AH": The objectives of Islamic law. *Islamic Studies, 38*(2), 193–208. https://www.jstor.org/stable/20837037. DOI: 10.52541/isiri.v38i2.6127

Kamali, M. H. (2008). *Shari'ah law: An introduction.* Simon and Schuster.

Kamali, M. H. (2010). *Environment in Islam* [Paper presentation]. *International Conference on Environment in Islam*, Amman, Jordan.

Kamarzaman, N., Ahmad, A. A., Zain, M. N. M., & Muda, M. Z. (2024). Peranan Wakaf dalam Penggerak Ekonomi Islam bagi Menangani Keterbatasan Dana dalam Penyelidikan dan Inovasi di Sektor Pendidikan TVET [The Role of Waqf in Driving Islamic Economics to Address Funding Limitations in Research and Innovation Within The TVET. *BITARA International Journal of Civilizational Studies and Human Sciences (e-ISSN: 2600-9080), 7*(2), 290–308.

Kamarzaman, N., Mat Zain, M. N., & Azlin Alisa, A. (2025). Funding shortages impact on research and innovation in TVET institutions: A qualitative analysis. *Online Journal for TVET Practitioners, 10*(1), 1–11. DOI: 10.30880/ojtp.2025.10.01.001

Kamil, W. R., Mohd Bakho, S. S., SC, Zhang, W., Aziz, A. A., Reddy, R., & Osman, M. R. (2020, May). Islamic Finance: A Catalyst for Financial Inclusion [pdf]. Kuala Lumpur: Securities Commission Malaysia.

Kamla, R. (2009). Critical insights into contemporary Islamic accounting. *Critical Perspectives on Accounting, 20*(8), 921–932. DOI: 10.1016/j.cpa.2009.01.002

Kang, J., & Park, S. (2022). Commercialization of TVET innovations: The South Korean model for intellectual property management. *The Journal of Technology Transfer, 47*(3), 582–601.

Kanter, A. S. (2014). *The development of disability rights under international law: From charity to human rights.* Routledge. DOI: 10.4324/9780203711712

Karakulah, M., & Muneeza, A. (2024). Exploring the Role of Donation-Based Crowdfunding in Islamic Social Finance. *International Journal of Islamic Economics and Finance Research, 7*(1 July), 42-58.

Karim, R. A. A., & Hossain, M. (2020). The role of sadaqah in community development during crisis: A case study on COVID-19. *Journal of Islamic Finance and Business, 8*(1), 16–27.

Karyanto, B., Aziz, L. H., Yusuf, M., Muzayyanah, M., Putra, A. R., & Darussalam, A. Z. (2021). *Pengantar ekonomi syariah* (Fasa, M. I., Ed.). Widina Bhakti Persada Bandung.

Kasdi, A., Karim, A., Farida, U., & Huda, M. (2022). Development of Waqf in the Middle East and its Role in Pioneering Contemporary Islamic Civilization: A Historical Approach. *Journal of Islamic Thought and Civilization*, *12*(1), 140–153. DOI: 10.32350/jitc.121.10

Kasmon, B., Ibrahim, S. S., Daud, D., Raja Hisham, R. R. I., & Dian Wisika Prajanti, S. (2025). FinTech application in Islamic social finance in Asia region: A systematic literature review. *International Journal of Ethics and Systems*, *41*(1), 213–237. DOI: 10.1108/IJOES-07-2023-0155

Kasmon, B., Ibrahim, S. S., Daud, D., Raja Hisham, R. R. I., & Ratnasari, R. T. (2024). Future behavior in waqf digitalization: Integrating UTAUT and DIT theories. *Journal of Islamic Marketing*. Advance online publication. DOI: 10.1108/JIMA-03-2024-0111

Kasri, N. S., & Hilmi, M. H. (2020). International best practices in existing corporate waqf models: a retrospective–introduction, chapter content, best practices. In *Challenges and Impacts of Religious Endowments on Global Economics and Finance* (pp. 223–253). IGI Global Scientific Publishing. DOI: 10.4018/978-1-7998-1245-6.ch011

Kassim, S., Redzuan, N. H., & Zakariyah, H. (2024). *IMPORTANCE OF FINANCIAL LITERACY AND AWARENESS IN MICROTAKAFUL : IMPLICATIONS FOR INDUSTRY. 2024*.

Kassim, S., & Wulandari, P. (2016). Issues and challenges in financing the poor: Case of Baitul Maal Wa Tamwil in Indonesia. *International Journal of Bank Marketing*, *34*(2), 216–234. DOI: 10.1108/IJBM-01-2015-0007

Kaur, P., Dhir, A., Tandon, A., Alzeiby, E. A., & Abohassan, A. A. (2021). A systematic literature review on cyberstalking. An analysis of past achievements and future promises. *Technological Forecasting and Social Change, 163*(June 2020), 120426. DOI: 10.1016/j.techfore.2020.120426

Kaweesa, Y., Rosman, R., Syahira, S., & Yusoff, M. (2024). Examining the Trend of the Research on Islamic Financial Literacy from 2016-2023: A Bibliometric Review. *Journal of Islamic Finance*, *13*(1), 70–90. https://journals.iium.edu.my/iiibf-journal/index.php/jif/article/view/886

Kazemi, H., & Rahmani, F. (2013). Relationship between information asymmetry and cost of capital. *Management Science Letters*, *3*(1), 321–328. DOI: 10.5267/j.msl.2012.10.026

Khalil, M. (2020). Financial citizenship as a broader democratic context of financial literacy. *Citizenship. Social and Economics Education*, *20*(1), 3–16. DOI: 10.1177/2047173420948411

Khambule, I. (2021). COVID-19 and the counter-cyclical role of the state in South Africa. *Progress in Development Studies*, *21*(4), 380–396. DOI: 10.1177/14649934211030457

Khamis, M. R., Jameelah Hashim, M., & Ab Rahman, A. (2024). Effectiveness Role of zakat in Reducing Income Inequality Among Muslim Society. *Ulum Islamiyyah*, *36*(03), 26–37. DOI: 10.33102/uij.vol36no03.604

Khando, K., Islam, M. S., & Gao, S. (2023). The Emerging Technologies of Digital Payments and Associated Challenges: A Systematic Literature Review. *Future Internet*, *15*(1), 21. Advance online publication. DOI: 10.3390/fi15010021

Khan, L., & Arif, I. (2022). Islamic financial literacy and intention to use Islamic banking: A role of financial considerations. *Journal of Finance and Economics Research*, *7*(1), 47–59. DOI: 10.20547/jfer2207104

Khan, M. (2011). Islamic microfinance and poverty alleviation: A case study of the Islamic Microfinance Network. *Journal of Islamic Economics*, *28*(2), 95–110.

Khan, M. S., Azad, I., Moosa, S., & Javed, M. Y. (2024). Do we really need financial literacy to access the behavioral dynamics of generation Z? A case of Oman. *Heliyon*, *10*(13), e32739. DOI: 10.1016/j.heliyon.2024.e32739

Khan, T., & Badjie, F. (2020). Islamic blended finance for circular economy impactful SMEs to achieve SDGs. *The Singapore Economic Review*, *67*(1), 219–244. DOI: 10.1142/S0217590820420060

Kholisha, N., Purwantob, M. R., Muhammad, S., Mukharromd, T., & Marazi, H. (2020). The significance of Maqasid Syariah principles in improving Islamic economics and finance. *International Journal of Innovation, Creativity and Change*, 13(3).

Khoshakhlagh, M., Amini Milani, M., & Abolhasani Hastiani, A. (2024). Investigating the Impact of Qard al-Hasna (Interest-Free Loan) Facilities on the Misery Index in Iran: An ARDL Approach. *Iranian Journal of Economic Studies*, *12*(2), 531–550. DOI: 10.22099/IJES.2025.52171.1991

Klucarova, S., & He, X. (2023). Cash is the king: Conspicuous consumption and preference for cash payment in restaurants. *Journal of Hospitality and Tourism Management*, *54*, 357–360. Advance online publication. DOI: 10.1016/j.jhtm.2023.01.010

Kock, N. (2015). Common method bias in PLS-SEM: A full collinearity assessment approach. *International Journal of e-Collaboration, 11*(4), 1–10. DOI: 10.4018/ijec.2015100101

Kosim, B., Safitri, E., & Sindi, S. (2021). Pengaruh inklusi keuangan dan peran lembaga keuangan mikro terhadap kinerja UMKM di Kecamatan Seberang Ulu I Kota Palembang. *Motivasi, 6*(2), 144. DOI: 10.32502/mti.v6i2.3797

Koskelainen, T., Kalmi, P., Scornavacca, E., & Vartiainen, T. (2023). Financial literacy in the digital age - A research agenda. *The Journal of Consumer Affairs, 57*(1), 507–528. DOI: 10.1111/joca.12510

Krathwohl, D. R. (2002). A revision of Bloom's taxonomy: An overview. *Theory into Practice, 41*(4), 212–218. DOI: 10.1207/s15430421tip4104_2

Krishnaveni, V., Jusoh, Z. M., Othman, M. A., & Zainudin, N. (2024). Financial security in retirement: The importance of savings vs earnings in Malaysia. *International Journal of Academic Research in Business & Social Sciences, 14*(10), 1671–1683. DOI: 10.6007/IJARBSS/v14-i10/23273

Kunhibava, S., Muneeza, A., Mustapha, Z., Khalid, M., & Kiran, G. (2024). Blockchain Use Case in Islamic Social Finance. *ISRA International Journal of Islamic Finance, 16*(1), 93-110–193 – 110. DOI: 10.55188/ijif.v16i1.659

Kurniawati, Y., Alfin, A., Suseno, F., Hanifa Seftiani, F., Islam Negeri Sjech Djamil Djambek Bukittinggi, U. M., Gurun Aua, J., Putiah, K., Banuhampu, K., Bukittinggi, K., Barat, S., Djambek Bukittinggi, D., & Author, C. (2024). The Role of Ziswaf in Improving Financial Literacy and Reducing Unemployment for Economic Growth. *ICEFS Proceeding, 2*, 102–107. https://doi.org/DOI: 10.30983/iciefs.v2.763

Lahnech, A., & Chami, M. (2025). Exploring the Synergy Between Microfinance and Poverty: A Bibliometric and Comprehensive Systematic Literature Review. *SAGE Open, 15*(2), 21582440251340771. Advance online publication. DOI: 10.1177/21582440251340771

Lahsasna, A. (2016). Framework of Islamic financial education and literacy. *Journal of Wealth Management and Financial Planning, 3*(6), 1–14.

Laldin, M. A., & Furqani, H. (2013). Developing Islamic Finance in the Framework of Maqasid al-Shariah: Understanding the Ends (Maqasid) and the Means (Wasa'il). *International Journal of Islamic and Middle Eastern Finance and Management, 6*(4), 278–289. DOI: 10.1108/IMEFM-05-2013-0057

Lambert, R., Leuz, C., & Verrecchia, R. E. (2007). Accounting information, disclosure, and the cost of capital. *Journal of Accounting Research*, *45*(2), 385–420. DOI: 10.1111/j.1475-679X.2007.00238.x

Latifah, L., Rodoni, A., & Aziz, R. M. (2025). The Empowerment of MSMEs through Islamic P2P Financing: A Value-Based Social Entrepreneurship Framework. [IJIEF]. *International Journal of Islamic Economics and Finance*, *8*(2), 246–267. DOI: 10.18196/IJIEF.V8I2.27985

Law, C. (2024). *Maqasid Al-Shariah And The Sustainable Development Goals In The Practice Of Takaful: An Analysis.* https://conventuslaw.com/report/malaysia-maqasid-al-shariah-and-the-sustainable-development-goals-in-the-practice-of-takaful-an-analysis/

Lee, K. C. (1997). The Malaysian government pension scheme. Whither its future direction? *Jurnal Ekonomi Malaysia*, *31*, 87–106.

Lee, Y. Y., Gan, C. L., & Liew, T. W. (2023). Do E-wallets trigger impulse purchases? An analysis of Malaysian Gen-Y and Gen-Z consumers. *Journal of Marketing Analytics*, *11*(2), 244–261. DOI: 10.1057/s41270-022-00164-9

Lin, C. A., & Bates, T. C. (2022). Smart people know how the economy works: Cognitive ability, economic knowledge and financial literacy. *Intelligence*, *93*, 101667. DOI: 10.1016/j.intell.2022.101667

Lisa, O., Nugroho, L., Ildiko, O., Utami, W., & Nugraha, E. (2023). The performance of Islamic microfinance institutions in the COVID-19 pandemic: Is asset quality important? *Sosyoekonomi*, *31*(58), 145–160. DOI: 10.17233/sosyoekonomi.2023.04.07

Littlefield, E., & Kneiding, C. (2009). The Global Financial. *Crisis*, *52*, 1–8.

Liu, J., Chen, Y., Chen, X., & Chen, B. (2024). Digital financial inclusion and household financial vulnerability: An empirical analysis of rural and urban disparities in China. *Heliyon*, *10*(15), e35540. DOI: 10.1016/j.heliyon.2024.e35540 PMID: 39170403

Liu, T., Fan, M., Li, Y., & Yue, P. (2024). Financial Literacy and Household Financial Resilience. *Finance Research Letters*, *63*, 105378. DOI: 10.1016/j.frl.2024.105378

Luntajo, M. M. R., & Hasan, F. (2023). Optimalisasi Potensi Pengelolaan Zakat di Indonesia melalui Integrasi Teknologi. *Al-'Aqdu. Journal of Islamic Economics Law*, *3*(1), 14–28.

Lusardi, A. (2015). Financial literacy: Do people know the ABCs of finance? *Public Understanding of Science (Bristol, England)*, *24*(3), 260–271. DOI: 10.1177/0963662514564516

Lusardi, A., & Mitchell, O. S. (2011). Financial literacy around the world: An overview. *Journal of Pension Economics and Finance*, *10*(4), 497–508. DOI: 10.1017/S1474747211000448

Lusardi, A., & Mitchell, O. S. (2014). The economic importance of financial literacy: Theory and evidence. American Economic Journal. *Journal of Economic Literature*, *52*(1), 5–44. DOI: 10.1257/jel.52.1.5

Lusardi, A., & Mitchell, O. S. (2017). How Ordinary Consumers Make Complex Economic Decisions: Financial Literacy and Retirement Readiness. *The Quarterly Journal of Finance*, *7*(3), 1750008. Advance online publication. DOI: 10.1142/S2010139217500082

Lu, Z., Wu, J., Li, H., & Galloway, B. (2024). Digital finance and stock market participation: The case of internet wealth management products in China. *Economic Systems*, *48*(1), 101148. DOI: 10.1016/j.ecosys.2023.101148

MacCallum, R. C., Widaman, K. F., Zhang, S., & Hong, S. (1999). Sample size in factor analysis. *Psychological Methods*, *4*(1), 84–99. DOI: 10.1037/1082-989X.4.1.84

Madani, R. I., Nurhidayati, N., & Thomafy, K. (2024). Examining The Potential of Cash Waqf and Development Model. *Munazzama: Journal of Islamic Management and Pilgrimage*, *4*(2), 83–103.

Maduku, D. K., & Mbeya, S. (2024). Understanding family takaful purchase behaviour: The roles of religious obligation and gender. *Journal of Financial Services Marketing*, *29*(2), 440–458. DOI: 10.1057/s41264-023-00213-z

Mahayudin, Y. (2004). *Tamadun Islam*. Penerbit Fajar Bakti Sdn.Bhd.

Mahdzan, N. S., Zainudin, R., & Au, S. F. (2017). The adoption of Islamic banking services in Malaysia. *Journal of Islamic Marketing*, *8*(3), 496–512. DOI: 10.1108/JIMA-08-2015-0064

Mahdzan, N. S., Zainudin, R., Wan Ahmad, W. M., & Hanifa, M. H. (2024). Does Islamic financial literacy and motives influence the holdings of Islamic financial products? A study on bank customers in Klang Valley, Malaysia. *Journal of Islamic Marketing*, *15*(9), 2286–2309. DOI: 10.1108/JIMA-05-2022-0158

Mahmud, M. S., Foziah, N. H. M., Abdul Kareem, I. A., Jamal, A., & Nasir, M. (2021). Retirement planning in perspective of Islamic wealth management. *Journal of Islamic Banking & Finance*, *38*(1).

Maîtrot, M. (2018). Understanding social performance: A 'practice drift' at the frontline of microfinance institutions in Bangladesh. *Development and Change*, *50*(3), 623–654. DOI: 10.1111/dech.12398

Malaysia., G. of. (2021). *Twelfth Malaysia Plan, 2021-2025: Sustainable growth for Malaysia's future.*

Malaysian Qualifications Agency. (2022). *TVET Quality Assurance Framework.* MQA.

Malaysian Science and Technology Information Centre. (2025). *Research and development (R&D) indicators.* Ministry of Science, Technology and Innovation. https://mastic.mosti.gov.my/statistic/research-and-development-rd-indicators/

Malaysian Technology Development Corporation. (2023). *Commercialization Pathways for Technical Innovation in Malaysia.* MTDC.

Mancone, S., Tosti, B., Corrado, S., Spica, G., Zanon, A., & Diotaiuti, P. (2024). Youth, money, and behavior: the impact of financial literacy programs. *Frontiers in Education, 9*(2014). DOI: 10.3389/feduc.2024.1397060

Maniam, S. (2024). Determinants of Islamic Fintech Adoption: A Systematic Literature Review. *Journal of Islamic Marketing*, *15*(11), 2916–2936. DOI: 10.1108/JIMA-11-2023-0373

Mansori, S., Safari, M., & Mohd Ismail, Z. M. (2020). An analysis of the religious, social factors and income's influence on the decision making in Islamic microfinance schemes. *Journal of Islamic Accounting and Business Research, 11*(2), 361–376. DOI: 10.1108/JIABR-03-2016-0035

Mansor, M., Sabri, M. F., Mansur, M., Ithnin, M., Magli, A. S., Husniyah, A. R., Mahdzan, N. S., Othman, M. A., Zakaria, R. H., Satar, N. M., & Janor, H. (2022). Analysing the predictors of financial stress and financial well-being among the bottom 40 percent (B40) households in Malaysia. *International Journal of Environmental Research and Public Health, 19*(19), 12490. Advance online publication. DOI: 10.3390/ijerph191912490

Mansour, W., & Jlassi, M. (2014). The effect of religion on financial and investing decisions investor behavior. *The Psychology Of Financial Planning And Investing*, 135-151.

Maravilla, V. S.Jr, & Flores, G. (2025). Entrepreneurial competency, resilience, and financial literacy: Drivers of sustainable performance in SMEs for societal welfare. *Journal of Sustainability, Society, and Eco-Welfare*, *2*(2), 159–176. DOI: 10.61511/jssew.v2i2.2025.1374

Marwah, A., Sapa, N. bin, & Syatar, A. (2025). Integrating Maqashid al-Shariah into Islamic Economic Practices: A Contemporary Analytical Framework and Its Applications. *El-Kahfi | Journal of Islamic Economics, 6*(01), 36–44. https://doi.org/DOI: 10.58958/ELKAHFI.V6I01.456

Masrizal, S., Sukmana, R., & Trianto, B. (2024). The effect of Islamic financial literacy on business performance with emphasis on the role of Islamic financial inclusion: Case study in Indonesia. *Journal of Islamic Marketing*, *16*(1), 166–192. DOI: 10.1108/JIMA-07-2022-0197

Mat, M., Shamsuddin, J., Sitiris, M., Yunus, S. M., Abu, A. H., & Kulliyyah, S. (2022). E-Wallet in Malaysia: A Proposed Structure of Contracts According to The Juristic Adaptation (Takyif Fiqhi). *Malaysian Journal Of Islamic Studies (MJIS), 6*(2), 15–37. https://journal.unisza.edu.my/mjis/index.php/mjis/article/view/203

Maulida, S., & Ali, M. M. (2023). Maqasid shariah index: A literature review. *Maqasid al-Shariah Review*, 2(1).

Maulina, R., Dhewanto, W., & Faturohman, T. (2023). The Integration of Islamic Social and Commercial Finance (IISCF): Systematic Literature Review, Bibliometric Analysis, Conceptual Framework, and Future Research Opportunities. *Heliyon*, *9*(11), e21612. DOI: 10.1016/j.heliyon.2023.e21612

McKee, M., & Stuckler, D. (2020). If the world fails to protect the economy, COVID-19 will damage health not just now but also in the future. *Nature Medicine*, *26*(5), 640–642. DOI: 10.1038/s41591-020-0863-y PMID: 32273610

Md Husin, M., & Ab Rahman, A. (2013). What drives consumers to participate into family Takaful schemes? A literature review. *Journal of Islamic Marketing*, *4*(3), 264–280. DOI: 10.1108/JIMA-04-2012-0019

MD Said, M.H., & Jumri, M.F. (2017). *Tamadun Islam*: Politeknik Port Dickson, Negeri Sembilan. h.h. 60.

Mightyn, A., Nugroho, L., & Hidayah, N. (2022). Kajian usaha pemerintah dalam mempertahankan keberlangsungan UMKM di masa pandemi Covid-19. *Jurnal Cakrawala Ilmiah*, *2*(4), 1553–1564. DOI: 10.53625/jcijurnalcakrawalailmiah.v2i4.4281

Milosevic, D., & Kanter, R. (2019). Collaborative Advantage: The Art of Alliances. *Harvard Business Review*, *72*(4), 97–101.

Ministry of Education Malaysia. (2015). *Malaysia Education Blueprint 2015–2025 (Higher Education).* Ministry of Education Malaysia. https://www.kooperation-international.de/uploads/media/3._Malaysia_Education_Blueprint_2015-2025__Higher_Education__.pdf

Ministry of Finance Indonesia. (2022). *Green Sukuk Allocation and Impact Report.* Ministry of Finance of the Republic of Indonesia.

Ministry of Finance Malaysia. (2024, October 26). *AKPK reports 53,000 under-30s owe RM1.9 billion – Amir Hamzah.* https://www.mof.gov.my/portal/en/news/press-citations/akpk-reports-53-000-under-30s-owe-rm1-9-bln-amir-hamzah

Ministry of Finance Malaysia. (2025, January 8). *AKPK benefits 1.4 million individuals as at December 2024: MoF.* https://www.mof.gov.my/portal/en/news/press-citations/akpk-benefits-1-4-million-individuals-as-at-december-2024-mof

Ministry of Finance Malaysia. M. (2024, January 9). *eMADANI | Portal Manfaat.* Ministry of Finance Malaysia. https://manfaat.mof.gov.my/individu/emadani

Ministry of Higher Education. (2023). *Research Grant Distribution Report 2022.* MOHE.

Ministry of Human Resources. (2023). *Technical and Vocational Education and Training Report 2023.* MOHR.

Miroshnychenko, I., Torres de Oliveira, R., De Massis, A., & Überbacher, R. (2024). Family Involvement and Firm Performance: A Worldwide Study Unveiling Key Mechanisms. *Family Business Review*, *37*(4), 449–475. DOI: 10.1177/08944865241290856

Mishra, D., Kandpal, V., Agarwal, N., & Kumar, R. singh, R., Priyadarshi, N., & Twala, B. (2024). Digital and Financial Literacy for Uplifting Women and Achieving Sustainable Development Goals. *F1000Research 2024 13:1364, 13*, 1364. DOI: 10.12688/f1000research.156744.1

Modigliani, F., & Brumberg, R. (1954). Utility analysis and the consumption function: An interpretation of cross-section data. *Franco Modigliani*, *1*(1), 388–436.

Mohamad, M., & Saravanamuttu, J. (2015). Islamic banking and finance: Sacred alignment, strategic alliances. *Pacific Affairs*, *88*(2), 193–213. DOI: 10.5509/2015882193

Mohamad, N., Affandi, H. M., Sohimi, N. E., Kamal, M. F. M., Herrera, L. M., Zulkifli, R. M., & Abas, N. H. (2023). Exploring TVET Institution Directors' Barriers in Managing Malaysian TVET Institutions-Industry Partnership. *Journal of Technical Education and Training*, *15*(1), 277–287. DOI: 10.30880/jtet.2023.15.01.024

Mohamad, S., Othman, J., Lehner, O., & Muda, R. (2017). Social sukuk: A new mechanism to fund social services. *Journal of Emerging Economies & Islamic Research*, *5*(1), 1–13. DOI: 10.24191/jeeir.v5i1.6252

Mohamed, H. A., & Otake, T. (2025). The role of Islamic FinTech in digital financial inclusion and sustainable development post covid-19: Cross-country analysis. *International Journal of Islamic and Middle Eastern Finance and Management*, *18*(3), 649–671. DOI: 10.1108/IMEFM-02-2024-0100

Mohammadi, S., & Esmaeilioghaz, H. (2017). A Study of the Impact of Accounting Information Quality and Information Asymmetry on Underinvestment in Iran. *Journal of Industrial Distribution & Business*, *8*(1), 33–39. DOI: 10.13106/ijidb.2017.vol8.no1.33.

Mohapatra, N., Das, M., Shekhar, S., Singh, R., Khan, S., Tewari, L. M., Félix, M. J., & Santos, G. (2025). Assessing the Role of Financial Literacy in FinTech Adoption by MSEs: Ensuring Sustainability Through a Fuzzy AHP Approach. *Sustainability 2025, Vol. 17, Page 4340*, *17*(10), 4340. DOI: 10.3390/su17104340

Mohd Ali, A.N., Yeon, A.L., & Hussain, M.A. (2016), Private retirement scheme in Malaysia: Legal analysis. *International Journal of Economics and Financial Issues*, 6(7) Special Issue, 290–295.

Mohd Noor, A. (2021). Industry-academia collaboration through CREST: Impacts on TVET research funding in Malaysia. *Malaysian Journal of Technical Studies*, *8*(2), 112–129.

Mohiuddin, M. (2017). Islamic social enterprises in Bangladesh: Conceptual and institutional challenges. *International Journal of Islamic and Middle Eastern Finance and Management*, *10*(2), 246–263. DOI: 10.1108/IMEFM-09-2015-0103

Mohsin, M. I. A. (2013). Financing through cash-waqf: a revitalization to finance different needs. *International Journal of Islamic and Middle Eastern finance and management*, *6*(4), 304-321.

Mokhtar, N., Sabri, M. F., Ho, C. S. F., & Dass, T. A. M. (2018). Profile and differences in financial literacy: Empirical evidence. *Malaysian Journal of Consumer and Family Economics*, *21*, 164–185. http://psasir.upm.edu.my/id/eprint/73653/

Muflih, M., Iswanto, B., & Purbayati, R. (2024). Green loyalty of Islamic banking customers: Combined effect of green practices, green trust, green perceived value, and green satisfaction. *International Journal of Ethics and Systems, 40*(3), 477–494. DOI: 10.1108/IJOES-03-2023-0062

Muhammad, A. A., Shariff, I. A., & Umar, A. (2023). The Impact of Islamic Models of Zakat and Waqf in Reducing Poverty Among Vulnerables During The Pandemic Era in Bauchi State, Nigeria. *AZKA International Journal of Zakat & Social Finance, 4*(1), 69–90. Advance online publication. DOI: 10.51377/azjaf.vol4no1.143

Mujiatun, S., Trianto, B., Cahyono, E. F., & Rahmayati. (2023). The Impact of Marketing Communication and Islamic Financial Literacy on Islamic Financial Inclusion and MSMEs Performance: Evidence from Halal Tourism in Indonesia. *Sustainability 2023, Vol. 15, Page 9868, 15*(13), 9868. DOI: 10.3390/su15139868

Muslim ibn al- ajjāj. (n.d.). *a ī Muslim*, Hadith no. 1619.

Mustaffa, J., Isa, M. Y. B. M., & Mohammed, Z. (2022). Governance structures: Dependability and efficiency of the waqf institutional system in Malaysia. *Journal of Economics and Business Aseanomics, 7*(2), 058-070.

Mustapha, F., & Hasbullah, M. (2021). Kemasukkan Sains dan Teknologi dari Barat ke dalam Kerajaan Uthmaniyah pada Abad ke-18 dan Abad ke-19: Satu Penilaian Sejarah. *Journal of History Department, 30*(1), 20–42.

Muthmainnatun, A. T., Nugroho, L., & Sugiarti, D. (2022). Analisa prosedur penyaluran pembiayaan murabahah pada lembaga keuangan mikro syariah (Studi kasus pada BMT Syarif Hidayatullah Gunungwungkal). *Jurnal Cakrawala Ilmiah, 2*(3), 1121–1129. DOI: 10.53625/jcijurnalcakrawalailmiah.v2i3.4111

Mutmainah, L. L., Nurwahidin, N., & Huda, N. (2025). Optimizing productive waqf for halal tourism development. *Journal of Islamic Accounting and Business Research.*

Mydigital Investment Office. (2023). *Islamic Digital Economy - Driving Investments Through Islamic Digital Economy*. Retrieved from https://mydigitalinvestment.gov.my/islamic-digital-economy

Nanda, A. P., & Banerjee, R. (2021). Consumer's subjective financial well-being: A systematic review and research agenda. *International Journal of Consumer Studies, 45*(4), 750–776. Advance online publication. DOI: 10.1111/ijcs.12668

Napitupulu, R. M., Sukmana, R., & Rusydiana, A. S. (2024). Governance of Islamic Social Finance: Learnings from Existing Literature. *International Journal of Islamic and Middle Eastern Finance and Management, 17*(3), 552–571. DOI: 10.1108/IMEFM-06-2023-0222

Nasdaq Dubai. (2019). Majid Al Futtaim lists world's first benchmark corporate Green Sukuk on Nasdaq Dubai. https://www.nasdaqdubai.com/exchange/media/press-releases/majid-al-futtaim-lists-worlds-first-

Nasira, N. F., Roslin, R. M., Nasir, M. N. F., Nasir, M. F., Nasir, M. A., & Mohamed, N. A. (2021). Investigating Knowledge as a Possible Predictor of Purchase Intention among Muslims in Malaysia for Life Insurance and Takaful. *International Journal of Academic Research in Business & Social Sciences, 11*(2), 727–740. DOI: 10.6007/IJARBSS/v11-i2/8880

Nasution, S. (2002). *Sejarah Peradaban Islam*, Yayasan Pustaka Riau: Riau, h.h. 102.

Nasution, A. M. (2020). Pengelolaan Zakat Di Indonesia. *Journal of Islamic Social Finance Management, 1*(2), 293–305. DOI: 10.24952/jisfim.v1i2.3589

Nawi, H. M., & Hussin, H. S. (2020). A good cop is never cold or hungry: Antecedents and consequences of financial literacy among members of the royal Malaysia police, International *Journal of Academic Research in Accounting. Finance and Management Sciences, 10*(1), 270–289.

Nawi, H. M., Siong, O. H., Tanaraj, K., Sapiai, N. S., Nee, C. Y., & Jusoh, M. A. (2024). Visualising the research landscape on financial issues among special needs children: A bibliometric analysis from 1992 to 2024. *Edelweiss Applied Science and Technology, 8*(6), 5214–5235. DOI: 10.55214/25768484.v8i6.3146

Nayan, M.A., and Othman, Y.H. (2019). The Important of Islamic Retirement Planning in Malaysia. Unishams-INTERNATIONAL CONFERENCE 2019/ E-PROCEEDINGS

Netemeyer, R. G., Warmath, D., Fernandes, D., & Lynch, J. G.Jr. (2018). How Am I Doing? Perceived Financial Well-Being, Its Potential Antecedents, and Its Relation to Overall Well-Being. *The Journal of Consumer Research, 45*(1), 68–89. DOI: 10.1093/jcr/ucx109

Ningrat, R. G., & Nurzaman, M. S. (2019). Developing Fintech and Islamic Finance Products in Agricultural Value Chain. *Journal of Islamic Monetary Economics and Finance, 5*(3), 491–516. DOI: 10.21098/jimf.v5i3.1077

Noordin, K. A., Ahmad, S., Ismail, Z., & Wahid, H. (2022). Regulatory challenges in international waqf transactions: A comparative analysis. *International Journal of Islamic and Middle Eastern Finance and Management, 15*(3), 356–371.

Nopiardo, W. (2019). Perkembangan Peraturan Tentang Zakat Di Indonesia. [Jurnal Ilmiah Syariah]. *JURIS, 18*(1), 65–76. DOI: 10.31958/juris.v18i1.1369

Nor, S. M., Yaacob, S. E., Rahman, A. A., & Zainal, H. (2024). Digitizing zakat Distribution in Malaysia: A Case Study on Application Process at Kedah State zakat Board. *Samarah: Jurnal Hukum Keluarga dan Hukum Islam, 8*(3), 1901-1927.

Nouman, M., Siddiqi, M. F., Ullah, K., & Jan, S. (2021). Nexus between higher ethical objectives (Maqasid Al Shari'ah) and participatory finance. *Qualitative Research in Financial Markets, 13*(2), 226–251. DOI: 10.1108/QRFM-06-2020-0092

Nugraha, A. L., & Sudrajad, O. Y. (2025). *Pesantrenpreneur: The Fusion of Piety, Profit and Progress*. Islamic Bussiness Review. https://islamicbr.com/read_article/pesantrenpreneur-the-fusion-of-piety-profit-and-progress

Nugraheni, P., & Widyani, F. N. (2021). A study of intention to save in Islamic banks: The perspective of Muslim students. *Journal of Islamic Marketing, 12*(8), 1446–1460. DOI: 10.1108/JIMA-11-2019-0233

Nugroho, L. (2014). Challenges sharia microfinance institutions: Evidence from Indonesia. *EJIF – European Journal of Islamic Finance, 3*, 1–6. http://www.ojs.unito.it/index.php/EJIF/article/view/793/766

Nugroho, L., & Chowdhury, S. L. K. (2015). Mobile banking for empowerment Muslim women entrepreneur: Evidence from Asia (Indonesia and Bangladesh). *Tazkia Islamic Finance and Business Review, 9*(1), 83–100. https://tifbr-tazkia.org/index.php/TIFBR/article/view/79

Nugroho, L., Melzatia, S., & Indriawati, F. Nurhasanah, & Safira. (2022). *Lembaga keuangan syariah dari konsep ke praktik*. Widina Bhakti Persada. https://books.google.co.id/books?id=w4uREAAAQBAJ

Nugroho, L., Suganda, A. D., Febrianty, F., Hamid, M. A. L., Ihwanudin, N., & Trimulato, T. (2020). *Pengantar perbankan syariah*. Widina Bhakti Persada Bandung. www.penerbitwidina.com

Nugroho, L. (2014). Challenges sharia microfinance institutions: Evidence from Indonesia. *European Journal of Islamic Finance, 1*, 1–6. http://www.ojs.unito.it/index.php/EJIF

Nugroho, L. (2015). Islamics principles versus green microfinance. *European Journal of Islamic Finance, 3*, 1–10. http://www.ojs.unito.it/index.php/EJIF

Nugroho, L. (2022). The relationship between maqasid sharia and profitability ratio in Islamic banking industries performance. *Sosyoekonomi, 30*(53), 243–259. DOI: 10.17233/sosyoekonomi.2022.03.13

Nugroho, L., Badawi, A., Hidayah, N., & Ahmad, N. (2020). Pancasila (five principles of Indonesia nation) snapshot in customer deposit of Islamic bank (religion, age and gender perspective of Bank Mandiri Syariah). *Journal of Research in Business*, *5*(1), 74–95. https://dergipark.org.tr/en/pub/jrb/issue/55478/670229. DOI: 10.35333/JRB.2020.177

Nugroho, L., Mor, S., Iskandar, D., Setiany, E., Asih, D., & Mellin, F. (2024). The urgency of digitalization vis-a-vis business trends (Indonesia case). In *Proceeding International Annual Conference Economics* (pp. 1–13). Management, Business, and Accounting., https://proceeding.inacemba.org/index.php/eproceeding-inacemba/article/view/1

Nuraini, I. (2022). Analysis of Zakat Management Performance Based on The National Zakat Index Approach: A Case Study. *Islamic Social Finance, 2*(2).

O'Cass, A. (2004). Fashion clothing consumption: Antecedents and consequences of fashion clothing involvement. *European Journal of Marketing*, *38*(7), 869–882. DOI: 10.1108/03090560410539294

Obaidullah, M. (2019). *Islamic Social Finance Report 2019: Current Trends and Future Pathways*. Islamic Research and Training Institute (IRTI), IDB Group.

Obaidullah, M., & Khan, T. (2008). Islamic Microfinance Development: Challenges and Initiatives. In *Islamic Research & Training institute Policy Dialogue Paper, (2)*. (Issue 2).

Obaidullah, M., Shirazi, N. S., Muljawan, D. S., & Izhar, H. (2014). Islamic Social Finance Report 2014.

Obaidullah, M. (2015). Enhancing Food Security with Islamic Microfinance: Insights from Some Recent Experiments. *Agricultural Finance Review*, *75*(2), 142–168. DOI: 10.1108/AFR-11-2014-0033

Obaidullah, M. (2021). *Islamic Social Finance for Climate Resilience: A Framework for Action*. Islamic Development Bank Institute.

Obaidullah, M., & Khan, T. (2008). *Islamic Microfinance Development: Challenges and Initiatives*. Islamic Research and Training Institute.

OECD. (2011). *Measuring financial literacy: Questionnaire and guidance notes for conducting an internationally comparable survey of financial literacy*. International Network on Financial Education.

OECD. (2020). *Developing Sustainable Finance Definitions and Taxonomies, Green Finance and Investment*. OECD Publishing.

OECD. (2023). *Increasing Development Finance Efforts to Scale Private Finance Mobilised and Its Impact.* https://www.oecd.org/en/publications/increasing-development-finance-efforts-to-scale-private-finance-mobilised-and-its-impact_345b768b-en/full-report/component-2.html

OECD. (2025). Vocational education and training systems in nine countries: Germany. OECD Publishing. https://www.oecd.org/en/publications/vocational-education-and-training-systems-in-nine-countries_1a86eb6c-en/full-report/vocational-education-and-training-in-germany_dae78944.html

OECD/INFE. (2021). *Supporting the financial resilience of citizens throughout the COVID-19 crisis.* Organisation for Economic Co-operation and Development. https://www.oecd.org/financial /education/ supporting-the-financial-resilience-of-citizens-throughout-the-covid-19-crisis-38a2ffd5-en.htm

OJK. (2022). *Survei Nasional Literasi dan Inklusi Keuangan Tahun 2022.* https://ojk.go.id/id/berita-dan-kegiatan/siaran-pers/Pages/Survei-Nasional-Literasi-dan-Inklusi-Keuangan-Tahun-2022.aspx

Oliver, R. L. (1980). A cognitive model of the antecedents and consequences of satisfaction decisions. *JMR, Journal of Marketing Research, 17*(4), 460–469. DOI: 10.1177/002224378001700405

Omar, N., & Khairi, K. F. (2021). Zakat and Blockchain: A Review. *International Journal of Islamic Economics and Finance Research, 4*(2 December), 60–66. DOI: 10.53840/ijiefer53

Ooi, K. B., & Tan, G. W. H. (2016). Mobile technology acceptance model: An investigation using mobile users to explore smartphone credit card. *Expert Systems with Applications, 59*, 33–46. Advance online publication. DOI: 10.1016/j.eswa.2016.04.015

Osman, I., Syed Alwi, S. F., Rehman, M. A., Muda, R., Hassan, F., Hassan, R., & Abdullah, H. (2024). The dilemma of millennial Muslims towards financial management: An Islamic financial literacy perspective. *Journal of Islamic Marketing, 15*(1), 59–78. DOI: 10.1108/JIMA-09-2021-0283

Othman, M. N. A., Rashid, M. A. A., Maura, A. A., & Seman, S. A. (2024). Factors influencing the retirement planning among private sector workers in Malaysia. *Journal of Ecohumanism, 3*(7), 1141–1153I. DOI: 10.62754/joe.v3i7.4283

Ouachani, S., Belhassine, O., & Kammoun, A. (2021). Measuring financial literacy: A literature review. *Managerial Finance, 47*(2), 266–281. DOI: 10.1108/MF-04-2019-0175

Ozili, P. K. (2023). Impact of Monetary Policy on Financial Inclusion in Emerging Markets. *Journal of Risk and Financial Management, 16*(7), 303. Advance online publication. DOI: 10.3390/jrfm16070303

Panos, G. A., & Wilson, J. O. S. (2020). Financial literacy and responsible finance in the FinTech era: Capabilities and challenges. *European Journal of Finance, 26*(4–5), 297–301. DOI: 10.1080/1351847X.2020.1717569

Pati, A. P. (2021). Structural Transformation, Profit and Cost: What Drive(s) Mission Drift in Indian Microfinance? *International Journal of Rural Management, 17*(1), 75–92. DOI: 10.1177/0973005220967223

Penang Institute. (2023). *TVET in Malaysia: Current situation, challenges and recommendations*. Penang Institute. https://penanginstitute.org/publications/issues/tvet-in-malaysia-current-situation-challenges-and-recommendations/

Penrose, E. T. (1952). Biological analogies in the theory of the firm. *The American Economic Review, 42*(5), 804–819.

Peterson, T. L. (2018). Future care planning by older grandparents raising adolescent grandchildren. *Families in Society, 99*(1), 67–77. DOI: 10.1177/1044389418756615

Podsakoff, P. M., MacKenzie, S. B., Lee, J.-Y., & Podsakoff, N. P. (2003). Common method biases in behavioral research: A critical review of the literature and recommended remedies. *The Journal of Applied Psychology, 88*(5), 879–903. DOI: 10.1037/0021-9010.88.5.879

Pokharel, J., & Maharjan, I. (2024). Financial Behavior of Generation Z and Millennials. *Journal of Emerging Management Studies, 1*(2), 148–170. DOI: 10.3126/jems.v1i2.71522

Potrich, A. C. G., Viera, K. M., & Silva, W. M. D. (2016). Development of a financial literacy model for university students. *Management Research Review, 39*(3), 356–376. DOI: 10.1108/MRR-06-2014-0143

Prabhakaran, S., & Mynavathi, L. (2025). Does Fintech Usage Alter the Relationships Between Financial Literacy, Behaviour and Well-Being? Evidence from India. *Organizations and Markets in Emerging Economies, 16*(1(32)), 133–154. DOI: 10.15388/omee.2025.16.6

Prasetyo, A., Effendi, J., & Nursyamsiah, T. (2018). The Effectiveness of Islamic Microfinance Distribution on Microbusiness Owner's Poverty Alleviation (Case Study: BMT Bina Masyarakat Purworejo). *Jurnal AFKARUNA, 14*(1), 1–26. DOI: 10.18196/AIIJIS.2018.0078.1-26

Prasojo, S. L., & Muhfiatun. (2024). Harmonizing Sustainable Development Goals and Maqasid Shariah: A Strategic Framework for Indonesian Islamic Banks (Case Study on Bank Syariah Indonesia). *Journal of Islamic Finance, 13*(2), 106–117. https://journals.iium.edu.my/iiibf-journal/index.php/jif/article/view/928

Preacher, K. J., & Hayes, A. F. (2008). Asymptotic and resampling strategies for assessing and comparing indirect effects in multiple mediator models. *Behavior Research Methods*, *40*(3), 879–891. Advance online publication. DOI: 10.3758/BRM.40.3.879

Private Pension Administrator Malaysia. (2025, June 14). *PPA.my*. https://www.ppa.my

Purwanti, T., Ristiyana, R., Libriantono, B., Widayati, T., Budiman, N. A., & Nugroho, L. (2022). *UMKM membangun ekonomi kreatif.* Global Eksekutif Teknologi. https://books.google.co.id/books?id=IaqmEAAAQBAJ

Pusat Pungutan Zakat - Majlis Agama Islam Wilayah Persekutuan. (2023). *Laporan Tahunan 2023*. Pusat Pungutan Zakat Wilayah Persekutuan.

Pusparini, M. D. (2023). Maqasid Sharia-Based Financial Plan to Prevent Conspicuous Consumption Among Muslim Household. *Al-Tijary*, *8*(1), 15–30. DOI: 10.21093/at.v8i1.5040

Puspitasari, I., Wiambodo, A. N. R., & Soeparman, P. (2021). The impact of expectation confirmation, technology compatibility, and customer's acceptance on e-wallet continuance intention. *AIP Conference Proceedings*, *2329*, 050012. Advance online publication. DOI: 10.1063/5.0042269

Qur'an. (n.d.)... *Surah Al-A zāb*, (33), 72.

Qur'an. (n.d.)... *Surah Al-Baqarah*, (2), 261.

Qur'an. (n.d.)... *Surah Al-Furqān*, (25), 67.

Qur'an. (n.d.)... *Surah Al-Isrā*, (17), 26–27.

Qur'an. (n.d.)... *Surah Al-Mā'idah*, (5), 2.

Qur'an. (n.d.)... *Surah An-Nisā*, (4), 11.

Qutaiba, M., Owais, M., & Muharam, A. S. (2024). The current issue of reporting zakat in Indonesia: A critical analysis. *Journal of Islamic Economic and Business Research*, *4*(1), 1–25. DOI: 10.18196/jiebr.v4i1.227

Rabinovich, A., Morton, T., & Postmes, T. (2010). Time perspective and attitude-behaviour consistency in future-oriented behaviors. *British Journal of Social Psychology*, *49*(1), 69–89. DOI: 10.1348/014466608X401875

Rachman, R., & Nugroho, L. (2024). Understanding the drivers of customer interest in Islamic banks in Bali: Challenges and strategic solutions. In *International Seminar Conference of Economics and Business Excellence* (pp. 61–67). DOI: 10.33830/iscebe.v1i1.3604

Radelet, S., & Sachs, J. (1998). *The onset of the East Asian financial crisis* (No. w6680).

Rafiki, A. Syahrial, H., & Andika, S. (2024). A Review on Digital Zakat Management Research. *Information Management and Business Review*, 16(3)(S): 167-174.

Rahardja, U., Sigalingging, C. T., Putra, P. O. H., Nizar Hidayanto, A., & Phusavat, K. (2023). The Impact of Mobile Payment Application Design and Performance Attributes on Consumer Emotions and Continuance Intention. *SAGE Open*, *13*(1), 1–18. DOI: 10.1177/21582440231151919

Rahayu, N. W. I., Rahayu, N. W. I., Al Ahsani, N., Suroyya, D., & Yudiawan, A. (2025). A Bibliometric Analysis of Blockchain-Based Zakat System Design: Solutions for Transparency and Oversight of Zakat Funds in the Digital Era. *Academic Journal of Interdisciplinary Studies*, *14*(1), 346. DOI: 10.36941/ajis-2025-0023

Rahim, N., Bakri, M. H., Fianto, B. A., Zainal, N., & Hussein Al Shami, S. A. (2023). Measurement and structural modelling on factors of Islamic Fintech adoption among millennials in Malaysia. *Journal of Islamic Marketing*, *14*(6), 1463–1487. DOI: 10.1108/JIMA-09-2020-0279

Rahim, S. H. A., Rashid, R. A., & Hamed, A. B. (2016). Islamic financial literacy and its determinants among university students: An exploratory factor analysis. *International Journal of Economics and Financial Issues*, *6*(7), 32–35. DOI: 10.15405/epsbs.2016.08.58

Rahman, M. H., Abdullah, M. F., Osmani, N. M., & Aziz, N. S. Z. (2024). Application of tàawun (mutual assistance) in cross-subsidisation of surplus among different takaful operators: An exploratory study in Malaysia. *International Journal of Islamic and Middle Eastern Finance and Management*, *17*(6), 1136–1154. DOI: 10.1108/IMEFM-12-2023-0479

Rahman, S. A., Tajudin, A., & Tajuddin, A. F. A. (2018). The significance of Islamic financial literacy among youth in Malaysia. *International Journal of Business and Management Invention*, *7*(10), 27–31.

Rahman, Z. A., & Abdullah, A. (2023). From innovation to commercialization: Challenges and opportunities for Malaysian TVET institutions. *International Journal of Technology and Vocational Education, 12*(1), 34–52.

Rahman, Z. A., & Ahmad, S. (2023). Waqf-linked sukuk for TVET infrastructure development: Structural analysis and performance metrics. *Journal of Islamic Monetary Economics and Finance, 9*(1), 123–142.

Rahman, Z. A., & Haneef, M. A. (2020). Comparative analysis of waqf regulations: A study of Malaysia, Indonesia and GCC countries. *Islamic Economic Studies, 28*(1), 55–74.

Raimi, L., Abdur-Rauf, I. A., & Ashafa, S. A. (2024). Does Islamic Sustainable Finance Support Sustainable Development Goals to Avert Financial Risk in the Management of Islamic Finance Products? A Critical Literature Review. *Journal of Risk and Financial Management 2024, Vol. 17, Page 236, 17*(6), 236. DOI: 10.3390/jrfm17060236

Ramdhani, A. F., Mulyana, R., & Afendi, F. M. (2022). Analysis Of Factors Influencing The Cash Waqf Receiving: Electronic Money Transaction. *Journal of Islamic Economics. Finance and Accounting Studies, 1*(1), 1–17.

Ramli, F. A. A. (2021). Mobile payment and e-wallet adoption in emerging economies: A systematic literature review. *Journal of Emerging Economies and Islamic Research, 9*(2), 1–39.

Rantaprasaja, L. (2025). Economic Empowerment Through Islamic Financial Inclusion: The Strategic Role of Universities in Synergy with Islamic Financial Institutions. *Diversity: Jurnal Ilmiah Pascasarjana, 5*(1), 73–83. DOI: 10.32832/diversityjournal.v5i1.19304

Rapi, M. Z. H., Salaudeen, A. O., Ravi, M. I. R., Wongsangiam, R., & Redzuan, N. H. (2022). Micro *Takaful* programs for the poor: The Malaysian experience. *The International Journal of Accounting, 7*(45), 65–81.

Rasul, N. M., & Awang, M. S. (2024, December). Faraid And Hibah as Islamic Estate Planning Tools Among Muslim Society in Malaysia, The Concept, Importance and Issues. In *Salam Digest: Syariah and Law Undergraduate Symposium* (Vol. 2, No. 1, pp. 104-122).

Raza, A., Rehmat, S., Ishaq, M. I., Haj-Salem, N., & Talpur, Q. (2024). Gamification in financial service apps to enhance customer experience and engagement. *Journal of Consumer Behaviour, 23*(4), 1653–1670. DOI: 10.1002/cb.2294

Razali, M., Mohd, N., Hadigunawan, N., & Saidon, R. (2021). Maqasid shariah hifz mal in e-wallet application. *Islamiyyat. International Journal of Islamic Studies*, *43*(1).

Reeder, N., Rocyn Jones, G., Loder, J., & Colantonio, A. (2021). *Social impact bonds: The role of outcome-based financing in social innovation.* Routledge.

Rexhepi, G. (2016). The architecture of social finance. In *Routledge handbook of social and sustainable finance* (pp. 35–49). Routledge.

Ridgway, N. M., Kukar-Kinney, M., & Monroe, K. B. (2008). An Expanded Conceptualization and a New Measure of Compulsive Buying. *The Journal of Consumer Research*, *35*(4), 622–639. DOI: 10.1086/591108

Ridzuan, A.A., Zainol, M.N.A., Hai Liaw, J.O., Mohaiyadin. N.M., & Yaacob, S. (2018). Dimensi-dimensi Kejayaan Sultan Muhammad Al-Fateh Arkitek Penaklukan Kota Konstantinopel, e-Prosiding Persidangan Antarabangsa Sains Sosial dan Kemanusian pada 23-24 April 2018.

Rifansyah, M., & Suradi, R. (2024). Analysis of the Receipt and Distribution of Zakat, Infaq, and Sadaqah Funds through the National Zakat Amil Agency in Pontianak in 2016-2021. *Journal of Economics. Management and Trade*, *30*(7), 65–79. DOI: 10.9734/jemt/2024/v30i71226

Riyanda, A. R., Jalinus, N., Abdullah, R., Ranuharja, F., Islami, S., Adi, N. H., & Aminuddin, F. H. (2022). The New Paradigm of Technical and Vocational Education and Training (TVET). EDUKATIF: jurnal ilmu pendidikan, 4(1), 364-371.

Rook, D. W. (1987). The buying impulse. *The Journal of Consumer Research*, *14*(2), 189–199. DOI: 10.1086/209105

Rook, D. W., & Fisher, R. J. (1995). Normative influences on impulsive buying behavior. *The Journal of Consumer Research*, *22*(3), 305–313. DOI: 10.1086/209452

Rosman, R., Redzuan, N. H., Mokhtar, N. Z. N., Engku Ali, E. R. A., & Mohammed, M. O. (2022). Islamic Social Finance and Sustainable Development Goals: Issues and Challenges. *Journal of Islamic Finance*, *11*(2), 56–67. DOI: 10.31436/jif.v11i2.690

Rusli, N. A. (2024a). A Comparative Analysis of Technical and Vocational Education and Training (TVET) for Special Needs Students in Malaysia and Hungary. *Online Journal for TVET Practitioners*, *9*(1), 14–23. DOI: 10.30880/ojtp.2024.09.01.002

Rusydiana, A. S., & Ali, M. M. (2022). The application of Maqasid Shariah on banking industry. *Maqasid al-Shariah Review*, 1(1).

Rusydiana, A. S., Sukmana, R., & Laila, N. (2023). *Waqf Development Model for SDG-16 (Peace, Justice and Strong Institutions). Islamic Social Finance, 3(2).* SMART Insight.

Sa'adah, T. P., Ritonga, I., Latifah, F. N., & Mugiyati, M. (2025). Systematic Literatur Review of Productive Waqf in Indonesia and Their Contribution to SDGs. *Perisai : Islamic Banking and Finance Journal*, *9*(1), 27–48. DOI: 10.21070/perisai.v9i1.1802

Sabri, M. F., & Falahati, L. (2014). Toward a framework of financial wellness determinants: Investigating the moderating effect of religion. *Australian Journal of Basic and Applied Sciences*, *8*(9), 275–281. https://api.semanticscholar.org/CorpusID:154287518

Safei, A. A. (2021). The Formula of Islamic Community Development in Indonesia Through the Social Entrepreneurship Approach. *Religious: Jurnal Studi Agama-Agama Dan Lintas Budaya*, *5*(1), 47–58. DOI: 10.15575/rjsalb.v5i1.9685

Saidurrahman, S. (2013). The politics of zakat management in Indonesia: The tension between BAZ and LAZ. *Journal of Indonesian Islam*, *7*(2), 366–382. DOI: 10.15642/JIIS.2013.7.2.366-382

Saladin, M., Azmil, M., & Ali, S. M. (2020). Well-being of the society: A Maqasid Shariah approach. *Afkar*, *1*(Special Issue), 25–46.

Saleh, M. N. A. H., & Hassan, H. H. (2022). Determinants of Secured Post-Retirement Lifestyle in Klang Valley. *International Journal of Early Childhood Special Education*, *14*(3).

Salik, I. (2024). *The Islamic Guide to Depression: 10 Spiritual Reflections*. Goodly Word Books.

Salivio, M. P., Rillo, A. C., & Rosete, M. A. (2024). Cashless Commerce: A Study on the Interplay between Digital Payments and Luxury Consumption among Private Enterprises' Employees. *Journal of Business and Strategic Management*, *9*(9), 20–48. DOI: 10.47941/jbsm.2398

Salleh, S., Shafii, Z., Hanefah, M. M., Kamaruddin, M. I. H., Zakaria, N., & Sabri, N. A. M. (2022). Development Of Shariah Governance And Audit In Islamic Co-operative Sector. *Seminar Antarabangsa Islam Dan Sains 2022*.

Salleh, N. M., Shukry, S. N. M., Maylyn, V., & Jokinol, C. (2023). Analyzing the challenges, effects, and motivations of gig economy workers. *International Journal of Academic Research in Business & Social Sciences*, *13*(6), 2125–2142. DOI: 10.6007/IJARBSS/v13-i6/17514

Salman, M. J., Mohamad, N. A., & Sadique, M. A. (2021). E-WAQF IMPLEMENTATION: A PARADIGM SHIFT IN NIGERIA WAQF SYSTEM. *Journal of Asian and African Social Science and Humanities*, *7*(4), 41–53. DOI: 10.55327/jaash.v7i4.255

Samad, R. R., & Shafii, Z. (2016). Adoption of Shari'ah Governance in Cooperative Sector in Cooperative Sector in Malaysia: Case of Cooperative Banks and Credit Unions. *In The Fourth International Tunisian Conference for Islamic Wealth*, 1–21.

Samsi, S., Martomo, Y. P., & Anafih, E. S. (2024). BAZNAS leadership commitment in harnessing zakat potential and strengthening the community economy. *Society*, *12*(2), 927–942. DOI: 10.33019/society.v12i2.750

Sari, M. D., Bahari, Z., & Hamat, Z. (2013). Review on Indonesian zakah management and obstacles. *Social Sciences*, *2*(2), 76–89. DOI: 10.11648/j.ss.20130202.18

Sari, R. C., Fatimah, P. R., Ilyana, S., & Hermawan, H. D. (2021). Augmented reality (AR)-based sharia financial literacy system (AR-SFLS): A new approach to virtual Sharia financial socialization for young learners. *International Journal of Islamic and Middle Eastern Finance and Management*, *15*(1), 48–65. DOI: 10.1108/IMEFM-11-2019-0484

Saro, N., Bhari, A., Rani, M. A. M., & Yusof, M. F. M. (2023). *Analysis of Digital Zakat Payment Implementation: A Comparison in Southeast Asia*. https://www.researchgate.net/publication/371039191_Analysis_of_Digital_Zakat_Payment_Implementation_A_Comparison_in_Southeast_Asia

Saunders, M., Lewis, P., & Thornhill, A. (2019). *Research Methods for Business Students*. Pearson Deutschland. https://elibrary.pearson.de/book/99.150005/9781292208794

Saylani Welfare. (2020). *COVID-19 relief efforts in Pakistan*.

Schomburgk, L., Belli, A., & Hoffmann, A. O. I. (2024). Less cash, more splash? A meta-analysis on the cashless effect. *Journal of Retailing*, *100*(3), 382–403. DOI: 10.1016/j.jretai.2024.05.003

Securities Commission Malaysia. (2017). Malaysia'a Green Sukuk Under the SC's Sustainable and Responsible Investment Sukuk Framework. *Malaysian ICM*, 12(2), 5-6. https://www.sc.com.my/api/documentms/download.ashx?id=1316fd32-1993-44cb-9669-5d5687adda35

Securities Commission Malaysia. (2022a). *SRI Roadmap for the Malaysian Capital Market: Mid-Term Review*. Securities Commission Malaysia.

Securities Commission Malaysia. (2022b). *SRI Sukuk and Tax Incentives Framework.* Securities Commission Malaysia.

Sedikides, C. (2010). Why does religiosity persist? *Personality and Social Psychology Review, 14*(1), 3–6. DOI: 10.1177/1088868309352323

Seibel, H. D., Agung, W. D., Siebel, H., & Agung, D. (2006). Islamic Microfinance in Indonesia. In *Deutsche Gesellschaft für Technische Zusammenarbeit (GTZ) GmbH: Vol. No.2* (Issue February). DOI: 10.1355/sj23-1d

Sen, S., Antara, N., & Sen, S. (2020). The determinants of opening account with Islamic banks. *Journal of Islamic Marketing, 12*(9), 1709–1733. DOI: 10.1108/JIMA-04-2020-0110

Septianingsih, R., Abdullah, A., & Salleh, M. Z. M. (2024). A Systematic Review: Challenge of Islamic Microfinance Baitul Maal Wat Tamwil in Indonesia. In *Islamic Finance*. New Trends in Law and Regulation. DOI: 10.1007/978-3-031-48770-5_3

Setianingrum, A., Madjid, S., & Asaari, M. (2018). Zakat As Tax Credit for Harmonize Fiscal Setting in Indonesia. *Jurnal Ekonomi Pembangunan (Balai Penelitian dan Pengembangan Ekonomi, Fakultas Ekonomi Universitas Muhammadiyah Surakarta), 16*(1), 57–72.

Setiawan, A., & Nurzaman, M. S. (2022). Application of Blockchain and Smart-Contract on Waqf Asset Management: Is It Necessary? *EL DINAR: Jurnal Keuangan Dan Perbankan Syariah, 10*(2), 85–101. DOI: 10.18860/ed.v10i2.15529

Setiawati, R., Nidar, S. R., Anwar, M., & Masyita, D. (2018). Islamic financial literacy: Construct process and validity. *Academy of Strategic Management Journal, 17*(4), 1–12. https://www.proquest.com/scholarly-journals/islamic-financial-literacy-construct-process/docview/2124080881/se-2

Setyowati, A., Harmadi, H., & Sunarjanto, S. (2018). *Islamic financial literacy and personal financial planning: A socio-demographic study. 22*(1), 63–72. DOI: 10.26905/jkdp.v22i1.1625

Shafie, Z. B., Premier, U. O., Karamah, Z., Baharul, A., Technology, I., & Premier, U. O. (n.d.). *Chapter 7 : ANALYSIS OF LECTURERS ' INVOLVEMENT IN FOR POLYTECHNIC*. 147–166.

Shafik, A. S. M., & Ahmad, W. M. W. (2019). Financial literacy among Malaysian Muslim undergraduates. *Journal of Islamic Accounting and Business Research, 11*(8), 1515–1529. DOI: 10.1108/JIABR-10-2017-0149

Shahariman, A. A. B., Asari, N. A. M. B., Sulaiman, N. A. A. B., & Marzuki, N. A. A. B. (2024). Islamic principles and their application in personal financial decision making. *Accessed*, (Dec), 15.

Shahmi, M. A., Putra, M. D., Fahlefi, R., Arifah, L., & Mansur, M. (2025). Energy Waqf and the Environmental Crisis: Advancing Islamic Philanthropy for Sustainability. *Economica: Jurnal Ekonomi Islam*, *16*(1), 1–17. DOI: 10.21580/economica.2025.16.1.23549

Shah, N. A. M. A., Nasrul, M. A. D., Rahman, S. F. A., & Seviyana, D. (2023). Comparative analysis of Malaysian and Indonesian retirement plan. *Lex Scientia Law Review*, *7*(2), 659–708. DOI: 10.15294/lesrev.v7i2.69847

Shaikh, S. A. (2020). Waqf and Sustainable Development: A Critical Appraisal of the Potentials and Governance Challenges. *Islamic Economic Studies*, *28*(1), 57–77. DOI: 10.1108/IES-09-2020-0052

Sham, F. M., & Yusof, S. (2015). Religiosity of Muslim adolescents from single parent families living in government-subsidised settlement. *Global Journal Al-Thaqafah*, *5*(2), 31–42. DOI: 10.7187/GJAT882015.05.02

She, L., Rasiah, R., Weissmann, M.A. & Kaur, H. (2023). Using the theory of planned behaviour to explore predictors of financial behaviour among working adults in Malaysia. *FIIB Business Review*, 1–18

Sheikh, R. (2025), Developing ethical investment criteria based on Maqasid Shariah. *Qualitative Research in Financial Markets*, Vol. ahead-of-print No. ahead-of-print. https://doi-org.ezaccess.remotexs.co/10.1108/QRFM-04-2025-0103

Shirazi, N. S., Kuanova, L. A., Ryskulov, A., & Mukusheva, A. G. (2022). The experience and the prospects of Islamic finance in Kazakhstan. *Qualitative Research in Financial Markets*, *14*(3), 461–482. DOI: 10.1108/QRFM-03-2020-0023

Sholihin, M., Shalihin, N., & Addiarrahman, . (2023). The Scale of Muslims' Consumption Intelligence: A Maqā id Insight. *ISRA International Journal of Islamic Finance*, *15*(2), 98–118. DOI: 10.55188/ijif.v15i2.544

Shrigley, R. L., Koballa, T. R.Jr, & Simpson, R. D. (1988). Defining attitude for science educators. *Journal of Research in Science Teaching*, *25*(8), 659–678. DOI: 10.1002/tea.3660250805

Shupe, C., Li, G., & Fulford, S. (2023). Consumer Use of Buy Now, Pay Later Insights from the CFPB Making Ends Meet Survey. *Consumer Financial Protection Bureau ....* https://papers.ssrn.com/sol3/papers.cfm?abstract_id=4399626

Siddiqi, M. N. (2005). *Teaching Islamic Economics*. Islamic Economics Research Centre, King Abdul Aziz University.

Sirgy, M. J., Lee, D.-J., Grace, B. Y., Gurel-Atay, E., Tidwell, J., & Ekici, A. (2016). Self-expressiveness in shopping. *Journal of Retailing and Consumer Services, 30*, 292–299. DOI: 10.1016/j.jretconser.2016.02.008

Siswantoro, D. (2013). Regulatory Compliance and Experiences of Islamic Cooperatives in Competitive Business in Indonesia. *International Journal of Excellence in Islamic Banking and Finance, 3*(1), 1–14. DOI: 10.12816/0001418

Siswantoro, D., & Nurhayati, S. (2012). Factors affecting concern about zakat as a tax deduction in Indonesia. *Int. J. Manag. Bus. Res, 2*(4), 293–312.

Smolo, E., & Mirakhor, A. (2010). The global financial crisis and its implications for the Islamic financial industry. *Journal of Islamic and Middle Eastern Finance and Management, 3*(4), 372–385. DOI: 10.1108/17538391011093306

Srinivas, Y. (2005). Bank finance to the SME sector-Issues and perspectives. Chartered Accountant- New Delhi, 54 (3), 436

Sriram, M. S. (2012). The AP Microfinance Crisis 2010: Discipline or Death? *Vikalpa, 37*(4), 113–128. DOI: 10.1177/0256090920120407

Strömbäck, C., Lind, T., Skagerlund, K., Västfjäll, D., & Tinghög, G. (2017). Does self-control predict financial behavior and financial well-being? *Journal of Behavioral and Experimental Finance, 14*, 30–38. DOI: 10.1016/j.jbef.2017.04.002

Sudirman, A., Alaydrus, S., Rosmayati, S., Syamsuriansyah, S., Nugroho, L., & Arifudin, O. (2020). *Perilaku konsumen dan perkembangannya di era digital*. Widina Bhakti Persada Bandung. www.penerbitwidina.com

Suhaimy, K. A., & Hassan, M. K. (2023). Artificial intelligence in waqf portfolio optimization: Empirical evidence from Malaysian institutions. *Journal of Islamic Finance, 12*(2), 178–194.

Suharti, F. (2018). Sinergitas Islamic microfinance institution (IMFI): Pemberdayaan dan Peningkatan Usaha Mikro Kecil Menengah (UMKM). *El-Jizya Jurnal Ekonomi Islam, 5*(1), 52–80. DOI: 10.24090/ej.v5i1.1626

Sulaiman, S., Hasan, R., & Mohammad, M. T. S. (2019). Integration of waqf and sukuk for educational infrastructure financing: A proposed model. *International Journal of Islamic Economics and Finance Research, 2*(2), 1–15.

Sullivan, A. (2011). The role of waqf in Islamic social finance: The impact of endowments on public services. *Journal of Social Finance, 5*(2), 71–84.

Sulong, A.R. (2013). Pemikiran Turki Uthmaniyah Menurut Syeikh Wan Ahmad bin Muhammad Zain Al-Fatani dalam bukunya Hadiqat Al-Azhar Wa Al-Rayahin, Tesis yang diserahkan untuk memenuhi keperluan bagi ijazah Doktor Falsafah yang diambil pada Jun 2013.

Sun, J., & Zhang, J. (2024). Digital Financial Inclusion and Innovation of MSMEs. *Sustainability 2024, Vol. 16, Page 1404, 16*(4), 1404. DOI: 10.3390/su16041404

Sun, Y., Liu, L., Xu, Y., Zeng, X., Shi, Y., Hu, H., Jiang, J., & Abraham, A. (2024). Alternative data in finance and business: Emerging applications and theory analysis [review]. *Financial Innovation, 10*(1), 127. Advance online publication. DOI: 10.1186/s40854-024-00652-0

Swandaru, R., & Muneeza, A. (2022). Can fraud in Islamic financial institutions be prevented using high standards of Shariah governance?. *International journal of law and management, 64*(6), 469-485. https://doi.org/DOI: 10.1108/IJLMA-07-2022-0162

Syed Azman, S. M. M., & Engku Ali, E. R. A. (2019). Islamic Social Finance and the Imperative for Social Impact Measurement. *Al-Shajarah: Journal of the International Institute Of Islamic Thought & Civilization,* ISSN 1394-6870, pp. 43-68.

Syed Chear, S. L. (2023). *Governance of TVET in Malaysia: Gaps and opportunities for researchers*. TVET-Online Journal.

Tahiri Jouti, A. (2019). An integrated approach for building sustainable Islamic social finance ecosystems. *ISRA International Journal of Islamic Finance, 11*(2), 246–266. DOI: 10.1108/IJIF-10-2018-0118

Talavera, C., & Sanchis, J. R. (2020). Alliances between for-profit and non-profit organizations as an instrument to implement the economy for the common good. *Sustainability (Basel), 12*(22), 9511. DOI: 10.3390/su12229511

TalentCorp Malaysia. (2023). *Industry-Academia Collaboration Report: Bridging the Gap in Malaysia's Talent Development*. TalentCorp.

Talwar, S., Dhir, A., Khalil, A., Mohan, G., & Islam, A. K. M. N. (2020). Point of adoption and beyond. Initial trust and mobile-payment continuation intention. *Journal of Retailing and Consumer Services, 55*, 102086. https://doi.org/https://doi.org/10.1016/j.jretconser.2020.102086. DOI: 10.1016/j.jretconser.2020.102086

Tambunan, T. (2019). Recent evidence of the development of micro, small and medium enterprises in Indonesia. *Journal of Global Entrepreneurship Research, 9*(1), 18. DOI: 10.1186/s40497-018-0140-4

Tam, C., Santos, D., & Oliveira, T. (2020). Exploring the influential factors of continuance intention to use mobile Apps: Extending the expectation confirmation model. *Information Systems Frontiers*, *22*(1), 243–257. DOI: 10.1007/s10796-018-9864-5

Tang, A. K. Y. (2019). A systematic literature review and analysis on mobile apps in m-commerce: Implications for future research. *Electronic Commerce Research and Applications*, *37*(August), 100885. DOI: 10.1016/j.elerap.2019.100885

Tarique, K. M., Islam, R., & Mohammed, M. O. (2021). Developing and validating the components of Maqasid al-Shari'ah-based performance measurement model for Islamic banks. *International Journal of Islamic and Middle Eastern Finance and Management*, *14*(2), 366–390. DOI: 10.1108/IMEFM-12-2018-0432

Terzi, M. Z. Hz. (2017) *Peygamber ve Hulefâ-yi Râşidîn Döneminde Askeri Teşkilat*. Istanbul: Siyer Yayınları.

The Asia Foundation. (2022). *Recommendations towards improving technical and vocational education and training in Malaysia*. The Asia Foundation. https://asiafoundation.org/wp-content/uploads/2024/08/Recommendations-Towards-Improving-Technical-and-Vocational-Education-and-Training-in-Malaysia.pdf

Thomas, S. N., Zacharia, A., Thomas, A. C., Mathew, P. C., & Joseph, M. (2024). The Role of Digital Payments in Enhancing Financial Inclusion: Analysing and Visualizing Research Trends. *Library of Progress-Library Science, Information Technology & Computer, 44*(3).

Thomson Reuters. (2017). *The rise of green sukuk: Islamic finance for a sustainable future*. Thomson Reuters Islamic Finance.

Thoumrungroje, A. (2018). A cross-national study of consumer spending behavior: The impact of social media intensity and materialism. *Journal of International Consumer Marketing*, *30*(4), 276–286. DOI: 10.1080/08961530.2018.1462130

Thurstone, L. L. (1928). Attitudes can be measured. *American Journal of Sociology*, *33*(4), 529–554. https://www.journals.uchicago.edu/doi/epdf/10.1086/214483. DOI: 10.1086/214483

Tiwari, S. K.Sujeet Kumar Tiwari. (2024). The Future of Digital Retirement Solutions: A Study of Sustainability and Scalability in Financial Planning Tools. *Journal of Computer Science and Technology Studies*, *6*(5), 229–245. DOI: 10.32996/jcsts.2024.6.5.19

Tripathi, S. (2023). Determinants of Continuance Intention to Use Mobile Wallets Technology in the Post Pandemic Era: Moderating Role of Perceived Trust. *Journal of International Technology and Information Management*, *31*(3), 128–170. DOI: 10.58729/1941-6679.1570

Tuan Pham, M., & Chang, H. H. (2010). Regulatory Focus, Regulatory Fit, and the Search and Consideration of Choice Alternatives. *The Journal of Consumer Research*, *37*(4), 626–640. DOI: 10.1086/655668

Uddin, S. M., Abedin, M. Z., & Afroz, N. (2020). Islamic Financial Inclusion: An Alternative Approach to Reach the Unbanked of Bangladesh. In Rafay, A. (Ed.), *Growth and Emerging Prospects of International Islamic Banking* (pp. 155–173). IGI Global Scientific Publishing., DOI: 10.4018/978-1-7998-1611-9.ch009

UNCTAD. (2024). *Financing for Sustainable Development Report 2024: Financing for Development at a Crossroads*. https://unctad.org/publication/financing-sustainable-development-report-2024

Underdown, K., & Tamara, D. (2025). Digital wallets: a study on the influence of consumer perceptions and attitudes on impulsive consumer behaviour. *Frontiers in Human Dynamics, Volume 7-2025*. DOI: 10.3389/fhumd.2025.1545141

UNDP & IsDB. (2019). *Islamic Finance for the Sustainable Development Goals*. United Nations Development Programme and Islamic Development Bank.

UNEP. (2023). *Adaptation Gap Report 2023*. United Nations Environment Program. https://www.unep.org/resources/adaptation-gap-report-2023

UNESCAP. (2020a). *Green Microfinance: Trends, Challenges, and Opportunities in Asia-Pacific*. United Nations Economic and Social Commission for Asia and the Pacific.

UNESCAP. (2020b). *Leveraging Islamic Finance for Climate-Smart Agriculture*. United Nations Economic and Social Commission for Asia and the Pacific. https://www.unescap.org

Usman, A. S., & Tasmin, R. (2016). The role of Islamic micro-finance in enhancing human development in Muslim countries. *Journal of Islamic Finance*, *5*(1), 53–62. DOI: 10.31436/jif.v5i1.111

Usmani, M. T. (2002). An introduction to Islamic finance. *Language, 17*(397p), 22cm.

Varaprasad, N. (2021). Technical and Vocational Education Trends and Issues in Singapore. In Trends and Issues in International Technical and Vocational Education in the Indo-Pacific Region (p. 287).

Veblen, T. (2017). *The theory of the leisure class*. Routledge. DOI: 10.4324/9781315135373

Venkatesh, V., Morris, M. G., Davis, G. B., & Davis, F. D. (2003). User acceptance of information technology: Toward a unified view. *Management Information Systems Quarterly*, *27*(3), 425–478. Advance online publication. DOI: 10.2307/30036540

Verma, R., & Chatterjee, D. (2025). Relative Impact of Digital and Traditional Financial Inclusion on Financial Resilience: Evidence from 13 Emerging Countries. *Journal of Economics and Business*, *133*, 106233. DOI: 10.1016/j.jeconbus.2025.106233

Verplanken, B., & Herabadi, A. (2001). Individual differences in impulse buying tendency: Feeling and no thinking. *European Journal of Personality*, *15*(1, suppl), S71–S83. DOI: 10.1002/per.423

W. Ahmad, W.Y. (n.d). Sistem Ketenteraan Kerajaan Madinah Pada Zaman Nabi Muhammad SAW, *Jurnal Usuluddin*, 134-145.

Wahab, N. A., Bin-Nashwan, S. A., Chik, M. N., & Hussin, M. Y. M. (2023). Islamic Social Finance Initiatives: An Insight into Bank Islam Malaysia Berhad's Innovative BangKIT Microfinance Product. *ISRA International Journal of Islamic Finance*, *15*(1), 22–35. DOI: 10.55188/ijif.v15i1.483

Wahab, N. A., & Rahman, A. R. A. (2011). A framework to analyse the efficiency and governance of zakat institutions. *Journal of Islamic Accounting and Business Research*, *2*(1), 43–56. DOI: 10.1108/17590811111129508

Wahab, N. A., & Rahman, A. R. A. (2013). Determinants of efficiency of zakat institutions in Malaysia: A non-parametric approach. *Asian Journal of Business and Accounting*, *6*(2).

Wahid, F. N., Rosli, M. S. D. A., Afandi, M., Rani, M., & Arif, M. I. A. M. (2023). Catalysing National Health Security by The Islamic Micro Endowment Mechanism Through Financial Technology Platform. *International Journal of Academic Research in Business & Social Sciences*, *13*(7), 39–46. DOI: 10.6007/IJARBSS/v13-i7/17672

Wahyudi, I. (2014). Commitment and trust in achieving financial goals of strategic alliance. *International Journal of Islamic and Middle Eastern Finance and Management*, *7*(4), 421–442. DOI: 10.1108/IMEFM-10-2013-0113

Wahyudi, I. (2015). Realizing knowledge sharing in strategic alliance: case in Islamic microfinance Realizing knowledge sharing in strategic alliance: case in Islamic microfinance. *Journal of Islamic and Middle Eastern Finance and Management*, *31*(4), 260–271.

Wahyudi, I., Yama, I., & Said, M. (2025). Islamic Social Finance as a Catalyst for SDGs: A Systematic Analysis of Implementation Models and Digital Innovation. *Falah: Jurnal Ekonomi Syariah, 10*(1), 54–70. DOI: 10.22219/jes.v10i1.37591

Wahyuni, E. T. (2008). The Accountability of Islamic Microfinance Institution: Evidence From Indonesia. *The Winners, 9*(1), 22–34. DOI: 10.21512/tw.v9i1.728

Wan, C. D. (2025). *TVET in Malaysia's human resource development plans: Realities and "game changers"* (ISEAS Perspective No. 2025/5). ISEAS–Yusof Ishak Institute. https://www.iseas.edu.sg/articles-commentaries/iseas-perspective/2025-5-tvet-in-malaysias-human-resource-development-plans-realities-and-game-changers-by-wan-chang-da/

Wang, J., Bouri, E., & Ma, F. (2022). Which Factors Drive Bitcoin Volatility: Macroeconomic, Technical, or Both? SSRN *Electronic Journal*, 1–38. DOI: 10.2139/ssrn.4080107

Wardiwiyono, S. (2012). Internal control system for Islamic micro financing. *International Journal of Islamic and Middle Eastern Finance and Management, 5*(4), 340–352. https://doi.org/doi:10.1108/17538391211282836. DOI: 10.1108/17538391211282836

Warmath, D., & Zimmerman, D. (2019). Financial literacy as more than knowledge: The development of a formative scale through the lens of Bloom's domains of knowledge. *The Journal of Consumer Affairs, 53*(4), 1602–1629. DOI: 10.1111/joca.12286

Wediawati, B., Adriani, Z., Setiawati, R., Ratnawati, R. T. S., & Dewi, E. (2025). The Impact of Entrepreneurial, Financial, and Digital Literacy on MSME Performance. *Jurnal Ilmiah Manajemen Kesatuan, 13*(4), 2643–2658. DOI: 10.37641/jimkes.v13i4.3411

Widiastuti, T., Robani, A., Sukmaningrum, P. S., Mawardi, I., Ningsih, S., Herianingrum, S., & Al-Mustofa, M. U. (2022). Integrating sustainable Islamic social finance: An analytical network process using the benefit opportunity cost risk (ANP BOCR) framework: The case of Indonesia. *PLoS One, 17*(5), e0269039. DOI: 10.1371/journal.pone.0269039 PMID: 35617300

Widityani, S. F., Faturohman, T., Rahadi, R. A., & Yulianti, Y. (2020). Do sociodemographic characteristics and financial literacy matter for selecting Islamic financial products? *Journal of Islamic Monetary Economics and Finance, 6*(1), 51–76. DOI: 10.21098/jimf.v6i1.1057

Widyastuti, M., Ferdinand, D. Y. Y., & Hermanto, Y. B. (2023). Strengthening formal credit access and performance through financial literacy and credit terms in micro, small and medium businesses. *Journal of Risk and Financial Management, 16*(1), 52. DOI: 10.3390/jrfm16010052

Widyastuti, U., Febrian, E., Sutisna, S., & Fitrijanti, T. (2022). Market discipline in the behavioral finance perspective: A case of Sharia mutual funds in Indonesia. *Journal of Islamic Accounting and Business Research, 13*(1), 114–140. DOI: 10.1108/JIABR-06-2020-0194

Wijaya, H. R., Hati, S. R. H., Ekaputra, I. A., & Kassim, S. (2024). The Impact of Religiosity and Financial Literacy on Financial Management Behavior and Well-Being Among Indonesian Muslims. *Humanities & Social Sciences Communications, 11*(1), 1–13. DOI: 10.1057/s41599-024-03309-6

Wijaya, I. F., Hakim, A. R., Saputro, N., & Mulyadi, M. (2019). Religiosity level and saving decisions in Baitul Maal wat Tamwil: The case of Indonesia. *Journal of Islamic Marketing, 11*(6), 1465–1483. DOI: 10.1108/JIMA-09-2018-0160

Wildana, M. D. A., & Imamia, T. L. (2022, April). Waqf in the 21st Century: The Implementation of Blockchain and Smart Contract Technology. *Journal of International Conference Proceedings, 5*(1), 456–466. DOI: 10.32535/jicp.v5i1.1774

Wilson, J., & Lederer, E. M. (2025). *US Skips Global UN Meeting Aimed at Raising Trillions to Combat Poverty.* https://apnews.com/article/poverty-inequality-development-financing-un-spain-e7b965e2a160b7c51f7da6fcf58edc29

Windasari, N. A., & Lin, F. (2021). Why Do People Continue Using Fitness Wearables? The Effect of Interactivity and Gamification. *SAGE Open, 11*(4), 21582440211056606. Advance online publication. DOI: 10.1177/21582440211056606

Wohlstetter, P., Smith, J., & Malloy, C. (2005). Strategic Alliances in Action: Toward a Theory of Evolution. *Policy Studies Journal: the Journal of the Policy Studies Organization, 33*(3), 419–442. DOI: 10.1111/j.1541-0072.2005.00123.x

Wong, K. T., Lim, S. Y., & Hassan, F. (2022). Geographical disparities in TVET research funding: A longitudinal analysis of Malaysian institutions. *Education Sciences, 12*(3), 235–251.

Worldpay. (2025). *Global Payments Report | Payment Insights | Worldpay.* https://worldpay.com/en/global-payments-report

Worokinasih, S., Nuzula, N. F., Damayanti, C. R., & Sirivanh, T. (2023). The resilience of youth entrepreneur: The role of social capital, financial literacy, and emotional intelligence on SMEs' performance in Indonesia. [Bisnis Dan Manajemen]. *BISMA, 16*(1), 1–27. DOI: 10.26740/bisma.v16n1.p1-27

Wudil, A. A., Saad, N. M., Omercic, J., Zakaria, L., & Muhammad, R. (2025). Islamic Finance and Poverty Reduction in African Countries: An Empirical Analysis. *International Journal of Economics, Management and Accounting, 33*(1), 77–97. DOI: 10.31436/ijema.v33i1.1299

Xiao, J. J. (2008). Applying behavior theories to financial behavior. In *Handbook of Consumer Finance Research* (pp. 69–81). Springer., DOI: 10.1007/978-0-387-75734-6_5

Xiao, J. J., & Porto, N. (2017). Financial education and financial satisfaction: Financial literacy, behavior, and capability as mediators. *International Journal of Bank Marketing, 35*(5), 805–817. DOI: 10.1108/IJBM-01-2016-0009

Yaacob, N. M., Abu Bakar, N., & Alias, M. (2021). Reviving Waqf for Environmental Sustainability: Issues, Challenges, and Prospects in Malaysia. *Journal of Fatwa Management and Research, 26*(1), 87–104.

Yadav, M., Banerji, P., & Garg, A. (2025). Digital financial literacy and retirement planning with mediating effect of saving behaviour. *American Journal of Business, 40*(June), 127–143. Advance online publication. DOI: 10.1108/AJB-12-2023-0221

Yahya, M. H., Muhammad, J., Abdullah, A., & Nasir, A. M. (2013). Chinks in the capitalism system-the pertinence of Islamic finance. *Journal of International Business and Cultural Studies, 7*, 1–16.

Yapilami, A., & Adamu, Z. Balami. (2024). *ISSN : 2204-012X African Journal of Innovative Research and Advanced studies ISSN : 2204-012X African Journal of Innovative Research and Advanced studies. 14*(4), 9–20.

Yayasan Wakaf Malaysia. (2023). Cash Waqf Collection and Distribution Report 2018-2023. Kuala Lumpur: YWM.

Yoganandham, G. (2025). Mastering Economic And Financial Sources With Reference To Budgeting, Savings, Early Investing, Debt Management And The Power Of Financial Planning-A Comprehensive Analysis. *Degres Journal, 10*(1), 19-33. Retrieved from https://degres.eu/wp-content/uploads/2-DEJ1457.pdf

Yong, C., Yew, S., & Wee, C. (2018). Financial knowledge, attitude and behaviour of young working adults in Malaysia. *Institutions and Economies, 10*(4), 21–48. https://ijie.um.edu.my/article/view/13444

Yousef, F. (2024). The Impact of E-Wallets on Consumer Spending Behavior and Financial Management. *International Journal of Scientific Research, 3*(12), 429–456. DOI: 10.59992/IJSR.2024.v3n12p12

Yuan, W., Gong, S., & Gao, J. (2021). How Does House Demolition Affect Family Conspicuous Consumption? *Frontiers in Psychology, 12*, 741006. Advance online publication. DOI: 10.3389/fpsyg.2021.741006

Yumna, A., Marta, J., & Yanuarta RE, R. (2025). The Impact of Financial and Social Inclusion on Well-Being: Evidence from a Waqf-Based Microfinance Institution in Indonesia. *International Journal of Ethics and Systems*. https://doi.org/DOI: 10.1108/IJOES-08-2024-0243/1253232/THE-IMPACT-OF-FINANCIAL-AND-SOCIAL-INCLUSION-ON

Yunus, M. (2007). *Creating a world without poverty: Social business and the future of capitalism*. Public Affairs.

Yusfiarto, R., Nugraha, S. S., Mutmainah, L., Berakon, I., Sunarsih, S., & Nurdany, A. (2023). Islamic Capital Market Adoption from a Socio-Psychological Perspective and Islamic Financial Literacy. *Journal of Islamic Accounting and Business Research, 14*(4), 574–594. DOI: 10.1108/JIABR-02-2022-0037

Yusoff, N. D., Ismail, S., Abd Razak, N., Rafien, N. S. M., & Yaakub, W. (2024). Retirement Preparedness among Malaysia's Low-Income Private Sector Employees: A Conceptual Model. *Information Management and Business Review, 16*(3(I)S, 3 (S)), 613–627. DOI: 10.22610/imbr.v16i3(I)S.4088

Yusof, M. A., & Ab. Aziz, M. R. (2015). Scrutinizing the Method of Contribution for Islamic Waqf Bank Fund. *Journal of Islamic Economics Banking and Finance, 11*(1), 181–192. DOI: 10.12816/0026024

Yusof, M. A., Ridhwan, M., Aziz, A., & Ramli, Y. (2013). Exploring New Opportunity and Mechanism for Islamic Waqf Bank Model. *2nd Applied International Business Conference (AIBC2013)*, 805–816.

Zailani, M. N., Satar, N. H. M., & Zakaria, R. H. (2022). Maqasid Al-Shariah based index of socio-economic development: A literature review. *The Journal of Muamalat and Islamic Finance Research,* 47-62.

Zailani, M. N., Mohd Satar, N., & Zakaria, R. H. (2022). A Review of indicators for the preservation of wealth (hifz al-mal) based on maqasid al-shariah. *Journal of Islamic Philanthropy & Social Finance, 4*(1), 23–29. DOI: 10.24191/jipsf.v4i1.3429

Zainalaludin, Z., Saidi, N., Foong, H. F., & Abdullah, S. F. Z. (2021). Relationship between poverty levels and age categories among male and female consumers in Malaysia. *Jurnal Pengguna Malaysia*, *37*, 90–110.

Zainal, N., Nassir, A., Kamarudin, F., & Law, S. H. (2020). Does bank regulation and supervision impede the efficiency of microfinance institutions to eradicate poverty? Evidence from ASEAN-5 countries. *Studies in Economics and Finance*, *38*(2), 272–302. DOI: 10.1108/SEF-10-2019-0414

Zain, N. M., Aspah, V., Abdullah, N., & Ebrahimi, M. (2017). Challenges and evolution of higher education in Malaysia. *UMRAN-Journal of Islamic and Civilizational Studies*, *4*, 1–1.

Zain, N. S., Hassan, R., & Marwan, S. (2023). Social Impact Measurement as a Tool of Governance and Accountability for Waqf Organisations. *International Journal of Islamic Economics and Finance Research*, *1*(1), 132–148. DOI: 10.53840/ijiefer122

Zakariyah, H., Salaudeen, A. O., Othman, A. H. A., & Rosman, R. (2022). Enhancing waqf management through fintech in Malaysia. *Journal of Emerging Economies and Islamic Research*, *10*(2), 62–73.

Zakat and Sadaqat Foundation. (2022). *Annual Impact Report 2021–2022*. Nigeria.

Zakat Foundation. (2021). *Zakat Foundation of America: Impact report*.

Zalim, S. N. A. (2021). Performance measurement in Islamic microfinance institutions: Does it change social norms and values? *Qualitative Research in Financial Markets*, *14*(2), 306–323. DOI: 10.1108/QRFM-09-2020-0186

Zamroni, M. A., Toha, M., Zuana, M. M. M., & Isbahi, M. B. (2023). Exploring Zakat Distribution Via Blockchain in Indonesia Perspective of Maslahah Mursalah Wahbah Zuhaili. [IIJSE]. *Indonesian Interdisciplinary Journal of Sharia Economics*, *6*(3), 3544–3555. DOI: 10.31538/IIJSE.V7I3.5821

Zavolokina, L., Dolata, M., & Schwabe, G. (2017). FinTech transformation: How IT-enabled innovations shape the financial sector. *Lecture Notes in Business Information Processing*, *276*, 75–88. DOI: 10.1007/978-3-319-52764-2_6

Zetzsche, D. A., Arner, D. W., & Buckley, R. P. (2020). Decentralized finance. *Journal of Financial Regulation*, *6*(2), 172–203. DOI: 10.1093/jfr/fjaa010

Zhao, X., Lynch, J. G.Jr, & Chen, Q. (2010). Reconsidering Baron and Kenny: Myths and truths about mediation analysis. *The Journal of Consumer Research*, *37*(2), 197–206. Advance online publication. DOI: 10.1086/651257

Zhou, T. (2014). Understanding the determinants of mobile payment continuance usage. *Industrial Management & Data Systems, 114*(6), 936–948. DOI: 10.1108/IMDS-02-2014-0068

Zia, I. Z., & Prasetyo, P. E. (2018). Analysis of financial inclusion toward poverty and income inequality. *Jurnal Ekonomi Pembangunan (Balai Penelitian dan Pengembangan Ekonomi, Fakultas Ekonomi Universitas Muhammadiyah Surakarta), 19*(1), 114. DOI: 10.23917/jep.v19i1.5879

Ziderman, A. (2018). *Funding Mechanisms for Financing Vocational Training: An Analytical Framework*. DOI: 10.1007/978-3-319-90388-0_8

Zin, M. M., & Abidin, A. (2018). Islamic microfinance for poverty alleviation: A case study of Bank Rakyat Indonesia. *Journal of Islamic Finance*, *7*(3), 56–68.

Zin, R. H. M. (2012). Malaysia: Towards a social protection system in an advanced equitable society. *ASEAN Economic Bulletin*, •••, 197–217.

Zulfikri, Z., Adam, A., Kassim, S., & Hassan, A. (2022). Trust Enhancement in Zakat Institutions using Blockchain Technology: A Qualitative Approach. *European Journal of Islamic Finance*, *9*(1), 31–36. DOI: 10.13135/2421-2172/6312

About the Contributors

Muhammad Ridhwan Ab. Aziz is a Professor of Islamic Banking and Finance at the Faculty of Economics and Muamalat, Universiti Sains Islam Malaysia (USIM). He received his Bachelor Degree of Business Administration (Hons.) in 2001, Master Degree in Islamic Studies, specializing in Islamic Banking in 2008 and Doctorate in Islamic Banking in 2011 from University of Malaya. He is an Assessor for academic program accreditation of Malaysian Qualification Agency (MQA) in the field of Islamic banking and Islamic finance. He is also a Shariah Committee Member for Export-Import Bank of Malaysia Berhad (EXIM Bank) and Citibank Berhad (Malaysia), Internal Shariah Advisory Board for Citibank N.A. Labuan Branch, Shariah Supervisory Board Member for Shuaa Funds OEIC ICC Limited in United Arab Emirates, Registered Shariah Adviser for Labuan Financial Services Authority (LFSA) as well as an Arbitrator (Hakam) for Negeri Sembilan Syariah Judiciary Department. He is also Academic Advisors for Islamic finance program in various colleges, university colleges and university as well as Members of Editorial Board for local and international journals. He also involves as Panel of Interview for Biasiswa Yang Dipertuan Agong, Public Service Department/Jabatan Perkhidmatan Awam (JPA), Malaysia and Biasiswa Kementerian Pendidikan Malaysia, Ministry of Education Malaysia. He actively involves in the popular writing in various platforms such as Islamic Finance News (IFN), Harian Metro, Berita Harian, BERNAMA, Utusan Malaysia, Dewan Ekonomi and The Newsletter of Muamalat. His area of expertise is in the field of Islamic banking and finance, Islamic commercial law, Islamic money and capital market as well as Islamic social finance. Until now, he has supervised and graduated eighteen (18) master's and Phd graduates mainly in the field of Islamic banking and finance as well as in Islamic social finance. He involved as examiner in thesis examination for thirty-nine (39) master's and Phd candidates in his area of expertise. He has been invited as speaker for keynote speaker, guest speaker, guest lecture, public lecture as well as inaugural lecture from local and international universities and institutions. He has been awarded for various research and innovation awards such as best paper award, USIM top 100 researchers award, award for most selling book, publication award for prolific writer in social science cluster, active book writer award for English category as well as best research award in social science and ihtisas arts. He also won gold and silver medal awards in local and international research and innovation competitions. He obtained certificate of copyright from Intellectual Property Corporation of Malaysia or Perbadanan Harta Intelek Malaysia for two innovative products namely Bank Wakaf and Wakaf Kepakaran Profesional for duration of 100 years. He also involved in various consultancy projects with external parties and collaborators such as Islamic Banking & Finance Institute Malaysia (IBFIM), Association of Islamic Banking Institutions Malaysia (AIBIM), Lembaga Kemajuan Johor Tenggara (KEJORA), Malaysia Productivity Corporation (MPC) and Perbadanan Wakaf Negeri Sembilan Sdn. Bhd. (PWNS/MAINS). Until now, he has authored thirty (30) books and thirty-five (35) chapters in book. He has also presented thirty-three (33) papers and published one hundred and twenty-eight (128) articles in various national and international conferences and indexed journals. He is actively conducting research in forty-six (46) research projects in his area of expertise and funded by various internal and external parties such as Ministry of Higher Education Malaysia, Majlis Agama Islam Negeri Sembilan (MAINS), Pusat Zakat Negeri Sembilan (PZNS), Yayasan Tun Ismail Ali, Permodalan Nasional Berhad (YTI/PNB), Yayasan Pembangunan Ekonomi Islam Malaysia (YAPEIM), Albukhary International University (AIU) and Bank Pembangunan Malaysia Berhad (BPMB). Currently, total research funding obtained is RM2,364,530.00. He can be reached at ridhwan.aziz@usim.edu.my.

***

Nurul Asikin is a PhD candidate in the field of Shariah Muamalah at the Centre for Shariah Studies, Faculty of Islamic Studies, National University of Malaysia (UKM). Currently pursuing advanced studies in Islamic commercial law, Nurul Asikin focuses on the complexities of financial transactions and legal frameworks under Shariah law. With a strong interest in the intersection of Islamic jurisprudence and modern economic practices, Nurul Asikin aims to contribute to the development of Shariah-compliant financial systems and practices. Throughout her doctoral research, Nurul Asikin has been involved in various academic activities, including seminars and research collaborations, to expand knowledge in Shariah Muamalah. She is committed to advancing the understanding and application of Islamic commercial law in contemporary settings, with a particular emphasis on its role in fostering ethical financial practices.

Dalila Abu Bakar Currently, she is an Assistant Professor and senior lecturer at department of Accountancy and Business, Faculty of Accountancy, Finance and Business in Tunku Abdul Rahman University of Management of Technology Pahang branch. Her research interest and specialization include earnings management, fraud detection and corporate governance. She active in research activities and innovation teaching and learning program.

Junaidah Binti Abu Seman is a Senior Lecturer at the Faculty of Economics and Muamalat, Universiti Sains Islam Malaysia (USIM), specializing in Islamic finance. She holds a PhD from the University of Salford (2017), an MA from INCEIF (2011), and a BA from USIM (2006). With extensive teaching and supervision experience, she has led and participated in numerous research projects, focusing on topics such as sustainable financing and financial literacy. Her publications include articles in reputable journals and contributions to books on Islamic finance and takaful. Junaidah is a lifetime member of the Malaysian Muamalat Association and an ordinary member of the Malaysian Muamalat Association (MMA). She has received several awards for excellence in service and research, including best paper awards at international conferences.

Aminuddin is a postgraduate alumnus of the Master of Sharia Economics Program at UIN Sunan Kalijaga Yogyakarta. His research interests include Islamic philanthropy, ZISWAF, the halal industry, and Islamic economics. He has conducted research on the empowerment of productive waqf, focusing on the development of strategic mosque-based models designed to promote economic independence, improve community welfare, and strengthen social functions.

Mohd Asyraf Bin Yusof is a dedicated academician and researcher at the Academy of Contemporary Islamic Studies (ACIS), Universiti Teknologi MARA (UiTM) Sarawak Branch, Campus 2. Specializing in Islamic finance, waqf, fintech, and sustainable development, he has significantly contributed to bridging traditional Islamic economic practices with modern technological innovations. His recent research focuses on leveraging e-wallet-based waqf funding for Technical and Vocational Education and Training (TVET) institutions to foster sustainable R&D funding and economic resilience. As the chairperson of the Borneo International Postgraduate Conference 2025, Dr. Asyraf is actively involved in promoting academic collaboration and knowledge sharing. Passionate about lifelong learning, he continues to enhance his skills in Arabic and English while maintaining a strong commitment to personal fitness and well-being.

Asma' Rashidah Idris is an economic lecturer, researcher, and educator with a passion for business and economics, entrepreneurship, and finance. She earned Bachelor of Economic majoring in Islamic Economics and Finance in 2004. She graduted with Master of Business and Administration (MBA) Finance from University Teknologi MARA and then she got PhD in Economics from Universiti Putra Malaysia (UPM) in 2019. She actively involved in academic writing and publication focusing on issues related to business and economics, student entrepreneurship, finance. Currently, she focuses on the topic of retirement planning.

Shafinar Ismail is a Finance Professor at Universiti Teknologi MARA (UiTM), Melaka, Malaysia. She holds a PhD in behavioral Finance from Brunel University, UK. Her research interests include behavioral finance and Islamic social finance. She is currently the chief editor of the International Journal of Business and Social Science (MyCite) and sits on the advisory board of several SSCI journals. She is active in scholarly communities and holds the President of the International of Economics and Business (IAEB) position. She also was the Finance Visiting Professor at the University of New Orleans, Louisiana, USA, and Princess Nourah bint Abd Rahman University, Riyadh, Saudi Arabia. Her publications stand for more than 200 articles and four books, besides chapters in books, conference proceedings, working papers, newsletters, and newspaper articles. Her excellence in research has brought her several award-winning awards, including the UiTM Malaysia Best Researcher Award (Business and Management) in the year 2018, the UiTM Malaysia Excellent Researcher Award (2021), the Faculty of Business Management (FBM) UiTM Malaysia Jewel In The Crown best supervisor awards for 2020 and 2021, the UiTM Melaka Best Researcher Award for eight (8) years, and the UiTM Melaka Best Supervisor Award for seven (7) years.

Norhanizah Johari (Dr.), (A.M) Current position and institution: An accounting lecturer in the Department of Accounting, Universiti Islam Selangor, Malaysia Academic qualifications: Ph.D in Islamic Finance and Muamalat, The Accounting Research Institute, UiTM Shah Alam, Malaysia. Master's in Accountancy, UiTM, Shah Alam, Malaysia. Bachelor of Accountancy (Hons), UiTM, Shah Alam, Malaysia. Diploma in Accountancy, UiTM Shah Alam, Malaysia. Research interests or areas of specialization: Financial accounting and reporting Internal control Governance Accounting education Publications, research projects, or contributions: FRGS Grant (2022) GPIK Grant (2022) FRGS Grant (2018) GPIK Grant (2016) ICIFE-UUM Grant (2014) Awards, recognitions, or grants: Best Paper Awards Best Presenter Awards Best Employee Awards GoT Award (Ph.D) Best Research Award (Ph.D) Professional affiliations or memberships: Associate Member of Malaysian Institute of Accountants (MIA) Any other relevant achievements or roles: Managing Editor of IJIEFER (current)

Mohd Abdullah is a professor in accounting. His expertise is in auditing and corporate governance.

Norshahira Kamarzaman is a full-time student at the Centre for Shariah Studies, National University of Malaysia (UKM). She is also a lecturer in the field of Shariah, teaching at Polytechnic/Community Colleges under the Department of Polytechnic and Community College Education, Ministry of Higher Education Malaysia. She holds a Bachelor's Degree in Shariah and has expertise in Islamic law, Islamic finance, Maqasid al-Shariah, and Waqf. She has published several articles in academic journals and is currently involved in research on the Waqf model for TVET institutions in Malaysia.

Zarina Kassim is currently a Senior Lecturer at the Faculty of Defence Studies and Management, National Defence University of Malaysia (NDUM). She earned a Bachelor of Economic (honour) in 2010 and Master's in Economics in 2013 from Faculty of Economics and Management, the National University of Malaysia (UKM) and also completed Doctor of Philosophy (PhD) in Economics Education from Faculty of Education at the same university in 2019. Her research interests include Economics Development, Economic and Social Well-being, Defence Economics, and Economics Education. She is an ambitious person that interested in professional development and researching, ongoing learning and growth, who likes to communicate and working with new ideas and people.

Maksud A.Madraswale working as an Associate Professor, Department of Management, Presidency University, Bengaluru. For few years he served at Oman and other Arab Countries. To his credit he published five articles in Scopus Indexed journals.

Hafizah Mat Nawi is currently a senior lecturer at the Faculty of Defence Studies and Management, National Defence University of Malaysia. She earned her PhD in Accounting & Finance from Brunel University London, UK, in 2015, an MBA (Finance) from the University of Malaya in 2007; and a Bachelor of Accounting from the International Islamic University of Malaysia in 2004. She is an associate member of the Malaysian Institute of Accountants (MIA) and a Registered Shariah Financial Planner under the Malaysian Financial Planning Council (MFPC). Her research interests encompass accounting, personal and corporate finance, entrepreneurship, and management. Currently, she actively conducts research in the fields of personal financial education and personal financial planning involving military personnel and families with special needs children (SNC). She is also experienced in producing review articles and bibliometric studies.

Hj. Hasan Al-Banna Mohamed is a Professor in Department of Management, Faculty of Management and Defence Studies, National Defence University of Malaysia (NDUM), Kuala Lumpur. He obtained his PhD from Malaya University in Islamic Quality Management in 2015. In addition to the academic post, he has experience working as the Director for the Division of Quality Assurance and Data Management, NDUM, from 2010 until 2022. After that, he has been appointed as a Senior Director for the Project Management and Strategic Planning Division, in the Assistant Vice Chancellor Office (Project Management and Strategic Development), NDUM. His areas of expertise and research are in Islamic Management, Quality Management, Human Resource Development and HRM, Islamic Studies.

Noor Azila Mohd Zaid is a Senior Lecturer with a strong academic background and professional focus in the field of finance. She holds a degree and Master in Finance and has built a career centered on both teaching and research within this discipline. Her research interests and expertise lie primarily in finance, where she actively contributes to academic discourse and innovation. Committed to advancing financial knowledge and fostering analytical thinking among her students, Noor Azila continues to play a pivotal role in shaping future professionals in the field.

Salwa Muda is a senior lecturer in Universiti Teknologi MARA (UiTM) Negeri Sembilan, Malaysia. She obtained her PhD in Accounting from Universiti Kebangsaan Malaysia (UKM) in 2018, MBA (Accounting) from Universiti Utara Malaysia (UUM) in 2003 and Bachelor in Accounting (Hons) from Universiti Utara Malaysia in 2001. She is actively engaged in academic writing and publishing, particularly in intellectual capital and entrepreneurship.

Nazifah binti Mustaffha (Dr.). Current position and institution: An accounting lecturer in the Department of Accounting, Universiti Islam Selangor, Malaysia Academic qualifications: Ph.D. in Accountancy, Faculty of Accountancy, UiTM Shah Alam, Malaysia. Master of Science (Accounting) and Bachelor of Accounting (Hons) from the International Islamic University Malaysia. Research interests or areas of specialization: risk management, accounting for Islamic institutions, and Zakat and Waqf accounting and governance. Publications, research projects, or contributions: FRGS Grants (2015 and 2021), GPIK Grant (2022). Currently as editor of the International Journal of Islamic Economics and Finance Research (IJIEFER)

Nasrudin is a lecturer in the Department of Communication at Universitas Islam Kalimantan Selatan Muhammad Arsyad Al-Banjari, Banjarmasin. He specializes in communication studies and is involved in teaching and research. Email: nasruddin3100@gmail.com

Nofriansyah Nofriansyah He earned a Bachelor's degree in Economics Education from Universitas Sriwijaya in 2017 and a Master's degree in Economics Education from Universitas Negeri Padang in 2019. Currently, the author is pursuing a doctoral degree in economic education at Universitas Pendidikan Indonesia (UPI) with an LPDP scholarship in 2024 until now. His areas of expertise include education (evaluation, learning models, instructional media, and learning strategies) and economics, microeconomics, macroeconomics, and management). He can be reached via: nofriansyah10@upi.edu/nofriansyah10@gmail.com.

Lucky Nugroho is a highly experienced expert in Islamic banking, financial strategy, and microfinance, with over two decades of combined professional and academic service. He has held key strategic positions at Bank Syariah Mandiri and Bank Syariah Indonesia, including roles in corporate planning, financial analysis, micro banking development, and treasury management. He is currently an Associate Professor lecturing at Universitas Mercu Buana and Universitas Terbuka, focusing on Islamic banking and finance. Dr. Nugroho holds advanced degrees from leading institutions in Indonesia, Belgium, and the Netherlands. He is also certified as a Certified Human Resources Professional (CHRP) from Universitas Atmajaya and holds a Level 3 Risk Management Certification, which strengthens his capability in managing strategic and operational risks within financial institutions. His expertise lies in Islamic microfinance, sustainable development, and strategic management of Islamic financial institutions.

R.Bhuvaneswari working as an Assistant Professor of English at Dr.Mahalingam College of Engineering and Technology, Pollachi. To her credit she completed 10 NPTEL / SWAYAM and published few articles in Scopus indexed journals.

R. Velmurugan presently working as an Associate Professor in Commerce, Karpagam Academy of Higher Education, Coimbatore. He started his career as a Project Fellow under UGC Sponsored Major Research Project at NGM College, Pollachi. He has 18 years of teaching experience has 15 years of research experience. To his credit he produced 22 Ph.D. Scholars and 5 M.Phil. Scholars. At present 1 scholar submitter his thesis, 6 Ph.D. Scholars are under his guidance. Moreover, to his credit he published 168 articles in various International Journals, of which 85 articles are published in Scopus Indexed Journals and 15 articles in Web of Science and 76 articles in edited volumes. He also participates and presented 27 papers in various International Seminar / Conference and 54 National Seminar / Conference. He acted as an external examiner for various M.Phil. and Ph.D. Viva voce examinations. He acted as a Vice Chancellor nominee for Doctoral Committee Expert at Bharathiar University, Coimbatore and Periyar University, Salem. He acted as a Chairperson at various National Level Conferences. He also acted as an Expert for Syllabus Scrutiny Committee, Question Paper Scrutiny Committee and Expert members for Board of Studies at various reputed Colleges. Considering his meritorious contribution, he received awards like Best Paper Presenter, Best Research Supervisor and Best Faculty Awards from various research foundations and councils. He too acted as a resource person for 27 Guest Lectures, 30 Workshops and 10 faculty development programmes.

lRahmawati Rahmawati - Contributing AuthorlRahmawati Rahmawati is a lecturer at the Department of Accounting, Faculty of Economics and Business, Islamic State University Syarif Hidayatullah Jakarta, Indonesia. Her areas of research interest are Islamic accounting, financial accounting, and reporting, Islamic cooperative governance, internal audit, and finance in Islamic cooperative.

Endang Supardi author is a professor in the Office Management Study Program at the Faculty of Economics and Business Education, Indonesian Education University (UPI), Bandung, Indonesia. The field of expertise is the science of learning entrepreneurship. The author is active in teaching, research, and scientific publication activities. The author can be contacted via email: endang-supardi@upi .edu

Ravi Thirumalaisamy working as an Assistant Professor, Department of Business and Economics, Modern College of Business and Science. To his credit, he published more than 16 articles in Scopus indexed journals.

Rendika Vhalery is a lecturer in the Department of Economics Education at Universitas Indraprasta PGRI, Jakarta, Indonesia. He earned a Bachelor's degree in Economics Education from Universitas Sriwijaya in 2016 and a Master's degree in Economics Education from Universitas Negeri Padang in 2018. He is currently pursuing a Doctoral degree in Economics Education at Universitas Negeri Malang. His areas of expertise include education (evaluation, learning models, instructional media, and learning strategies) and economics (personal financial management, microeconomics, and macroeconomics). He can be reached via rendikavhalery31@ gmail.com

Wahyu Wibowo is a postgraduate alumnus of the Master of Sharia Economics Program at UIN Sunan Kalijaga Yogyakarta. His academic interests include the halal industry, Islamic philanthropy, and economic literacy. She received four PKM grants funded by DIKTI (2012–2014), three of which focused on community service- ranging from Jarimatika training to literary-mathematics education for orphans, one of which was selected as a national finalist. She also initiated an entrepreneurship project titled IBU SASTIKA (Innovative Mathematics Literature Book) which combines educational innovation with creative content. Wahyu Wibowo is a postgraduate alumnus of the Master of Sharia Economics Program at UIN Sunan Kalijaga Yogyakarta. His academic interests include the halal industry, Islamic philanthropy, and economic literacy. She received four PKM grants funded by DIKTI (2012–2014), three of which focused on community service—ranging from Jarimatika training to literary-mathematics education for orphans, one of which was selected as a national finalist. She also initiated an entrepreneurship project titled IBU SASTIKA (Innovative Mathematics Literature Book) which combines educational innovation with creative content.

Index

A

B

C

D

E

F

H

I

M

O

P

R

S

T

U

V

W

Z

www.ingramcontent.com/pod-product-compliance
Lightning Source LLC
LaVergne TN
LVHW062329300926
849161LV00007B/1634